Snelling Thomas

A View of the Silver Coin and Coinage of England

From the Norman Conquest to the Present Time

Snelling Thomas

A View of the Silver Coin and Coinage of England
From the Norman Conquest to the Present Time

ISBN/EAN: 9783337173357

Printed in Europe, USA, Canada, Australia, Japan

Cover: Foto ©Suzi / pixelio.de

More available books at **www.hansebooks.com**

A VIEW OF THE SILVER COIN AND COINAGE OF ENGLAND, FROM THE NORMAN...

Thomas Snelling

A VIEW OF THE SILVER COIN AND COINAGE OF *ENGLAND*.

THE Coins of William the Conqueror, and his ſon William Rufus, are here deſcribed together, as there is not, even to this day, any juſt criterion whereby to diſtinguiſh one of them from the other. WILL. I. 1066. WILL. II. 1087.

However, from ſeveral of No. 1. being found with ſome of Harolds, having the ſame mint-maſter's name on both, that is ſuppos'd to be the Conqueror's, as is alſo No. 3. he being thus drawn in doomſday-book; and likewiſe No. 7. from the two ſcepters, as Rufus had a right but to one; No. 11, 12. are ſuppos'd to be of Rufus, as the ſtars are found on his great ſeal.

Each of the Williams have their Buſt (*a*) on one ſide, which generally extends to the edge of the Coin, except No. 7. 11. which are bounded by the inner circle, HEAD SIDE. Type.

(*a*) A ſeries of the heads of the Monarchs of England, from the Conqueſt to the preſent time, or for near 700 years, are to be found on their ſilver coin, and all of them of good ſilver, a circumſtance peculiar to the Engliſh collection, and which that of no other nation in Europe beſides can exhibit. We have therefore called one ſide, throughout this work, the head ſide.

B ſhew-

WILL. I. WILL. II. shewing the head, neck, and breast; but the head is differently posited, as on No. 1. it is half-faced, looking to the right; on No. 2. it regards the left, all — A. the rest exhibit the full face.

He appears with a sword in his right hand on No. 3. and with a scepter on No. 1, 2, 8, 9. there is a scepter on each side the head on No. 7. and on No. 8. a scepter on one side and a star on the other; a star or mullet is on each side the head on No. 11, 12. the latter of which is sometimes without them, and on others they are enclosed in an annulet: lastly, the head of No. 6. is within a sort of portal or canopy.

All the heads are crowned, No. 3. 8. 12. have a sort of diadem of pearls, with three pearls rais'd on points over it, the others have all of them a sort of arch; No. 10. has also pearls or bobs hanging to each ear.

Legend. Round the head is the name and title, but with some variety, as No. 1. reads PILLEMUS REX A, others have AN, ANG. ANGL. ANGLO, ANGLOR, also PILEM, PILLEM, PILLEMU, PILELM, PILLELM, with the P (being the Saxon w) but No. 1. sometimes wants it, reading only ILLEMU.

REVERSE. Type. The Types of the reverses are very different, some having only one cross, as No. 1. 2. 4. 9. others, as No. 5. 7. 12. a cross and saltier; a sort of lozenge, with arched sides, appears on No. 6. which on No. 3. is join'd with a cross, as are also the lozenge-like figures on No. 8. 10. 11. tho' differing in form and position.

The cross on No. 1. is terminated in a kind of knot, as are also the lozenges on No 3. 6. the crosses on No. 7. 8. are fleury; that on No. 1. and the saltier on No. 7. are bottoné, and that on No. 12. is terminated with annulets; those on No. 10. 12. are voided; the lozenge-like figures on No. 8. 10. have a pellet on each angle.

The cross on No. 4. is enclosed in a kind of compartment, each angle of which has a pellet on it, a sort of knot like those on No. 1. 3. 6. issues from the inner circle into the quarters of the cross on No. 2. they have mostly an annulet in the centre; and No. 9. has also one in each quarter, with the letters P A X S in them (*b*).

Heraldric terms are here made use of for want of knowing others which would convey juster ideas, but we do not think any description can equal the bare inspection of the figures on the plates.

Legend. The inscription on the reverse is the name of the moneyer, or mint-master, and that of the place where coined, with the particle ON signifying IN or OF * between them, as No. 9. Sideloc on Pell, No. 11. Ontheorn on Co; that is, Sideloc in Wells, Ontheorn in Colchester, &c. (*c*)

Specimens of both sorts of names are contain'd in the two following lists, which

(*b*) The Conqueror continued to coin in the taste of his predecessors Harold, Edward the Confessor, the Canutes, and Ethelred, each of which have their head on their coins some half-faced, others full-faced, with different crowns or ornaments, also with and without a scepter; and the reverse have also different crosses.

(*c*) The names of the moneyers and towns had also been on the coins of his predecessors just mentioned, and appears to have been a method particular to the English Silver-coin; being constantly found on them for near three centuries.

The only foreign coins we meet with, wherein this method was imitated, are in Olaus and Anund, kings of Sweden, Swain, king of Denmark, and Sithric, king of Dublin †; all cotemporary with Ethelred, also on the first pennies of the kings of Scotland, as David I. William I. and Alexander II. as will appear when we come to the Scotch series.

* See No. 40. † Kederi Nummi Aliquot, p. 7, 55, 56. Simons Irish Coins, p. 6.

A. [illegible]

which admit of great additions by carefully inſpecting the pennies of theſe two kings. Will. I. Will. II.

NAMES of MONEYERS on the PENNIES of the two WILLIAMS.

Aelfſi	Ceoli	Gifpard	Man	Sdrott	Thorn
Afarve	Ceorl	Godi	Manna	Sefparth	Thorſtan
Aglfine	Ceati	Godic	Marepil	Segparth	Ulfiel
Alef	Cintſpine	Godric	Munpine	Segpine	Ulfri
Aleif	Colſpegen	Godrici	Murñn	Sepi	Pelſpine
Alfrad	Cuiric	Godpi	Od	Sepine	Petpi
Aldpine	Didric	Godpine	Odbeurn	Sideloc	Pimer
Aleſmer	Dilmun	Goldman	Odthnorin	Sidemin	Pinſpine
Aleſtmaer	Dinnic	Goldpine	Onthreorn	Siferth	Pine
Anderbode	Dunnic	Guthrien	Opitrern	Siepine	Pinthborne
Antholf	Dor	Hargod	Ordpi	Sipioe	Pinuric
Arthur	Duregrim	Harmil	Orgur	Sifred	Pujerered
Auderine	Driman	Huſpal	Oſberth	Sipord	Pulſpord
Auine	Eadpi	Jecelbrent	Oſpold	Speatline	Pulfred
Beriteri	Eadpine	Jedgpord	Oter	Spentline	Pulfgmet
Boda	Eadpeard	Jegelbrht	Outhreorn	Spott	Pulfmaer
Bratmer	Edpi	Jegelric	Refpine	Spottine	Pulfmer
Brintred	Elfſi	Jeſthn	Reſpine	Sprtic	Pulſpi
Brentric	Eorpine	Leigten	Roger	Stiepin	Pulſpic
Brumman	Eſderne	Leofpine	Rosfetel	Theolric	Pulſpini
Brummic	Folgard	Lifpine	Rulepi	Theodred	Pulſric
Bruntui	Forna	Lufred	Rulfspi	Threorn	Pulſspi.
But					

NAMES of TOWNS on the PENNIES of the two WILLIAMS.

Ae	Elrpic	Hreli	Lund	Oxnef	Snottin
Aeſh	Eof	Hunten	Lunde	Oxnei	Stan
Aeſt	Eofe	Je	Lundei	Orthpï	Stotic
Bric	Eofer	Jex	Lundene	Orthri	Su
Bricſtow	Eofr	Jexce	Lundne	Ric	Sud
Brigetſo	Exce	Jexfe	Lundnei	Ricom	Suel
Brigſtſo	Exceer	Jexfei	Lundnde	Rltune	Suthbï
Ca	Excer	Jexec	Lundnen	Rofi	Sutheper
Can	Execes	Jexeci	Luned	Rufei	Suthrï
Cant	Exeter	Lepi	Luni	Tan	Suterk
Cantu	Gepi	Licae	Ludeic	Tant	Palice
Cantuï	Gi	Liepen	Lyndr	Tanu	Pell
Canterbir	Gif	Linco	Maint	Thiotford	Perni
Cnt	Giſle	Lincol	Meigt	Thofred	Pi
Cntle	Gip	Lincoln	Mifgt	Shaeftiſbir	Pin
Cati	Gipe	Lini	Norp	Sced	Pinc
Co	Glei	Lofec	Ox	Shiefe	Pinire
Col	Glouces	Loync	Oxen	Shine	Pinre
Dou	Hardfrd	Londini	Oxenefo	Sinfl	Pltune
Dori	Here	Lun	Oxeneſo	Snotin	Pigri
Dorces	Herefor				

Sorts. These two kings coin'd no other money than the penny.

Rarity. The Coins of the two Williams are none of them very common, but No. 3. 9. are something scarcer, and No. 2. 6. are very rare.

Weight. The pound weight at this time in use in the English mints, and which is suppos'd also to be the same as that us'd by the Saxons *, was that call'd the Tower or Moneyers Pound, which consisted of 12 ounces, each of 20 pennyweights or 240 pennyweights; the first of which subdivisions was in use with the Romans, but the second introduced into France by Charlemagne †; and from thence, as is suppos'd, brought into England by the Conqueror; but the penny itself would support an opinion of its being known here long before *(d)*.

This pound contained 15 sixteenths of the pound Troy, or 11 ounces 5 pennyweights Troy ‡, and therefore the pennyweight and penny, at this time, weighed 22½ Troy grains.

Fineness. These pennies were made of mixed silver, one pound, or 12 ounces, of which contained 11 ounces two pennyweights of fine silver, and eighteen pennyweights of copper or alloy: and silver of this fineness, in the most early indenture of the mint, viz. that of 28 Edw. I. is called OLD STANDARD §, and in this sense only of the word standard we shall use it throughout this work, and it is the pound weight of this standard silver all our calculations are built upon (*e*).

Value. The Money Pound, or Pound Tale, consisted likewise of 240 pennies, that is, of 20 shillings, each of 12 pennies, and each of these pennies, at this time, poised a pennyweight of the Tower pound, and therefore 240 of them weighed the Tower pound; and consequently the pound tale of equal value with the pound weight *(f)*.

Henry I. 1100. The same difficulty attends the true placing of the Coins of the first and second Henry, as did that of the two Williams, it being done only by conjecture; and we are not certain that some we have here put to the first Henry may not be of the second, or even of his son Henry junior, if he coined any.

Head Side. Type. Henry is exhibited with more variety than his father and brother, for besides the profile head to the right, as on No. 19. 20. 22. and the full face on No. 14, 15, 18. 23; he is represented almost full-faced, but something inclined to the right on No. 24, and to the left on No. 16, 17.

He has a scepter in his hand on No. 16, 17, 18. 22, 23, 24. that on No. 18,

(d) England at present is the only nation which still retains the use of these ancient subdivisions of the pound weight, or where the pennyweight is the same part of its pound weight; as the money penny is of the money pound.

(*e*) Besides the sense the word standard is taken in above, and which it is probable was the only one it had for some ages, it at present likewise is synonymous with the word FINENESS in general, thus silver of 10 or 11 oz. FINE, is said to be of the STANDARD of 10 or 11 oz. (both which significations it has also in gold) and 3dly, it is used to signify the QUANTITY OF FINE SILVER IN THE POUND STERLING, thus altering of the standard, or debasing of the standard, are the same as altering or lessening the quantity of fine silver in the said pound.

(f) Money was paid into the Exchequer ‖ 1st, de Numero, by pounds tale of 20 shillings, 2dly, ad Scalam, or in pounds of twenty shillings and sixpence, 3dly, ad Pensam, or as many pennies as weighed 12 oz. 4thly, Arsure, in pounds of 12 oz. to undergo the tryal by combustion or assay.

And it is said, that if it was lawful money the pound would lose but six pennies in the examination or trial, but if by lawful money we understand that made of standard silver, it certainly would be such even if it had lost 18 pennies instead of six; we submit the solution of this difficulty to the curious in these enquiries.

* Folkes, p. 3. † Le Blanc, p. xviii. 96. ‡ Folkes, p. 3. § Lowndes, p. 34. ‖ Ancient dialogue concerning the Exchequer, p. 19, 20.

very fingular, as terminating in a kind of rofe, whereas the others are fleury. No. 23. has a ftar on one fide the head, No. 16. has two ftars, and No. 17. three ftars before the face, No. 19. has a rofe before the face, No. 13. has on each fide the head an annulet, and No. 14. has bobs or pearls from each ear, as No. 10. of the Williams. HENRY I.

They read differently, as No. 12. HENRI REX NL. alfo HENRI, HENRIC, HENRICUS, and R, RE, A, AN. Legend.

We have ftill the crofs, faltier, compartment, &c. but with more variety than before, thus No. 13, 18, 19, 20. have a fingle crofs, No. 16, 17. a crofs and faltier, No. 22, 24. have the lozenge-like figure, both of them fleury; the firft has a ftar in the center, the laft is joined with a faltier, and has a pellet in each quarter, made by the interfection. No.131. has a compartment, whofe angles terminate in three pellets very near the center. No.213. has the compartment without any pellets on its angles, but has five annulets in crofs in the area; that of No. 18. is fmall and does not touch the inner circle, like the others, having alfo an annulet on each arch, and angular point, each angle is alfo fill'd with a fort of rofe. The compartment of No. 23. has a fort of rofe like thofe on the quarters of No. 18. with a fmall crofs and ftar in the center, and three fleurs-de-lis iffuing from the inner circle. No. 14. has alfo a fort of compartment, with a large annulet in the center. No. 19. 20. have an annulet in each quarter of the crofs, the firft inclofes a pellet. No. 15. is the only coin we have met with in the Englifh fuite from the Conqueft to Henry VIII. without a crofs on its reverfe, as there is none on this, but it has the word PAX in the center, with two bars and two annulets both above and below it. REVERSE.

The infcriptions, as before, have the name of the moneyer, and that of the town, but with lefs variety than the two Williams, as there are fewer Coins of this King. Legend.

NAMES of MONEYERS on the PENNIES of HENRY I.

Alen	Eturi	Gol	Ofbr	Rolland	Palford
Alfpine	Fucred	Hermer	Ordgur	Sain	Pintured
Algar	Geraud	Jelfpine	Orim	Sam	Pulfrine
Arcil	Goefrei	Jordan	Ofulf	Sigar	Pulfpine
Cinri	Godric	Lefpard	Rauf	Smiene	Pulfpord
Edmund	Godpine	Morus	Richard	Smiorne	Witt

NAMES of TOWNS on the PENNIES of HENRY I.

Bado	Gipe	Lund	Norpic	Rufa	Sut
Bifes	Here	Lunde	Norwic	Sedm	Pelligli
Brifto	Le	Lundene	Ric	Stanf	Pin
Cant	Linc	Lundon	Rofi	Su	Pintrfir
Canter	Lun				

The penny only of this king is to be found in collections, neither the half-penny or farthing, faid to have been coin'd by him *, having reach'd our time. SORTS.

All the Coins of this king are very fcarce, but efpecially No. 16, 17. 21. and No. 14. 18. have never before been publifh'd. RARITY.

* Stow's Annals, p. 101.

Weight. The penny ſtill weigh'd one pennyweight tower, or 22½ Troy grains (*g*).

Fineness. Standard, or 11 oz. 2 pennyweights fine ſilver, and 18 pennyweights alloy.

Value. The pound tale of the ſame value as the pound weight.

Stephen. 1135. HeadSide. Type. Stephen is repreſented on No. 25. with the almoſt full face, regarding the right, and on No. 26, 27, 28, with a profile head turn'd to the left.

He has a ſcepter fleury in his right hand on No. 25, 26. 29, but on No. 27. he holds a flag with a croſs fitche on it, and on No. 28. he holds a ſort of horſeman's mace, headed with points like a mullet, both of which are without other example in the Engliſh ſeries.

Stephen appears crown'd on all his coins, that on No. 25. is arched, the others all open and fleury; No. 30, is very ſingular, repreſenting two figures with their hands join'd, ſuppos'd to be Stephen and Henry, with a ſort of ſcepter fleury between them, and this is the only Coin without a head from the Conqueſt till Henry VIII.

Legend. His name is round the head, but with ſome difference, and always miſ-ſpelt, as STEFN, STEFNE, STIEFNE, STIEN, ſometimes alſo with R, RE.

Reverse. Type. A croſs voided, with a pellet in the center, and on the point of each limb of the croſs, appears on No. 25, with a fleur-de-lis iſſuing from the inner circle into the quarters (*b*); another has a mullet iſſuing from the inner circle, inſtead of the fleur-de-lis, the croſs is alſo broader and patee; as is ſhewn in the ſmall figure. No. 26, 27, 28, 29. have a croſs join'd to a compartment, whoſe angles end in fleurs-de-lis in the quarters. No. 29, 30. have a croſs and ſaltier, but entirely different from each other, and inſtead of the uſual legend have the circle fill'd with roſes and other figures.

The ſame is alſo obſervable on a Coin of his ſon Euſtace (A), and alſo on a Robert (B), heretofore ſuppos'd to be the Conqueror's ſon, duke of Normandy, but

(*g*) In France, between the years 1075 and 1093, the pound weight of 12 ounces of Charlemagne was laid aſide intirely *, and the mark of eight ounces, or two thirds of it, introduced in its ſtead.

We find the ſame thing to have happen'd in Germany, about the ſame time, occaſion'd, we are inform'd † by the uncertainty of the pounds there in uſe.

And although in England the Pound ſtill continued to be uſed, yet the Mark was alſo admitted, computations and payments by weight and by tale being made in both.

(*b*) We have here brought two pennies, (C. D.) to plead for admittance among thoſe of Stephen, and we think the reaſon of their not having been amongſt them before, is owing to their blunder'd inſcriptions; for their type, both head and reverſe, ſtrongly ſupport this opinion, that round the head of (D) being ANFILEM REX ‡ different from all the Williams. And the reverſe is ✠ NI . . . . OBINA; the type differs from No. 25. in having the voided croſs continued to the edge of the Coin inſtead of the inner circle

* Le Blanc, p. 150. † Tieman Frieſens Muntz Spiegel, p. 111. Hoffman's Muntz Schluſſel, p. 129. ‡ Ducarrel Anglo Gallic Coins, pl. 6. No. 72.

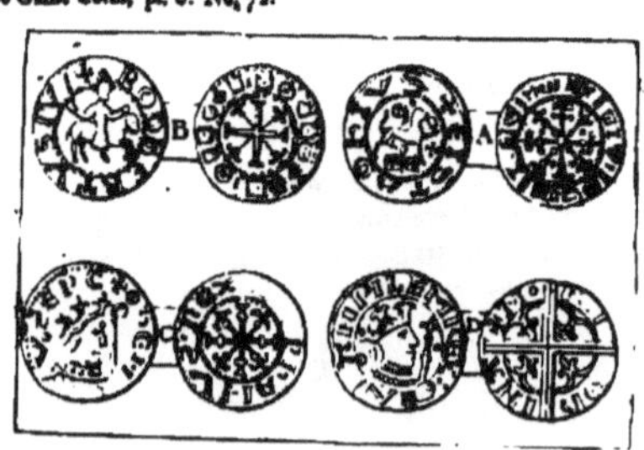

but Mr. North, with more propriety, gives it to Robert, Earl of Gloucester, which opinion we think is farther supported by the similitude of the border with that of Eustace, and with No. 29, 30. of Stephen, and more so as this Coin, the Eustace, and that of Stephen and Henry were all found together †. STEPHEN.

We have but short lists of this king to present the reader with, occasion'd not only by the few Coins of his now remaining, but also from the indifferent preservation those are generally in. Legend.

NAMES of MONEYERS on the PENNIES of STEPHEN.

Aelmar	Ferris	Sptidets	Tomas	Paen	Wlr
Ericus	Roberd	Thobi	Tovi	Pillem	

NAMES of TOWNS on the PENNIES of STEPHEN.

Ca	Le	Lu	Lunde	Snot	Pilt
Co	Lewes	Lund	Norwic	Su	Piltu
Here	Linco				

This king coined only the penny. SORTS.

All this king's money is very scarce, but especially No. 28, 29, 30. which are extremely rare; and No. 28. never before publish'd. RARITY.

The weight of the penny still a pennyweight of the Tower Pound, or 22½ Troy grains, but very unequally coin'd. WEIGHT.

Standard, or 11 oz. 2 pennyweights fine silver, and 18 pennyweights alloy. FINENESS.

The pound tale and pound weight the same, and of equal value. VALUE.

This king is represented on No. 32. with an almost full face, but a little inclining either to the right or left, much like No. 25. of Stephen, which type was used to be placed to Henry I. ‡ but in the present method of classing the series, it is adjudged to this king, however the point is still doubtful, and the discovery of a just criterion, whereby to distinguish the Coins of these two kings, would give us very sensible pleasure. HENRY II. 1154. HEAD SIDE. Type.

Number 31. is certainly of the same Henry as No. 32. exhibiting the side face to the left, like the other type of Stephen, especially No. 29.

He has a scepter patee in his hand on No. 32. nearly upright, as usual; but on No. 31. it lies on his shoulder different from any, either before or since. He is crown'd on both with a crown fleury.

Number 31. reads only .... RI REX ANGL. HEN being obliterated, and No. 32. HENRI R, A, sometimes RE, REX, also AN, ANG. Legend.

The reverse of both No. 31, 32. the same, that is a cross patee, with a small one of the same in each quarter. REVERSE.

There are but few legends perfect on these coins, being struck in such a manner as to have scarcely three letters legible together. Legend.

circle. (C) * reads O HENUIEPC (the bust filling that part where the RIC is supplied), the crosier, we apprehend, may be an imperfect fleury scepter, or one badly struck; the reverse reads .... PHANUS REX, and its type is nearly that of No. 29. differently posited, but we submit these conjectures to better judgements.

* Pembroke, p. 4. t. 23. Folkes, p. 5. Leake, first series, pl. 1. No. 4. † Thoresby, p. 350, 351. ‡ Thoresby's plate, No. 128.

HENRY II.

NAMES of MONEYERS on the PENNIES of HENRY II.

Edmund, Funere, Jordan, Ricard, Robert, Wiler, Willeme, Willelme, William.

NAMES of TOWNS on the PENNIES of HENRY II.

Cardic	Everwi	Glou	Nor	Sedm	Win
Cant	Gipe	Lund	Nucas	Stan	

WEIGHT. The penny or sterling equal a penny weight of the Tower Pound, or $22\frac{1}{2}$ Troy grains.

FINENESS. Standard, or Sterling, or 11 oz. 2 pennyweights fine silver, and 18 pennyweights alloy.

VALUE. The pound Tale, or Sterling (*i*), the same as the pound weight Tower.

A RICHARD I. 1189. The two pennies we have here given of this king were lately found, with many more, near Leeds in Yorkshire, to the great satisfaction of all lovers of this study; as those which were before produc'd for this king's were no other but double-struck blunder'd Coins of Edward the Confessor, Henry III. and Edward I. as may be seen in Speed, Thoresby, Leake, and Rapin.

HEAD SIDE. Type. He is represented on No. 33. full faced, with a scepter in his right hand, held a-cross his left breast, much in the taste of No. 9. of the Conqueror's; on No. 34. he is also full faced, much like No. 23. a cross appears on one side the head, and a scepter fleury on the other.

Legend. Number 3. reads RICARDUS REX ANG. but on No. 34. no more remains than RICARDUS.

REVERSE. Type. There is on No. 33, a small cross pattee in the center, and a pellet at a small distance from each of its ends, enclosed within a compartment, much like that of No. 18. but without its ornaments. No. 34. has a cross and saltier, but different from any before, altho' much like No. 7. 29.

Legend. We can read on No. 33. GEOFRIC ON EVE, but on No. 34. only LUN.

SORTS. The penny, or sterling, only.

RARITY. The rarest Coin in the English collection.

WEIGHT. The penny still equal to the pennyweight Tower, or $22\frac{1}{2}$ Troy grains.

FINENESS. Standard, or Sterling, or 11 oz. 2 pennyweights fine silver, and 18 pennyweights alloy.

VALUE. The pound sterling of equal value with the pound weight Tower (*k*).

This

(*i*) The appellation of STERLING given to our penny, and from that to its aggragates the shilling and pound, as also to silver of that particular fineness of which it was made; although mention'd before this king's reign *, yet is first found in our records in his time †; but other authors again ‡ refer it to the reign of Richard or John.

To the great credit of this nation, in the conduct of its mint, our POUND STERLING is at this day the most valuable of any of the NOMINAL, TALE, or MONEY POUNDS in Europe; that is, it has deviated less from its original, the POUND WEIGHT, or contains a greater quantity of FINE SILVER, it being still about $\frac{1}{3}$ of a pound, whereas that of France is reduced to about [illegible].

(*k*) This king's ransom was 150000 marks of fine silver, Cologne weight, which Cologne mark was 19 twentieths of the Troy mark of the Low Countries §, and that is equal to the mark of France or Paris ‖, which is 63 sixty-fourths of the English Troy mark ¶, or 3591 Troy grains. Eisenschmidt makes

* Nicholson's English Historical Library, p. 264. † North's Remarks on Clerke's conjectures, p. 27. ‡ Cambden's Remains, chap. money. § Budelius de Monetis, p. 64. ‖ Boizard Traite des Monnoyes, p. 259. ¶ Philosophical Transactions, No. 465. Magens's Universal Merchant, p. 126.

A. The pennies of this king are forgeries of the [illegible]

This king had mints in many places of England §, and yet not one of his Coins are now to be found, from whence we might tell what were its type and legend. JOHN. 1199.

We are therefore obliged to fill the gap with those coin'd by him in Ireland.

In his first Coinage, No. 35. he is represented with a round face, like a full moon, on the others he is full-fac'd, and crown'd fleury, with a scepter in his hand, terminated with four pellets in cross, with a kind of rose on one side the head on the penny; but on the halfpenny and farthing with stars on each side, and all three sorts within a triangle. HEAD SIDE. Type.

JOHANES DOM appears on No. 35. being coin'd whilst only Lord of Ireland, on No. 37. JOHAN REX, and No. 38. JOHANNES REX, but No. 36. has the moneyer's name WILLEM ON; his own name, and that of the place where coin'd, being on the reverse, viz. Johanes, Dw, for Dublin. Legend.

There is a cross voided on No. 35. very much like that on No. 25. but instead of fleurs-de-lis has an annulet in each quarter; the type of No. 36, 37, 38. are different from any thing on either English or Irish Coin either before or since, that is, a crescent and star on the penny *(l)*, the halfpenny a crescent and cross, and the farthing a star, all of them within a triangle. REVERSE. Type.

The inscription on No. 35. is NORMAN ON DIW. on No. 37. is WILLEM ON WA. and on No. 38. WILLEM ON LIME. they being coin'd at Dublin, Waterford, and Limeric. Legend.

The first farthing and halfpenny we meet with, of any English monarch, are of this king, as No. 36. No. 35. and No. 37. but it must be remembred that they are Irish, and that no English ones are to be found, in any cabinet, till those of Edward I. SORTS.

The weight of the penny equal that of the pennyweight Tower, or 22½ Troy grains. WEIGHT.

Standard, or 11 oz. 2 pennyweights fine silver, and 18 pennyweights alloy. FINENESS.

The pound tale weigh'd, and was of equal value with the pound weight. VALUE.

There are two sorts of pennies of this king, called his first Coinage, before his 32d year, and the second Coinage, after his 32d year, or those of the short cross *(m)* and the long cross; the former of which have heretofore †† been assign'd to Henry II. as having no Number after the name, as the latter always have, both being consider'd with attention, soon appear to be of the same king, and is further confirm'd by the agreement of the moneyers names on both. HENRY III. 1216.

This king is represented full-faced upon all his coins, but different from any HEAD SIDE. Type.

makes the Cologne mark 3611 Troy grains *, and Mr. Magens 3605 †, the medium of which is 3602, which exceeds the Tower mark, or 15 sixteenths of the Troy mark, but by two grains; which Tower mark, in a register of the Chamber of Accompts at Paris, is called the mark of Rochelle, or of England ‡.

(l) Du Fresne, in his Glossary, t. 2. p. 650. has engrav'd one much like it, of a Count of Tholouse, very probably of that Raymond who married this king's youngest sister ‖.

(m) A Silver Coin minted at Cologne, of Otho, Emperor of Germany, and which by Tileman Friesens, who engraved it, is placed to Otho III. ¶ is at once determin'd by its having this reverse of the short cross of No. 39. to be of Otho IV. first cousin to this king, and the great patron of the famous Gervaise of Tilbury **.

* De Ponderibus, p. 9. 14. † Universal Merchant, p. 49. ‡ Du Fresne Gloss. voce Marca. Boizard, p. 249. Folkes, p. 3, 4. § Stow's Survey, chap. Tower. ‖ Sandford, p. 70. ¶ Muntz Spiegel, p. 109. ** Medox's Epist. Dissert. to Lord Hallifax, p. viii. †† Thoresby's pl. No. 135. Leake's first series, pl. 1. No. 7, 8.

HENRY III. of his predeceſſors, as having the face or maſk, with only a kind of circle for the neck on No. 39. but on No. 41, 42. without either the neck or ſhoulder, and both ſorts are encloſed within the inner circle.

On No. 39. or the firſt coinage, he has always a ſcepter in his hand, terminated with four pellets in croſs, like thoſe on the reverſe, and like that of his fathers; but on No. 41, 42. of the ſecond Coinage, he is ſometimes with and ſometimes without it.

He is crown'd on all, but the crowns differ from each other, and from any before or ſince.

Legend. The firſt Coinage always read HENRICUS REX, but the ſecond read HENRICUS REX III. HENRICUS REX TERCI, and HENRICUS REX ANG. and the reverſe of No. 42. ſeems to have the remainder of the title, viz. LIE. TERCI LON. the laſt word for London, where we may ſuppoſe it was coin'd.

REVERSE. Type. The croſs of the firſt Coinage, No. 39. is form'd of double lines, ending in pellets, with four pellets in croſs in each quarter, much like that of Stephen, No. 25. and No. 33. of John, excluſive of what is in the quarters.

The croſs of No. 41. the ſecond Coinage, only differs in being carried quite to the edge of the Coin, and is the firſt long croſs we meet with ſince the Conqueſt (except the blunder'd Stephen) but continued to be the only one from this time till about the middle of Charles the Firſt's reign; there are only three pellets in each quarter upon theſe; and they are not joined as in the other Coinage.

Legend. We have more names of moneyers and towns of this king's, than of any ſince the Conqueror, ſeveral of the firſt coinage have the letters B. FR. L. M. T. after the moneyers name, but the meaning of thoſe letters is not clear, but we think that opinion which ſuppoſes they are initials of the moneyer's ſurname, is ſtrengthned by No. 39. which has the ſurname of CHIC at length on it. No. 40. is ſingular in having OF inſtead of ON, and is the only Coin we remember to have ſeen with it.

NAMES of MONEYERS on the PENNIES of HENRY III.

Abel	Colwine	Gifre	Ilger	Jurden	Piers
* Adam	* Davi	Gicelm	Joa	Lenolf	Piers M
Aimer	Davion	Gilbert	Joan	* Lucas	Randul
Aimes	Docelm	Goldwin	Joan Chic	Meinir	Rauf
Alain	Eadmund	Goldwine	Joanas	Melnir	Reicu
* Alein	Edmund	Halli	Job	Miles M	Reinald
Alenre	Edrich	Helis	Joh	Nichole	Renauld
Aliſand	Einadi	Henry	Johan	Nicol	Renaud
Allen	* Elis	Hernaud	Johan B	Nicole	Rener
Allwine	Ernaud	Hub	Johan M	Oſber	Ricard T
Alwine	Everard	Hue	Johan FR	Oſmund	Richard
Andrew	Filemer	Hugo	* John	Oſnund	Roberd
Arnaud	Fimer	Hugon	Johas	Owein	Robert
And	Fulre	Hunfrei	Johs	Paul	Rodbert
Bartelme	Gefard	Jacob	Jolie	Phelip	Roger
Beneit	Gefrei	Jefrei	Jon	Philip	Roger T
Caldwine	Gerard	Jeremiah	Jonons	Philaimer	Salemun
Colwein	Giffrei	Ilgar	Iſac	Pieres	Samuel

Simon

Pennies or Sterlings from WILLIAM the Conqueror to HENRY the Third.

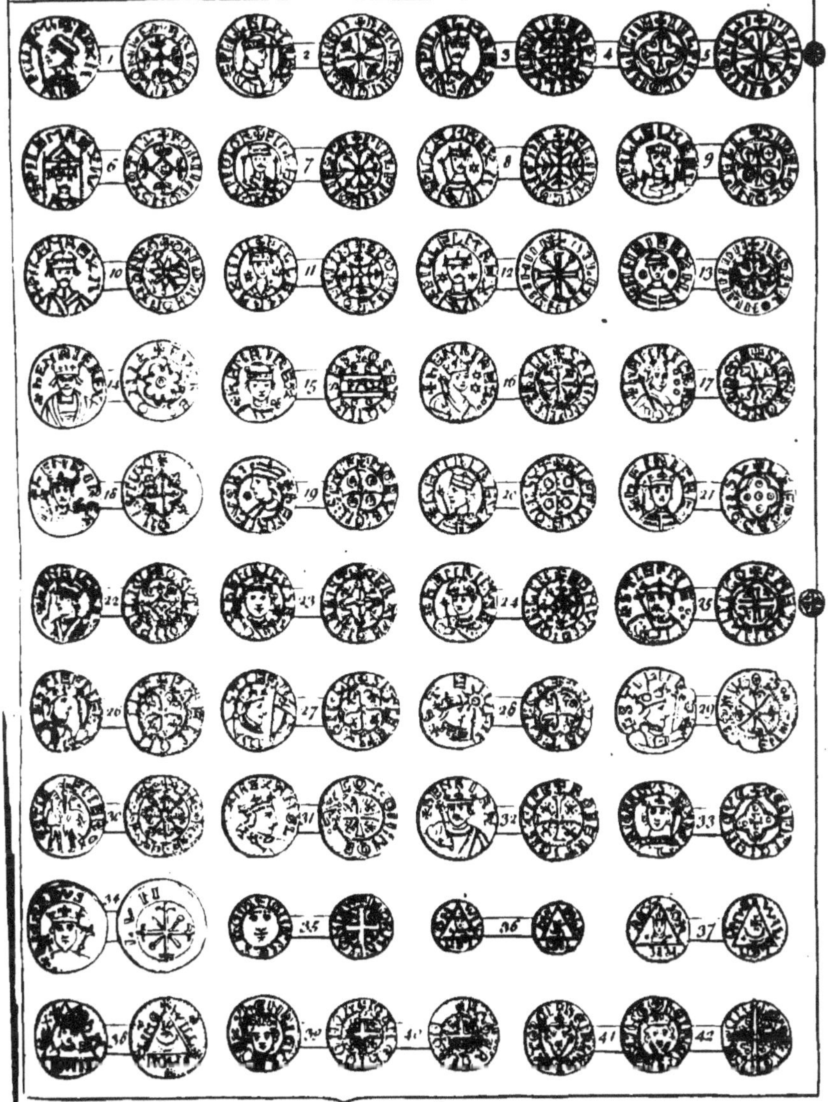

1 2 3 4 5 6 7 8 9 10 11 12 13 14 15 16 17 18 19 20 21 22 23 24 25 26 27 28 29 30 31 32 33 34 35 36 37 38 39 40 41 42

'ȣ

HENRY III.

Simon	Stivene	Turril	Wicion	Willelm T	Willem
Simond	Thomas	Vlerd	* Willelm	Willelm L	Willera
Simun	Tomas	* Walter			

* These names to both Coinage.

NAMES of TOWNS on the PENNIES of HENRY III.

Bruſt	Ever	Linc	No	Oxen	Scinted
Burſt	Everw	Lincoln	Nor	Oxene	Sented
Ca	Everwi	Lind	Nora	Oxon	Tande
Can	Evi	Lu	Norh	Oxonſó	Und
Cant	Ecce	Lun	Norha	Ork	W
Canta	Ex	Lund	Northa	Ro	Wi
Cante	Exc	Lunde	NNor+t	Ronce	Win
Canter	Exce	Lunden	Norw	Ruſa	Winc
Car	Glo	Lundon	Norwi	Rula	Wilt
Cardv	Glouce	Nic	Norwic	Sadmund	Wilton
Cice	Gloucet	Nica	Norwich	Sed'm	Wirce
Dur	Hereof	Nicol	Ocs	Sedmund	Wiric
Ev	Lenc				

In the records of the ſixth year of this king it appears, the halfpenny and farthing were then coined *, but we have never been ſo fortunate as to ſee one of either ſort, or to hear of any cabinet that can boaſt of being poſſeſs'd of either of them (*n*). SORTS.

This king's pennies very common, except thoſe with TERCI and ANG. which are very ſcarce. RARITY.

The penny, or Sterling, ſtill weighs the pennyweight Tower; or 22½ Troy grains. WEIGHT.

Standard, or Sterling, or 11 oz. 2 pennyweights fine ſilver, and 18 pennyweights alloy. FINENESS.

The pound Sterling equal the pound weight Tower. VALUE.

The only criterion uſed to diſtinguiſh the pennies of Edward I. from Edward II. is the difference of the name; as thoſe with EDW are thought to be the fathers, and thoſe with EDWA, EDWAR, EDWARD, the ſons †. EDWARD I. 1272.

They are repreſented full-faced, with ſpreading hair, and crown'd fleury, ſhewing only the neck, and barely the ſhoulder, and contained within the inner circle, appearing to be an improvement of the laſt Coinage of Henry III. and therefore, like them, differing from almoſt all his predeceſſors, whoſe buſts generally HEAD SIDE. Type.

(*n*) The collection of Engliſh Silver Coins may, with great propriety, be divided into four claſſes; the firſt from William the Conqueror to Henry II. inclusive, during which interval the type, both of the head and reverſe, continually vary, and afford beſides a great variety of names both of moneyers and towns ‡. The ſecond are thoſe compriſed between Edward I. and the 18th of Henry VII. during which period there is as remarkable a ſameneſs in them, as there was variety before, and have only one moneyer's name, and but few towns §. The third commences with the Coinage of the 18th of Henry VII. when he changed the full-face for the profile one, and the three pellets for the royal arms on the reverſe, and terminates with the hammer'd money; and the fourth contains all the milled money, or preſent currency from the firſt introducing the mill and ſcrew to the preſent time.

* Folkes, p. 7. North's Remarks, p. 27. † Archbiſhop Sharpe Of the Engliſh Silver Coins, ſect. 6. p. 32. MS. Nicholſon, p. 235. Thoreſby, p. 353. Folkes, p. 10. ‡ See plate 1. § See plate 2.

extend

EDWARD I. extend to the edge of the Coin, and shew the neck and breast also; this type was continued, without any material difference, till the 18th of Henry VII. or for 232 years.

A The head on the groat, No. 10. is enclosed within a compartment, like those on the reverses of No. 18, 21, 23. plate 1. but form'd of dotted lines, having a star on each side the head, and another on the breast, with four roses in the angles, much like those on No. 18.

Legend. The legend round the head on the halfpenny and penny is EDW. R. ANG. DNS. HYB. others have EDWA, EDWAR, EDWARD, and a very neat one has REX, instead of R. the farthing has E. R. ANGLIE. and the groat EDWARDUS DI GRA. REX ANG. having the rest of the titles on the exterior circle of the reverse.

REVERSE. Type. The reverse has a cross patee, extending to the edge of the Coin quite thro' the legendary circle, with three pellets in each quarter of the cross, as the last Coinage of Henry III. the groat differs from the smaller pieces only in having two letter'd circles instead of one, and this reverse, as well as the head, remain'd the same for more than two centuries. No. 3. is very remarkable for having only one pellet instead of three in each quarter; No. 4. for the boar's head in the second quarter; No. 6. for a cross in the said quarter, and we have seen another likewise with a sort of thistle in the same place.

Legend. There is only one moneyers name on the Edward's pennies, which has DE after it instead of ON, as ROBERT DE HADELEIE, and ROBERTUS DE HADL', all their other money having the name of the city or town, with CIVITAS or VILLA before it, the last sometimes wrote Vil' or Vill. and the groat has only CIVI instead of CIVITAS.

NAMES of TOWNS on the MONEY of EDWARD I. and EDWARD II.

Berewici	Cestrie	Eboraci	Hadeleie	Lincol	Novicastri
Bristolie	Dureme	Exonie	Kyngeston	London	Sciedmundi
Cantor					

Sometimes spelt Bristollie, Dunelm. Sedmundi, the farthing Londoniensis, and the groat Londonia, and on the exterior circle DUX AQUT. DNS HIBNE.

MintMarks. There is generally on all our money, from the Conquest (and even before) a plain cross at the beginning of the legend, both on the head and reverse, and it was placed there no doubt by our ancestors, for no other reason than the great veneration they had for that figure, and we meet with no other signature in that place till on No. 33, 40. plate 1. which have a star; and No. 42. a star and crescent; No. 8. plate 2. of Edwards have a lion rampant; and No. 9. a flourished cross, both of the Durham mint.

These have since been called private marks, or mint marks, placed there not only to distinguish the money of different mints from each other, but also the several Coinages of the same mint. We meet with them in every reign, without being certain in what part of those reigns to place them, or how many years they continued, or indeed any thing at all in relation to them, until Elizabeth, and when the milled money began to be coin'd they were quite laid aside.

SORTS. Besides the penny, collections now first exhibit the farthing, No. 1. and the halfpenny, No. 2, 3, 4. coin'd in an English mint, in the 7th of Edward I.*

Number 10. is suppos'd to be a pattern for a larger sort of Coin than any then current, not nicely adjusted in its weight, so that those now remaining, by their

* Stowe's Annals, p. 201. Survey, chap. tower.

weight

A. Mr. Cuff had three varieties of this pattern No. 10. ... HIBNE star under bust; HIBNE ... small pellets under bust; HIBNE without either star or pellets.

weight are ſuppoſed to have been intended for three-penny, five-penny, or ſix-penny pieces, as well as groats; but we think they were deſign'd only for groats, altho' impreſs'd on pieces of different weights, however that be the Coin now before us, upon the firſt ſuppoſition, claims that name; as it weighs 88 Troy grains, and its true weight, if coin'd before his 28th year, was 90, but if after his 28th year it was 88$\frac{8}{9}$ Troy grains. EDWARD I. EDW. II. 1307.

The money of theſe two kings very common, if we except the pennies of Hadeleie, Exonie, Ceſtrie, and Kyngeſton, which are very ſcarce (*o*,) the farthing, and halfpenny not ſo often found as the penny, but the groat is one of the rareſt Coins in the Engliſh ſeries. RARITY.

The money of Edward I. before his 28th year, weigh as all the former, that is the penny 22$\frac{1}{2}$, the halfpenny 11$\frac{1}{4}$, and the farthing 5$\frac{5}{8}$ Troy grains, but afterwards 22$\frac{2}{9}$, 11$\frac{1}{9}$, 5$\frac{5}{9}$ Troy grains. WEIGHT.

In the 28th of Edward I. an indented trial piece of the fineneſs of 11 oz. 2 dwt. of fine ſilver, and 18 dwt. of alloy, was lodged in the exchequer, and FINENESS.

(*o*) The pennies in the following liſt were all found together, under a barn floor, near Newbury in Berkſhire, in the year 1756, and afterwards came into our hands, and are here ſubjoined, as a ſupport to what has been ſaid above, in relation to the plenty of ſome ſorts and ſcarcity of others; being 3520 in number, weighing 155 oz. 15 dwts. or about 21$\frac{1}{4}$ Troy grains each penny at a medium.

Berewici	37	Eboraci	58	Lincol.	76	Iriſh	35
Briſtolie	85	Exonie	5	London	1660	Scotch	28
Cantor	1017	Hadeleie	6	Novicaſtri	32	Foreign	51
Ceſtrie	3	Kyngeſton	10	Sciedmundi	128	Obliterated	31
Dureme	317						

The Engliſh and Iriſh were all of Edward I. and Edward II. the Scotch were moſtly of Alexander III. and a few of John Baliol; and the foreigners all of them imitations of the type of the Engliſh ſterling; that they might by that means paſs undiſtinguiſhed amongſt them, they being a famous and well known coin †, four of which we have cauſed to be engraven, viz. (A. B. C. D.) of which (A. B.) were coined by the ſame LORD, and at the ſame place, viz. SERAIN, (C) was minted at Aloſt in Flanders, and (D.) at Mons in Hainault. The head ſide of (B.) is like that of the Iriſh Edward, and that of (C.) like the Scotch Alexander III. the money of both thoſe nations running then current with the Engliſh ‡. The legend on the head ſide of (D.) is exactly like that on the Edwards (only AGNL. inſtead of ANGL.) but on the reverſe it has MONETA MONTES, and therefore we may ſuppoſe it one of thoſe counterfeit ſterlings prohibited to be imported at this time §. All the above are of good ſilver, but how much worſe than ſtandard we cannot determine; but more of theſe Coins hereafter.

We have never been ſo fortunate as to ſee any piece that could ſtrictly be called a Crokard, Pollard, Eagle, Lionine, Mitre, Roſary, Steping, or Stalding, of theſe times.

† Le Blanc, p. 166. ‡ Statute of great money. § Stat. of ſmall money, 20 E. I.

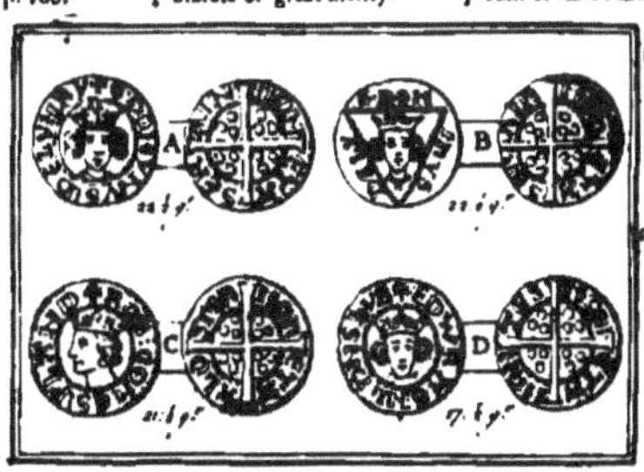

EDWARD I. EDW. II. was, at that time, called the OLD STANDARD, or that of the OLD STERLINGS *.

VALUE. In the 28th of Edward I. the Tale Pound, or Pound Sterling, first began to differ or come short of the Pound weight Tower, from which it drew its origine; and to which until now it was equal, for by indenture of that year the pound weight was to contain twenty shillings and three-pence in Tale, that is $1\frac{1}{80}$ pounds sterling, by which means the pound sterling was reduced to $\frac{80}{81}$ of a pound weight, or to 11 oz. $17\frac{1}{27}$ dwt. Tower.

The pound weight being thus nominally increas'd $\frac{1}{80}$, and the pound sterling as much debas'd, or $1\frac{1}{4}$ per cent. *(p)*

EDW. III. 1326. HEADSIDE. Type. The type of the farthing, halfpenny, and penny of this king, are the same as those of his father and grandfather, that of the half groat and groat have the same head, within a compartment, not of four arches and plain, like Edward I. but of nine arches, and the angles fleury; they continued to be coin'd thus till the 18th of Henry VII. as we observed before under Edward I. in relation to the penny.

Legend. The farthing and halfpenny read EDWARDUS REX, and some have also A. AN. ANG. the penny, in common, EDWARDUS REX ANGLI, or ANGLIE, but we have them also with EDWARD DI GRA. REX ANG. EDWARD ANG. REX DNS. HYB. and EDWAR REX ANG. DNS. HYB. the half groat has EDWARDUS REX ANGLI DNS. HYB. or EDWARDUS REX ANGLI Z FRACI, or FRANCI, the groat EDWARD DEI. G. REX ANGL. DNS. HYB. Z AQT. or EDWARD D. G. REX ANGL. Z FRANCIE, there are some also with DI. GRA. and others have A, AT. the half groat and groat, with the titles of HYB. Z AQT. were coined before 1360, or after 1369, and those with that of FRANCIE between those two years †.

REVERSE. Type. The impress on the reverse of the money of this king, is the same as upon those of the two first Edwards, one of the Durham pennies has the top of the cross turn'd like a crozier, to the left, and we meet with the same also on another of the same mint of Edward I. but it is there turn'd to the right, both it is probable were of the bishops mint, and thus distinguished from those of the kings at the same place.

Legend. The places of mintage are but few on the Coins of this king, being only CALESIE, DUREME, EBORACI, LONDON. A remarkable penny of the second reads DUREMMIE, and has VILLA instead of CIVITAS; another reads DUNELMIE: And we think it worth remarking, that during this long reign we have no money coined at Canterbury, no more than in the next, and only a few half groats of the 4th, 5th, and 6th Henrys.

The inscription chosen for the exterior circle of the half groat and groat was

(p) These alterations are called RAISING OF THE COIN, or RAISING OF THE VALUE OF THE COIN, but in reality the quite contrary effect is produced from them. Value in Coin arises from the quantity of fine metal it contains, (as in the case before us of fine silver) and increasing of this quantity does, at the same time, raise the value of it, but these alterations have continually lessen'd this quantity, therefore its value has continually been diminished with it, instead of increased, as in the above example by $\frac{1}{81}$.

It is also called RAISING THE VALUE OF THE SILVER IN THE COIN; but this is not the case neither, it should be termed RAISING THE DENOMINATION OF THE SILVER IN THE COIN; as in the case above, the same quantity, that is, the pound weight is raised $\frac{1}{80}$ or from 240 10 243 pennies; but remains of the same value as before.

* Lowndes, p. 34. Folkes, p. 5. † Leake, p. 98. Folkes, p. 12. 157.

POSUI

POSUI DEUM ADJUTOREM MEUM, ſome of the half groats want the laſt word, and ſome have only ME. and this inſcription is found on them in every reign afterwards, till James I. or for near three centuries. EDW. III.

MintMarks. There are a croſs patee, a coronet, a bell, and an halfpenny with a ſmall ſtar.

SORTS. The farthing, No. 11. (*q*), halfpenny, No. 12. penny, No. 13. and after this 27th year the half groat, No. 14. and groat, No. 15. (*r*). There is none but the penny of Durham, the half groat and groat of Calais, of York all but the farthing, and of London all.

RARITY. The money of this king common, however the farthing and halfpenny ſomething ſcarcer than the others, but the half groat and groat of Calais are very rare.

WEIGHT. Before his 18th year the farthing weighed 5$\frac{1}{8}$, the halfpenny 11$\frac{1}{4}$, the penny 22$\frac{1}{2}$ Troy grains, from the 18th to the 20th year they were 5$\frac{1}{13}$, 10$\frac{2}{13}$, and 20$\frac{4}{13}$ Troy grains, from the 20th (*s*) to the 27th year they were 5, 10, and 20 Troy grains, and after his 27th year they were 4$\frac{1}{2}$, 9 and 18, and the half groat and groat 36 and 72 Troy grains.

FINENESS. Standard, or 11 oz. 2 pennyweights fine ſilver, and 18 pennyweights alloy.

VALUE. In his 18th year the pound weight Tower, of ſtandard ſilver, was to contain 22 ſhillings and two-pence in Tale ‡‡, or 1$\frac{13}{120}$ pound Sterling; therefore the pound Sterling reduced to $\frac{120}{133}$ of a pound weight, or 10 oz. 16$\frac{72}{133}$ dwt. Tower.

Which raiſed the pound weight nominally near $\frac{1}{10}$, and debas'd the pound Sterling as much, or about 9$\frac{3}{4}$ per cent.

By indenture of his 20th year §§ the pound weight was to contain 22 ſhillings and ſix-pence in Tale, or 1$\frac{1}{8}$ pound Sterling, therefore the pound Sterling reduced to $\frac{8}{9}$ of a pound weight, or to 10 oz. 13 dwt. 8 grains Tower, which rais'd the pound weight nominally $\frac{2}{133}$, and debas'd the pound Sterling as much or 1$\frac{1}{2}$ per Cent.

(*q*) In his 18th year * the commons petition that the king's officers may receive the Coin of farthings, and that they might be of good Sterling and not utterly revoked, and in his 37th year they petition to have half the ſilver coin'd into halfpence and farthings, for the uſe of the poor; ‖ the only indentures that mention them are of the 23d and 30th years of his reign †.

(*r*) The firſt groſs, or groat, was coin'd at Tours, anno 1226 ‡, the next was that of Bohemia, anno 1290; and thoſe of Saxony and Miſnia about 1307 §, all of which paſſed on the footing of the ſol, or ſhilling, that is, 12 deniers or pfennings; but that of Edwards was current but for four pennies or $\frac{1}{3}$ of a ſhilling, notwithſtanding it was of more value than any of them, as it was about the 54th of the Tower Mark of fine ſilver, and that of Tours only the 61ſt of the Paris Mark, and the other two ‖ the 68th of the Cologne Mark of fine ſilver.

There has been none of the former coin'd ſince 1473, nor the term uſed, the preſent weiſs, or white groſs of Bohemia, reckon'd at $\frac{1}{2}$ of the Kayſer groſch ¶ is but the 480th of the Cologne Mark of fine ſilver, and that of Saxony, or the gute groſch only the 288th of the ſame Mark on the Leipſick foot. But our Sterling groat is ſtill the 124th of the Tower Mark of fine ſilver, or more than double the gute groſch, about treble the Kayſer groſch, and quadruple the Bohemian, and ſtill remains of the ſame fineneſs as at its firſt coinage four centuries ſince.

(*s*) In his 23d year the pound weight was ſhered into 9 pennies more in halfpence, and 11 pennies more in farthings than it was in ſingle pennies; that is, it was cut into 270 pennies, 558 halfpennies, and 1124 farthings, and it appears the maſter had theſe extra halfpence and farthings added to his allowance for workmanſhip **. But this is the only inſtance we have obſerved of this kind, as in all the other indentures, the number of halfpennies are juſt double the pennies, and thoſe of the farthings quadruple.

* Cotton's Abridg. p. 81. ‖ Ibid. p. 97. † Lowndes, p. 36, 37. ‡ Le Blanc, p. 2, 315. § Wagner's Nachricht vom groſch. p. 16, 32. ‖ Ibid. Ta. B. p. 31. ¶ Praun's Nachricht vom Muntz Weſen, p. 428. ** A briefe collection of alterations which have been made in the monies of this realm, ſince the time of king Edward I. MS. ‡‡ Ibid. Folkes, p. 11. §§ Lowndes, p. 36.

Again

Edw. III. Again, by indenture of his 27th ‖‖ year the pound weight was to contain 25 shillings in Tale, or $1\frac{1}{4}$ pound Sterling, and therefore the pound Sterling was now but $\frac{4}{5}$ of the pound weight or 9 oz. 12 dwts. Tower.

And here the pound weight was raised $\frac{1}{9}$, and the pound Sterling debas'd as much, or $11\frac{1}{9}$ per Cent. (*t*)

Rich. II. 1377. The head of this king on his coin no way to be distinguished from those of his four immediate predecessors.

Head Side. Type. Legend. The farthing reads Ricard. Rex Ang. the halfpenny have Ang. Anglie, the penny Ricardus Rex Anglie, the half groat Ricard. Di Gra. Rex Anglie, and the groat the same with z Francie.

Reverse. Type. Legend. The cross and pellets as before, with the usual legend, of the name of the place of mintage, which in this reign are but two, viz. Eboraci and London, and on the outward circle of the half groat and groat Posui Deum Adjutorem Meum.

Sorts. The farthing, No. 16. (*u*), halfpenny, No. 17. penny, No. 18. half groat, No. 19. and groat, No. 20.

Rarity. All this king's money is very rare, except the halfpenny, which is pretty common, and next to that the penny, but it is generally very much clipped.

Weight. The farthing $4\frac{1}{2}$ gr. the halfpenny 9 gr. the penny 18 gr. the half groat 36 gr. and the groat 72 grains Troy.

Fineness. Standard, or 11 oz. 2 pennyweights fine silver, and 18 pennyweights alloy.

The

(*t*) The first alteration in the money above, was in his 17th year, for in that same year it was afterwards enacted, that silver shall be coined according to the old Sterling, in poize and alloy, and to enable the king to do this, that is, to increase the goodness of money, (or make the penny heavier again) he was to have 40 shillings on each pack of wool, more than the old custom *, but for all this, in his 20th year, it was again debased; and although in his 25th year it is enacted, that the silver money, which then remained, should not only be unimpaired in weight and alloy, but as soon as possible be restor'd to its ancient estate, as in the Sterling; yet instead of this being done, in his 27th it is once more debas'd, and notwithstanding that the commons petition the same year, that the coin may be reduced to the old Sterling †; and the next year again, that the king would fix a time to make the money finer, ‡ (that is the pound Sterling, for the pound weight remain'd still 11 oz. 2 dwts.) yet both of them without effect, as it remain'd on that footing all the rest of his reign.

This king continued to provide against the bringing in of foreign money made in imitation of *English*, which is termed false money and counterfeit Sterling ‡, and another sort, called *Black-Money*, which had obtained a currency, was cry'd down §, and was probably the base money of *Flanders*, *Burgundy*, *Britany*, &c. which were strictly black, as being worse than the basest of our Henry VIII. ‖

Transportation of money and bullion was likewise forbid ¶, as also to melt the coin, *i. e.* halfpennies and farthings to make into plate **. For to help the want of money it was thought good that every merchant, for every sack of wool, should bring in 40 shillings in bullion to be stamped within the realm ††. It was also enacted, in his 14th year ‡‡, that two marks of silver should be brought to the king's exchange for every sack of wool, &c. that was exported, and the same again, or four nobles, in his 17th year §§; but in his 22d year the commons petition to have the act repealed, for that carrying away of bullion was forbidden in Flanders ¶¶.

(*u*) The commons petition in his 2d year *** that farthings and halfpence may be coined, and commandment given to sell according to the same, and in his 4th year that they may be coined according to the Sterleage (Sterling) †††.

‖‖ Lowndes, p. 36. * Cotton, p. 37, 38. † Ibid. p. 82. ‡ Ibid. p. 87. ‡ St. 9. E. III. cap. 2. 9. § Ibid. cap. 4. ‖ Du Fresne Gloss. tom. 2. p. 652. Le Blanc, p. 198. ¶ 9 E. III. cap. 9. 38 E. III. cap. 2. ** 9 E. III. cap. 3. †† Cotton, 13 E. III. p. 18. ‡‡ Cap. 21. §§ Cotton's Abridg. p. 37. ¶¶ Ibid. p. 70. *** Ibid. p. 171. ††† Ibid. p. 192.

The pound weight Tower $1\frac{1}{4}$ pound Sterling, and the pound Sterling $\frac{4}{5}$ of a pound weight Tower, or 9 oz. 12 dwts. Tower (*w*). VALUE.

The money coined by Henry IV. before his 13th year, and that coined by Henry VI. after his 49th year, are by the balance placed to their right owners; but that of the former, coined after his 13th year, and of the latter before his 49th, are blended with those of Henry V. being of the same weight, type and legend, and not having any number after the names are not to be distinguished from each other, the usual distinction, of those with the annulets or eylet holes on each side the head to Henry V. being by no means satisfactory ||||. HENRY IV. 1399. A. HENRY V. 1413. B. HENRY VI. 1425.

The type of these three kings the same full face as those of the four preceding ones, some of which have the eylet hole on each side the head, others a fleur-de-lis, and a third sort have three pellets. HEAD SIDE. Type.

The two farthings, No. 30, 31. both read different, as H. D. G. ANG. z FRANSIE REX, and HENRIC. DI GRA. REX AN[illegible] the halfpennies, No. 2[illegible]. 22. both HENRIC. REX AN[illegible] the pennies in common HENRICUS REX ANGLI. or ANGLIE, and also some HENRIC. but we have one with HENRIC. DI GRA. REX ANG. and another HENRIC. REX ANG. z FRANC. both of the YORK mint. The half groat HENRIC. DI GRA. REX ANG. z F. or FRA. and the groat HENRIC. DI GRA. REX ANGLIE z FRANC. some have ANGLI. Legend.

The cross and pellets, as in the four preceding reigns, a small annulet joins the three pellets in the second and third quarters of the cross on No. 26, 27, 28, and 29. there is an M on the center of No. 23. and on No. 3[illegible] a rose, which is common to all those of the York mint since Edward I. there being some of that king's with and some without it. REVERSE. Type.

These three kings minted only in the following towns, CALESIE, CANTOR. DUREME, EBORACI, LONDON, we have never seen either DONWIC or BRISTOL, the exterior circle have as usual, POSUI DEUM ADJUTOREM MEUM. Legend.

We have observed only the rose on No. 33. and the fleur-de-lis on No. 3[illegible] and a few different crosses. Mint Marks.

The farthing, No. 21. the halfpenny, No. 22. 26. 30. 31. the penny, No. 23. 27. 32. the half groat, No. 24. 28. 33. and the groat, No. 25. 29. 34. SORTS.

The mult of the pennies of these three kings seem to have been coined at York, in the Archbishop's mint, and have generally some Signature on each side of the head, as a rose, cross, star, annulet, three pellets, C, Key, and a pellet;

(*w*) Altho' the Coin received no alteration in its value in this reign, yet we find proposals were made in his 9th year * to raise it, to prevent its being transported.

No foreign coins, nor those of Scotland, to be current, which last had continued on the same footing with the English till 45 E. III. when the commons petition that all Scotch monies might be brought into the exchequer by a day †; and in his 47th year ‡ they were to pass but for $\frac{3}{4}$ of the English, in the 14 R. II. § they were reduced to $\frac{1}{2}$ the English, and in his 17th year || entirely forbidden.

No money was to be exported ¶, nor half groat or groat to be melted **.

It was enacted that every merchant should bring an ounce of gold †† into the Tower of London, for every sack of wool, &c. but they require to have this act repealed, as the Duke of Burgundy had forbid the carrying of bullion out of Flanders ‡‡; however, in the 1 H. IV. we find it was to be brought to Calice §§.

* Cotton, p. 309. † Ibid. p. 114. ‡ St. 47. E. III. cap. 2. § St. 14. R. II. cap. 12. || St. 17. R. II. cap. 1. ¶ 5 R. II. cap. 2. ** 17 R. II. chap. 1. †† Cotton, 20 R. II. p. 362. ‡‡ Ibid, 21 R. II p. 375. §§ Ibid. p. 393. |||| Archbishop Sharpe, Sect. 6. Nicholson, p. 387. Thoresby, p. 357. Leake, p. 139. Folkes, p. 13.

F being

A. The heavy groat of H. IV is not known: Mr Martin of [illegible] has the heavy halfgroat wt. 33 grs which has evidently lost 3 grs by circulation [illegible] !!! –

B. The annulets are no proof of the coins belonging to H. V. as Mr Cuff has two halfgroats with these marks, weighing respectively 31 and 28 grs. the latter must therefore belong to H IV.

HENRY IV. HENRY V. HENRY VI. being in general sadly defaced and horribly clipped, much more than either those of London, Calais, or Durham: The groats are mostly of London and Calais, there being very few of York, there are no other but half groats of Cantor, and pennies of Durham.

RARITY. The groat and half groat are very common, excepting the light groat, No. 34. of Henry VI. which is scarce, and the heavy groat of Henry IV. which is extremely rare; a fair and round penny, either of London or Eboraci are far from being common, any more than the farthing (*x*), but there are many halfpennies.

WEIGHT. Those of Henry IV. before his 13th year, the farthing weighs 4½ gr. the halfpenny 9 gr. the penny 18 gr. the halfpenny 36 gr. and the groat 72 gr. Troy; between that and the 49 H. VI. which are those we have in common, they weigh 3¾ gr. 7½ gr. 15 gr. 30 gr. and 60 grains Troy; those of 49 H. VI. are 3 gr. 6 gr. 12 gr. 24 gr. and 48 Troy grains.

FINENESS. Standard, or 11 oz. 2 pennyweights fine silver, and 18 pennyweights alloy.

VALUE. By an act of 13 Henry IV. (*y*) the pound weight of Standard silver was to contain thirty shillings in Tale, or 1½ pound Sterling, therefore the pound Sterling reduced to ⅔ of a pound weight, or 8 oz. Tower.

By which the pound weight was nominally raised ⅕, and the pound Sterling debased in the same proportion, or 20 per Cent.

(*x*) The provision made by St. 2 H. IV. against the currency of foreign money, had no effect for want of a sufficient quantity of small English, and we find that two years afterwards the commons pray an ordinance to remedy the want of halfpence and farthings *, and by St. 4. H. IV. cap. 10. of that same year, one third of the bullion brought into the mint was to be coined into halfpence and farthings in equal quantities. But in the 1 H. VI. there was but ⅓ of the bullion coined into halfpence and farthings, that is, ¼ into halfpence or mailes, and 1/12 into farthings or ferlings, of the remainder ½ were to be pennies or easterlings, ¼ half groats, and ¼ groats. † In 23 H. VI. was an act ‡ for coining and making current halfpence and farthings to continue for two years.

(*y*) It is enacted that the mint-master within the Tower of London, and all other minters, by the king's grant may, during two years, of every pound Tower of silver, coin 30 shillings Sterlings, so as the silver be of as good alloy as the old coin was ‖.

The St. 2. H. VI. cap. 6. forbids the bringing in or currency of foreign money, as those of Flanders and Scotland; and the commons in 8 H. IV. petition that those who brought Scotch money or Galley halfpence into the realm, might incur the loss of life §; and in his 11th and 13th years they were utterly forbidden. Yet for all this, the St. 2. H. V. cap. 1. again provides against their currency, and with them also are joined Suskins and Dodkins, the first of which was certainly the Flemish Seskin or piece of six mites, and the other the Holland Duitkin or Doitkin of two penningens. The last foreigner we find mentioned is the Blanc in 2 H. VI. said by Nicholson to be that coined by his father in France.

Transporting of coin or bullion is forbid by St. 2. H. IV. cap. 5. 4 H. IV. cap. 16. and 2 H. VI. cap. 6. and the melting of it is provided against by St. 4. H. IV. cap. 10.

By St. 8. H. V. cap. 2. merchant aliens had liberty to carry wool to any other place, besides the staple, upon paying the master of the mint in the Tower 1 oz. of gold bullion, or its value in silver (which was about two marks as before) for every sack ¶. And by St. 8. H. VI. cap. 18. ** there was to be brought to the mint in Calais, for every sack of wool of the price of twelve marks, ten pounds, of ten marks, five pounds, and of eight marks, four pounds, to be forged in the king's coin, which was just ¾ of the value of each, and much more than by any act before, and is no doubt the reason of the plenty of the Henries Calais money found at this time.

The price of uncoined silver being 32 shillings the pound Troy, or one shilling above the mint price, occasion'd a great scarcity of white money, therefore an act was made †† to restrain the price to 30 shillings, or one shilling under the mint price, the difference being 1/31 or about 3¼ per cent. but at present the price of bullion is about ⅛ above the mint price, or 12½ per cent.

* Parl. Rolls, 4 H. IV. Leake, p. 128. † Clause 1. H. VI. M. 1. Leake, p. 148. ‡ Cotton, p. 631. ‖ Cotton, 13 H. IV. p. 481. Leake, p. 130. § Cotton, p. 461. ¶ Rastal, vol. 1. p. 214. ** Ibid. p. 235. †† Rastal, 2 H. VI. cap. 13. vol. 1. p. 222.

The

The head of this king as before on all the pieces, but on some accompanied with an annulet on each side, on others with a rose, on others with four pellets, some have a rose on the breast, and those of the country mints the initial of the town where coined on the same place. EDWA. IV. 1460. HEAD SIDE. Type.

The halfpenny generally reads EDWARD. DEI GRA. REX, and the penny EDWARD. DI GRA. REX ANG. the half groat EDWARD. DI GRA. REX ANG. z FRA. and the groat EDWARD DI GRA. REX ANG. z FRANC. sometimes DEI. Legend.

The reverse of this king as before, the cross and pellets. REVERSE. Type.

There are more towns in which this king coined than any since Edward II. as BRISTOL, CANTOR, COVETRE, DUREME, EBORACI, LONDON, NORWIC, the third town now first makes its appearance on an English Coin, the last had been on none since Henry II. the exterior circle POSUI DEUM ADJUTOREM MEUM, sometimes the first is spelt Bristol, Bristow, and the last Norwic. Legend.

There are more privy, or mint marks, of this king than any before him, as rose, cinquefoil, sun or star, crown, single annulet, pellet and annulet, besides the cross with some variety. Mint Marks.

The farthing, No. 35. the halfpenny, No. 36. the penny, No. 37. the half groat, No. 38. and the groat, No. 39. the pennies, like those of the Henries, are generally of the York mint, badly preserved and most sadly clipt; having signatures on them as those have, as a G. or T. on one side the head, and a key on the other; those of the Durham mint appear likewise to be of the bishops, some having a B. others a D. and V. by the side of the head; also a D. on the center of the cross in the reverse, and some have a rose in the same place. SORTS.

The groats of this king very common, if we except those of Norwic and Covetre, and the heavy one before his fourth year, which are very scarce; the half groats are none of them common, and a fair round legible penny a great curiosity, as is also the farthing. RARITY.

Until his 4th year the farthing weighed 3¾ gr. the halfpenny 7½ gr. the penny 15 gr. the half groat 30 gr. the groat 60 Troygrains, after his 4th year they weighed 3 gr. 6 gr. 12 gr. 24 gr. and 48 grains Troy. WEIGHT.

Standard, or 11 oz. 2 pennyweights fine silver, and 18 pennyweights alloy. FINENESS.

By indenture of his 4th year *, the pound weight of Standard silver to contain 37 shillings and six-pence, or 1⅞ pound sterling, therefore the pound sterling reduced to $\frac{8}{15}$ of a pound weight, or 6 oz. 8 dwt. Tower. VALUE.

By which the pound weight was nominally rais'd ¼, and the pound sterling debas'd as much, or 25 per cent. (z)

The head on the money of this king the same as before, that is, still the full face. RICHA. III. 1483. HEAD SIDE. Type.

The halfpenny has RICARD. DI GRA. REX, the penny RICARDUS REX ANGLI, the half groat RICARD. DI GRA. REX ANGL. z FRA. and the groat RICARD. DI GRA. REX ANG. z FRANC. Legend.

The reverse still as before, the cross and pellets. REVERSE. Type.

There are but three towns in which this king had mints, that is, DUNOLM, Legend.

(z) By St. 17. E. IV. cap. 1. no Irish money to be current, and in the said act provision is made against transporting and melting the Coin. And by St. 3. E. IV. cap. 1. Every merchant of the staple was obliged, in the sale of his staple wares to receive half the value in English coin, bullion, or plate, and to have the two latter immediately coin'd in the mint of Calais.

* Lowndes, p. 40.

EBORACI,

RICH. III. EBORACI, and LONDON, and there are only the penny of the first, and groat of the second, and on the exterior circle POSUI DEUM ADJUTOREM MEUM.

Mint Marks. The mint marks are but two, that is, the rose and the boar's head.

SORTS. The farthing, the halfpenny, No. 40. the penny, No. 41. the half groat, No. 42. and the groat, No. 43.*

RARITY. All the Coins of this king's are very rare, but especially the farthing, halfpenny, penny, and half groat.

WEIGHT. The farthing weighs 3 gr. the halfpenny 6 gr. the penny 12 gr. the half groat 24 gr. and the groat 48 grains Troy.

FINENESS. Standard, or 11 oz. 2 pennyweights fine silver, and 18 pennyweights alloy.

VALUE. The pound weight Tower of Standard Silver contained $1\frac{7}{8}$ pounds Sterling, and the pound Sterling contained $\frac{8}{15}$ of a pound weight, or 6 oz. 8 dwt. as the latter Coinage of Edward IV.

HENRY VII. 1485. 1st Coinage. HEAD SIDE. Type. The money coined by this king before he changed the type of it, in his 18th year, differs from that of the three last Henries, in the crown having an arch on it, instead of being open, which peculiar type has heretofore been assign'd to Henry VI. * but as these, by their weight, are confined to those coined by him in his 49th year, the number of them still remaining, will not admit of their being coined during that short-liv'd restoration.

Some of the half groats have a key on each side of the head at bottom, and another, No. 45. is likewise without the compartment.

Legend. The halfpenny reads H. D. G. REX ANGLIE z FR. or HENRIC. DI GRA. REX A. the half groat HENRIC. DI GRA. REX ANG. and the groat HENRIC. DI GRA. REX AGL. z FR. some have ANGL. † ANGLI. as also FRA. FRAN. FRANCI. the farthing is obliterated, nor did we know any cabinet that had a perfect one.

REVERSE. Type. The reverse differs in nothing from the preceding ones, having still the cross and pellets, only No. 47. has a sort of lozenge on the center of the cross.

Legend. There are but three towns to be found on the money of this king, CANTOR. EBORACI, LONDON. and on the exterior circle POSUI DEUM ADJUTORE MEUM, some have DEU ADJUTOE MEU.

Mint Marks. The privy marks on the groats are an anchor, cinquefoil, cross croslet, double fleur-de-lis, escallop-shell, hounds-head, and leopards-face, all of the London mint, and on the half groats of the same mint only a fleur-de-lis and ton; and on the half groats of Cantor. and Eboraci a Martlet and Ton.

SORTS. Of this type are only found the farthing, No. 43. the halfpenny, No. 44. the half groat, No. 45. 46. and the groat, No. 47. having never heard of or seen the penny.

RARITY. All the sorts of this coinage are common, except the farthing, which is very rare.

2d Coinage. HEAD SIDE. Type. In the 18th year of this king, the old familiar type of the full face, which had been so long exhibited on our silver money was laid aside, for that of the profile face turned to the left; on the half groat and groat of the old sorts, and on that of the shilling now first coined; the penny had the king setting in a chair or throne, having the scepter in his right hand, and the orb in his left, which was borrowed no doubt from the gold sovereign; but the halfpenny still retained the full face.

* Selden's Titles of Honour, p. 135. Archbishop Sharpe, sect. 6. Nicholson, p. 298. Thoresby, p. 357. No. 217. Leake, p. 154. † See Archbishop Sharpe, sect. 5. in relation to the want of the N in this word.

The

A

Full Fac'd Coins from EDWARD the First to HENRY the Seventh.

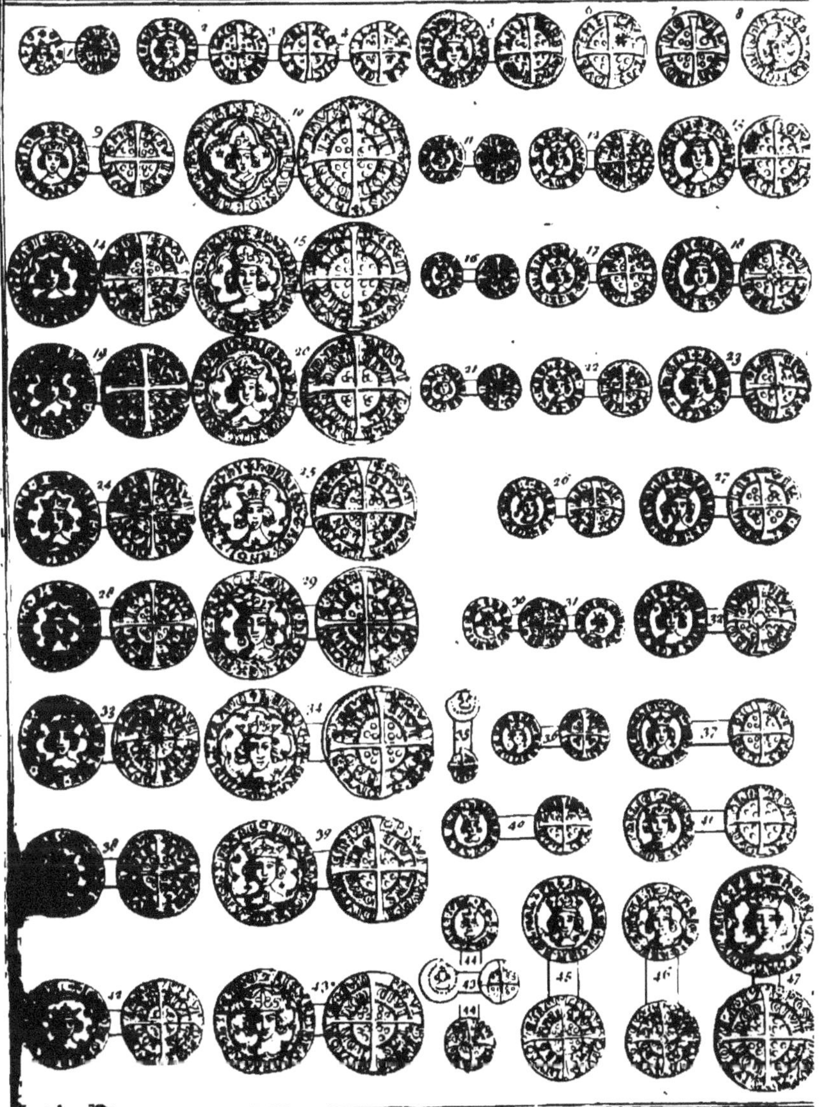

The penny has HENRIC. DI GRA. REX A. AL. or AGL. the half groat reads HENRIC. VII. DI GRA. REX AGL. z, some have AL. the groat HENRIC. VII. DI GRA. REX AGL. z F. sometimes ANG. FR. these are the first English Coins which have the number after the name; the shilling is inscribed in three different manners, as HENRIC. DI GRA. REX ANGLIE z FR. HENRIC. VII. DI GRA. REX ANG. z FR. and HENRIC. SEPTIM. DI GRA. REX ANGL. z FR. Legend. A

The type of the reverse was changed at the same time as that of the head, the three pellets so well known on our money, was taken away, and with them also the letter'd circle, that immediately enclosed it, and in their stead the royal shield, with the quarter'd arms of France and England, was put on the same cross. The reverse of the halfpenny still shewed the cross and pellets, for very near a century. REVERSE. Type.

The halfpenny and penny still have the place of mintage on them, which are only three, that is, DIRHAM, EBORACI, LONDON, the pennies of the first of which places have T. D, D. S, D. R, or some other letters on each side of the arms, and No. 3. has a miter over the arms on the top of the cross, which cross on No. 2. is also turned like a crozier, and a crozier likewise appears on the left arm of the chair on the other side, those of Eboraci have only the keys at the bottom of the shield. Legend.

The half groat, groat, and shilling, have only the outward circle left, with its old inscription, POSUI DEUM ADJUTOREM MEUM.

The fleur-de-lis we conceive to be the first used in this Coinage, and is found on all the pieces, from the halfpenny to the shilling, as on No. 4. 5. 6. 7. 8. but the pheon is only on the half groat and groat, and the cross croslet and hounds-head only on the groat. Mint Marks.

The half groat of the two Archbishops mints of Canterbury and York, have the martlet and cinquefoil.

The farthing, (see No. 33. pl. 2.) the halfpenny, No. 4. the penny, No. 1, 2, 3, 5. the half groat, No. 6. the groat, No. 7. and the shilling (*a*), No. 8. this last sort now first coined, and of them but very few. SORTS.

All the pieces of this Coinage are very common, except the shilling, which is one of the rarest Coins in the English series, the groats with the fleur-de-lis and the hounds-head not so common as the others. RARITY.

Both Coinages weigh the same, that is, the farthing 3 gr. the halfpenny 6 gr. the penny 12 gr. the half groat 24 gr. the groat 48 gr. and the shilling 144 grains Troy. WEIGHT.

Standard, or 11 oz. 2 pennyweights fine silver, and 18 pennyweights alloy. FINENESS.

The pound weight Tower of Standard silver contained 1⅞ pounds Sterling, VALUE.

(*a*) The shilling had hitherto been only a money of accompt, or an aggregate of pennies, and that ever since the conquest, but never till now an effective Coin; and was now struck at something more than [illegible] half its original value, or 1/40 of a pound weight Tower of Standard silver; at present there are 58⅛ of them in the said pound, or it is still more than ⅔ of its original value.

The first piece of money coined under this name was that of Hamburgh, anno 1407,* or near 100 years before that of Henry VII. at about 1/60 of the Cologne fine Mark, or a trifle more than three-pence Sterling, but when ours began to be coined it contained no more than about the 205th part of the said fine Mark †, or about 1½ Sterling, and ever since the year 1728, it has been the 576th of the said fine Mark, or not quite the penny Sterling; that of Denmark is about ⅓ of that of Hamburgh, that of Prussia about ¾ of a farthing Sterling, and that of Poland ½. The Bern shilling is about three farthings, and those of Lucern and Zurich about one halfpenny Sterling. Those of Holland and Flanders approach the nearest to the English of any, being something more than half of it.

* Rademan's Wechsel Baum, p. 100. Ibid. p. 101. † Laverentzen's Museum Regium, B'13.

A. The B.M. has a groat ending Septim; and also one without the numerals or Septim, type of the Shilling Reading p. 20. both are unique !!!

HENRY VII. and the pound Sterling weighed $\frac{1}{15}$ of a pound weight, or 6 oz. 8 dwt. Tower (*b*).

HEN. VIII. 1509. 1st Coinage. HEAD SIDE. Type. Legend.

The money coined by Henry VIII. before his 18th year, are no other way diſtinguiſhed from thoſe of his father, than by having VIII. after the name inſtead of VII. the head being the ſame in both; we ſhall therefore refer to that Coinage both for deſcription and inſcription. We muſt however except the Tournay groat, which has no number after the name, and reads HENRIC. DI GRA. REX FRANC. Z ANGLIE.

REVERSE. Type. The type of the reverſe the ſame as the laſt Coinage of his fathers.

Legend. The legend of the half groats of that Coinge, had none of them the name of the place of mintage, only POSUI, &c. like the groat; but here we have them both ways, ſome of Archbiſhop Warham, and that of Bainbrigge, have POSUI, &c. but others of Cranmer, and thoſe of Wolſey, have CIVITAS, CANTOR. and CIVITAS, EBORACI, with the initials X. B, W. A. and T. W. on the ſide of the ſhield, and on the latter the Cardinal's hat at bottom, and his penny the ſame. The Tournay groat has likewiſe the name of the place where coined, viz. CIVITAS TORNACEN, and is the firſt groat we meet with thus inſcribed, of thoſe with the ſingle legendary circle.

MintMarks. We think he firſt coined with the pheon, uſed by his father, and continued it without any other alteration than the VII. made into an VIII. and we have only the groat with this mint mark, nor of that with a caſtle, but of the portcullis we have all from the groat to the halfpenny; the half groats of Cantor and Eboraci have a martlet, a bird's-head, long-croſs, eſcallop-ſhell and flower.

SORTS. The farthing, (ſee No. 43. pl. 2. as it is not known from his father's.) The halfpenny, No. 9. the penny, No. 10. the half groat, No. 11. and the groat, No. 12, 13. (*c*)

The farthing and halfpenny not being eaſily diſtinguiſh'd from each other, therefore the St. 14 and 15 H. VIII. cap. 12. enacts, that the farthing ſhould have on one ſide a portcloſe, and on the other a croſs with a roſe †; but no farthing, with this type, is at preſent to be found in any cabinet that we know of, they are of Standard ſilver, and weigh but three grains Troy, but few could have been coined, as the ſtatute directs only $\frac{1}{10}$ of any quantity of bullion brought to the mint, was to be coined into farthings, and $\frac{1}{15}$ into halfpence, but half of it was to be in pennies, $\frac{1}{6}$ in half groats, and $\frac{1}{6}$ in groats.

RARITY. The groats of this Coinage very common, except that of Tournay, No. 13. and that with the pheon, which are very ſcarce; the half groats not near ſo common as the groats, but that of Archbiſhop Bainbrigge, No. 17, and that of

(*b*) This king permitted foreign money to be current, and by St. 4. H. 7. cap. 8. it is made treaſon to counterfeit any ſuch.

Tranſporting of money, plate, or bullion is forbid by cap. 23. of the ſame ſtatute, as it is alſo to pay either of them, to any merchant ſtranger for their wares.

Refiners are forbid alſo by cap. 2. of the ſame Statute, to alay, or ſell any alayed gold or ſilver, none but ſilver that was at leaſt 6 dwt. better than Standard, and that only to the officers of his majeſty's mints, changes and goldſmiths.

(*c*) Two very ſingular groats, appearing to us intended only as for patterns, but never current, we have here omitted, as we propoſe to exhibit them altogether in a future work. There is alſo a third piece of this king, which if a pattern for a coin, muſt have been for a four ſhilling piece *, but we are rather inclined to think it a medal, for in this king's time the firſt Engliſh medals make their appearance.

* Folkes, p. 26. † Ibid. p. 23.

Car-

Cardinal Wolsey with T. W. No. 19. are also very rare; to which we may add also his penny of this Coinage, No. 18. HEN. VIII.

WEIGHT. The farthing weighs 3 gr. the halfpenny 6 gr. the penny 12 gr. the half groat 24 gr. and the groat 48 grains Troy.

FINENESS. Standard, or 11 oz. 2 pennyweights fine silver, and 18 pennyweights alloy.

VALUE. The pound weight Tower contained $1\frac{7}{8}$ pound Sterling, and the pound Sterling only $\frac{8}{15}$ of a pound weight Tower.

18th Year. HEAD SIDE. Type. This Coinage has his face in profile to the left, as before, but a new dye, and younger, generally called by collectors, his own face, to distinguish it from the former Coinage; and it must be remembred that this relates only to the half groat and groat, the other sorts remaining as before, only the halfpenny has the initials of the Archbishops who coined them, as W. A. T. C. and E. L. on the side of the head.

Legend. The halfpenny and penny read H. D. G. ROSA, SINE SPINA, some also SIE SPI, they are said to be known * by this from the former Coinage, and from Henry VII. but No. 33. overthrows this observation, as it reads HENRIC. DI GRA. REX AGL. and yet is undoubtedly of this Coinage, as Cranmer was not made Archbishop until 1533.

The half groat is inscribed HENRIC. VIII. D. G. R. AGL. z F. and the groat HENRIC. VIII. D. G. R. AGLIE. z FRANCE, we have them also with DI GR. GRA. REX. AGL. FR. FRA. FRAN. FRANC.

REVERSE. Type. Legend. There is no difference in the type of the reverse from that of the former, only in the initials of the Archbishops, which besides the W. A. and T. W. as on the last, there are also T. C, L. E, and E. L. on the half groats, also T. W. on the groat of Cardinal Wolsey, with CIVITAS EBORACI; the half groats of the Tower mint, and all the groats but that of Wolsey's, have POSUI DEU' ADJUTORE' MEU', some ADJUTOE'.

MintMarks. On the groats we have the rose, bolt, fleur-de-lis, cloud and pheon, all which it is probable were of the Tower mint, and we have all the pieces from the halfpenny to the groat with the three first, but only groats of the cloud and pheon, there is the greatest variety in those of the rose, in respect to the stops of the inscription, and in the inscription itself, from whence we may suppose it was longer used than any of the rest, there are three or four different ones on the half groats of W. A, T. C, and T. W. as the wheel, tau, star, cross, &c. but only one on that of L. E. viz. the key.

SORTS. The halfpenny, No. 21. the penny, No. 22. the half groat, No. 23. and the groat, No. 24. the must of the half groats are of Cantor. and Eboraci, and the pennies of Dirram either with T. W. or C. D.

RARITY. The pieces of this Coinage, which are not common, are the pheon groat with the Arabic 8, the half groats of the three London mint marks above, and the halfpennies with T. C, W. A, and E. L.

WEIGHT. The pound weight Tower (*d*), which had been the only one used in the English mints since the Conquest, was laid aside in the 18th year of this king's

(*d*) An anonymous author, who wrote in the year 1506, thus expresses himself in relation to the use of the pound Tower, "but I say, who wrote this book, that it is a right great untruth and deceit, that any such pound TOWERES should be occupied, for that thereby the merchant is deceived subtilly, and the mint master is thereby profited." †

* Thoresby, p. 361. Folkes, p. 18.

† A treatise declaring many notable instructions, very necessary and convenient to be had of all estates, especially to those which will be a master, or warden, or any other minister within the king's mint; and beginneth with the diversity of the pound Troy and pound Toweres, MS.

reign,

HEN. VIII. reign, and the pound Troy (*e*) was introduced in its ſtead, being heavier by one ſixteenth than the Tower pound.

WEIGHT. The halfpenny weighs $5\frac{1}{3}$ gr. the penny $10\frac{2}{3}$ gr. the half groat $21\frac{1}{3}$ gr. and the groat $42\frac{2}{3}$ grains Troy.

FINENESS. Standard, or 11 oz. 2 dwt. fine Silver, and 18 dwt. alloy.

VALUE. One pound weight Troy of Standard Silver was to contain 45 ſhillings in Tale **, or $2\frac{1}{4}$ pounds Sterling, which rais'd the ſaid pound weight Troy nominally $\frac{1}{8}$, for before the riſe there was but two pound Tale, or Sterling, to the pound weight Troy, and the pound Sterling was but half the pound weight, or but 6 oz. Troy; but now being leſſen'd $\frac{1}{9}$ it became but $\frac{4}{9}$ of it, or 5 oz. 6 dwt. 16 gr. Troy.

From the 4th of Edward IV. till this riſe, the pound weight Tower was equal to $1\frac{7}{8}$ pound Sterling, and the pound Sterling but $\frac{8}{15}$ of the pound weight Tower, but it is now rais'd to $2\frac{7}{64}$ pound Sterling, and the pound Sterling reduc'd to $\frac{64}{135}$ of the pound weight Tower, or 5 oz. 13 dwt. $18\frac{2}{3}$ grains.

Had the pound weight not been changed, and 45 ſhillings cut out of the pound Tower, the riſe would have been $\frac{1}{5}$ inſtead of $\frac{1}{8}$.

34th Year. HEAD SIDE. Type. The head in this Coinage is almoſt full-faced, but a little inclined to the left, and this alſo is confined to the groat and half groat, for the Teſtoon is full-faced.

Legend. The half groat is inſcribed HENRIC. 8. D. G. AGL. FR. z HB. REX, but the groat has FRA. z HIB. the Teſtoon HENRIC. VIII. DI GRA. AGL. FRA. z HIB. REX.

REVERSE. Type. The reverſe is no way different from the former on the half groat and groat, but in having an annulet, commonly called a gun-hole, at each end of the croſs, which alſo proves that No. 35. which has been ſuppos'd a penny of this Coinage, is not, however that may eaſily be determin'd by the goodneſs of the ſilver.

The type of the teſtoon is quite new in the ſilver Coinage, and ſeems borrow'd from that of the gold crown.

All three ſorts have the old inſcription of POSUI DEU' ADJUTORE' MEU', ſome have ADJUTOE', and the teſtoon has ADJUTORIUM MEUM.

Mint Marks. There is no other to this Coinage than the fleur-de-lis.

SORTS. The farthing, the halfpenny, the penny, the half groat, No. 36. the groat, No. 37. and the teſtoon *(f)*, or twelve-penny piece, No. 38.

The

(*e*) Charlemagne changed the Roman pound weight for another, call'd by Le Blanc * the GAULISH pound, but we could never find it had the appellation of TROY given to it, but its mark; which immediately ſucceeded it, always has; however, it appears highly probable that the Engliſh pound Troy is derived from this, altho' not uſed till long after that was laid aſide, and at its firſt being introduced here, the mark was of the ſame weight as the mark weight Troy or of Paris, and that of the Low Countries was the ſame. An old book concerning mint matters, in the time of Edward III. ſays, the Engliſh Troy mark was heavier than that of France and Flanders, by 2¼ dwt. † in the 14 E. IV. it was found heavier 1½ dwt. in the 22 H. VII. anno 1506, it was heavier by 3 dwt. ‡ and the ſame again in the 17th Eliz. 1575. § in the 30th Eliz. 1588, ‖ it being of the ſame weight as at this time, therefore it was then, as well as now ¶ 2⅛ dwt. heavier than that of Paris.

(f) Teſtoons were thus called, Le Blanc informs us, from the head of the king (Lewis XII.) being on them, but that they had their original in Italy, which makes Vittori very juſtly obſerve, that as they bear the heads of ſeveral Italian princes on them prior to that of Lewis XII. therefore they may more properly be ſaid to have received their name from them; ‡ the French adopted the term, they having as few

* p. 96. † Malyne's Lex Mercatoria, p. 2. cap. 8. ‡ A treatiſe declaring many notable inſtructions, &c. MS. § Sundry notes of weights and meaſures of England, by Tho. Langton, MS. ‖ Report from the committee appointed to enquire into the original ſtandard of weights and meaſures, p. 58. ¶ Philoſophical Tranſactions, No. 465. ‡ Il Fiorini D'Oro Antico Illuſtrato, p. 260. ** Grafton, p. 1128. Stowe, p. 526. Folkes, p. 20.

Coins of HENRY the Seventh and HENRY the Eighth.

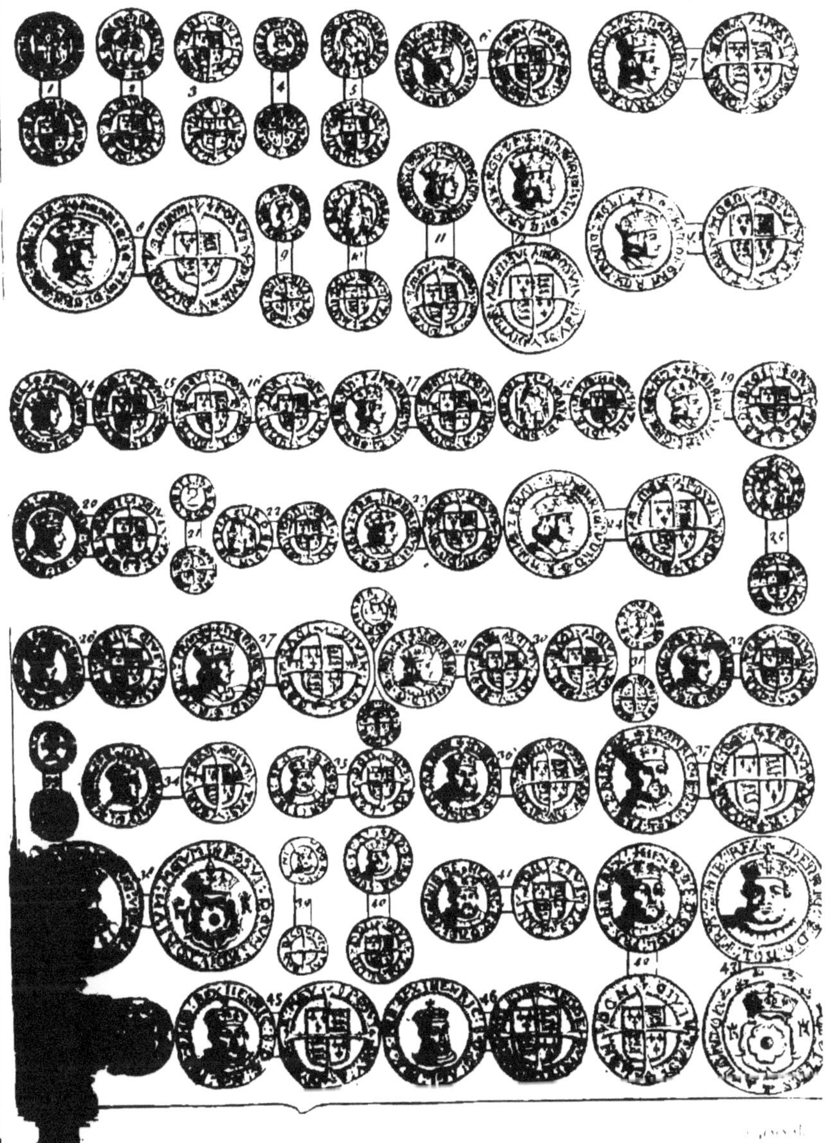

The half groat and testoon very scarce, the groat common, the farthing, halfpenny and penny we have never seen. RARITY.

The farthing weighs 2½ gr. the halfpenny 5 gr. the penny 10 gr. the half groat 20 gr. the groat 40 gr. and the testoon 120 grains Troy. WEIGHT.

Hitherto the pound Sterling had been lessen'd or debas'd seven different times from the Conquest *, which was always done by lessening the weight each time, and leaving the fineness or standard untouch'd; but now we find not only the weight, but also the standard is altered from 11 1/10 oz. fine, and 9/10 oz. alloy, to 10 oz. fine and 2 oz. alloy: or a debasement of near 10 per cent. FINENESS.

By indenture † the pound weight Troy of silver 10 oz. fine was to contain 48 shillings in Tale, therefore the same pound weight of Standard, or of 11 1/10 oz. contains 53 7/25, which if 53 3/11 or 53 1/3 makes 2 2/3 pound Sterling in one pound Troy, and the pound Sterling now but 3/8 of the pound weight Troy, or 4 oz. 10 dwt. which was an advance of 17 1/3 per cent. VALUE.

By this means the pound weight Tower became nominally 2½ pound Sterling, and the pound Sterling no more than 2/5 of the pound weight, or 4 oz. 16 dwt. Tower.

36th and 37th year. Type. The type of these two Coinages the same as the last, but with more variety in the head, the halfpenny, penny, and testoon are full-faced, the reverse as before.

Legend. There are upon some of the half groats and groats POSUI, &c. as in the last Coinage, and these we suspect if not all, yet the greater part of them, to have been of the 36th year, as being generally not so base as those with the cities, which are BRISTOLIE, CANTOR, EBORACI, and LONDON upon all the pieces, from the halfpenny to the testoon, except the testoon of the second, which we have never seen, No. 46. has this remarkable legend REDDE CUIQUE QUOD SUUM EST. A.

The mint marks of these two Coinages are mostly on the posui groats, as a bow, bolt, anchor, fleur-de-lis, martlet, &c. MintMarks.

The farthing, the halfpenny, No. 39. the penny, No. 40. the half groat, No. 41, 44. the groat, No. 42, 45, 46. and the testoon, No. 43. SORTS.

All the pieces of this Coinage are common, except the halfpenny and testoon, the half groat, No. 4. and the groat, No. 46. which are very rare. RARITY.

The halfpenny weighs 5 gr. the penny 10 gr. the half groat 20 gr. the groat 40 gr. and the testoon 120 grains Troy. WEIGHT.

In his 36th year the fineness is again debased, it being now but 6 oz. fine, or just half fine and half alloy, being a debasement of 66⅔ per cent. FINENESS.

In his 37th year the fineness is reduced to 4 oz. fine and 8 oz. alloy, or one part fine to two of alloy, being a debasement of 50 per cent.

By indenture of his 36th year the pound weight Troy still contained 48 shillings, but the silver only 6 oz. fine, instead of 10 oz., here was an augmentation of 2/3 of a pound Sterling in a pound weight, which contained now 4 4/9 pound Sterling, and the pound Sterling at the same time was reduced to 9/40 of the pound weight, or 2 oz. 14 dwt. Troy. VALUE.

few Coins with the head of their princes as the Italians had, but it was very improper here in England, where the silver money of every king from the Conquest have their head on it. The shilling of Henry VII. was strictly a testoon in type (most of them at that time having profile faces, either to the right or left) as well as value, it being about 1/15 of the Tower mark fine, and that of Lewis XII. about 1/25 of that of Paris, but this of Henry VIII. differed in both, having a full face, and not being above ¾ of the value, or 1/15 of the Tower mark.

* 28 E. I. 18 E. III. 20 E. III. 27 E. III. 13 H. IV. 4 E. IV. and 18 H. VIII. † Lowndes, p. 43.

The

A. Halfgroat [illegible]

HEN. VIII. The pound weight Tower became rais'd to 4⅙ pound Sterling, and the pound Sterling reduced to $\frac{6}{25}$ of the pound weight Tower, or to 2 oz. 17⅗ dwt. Tower.

The next years indenture * kept still 48 shillings to the pound weight Troy, but reduced the fineness again from 6 oz. to 4 oz. which was raising the pound weight nominally ½ or 50 per cent. and now it consisted of 6⅔ pounds Sterling, and the pound Sterling reduced to $\frac{3}{20}$ of the pound weight, or 1 oz. 16 dwt. Troy.

This rais'd the pound weight Tower to 6¼ pounds Sterling, and the pound Sterling was reduced to $\frac{4}{25}$ of the said pound weight Tower, or to 1 oz. 18⅖ dwt. Tower.

EDWA. VI. 1547. Base Money. Head Side. This king appears on his first Coins with a profile head, as on the last Coinage of his grandfather, and the first of his fathers, and that on all the pieces from the testoon to the penny inclusive.

Type. Legend. The penny is inscribed ED. 6. D.' G.' ROSA SINE SPINA (on No. 6. it is SPIPA) or E. D. G. ROSA SINE SPI, the half groat EDWARD 6. D.' G.' AGL. FRANC. z HIB. REX, and the groat EDWARD. 6. D.' G.' AGL. FRA. z HIB. REX. The testoons read the same, only have the Roman VI. instead of the Arabick 6. but it is to be observ'd of these testoons, that some of them have these titles on the reverse, as No. 9, 10. pl. 4. and the legend of the reverse is round the head.

REVERSE. Type. The penny, the half groat, and the groat have the cross and arms, as before, but the testoon has the arms in an oval shield garnish'd, with E. R. on the side of it, and this is the first time we meet with this sort of shield on an English Coin; we meet with it again on the half shilling and shilling of Philip and Mary, and likewise on many pieces of Charles the First.

Legend. The penny has on it the name of the town where coined, which are no other than BRISTOLIE or LONDON that we have seen, some of the half groats and groats also have the place of mintage, as CANTOR. and LONDON, but others again have the old inscription of POSUI DEU' ADJUTORE' MEU', instead of it.

The inscriptions on the testoons of this king are peculiar to his money only, some having TIMOR DOMINI FONS VITE MDXLIX. others have M. D. L. M. D. L. I. Some have INIMICOS EJUS INDUAM CONFUSIONE, but these have not the date after them; both these inscriptions are sometimes found on the head side, as we just now observed, and the titles round the arms on the reverse, as No. 9, 10. pl. 4.

These are likewise the first English Coins which have the date of the year on them.

MintMarks. The testoons coined before his 5th year have an arrow or bolt, a bow, a swan, the letter Y, &c. but the very base ones of that year, have a lyon, a rose, a fleur-de-lis, or harp, as we learn from Queen Elizabeth's † proclamation of 28th Sept. 1560.

SORTS. The farthing and half-penny still mention'd in the indentures ‡, but not one to be found in any cabinet, no more than the Testoon of his first year, those we have are the penny, No. 6, 7. pl. 3. the half groat, No. 1, 4. the groat, No. 5, 8. all of the first Coinage. The testoons, before his 5th year, are No. 9, 10, 11, 12. and those of that year, or the basest sort, are No. 13, 14.

RARITY. The penny, the half groat, and the groat, are all of them extremely rare. The testoons, No. 9, 10. are far from being common, especially the former, and those with the counter mark, No. 12. 14. are likewise extremely rare.

* Lowndes, p. 44. † Folkes, p. 50. Leake, p. 234. ‡ Folkes, p. 24.

The

The farthing should weigh $2\frac{1}{2}$ gr. the halfpenny 5 gr. the penny 10 gr. the half groat 20 gr. the groat 40 gr. and the testoon of this Coinage, if it ever comes to hand, should weigh 120 gr. and the common testoon weighs 80 gr. WEIGHT.

There are likewise some testoons which weigh 60 gr. supposed to be 8 oz. fine *, others that weigh 53 gr. suspected to be of 9 oz. fine, and one dated MDXL7. which weighs 46 gr. supposed to be 10 oz. fine, whose just weight, on that supposition is 48 gr. There is likewise a piece weighing 5, and another 10 of these last, of the same type, nearly and therefore supposed to have been intended as patterns for 5 shilling, and 10 shilling pieces, for which reason we have omitted them here.

The silver of his first Coinage was of the same fineness as the last of his father's, or 4 oz. fine, and 8 oz. alloy; the testoons, until his 5th year, were of 6 oz. and fine 6 oz. alloy, but those of his 5th year are only 3 oz. fine, and 9 oz. alloy. FINENESS.

The indenture of his 1st year † was the same as the last of his father's, and altho' that of the 3d year ‡, has 72 shillings of 6 oz. fine, instead of 48 testoons of 4 oz. fine, in the pound weight; no difference is thereby made in value of the pound Sterling, it being still $\frac{3}{20}$ of the pound weight Troy; but by the indenture of the 5th year §, the testoons are to be no more than 3 oz. fine, instead of 6 oz. as they were before, and of the same weight: Therefore here was a debasement of the pound Sterling cent. per cent. it being now but $\frac{3}{40}$ of the pound weight Troy, or 18 dwt. and the said pound weight was nominally doubled, containing now $13\frac{1}{3}$ pound Sterling. VALUE.

The pound weight Tower was also doubled in denomination, or contained $12\frac{1}{2}$ pound Sterling, and the pound Sterling was now reduced to $\frac{2}{25}$ of the pound weight Tower.

The pound weight Troy of Standard silver was risen in its nominal value anno 5 E. VI. to five times what it was in 36 H. VIII. before the debasement, or, from $2\frac{2}{3}$ to $13\frac{1}{3}$ pounds Sterling, in one pound weight Troy, and the pound Sterling by the same means reduced from $\frac{3}{8}$ to $\frac{3}{40}$ of a pound weight.

The two proclamations of the 9th of July, and the 17th of August this same year, reduced the nominal value to $\frac{1}{4}$ what it then was at, or to $3\frac{1}{3}$ pound Sterling, and at the same time quadrupled the intrinsic or true value of the pound Sterling, making it $\frac{3}{10}$ of a pound weight, instead of $\frac{3}{40}$ as it was before.

Which left still an advance upon the 34 H. VIII. of $\frac{1}{4}$ or 25 per cent.

The king, in this Coinage, is represented full-faced and crowned, having a full-blown rose on one side the head, and the value in pence on the other, as III for the $\frac{1}{4}$ shilling, VI for the half shilling, and XII for the shilling, and they are the first English Coins which have their value on them, and have continued in use on some sorts or other of our money (except Elizabeth, none of whose money has it) till the present time, being still found on the reverse of the penny, half groat, quarter shilling and groat. Fine Money. HEAD SIDE. Type.

This is the last full-face to be found on an English Coin.

The half crown and crown exhibit him on horseback, with a sword in his hand, having his horse caparisoned, and the date under him, as 1551, 1552, 1553. The horse on some of the half crowns appears as on a trot, but is generally in a galloping posture; this type was quitted by Queen Elizabeth, but resumed again by James the First and Charles the First.

* Folkes, p. 22. † Lowndes, p. 45. ‡ Ibid. p. 46. § Ibid. p. 47.

The

Edw. VI. The penny shews him in a chair, as those of his father and grandfather, the base farthing has a portcullice, but the halfpenny and the penny a rose.

Legend. The halfpenny and penny are inscribed E. D. G. Rosa Sine Spina, all the other sorts have Edward. VI. D.' G.' Agl'. Fra. z Hib'. Rex, some have Ao. Fr. Fran'. Hiber.

Reverse. The reverse has the cross and arms, as those of his father and grandfather, on all the pieces, both fine and base, except the farthing, which has the cross and pellets.

Legend. The base farthing and halfpenny, and the fine penny still retain the old legend, viz. the place of mintage, that is, Eboraci and London, there are also a quarter shilling and half shilling with Eboraci, some of the base monies were to have been coined also at Canterbury, but we have never seen any of that mint. The common legend on all the other pieces, from the crown to the quarter shilling, is Posui Deu' Adjutore' Meu'.

MintMarks. The mint marks of this Coinage are the Ton and Y, the first being that used by Throgmorton, in the Tower of London, the other by Yorke, in the borough of Southwark, those coined at York have a pierced mollet.

Sorts. The farthing now for the last time found in the indentures *, but no cabinet is possess'd either of that or the halfpenny. The sorts we have are, the penny, No. 20. the quarter shilling, No. 17. the half shilling, No. 16. the shilling, No. 15. the half crown, No. 19. and the crown *(d)*, No. 18. The quarter shilling, half shilling, half crown and crown were now first coined.

The base farthing, No. 21. and the halfpenny, No. 2, 3.

Rarity. All the pieces of the good silver, from the quarter shilling to the crown, are common, but the penny is extremely rare, as is also the base farthing, the halfpenny is also scarce, but the penny we have never seen.

Weight. The farthing should weigh 2 gr. the halfpenny 4 gr. the penny 8 gr. and the quarter shilling 24 gr. the half shilling 48 gr. the shilling 96 gr. the half crown 10 dwt. and the crown 1 oz. Troy.

The base money, if coined up to the just value of the good silver, should weigh 22 gr. the halfpenny 11, and the farthing 5 gr. Troy.

Fineness. The purity of our silver again restored to 11 oz. 1 pennyweight fine silver, and 19 pennyweights alloy, or within $\frac{1}{222}$ of standard.

The base monies were 4 oz. fine silver, and 8 oz. alloy §.

Value. By indenture of the 6 E. VI. ‖ the poundweight Troy of silver, 11 oz. 1 dwt. fine, was to contain 60 shillings in Tale, by which the said poundweight of Standard silver contained $3\frac{3}{221}$ pound Sterling, and the pound Sterling was $\frac{221}{666}$, or a trifle less than $\frac{1}{3}$ of a pound weight, or 3 oz. $19\frac{71}{111}$ dwt. Troy.

In the last Coinage of Standard silver, or that of 18 H. VIII. the poundweight contained 45 shillings, and in this there was 60, which had these been Standard, would have been a nominal rise of $\frac{1}{3}$ exactly in the poundweight, in this Coinage, more than in that, and a debasement of $33\frac{1}{3}$ per cent. in the pound Sterling.

(d) This piece contained as much silver as made it of equal value with the piece of gold of this name, and was therefore properly a silver crown, as that was a gold crown.

And this method was made use of, upon the first coinage of these large silver pieces in other places, they being made of the value of the best current gold coins, and receiving their name from them; as in Germany the Gold Gulden gave its name to the piece of silver current fos it, being called a Gulden Groschen † or Great Gulden; in Italy the silver piece of the value of the gold Ducat, was called a Ducatone or great Ducat; and the large Genoese piece, of the value of a Scudo d'Oro, was called a Scuto d'Argento ‡, or silver Scudo, and sometimes by a similar name of Mezzo Doppia d'Argento.

* Lowndes, p. 48. † Locio's Muntz Tractat von Guldinern, p. 6. ‡ Saggi Cronologici o sue Genoua nelle sue AntichitaRicercati, p. 121. § Folkes, p. 43. ‖ Lowndes, p. 48.

She

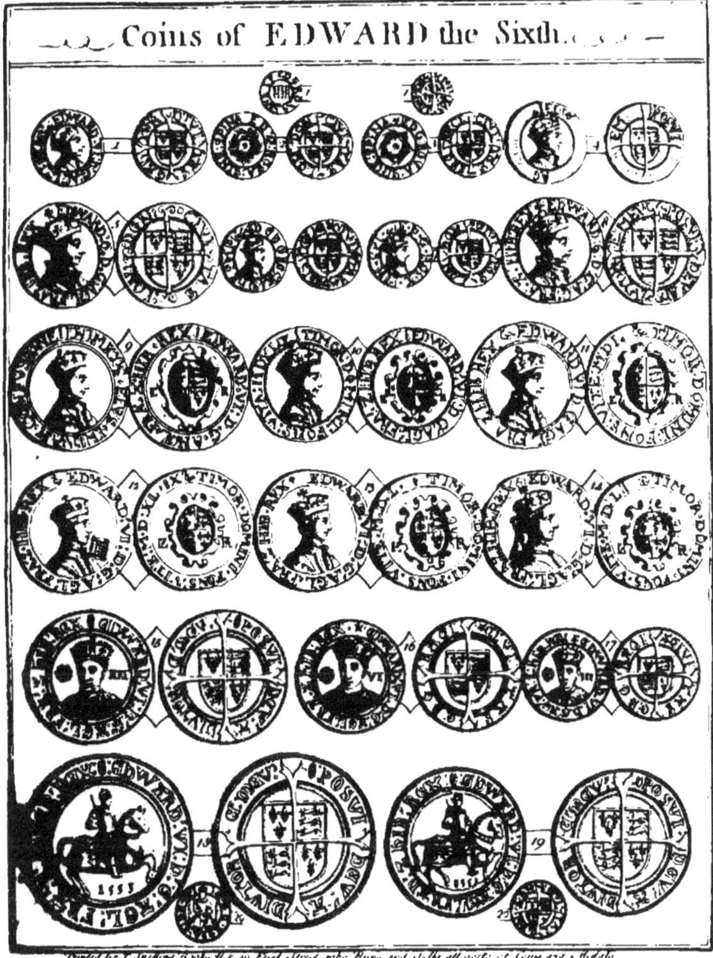
Coins of EDWARD the Sixth.

Coins of PHILIP and MARY.

Mary. Head Side. 1553. Type.

This queen appears with a profile head crowned, regarding the right on the penny, half groat, and groat, both before and after her marriage, but the half ſhilling and ſhilling, after her marriage, have both their heads looking at each other, with a crown above them, having the date on each ſide of it on ſome of them, as 1554, 1555, 1557, another ſort has the date at the bottom; others again there are which have no date at all.

The half crown has his head, with a crown over it, on one ſide, and hers on the other, in the ſame manner, and the baſe halfpenny has a roſe.

Legend.

The halfpenny and penny, before her marriage, have M. D. G. Rosa Sine Spina, and thoſe after have P. z M. the half groat, of the firſt Coinage, has Maria D. G. A. Fr. z Hib. Regi. the groat has Ang. Fr. After her marriage the half ſhilling and ſhilling reads Philip et Maria D. G. R. Ang. Fr. Neap. pr. Hisp. or His. and theſe are the firſt pieces coined after their marriage, the next having Philip et Maria D. G. Rex et Regina Ang. others have An. Angl. the half groat and the groat reads the ſame as theſe laſt, only want the word Ang. and ſome have z inſtead of et, others read Reg. Regi. Regin. and we never ſaw either the half groat or groat with the legend of the firſt ſhilling.

The half crown reads Philipus D. G. R. Ang. Fr. Neap. pr. Hisp. with the date 1554 under the head *, another reads Philip.

Reverse. Type.

The halfpenny, penny, half groat and groat in both Coinages, have the croſs and arms as uſual, the half ſhilling and ſhilling have the arms of Spain impaled with thoſe of England crown'd, in an oval ſhield garniſh'd, with the values VI. and XII. generally over it, but on ſome it is omitted, and theſe are the only Coins we have with their values placed in this manner.

Legend.

We now find no other place of mintage on the Coin but London, and that only on the halfpenny and penny. Before her marriage, the groat has Veritas Temporis Filia, the half groat the ſame, only Tempo', inſtead of Temporis, thoſe after her marriage have Posuimus Deum Adjuto' Nos: ſome have No, the half ſhilling and ſhilling read Posuimus Deum Adjutorem Nostrum, No. 12. has Adjutorium, No. 15. Nostrem, and No. 19. only Nos.

The half crown has only her name and titles Maria D. G. R. Ang. Br. Neap. pr. Hisp. and the date 1554 above it.

Mint Marks.

The groat, before her marriage, has a pomegranate either after Veritas or Temporis, thoſe after her marriage have all of them the fleur-de-lis, but we have obſerved it upon no other half ſhilling than that of 1557, nor could we ever procure the ſhilling with this privy mark on it.

Sorts.

Before her marriage there are the halfpenny, No. 6. the penny, No. 2. the half groat, No. 1. and the groat, No. 5. after which we have the halfpenny, No. 7. the penny, No. 3. the half groat, No. 4. the groat, No. 8. to which were then added the half ſhilling, No. 14. 16, 17. 19. the ſhilling, No. 9, 10, 11, 12, 13. and 15. and the half crown, No. 18.

Rarity.

The groats are the only Coins of this Queen that are common, the half ſhillings and ſhillings are often met with, but generally in bad preſervation, thoſe which are the moſt common are with Pr. Hisp. there being few with Rex Ang. thoſe without either date or value are very ſcarce, thoſe with the date under the head are the rareſt of any.

The baſe halfpenny is alſo rare, but the fine penny and half groat are extremely rare, and we know of but one half crown.

* Die Ongevaluweerde Ghouden & Silveren Munte, 1559.

WEIGHT. The weight of the penny is 8 gr. the half groat 16 gr. the groat 32 gr. the half shilling 48 gr. the shilling 96 gr. and the half crown 10 dwt.

A pound weight Troy of the base halfpennies was shered into 40 shillings *, from whence the weight of each is 12 gr.

FINENESS. The fineness was now but 11 oz. fine silver, and 1 oz. alloy, being worse than the last Coinage by $\frac{1}{222}$.

VALUE. By indenture of her 1st year, the pound weight Troy of silver 11 oz. fine was to contain 60 shillings in Tale, and therefore the said pound weight of Standard silver contained $3\frac{1}{110}$ pound Sterling, and the pound Sterling reduced to $\frac{110}{331}$ of a pound weight, or 3 oz. 19 $\frac{251}{331}$ dwt. Troy.

The pound weight was here nominally rais'd $\frac{1}{110}$, and the pound Sterling debas'd in the same proportion.

The pound weight Troy of silver 3 oz. fine, contained 20 shillings in Tale, therefore the said pound weight of Standard silver, contained $3\frac{7}{10}$ pounds Tale or Sterling, whereas the fine money above was coined into no more than $3\frac{1}{110}$ pound Sterling in the pound weight, by which means here was a profit of 23 per cent. to be made by exchanging the base for the fine money, and it is to be observed that this, (and the 6 E. VI.) were the only instances in the English Coinage of the small money being of base, and the large of good silver, and shews how ill the attempt now succeeded, when put into execution.

ELIZAB. 1558. Hammer'd Money. HEAD SIDE. Type. All the money of this queen, from the three farthing piece to the crown, inclusive, have her head crown'd in profile like her sister's, and on the half crown and crown she has the scepter in her right hand, and the orbe with the cross, in her left, and this is the first time we see the scepter since Henry III. the half shilling, with its $\frac{1}{2}$, $\frac{1}{4}$, and $\frac{1}{8}$, or the three-penny, three-halfpenny, and three-farthing, piece have each of them a rose behind the head, and by that are distinguished from the penny, half groat, groat, and shilling. The head on No. 15. is the best perform'd of all the hammer'd half shillings, the halfpenny has a portcullis.

Legend. The three-farthing piece, the penny, the three-halfpenny piece, and latter half groat, are all inscribed E. D. G. ROSA, SINE SPINA. The first half groat, and all the other pieces to the crown, in general read ELIZABETH D. G. ANG. FR. ET HIB. REGINA, but some have ELIZAB. AN. FRA. HI. HIBER. REGI. REGIN.

REVERSE. Type. The old shield with the royal arms and cross, appears upon the reverse of all the pieces, from the three-farthings to the crown; which last has its shield handsomely garnish'd, as is that also on No. 16. the date of the year is over the shield, on the three-farthing, the three-halfpenny, the three-penny, and the six-penny piece, and on no other. The halfpenny has the cross and pellets.

Legend. The name of the place of mintage, which had been on some or other of the pieces ever since the Conquest, is now, for the last time, to be met with in this reign, and that only on the penny, the three-farthing piece, the three-halfpenny piece and the latter half groat, all which have CIVITAS LONDON.

The other pieces are all inscribed POSUI DEU' ADJUTOREM MEU', except the half crown and crown, which have DEUM & MEUM.

Mint Marks. The M. M., are upon all the pieces from the half penny to the crown. We find more mint marks upon the money of this queen, than upon any of her predecessors, and from the dates upon the half shillings, we are informed in what years those other pieces were coin'd which have none; some of these private marks continued to be used for four or five years together, as the pheon and cross,

* Folkes, p. 48.

others

others for a leſs time, and very few but were continued more than one year, we ELIZ. are at a loſs for a reaſon why there ſhould be three different ones in the ſame year, as on the half ſhilling of 1582, we have ſeen a ſword, bell, and the letter A, and again on that of 1595, the ton, woolpack, and key, as appears from the following liſt of theſe marks, and their accompanying dates, on the half ſhillings, which have come under our obſervation.

Mark	Dates	Mark	Dates	Mark	Dates
Martlet, Croſs Croſlet, Fleur-de-lis	No half ſhilling	Acorn - -	1573, 1574	Hand - -	1590, 1591, 1592
Pheon - -	1561, 1562, 1563, 1564, 1565	Cinquefoil -	1574, 1575, 1576	Ton - - -	1592, 1593, 1594, 1595
Roſe - - -	1565	Croſs - -	1577, 1578, 1579, 1580, 1581	Woolpack -	1594, 1595, 1596
Portcullis - -	1566	Sword - -	1582	Key - - -	1595, 1596
Lyon - -	1566, 1567	Bell - -	1582, 1583	Anchor - -	1597, 1598, 1599
Coronet - -	1567, 1568, 1569, 1570	A - - -	1582, 1583, 1584	Annulet - -	1600
Caſtle - -	1569, 1570, 1571	Eſcallop Shell	1584, 1585, 1586	.1. - - -	1601, 1602
Ermyn Spot	1572, 1573	Creſcent - -	1587, 1588, 1589	.2. - - -	1602

The firſt Coinage from 1558 to 1560, was only of the penny, No. 1. 5. the SORTS. half groat, No. 2. 6. the groat, No. 3, 4. 8. and the ſhilling, No. 7. 9, 10. the groat and ſhilling were diſcontinued the next year, and in their ſtead was coin'd the half ſhilling, No. 14, 15. the quarter ſhilling, No. 13. the three-halfpenny piece, No. 12. and the three farthing piece, No. 11. this is the firſt appearance of theſe two laſt ſorts, in the Engliſh ſeries, and they were continued untill 1582, when they and the quarter ſhilling were laid aſide. The ſhilling was again added, anno 1582, as alſo the halfpenny (*e*), No. 17. which continued to be minted during the remainder of her reign, in the two laſt years of which 1601 and 1602, were alſo added the half crown, No. 21, and the crown, No. 22.

The money of this queen in general very common, but we muſt however ex- RARITY. cept the three-farthing piece, which is very ſcarce; the half ſhillings of 1563,

(*e*) That moſt excellent method, of having the ſmall money of Standard ſilver, as well as the large, had hitherto been the conſtant practiſe in the Engliſh mint, (except the laſt year of Edward VI. and the ſhort reign of queen Mary;) thus when the groat was firſt coined, the farthing was the 16th part of it, in weight as well as in value, and alſo the 48th of the ſhilling, when that firſt appeared; the ſame tract was purſued by this queen, all the above pieces weighing in proportion to their value, as the halfpenny the 120th part of the crown, and the penny at this time is ſtill the 60th. The many diſadvantages ariſing from the contrary method, is beſt known to thoſe ſtates who have purſu'd it.

1597.

ELIZ. 1597, 1598, and 1599. are alſo rare, as are alſo the ſhilling with the annulet, and the half crown of her laſt year.

WEIGHT. Until her 43d year the halfpenny weighs 4 gr. the three-farthing piece 6 gr. the penny 8 gr. the three-halfpenny piece 12 gr. the half groat 16 gr. the quarter ſhilling 24 gr. the half ſhilling 48 gr. the ſhilling 96 gr. and after her 43d year the halfpenny weighs $3\frac{27}{31}$ gr. the penny $7\frac{23}{31}$ gr. the half groat $15\frac{15}{31}$ gr. the half ſhilling $46\frac{14}{31}$ gr. the ſhilling $92\frac{28}{31}$ gr. the half crown 9 dwt. $16\frac{8}{31}$ gr. and the crown 19 dwt. $8\frac{16}{31}$ gr. Troy; they have remain'd of the ſame weight until this day.

FINENESS. In the 2d year of this queen * the purity of the ſilver was again reſtored to its old footing of STANDARD, or 11 oz. 2 dwt. fine ſilver, and 18 dwt. alloy; and has remain'd thus, unalter'd to this day.

VALUE. By indenture of her 2d year, as alſo of her 19th, 25th, and 35th years one pound weight Troy of Standard ſilver, was to contain 60 ſhillings in Tale, or 3 pound Sterling; whereby the pound Sterling was now juſt $\frac{1}{3}$ of the pound weight Troy, or 4 oz.

And here the nominal value of the pound weight was reduced $\frac{1}{111}$, and the intrinſic or real value of the pound Sterling as much increaſed, or $0\frac{10}{11}$ per cent.

By the indenture of her 43d year, the pound weight Troy of Standard Silver was to contain 62 ſhillings, or $3\frac{1}{10}$ pound Sterling; whereby the pound Sterling was now reduc'd to $\frac{10}{31}$ of the pound weight, or 3 oz. 17 dwt. $10\frac{2}{31}$ gr. Troy, as it has remain'd ever ſince.

By which means the pound weight Troy was nominally raiſed $\frac{1}{30}$, and the pound Sterling as much debaſed, or $3\frac{1}{3}$ per cent.

The pound weight Tower of Standard ſilver was now nominally raiſed to $2\frac{29}{32}$ pound Sterling, and the pound Sterling but $\frac{32}{93}$ of the pound weight, or 4 oz. 2 dwt. $13\frac{2}{31}$ gr. Tower, as it remains at this time.

And the true proportional values of the pound Sterling, as it was at the Conqueſt, and as it is at this time, are truly expreſs'd by the ratio of 93 to 32.

Mil'd Money The milled money does not vary in its type, from that of the hammer'd, the only difference being in their ſuperior neatneſs, and in the letters being ſquarer and better made; the pieces are alſo rounder, and more uniform; and have the edges grained, the inner circle is alſo taken away.

There are two or three varieties in the head, on the quarter and half ſhillings of 1562, but thoſe of 1574 and 1575, by far exceed all the others, having a larger and more elegant buſt, extending to the letter'd edge; the croſs on the reverſe is likewiſe broader and neater, having flat ends, inſtead of being open and flouriſhed, as they generally are, except thoſe of 1564, No. 3. 11. which are likewiſe flat.

The half ſhilling of 1570 and 1571, No. 13, 14, 15, are ſingular, for having a break in the inſcription, under the head, which none of the others, either milled or hammer'd have, the inſcription itſelf is alſo different, as it reads ELIZABETH D. G. AN. F. & HI. REGINA; and thoſe of 1574 and 1575, are the ſame, the common inſcription being ELIZABETH D. G. ANG. FRA. ET HIB. REGINA.

MintMarks. The two mint marks on this money, are the mollet of 6 points, and the fleur-de-lis; of the former there are half ſhillings dated 1561, 1562, 1563, 1564, and 1566, and quarter ſhillings of all but the laſt. No. 13. has likewiſe the ſame

* Lowndes, p. 50.

mark,

Hammer'd Coins of ELIZABETH.

Printed for T. Snelling Bookseller in Fleet Street.   J. Perry Sculp.

Mill'd Coins of ELIZABETH.

Printed for T. Snelling Bookseller, in Fleet Street, who Buys & Sells all Sorts of Coins and Medals.

mark, but appears to be of a different Coinage, as are alſo No. 4. 16. altho' with the ſame mint mark. With the fleur-de-lis we have only ſeen half ſhillings of 1567, 1568, and 1570, the latter of a different mint from the two firſt, nor have we ever ſeen any quarter ſhilling with this privy mark. No. 15. has the mint mark of the hammer'd money of that year. ELIZAB.

The only pieces now found with the mollet are the three-farthing piece, No. 6. the half groat, No. 5. the groat, No. 7. the quarter ſhilling, No. 1. 2. 3. 4. the half ſhilling, No. X, 8, 9, 10, 11, 12, 13, 14, 15, 16. and the ſhilling, No. 17. SORTS.

Mr. Folkes informs us, he had ſeen the penny and three-halfpenny piece of thoſe with the mollet, but unluckily has left us no impreſſion of them, nor could we procure one of either, from any cabinet we had acceſs to.

The pieces with the fleur-de-lis are the penny, No. 20. the half ſhilling, No. 12. the ſhilling, No. 18. and the half crown, No. 21.

The half ſhilling of 1561, 1562, 1567, and 1568, and the quarter ſhilling of the two firſt dates, as alſo the groat, No. 7. and the ſhilling, No. 17. are very common. The dates of 1563, 1564, 1566, are ſomething ſcarcer, thoſe of 1570, 1571, No. 13, 14, 15. are very rare, as are alſo the penny, No. 20. and the ſhilling, No. 18. thoſe of 1574, and 1575. are extremely rare, and we know of but one of the half crowns, No. 21. RARITY.

This king appears with a profile head to the left, on all his half ſhillings and ſhillings, as he does alſo on the penny and half groat of his firſt Coinage, and behind the head is the value of each, in pence, as I. II. VI. XII. On his half crown and crown he is repreſented on horſe-back in armour, with a ſword in his hand, a crown'd roſe appears generally on the trappings of the horſe, but No. 17. has a crown'd thiſtle. The halfpenny, like that of Elizabeth, has a portcullis, and is only known from hers by the M. M. over it, the halfpenny of the ſecond Coinage has a roſe without any legend, the penny the ſame, but with a legend, and the halfpenny has the roſe crown'd. JAMES I. 1603. HEAD SIDE. Type.

The firſt Coinage read JACOBUS D.' G.' ANG. SCO. FRA. ET HIB. REX, and the ſecond JACOBUS D.' G.' MAG. BRIT. FRA. ET HIB. REX, ſome have JACOB. BRI. FRAN. the halfpenny and penny of both read J. D.' G.' ROSA SINE SPINA. Legend.

The royal arms quarter'd appears upon all his Coins, (except the penny and the half groat of his ſecond Coinage,) that is France and England in the firſt and fourth, Scotland in the ſecond, and Ireland in the third quarter, but without the croſs, which had been conſtantly upon all the Engliſh Coins ſince the Conqueſt until now, (except only the teſtoon of Edward VI. and the half ſhilling and ſhilling of Philip and Mary) the half ſhilling and ſhilling are in a plain ſhield, but thoſe of the half crown and crown are garniſhed. The halfpenny, the penny, and the half groat of the ſecond Coinage have a thiſtle, and on the laſt it is crowned. REVERSE. Type.

The half ſhillings, like thoſe of Elizabeths, and the firſt years of his ſon Charles I. have the dates over the ſhield, ſome of the ſhillings, half crowns and crowns, of the ſecond Coinage, have the feathers over the ſhield, but none of the half ſhillings, as that place was filled with the date.

The penny and half groat of the firſt Coinage have no legend, thoſe of the ſecond Coinage have TUEATUR UNITA DEUS, all the other pieces of the firſt Coinage have EXURGAT DEUS DISSIPENTUR INIMICI, and of the ſecond Coinage QUÆ DEUS CONJUNXIT NEMO SEPARET. Legend.

MintMarks. The trial of the Pix seems to have been very regular during this reign, and in consequence of that, the privy marks appear in general to have been changed every year. The following List shews when each began to be used *,

Thistle, - 21 May, 1603	Mollet, - - 9 May, 1611	Plain Cross, 15 May, 1618
Fleur-de-lis, 22 May, 1604	Tower, - 22 May, 1612	Saltyre Cross, 9 June, 1619
Rose, - - 20 June, 1605	Trefoil, - 28 April, 1613	Spur Rowel, 20 Aug. 1619
Escallop shell, 10 July, 1606	Cinquefoil, 20 Oct. 1613	Rose, - - 23 June, 1620
Grapes, - 30 June, 1607	Ton, - - 17 May, 1615	Thistle, - 8 June, 1621
Coronet, - 11 Nov. 1607	Book, - 15 Nov. 1616	Fleur-de-lis, 3 July, 1623
Key, - - 17 May, 1609	Half Moon, 23 Aug. 1617	Trefoil, - 17 June, 1624
Bell, - - 11 May, 1610		

These marks are upon all the pieces from the halfpenny to the crown, there are half shillings with dates from 1603 to 1615 inclusive, but none after until 1621, and from thence to 1624, both inclusive, those of 1604, have some of them EXURGAT, and others QUÆ DEUS, both with the thistle and fleur-de-lis; we have likewise the half shilling of 1607, with the escallop-shell, grapes and coronet. The shillings are found with all of them, except the cross, saltyre and crescent; but of the half crowns and crowns we have only the thistle, fleur-de-lis, rose, escallop-shell, 2d thistle, 2d trefoil, and 2d fleur-de-lis, there being none between the years 1607 and 1620 inclusive, owing, no doubt, to the great scarcity of silver.

SORTS. The halfpenny, No. 1. the penny, No. 2. the half groat, No. 3. the half shilling, No. 4. the shilling, No. 5. the half crown, No. 6. and the crown, No. 7. all these of the first Coinage, and of the second Coinage the halfpenny, A. No. 8. the penny, No. 9. the half groat, No. 10. the half shilling, No. 11. the shilling, No. 12, 13. the half crown, No. 14, 15. and the crown, No. 16, 17.

RARITY. The Coins of this king are all of them very common, if we except the first half crown, No. 6. which is very rare; those with the feathers over the arms are not so common as those without.

WEIGHT. The half-penny weighs $3\frac{27}{31}$ gr. the penny $7\frac{23}{31}$ gr. half groat $15\frac{15}{31}$ gr. the half shilling $46\frac{14}{31}$ gr. the shilling $92\frac{28}{31}$ gr. the half crown 9 dwt. $16\frac{8}{31}$ gr. and the crown 19 dwt. $8\frac{16}{31}$ Troy grains.

FINENESS. Standard, 11 or oz. 2 pennyweights fine silver, and 18 pennyweights alloy.

VALUE. There was no alteration in the value of the silver money, during this reign, it remaining the same as the 43d of Elizabeth, † that is, the pound weight Troy of Standard silver is $3\frac{1}{10}$ pound Sterling, and the pound Sterling $\frac{10}{31}$ of the pound weight Troy *(g)*.

This

(g) In order to keep the money within the land, and to encourage more to be brought in, it was appointed by proclamation ‡, that certain foreign coins should be current, at fixed rates; that no coin, plate or bullion, should be transported; that no goldsmith should make any profit by exchange of monies §, that no goldsmith should make plate of English money, but only of old broken plate, bullion, foreign coin, or burnt lace; that no Finour should allay, or sell, any silver in mass, to any but to the officers of his majesty's mint, exchanges or goldsmiths, that no foliate should be used for guilding or silvering, that no gold or silver thread should be made, and the company of gold wire-drawers was dissolved.

The

* Folkes, p. 69. † Lowndes, p. 53. ‡ 18 May, 9th James. 14 May, 10th Ja. 20 March, 13th Ja. 4 Feb. 16th Ja. 11 June, 20th Ja. 22d Ja. § See St. 5 and 6 Ed. 6. cap. 16.

A. No. 9th are known with TVEATVR on both sides very rare

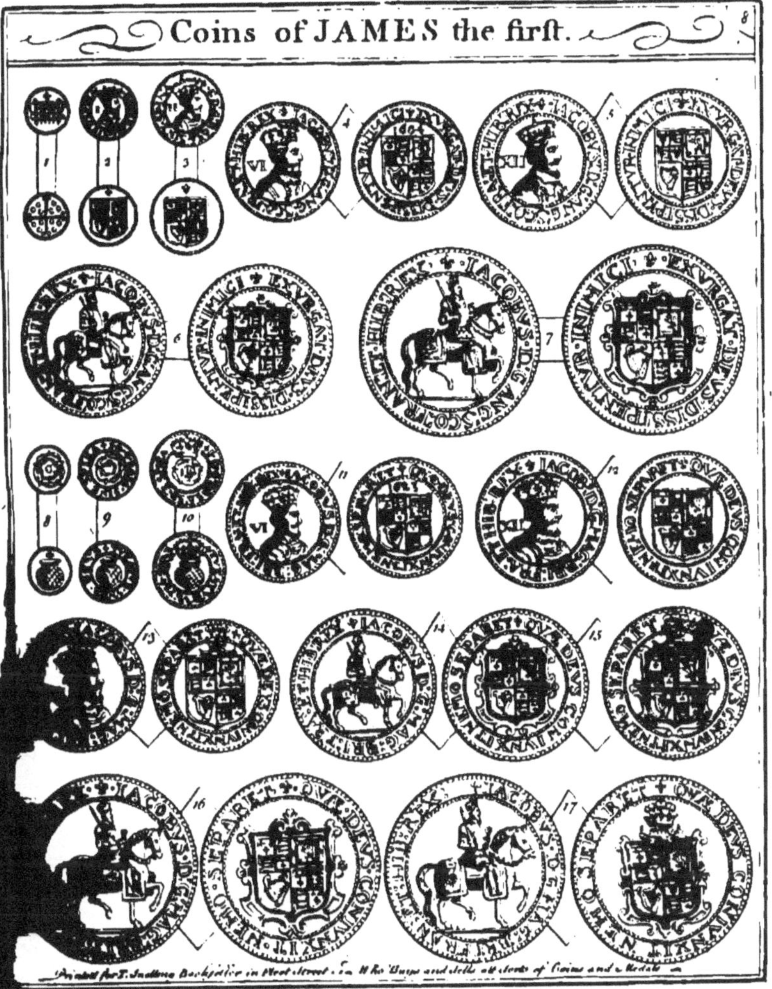
Coins of JAMES the first.
8

CHARLES I. 1625. Tower Mint HEAD SIDE. Type.

This king is exhibited with a profile head turned to the right, upon all his money (except the halfpenny, the penny, and the half groat of his firſt five years, which have a roſe like his father's) but with very great variety in relation to the workmanſhip, according to the ſkill and care of the performer. He was at firſt repreſented with a ruff, but ſomething different in its form, until 1630 or 1631,

The great ſcarcity of ſilver coin in this reign appears if not to have taken its riſe yet to have been much increaſed by the enhancing the value of the gold by proclamation of 20 Nov. 1611.** And, in order to make it more plenty, we find a propoſal made by capt. Hayes for raiſing the price of the ſilver, in a paper dated 12 May, 1612,†† by coining the ſilver at 10 oz. 10 dwt. fine, and 64 ſhillings to the pound Troy. In two other papers, dated 20 July, and 5 March, 1612,‡‡ it is propoſed to cut 64 ſhillings out of the ſaid pound of Standard. And Mr. Folkes ‖‖ informs us, "That directions were actually given to the attorney-general, the 21ſt Feb. 1619, to prepare new indentures of the mint, whereby the pound weight Troy of Standard ſilver ſhould be coined into 66 ſhillings; but theſe directions were ſoon after recalled, and the deſigned alteration of the ſilver Coin was ordered to be ſuſpended for twelve months; upon a report made to the council, the 25th of the following April, by ſeveral eminent merchants, whoſe advice had been deſired in a conſultation with the miniſters on that occaſion." And we find, ſome years before this, in a paper called by Sir Julius Cæſar §§, Mr. Solicitor's Report, and ſigned Tho. Parry, Fr. Bacon, that in purſuance of letters by them received, to enquire into the cauſe of the great ſcarcity of ſilver; they had called to them the officers of the mint, and ſome principal merchants, and that the expedient of raiſing the price of the ſilver being mention'd, the reſult was as follows, "and upon this point it is fit we ſhould give your lordſhips to underſtand, what the merchants intimated unto us, that the very voycing, and ſuſpecte of rayſing the price of ſilver, if it be not cleere, would make ſuch a deadneſs and retencion of money, this vacation, (as to uſe their own words) would be a miſerie to the merchants; ſo that we were forced to uſe proteſtation, that there was no ſuch intent."

Sir Richard Martin declared it as his opinion, in a paper dated 18 Oct. 1600, to the Lord Privy Seal, and Lord High Treaſurer *, and in two others to Sir Julius Cæſar, dated the 15 July, 1609, and 12 Oct. 1611, † that the pound weight Troy of England being heavier than that of France, Flanders, Germany and Spain, was one of the reaſons that kept bullion from coming to the mint, but in a conference he had by order of the Lord Treaſurer, on this (among other) ſubjects, with Sir William Herick, Alex. Preſcot and John Williams, Eſqrs. his majeſty's goldſmiths, Oct. 18, 1611. they report the reſult of it to have been as follows, "we are of opinion that the alteration of the pound weight Troye being the publique meaſure uſed in this lande for gold, ſilver, &c. will be hurtful manie ways, neither will it alter the value of the bullion; but the name of a quantity, nor is it poſſible for this land to agree therein with everie neighbour kingdom, becauſe they differ among themſelves." ‡ How juſt this determination was, appears, when we conſider, that the Troy mark of France, tho' ſaid to be of the ſame weight as that of Germany (i. e. Cologne) and that of Spain; yet was 5 per cent. heavier than the former §, and 6¼ per cent. heavier than the latter of them ‖.

The abuſe of exchange by bills, is likewiſe put down by Sir Richard Martin, as another reaſon of the tranſportation of money, and is ſtrongly inſiſted on by Malynes, in moſt of his writings, who urges the re-eſtabliſhing a royal-exchanger, and it ſeems that the company of goldſmiths were under apprehenſions that ſuch an officer was to be appointed, as appears in their petition to the Chancellor of the Exchequer as follows ¶, "whereas your petitioners underſtand that the Right Hon. Lord Knevet (pretending himſelf by patent to be warden of his majeſties exchange) ſeeketh by that means to erect an exchange, and to obtain a permiſſion from his majeſtie, by proclamation to all perſons, other than himſelf, to buy gold or ſilver bullion, or to exchange gold monies for profit." And they ſhew, in ſeventeen articles, the damage that would accrue to the kingdom in general, and to themſelves in particular, if ſuch an officer ſhould be appointed.

The executing the ſtatute of employment was alſo propoſed, as a means to prevent tranſportation of money; and we find his majeſty was petition'd ‡ for a grant to erect an office for putting this ſtatute in execution, in conſideration of 100 pounds Sterling per annum, paid by the petitioners into the exchequer, and they to take of the merchant ſtrangers three-pence in the pound, towards defraying their expence, &c.

** Mun's England's Treaſure, c. 8. Malyne's Lex Mercat. p. 323. †† Sir Julius Cæſar's Collection of Papers relating to Mint Affairs, MS. p. 68. ‡‡ Ibid. p. 174, 185. ‖‖ p. 70. §§ Collection, p. 187. * Sir Julius Cæſar's Collection, &c. p. 149. † Ibid. p. 112. 133. See alſo Malyne's Lex Mercatoria, p. 2. c. 8. p. 3. c. 10. ‡ Sir Julius Cæſar's Collect. p. 115. § Bodelius, p. 64. ‖ Vayrac Etat preſent de l'Eſpagne, tom. 3. p. 282. Greaves's Table of Weights. ¶ Sir Julius Cæſar's Collection, &c. p. 125. 223. ‡ To the King's moſt excellent Majeſty, The humble Petition of the Hon. Patrick Leſlie, Lord Lundores, and Sir Robert Stewart, Knt. MS.

when

CHARLES I. when he is in a laced band, which continued to the end of his reign, all which pieces have the value on them behind the head, as those of his father; that is, I. II. VI. and XII. for so many pence.

On the half crown and crown he is represented on horse-back, in armour, with a broad-sword in his hand, as if lifted to strike, the horse is caparizon'd, and has a plume of feathers both on his head and on his rump, but two years after he is represented with a smaller sword, which rests on his shoulder, and the feathers is taken from the horse's rump, and both these sorts are peculiar to those of the Tower mint; this type continued till about 1630 or 1631, when it was again alter'd, he holding the sword nearly upright, the caparizon is taken away from the horse, as is the feathers also from his head; and the king's scarf over his armour appears more conspicuous than on the former, and flies behind him, and this is the common type as well of Briots, as of all the country mints.

Legend. The rose penny and half groat read C. D. G. ROSA SINE SPINA, those with the head CARO. or CAROLUS D. G. MA. BR. FR. ET HI. REX, some have M. B. F. H. the larger pieces are inscribed, in general, CAROLUS D. G. MAG. BRIT. FRA. ET HIB. REX, some have MA. BRI. FR. FRAN.

Reverse. Type. The reverses of this king's money have all of them the royal arms, from the penny to the crown, (except as before, the halfpenny, the penny, and the half groat of his first five years, which have a rose) which on the first Coinages were in a square shield and the cross, nearly as on its first appearance on our silver Coins, and the half shilling had the date over the shield, as in the two preceding reigns, but about 1630 or 1631, it was omitted, the shield being at that time alter'd to an oval one garnished, with C. R. at the top, which soon gave place to another not so neat, tho' still oval, the C. R. being now on the side of the shield, and this was a third time changed for another, much ruder, being rounder and shorter, which continued, till his death, on all the pieces, except the half shilling and shilling, on which the old square shield and cross was again introduced, which, besides the badness of the work, has the cross different, being contained within the inner circle instead of extending to the edge of the Coin, as it had done ever since the time of Henry the Third.

Legend. The penny and the half groat are inscribed JUSTITIA THRONUM FIRMAT. all the other pieces, from the half shilling to the crown, have CHRISTO AUSPICE REGNO.

MintMarks. The time when the M. M. in the following list began to be used is taken from the register of the several trials of the Pix. *

Trefoil, -	1 April, 1625	Rose, - -	30 June, 1631	Δ in a circle,	15 June, 1641
Fleur-de-lis,	7 July, 1625	Harp, - -	21 June, 1632	.P. - -	29 May, 1643
Blackmoor's head, - Long Cross	29 June, 1626	Portcullis, -	11 July, 1633	.R. - -	15 July, 1644
		Bell, - -	27 June, 1634	Eye, - -	12 May, 1645
		Crown, -	18 June, 1635	Sun, - -	10 Nov. 1645
Castle, -	27 April, 1627	Ton, - -	14 Feb. 163$\frac{6}{7}$	Scepter,	15 Nov. 1646 to the king's death.
Anchor, -	3 July, 1628	Anchor, -	8 May, 1638		
Heart, - -	26 July, 1629	Triangle, -	4 July, 1639		
Feathers, -	23 June, 1630	Star, - -	26 Jan. 1640		

We have never seen any piece of this king's money marked with a trefoil. The first change in the half crown and crown, just mentioned, was in those mark'd with

* Folkes, p. 77.

Coins of CHARLES the First.

CHARLES I.

with the castle, and the second was in the crown mark'd with the portcullis, the half crown with that M.M. remaining unchang'd. The type of the penny and half groat was changed during the time that the feathers was the M.M. there being half groats both with the rose, and the head, with that M. M. on them; and at the same time the square shield was changed for the oval one, and the dates, which had been constantly over the shield on the half shillings, (as 1625, 1626, 1627, 1628, 1629 and 1630.) were now omitted. The king first appears with a band on those with a harp M. M. those with the square shield and short cross first appear on the half shilling and shilling, with the ton M. M. and those with that M. M. are the last of this kings on which we see the feathers over the arms. The only M.M. on any of the rose pennies is the fleur-de-lis. And no other than the feathers, rose, harp, and triangle on the pennies which have the head, but there are half groats, half shillings, shillings, half crowns and crowns with all of them.

SORTS.

There are the halfpenny, No. 1. the penny, No. 2. 8. 14. the half groat, No. 3. 9. 15. the half shilling, No. 4. 10. 16. the shilling, No. 5. 11. 17. the half crown, No. 6. 12. and the crown, No. 7. 13. all of them on plate 9.

RARITY.

The money of this king is very common, but with relation to the particular M. M. we have observed those with the blackmoor's head to be very scarce all of them, but in particular the half crown and crown, as are those pieces also with the castle, first anchor, and heart.

BRIOT'S MINT.

This celebrated artist was authorised, to engrave the king's effigies for his coins, by patent, dated the 16th of December, 1628;* and by a warrant dated the 11th of February 1629, was to have lodgings in the mint, but it is probable it was towards the close of the year 1631, before he was settled there, as the commission appointed to see it perform'd, (in consequence of his petition of the 2d of Octob. 1630) bears date the 13th of June that same year;† he had afterwards a grant, dated the 2d of January, 1633,‡ to be one of the chief engraver's within the Tower, but his famous pattern shilling is not dated before 1635.

HEAD SIDE. Type.

A very neat profile head crowned of the king, looking to the right, with a laced band, appears on the penny, the half groat, the half shilling, and the shilling, which band is not seen on the Tower money until the year 1632, which being about the time of Briot's establishment in the mint, makes it doubtful which was the proto type.(i)

The half crown and crown represent the king on horse-back as usual, with his drawn sword held nearly upright, like the third type of the Tower mint, which was not introduced until the year 1633, and therefore it is probable, these of Briots were the first designs. The ground under the horse is here properly represented

Legend.

The penny is inscribed CAR. D.' G.' MAG'. BRIT. FR. ET H'. R. the half groat has CAROLUS. HIB. the larger pieces read CAROLUS D. G. MAG. BRITAN. FRAN. ET HIBER. REX.

REVERSE. Type.

The penny and the half groat have the square shield and long cross, which are not found on those of any other mint besides this, the others having all of them the oval shield. The half shilling and shilling No. 3. 4. pl. 10. have the same shield, which was the only one in use from this king's accession till the

* Rymer, Tom. 19. p. 40. † Ibid. p. 287. ‡ Ibid. p. 526.

(i) An emulation seems to have been rais'd about this time in the Tower, as there are some very fine neat half shillings and shillings, with the rose and harp M. M. and we take the penny, No. 5. pl. 14. to be one of this sort.

CHARLES I. year 1630, on the pieces which came out of the Tower mint. The half shilling and shilling, No. 7, 8. have the same shield, but the short cross, which is not found on any of those minted in the Tower until about the year 1638, but which of them were the first struck, those by Briot or those in the Tower is not yet determin'd; the half crown and crown have a handsome oval garnish'd shield crown'd, (which none of those coin'd in the Tower have) and the initials C. R. also crown'd on the sides.

Legend. The penny and half groat are inscribed JUSTITIA THRONUM FIRMAT. but No. 2. has it, FIRMAT JUSTITIA THRONUM; all the other pieces have CHRISTO AUSPICE REGNO.

Mint Marks. There are two belonging to this Coinage, viz. a sort of emony flower and small B, which appear to have been first used, and an anchor and the small B, which we think did not take place until some years after the other, from the manner of the cross on the reverse. The B is sometimes wanting, and we find it alone upon the half shilling, just within the inner circle on the reverse, and on the small pieces just under the head.

Sorts. This mint only produced the penny, No. 2. (pl. 10.) the half groat, No. 1. the half shilling, No. 3. 7. the shilling, No. 4. 8. the half crown, No. 5. 9. and the crown, No. 6.

Rarity. These Coins are all of them common *(b)*.

York Mint. A mint was erected in this city about the year 1629, but nothing certain can be gather'd in relation to the particular years, in which any of the following Coins were struck, however some of them are suppos'd to have been coined there in the year 1633. †

Head Side. Type. The king appears with a profile head crowned, in a laced band, and regarding the right; with the value behind the head, viz. III. VI. XII. for the quarter shilling, half shilling, and shilling. No. 3. pl. 14. is very remarkable, as having neither value nor inner circle. The half crown and crown exhibit him on horse-back in armour, with his drawn sword as usual, some of which have EBOR under the horse, who treads on a ground line, on some, but on others on the inner circle.

Legend. The quarter shilling is inscribed CAROLUS D. G. MA: BR. FR. ET HI. REX, the other pieces generally CAROLUS D. G. MAG. BR. FR. ET HIB. REX, some have FRAN.

Reverse. Type. The old square shield and cross, with the word EBOR. over it, appears on No. 10. 13. (pl. 10.) the same shield, but without the cross, is also found on No. 16. 19. both which have the letters C. R. on the side of it, and the first is also crowned. No. 11, 12. 15. 17. 20. shew the oval garnished shield crown'd, the second and the fourth of which have also C. R. on the side of the shield. The common oval shield not crown'd, is found on No. 14. 18. and on No. 3. (pl. 14.) but we have never seen that where the shield is held by lions paws *.

Mint Marks. The only one on these Coins is the lion passant-gardant, but on No. 3. (pl. 14.) this M. M. is only on the reverse, it having a fleur-de-lis on the head-side, and No. 1. 2. the same, all which are supposed to be of this same mint, but we think of a later date.

(b) Besides the current monies above described this great artist left behind him, many fine pattern pieces, jettons, and medals, some of which are extreamly rare.

† Folkes, p. 79. * Leake, p. 317.

All

Coins of CHARLES

7

Printed for J. Snelling Bookseller in Fleet Street [illegible]

Coins of CHARLES the First.

Printed for T. Snelling Bookseller in Fleetstreet. Who Buys & Sells all Sorts of Coins & Medals.

Legend. All the pieces have the uſual inſcription, of CHRISTO AUSPICE REGNO, there are flowers between each word on No. 16, 17.

Rarity. The above Coins are all common, except the half crown, No. 16. 18, 19. and the ſhilling, No. 3. (pl. 14.) which are very ſcarce.

Aberistwith Mint. The money coined out of the ſilver, drawn from the lead-mines in the Principality of Wales, was diſtinguiſhed by having the feathers over the arms on the reverſe of the ſhilling, half crown and crown, both of James the Firſt, and thoſe of the firſt 12 years of this king, thoſe with the ton M. M. being the laſt which has them on it.

On the 30th of July, 1637. a particular mint was erected for this purpoſe at the caſtle of Aberiſtwith in Wales, from whence the officers and workmen were removed to Oxford, towards the cloſe of the year 1642. †

Head Side. Type. The money which came from this mint have the profile head of the king in a laced band, looking to the right on all the pieces from the penny to the ſhilling, with the value behind the head, as I. II. III. IIII. VI. and XII, they have alſo the feathers before the head on all but the two ſmalleſt pieces. The half crown has the king on horſeback as uſual in armour, with his drawn ſword, and feathers behind his back; the half-penny has a roſe.

Legend. The ſmall pieces read, CARO or CAROLUS D. G. M. B. F. ET H. REX, the larger pieces have CAROLUS D. G. MAG. BR. FR. ET HI. REX, the half Crown has BRIT. FRA.

Reverse. Type. The area of the reverſe, of the half-penny, penny, and half-groat, is filled with the Feathers, all the other pieces from the ſhilling to the half-crown, have the royal arms in the oval garniſhed ſhield, ſurmounted with the feathers.

Legend. The half-penny has no inſcription, the penny and half-groat have JUSTITIA THRONUM FIRMAT, and all the reſt CHRISTO AUSPICE REGNO.

Mint Marks. The M. M. is on all theſe Coins, from the penny to the half-crown, being an open book, there is beſides, a quarter ſhilling and groat, with a crown, the ſhield on the reverſe of which, is a ſmaller one than uſual.

Sorts. There are the half-penny, No. 21. pl. 10. the penny, No. 22, 23. the half-groat, No. 24, 25. the quarter ſhilling, No. 26, 27. the groat, No. 28, 29. the half ſhilling, No. 30. the ſhilling, No. 31. and the half-crown, No. 32.

Rarity. The half-penny and half-crown are both very ſcarce, and the half groat, No. 25. is exceeding rare and intereſting, as it proves this Mint exiſted at the ſame time as that at Oxford; all the reſt are common.

Oxford Mint. This Mint was ſet up on the king's coming to Oxford, towards the cloſe of the year 1642; (the officers and moneyers of that of Aberiſwith, being removed from thence hither by the king) and is ſuppoſed to have continued till the taking of Oxford, on the 24th of June, 1646.*

Head Side. Type. The king's head in profile crowned, in a laced band, and turned to the right, is as uſual, on all the pieces from the penny to the ſhilling; with their value behind the head. Some have the feathers before the head, and ſome are without them; the buſt of the groats, No. 9, 10, 14, 15. are different from the reſt, as they extend to the Edge of the Coin, and the laſt, has no inner circle.

The half-crown, the crown, the half pound, and the pound pieces, have the king on horſeback in Armour, with his drawn ſword, as before; ſome have the

† Folkes, p. 70, 82.

* Ibid. p. 85.

The

CHARLES I. feathers behind the back of the king, and some have not; on No. 9. they are under the horse, who treads on the inner circle; on some he treads on a ground line, on others again, there appears nothing to support him; on many he treads on several sorts of armour and weapons: those on No. 17. are the best represented, and the neatest dye, but yet not equal to No. 10, which is usually call'd by way of distinction, The OXFORD CROWN, from the fine perspective View of the City of Oxford, which appear on it, under the horse.

Legend. The small Coins are inscribed, CAROLUS D. G. M. B. FR. ET H. REX, some MAG. BR. F. HI. the large Coins read, CAROLUS D. G. MAG. BRIT. FRA. ET HIBER REX, some have MAGN. BRI. FRAN.

REVERSE. Type. The area on the reverse of the Coins of this Mint, is filled with the inscription, REL. PRO. LEG. ANG. LIB. PAR. but with great variety, as RE. RELI. RELIG. PR. PROT. LE. AN. LI. LIBER PA. this inscription from the penny to the shilling inclusive, is contained in three lines; but on allthe rest it consists but of two. A streight line is commonly above it, and another below it; but some have also two other lines in the middle, as No. 17, 18, and 24. instead of the top line on No. 6, 14, 16, 23, 35. pl. 11. and No. 9. pl. 12. there are two scrolls, and the same at bottom also; on No. 31. pl. 11. and No. 10. pl. 12. the inscription is in a compartment, on No. 15. pl. 11. and No18. pl. 12. There is generally 3 feathers over the top; but on some, as No. 5, 6, 14, 15, pl. 11. and No. 16, 18. pl. 12. there is but one; the three largest pieces have likewise their value, in the same place, as V, X and XX †. At the bottom of the inscription, is generally the date, as 1642, 1643, 1644, 1645, and 1646. Some under the Date have OX. or OXON. and some have also BR. and No. 34. has the letter A. there are no earlier date than 1644, on any piece less than the half shilling; no ten shilling piece after 1643, nor twenty shilling piece after 1644.

Legend. The Legend on all these pieces is EXURGAT DEUS DISSIPENTUR INIMICI; (from whence they are frequently called the EXURGAT Money) but No. 20. is very remarkable, having the common legend of the other Money of this king, viz. CHRISTO AUSPICE REGNO.

MintMarks. Some of these pieces have the open book, others a fleur-de-lis, B, BR, the feathers, and No. 34. has a blackamoor's head; but most of them are without any at all.

SORTS. We have the penny No. 1. the half groat No. 2, 3. the quarter shilling, No. 4, 5, 6, 7, 8. the Groat, No. 9, 10, 11, 12, 13, 14, 15, 16, the half shilling No. 17, 18, 19, 20, 21, 22, 23. the shilling, No. 24, 25, 26, 27, 28, 29, 30, 31, 32, 34, 35, all in pl. 11, the half-crown, No. 1, 2, 3, 4, 5, 6, 7, 8, 9. the crown, No. 10, 11, 12. the ten shilling piece or half pound, No. 13, 14. and the twenty shilling or pound piece, No. 15, 16, 17, 18.

This was the first and the last time we had a piece of the value of a pound sterling in silver, but in gold they had been coined in every reign (but Mary's) since Henry VIII.

RARITY. This money is in general, common enough, however, we must except the half groat, the quarter shilling, No. 5. dated 1645, and the shilling, No. 34. which are very scarce; the fine pound piece, No. 18. is also very rare, but the OXFORD Crown, No. 10. and the penny No. 1. are two of the rarest Coins in the English Collection.

† At the close of the article REVERSE of Mary, page 30. should have been added, "Except the larger pieces coined at Oxford and all the commonwealths."

The

RELIG PRO LEG
ANG LIBER PAR
1642
1643
1642

CHARLES I. feathers behin
der the horse,
on others agai
veral sorts of
the neatest d
distinction, T
Oxford, whic

Legend. The small
MAG. BR. F
ET HIBER R

REVERSE. Type. The area o
tion, REL. P
RELIG. PR.
the shilling in
two. A strei
also two othe
No. 6, 14, 16
at bottom a
compartment
over the top;
is but one; tl
V, X and XX
1643, 1644,
some have al
1644, on an
nor twenty sh

Legend. The Lege
(from whenc
very remark
viz. CHRIST

MintMarks. Some of tl
thers, and
any at all.

SORTS. We have
4, 5, 6, 7,
No. 17, 18,
32, 34, 35,
No. 10, 11,
shilling or p

This was
sterling in
since Henry

RARITY. This mo
groat, the q
are very sca
Crown, No
Collection.

† At the clos
coined at Oxfor

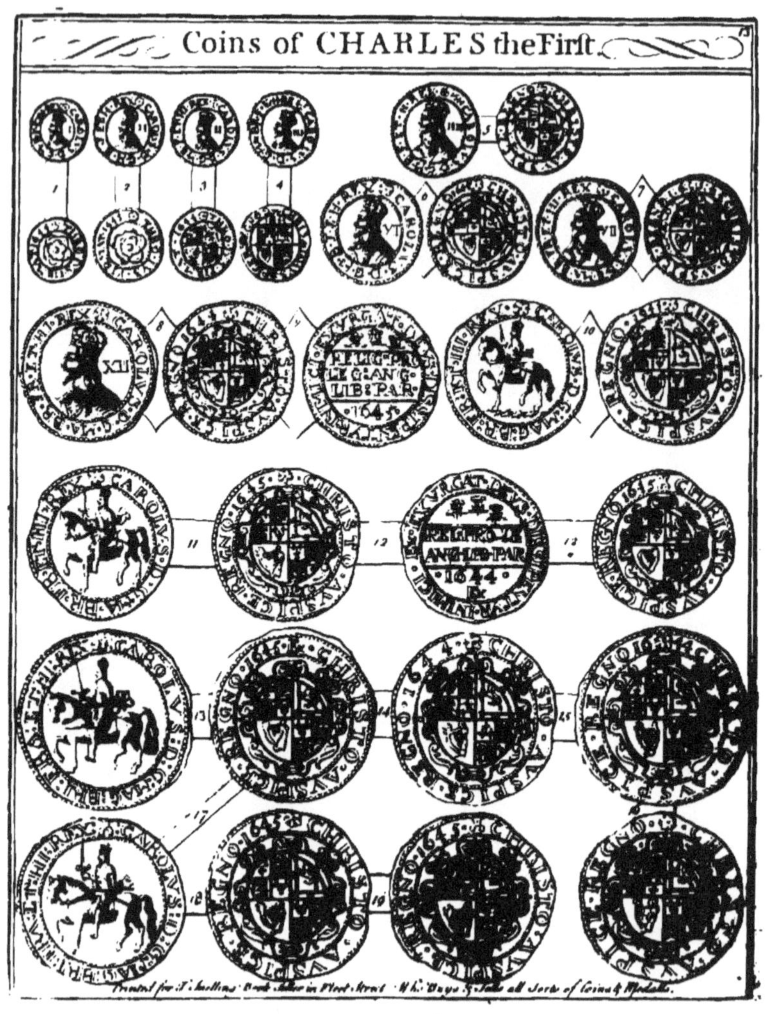
Coins of CHARLES the First.
RELIG·PRO
LEG·ANG·
LIB·PAR
1645
1644

The reason which has induced us to suppose that all the pieces in pl. 13. have been struck in this City, is the sameness observable in the half crowns and crowns, and that two of them, viz. No. 12, 13. have Ex on them, and have also the rose for their M. M. on one side, which is common to all the other pieces in that plate. EXETER Mint.

All the coins of this Mint, from the penny to the shilling, have as usual, the king's profile head crown'd, in a laced Band, with the value behind it. The half crown and crown have the king on horseback in Armour, with his drawn sword. HEAD SIDE. Type

Some of the small pieces are inscribed, CAROLUS D. G. M. B. F. ET H. REX, others have, MA. BR. FR. HI. RE. and No. 5. has also the date 1644. The larger pieces read CAROLUS D. G. MAG. BRI. FRA. ET HI. REX. Legend.

The penny and the half groat, No. 2. have the area fill'd with a rose; the half groat No. 3. and the rest of the pieces, (except No. 9, 12, and the quarter shilling) have all the oval garnish'd shield, but the quarter shilling has the square shield, with the date 1644, over it; No. 9, and 12. have the inscription hitherto thought to be peculiar to the Oxford Money, viz. RELIG. PRO LE ANG. LIB. PAR, 1645, and the other, REL. PRO LEG. ANG. LIB. PAR, 1644 Ex. REVERSE. Type.

We find, THRO. JUS FIRMAT 1644, on the penny and half groat, all the other pieces, except No. 9. 12. have CHRISTO AUSPICE REGNO 1644, or 1645; but they have EXURGAT DEUS DESSIPENTUR INIMICI. Legend.

The rose appears as a M. M. on both sides of most of the pieces, from the penny to the crown; however, a castle is also seen on some of the half crowns and crowns, on one side, and the rose on the other, as in No. *12, and 19. MintMarks.

We should suspect from the M. M. of No. 19. pl. 14. that it came out of this mint, but Mr. Folkes is of opinion it was coined at York.

There are the penny No. 1. the half groat, No. 2, 3. the quarter shilling, No. 4. the groat, No. 5. the half shilling, No. 6, 7. the shilling, No. 8, 9. the half crown, No. 10, 11, 12, *12, and the crown, No. 13, 14, 15, 16, 17, 18, 19. SORTS.

The most common coins of this mint are the crowns, as also the groat No. 5, the half shilling, No. 6. 7. and the shilling No. 8. the penny and the two half groats are very scarce, together with the half crowns; but the shilling, No. 9. and the half crown, No. 12. are extremely rare and valuable, as they clearly prove, that all the Exurgat money was not coined at Oxford‡, as has hitherto been supposed. RARITY.

The half crown, No. 15. pl. 14. is the only piece that at present is to be found of this mint, and it is proved to have been struck there, by its having CHST under the horse, and instead of a mint mark, the three garbs, part of the arms of the city, it has also the feathers behind the king's back; it is extremely rare. CHESTER Mint.

That the half crown, No. 17. pl. 14. was coin'd in this mint, appears from the 3 pears over the shield on the reverse, being the arms of that city, there is also one pear on the other side, instead of a mint mark; it differs in nothing else from the other half crowns, and also is a very rare coin. WORCESTER Mint.

The king appears on horseback, on No. 19. pl. 14. with a truncheon in his hand, and riding full speed over several sorts of weapons, which together, with the date under the shield on the reverse, is what it differs in from the other half crowns; the M. M. of the rose is conspicuous on it, and does plead for its being Unknown Mints.

‡ Folkes, p. 90.

CHARLES I. admitted amongst those we have supposed to be struck at Exeter, but Mr. Folkes thinks it was coined at York, when the king set up his standard there; it is very rare.

We should immediately conjecture from the reverse of the half crown, No. 12. pl. 14. that it came out of the Tower Mint, when the rose was the mint mark, it being exactly the type then used there, but then on the other side, we find no feathers on the horse's head, nor any trappings on his back, nor does the king rest his sword on his shoulder, as usual on the Tower half crown, and therefore it did not come from thence; the figure of the king appears as if falling backward.

The two half crowns, No. 14, 16. are very singular, and its probable may have both come out of the same mint, as also No. 7, 8, 9, 10, 11. on the last of which appears as a mint mark a helmet, a lyon, &c. and over the shield, between C R, a castle; and as we find the helmet on No. 7, 8, 9, 14. the castle on No. 7. also the lyon appearing in the legend of No. 16. and the agreement of the shield on No. 7. makes it probable that they are all the production of the same mint.

Amongst the very great variety of this king's money, altho' we meet with many very rude, and of bad workmanship, yet we think none of them comes up to the half crown, No. 13. the barbarous work of which, was certainly that of a smith, and not of an engraver.

The quarter shilling, No. 4. is the only coin we have met with of this king's, with the square shield without a cross, like those of his father's, but where coin'd we cannot determine, nor what is its mint mark.

SIEGE Money.

This king's reign was the first and only one which has produced any obsidional pieces, but here we have a great variety of them, but are ignorant of the places where many of them were struck.

Newark.

The obverse of these Coins have a crown, with the initial letters C. R. on the sides of it, and under it the respective values, as VI, IX, XII, and XXX. for so many pence, and these are all the sorts we have seen of them.

The reverse is filled with the words, OBS NEWARK, or NEWARKE, 1645, or 1646. They are all in form of a lozenge, and are very common.

Carlisle.

The Obverse of this money has, like that of Newark, a crown, with the initial letters C. R. but they are under it, and not on the side, and under them is the value, as XII or IIIs. which are the only two sorts we have seen, and are both round.

The reverse is filled with OBS CARL. 1645, on some of them, in two lines, in others it forms but one line.

Pontefract.

The obverse of these, are commonly like the others just mentioned, having the letters C. R. crown'd, but with the legend, DUM SPIRO SPERO round them; another sort, instead of the C. R. has under the crown, HANC DEUS DEDIT, 1648, and round it, CAROLUS II. D. G. MAG. B. F. ET H. REX, being struck after the death of his father.

The reverse shews the castle of Pontefract with the flag flying on the top of it, on all of them but No. 19, which is without; they have all of them, on the dexter side, the letters O B S. and No. 18, 19. have the date 1648 also at bottom. No. 18. has on the sinister side of the castle, a hand issuing out of it, holding a sword; No. 20, 21. have a gun, issuing from the same place, and No. 19. has ԏ XII. ○ No. 20, 21. have also round them, the first, CAROLUS SECUNDUS, 1648; the other, POST MORTEM PATRIS PRO FILIO.

There are said to have been half crowns and crowns of this sort, but we never could procure either of them, or even a drawing of them.

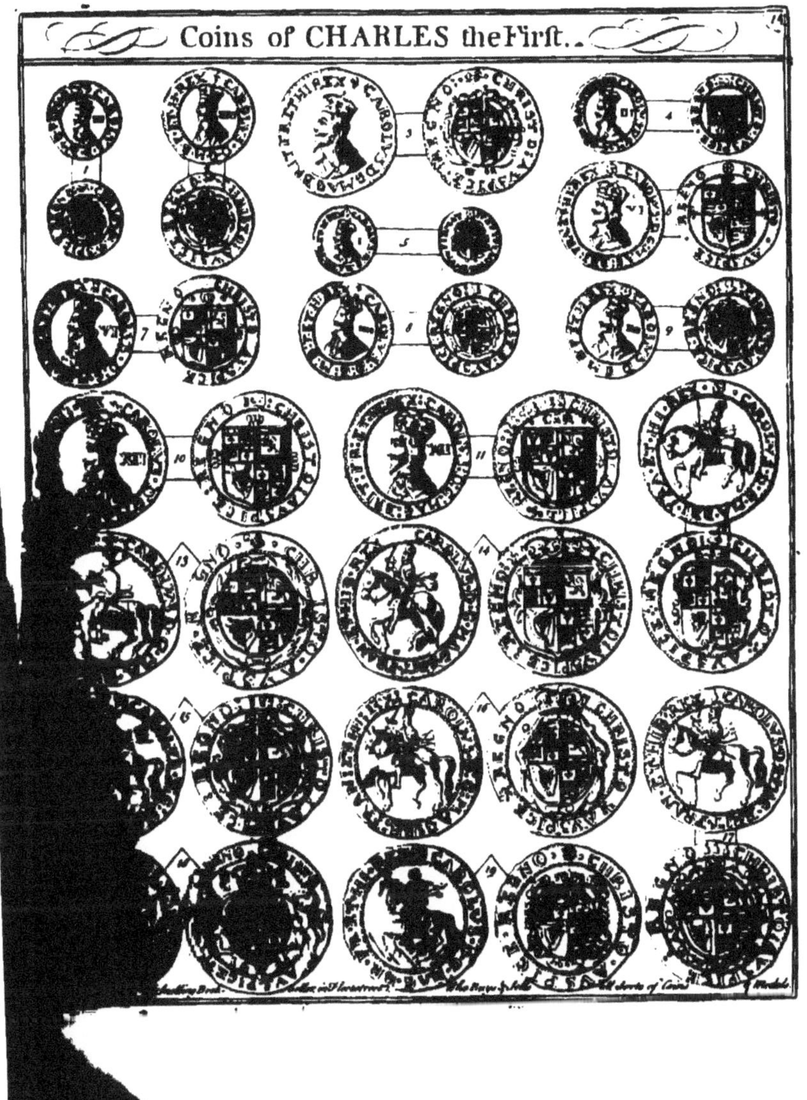
Coins of CHARLES the First.

rborough

chester.

cnown
tles.

IGHT.
ENESS.
LUB.

CHARLES the first and second.

3 D XI

4 S I

5 D II

6 S I

9 S II

OBS Scarborough 1645 10 S D II VI

11 S V

C R III 13 S OBS CAR 1645

OBS: NEWARK 1646 15 C R IX

OBS: NEWARK 1645 16

C·R DUM:SPIRO:SPERO 18 OBS 1648

CR DUM:SPIRO:SPERO 19 OBS

21

seller in Fleetstreet - Who Buys & Sells all Sorts of

These pieces are some of them in shape of a lozenge, others of them are octangular; from which last are formed, the round ones we sometimes meet with, being made by taking off the angles, and are therefore always lighter; and are all very scarce. CHARLES I.

The pieces said to have been stamped at this Castle, are No. 10, 11. being thin plates of silver, with the value punched on them, of IIs, VId, and Vs. the former has upon the back of it OBS SCARBOROUGH 1645, engraved on it, the other is quite plain, and are both extremely rare. Scarborough

Number 7, 8. are likewise stamped with a castle, and have had engraved round them, CAROLI FORTUNA RESURGAM: the first is octagonal, the other is round, and are also very rare. Colchester.

The three pieces, No. 3, 4, 5. appear by the likeness of the castle on them, to have been stamped at the same place, and have their respective values of XId. Is. and Is. IId. upon them, and weigh 80 gr. 91 gr. and 99 gr. and are r. r. r. Unknown Castles.

The castles represented on No. 1, 2, 6. are entirely different from each other, and we may therefore suppose, stamped at different places, as also the two castles on No. 9. they have all their values on them, of VId, VIId. Is. and Is, IId. and the three first weigh 49 gr. 53 gr. and 85 gr. these also are r. r. r.

During all this reign, remain'd on the same footing as the 43d of Elizabeth. *(a)* WEIGHT. FINENESS. VALUE.

This

(a) An alteration in the value of the coin, was intended to have been made in the 2d year of this king, by cutting the pound weight Troy of standard Silver, into 70s. 6d. as appears by a commission dated August the 11th, and by another of the 2d of September that same year, * which would have been an advance of 14 per Cent. ——— And again in 1640 it appears, that other proposals on the same subject had been made, which occasioned the famous speech said to have been spoken at the council table, in July this year, by Sir Tho. Rowe; † but we find in the Cottonia Posthuma, ‡ that Sir Robert Cotton had spoken it at the said table, 14 years before.——As to the alteration itself, it is said; 1st, That three pence in silver, added to a quantity of copper, should be made to go current for 12 pence; 2dly, The Cottonia says, that the loss to his majesty in 100l. tale (N. B. It should be weight) would be 59 oz. making 14l. 17s. Rushworth and the other say, not 100l. but 700l. tail; And, 3dly, they all agree that the said loss, would be but one fourteenth: which three articles contradict one another, and are by no means to be reconciled together.

The office of Royal Exchanger so much contended for in the last reign, as a principal means to put a stop to the transportation of money, was granted 26 December, 1626, to Henry Earl of Holland, for 31 years§; but several complaints of the inconveniencies arising from it, and of abuses committed by his deputies, being laid before the parliament ‖; occasioned it, we apprehend, to be soon after discontinued: yet Violet was for having it restored again, affirming, that the warden of the mint, was by law the states exchanger ¶.

Foreign coin and bullion were, during all this reign, bought and sold at 1d, 2d, 3d. &c. per oz. above the mint price**, notwithstanding the king's proclamation ††, to the contrary; and this occasioned the culling and melting of the heavier Silver coin; 30,000l. of which, in six-pences, shillings, and half crowns, were melted by one single goldsmith-banker, every year, for six years together, or from 1624 to 1630 ‡‡ and many more followed the same trade, all of which was transported by the merchant, or work'd up by the manufacturer; several of whom, in the 12th Car. were fined in the Star-chamber to the value of 24,100l. §§ as others had been before: towards the close of the late reign, in 200,000l. for the same offence ‖‖. The parliament took it into consideration in the year 1640, as appears by their order of the 18th of March ¶¶, by which Violet was commanded to prosecute the business, and in consequence of that order, delivered in his humble declaration, dated 12 April, 1643. By another order of parliament, of the 1st of September 1647***, the commissioners of the navy are required to consider the subject, who the next day sent their order to the commissioners of the customs; and on December 3, to the officers of the mint,

who

* Rymer, tom. 18. p. 740, 752. Cottonia Posthuma, 8vo. 1651, p. 300. † Speeches and Passages in this happy Parliament, 4. 1641, p. 353. Rushworth, vol. 3. p. 1216. ‡ Page 283. § Rymer, tom. 18. p. 867. ‖ Journals of the House of Commons, vol. 1. p. 507. ¶ Most exact Letter, p. 57. ** Violet's humble Declaration, &c. 4to. 1643. p. 23. †† May 26, 1627. Rymer, tom. 19. p. 6. ‡‡ Violet's Proposals to Oliver Cromwell, Fol. 1656, p. 89. §§ True Discovery, 12mo. 1650, p. 6. Rushworth, vol. 2. p. 350. ‖‖ Violet's Petition against the Jews, p. 1. A. Appeal to Cæsar, p. 12. ¶¶ Journals, vol. 2. p. 106. *** Ibid. vol. 4. p. 286.

COMMON-WEALTH. 1649. This money was coined in pursuance of an ordinance of parliament, of the 17th of July, 1649§, and continued to be coined until the restoration: but there are none found either of 1657 or 1659, and but very few of 1658 and 1660.

OBVERSE. The obverse has the cross of St. George in an antique shield, encircled with a branch of laurel, and the four largest pieces have inscribed round them, THE COMMONWEALTH OF ENGLAND, but the other three pieces have no inscription at all.

REVERSE. The reverse has the two shields of England and Ireland conjoined, and encircled as before, which has given occasion to the name of breeches money; by which it is often distinguished. The four largest pieces are inscribed, GOD WITH US, and the date of the year, as 1649, 1650, 1651, 1652, 1653, 1654, 1655, 1656, 1658, and 1660. They have also their respective values at the top of the shields, as I, II, VI, XII, II VI, and V.

MintMarks. The sun is the M. M. used until 1656 inclusive, and afterwards on those of 1658 and 1660, the anchor.

SORTS. Are the half-penny, No. 1. pl. 16. the penny, No. 2. the half groat, No. 3. the six-pence, No. 4, the shilling, No. 5. the half crown, No. 6. and the crown, No. 7.

RARITY. All these coins are very common, *(b)* if the collector does not confine himself to dates, for those of 1658 and 1660 are very scarce, especially the half crown of the last, the crown of which we have never seen, nor any other sort but the half shilling of 1658.

WEIGHT. FINENESS. VALUE. The same as that of the 43d year of Queen Elizabeth, in all the three Articles *(c.)*.

OLIVER, Protector. 1656. All the pieces coined by the Protector, are very beautiful, being the performance of the incomparable SIMON, and worked off by the mill and screw, and if we admit them to have been current money, the half-crown and crown are the first that shew an inscription on their rim; which all the succeeding milled money have constantly had ever since, serving as a pattern to them in this particular, as well as in the taste of the head.

HEADSIDE. The Protector appears with a profile bust laureat, regarding the right, being the first English coin with the head thus adorned, and the only one to be found on any of the milled money since, but looking different ways.

It is inscribed, OLIVAR D. G. R. P. ANG. SCO. HIB. &c. PRO. with the date at top, which is generally 1658, but there are a few half crowns and shillings with 1656.

The

who severally report their opinion in relation to this affair*; and in November the City of London petitioned the parliament on the same account: and this is all we can find was done in this matter, till after the king's death.

(b) The dispute between the corporation of the moniers belonging to the mint, and Blondeau, produced several fine pattern pieces, which are exceeding rare, amongst which the half crown was the first piece we ever had coined in England, with an inscription on its rim.

(c) The 18th of August, 1649, the council of state ordered that a committee should be appointed to consider the state of the coin, that means might be found to put a stop to its transportation, and to set the mint at work†. An Act was accordingly drawn up by them for this purpose, and laid before the parliament, which was twice read there, and on the 15th of April, 1653, was called for again, and ordered to be reported ‡ on the 21st, but the day before, or on April the 20th, Oliver broke up the parliament.

* Violet's true Discovery, p. 68. Corporation of Moniers Answer to Blondeau, p. 32. † Violet's Proposals, p. 109. ‡ Journals, vol. 5. p. 278.

§ Scobel's Acts, Part 2, page 65:

The reverse has a crowned shield, with St. George's cross in the 1st and 4th quarter for England, St. Andrew's cross in the second for Scotland, and the harp for Ireland in the 3d, and on the center over all, his paternal coat. REVERSE.

The inscription on all the pieces, is PAX QUÆRITUR BELLO, and on the edge of the half crown and crown, are HAS NISI PERITURUS MIHI ADAMAT NEMO.

Are the half shilling, No. 8. pl. 16. the shilling No. 9. the half crown No. 10. and the crown, No. 11. SORTS.

These coins are all of them very scarce, but in particular, the half shilling is exceeding rare. RARITY.

They exactly answer that of the other money of this time, or of all since the 43d year of Queen Elizabeth. WEIGHT. FINENESS. VALUE.

The first money coined by this king after his restoration, have his head crowned in profile, looking to the right, much like those of his father's, but neater by far, and more uniform; these at first had neither inner circle nor value, but the latter was afterwards added by warrant of the 28th of November, 1661;* these sorts were soon after followed by those with the inner circle also, which were not so well performed as the two first; and besides, were very irregular in their form. CHAR. II. 1660. Hammer'd Money. HEAD SIDE. Type.

They are mostly inscribed, CAROLUS II. D. G. MAG. BRIT. FR. ET HIB. REX, but some have, M. B. BR. BRI. FRA. FRAN. H. HI. Legend.

The reverse has the same square shield and short cross, as was on the latter half shilling and shilling of his father's and like those also are inscribed, CHRISTO AUSPICE REGNO on all the pieces, the penny and half groat included, and in this differ from those two pieces of his father's. REVERSE. Type. Legend.

The only one we find on these pieces is a crown, and these are the last pieces, on which we meet with any mint mark on them. Mint Marks.

The first coinage without either inner circle or value, consisted of the same sorts as had been struck in the Tower, by the two last king's, (except the half penny and crown) that is the penny, No. 12. pl. 18. the half groat, No. 13, the half shilling No. 14. the shilling, No. 15. and the half crown, No. 16. the crown altho' mentioned in the indenture was never coined, no more than the half-penny, except this last was with the rose, and therefore not known from his father's:† and the same pieces, all but the penny, were coined when the value was added to them, as No. 17, 18, 19, and 20. The 4 smaller pieces, No. 28, 29, 30, 31. seem to have been coined about the same time, but their inscription beginning at the bottom, and all the others at the top, induced us to put them separate. There are of those with the inner circle besides the former mentioned pieces, a quarter shilling No. 23, and a groat, No. 24. SORTS.

The second coinage, or those with the value, but without the inner circle, are the scarcest of the three, and with respect to the particular sorts, the half crowns are by far scarcer than the others, especially the two first, No. 16. and No. 20. which are very rare. RARITY.

This money first began to be coined on February the 6th, 166 1/2, in consequence of two warrants of November the 5th, and January the 19th, and were made current by proclamation of the 27th of March, 1663,‡ and has all of it the king's head in profile, looking to the left, like that on the hammer'd money, but not crown'd, as had hitherto been the constant practice, but laureat like that of Oliver. Milled Money. HEAD SIDE. Type.

* Folkes, p. 103. † Ibid. ‡ Ibid. 107.

CHARLES II. The first crown has a rose under the king's head, another sort has an elephant, as also an half crown and shilling, and there are shillings with the feathers.

Legend. They are all inscribed, CAROLUS DEI GRATIA.

REVERSE. Type. The type of the reverse was quite in a new taste, consisting of four crown'd shields, formed into a cross, whose center exhibits the radiated cross of St. George or the Garter Star, and the spaces between the shields fill'd with two interlink'd C's. On the first crown piece of this king, France and England quarterly, were placed at top and bottom, or in the 1st and 4th shields, Ireland on the dexter side, being properly the 2d shield, and Scotland on the sinister side, or the 3d shield, and therefore were wrong marshalled*. All the other monies of this reign and until the Union, have England at top, and France at bottom, Ireland remaining on the dexter, and Scotland on the sinister side as before.

Legend. They are inscribed, MAG. BR. FRA. ET HIB. REX, with the date of the year divided at the top, and there are on some or other of the pieces every date, from 1662 to 1684.

The half crown and crown are inscribed on the rim, DECUS ET TUTAMEN, and the year of the king's reign.

SORTS. Are the penny, No. 1. pl. 17. the half groat No. 4. the quarter shilling, No. 7. the groat No. 10. the half shilling No. 13, the shilling No. 20, the half crown, No. 27. and the crown No. 35.

RARITY. These pieces being still in currency, therefore those only may be said to be scarce, that are in fine preservation, to which we may add those with the feathers, and with the elephant, which are not so common as the others, we have seen the last with no other dates but 66 and 81: and the former with 70, 71, 74, 75, and 79.—There are but few crowns of 65, 70, 74, 75, 78, 83, or 84; as few half crowns of 62, 65, 67, 68, or 78: or shillings of 62, 64, 65, 67, 69, 74, or 75. There are no half shillings before 1674, that have come under our inspection, but they are to be found with every date afterwards. The small pieces seem mostly coined after 1670.

WEIGHT. FINENESS. VALUE. WEIGHT, FINENESS, and VALUE, continued the same as those of the 43d of Queen Elizabeth. (e)

JAMES II. 1685. HEAD SIDE. The head of this king is in profile, and laureat, looking to the left, the contrary way to that of his brother's. The inscription round it is JACOBUS DEI GRATIA.

REVERSE. The reverse has the 4 shields in cross, as his brother's, but the void spaces of the cross, have no interlink'd letters in them, but are quite plain.

(e) The old statutes against the exportation of money and bullion, buying and selling of gold and silver above the mint price, culling, &c. are enforced by a proclamation of the 10th of June, 1661; and the same thing is done with regard to melting the Coin, by Stat. 13 and 14. 2 Car. c. 31. but by the Stat. 15. 2 Car. c. 3. permission being given to export foreign coin and bullion; the East-India Company not being restrained in quantity, soon seized on this opportunity, to export about 8 or 10 times more, annually, than they were used to do, or to the value of 400,000 or 500,000l. instead of their former sum of about 40,000 or 50,000l. † which appears to be the principal cause of the high price Silver has risen to, as such a quantity still makes the demand exceed the supply. By Stat. 18. 2 Car. c. 5. the government took the expence of coinage upon themselves, in order to encourage the bringing bullion to the mint, but the good effects of this act, have been likewise frustrated, by the same causes as occasion'd the rise of the price of the Silver.

* See Leake, p. 361.

† Pollexfen's Discourse on Trade, p. 98, 127, &c.

JAMES II.

SORTS.

WEIGHT.
FINENESS.
VALUE.

W. and M.
1689.
HEADSIDE.

REVERSE.

SORTS.

RARITY.

WILL. III.
1694.
HEADSIDE.

REVERSE.

CHARLES II.

Legend.

REVERSE.
Type.

Legend.

SORTS.

RARITY.

WEIGHT.
FINENESS.
VALUE.

JAMES II.
1685.
HEAD SIDE.

REVERSE.

It is inscribed, MAG. BR. FR. ET HIB. REX, with the date, and on the rim of the half crown and crown, are DECUS ET TUTAMEN, with the year of the king's reign, JAMES II.

The 4 smaller pieces have as many of the initial letters of the king's name crown'd, as they contain pennies, as I. II. III. IIII.

Are the penny, No. 2. the half groat, No. 5. the three-pence, No. 8. the groat, No. 11. the six-pense, No. 14. the shilling, No. 21. the half crown, No. 28. and the crown, No. 36. SORTS.

WEIGHT, FINENESS, and VALUE, continued the same as the 43d of Queen Elizabeth. WEIGHT. FINENESS. VALUE.

Both their busts are exhibited together in profile, looking the same way, or to the left, that of the king is laureat, and the queen is in her hair. W. and M. 1689. HEADSIDE.

They are inscribed, GULIELMUS ET MARIA DEI GRATIA.

The reverse of the first pieces coined by them, (which were only half crowns) have the arms in a single shield, quarterly, and of which there are two sorts, one of which have France and England quarterly, in the first and 4th, Scotland is in the 2d, and Ireland is in the 3d quarter; but on other sorts, England is in the 1st quarter, and France in the 4th; Scotland and Ireland remaining as before. All the other coinages have the 4 shields in cross, as in the two former reigns, with WM. interlink'd in the void spaces of the cross, and the arms of Nassau in the center, instead of the radiated cross of St. George as was before. REVERSE.

They are inscribed, MAG. BR. FR. ET HIB. REX ET REGINA, with the date, not at top as is the usual manner, but round the center.

The rim of the half crown and crown are inscribed as usual, DECUS ET TUTAMEN, with the year of their reigns.

The 4 smaller pieces have the figures 1, 2, 3, 4, on them, for their respective values, which has been the method continued on all these pieces, to the present time.

Are the penny, No. 3, the half groat No. 6, the three-pence, No. 9, the groat No. 12, the six-pence, No. 15, the shilling, No. 22, the half crown, No. 29, 30. and the crown, No. 37. SORTS.

The half crowns with the arms in a single shield, (being those of 1689 and 90) are the most common, not only of the half crowns, but also of all the current sorts, the reason of which, is the great quantity of them that were coined, there being treble as much in value coined in them, as were in all the other pieces taken together, that were coined in the years 1691, 1692, 1693, and 1694; as appears from the comptrolment rolls. RARITY.

He appears with his bust in profile, looking to the left as before, and laureat. There is an half crown with an elephant under the head, a six-pence and a shilling, No. 16, 23. with the feathers, but very small; and the pieces coined at the Country Mints in the grand re-coinage, have the initial letters of those places under the head, as B, C, E, N, Y. for Bristol, Chester, Exeter, Norwich, York. WILL. III. 1694. HEADSIDE.

The inscription is GULIELMUS DEI GRATIA.

The reverse continues still as before, the four shields of England, Ireland, Scotland REVERSE.

WILL. III. land, and France; with that of Naſſau in the center, and in common the ſpaces between the ſhields are plain.

There are ſome ſix-pences, ſhillings and half crowns, coined of the Welch Silver, which have the feathers, in each of the void ſpaces of the ſhields, and are the firſt we meet with wherein they are thus placed, they being in the center on the ſhilling of Charles II.

Other ſix-pences and ſhillings there are, which being coined out of the Silver produced from the lead mines in the Weſt of England, have a roſe in the ſaid ſpaces, which are alſo the firſt that are found in this manner, it being under the head, on the crown of Charles II.

SORTS. Are the penny, the half groat, the three-pence, the groat, the ſix-pence, No. 16. the ſhilling, No. 23. the half crown, No. 31. and the crown, No. 38.

RARITY. The half crown with the elephant, and thoſe pieces with the roſe and the feathers, are not ſo common as the other coins of this king: the two laſt ſeem to have been only coined in the years 1699 and 1701: and thoſe with the ſmall feathers under the head, No. 16. and 23. are both dated 1701.

WEIGHT. FINENESS. VALUE. WEIGHT, FINENESS, and VALUE, the ſame as thoſe of the 43d of Queen Elizabeth (*c*).

ANNE, 1702. HEAD SIDE. This queen is repreſented with a profile face, looking to the right, in her hair, which is tied up behind with a fillet.

Thoſe coined out of the Silver taken at Vigo, have that word under the queen's head, and thoſe coined at Edinburgh, have ſome of them an E. and others the ſame letter with a ſmall *.

The inſcription round the head is ANNA DEI GRATIA.

REVERSE. The reverſe until the Union, was the ſame four ſhields in croſs, and the center again filled as at firſt, with the radiated croſs of the garter; but the Union occaſioned an alteration in the diſpoſition of the ſhields; England and Scotland impal'd, being placed at top and at bottom, Ireland ſtill remaining on the dexter ſide, and France was poſited on the ſiniſter ſide.

They are inſcribed, MAG. BR. FR. ET HIB. REG[illegible] and on the rim of the half crown and crown, DECUS ET TUTAMEN, with the year of the queen's reign.

SORTS. Are the penny, the two-pence, the three-pence, the groat, the ſix-pence, No. 17. the ſhilling, No. 24, the half-crown, No. 32. and the crown, No. 39.

(*c*) The heavy hammer'd money being all culled and melted, and none but the light clipped, being left in currency with the milled, they were therefore all call'd in to be re-coined. The clipping trade had long been carried on, but grew worſe and worſe every day, for altho' by an ordinance of parliament of the 6th of September 1647,* no clipped money was to be taken, and in conſequence thereof, much of it was ſold to the goldſmiths by weight, yet they, inſtead of breaking it, paid it away, and by that means bought it twenty times over;† ſo that in 1680, we find complaints ‡ that little elſe but clipped money was then current: but it might be ſaid to have been carried on with moderation until the year 1688, as not having loſt above 8 per cent. till then, but from that time they ſet about it in earneſt, ſo that in about 6 years, they had reduced it to about one half, and in this ſtate it nearly was, when it was recoined, nine millions of which, being then brought in, produced about 4,725933l. and it is thought would not have produced ſo much, but for ſome heavy money brought out of hoards at that time§.

* Scobel, Part I. p. 138. Journals, vol. 4. p. 298. † Violet's True Diſcovery, 12mo. p. 46. ‡ Britannia Languens, p. 227. § Davenant's new Dialogues, p. 70, 76. Lowndes, p. 159.

WEIGHT,

Veight.
Ineness.
Value.

George I.
1714.
HeadSide.

Reverse.

...orts.

George II.
1727.
HeadSide.

Reverse.

WILL. III. lar
be

ve
th
th

dt
w
th

SORTS.

1(

RARITY.

th
h:
fe

WEIGHT.
FINENESS. E
VALUE.

ANNE, 1702.
HEADSIDE.

w

h
lc

REVERSE.

a;
fi
p
fi

t.
tl

SORTS.

I
I

WEIGHT, FINENESS, and VALUE, as in the forty-third year of Queen Elizabeth. WEIGHT. FINENESS. VALUE.

This king is represented with his bust laureat, looking to the left, the shilling coined out of the Welch copper company's silver, has W. C. C. under the head. GEORGE I. 1714. HEADSIDE.

It is inscribed, GEORGIUS D. G. M. BR. FR. ET HIB. REX. F. D. differing from all the milled money, in having the titles on the head-side; and the F. D. for FIDEI DEFENSOR, is now for the first time found on our money.

The reverse contains still the 4 shields in cross, three of them the same as in the last reign, and one now first added, and are disposed as follows; that is, England and Scotland impaled at top, Brunswick, Lunenburgh and Westphalia on the dexter side, France on the sinister, and Ireland at bottom. REVERSE.

The spaces between the shields on some are plain, some have the rose and feathers alternately in them (but there are none with either sort of them alone) others have S. S. C. alternately, as being coined out of the Silver sent to the mint by the South-Sea company, and again some shillings that have the feathers and CC's alternately, as No. 25. were coined from Silver sent to the mint, by the Welch copper company.

They are inscribed only with the king's foreign titles, BRUN. ET L. DUX S. R. I. A. TH. ET EL. for BRUNSWIGÆ ET LUNENBERGÆ DUX SACRI ROMANI IMPERII ARCHI THESAURARIUS ET ELECTOR, whereas all the other milled money had the English ones.

Are the penny, the two-pence, the three-pence, the groat, the six-pence No. 18. the shilling, No. 25. the half crown, No. 33. and the crown, No. 40. 41. SORTS.

WEIGHT, FINENESS, and VALUE, the same as the 43d year of Queen Elizabeth (*i*).

This king is exhibited with a laureat head, looking to the right, those coined from the Lima Silver brought home by Lord Anson, have that word under the king's head. GEORGE II. 1727. HEADSIDE.

The inscription appears again in the old manner, GEORGIUS II. DEI GRATIA.

The reverse exhibits the same four shields in cross as his father's. REVERSE.

The spaces between the shields are on some of them plain; some have a rose in each of those spaces, others again are filled with the feathers, and others have them alternately in each quarter, and this is the only reign on the reverses of which we have all the three varieties.

(*i*) It appears that Silver was much scarcer anno 1717, than it had been in any year since the grand re-coinage, being in September, 5s. 11d. per oz.* and no doubt, was principally occasion'd by the East India Company's exporting 3,183763 oz. this year†, which was double their annual quantity, taken at a medium, of the preceding 18 years, and about as much as was work'd up into plate in 5 years, as appears from the quantity which had been made in the three last years, and which was laid before the parliament ‡. Another reason assign'd for this scarcity, was our giving a larger quantity of Silver in exchange for gold, than any of our neighbours, and much of it, therefore, exported on that account, to prevent which, a proclamation was published December the 22d, 1717, which lessen'd it 2½ per cent. that is, there was to be no more than 21 shillings in silver given for a guinea, instead of 21 shillings and six pence for which it pass'd before.

* Thoughts on our Silver Coin, 8vo. 1718, p. 19. † Trade to India critically and calmly consider'd, 8vo. 1720, p. 11. and the table. ‡ Journals, vol. 18. p. 174. 682. ‡ Ibid.

The inscription round them contains both the English and foreign titles that is. M. B. F. ET H. REX F. D. B. ET L. D. S. R. I. A. T. ET E.

SORTS. Are the penny, the two-pence, the three-pence, the groat, the six-pence No. 19, the shilling, No. 26. the half crown, No. 34. and the crown No. 42.

N. B. The six-pence, shilling, and half-crown, having the same reverse on all the milled money as the crown, we have therefore engraven the reverse of that only, the shilling, No. 25. being the only sort which has the feathers and ƆC's, and the two half crowns, No 29, 30. those only on which the single shield is found; we have engraven them also.

WEIGHT. FINENESS. VALUE. WEIGHT, FINENESS, and VALUE, as the 43d of Queen Elizabeth, that is,

The Weight of one pound sterling is [illegible] of a pound weight Troy, or 30 oz. 17 dwt. 10[illegible] gr. Troy.

The Fineness is 11 oz. 2 dwt. fine silver, and 18 dwt. alloy, as at the Conuest.

The Value of one pound weight Troy, is $3\frac{1}{10}$ pounds sterling, 62 shillings or 720 pennies. *(k)*

The rare Coins undermentioned are in the cabinets of the following gentlemen.

No. 1. pl. 11.	Rob. Bootle, Esq;
No. 18. pl. 1. No. 5. pl. 11.	Mr. Edw. Brent
No. 29. pl. 1.	Joseph Browne, Esq;
No. 20. pl. 4. No. 6, 18, 20. pl. 7.	Tho. Lee Dummer, Esq;
No. 11. pl. 1. No. 25. pl. 10.	Mr. Edw. Hodsoll
No. 42. pl. 2	Will. Sotheby, Esq;
No. 9. pl. 2.	Mark Cephas Tutet, Esq;
No 18. pl. 5. No. 2. 3. 4. 5. pl. 15.	James West, Esq;
No. 31, 34. pl. 11. No. 4. pl. 2. No. 9. 12. pl. 13.	Mr. John White

And we have in our own possession, No. 28, 39. 40, 42. pl. 1. A. B. C. D. page 13. No. 47. pl. 2. No. 2. pl. 9. and No. 4. pl. 14.

(k) The supply of Silver brought in by our trade, not being near sufficient, to answer the demand for it, by the merchant to export, (especially to the East Indies) and the manufacturer to work up; has at length so rais'd its price, that we have lately seen standard at 5s. 11d. per oz. whereas our mint price for the last century of years, has not been more than 5s. 2d. per oz. and the 60 years preceding that, but 5s. per oz. which difference, has caused all our unworn money to be melted or exported, and been productive of the great scarcity of it, so much felt at present, and seems to have reduced the legislature to the very disagreeable alternative either of not coining any more silver money, or to coin it on a different FOOT from the present; or 3dly, to give a less quantity of silver in exchange for gold, than is done at present; which last appears to be the most practicable, but at the same time to be but a partial remedy; however, we make no doubt but their wisdom will appear no less conspicuous on this, than on former occasions, and still further confirm the honourable character given us by a good judge of these matters, and one who can by no means be suspected of any design to flatter, viz. "That few nations (perhaps none) understand these affairs better than the English*."

* Le Blanc, p. 266.

A

A Table of the Number of Pounds Sterling contained in one Pound Weight, both Tower and Troy, the Quantity of Standard Silver contained in one Pound Sterling, and the Proportion the former Pounds Sterling bear to the present.

Name of the king and year of his reign.	Pounds sterling in 1 Pd. wt. Tower.			Tower wt. of standard in 1 pound sterling.			Pounds sterling in 1 pound wt. Troy.			Troy wt. of standard in 1 pound sterling.			Proportion of pounds sterling.			
	l.	s.	d.	oz.	dwt.	gr.	l.	s.	d.	oz.	dwt.	gr.		l.	s.	d.
Conquest - - 1066	1	0	0	12	0	0	1	1	4	11	5	0	2[illegible]	2	18	1[illegible]
28 Edward I. 1300	1	0	3	11	17	0[illegible]	1	1	7[illegible]	11	2	5[illegible]	2[illegible]	2	17	5
18 Edward III. 1344	1	2	2	10	16	13	1	3	7[illegible]	10	3	0[illegible]	2[illegible]	2	12	5[illegible]
20 ———— 1346	1	2	6	10	13	8	1	4	0	10	0	0	2[illegible]	2	11	8
27 ———— 1353	1	5	0	9	12	0	1	6	8	9	0	0	2[illegible]	2	6	6
13 Henry IV. 1412	1	10	0	8	0	0	1	12	0	7	10	0	1[illegible]	1	18	9
4 Edward IV. 1464	1	17	6	6	8	0	2	0	0	6	0	0	1[illegible]	1	11	0
18 Henry VIII. 1527	2	2	2[illegible]	5	6	16	2	5	0	5	6	16	1[illegible]	1	7	6[illegible]
34 ———— 1543	2	10	0	4	16	0	2	13	4	4	10	15	1[illegible]	1	3	3
36 ———— 1545	4	3	4	2	17	14[illegible]	4	8	10[illegible]	2	14	0	0[illegible]	0	13	11[illegible]
37 ———— 1546	6	5	0	1	18	9[illegible]	6	13	4	1	16	0	0[illegible]	0	9	3[illegible]
3 Edward VI. 1549	6	5	0	1	18	9[illegible]	6	13	4	1	16	0	0[illegible]	0	9	3[illegible]
5 ———— 1551	12	10	0	0	19	4[illegible]	13	6	8	0	18	0	0[illegible]	0	4	7[illegible]
6 ———— 1552	2	16	5	3	14	7[illegible]	3	0	3[illegible]	3	19	15[illegible]	1[illegible]	1	0	6[illegible]
1 Mary 1553	2	16	8	3	13	23[illegible]	3	0	6[illegible]	3	19	6[illegible]	1[illegible]	1	0	5[illegible]
2 Elizabeth 1560	2	16	3	3	14	16	3	0	0	4	0	0	1[illegible]	1	0	8
43 ———— 1601 and ever since	2	18	1[illegible]	3	12	6[illegible]	3	2	0	3	17	10[illegible]	1	1	0	0

N. B. The two last columns are the same, the last having the value of the Fraction reduc'd into shillings and pence.

A Table of the Weights of the English Silver Coins in Troy Grains.

	Farthing.	Half-penny.	Penny.	Half-Groat.	Quarter Shilling.	Groat.	Half Shilling.	Shilling	Half Crown.	Crown
Conquest -- 1066	—	—	22½	—	—	—	—	—	—	—
28 Edward I. 1300	5½	11	22	—	—	88⅔	—	—	—	—
18 Edward III. 1344	5	10	20[illegible]	—	—	—	—	—	—	—
20 ———— 1346	5	10	20	—	—	—	—	—	—	—
27 ———— 1353	4½	9	18	36	—	72	—	—	—	—
13 Henry IV. 1412	3¾	7½	15	30	—	60	—	—	—	—
4 Edward IV. 1464	3	6	12	24	—	48	—	—	—	—
18 Hen. VII. 1504	3	6	12	24	—	48	—	144	—	—
18 Hen. VIII. 1527	2⅔	5	10⅔	21⅓	—	42⅔	—	—	—	—
34 ———— 1543	2½	5	10	20	—	40	—	120	—	—
36 ———— 1545	2½	5	10	20	—	40	—	120	—	—
37 ———— 1546	2½	5	10	20	—	40	—	120	—	—
1 Edward VI. 1547	2½	5	10	20	—	40	—	120	—	—
3 ———— 1549	—	—	—	—	—	—	—	80	—	—
5 ———— 1551	—	—	—	—	—	—	—	80	—	—
6 ———— 1552	5½	11	8	—	24	—	48	96	240	480
1 Mary 1553	6	12	8	16	—	32	—	96	240	480
2 Elizabeth 1560	—	4	8	16	24	32	48	96	—	—
43 ———— 1601 and ever since	—	3[illegible]	7[illegible]	15[illegible]	22[illegible]	31	46[illegible]	92[illegible]	232[illegible]	464[illegible]

The three farthing piece of Q. Elizabeth weighs 6 grains, the three half-penny piece 12 gr. the X shilling piece of Charles I. 1 oz. 18 dwt. 17 gr. or 929 gr. and the XX shilling piece 3 oz. 17 dwt. 10 gr. or 1858 gr.

A Table of the king's Seignorage, the Master of the Mint's Allowance for Workmanship, and what the Merchant had paid him back, also the Quantity of fine Silver and Alloy; and the Remedy both in Weight and Fineness allowed, each estimated upon the Pound Weight‖.

	1 Pound weight. l.	s.	d.	To the king. s.	d.	To the master. s.	d.	To the king & the master. s.	d.	To the merchant. l.	s.	d.	Taken	Fine Silver. oz.	dwt	Alloy. oz.	dwt	Remedy. dwt.
28 Edward I.	1	0	3	0	9	0	5¼	1	2¼	the rest			[illegible]	11	2	0	18	
18 Edward III.	1	2	2	0	6	0	9	1	3	the rest			[illegible]	11	2	0	18	
19 ———	1	2	2	0	6	0	8	1	2	1	1	0	[illegible]	11	2	0	18	
20. 23 ———	1	2	6	0	9	0	6½	1	3½	the rest			[illegible]	11	2	0	18	
27 ———	1	5	0	0	4	0	6	0	10	the rest			[illegible]	11	2	0	18	
30 ———	1	5	0	0	4½	0	6¾	0	11¼	1	4	0¾	[illegible]	11	2	0	18	
18 Rich. II. / 4 Hen. IV.	1	5	0	0	3	0	7	0	10	1	4	2	[illegible]	11	2	0	18	
9 Hen. V.	1	10	0	0	3	0	9	1	0	1	9	0	[illegible]	11	2	0	18	2.
24 Hen. VI.				1	2	0	10	2	0	1	8	0	[illegible]	11	2	0	18	
49 ———				1	2	0	10	2	0	1	8	0	[illegible]	11	2	0	18	
4 Edw. IV.				3	4	1	2	4	6	1	13	0	[illegible]	11	2	0	18	
7. 22 ———	1	17	6	2	0	1	2	3	2	1	14	4	[illegible]	11	2	0	18	
8 ———				1	6	1	2	2	8	1	14	10	[illegible]	11	2	0	18	
19 Hen. VII.				0	2	0	10	1	0	1	16	6	[illegible]	11	2	0	18	
18 Hen. VIII.	2	5	0	0	2	0	10	1	0	2	4	0	[illegible]	11	2	0	18	
34 ———	2	16	0	5	8	2	4	8	0	2	8	0	[illegible]	10	0	2	0	
36 ———	4	16	0	———		———		40	0	2	16	0	[illegible]	6	0	6	0	
1 Edw. VI.	7	4	0	———		———		84	0	3	0	0	[illegible]	4	0	8	0	3.
3 ———				———		———		80	0	3	4	0	[illegible]	4	0	8	0	
4 ———	14	8	0	———		———		168	0	6	0	0	[illegible]	3	0	9	0	
6 ———				———		———		1	0	2	19	0	[illegible]	11	1	0	19	
1 Eliz.	3	0	0	0	4	1	2	1	6	2	18	6	[illegible]	11	2	0	18	
19 ———				0	10	0	8	1	6	2	18	6	[illegible]	11	2	0	18	
25 ———				0	8	1	2	1	10	2	18	2	[illegible]	11	2	0	18	
43 ———				0	8	1	4	2	0	3	0	0	[illegible]	11	2	0	18	2.
2 James I.				1	2	1	4	2	6	2	19	6	[illegible]	11	2	0	18	
2 Char. I.	3	2	0	0	10	1	2	2	0	3	0	0	[illegible]	11	2	0	18	
Char. II.				0	6	1	6	2	0	3	0	0	[illegible]	11	2	0	18	
18 ———				———		———		———		3	2	0	0	11	2	0	18	

It does not appear that any of our princes made any considerable advantage of the remedies until Q. Eliz. who in her 14th year, allow'd Lonison the master but 8 pence, instead of 14 pence, or 14 pence farthing, to bear all expences, which obliged him to avail himself of the said six-pence farthing, by means of these remedies, as appears by the report of the commissioners appointed to examine into this affair* : after which the Queen impowered him by commission dated Dec. 31, in her 21st year, to coin at 11 oz. 1 wt. in fineness, and 60s. 3d. in the pound weight † (which had been suggested to her majesty by the said commissioners) taking thus half the remedies, which amounted to about 6d. farthing as before. Other commissions to the said purpose, were granted in her 23d and 24th year; but in her 25th year, the subject was charged 22d. that is 4d. more, and the queen had but 8d. or 2d. less, which made up the 6d. which had been squeez'd out of these remedies.——Towards the latter end of her reign, and the 1st 17 years of James I. the money was again paid out by tale ‡, and therefore the profit of the shere came to the sovereign, which before was the Merchants.

The usual allowance to the moneyers for the workmanship of 1 pound of silver was 8d. but Sir Tho. Knevet,

‖ Briefe Collection of the Alterations, &c. MS. A Treatise declaring many notable instructions, MS.

* Stowe's Survey, by Strype, vol. 2, p. 100. † Folkes, p. 55. ‡ Ibid. 137.

Knevet, when he became Warden (the 41ſt of Eliz.) added 1d. more to have it better ſized and work'd neater;(z) and on the introduction of the milled money, 3d. more was allowed, making in the whole 18d. (including the 6d. for charges) and therefore the king had but 6d. or a little more than half his ſeignorage. Since which, 1d halfpenny has been taken off from the laſt mentioned 3d. which makes it 16d. halfpenny. —N. B. Only 14d. was allowed at the grand re-coinage, and they were ſhered at ſomething more than 62s. 3d. per pound.

A Table of the Fees and Salaries of the ſeveral Officers belonging to the Mint.

	1599. (a)			1649. (b)			1689. (c)			1739. (d)		
	l.	s.	d.	l.	s.	d.	l.	s.	d.	l.	s.	d.
Warden	100	0	0	100	0	0	400	0	0	400	0	0
Clerk	20	0	0	20	0	0	40	0	0	50	0	0
Comptroller	66	13	4	66	13	4	300	0	0	300	0	0
Clerk	13	6	8	13	6	8	40	0	0	50	0	0
Aſſay-Maſter	66	13	4	66	13	4	200	0	0	200	0	0
Clerk	10	0	0	10	0	0	20	0	0	25	0	0
Weigher and Teller	33	6	8	33	6	8	90	0	0	130	0	0
Clerk	10	0	0	10	0	0	10	0	0	12	10	0
Aſſiſtant Weigher	—			—			40	0	0	—		
Surveyor of the Meltings	26	13	4	26	13	4	} 110	0	0	} 132	10	0
Clerk of the Irons	13	6	8	13	6	8						
Clerk	10	0	0	10	0	0	10	0	0			
Chief Clerk	20	0	0	20	0	0	60	0	0	*60	0	0
Clerk of the Papers	20	0	0	20	0	0	40	0	0	40	0	0
2 Auditors	20	0	0	40	0	0	40	0	0	40	0	0
Smith of the Mint	10	0	0	10	0	0	—			—		
Porter	10	0	0	10	0	0	20	0	0	25	0	0
Chaplain	0	13	4	0	13	4	4	0	0	4	0	0
Sexton	0	4	0	0	4	4	1	0	0	1	0	0
							1425	0	0	1470	0	0
							1689.			1743. (e)		
							l.	s.	d.	l.	s.	d.
Maſter and Worker	—			—			500	0	0	500	0	0
3 Clerks	—			—			120	0	0	150	0	0
Aſſay Maſter	40	0	0	40	0	0	60	0	0	60	0	0
Purveyor	20	0	0	—			20	0	0	25	0	0
Chief Engraver	30	0	0	30	0	0	} 325	0	0	200*	0	0
2d ditto	40	0	0	40	0	0				80†	0	0
3d ditto	—			—						80‡	0	0
Aſſiſtant to Engravers	20	0	0	20	0	0	50	0	0	40	0	0
Provoſt of the Moneyers as Engineer‖‖	—			—			100	0	0	100	0	0
Clerk to the Warden §	—			—			—			100	0	0
Surveyor of Moneyers ‡	—			—			—			40	0	0
9 Moneyers ⅔ of a Year at 25l.‖ and ⅓ at 40l.¶	—			—			—			326	10	0
	600	17	4	600	17	8	1175	0		1701	5	

(z) Sir Julius Cæſar's Collect. p. 346. 350.
(a) Goldſmith's Storehouſe, p. 75. MS. (b) Journals vol. 5. p. 252. (c) Indenture of Tho. Neale, Eſq; MS.
(d) Warden's Account, MS. (e) Maſter's Acc. MS. * By Lett. Pat. 23 Ap. 1741. † By Warrant 16 Sept. 1727.
‡ By Warrant, 9 April, 1741. N. B. An extraordinary Engraver was appointed in 1761, at 100l. per Ann.
‖‖ Blondeau, by Letters Patent in 13 Car. 2. was appointed the firſt Engineer.
§ Warrant, 28 July, 1734. ‡ Warrant, 28 Sept, 1728. ‖ Warrant, 16 July, 1729. ¶ Warrant, 29 Mar. 1743.

An

An Account of Silver Monies coined from the 20th of July, 1660, to the 31st of December 1748, Year by Year, made out from the comptrollment Rolls and Books remaining in the Mint.

From July 20 to 31 Dec.	Weight. lb.	oz.	dwt.	gr.	Value. l.	s.	d. q.		Weight. lb.	oz.	dwt.	Value. l.	s.	d.
1660	543	0	0	0	1683	6	0	1704	4007	0	0	12421	14	0
1661	7484	0	10	0	23200	10	7¼	1705	429	7	15	1331	18	0½
1662	160218	8	0	0	496677	17	4	1706	932	0	0	2889	4	0
1663	98412	1	18	18	3305077	14	0	1707	1174	0	0	3639	8	0
1664	14301	0	0	0	44333	2	0	Edin.	103346	0	0	320372	12	0
1665	19910	3	0	0	61721	15	6	1708	3751	0	0	11628	2	0
1666	11982	0	0	0	37144	4	0	1709	25423	0	0	78811	6	0
1667	17131	2	0	0	53106	12	4	1710	817	0	0	2532	14	0
1668	40303	2	0	0	124939	16	4	1711	24768	0	0	76780	16	0
1669	14291	9	10	0	44304	11	1	1712	17848	8	0	55330	17	4
1670	46142	11	0	0	143043	0	10	1713	2333	0	0	7232	6	0
1671	38645	2	17	0	119800	4	8½	1714	1566	0	0	4854	12	0
1672	86673	8	17	0	268688	11	8½	1715	1643	0	0	5093	6	0
1673	101064	4	15	0	313299	12	6½	1716	1650	0	0	5115	0	0
1674	102886	3	15	0	31887	11	4½	1717	948	0	0	2938	16	0
1675	1856	2	5	0	5754	3	7½	1718	2295	0	0	7114	10	0
1676	101836	11	15	0	315694	12	8½	1719	1756	0	0	5443	12	0
1677	146034	0	13	0	452705	11	4½	1720	7832	0	0	24279	4	0
1678	7366	2	0	0	22835	2	4	1721	2313	0	0	7170	6	0
1679	87313	3	5	0	270671	2	9½	1722	1983	0	0	6147	6	0
1680	48204	0	10	0	180432	10	7	1723	48099	0	0	149106	18	0
1681	30782	11	10	0	95427	3	5	1724	1652	0	0	5121	4	0
1682	12759	0	0	0	39552	18	0	1725	2495	0	0	7734	10	0
1683	69851	0	0	0	216538	2	0	1726	836	0	0	2591	12	0
1684	17309	9	3	20	53660	5	6½	1727	661	0	0	2049	2	0
1685	30572	0	10	0	94773	6	7	1728	853	0	0	2644	6	0
1686	19294	10	5	0	59814	0	11½	1729	2055	0	0	6370	10	0
1687	80848	5	0	0	250630	1	10	1730	1122	0	0	3478	4	0
1688	24590	6	11	20	76230	14	0¼	1731	704	0	0	2182	8	0
1689	31152	6	15	17	96572	19	0¾	1732	845	0	0	2619	10	0
1690	643	5	0	0	1994	11	10	1733	1155	0	0	3580	10	0
1691	1203	5	7	18	3730	13	9¾	1734	1590	0	0	4929	0	0
1692	1341	10	17	3	4159	18	0¾	1735	1116	0	0	3459	12	0
1693	2992	6	1	0	9276	15	3	1736	1713	0	0	5310	6	0
1694	51	6	16	13	159	17	3¼	1737	1200	0	0	3720	0	0
1695	20	0	0	0	62	0	0	1738	Nil					
1696	810275	2	12	14	2511853	3	7	1739	3396	0	0	10527	12	0
1697	707160	0	0	0	2192196	0	0	1740	Nil					
1698	105364	0	0	0	326628	0	0	1741	3060	0	0	9486	0	0
1699	577996	0	0	0	1791787	12	0	1742	Nil					
Country	19498	0	0	0	60443	16	0	1743	2400	0	0	7440	0	0
1700	4805	10	6	16	14898	3	4½	1744	2528	0	0	7836	16	0
1701	37477	0	0	0	116178	14	0	1745	600	0	0	1860	0	0
1702	114	6	0	0	354	19	0	1746	44010	0	0	136431	0	0
1703	718	0	0	0	2225	16	0	1747	15000	0	0	46500	0	0
								1748	Nil					

COINED

COINED in each REIGN.

	WEIGHT. lb.	oz.	dwt.	gr.	VALUE. l.	s.	d.
By King Charles II. -	1200703	3	4	14	3722180	2	8
——— James II. - -	167198	10	6	20	518316	9	5¼
——— Will. and Mary	25492	4	18	8	79026	9	4¾
——— William III. -	2262596	0	19	6	7014047	16	11¾
— Queen Anne - -	170150	9	15	0	527467	10	4¼
— King George I. -	75176	0	0	0	233045	12	0
——— George II. to the 31ſt of Dec. 1748	88747	0	0	0	275115	14	0
	3990064	5	4		12369199	14	9

By the foregoing table it appears, that there has been coined ſince the reſtoration 12,369199l. ſterling, but as 544642l. of that ſum was coined with the hammer, therefore the total ſum that has been coined into milled, or our preſent current money, until December 31, 1748, is 11,824557l. ſterling, of which ſum it is very probable, that the 11 millions are gone, and no more left in currency than the eight hundred and odd thouſand pounds, to ſerve the purpoſe of ſmall change and commutation, which is the principal uſe, to which at preſent our ſilver money ſeems to be confin'd, and daily experience ſhews there is not a ſufficient quantity to anſwer that end.

The grand re-coinage between the years 1696 and 1699, amounted to the ſum of 6,404064l. ſter. which is the better half of what had been coined in the 89 years above, and will reduce what may be called the natural coinage to 5,965135l. which we will ſuppoſe, with what has been coined between 1748 and 1760, (to compleat the century) to amount to 6 millions, which is but 3-eighths of the ſum that was coined in the preceding century, or between 1558 and 1659, as that amounted to 16 millions§.—— There was coined during the reigns of Cha. II. James II. and Will. and Mary, in about 34 years and a half, the Sum of 4,319523l. 1s. 6d. or about 125203l. 8s. 11d. per ann. at a medium, but from the beginning of the reign of Geo. I. to 1748, or in about 35 years and an half, the ſum of 508161l. 6s. or no more than 14314l. 8s. per ann. at a medium—The plate brought in on encouragement in 1709 and 1711, amounted to 143056l. ſterling, or near 3-tenths of all Queen Anne's coinage.——The Silver ſent by the South-Sea Company in 1723, amounted to 3-fifths of all George the Iſt's, and the Lima to half of George the IId's coinage.

It appears from the comptrollment rolls, that there was no Silver coined between the 11th of June, the time of the acceſſion of George II. and the 31ſt of Dec. 1727, nor during the whole year 1740, and yet there are many pieces of this king's with the former date, and the 4 ſmalleſt pieces with the latter, which we may ſuppoſe were coined between the 1ſt of January and the 25th of March 1727-8 and 1740-1.

Davenant informs us, that between 1660 and 1688, there had been coined into milled money, 4,200000l. ſterling, but by what has juſt been ſaid, it appears, that only 3,774877l. was milled, and the the reſt hammer'd, which will therefore reduce the 2,200000l. he ſuppoſes to be left in 1688*, to leſs than 2000000l. another author† is of the ſame opinion in 1696, however, ſtates it at no more than half this ſum, or 1,000000l. and Mr. Lowndes‡ thought it did not exceed 563508l. which, if allowed to be true, ſix parts in ſeven of what had till then been coined, had diſappear'd.

§ Davenant's Diſcourſes on the Revenues, vol. 2. p. 31.—35. New Dialogues, p. 70. Lowndes, p. 104. Folkes, p. 71.

By Queen Elizabeth	4632932	3	8½	16050481 6 8½
James I. - -	1641004	13	3	
Charles I. - -	8776544	10	3	
Common Wealth	1000000	0	0	

* Diſcourſes, p. 33.—39. † Review of the univerſal Remedy for all Diſeaſes incident to Coin, p. 6. ‡ Page 185.

F I N I S.

E R R A T A.

PAGE 2. line 37. for Ontheorn, read, Onthreorn, p. 16. l. 14. add or Meu, p. 17. l. 15. inſtead of Ang. r. Angl. l. 19. add, others D. Hy. l. 22. after No. 23. add, and No. 33. p. 18. l. 6. after Henry IV. add, No. 25. line 25. Notes, inſtead of twelve r. twenty. p. 19. l. 13. r. Breſtol and Norvic. l. 6. and 7. inſtead of Ang. r. Anglie, p. 33. l. 28. and 31. for half-pennies, r. half-groats. p. 44. l. 8. for and encircle, r. not encircled, p. 45. l. 46. for like that, r. different from that, p. 54. againſt 1699, read, 19498——60443—16. and againſt Country, read, 577996—— 1791787 —— 12.

A

V I E W

OF THE

GOLD COIN

AND

COINAGE

OF

E N G L A N D,

From HENRY THE THIRD
To the PRESENT TIME.

Consider'd with Regard to

TYPE, LEGEND, SORTS, RARITY, WEIGHT, FINENESS, VALUE and PROPORTION.

With COPPER-PLATES.

L O N D O N:
Printed for T. SNELLING, next the *Horn Tavern*, in *Fleet-Street*.
MDCCLXIII.
Who buys and sells all Sorts of Coins and Medals.

INTRODUCTION.

T was the general receiv'd opinion, till within about 30 or 40 years, that Edward the third was the first of our monarchs that coined gold money in this kingdom, and this belief was founded, no doubt, on the inability of the curious in this study, to procure any piece of money prior to that prince, or to find any thing in our records relating thereto.

HENRY III. Gold Penny. 1257.

But, within that period of time, it has been discover'd, that gold money was coined here in the reign of Henry the third; which curious anecdote first appeared in the notes to the translation of M. Rapin de Thoyras's History of England *, published in the year 1732, the words are as follows, "The manuscript chronicle of the city of London, " says this king (Henry III.) in 1258 coined a penny of fine gold, of " the weight of two sterlings, and commanded it should go for 20 " shillings; if this be true, these were the first pieces of gold coined " in England." *N. B.* The date should be 1257, and the value 20 pence.

Mr. Maitland, in his History of London †, published, about seven years afterwards, in the year 1739, repeats nearly the same words from the same authority, i. e. " This year (anno 1257) the king caused to " be coined in London a penny of fine gold, weighing two sterlings, " which is supposed to be the first gold coin in England."

Lib. de Leg. in Rec. Guil.

The words of the said chronicle, as transcribed by him, are, " A. D. " 1257. Hoc anno creavit rex moneta aurea denar. pond. duos ster- " lingos de auro purissimo & voluit ut illo auro curreret in pond. " vinginti." Here seems, by some means, to be a mistake of the word *pond.* for *denar.* in the value.

* Vol. I. p. 347. Leake, p. 72. † Page 53.

Mr. Carte, in his History of England *, farther informs us, that this ancient manuscript § is preserved in the city Archives, and contains an historical account of what passed there during the latter part of the reign of Henry III. and the beginning of Edward I.——And, again, he says †, "It may, perhaps, appear strange that Henry, in "the height of his distress for want of money, should be the first "prince that ever struck gold in England. The piece he caused to "be struck was of pure gold, and weighed two sterlings; it was to "pass in the usual proportion of gold to silver at that time, for twenty "sterlings or pennies in silver. It is not said for what reason the "citizens of London made a representation against it, on Sunday, "Nov. 4; but the king was so willing to oblige them, that he pub-"lished a proclamation, declaring that nobody was obliged to take "it, and whoever did, might bring it to his exchange, and receive "there the value at which it had been made current, an half-penny "only being deducted probably for the coinage."

§ Liber de antiquis legibus.

This fortunate discovery occasioned the records in the Tower to be examined with great care, amongst which Mr. Holmes ‡ found the following precept, directed to the mayor and sheriffs of the city of London, to enforce the currency of this gold money.

DE MONETA AUREA.

Ro. Clauf. Ao. 41 Rs. Hen. III. m. 3.

Mandatum est majori & vicecomitibus London. Quod clamari faciant in civitate predicta. Quod *moneta regis aurea*, quam rex fieri fecit de cetero currat tam in civitate predicta, quam alibi per regnum Anglie tam ad empciones quam ad vendiciones faciendas. Viz. quilibet denarius pro xx denariis Sterlingorum. Et quod moneta regis argentea currat similiter sicut currere consuevit. Teste Rege apud Cestriam, 16mo. die Augusti.

Per Consilium Regis.

From whence it appears, that it was something less than three months after its publication, that the city petitioned against it. However, amongst the records just mention'd, there were likewise discover'd several Liberates, directed to the treasurer, barons and chamberlains of the Exchequer, in his 44th, 49th, 51st and 54th years, wherein this money is particularly mentioned, i. e.

* Vol. II. p. 23. † Ibid. p. 111.
‡ See Mr. Pegge's Letter to Dr. Taylor, in the Gent. Mag. 1756. p. 284.

REX

Rex Theſaurario & Camerariis ſuis ſalutem liberate de Theſaurario noſtro, Alberico de Fiſcamp & P. de Winton clericis. Garderobe noſtræ aurum in ſoleo ponderis XVIII Marcarum, & ijd. & LXII Biſancias Auri, VIIjd. & Ob. Auri de Muſc. & LXII *denar. Auri de nova moneta* reponend in Theſaurario noſtro. T. R. apud Weſtin. ij die Novembris. Ro. Liberat. 44 Hen. III. m. 11. & 7.

PRO WILLO FILIO RICI.

Rex Baronibus ſuis de Scaccario ſalutem. Allocate Willmo filio Ricardi cuſtodi Cambiorum noſtrorum in exitibus Cambii London. quadraginta ſolidos pro *viginti Denariis de Nova Moneta Auri*, quos per preceptum noſtrum emit & in Garderobam noſtram liberavit Nicholas de Lackenor Cuſtodi ejuſdem Garderobe die Mercurii proxim. poſt feſtum Sancti Luce Evangeliſte anno Regni noſtri XLmo. nono ad oblaciones noſtras inde faciendas. Teſte Rege apud Cantuariam 25to. die Octobris. Ro. Liberate A. 49. Rs. Hen. III. m. 1.

Rex Theſaurar. & Camerariis ſuis ſalutem Liberate de Theſauro noſtro Reginaldo de Cantebrigia Sexaginta Solidos pro *Triginta denariis Auri de Nova moneta* ab eo emptis & liberat. ad Oblaciones noſtras die ſancti Edwardi. Ro. Liberate Ao. 51. Rs. Hen. III. m. 10.

PRO BARTHO DE CASTELLO.

Rex Baronibus de Scaccario ſalutem. Allocate Bartho. de Caſtello cuſtodi Cambii noſtri London. & Cantuar. in exitibus ejuſdem Cambii viginti & quinque libras & ſeptem Solidos & quatuor Denarios, viz. Pro uno incenſario auri & opere ejuſdem Viginti & quinque Libras & viginti Denarios in quinque Obol de Muſc. Septem ſolidos & ſex denarios in uno beſanto & duos ſolidos & quatuor denarios in uno denario de Muſc. tres Solidos. *Et in uno Denario auri de Nova Moneta* duos Solidos per ipſum factis ad opus noſtrum ad oblaciones noſtras inde per diverſas vices faciendas. Teſte Rege 21mo die Julii. Ro. Liberate Ao. 54. Rs. Hen. III. m. 3.

By the three laſt of theſe records, or thoſe of his 49th, 51ſt and 54th years, we find that this money had been raiſed in its value from 20 pence to 24 pence, or two ſhillings; that is, in the firſt, 40 ſhillings are to be paid for 20 gold pennies, in the next, 60 ſhillings for 30 gold pennies, and, in the laſt, 2 ſhillings for 1 gold penny.

There has been alſo a diſcovery, lately made, of a bond * or inſtrument between two Jews, dated in his 46th year, wherein mention is made of a Jaku of gold, which is ſuppoſed to be this penny, but the reaſon why ſo called not eaſy to determine.

* Pegge's Letter to Mr. Da Coſta. Gent. Mag. 1756. p. 465.

Although

Although, as we have juſt now ſeen, there had been ſo many evidences (*a*) of the coinage of this money diſcovered, yet not one of theſe pieces, for ſeveral years after, was to be ſeen, it being but within a twelve-month that Mr. Hodſol has had the great good fortune to have his fine cabinet adorned with this truly curious and valuable piece.

OBVERSE. The obverſe exhibits the king ſitting on a chair or throne, in his royal robes crown'd, having, in his right hand, a very neat ſcepter, which paſſes under his arm, and is form'd of ſix pearls or pellets; in his left-hand he holds a globe or monde, ſurmounted but not touch'd, by a croſs compoſed of four of the ſame pearls or pellets, and a ſort of Moſaic work appears under his feet (*b*). It has inſcribed round it HENRICUS REX III.

REVERSE. The reverſe has the long croſs extending to the edge of the piece, dividing the lettered circle, as the ſterling after his 32d year; in the interſtices of the croſs are four very neat roſes between three ſmall pellets, whereas the ſterling has only three pellets, and thoſe much larger. It is inſcribed with the name of the Minter and Town, that is, WILLEM ON LUND, and we apprehend is the only inſtance of any gold coin with ſuch an inſcription.

WEIGHT. This piece weighs 45 grains Troy, or juſt two ſterlings or pennies of this king.

FINENESS. It appears to be fine gold, or at leaſt, of what is called the old ſtandard of 23 car. 3 $\frac{1}{2}$ gr. of fine gold, and $\frac{1}{2}$ carat gr. alloy.

VALUE OF PROPORTION. As the gold penny weighed two ſilver pennies, and was current for 20 of them; had they been of fine ſilver, as that was of fine gold, the proportion would have been as 1 to 10.

But, as the ſilver penny contained no more than 37 parts in 40 of fine ſilver, therefore the proportion was but $\frac{37}{40}$ ths of 10, or no more than 9 $\frac{1}{4}$.

Whereas, in the reigns of Henry I. * Stephen, Henry II. and John †, the proportion was only as 1 to 9,

Finally, when the gold penny was raiſed from 20 pennies to two ſhillings, or 20 per cent. the proportion was raiſed alſo from 9 $\frac{1}{4}$ to 11 $\frac{1}{10}$.

(*a*) In like manner not one farthing nor half-penny of this king have yet appeared ‖, altho' we have the following ſtrong evidence of their having been coined, i. e. "In Craſ-" tino Cinerium anno VI. regis traditi fuerunt prædictus VIII Cunei ad Obolos & Qua-" drantes rotundas faciendos.—Poſtea traditi fuerunt eiſdem die Jovis ante Paſcha VIII. " Cunei ad Quadrantes præter primos VIII. Cuneos ‡."

(*b*) This piece was properly a Ryal, and the firſt of the ſort coined in Europe, the petit ryal of Phillip le Belle being much in imitation of it, and he was the firſt king of France who coined them §, and began his reign A. D. 1285.

* North's Remarks, p. 42. † Madox's Hiſt. of the Exchequer, p. 189.
‖ See our View of the Silver Coin and Coinage, p. 11. ‡ Madox, p. 604.
§ Le Blanc, p. v. 180.

A VIEW OF THE GOLD COIN AND COINAGE OF *ENGLAND.*

HE first Gold Money coined by this king was the florin (*a*) or florence, which had for its type two leopards, and the half florin which had but one leopard; what was their legend we are not informed, * nor have one of either of them reached our time to satisfy us in that point, and no more than one of the quarter florins, which has semé of fleurs-de-lis, the royal helmet with a lion passant-gardant at top. EDW. III. 18th Year, 1344. FLORIN. OBVERSE Type.

The inscription round it is EDWR. R. ANGL. z FRANC. D. HIB. Legend.

(*a*) It is the most general opinion † that this famous money was first minted at Florence, anno 1252, and appears to be the first gold money of any note minted after the establishment of the modern states and kingdoms, and was so pleasing a coin, that others were made in France, Hungary, Bohemia, Bavaria, Rome, Mentz, Triers, Orange, Lubeck, &c. with the same type, but these of our Edwards entirely differed from them in that respect.

It was likewise in some places the common name for all sorts of gold money, and in Germany they made it a money integer or denomination in accompts, which still exists both there and in the Low-Countries, under its own proper name, and the synonymous one of Gulden.

* Rymer, tom. 5. p. 403. † Giovan. Villani Histor, lib. vi. c. liv. Borghini Moneta Fiorentina, p. 129. Vettori Fiorino d'Oro Antico Illustrato, c. 1. pt. 1.

Reverse Type. We are ignorant of the type and legend on the reverses both of the whole and the half florin, the type of the quarter No. 1. pl. 1. is a cross composed of treble lines of pearls or pellets, with a small rose on its center, and is very singular in having this cross surrounded with a sort of square figure, instead of the rose (*a*) or compartment, which, with some small variety, is found on most of the Gold money of this time.

Legend. It has for its legend EXALTABITUR IN GLORIA, which was continued on all the quarter nobles.

Sorts. The only sorts which were coined were the whole, the half, and the quarter.

Rarity. The quarter, which (as we have already observed) is the only one we have of the three, is the rarest coin in the gold series, and was formerly in the curious cabinet of the honourable Bryan Fairfax, Esq; from whence it passed to that of Martin Folkes, Esq; and is at this time in the collection of Mr. Hannot, of Woodford-bridge.

Weight. The quarter florin weighs 27 grains, the half florin should weigh 54 grains and the whole florin 108 grains Troy *(b)*.

Fineness. The gold of which these pieces were made consisted of 23 carats, 3 grains and a half pure gold, and half a grain alloy, that is 191 parts were fine and 1 part alloy, and this was the only sort of gold used in our mints until the eighteenth year of Henry the Eighth, anno 1527, or for more than 180 years, and in general is called the old standard of England.

Value or Proportion. The florin was current for six soldz or shillings, the half florin for three shillings, and the quarter florin for eighteen deniers or pence. Fifty florins were by indenture * to be cut out of one pound weight Tower of gold of the abovesaid fineness or proportion, which amounted to fifteen pounds sterling in tale, and therefore the nominal value of one pound weight of fine gold or of 24 carats was $15\frac{15}{191}$ pounds, or 15*l.* 1*s.* 6*d.* 3*qr.* sterling.

One pound weight Tower of standard silver was at this time coined into 22*s.* 2*d.* in tale or $1\frac{13}{120}$ pounds sterling, and therefore the pound weight of fine silver was coined into $1\frac{22}{111}$ pounds sterling *(d)*.

And from hence it appears that the proportion of fine silver to fine gold was as 1 to 12[illegible] *(e)* and the true value of one pound weight of fine gold was 12 lb. 8 oz. 14 dwt. $7\frac{1}{2}$ gr. of fine silver.

The

(*a*) The rose was a symbol of secrecy among the ancients, and from hence is deriv'd the adage UNDER THE ROSE when a secret is to be kept, and therefore with great propriety used on privy seals †, which came into use about the middle of the twelfth century, and from thence no doubt transferred to the gold money by way of ornament. It has always appear'd with eight leaves on our gold money, but on the French mostly with four.

(*b*) This florin weighed two of those of Florence ‡, and the half florin weighed one, being nearly the same weight as the double and single ducat have always weighed.

(*c*) The fineness of gold is calculated by twenty-fourth parts, call'd carats, each of which is divided into four parts, called carat grains, and each of these grains again is divided into four quarters, and fine gold without any alloy is said to be gold of 24 carats.

(*d*) Although the value of gold is always estimated by the pound sterling, and its component parts shillings and pence, yet the fine silver contained in it is the measure of that value, and therefore the quantity of fine silver in one pound sterling; or the number of pounds sterling contained in one pound weight of fine silver must first be known, before the value of fine gold can be found.

And where the requisite data for reducing the tale denominations to their weight of fine silver are wanting, which is too frequently the case, the proportion between gold and silver cannot be found, nor can the value of any sum of those denominations at different periods be compared together.

(*e*) But this value by no means pleased the people, they thought it too high, or that they gave too

* Lowndes, p. 35. † Menestrier Origine des Ornamens exterieurs des Armoires, p. 431. 12mo. Par. 1679. ‡ Rymer loc. cit.

many

The noble immediately succeeded the florin, and both in name *(f)* and type was different from any other, it exhibits the king standing upright in the middle of a ship in armour, with his sword erect in his right hand and his shield in his left, on which appears the quartered arms of France and England; those of France being semé of fleurs-de-lis. 18th Year. NOBLE. OBVERSE Type.

This Noble is inscribed EDWAR D. GRA. REX ANGL. Z FRANC. DNS. HYB. Legend.

The reverse has a cross formed of three lines, two of which are dotted, and are terminated with a sort of flourished ornament and a fleur-de-lis, having on its center a small rose or compartment, of four leaves or arches and four angles, whose points terminate in three pellets in the void spaces made by the cross: which have also in each of those spaces a lion with a crown over it, all contained within a compartment of eight arches dotted like the cross. In the center is an *L*, very probably for London, the place of its mintage. REVERSE. Type.

This noble is inscribed IHC TRANSIENS PER MEDIUM ILLORUM IBAT. Legend.

We know of but one of the nobles of this coinage, which is in the curious cabinet of Mr. Edward Hodsol. RARITY.

The noble weighs 138[illegible] grains Troy, the half noble should weigh 69[illegible] grains, and the quarter noble 34[illegible] grains. WEIGHT.

These pieces were 23 carats, 3 grains and a half fine gold, and half a grain alloy §. FINENESS.

The noble was made current for the well-known sum of half a MARK, or six shillings and eight-pence, the half or maile noble for three shillings and four-pence, and the quarter or ferling noble for twenty-pence. VALUE or PROPORTION.

By indenture ‖ the Tower pound was to be cut, into 39$\frac{1}{2}$ nobles, amounting to 13*l.* 3*s.* 4*d.* sterling, and the nominal value of the pound weight of fine gold was therefore equal to 13[illegible] pound, or 13*l.* 4*s.* 8*s.* 2*qr.* sterling.

The pound weight Tower of fine silver still contained as before 1[illegible] pound sterling.

And from hence it appears that the proportion of fine silver to fine gold was at this time, as 1 to 11[illegible], and the true value of *(g)* of one pound weight of fine gold was 11 lb. 11 dwt. 2 gr. of fine silver.

This noble differs from the type of the last only in having the initial letter *E* of the king's name in the center of the reverse, instead of the *L*, and which was continued on all of them afterwards till Edward the Fourth. 20th Year. NOBLE Type.

The

many sterlings or pennies for this florin, or which is the same thing, too many ounces or pounds of silver for one of gold, and therefore they were soon called in to be recoined or to be taken or refused at pleasure *.

(f) The gold money in general received their name from their type, the Royal being thus called as representing the king in his royal robes, the Masse from the scepter in his hand, the Chaise from the chair, and the same of the Angel, Salute, Sovereign, &c. † and it is very probable this coin received its name on the same account, its type being expressive of the king's NOBLE resolution to maintain the sovereignty of the sea, and at the same time commemorative of the NOBLE victory which he had obtain'd over his enemies some time before on that element, and this appears to have been the opinion of an ancient author in MS. in the Cottonian library ‡, who says,

> "For four things our NOBLE sheweth to me,
> "King, ship, and sword, and POWER OF THE SEE."

(g) This proportion was still thought too high, none were obliged to take this noble at first, except the sum exceeded twenty shillings, and above that sum none were to refuse it: those that purchased them of the king's exchanger for pennies paid 80$\frac{1}{2}$, and those that sold them to him were to have but 79 pennies.

* Rymer. † Le Blanc, p. v. ‡ Selden's Mare Clausum, p. 394. Archbishop Sharpe of the Gold Coins, sect. 3. Evelyn. p. 86. Leake, p. 109. § Lowndes, p. 20. ‖ Ibid. p. 35.

Legend. The inscription on the obverse and reverse are the same as the last, that is EDWAR. D. GRA. REX ANGL. z FRANC. DNS. HYB. and IHC TRANSIENS PER MEDIUM ILLORUM IBAT. being different from all the following ones of this king which have constantly on them EDWARD and AUTEM.

RARITY. This noble is likewise exceeding rare, and in the collection of Mr. Edward Hodsol.

WEIGHT. This noble weighs $128\frac{4}{7}$ Troy grains, the half noble should weigh $64\frac{2}{7}$ grains, and the quarter noble $32\frac{1}{7}$ grains.

FINENESS. Twenty-three carats, three grains and one half fine gold, and half a carat grain alloy.

VALUE or PROPORTION. The pieces also of this coinage were to pass current for the same as the last, that is the noble for 6*s.* 8*d.* the half noble for 3*s.* 4*d.* and the quarter for twenty-pence.

By indenture † there was 42 nobles to be cut out of one pound weight Tower, which amounts to 14 pounds sterling in tale, and the nominal value of the pound weight of fine gold was therefore equal to $14\frac{14}{191}$ pounds, or 14*l.* 1*s.* 5*d.* sterling.

The pound weight Troy of standard silver was at this time coined into 22*s.* 6*d.* in tale ‡ or $1\frac{1}{8}$ pounds sterling, and therefore the pound weight of fine silver was equal $1\frac{8}{37}$ pounds sterling.

And from hence it appears that the proportion of fine silver to fine gold was as 1 to 11 [illegible] and the true value of one pound weight of fine gold was 11 lb. 6oz. 16dwt. 7gr. of fine silver.

In this coinage the proportion was rais'd (*b*), for although the nominal values of the pound weight fine of both these metals had been advanc'd, yet that of the gold was the greatest, being about $\frac{1}{17}$, but the silver was no more than about $\frac{1}{18}$.

27th Year Noble. Obverse Type. The nobles of this coinage are like those of the former two, the only difference is that some of them have a flag flying on the mast, charg'd with St. George's cross at the stern of the ship, which neither of the others have, and this flag is also found on some of the half nobles, of this coinage, as being exactly of the same type as the whole. The quarter noble has only the royal shield, with the quarter'd arms of France and England within a compartment of eight angles, like that on the reverse, but its angles are fleury.

Legend. The noble and its half are inscribed EDWARD DEI G. REX ANG. z FRA. DNS. HYB. before and after the treaty of Bretigny, or before his thirty-fourth and after his forty-third year, but during that interval they are inscribed EDWARD D. G. REX ANG. DNS. HYB. z AQT. § the quarter reads nearly the same.

The type on the reverse of these nobles are like those of the two former coinages, and the half is exactly the same as the whole, that of the quarter differs from them only in having its cross form'd of but one line (the dotted ones being omitted) and that the lions have no crowns over them; there is one sort

pennies, however this was but for a short time, for soon after they were made current, and every person obliged to take them under the penalty of loss of body and goods *.

To prevent foreigners taking any advantage of this high price of the gold, none of their coins were to be current in England, and no other English money but this noble was to be exported, the king also procured them to be coined at Bruges, Ypres, &c.

(*b*) Raising the value of gold is giving a greater quantity of fine silver in exchange for the same quantity of fine gold (as for instance the pound weight) than was done before, as in the case above, and falling the value of gold is giving a less quantity.

* Rymer, t. 5. p. 416. 424. Leake, p. 101. † Lowndes, p. 36. ‡ Ibid. § Leake, p. 98.

which

Coins from Edward III. To Richard III.
Pl. I.

which wants the rose and letter in the center, and has four annulets in the interstices of the cross, as No. 2. plate 1. EDW. III.

The whole nobles have inscribed round them JHC AUTEM TRANSIENS P. MEDIU ILLORU YBAT. *(i)* (differing from the two former coinages in having Autem which both of them want) the half noble has DOMINE NE IN FVRORE TUO ARGUAS ME ‡, and the quarter noble has EXALTABITUR IN GLORIA, like the quarter florin: there are some little differences as TRANCIENS, PER, MEDIUM, ILLORUM, & IBAT. There is also a half Noble which wants the word NE. Legend.

Of this coinage there are the whole, No. 4. the half, No. 3. and the quarter, No. 2. the two last are also call'd Maille and Ferling Noble §, and likewise the halfpenny and farthing of gold, that of penny being given to the whole. SORTS.

They are all of them common, but the half and quarter not so frequent as the whole. RARITY.

The whole noble weighs 120 grains Troy, the half noble weighs 60 grains, and the quarter weighs 30 grains Troy. WEIGHT.

Twenty-three carats three grains and a half fine gold, and half a carat grain alloy. FINENESS.

This noble likewise pass'd for six shillings, and eight-pence, the half noble for three shillings and four-pence, and the quarter for twenty-pence, as before. VALUE OR PROPORTION.

By indenture ** one pound weight Tower was to contain 45 nobles, amounting to 15 pound sterling in tale, and one pound weight of fine gold was therefore equal to 15 [illegible] pounds or 15*l.* 1*s.* 6*d.* 3*qr.* sterling.

The pound weight of standard silver was cut into twenty-five shillings in tale or 1 $\frac{1}{4}$ pounds sterling, and the nominal value of the pound weight of fine silver was therefore equal to 1 [illegible] pounds sterling.

And from hence it appears that the proportion of fine silver to fine gold was as 1 to 11 [illegible], and that the true value of one pound weight of fine gold was 11 lb. 1 oz. 17 dwt. 22 gr. of fine silver.

Here the proportion was lessened, as the nominal value of one pound weight of fine gold was advanced but by [illegible], and that of the silver by $\frac{1}{5}$ or much higher.

But this value was yet thought too high, for in the 37th year of Edward the Third the commons petition ††, that the silver coin may be kept within the realm, and that gold may be paid to the merchant for his wares.

The money coined by this king no way differ from those of his grandfathers Edward the Third, on the obverse, but in the inscription, which on the whole Noble is RICARD DI GRA. REX ANGL. z FRANC. DNS. HIB. z AQT. on the half Noble we find RICARD DEI GRA. REX ANGL. DNS. HIB. and on the quarter RICARD DI GRA. REX ANG. RICH. II. 1377. NOBLE. OBVERSE.

(i) There are two opinions concerning the meaning of this text (John viii. v. 59.) the first is that of the alchymists, who say it alludes to the secret hermetical manner in which the gold was made, being as invisible to vulgar eyes as Jesus's passage thro' the midst of the Pharisees was to them; the other, which seems the most probable, is, that it had a secret virtue in it which secured those from danger who carried it about them. Camden * tells us it was the only amulet used in those days to escape dangers in battles, and the wonderful preservation of the king, as if by the invisible hand of providence he past unhurt through the midst of his enemies, in that extraordinary sea fight, which the type of this piece (both *coin* and *medal*) was intended to commemorate, Mr. Leake †, with great reason thinks was the occasion of its being us'd in that manner.

* Remains, Chap. Money. † P. 112. ‡ Psalm vi. and xxxviii. v. 1. § Rymer, t. 5. p. 403. ** Lowndes, p. 36. †† Cotton's Abridg. of the Records, p. 96.

REVERSE Type. The reverse is the same likewise on all the three sorts, except the initial letter of this king's name R. is in the center of the cross instead of an E. which was there before, but their inscriptions are the same, *viz.* on the whole Noble

Legend. IHC AUTEM TRANSCIENS PER MEDIU ILLORUM IBAT, on the half Noble it is DOMINE NE IN FURORE TUO ARGUAS ME, and on the quarter EXALTABITU IN GLORIA.

SORTS. This king coined no other than the Noble, No. 7. the half Noble, No. 6. and the quarter, No. 5. all in pl. 1.

RARITY. The money of this king is much rarer than those of his grandfather's after his 27th year, especially the half and the quarter.

WEIGHT. The Noble weighs 120 grains Troy, the half Noble 60 grains, and the quarter 30 grains like those of Edward the Third in common.

FINENESS. Twenty-three carats three grains and a half of fine gold, and half a carat grain alloy.

VALUE or PROPORTION. The proportion of fine silver to fine gold was as 1 to 11 [illegible], and the true value of one pound weight of fine gold was 11 lb. 1 oz. 17 dwt. 22 grains of fine silver.

HENRY IV. 1399. before his 13th Year. NOBLE. The money coined by this king during this interval of time, have the same type both on the obverse and the reverse, as those of the two preceding monarchs, only in the center of the cross on the reverse appears an H, the initial of his name, instead of the E. and the R. which was on theirs.

The inscription on the obverse is HENRIC. DI GRA. REX ANG. z FRANC. D. HYB. z AQT. and on the reverse the same as on all the preceding.

SORTS. There are the whole, No. 10. the half, No. 9. and the quarter Noble, No. 8. all in pl. 1.

RARITY. All the three sorts are extremely rare, the whole Noble without the flag, No. 10. hitherto unpublish'd, is in our own possession.

WEIGHT. The noble weighs 120 grains, the half Noble 60 grains, and the quarter 30 grains which is the weight of those of Edward and Richard, and by that are immediately known from all the other Henries.

FINENESS. Twenty-three carats three grains and a half of fine gold, and half a grain of alloy.

VALUE or PROPORTION. The proportion of fine gold to fine silver was still as 1 to 11 [illegible], and the true value of one pound weight of fine gold was 11 lb. 1 oz. 17 dwt. 22 grains of fine silver.

HENRY IV. 13th Year. 1412. HENRY V. 1413. HENRY VI. 1422. NOBLE. Type. In these coinages, which we do not know how to distinguish, but have great reason to believe very few are to be assign'd to that of Henry the Fourth, there appears to be some small difference, in the type of the obverse, from those that had been coined in the preceding reigns, as first the arms of France have now constantly but three fleurs-de-lis, whereas the former ones are semé, that is generally four, but sometimes five being as many as could conveniently be put in so small a space, the second difference is in the ship on these coins having in general but two ropes from the stern, instead of three, which appear upon all the others. Some of the quarter Nobles (*k*) have a fleur-de-lis over the top of the shield, and also

(*k*) There is a Noble and half Noble coin'd by Philip the Good, duke of Burgundy, in imitation of those of Henry Vth. and VIth. and of the same weight; we also find in the Placarts and Specie Books publish'd in the Low Countries *, a quarter Noble of the same coinage, agreeing both in type and legend

* Dongheualueerde Gouden & Silveren Muntz, Ant. 1575. Het Thresoor ost Schat van alle de Specien, Ant. 1580. Die Figueren van alle Goude ende Silvere Penningken, Ant. 1580.

also a half moon on one side, and rose on the other, likewise a fleur-de-lis in the center of the cross on the reverse. HEN. IV. V. VI.

The inscription on the obverse of the Noble, is HENRIC DI GRA. REX ANGL. z FRANC. DNS. HYB. on that of the half Noble it is the same all but the DNS. HYB. and the quarter has HENRIC. DI GRA. REX ANGL. or HENRIC. REX ANG. z FRANC. **Legend.**

That on the reverse of the Noble is IHC AUT. TRANSIENS PER MEDIUM ILLORU IBAT, the half Noble has DOMIN NE IN FURORE ARGUAS ME, and the quarter EXALTABITUR IN GLORIA.

The whole, No. 13, 16. the half, No. 12, 15. and the quarter Nobles, No. 11. 14. all in pl. 1. **Sorts.**

They are all three sorts very common. **Rarity.**

The Noble weighs 108 grains Troy, the half Noble 54 grains, and the quarter 27 grains, being the same as that of the Florin and its parts. **Weight.**

Twenty-three carats three grains and a half fine gold, and half a carat grain of alloy. **Fineness.**

The Noble still pass'd current for 6*s.* 8*d.* the half Noble for 3*s.* 4*d.* and the quarter for 20 pence, and by indenture of the 13th year of Henry IV.* the pound weight Tower was to be cut into 50 Nobles, amounting to 16*l.* 13*s.* 4*d.* sterling in tale, and the nominal value of one pound weight of fine gold was therefore equal to 16[illegible] pounds, or 16*l.* 15*s.* 3*qr.* sterling. **Value or Proportion.**

The pound weight of standard silver was, by the same indenture, to consist of 30 shillings in tale, or 1½ pounds sterling, and therefore the pound weight of fine silver was equal to 1[illegible] pounds sterling.

And from hence it appears that the proportion of fine silver to fine gold was as 1 to 10[illegible], and the true value of one pound weight of fine gold was 10lb. 3oz. 19dwt. 13½ grain of fine silver.

In this coinage the proportion fell again, as the nominal value of the pound weight of fine gold was rais'd only by [illegible], but that of the fine silver was advanced much more, or by [illegible].

During this king's short restoration to regal power he caused the Angel †, to be minted in imitation of those of Edward the Fourth's, who began the coinage of them a few years before. It only differs from that king's in the letter H and the fleur-de-lis, on each side of the mast instead of an E and a rose. **HENRY VI. 49th Year. 1470. Angel. Type.**

It is inscribed round the obverse HENRIC DI GRA. REX ANGL. z FRANC. the half or Angelet has only FR. and on the reverse of the whole PER CRUSE TUA SALVA NOS REDETORE, and on the half O CRUX AVE SPES UNICA, as on those of Edward the Fourth's. **Legend.**

There are only the whole, No. 21. and the half, No. 20. pl. 1. **Sorts.**

The whole Angel is rare, but the half is extremely rare. **Rarity.**

The Angel weighs 80 grains, and the half 40 grains Troy. **Weight.**

Twenty-three carats three grains and a half fine gold, and half a grain of alloy. **Fineness.**

gend with the whole Noble, whereas the quarter Nobles of our coinage entirely differ'd in both, and we should therefore suspect that very few, if any of them, had made their appearance in those countries, as not one of them are engraven in any of their Placart Books; and therefore as they found the quarter Noble of Burgundy was like the whole Noble, they suppos'd those coin'd here in England were the same, and accordingly have engrav'd them as such, those of the Henry's and Edward the Fourth's being found there in that manner, which shews how cautious we should be in crediting coins found only in those books, without any other authority.

* Folkes, p. 142. Lowndes, by mistake, places it to 9 H. V. † Lowndes, p. 39.

The

A [illegible] Angel. with B under the [illegible] for [illegible] Rayment [illegible] HENRICV, [illegible] HENRICVS

VALUE OF PROPORTION. The proportion of fine silver to fine gold was as 1 to 11 [illegible], and the true value of 1 pound weight of fine gold was 11lb. 1oz. 17dwt. 22gr. of fine silver, as in the fifth year of Edward the Fourth.

EDWA. IV. 1460. ROSE NOBLE or RYAL (*l*). The type of the obverse of the Noble and half Noble of this king, differs from those of all his predecessors, first in having constantly a square flag or standard on the stern of the ship, with the initial letter E of his name on it, which before always appeared on the center of the reverse, and secondly there is always a large rose on the side of the ship, which none of them before ever had. The rose or compartment likewise on the quarter Noble consists but of four leaves instead of eight, as all the former ones had, an E appears on the top of the shield, a rose on one side and sun on the other, with a fleur-de-lis at bottom.

Legend. There is inscribed on the whole EDWARD DI GRA. REX ANGL. z FRANC. DNS. HYB. on the half DNS. HYB. is wanting, and on the quarter both that and FRANC.

REVERSE. The type of the reverse is also changed, the cross with its small central compartment is now taken quite away, and in its stead appears a sun or star, with a full-blown rose on the center, the points or rays touching the flourish'd ornamented ends of the cross, and also the lyons, which were still left and enclosed within the same compartment of eight leaves, as all the former were.

Legend. They are inscribed nearly as all the former, that is the whole IHC AUT. TRANSIEN. PER MEDIUM ILLORUM IBAT, the half DOMINE NE IN FURORE TUO ARGUAS ME, and the quarter EXALTABITUR IN GLORIA.

ANGEL. Type. This king in his fifth year began to mint a new sort of money, on which appears the arch-angel St. Michael, having one foot on the dragon (which is flung on his back) and piercing him in at the mouth with a spear whose end terminates in a cross croslet.

Legend. The whole is inscribed EDWARD DI GRA. REX ANGL. z FRAN. but the half call'd an Angelet has only ANGL.

REVERSE. Type. The reverse shews a ship, with a large mast in the middle of it, the top of which is form'd into a cross, the royal shield, with the arms of France and

(*l*) The Noble having continued for 120 years at its original value of 6*s*. 8*d*. had given its name to that sum in accompts, but being now made current for half as much more, or ten shillings, it had the new name of RYAL given to it, which was the name the French had given to some of the first gold coins they struck, and was thus called from the figure of the king at length thereon in his royal robes, either sitting or standing, but generally the latter, which were imitated by Edward prince of Wales, call'd the Black Prince, as duke of Aquitain; the dukes of Burgundy and Brabant, and the counts of Flanders, but were about this time mostly disused, and giving place to the Ecu, they having coined none in France after Charles the VIIth, who died anno 1461.

It is sometimes also called by the name of a ROSE RYAL, but more frequently by that of ROSE NOBLE *, which seem'd to be most proper from the rose which it carried both on its obverse and reverse, which distinguished it from all the foregoing ones, and as they obtained great currency abroad; we find the two sorts constantly under the names of Henry Nobles and Rose Nobles, in the Cry's, Placcarts, and Ordonnances which made them current; which they were in most of the trading parts of Europe, as at † Liege, ‡ Juliers, Cleve, Berg, Cologne, Mentz, Triers, and other parts of Germany, in ‖ Sweden, § Prussia, ** Denmark (the toll of the sound being computed by rose Nobles about two centuries since) the †† Low-Countries, ‡‡ France, and many other places.

* Rymer, t. 12. p. 115. † Edicts des Monnoyes les quelles ont en cours par le Pays de Liege dez l'An. 1477. jusques a l'An. 1623. 4to. Liege. ‡ Budelius, B. 2. p. 256. ‖ Petter Diikman Observationer forna Swenskars och Gothers penninge Rachningz. Observat. xxv. 12mo. Stock. 1696. § Hartnoch Differt. de re nummar. Pruff. p. 313. ** Laverentzen Museum Reg. p. 2. sect. 5. c. 12. †† Der Cooplieden-Haud bouckkin, 12mo. Ghend. 1546. Het Thresoor oft Schat van alle de Specien, 12mo. Ant. 1580. Placcaets, 4to. Graven Haghe, 1603, 1606, 1613, 1619, 1623, and 1626. Ordonnantie, 4to. Ant. 1633. 1644. and 1652. ‡‡ Ordonnances, 12mo. Paris, 1571, 1577, 1615, and 1650.

Eng-

England is fixed on this maſt, having on the dexter ſide an E, the initial of the king's name, and on the ſiniſter a roſe.

The inſcription round the Angel is PER CRUCE TUA SALVA NOS XPE REDEMPT. and round the Angelet it is O CRUX AVE SPES UNICA. LEGEND.

There are as uſual the Noble or Ryal, No. 19. the half Noble or half Ryal, No. 18. and quarter Noble quarter Ryal or Ryal Farthing, No. 17. pl. 1. alſo the Angel, No. 23. and the half Angel, No. 22. pl. 1. which were now firſt coined. SORTS.

The Noble and its parts are very common, as is alſo the Angel, but the half Angel is very rare. RARITY.

The weight of the Noble of this king, and which is that of his fifth year, (having never ſeen or heard of any coin'd before that year, or of 108 grains,) is the ſame as that of the laſt Edwards, that is, 120 grains, the half Noble 60 grains, and the quarter Noble is 30 grains Troy. The Angel weighs 80 grains, and the half Angel 40 grains Troy; ſo that the Angel and half Angel juſt weighed the Noble or Ryal. WEIGHT.

The fineneſs of both theſe ſorts of money were the ſame as before, that is, twenty-three carats three grains and a half of fine gold, and half a grain of alloy. FINENESS.

This king, in the fourth year of his reign, rais'd the Noble from 6*s*. 8*d*. to 8*s*. 4*d*. being $\frac{1}{4}$ or 25 per cent. whereby the nominal value of one pound weight Tower of fine gold was advanced to 20*l*. 16*s*. 8*d*. ſterling; but this made no alteration in the true value of it, becauſe the nominal value of the ſilver was raiſed at the ſame time, and in the ſame ratio, the pound weight of fine ſilver being advanced to 2$\frac{1}{37}$ pounds ſterling, and therefore the proportion remain'd as before, as 1 to 10$\frac{100}{360}$. VALUE OF PROPORTION.

By indenture of his fifth year one pound weight Tower was to be cut into 45 Nobles * (as the 27th of Edward the Third) which were rais'd at the ſame time from 8*s*. 4*d*. to 10 ſhillings, and 67$\frac{1}{2}$ Angels, (*x*) at 6*s*. 8*d*. amounting to 22*l*. 10*s*. ſterling in tale, and thereby the nominal value of one pound weight of fine gold was equal to 22 [illegible] pounds, or 22*l*. 17*s*. 7*d*. 1*qr*. ſterling.

The pound weight of fine ſilver remain'd in this coinage without any alteration, being equal to 2$\frac{1}{37}$ pounds ſterling.

From hence it appears that the proportion of fine ſilver to fine gold was as 1 to 11 [illegible], and that the true value of one pound weight of fine gold was 11lb. 1oz. 17dwt. 22gr. of fine ſilver.

In this coinage the proportion is raiſed, being now the ſame as it was from the 27th of Edward the Third to the 13th of Henry the IVth, or before the laſt alteration, which was done by increaſing both the weight and the value of the Noble, but the latter more than the former, the value being rais'd by $\frac{1}{5}$, and the weight only by $\frac{1}{9}$.

In this reign there is the firſt break or gap in the ſeries of Nobles, from their firſt coinage under Edward the Third, there being none to be met with of this king, who coined only the angel, which no way differs from that of his brother's in type. RICH. III. 1483. ANGEL.

The whole Angel is inſcribed on the obverſe RICARD DEI GRA. REX ANGL. Z FRANC. and on the reverſe PER CRUCEM TUA SALVA NOS XPC REDEMPT. the half Angel has RICARD DI GRA. REX ANGL. and on the reverſe O CRUX AVE SPES UNICA.

(*x*) Called ſometimes by Authors Angel Noble, and Noble Angel, till it was rais'd to 7*s*. 6*d*. in the 18th H. VIII.

* *Lowndes*, p. 40.

SORTS. The Angel, No. 25. and the half Angel, No. 24. pl. 1. are the only two ſorts we have ever met with, and have a roſe and boars-head for mint marks.

RARITY. Both the whole and half are very rare, but eſpecially the latter.

WEIGHT. The Angel weighs 80 grains, and the half 40 grains Troy as before.

FINENESS. Twenty-three carats three grains and a half of fine gold, and half of a carat grain alloy.

VALUE or PROPORTION. The Angel paſs'd current for 6*s.* 8*d.* as before, the proportion between fine ſilver and fine gold was as 1 to 11 [illegible], and the true value of one pound weight of fine gold was 11 lb. 1 oz. 17 dwt. 22 gr. of fine ſilver.

HENRY VII. 1485. NOBLE or RYAL. OBVERSE Type. This king is repreſented on this piece as uſual in armour, ſtanding in a ſhip, with his ſword in his right hand and a ſhield in his left, which differs from that which appears on thoſe of his predeceſſors both in form and poſition, covering but very little of his body, a ſquare flag charg'd with a ſemy dragon appears at the ſtern of the ſhip, and another now, for the firſt time, at the head, on which is an H. the initial of his name: the ſide of the ſhip is ornamented with roſes, and the king is crown'd with an imperial arched crown, whereas on the former ones it is always open.

Legend. The inſcription round it is HENRIC DI GRA. REX ANGL. FRANC. DNS. IBAR.

REVERSE. Type. The reverſe differs more from the former Nobles than the obverſe, the ornamented ends of the croſs, the fleur-de-lis, the lions and crowns being now all taken away, together with the radiated roſe in the center, and the whole area quite to the letter'd circle, is filled with a large double roſe within a compartment of ten arches: having a feather iſſuing from each cavity of the roſe; on the center of which is the ſhield, with the arms of France alone, without thoſe of England, which is not to be found thus on any other piece, it is ſaid to have been coined abroad. See N. 1. pl. 2.

Legend. It is inſcribed round IHC AUTEM TRANSIENS PER MEDIUM ILLORUM IBAT as uſual.

SOVEREIGN OBVERSE Type. The double Ryal or Sovereign (*m*), as alſo the double Sovereign exhibit the king ſitting in a chair of ſtate, with a ſcepter in his right hand and the orbe in his left, on No. 2. pl. 2. the arms and back of the chair are plain, as is alſo the back ground; on No. 2. it is diaper'd with fleurs-de-lis; on No. 4. and 5. the chair is ornamented in the Gothic taſte, the back of which, on the former, extends to the edge of the coin, but on the latter no farther than the inner circle, and has on each of its arms a dragon, the ground in both being ſtrewed with fleurs-de-lis.

Legend. There is inſcribed round No. 2. HENRIC DI GRA. REX ANGL. FRANC. DNS. IBARNE, others have HENRICUS. DEI. GRACIA. ANGLIE. FRANCIE. IBAR. HIBNE.

REVERSE Type. The reverſe of No. 4. like that of the Ryal, has a double full-blown roſe, and on its center the royal ſhield, charg'd with the quarter'd arms of France and England; No. 3. is nearly the ſame, only ornamented with lyons and fleurs-

(*m*) This word appears to be of Engliſh original, and to have had its birth here, being derived from the type of the king or SOVEREIGN, who is exhibited on it ſitting in ſtate; which with ſome little difference, had been much in uſe for more than two centuries before, and ſeems to have grown out of uſe till reviv'd by the emperor Maximilian about this time; from which it is probable this of our Henry's was taken, but that was called by the old name of Ryal with the epithet of great joined to it, as being one of the largeſt coins which had till then appear'd abroad, where this piece of ours was conſtantly call'd by the name of Double Roſe Noble, and no other.

de-lis-

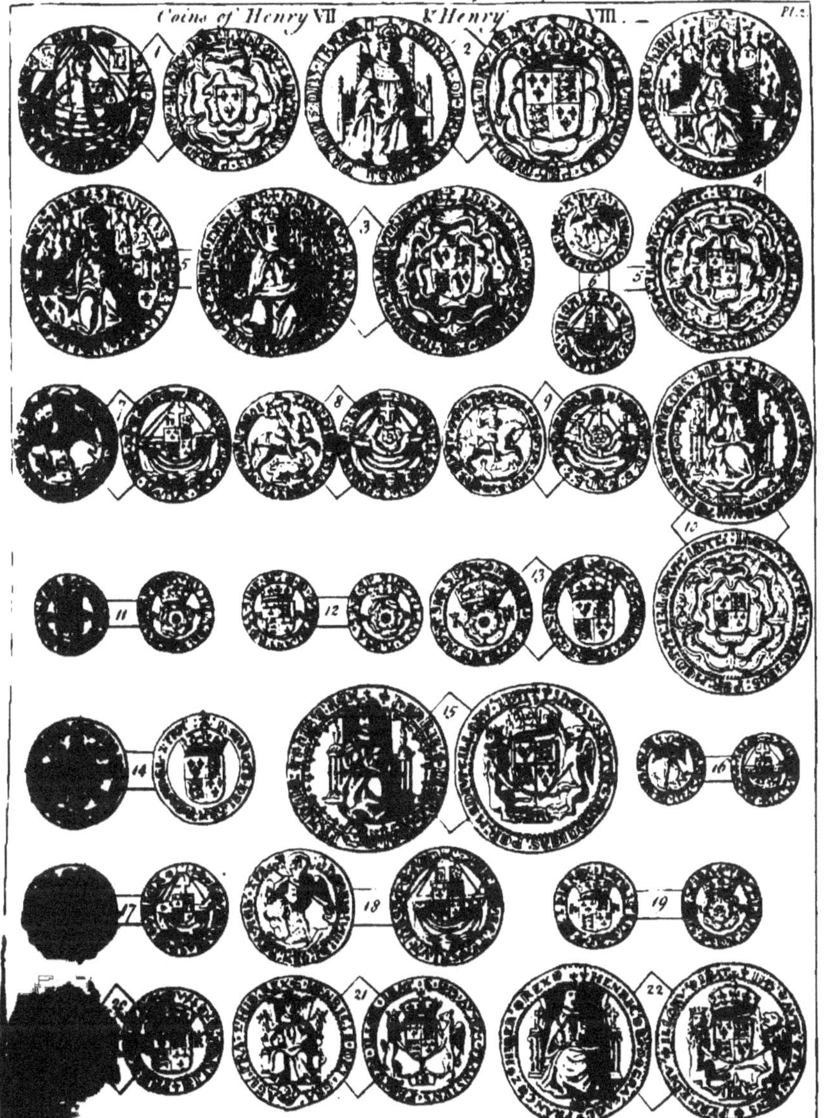
Coins of Henry VII & Henry VIII.
Pl. 2.

HENRY VII. de-lis between the rose and compartment, on that of No. 2. the rose is almost cover'd with the royal shield, which is also crown'd with a large imperial crown (*n*).

Legend. The inscription nearly as on the Ryal that is, IHS AUTE TRANCIENS PER MEDIU ILLORU IBAT, others have JHESUS, AUTEM, MEDIUM, ILLORUM, IBATNE.

ANGEL. Type. The Angel coined by this king is the same as the former ones, except the Arch Angels having both legs on the dragon instead of one, and the proper initial of his name on the reverse; it is inscribed HENRIC DI GRA. REX AGL. z FRA. the half the same, except z FRA. the inscription on the reverse the same as before.

Legend.

SORTS. The Ryal or Noble, the Sovereign and the double Sovereign, the half Angel and Angel.

RARITY. The half Angel and Angel are both common, the double Sovereign and Sovereign both very rare, but the Ryal is extremely rare.

WEIGHT. The half Angel weighs 40 grains, the Angel 80 grains, the Ryal 120 grains, as those of Edward the Fourth, the Sovereign 240 grains, or half an ounce, and the double Sovereign 480, or one ounce Troy.

FINENESS. The same as all his predecessors, that is, twenty-three carats three grains and a half fine gold, and half a carat alloy.

VALUE OF PROPORTION. The Ryal was current for 10*s.* the Sovereign for 20*s.* or one pound sterling (*o*), the double Sovereign for 40*s.* the half Angel for 3*s.* 4*d.* and the Angel for 6*s.* 8*d.* as before, and there being 45 Ryals, $67\frac{1}{2}$ Angels, &c. cut out of one pound weight, it amounted to 22*l.* 10*s.* sterling in tale, and the nominal value of one pound weight of fine gold was equal to 22*l.* 12*s.* 4*d.* 1*qr.* sterling, the proportion of fine silver to fine gold was as 1 to $11\frac{111}{111}$, and the true value of one pound weight of fine gold was 11 lb. 1 oz. 17 dwt. 22 gr. of fine silver.

HENRY VIII 1509. We have now another gap in the series of Nobles or Ryals, none of which having hitherto been found of this king, that have come to our knowledge.

18th Year. SOVEREIGN Type. The Sovereign or double Ryal, like that of his father, exhibits this king seated in his chair of state, with his scepter and globe; the chair is different from any of those of his fathers, and he has besides the portcullis at his feet, the interior part of the legendary circle is also ornamented, which is not seen on any of the others. The reverse is nearly as that of his fathers, but has the compartment differently ornamented.

Legend. It is inscribed on the obverse HENRICUS DEI GRACIA REX ANGLIE ET FRANC. DNS. HIB. and on the reverse IHESUS AUTEM TRANSIENS PER MEDIUM ILLORUM IBAT.

ANGEL. The Angel differs no way from his fathers, either in the type or legend, on the obverse or reverse, except in having the number VIII after the name.

GEORGE NOBLE. OBVERSE Type. This piece received its name from its type and value together, on the obverse of No. 8. it represents St. George on horseback, arm'd cap-a-pie, piercing the dragon under his horse with a spear, but on No. 9. he has a sword in his hand, lifted ready to strike him. The reverse of No. 8. is like that of the Angel, but has a large rose on the mast of the ship instead of the shield with the arms, and on the sinister side of the mast it has an R. instead of the rose, on that of No. 9. there is three masts instead of one.

(*n*) As there are but very few of these pieces to be met with, and those few mostly differing from each other, we should suspect several of them to have been rather pattern-pieces than current coin, especially as some of them exceed their indenture weight, but for want of a proper criterion we cannot distinguish one from the other. (*o*) This is the first pound sterling in specie in the English collection.

The

Legend. The inscription on the obverse of No. 8. is TALI DICAIT, SIG. MES. FLUCTUARI NEQI, but on No. 9. it is TALI DICATA SIGNO MENS FLUCTURI NEQ. on the reverse of No. 8. it is HENRIC. D. G. R. AGL. z. FRANC. DNS. HIBER. and of No. 9. it is HENRICUS D. G. REX ANG. z FRANC. DNS. HYB.

This is the first instance we meet with where the king's name and titles are put on the reverse, and the sentence usually chosen for the reverse is put on the obverse; we shall meet with it in the same manner again on some of the half crowns of this coinage, and frequently on those of his son Edward the Sixth.

CROWN (*o*) Type. This piece was now first introduced into the English series, having on its obverse a double rose crown'd between the letters H R. H A. H I. H K. the three last are the initials of the names of his queens, viz. Anne, Jane, and Katherine. The type of No. 14. (*p*) is quite singular, having a rose fix'd on the center of a cross fleury, with the letters H. R. crown'd in two of the quarters, and two lyons in the other two: the reverse on all of them is the royal shield, with the arms of France and England crown'd. Some have not any letters on the sides, but others have H. R. H. K. &c. as on the obverse (*q*).

Legend. The Crown is inscribed on the obverse HENRIC. VIII. RUTILANS ROSA SIE SPIA, sometimes SINE SPINA, and on the reverse DEI G. R. AGLIE z FRANC. DNS. HIBERNIE; the half crown on the contrary reads on the reverse HENRIC 8. DI G. ANGL. z FRA. or H. D. G. RUTILANS ROSA SINE SP. and on the obverse RUTILANS ROSA SINE SPINA, or SP.

SORTS. The Sovereign, the Angel, the half Angel, the George Noble, the Crown, and the half Crown, and although both the half Sovereign or Ryal, and the half George Noble are mentioned in the indentures, yet neither of them have reached our time.

RARITY. The Sovereign, the Angel and half Angel are common, the Crown and half Crown something scarcer, especially the latter, but the George Noble is very rare.

WEIGHT. The Sovereign weighs 120 gr. the Angel 80 gr. the half Angel 40 grains, and the George Noble $71\frac{1}{9}$ grains, being in proportion to their respective values; the Crown weighs $57\frac{3}{11}$, and the half Crown $28\frac{7}{11}$ grains Troy.

FINENESS. The Sovereign, Angel and George Noble were all of the antient standard of twenty-three carats three grains and a half fine gold, and half a carat alloy.

The Crown and half Crown had only twenty-two carats fine gold and two carats alloy, or 11 parts fine to one of alloy, and is frequently call'd CROWN GOLD, from the pieces of that name, being first made of this sort of gold, which has been the only sort used in our mints since the restoration.

VALUE or PROPORTION. The Sovereign was current for 22*s*. 6*d*. the Angel for 7*s*. 6*d*. the half Angel for 3*s*. 9*d*. the George Noble for 6*s*. 8*d*. the Crown for 5*s*. and the half Crown for 2*s*. 6*d*. By indenture the pound weight Troy was cut into 24 Sove-

(*o*) A gold coin had long been current in France, by the name of Escu-a-la-Couronne, but more generally by that of Escu d'Or, and was thus call'd from the shield, with the arms of France crown'd on its reverse, and in this they were follow'd by the Italians and Spaniards, who call'd it Scudo and Escudo; most latin authors who mention it, call it not Scutum from the shield, but Coronatus from the crown; which last was the name this king chose for this new species of coin; and in Germany and the Low-Countries they also call'd it Krone and Croone. It was about two per cent. better than that coin'd by the French anno 1524.

(*p*) We constantly meet with this coin in all the placarts publish'd in the Low-Countries between anno 1546 and 1650, and yet we esteem it the rarest piece minted by this king, nor have we ever had the pleasure of seeing one of them, it has a mint-mark peculiar to itself, and not to be met with on any other money of this king; whereas all the others have those common to this reign, as the bolt, rose, fleur-de-lis, wy, &c.

(*q*) The number after the name was now first introduced in the Gold, but had been in use in the Silver about twenty years.

reigns,

reigns, 72 Angels, 144 half Angels, and 81 George Nobles amounting to 27 pound sterling in tale, and the nominal value of one pound weight of fine gold was equal to 27 $\frac{9}{64}$ pounds or 27*l.* 2*s.* 9*d.* 3*qr.* sterling. By the same indenture there was to be 100 $\frac{1}{2}$ Crowns, and 201 half Crowns cut out of the same pound weight amounting to 25 $\frac{1}{8}$ pound sterling, and therefore the nominal value of one pound weight of fine gold was 27 $\frac{9}{22}$ pounds, or 27*l.* 8*s.* 2*d.* sterling. HEN. VIII.

One pound weight Troy of standard silver was now coined into 45*s.* sterling in tale, and therefore the nominal value of one pound weight of fine silver was 2 $\frac{16}{37}$ pounds sterling.

From hence it appears the proportion between fine gold and fine silver was as 1 to 11 $\frac{3}{19}$, and that the true value of one pound weight of fine gold was 11 lb. 1 oz. 17 dwt. 22 gr. of fine silver.

In this coinage the proportion or true value of gold was not altered, as the nominal values of the pound weight both of fine silver and fine gold were rais'd in the same ratio, that is $\frac{1}{8}$ or 12 $\frac{1}{2}$ per cent. but there was a change made at this time of the pound Tower for the pound Troy, which were in proportion to each other as 15 to 16, and occasions the rise to appear at the first view as $\frac{1}{5}$ or 20 per cent.

The Sovereign of this coinage shews the king in his chair of state, with his scepter and orbe, differing but little from the former: appearing on this fuller fac'd and with a beard, resembling the silver money now coined, and has likewise a rose at his feet instead of the portcullis. 34th Year. 1544. POUND SOVEREIGN. OBVERSE

It is inscribed HENRIC. 8. DI GRA. ANGLIE FRANCIE ET HIBE REX.

The type of the reverse is quite new on an English coin, exhibiting the royal shield with the quarter'd arms of France and England crown'd and supported, on the dexter-side by a lion, and on the sinister by a dragon, and has H. R. at the bottom of the shield. REVERSE. Type.

It is inscribed JHESUS AUTEM TRANCIENS PER MEDIUM ILLORU IBAT. Legend.

The only difference in the angel of this coinage from the last, is in its having an annulet on the side of the ship (commonly call'd a gun hole) which they have not. ANGEL. Type.

The whole angel is inscribed on the obverse HENRIC. 8. D. G. AGL. FRA. Z HIB. REX, the half Angel has HENRIC. 8. D. G. AGL. FR. Z HIB. RE. and the quarter HENRICUS VIII. DEI GRA. AGLIE, and on the reverse FRANCIE ET HIBERNIE RE. one sort has the same legend on the reverse as on the obverse, the whole and half have the same legend as usual on their reverses. Legend.

There are the Sovereign, No. 15. the Angel, No. 18. the half Angel, No. 17. and the quarter Angel, No. 14. all in plate 2. which last piece was now for the first time coin'd; the indentures also mention a half sovereign, but none have reached our times. SORTS.

These coins are all of them frequently met with, except the quarter Angel, which is not quite so common as the others. RARITY.

The Sovereign weighs 200 grains, the Angel weighs 80 grains, the half Angel 40 grains, and the quarter Angel 20 grain Troy. WEIGHT.

These pieces were all of twenty-three carats of fine gold and one carat of alloy, and this was the only time either before or since that such a standard was made use of in our mints. FINENESS.

The Sovereign was current for twenty shillings, or one pound sterling, the Angel for eight shillings, the half Angel for four shillings, and the quarter Angel for two shillings; by Indenture there was 28 $\frac{4}{5}$ Sovereigns, or 72 Angels in one pound weight Troy, amounting to 28*l.* 16*s.* sterling in tale, and therefore the nominal value of one pound weight of fine gold was 30 $\frac{1}{19}$ pounds, or 30*l.* 1*s.* 2*q.* sterling. VALUE or PROPORTION.

HEN. VIII. The pound weight Troy of fine ſilver was coined into $57\frac{1}{7}$ ſhillings or $2\frac{6}{7}$ pounds ſterling. And frum hence it appears that the proportion was as 1 to $10\frac{10}{17}$, and the true value of one pound weight of fine gold was 10lb. 5 oz. 4 dwt. 8 gr. of fine ſilver.

36th & 37th Years. POUND SOVEREIGN. The Sovereign of theſe two coinages differ but little from the foregoing, and are much eaſier diſtinguiſhed by their colour, (eſpecially the laſt) than by their type from thoſe of his 34th year, they are alſo a little ſmaller.

Type. The whole is inſcribed HENRIC. 8. D. GRA. AGL. FRANC. z HIB. REX.

Legend. the half Sovereign has HENRIC 8. DEI GRA. AGL. FRA. z HIB. REX. on the reverſe the legend is JHS AUTE TRANSIENS, PER MEDIU, ILLORU, IBAT, and on the half it is MEDI and ILLOR.

CROWN Type. The Crown and half Crown are the ſame as thoſe of his 18th year, only we do not meet with ſo many different letters, being no other but H. R. and H. K. on the ſides of the roſe and the ſhield.

Legend. The legend on the whole has the titles divided, part on the obverſe and part on the reverſe, as HENRIC. 8. ROSA SINE SPINE, and D. G. ANGLIE FRA. z HIB. REX, but that of the half has them all on one ſide HENRIC 8. D. G. ANG. FR. z HIB. REX. and on the reverſe RUTILANS ROSA SINE SPINA.

Sorts. There are the Sovereign, No. 22. the half Sovereign, No. 21. the Crown, No. 20. and the half Crown, No. 19. all in plate 2.

RARITY. Theſe pieces are not very common, eſpecially the half Sovereign and half Crown.

WEIGHT. The Sovereign weighs 192 grains, or 8 dwt. the half Sovereign 96 grains, or 4 dwt. the Crown 48 grains, and the half Crown 24 grains, or 1 dwt. Troy.

FINENESS. That of the 36th year was twenty-two carats fine gold, and two carats alloy, and that of the 37th was only twenty carats fine, and four carats alloy, and was the only inſtance of ſuch baſe gold being work'd in our mints.

VALUE or PROPORTION. The Sovereign was current for 20 ſhillings, or one pound ſterling, the half Sovereign for 10*s.* the quarter or Crown for 5*s.* and the half Crown for 2*s.* 6*d.*

By indenture of his 36th year the pound weight Troy was to conſiſt of 30 Sovereigns, amounting to 30 pound ſterling in tale, and the nominal value of one pound weight of fine gold to $32\frac{8}{11}$ pounds, or 32*l.* 14*s.* 6*d.* 2*q.* ſterling.

One pound weight Troy of fine ſilver contained 96 ſhillings, or $4\frac{4}{5}$ pounds ſterling; and from hence the proportion between fine ſilver and fine gold was as 1 to $6\frac{9}{11}$ *(q)*, and the true value of one pound weight of fine gold was no more than 6lb. 9 oz. 16 dwt. 13 gr. of fine ſilver.

Here the gold was rais'd only about $\frac{1}{10}$, but the ſilver near $\frac{3}{7}$, and as the medium proportion had been for a long while about 1 to 11, a profit was hereby to be made of near 60 per cent. by exchanging ſilver for gold.

In his 37th year there were ſtill 30 Sovereigns to the pound weight or 30 pound ſterling in tale, and the nominal value of one pound weight of fine gold was now 36 pound ſterling.

One pound weight of fine ſilver conſiſted now of 144 ſhillings, or $7\frac{1}{5}$ pound ſterling.

And from hence it appears that the proportion between fine ſilver and fine gold

(q) It is moſt certain that there could not have been any free exchange * of ſilver for gold from this year till the 6th year of Edward the Sixth, and we may with reaſon ſuppoſe that but little was coin'd, and that it was no ſooner deliver'd out of the mint, but immediately lock'd up.

* Folkes, p. 33.

was

HEN. VIII.

was as 1 to 5, and the true value of one pound weight of fine gold was no more than 5 lb. wt. Troy of fine silver.

Here the gold was rais'd only about $\frac{1}{10}$, but the silver most preposterously $\frac{1}{2}$, or 50 per cent. and the advantage by exchange of silver for gold was now about 220 per cent.

EDWA. VI. 1547. 1st Year. HALF SOVEREIGN. Type.

There appears to be but little alteration in this coinage from that of the 37th of Henry the Eighth, which was the last of his fathers, and was to consist of the same pieces which that consisted of; however, but two that I have heard of are at present to be met with, that is the half Sovereign and the half Crown.

He is exhibited on the obverse of the half Sovereign sitting on his throne or chair of state, with the scepter and orbe in his hands, on each elbow of the chair there is an angel, and a rose is likewise seen at his feet; on the reverse appears the royal arms crown'd and supported with a lyon and a dragon, as on his fathers, and E. R. at the bottom of the shield.

Legend.

It is inscribed on the obverse EDWARD 6. D. G. AG. FRAN. Z HIB. REX, and on the reverse JHS AUTE TRANSIE PER MED. ILLOR. IBAT.

HALF CROWN Type.

A rose crown'd between E. R. appears on the obverse of this piece, and on the reverse the royal shield crown'd with the arms of France and England quarterly between the same E. R. which letters make the only difference between this coin and that of his fathers.

Legend.

On the reverse we read EDWARD 6. D. G. AG. FR. Z HI. REX, and on the obverse RUTILANS ROSA SINE SPINA, as on No. 11. pl. 2. of the 18th year of his father.

SORTS.

We have just now observ'd there are none but the half Sovereign and half Crown, altho' both the Sovereign and Crown are mentioned in the indentures.

RARITY.

Both the aforesaid coins, No. 1.2. are extremely rare, especially the half Crown.

WEIGHT.

The half Sovereign weighs 96 grains, and the half Crown weighs 24 grains Troy (r).

FINENESS.

Twenty carats of fine gold and four carats of alloy, that is five parts fine to one of alloy, as in the 37th year of his father.

VALUE or PROPORTION.

The proportion was as 1 to 5, and the true value of one pound weight of fine gold was no more than 5 lb. weight of fine silver.

3d Year. 1549. POUND SOVEREIGN. Type.

The Sovereign of this coinage has the king sitting in his royal chair, having a sword in his right hand and the globe in his left, he appears in armour, but on all before in his royal robes; the reverse has the royal arms crown'd and supported as before.

Legend.

It has inscribed round it on the obverse EDWARD VI. DEI GRA. AGL. FRAN. ET HIBER. REX, and on the reverse JHS AUTEM TRANSIENS, PER, MEDI, ILLOR. IBAT.

$\frac{1}{2}$, $\frac{1}{4}$, and $\frac{1}{8}$ SOVEREIGN Type.

These are the first gold coins on which the heads of any of our princes are to be found (altho' we have them constantly on their silver money for 500 years before *.

There are two sorts of these pieces, one with the head bare, and which we conceive were the first attempts, and that No. 3. 7. and 8. were only patterns and not current money, the other sort have the head crown'd, as on the Sove-

(r) Mr. Folkes had observed more variety in the weights of the money of this king, than in that of any other, some being heavier and some lighter than they ought to have been of by indenture, and they were also as defective in their fineness, as he found, by experience, upon having some of them assayed.

* See our View of the Silver Coin and Coinage of England, p. 1.

reign,

EDWA. VI. reign, and are the proper half, quarter, and one-eighth of it, both ſorts of them have the ſame reverſe, that is, an oval ſhield with the royal arms garniſh'd and crown'd, with E. R. on the ſide of it differing from that on the teſtoons only in being crown'd; No. 3. has a full-blown roſe with four leaves, in which it differs from that of his fathers.

Legend. On the obverſe of No. 4, 5, 6. inſtead of the name and titles, as is uſual, we find SCUTUM FIDEI PROTEGET EUM, being the proper legenda of the reverſe, to which on No. 7. is added the date MDXLVIII (*s*), on No. 8. it is LUCERNA PEDIBUS MEIS VERBUM TUUM, on No. 3. we find EDWARD VI. REX ANGL. FRAN. HIB. on No. 10, 11. it is EDWARD VI. D. G. AGL. FRA. z HIB. REX, and on No. 9. contracted to AG. FR. HI. the legend on the reverſe of No. 4, 5, 6. are the ſame as theſe laſt, on No. 7. we find ANGL. & HIBER. and on No. 8. EDOVARD & ANGL. on No. 9, 10, 11. we have as uſual SCUTUM FIDEI PROTEGET EUM.

Number 4, and 9. are eighths, No. 3, 5. and 10. are quarters, and No. 6, 7, 8, and 11. are half Sovereigns, and we have ſeen a half Sovereign which differs very little from No. 3, but in having SCUTUM, &c. on the obverſe, and the titles on the reverſe.

RARITY. Theſe pieces are moſtly ſcarce, but No. 6, 11, and 12, we think are the ofteneſt met with, the $\frac{1}{4}$ and $\frac{1}{8}$ are very rare, eſpecially the latter, but No. 3, 7, and 8. are extremely rare.

WEIGHT. The Sovereign ſhould weigh 169$\frac{7}{17}$ grains, the half 84$\frac{12}{17}$, the quarter 42$\frac{6}{17}$, and the half quarter, or 8th, 21$\frac{3}{17}$ grains Troy.

FINENESS. All theſe ſpecies were Twenty-two carats fine gold, and two carats of alloy.

VALUE OR PROPORTION. The Sovereign was current for 20 ſhillings, or one pound ſterling, the half for 10*s*. the quarter for 5*s*. and the eighth for 2*s*. 6*d*.

One pound weight Troy was coined into 34 Sovereigns, that is, into 34 pounds ſterling, and the nominal value of one pound weight of fine gold was therefore equal to 37$\frac{1}{11}$ pounds, or 37*l*. 1*s*. 9*d*. 3*qr*. ſterling.

One pound weight of fine ſilver was coined into 144 Teſtoons or ſhillings, equal to 7$\frac{1}{5}$ pounds ſterling.

And from hence it appears that the proportion between fine ſilver and fine gold was as 1 to 5$\frac{1}{11}$, and the true value of one pound weight of fine gold was 5 lb. 1 oz. 16 dwt. 8$\frac{1}{2}$ gr. of fine ſilver.

Here was but little alteration, and that was in the gold alone, which was rais'd about one thirty ſixth.

4th Year FINE SOVEREIGN. 1550. The moſt material difference between the fine Sovereign or double Ryal of this king, and that of his father, No. 10. pl. 2. is the youthful countenance ſo apparent in his face on this piece, and there is alſo a great ſameneſs in their reverſes.

It has inſcribed round it on the obverſe EDWARD VI. D.G. ANGLIE FRANCIE z HIBERNIE REX, and on the reverſe JHESU AUTEM TRANSIENS, PER, MEDIUM, ILLORUM, IBAT.

ANGEL. This piece and its half are not materially different from thoſe of his fathers, the whole is inſcribed on the obverſe, EDWARD VI. D. G. AGL. FRA. z HIB. REX, the half is contracted to AG. FR. & HI. and the inſcription on the reverſe of both is the ſame as on all the preceding ones.

It is generally ſuppos'd that No. 15. was intended as a pattern for a piece of ſix angels, as its weight correſponds thereto; and if true not ſo proper for this work, as being confined only to current coins.

(*s*) This is the firſt gold coin in the Engliſh ſeries which has a date on it.

The type is different from the others and better perform'd, the arch-angel holding the ſpear with his right-hand, and has a ſhield with the royal arms in his left; the ſhip on the reverſe has likewiſe three maſts, with her ſails and tackling, and the ſhield with the arms is in this on the ſide of the ſhip. EDWA. VI.

It is inſcribed on the obverſe EDWARD VI. D. G. REX ANGL. FRAN. HIBER, zc. and on the reverſe PER CRUCEM TUAM NOS XRE RED.

It is very probable, that this piece and No. 3. came out at the ſame mint with the 5*s.* and 10*s.* pattern-pieces in ſilver, the ſame mint or private mark being on them all.

There are the Sovereign, No. 16. the Angel, No. 14. and the half Angel, No. 13. there were half Sovereigns mention'd in the indentures, but none of them at preſent to be found in any cabinet. SORTS.

N. B. All theſe pieces have the dragons head for the mint mark, and is peculiar to this coinage only, being on no other either in gold or ſilver.

Theſe pieces are all of them extremely rare. RARITY.

The Sovereign weighs 240 grains, the Angel 80 grains, the half Angel 40 grains, and the ſix Angel or Angel Sovereign 240 grains Troy. WEIGHT.

Theſe pieces were all of 23 carats 3 grains and a half fine gold, and half a carat grain of alloy. FINENESS.

The Sovereign was current for 24 ſhillings, the Angel for 8 ſhillings, and the half Angel for 4 ſhillings. VALUE OF PROPORTION.

By commiſſion (*t*) the pound weight Troy was coined into 28 [illegible] Sovereigns at 24 ſhillings each, amounting to 34*l.* 11*s.* 2*d.* 1*qr.* ſterling in tale: And the nominal value of one pound weight of fine gold was equal to 28 [illegible] Sovereigns, or 34*l.* 19*s.* ſterling.

The pound weight Troy of fine ſilver contained ſtill 144 teſtoons or ſhillings, or 7 $\frac{1}{5}$ pounds ſterling.

And from hence it appears that the proportion between fine ſilver and fine gold was now but 4 [illegible], and the true value of one pound weight of fine gold was no more than 4lb. 5dwt. of fine ſilver.

Here the nominal value of one pound weight of fine gold was leſſen'd about $\frac{1}{5}$ or 20 per cent. And as no alteration was made in the ſilver, the true value of conſequence fell in the ſame proportion, and this at a time, as we have already obſerv'd, when there was a gain of 220 per cent. to be made by exchanging of ſilver for gold, and which by this means was increaſed to more than 270 per cent (*u*).

By commiſſion (*x*) this year one pound weight of fine ſilver was doubled in its nominal value, and that of the gold left without alteration, which was therefore as much leſſen'd in its true value, and the proportion was now as 2 [illegible], and the true value of one pound weight of gold no more than 2lb. 2dwt. 12gr. Troy, and the profit ariſing from the exchange of the metals was now about 550 per cent (*y*). 5th Year. VALUE OF PROPORTION.

The Sovereign, the half, the quarter, and eighth, are in this coinage all of the ſame type, whereas in the former the three laſt ſorts differed from the firſt. 6th Year. 1551. POUND SOVEREIGN. OBVERSE.

(*t*) Lowndes, p. 47. (*x*) Ibid.

(*u*) It is not credible, that ſuppoſing theſe pieces had been coined, that they could be utter'd; but we rather ſuſpect that this coinage never took place, and that the above pieces are not of his 4th, but his 6th year, when the juſt proportion between the metals was reſtored.

(*y*) If the gold coinage of the 4th year did not take place, neither did this conſequence follow.

EDW. VI. The king is exhibited in this coinage half bodied, and in armour, looking to the left, with a ſword in his right hand, and a globe or orbe in his left.

REVERSE Round the circumference of the two largeſt ſorts are inſcribed EDWARD VI. D. G. AGL. FRA. z HIBER. REX, the quarter has HIB. and on the eighth it is EDWARD VI. D. G. A. FR. z HIB. REX.

The whole Sovereign has the ſame reverſe as that of his third year, and the half of his firſt year, as alſo thoſe of the 34th, 36th, and 37th of his fathers, that is, the ſhield, with the royal arms crown'd and ſupported with a lyon and a dragon, with the letters E. R. under it, and is the laſt time we meet with it in this manner, the three ſmaller pieces have only the ſame crown'd ſhield without ſupporters, with the aforeſaid initial letters on the ſides.

Legend. The whole and half Sovereign have the uſual legend of JHS. AUTE. TRANCI. PER MEDI. ILLOR. IBAT. and the quarter and eighth have SCUTUM FIDEI PROTEGET EUM.

SORTS. The Sovereign, the half Sovereign, the quarter, and the half quarter or eighth.

RARITY. The two largeſt of theſe pieces are common, the others are very ſcarce, eſpecially the eighth.

WEIGHT. The Sovereign weighs 178 $\frac{6}{11}$ grains, the half Sovereign 87 $\frac{3}{11}$ gr. the quarter Sovereign 43 $\frac{7}{11}$ gr. and the half quarter 21 $\frac{9}{11}$ grains Troy.

FINENESS. In this coinage the pieces were all of 22 carats fine gold and two carats of alloy.

VALUE or PROPORTION. The Sovereign was current for 20 ſhillings, or one pound ſterling, the half for 10 ſhillings, the quarter for five ſhillings, and the eighth for two ſhillings and ſix-pence, by indenture (y) the pound weight Troy was to be coined into 33 Sovereigns, amounting to 33 pounds ſterling, and therefore the nominal value of one pound of fine gold was equal to 36 pounds ſterling.

One pound weight Troy of ſilver 11 oz. 1 dwt. fine, was coined into 3 pounds ſterling in tale, and therefore one pound weight of fine ſilver was coined into 3 $\frac{57}{221}$ pounds ſterling.

And from hence it appears that the proportion between fine ſilver and fine gold was now as 1 to 11 $\frac{1}{20}$, and the true value of one pound weight of fine gold was 11 lb. 12 dwt. of fine ſilver.

MARY. 1553. Fine SOVEREIGN. The fine Sovereign or double Ryal of this queen differs but little from that of her fathers and brothers, ſhe being exhibited on it in her chair of ſtate, with the ſcepter and globe in her hands and the portcullis at her feet.

OBVERSE Type. Legend. This piece is inſcribed MARIA D. G. ANG. FRA. z HIB. REGINA MDLIII. being coined before her marriage, and is the firſt time we meet with the date of the year on the gold money.

REVERSE Type. The reverſe of the Sovereign is alſo nearly the ſame as all ſince Henry the Seventh, that is the large double roſe with the ſhield and royal arms on the center.

Legend. The inſcription on this piece is different from any of the preceding, being A DNO FACTUM EST ISTUD z EST MIRA IN OCUL NRIS. (Pſam. cxviii. v. 23.)

NOBLE or RYAL. The queen on this piece is repreſented as uſual in a ſhip, with a ſword in her right hand, and with her left hand ſhe holds the royal eſcutcheon with the arms

(y) Lowndes, p. 49.

of

Coins of Edward VI.

Plate

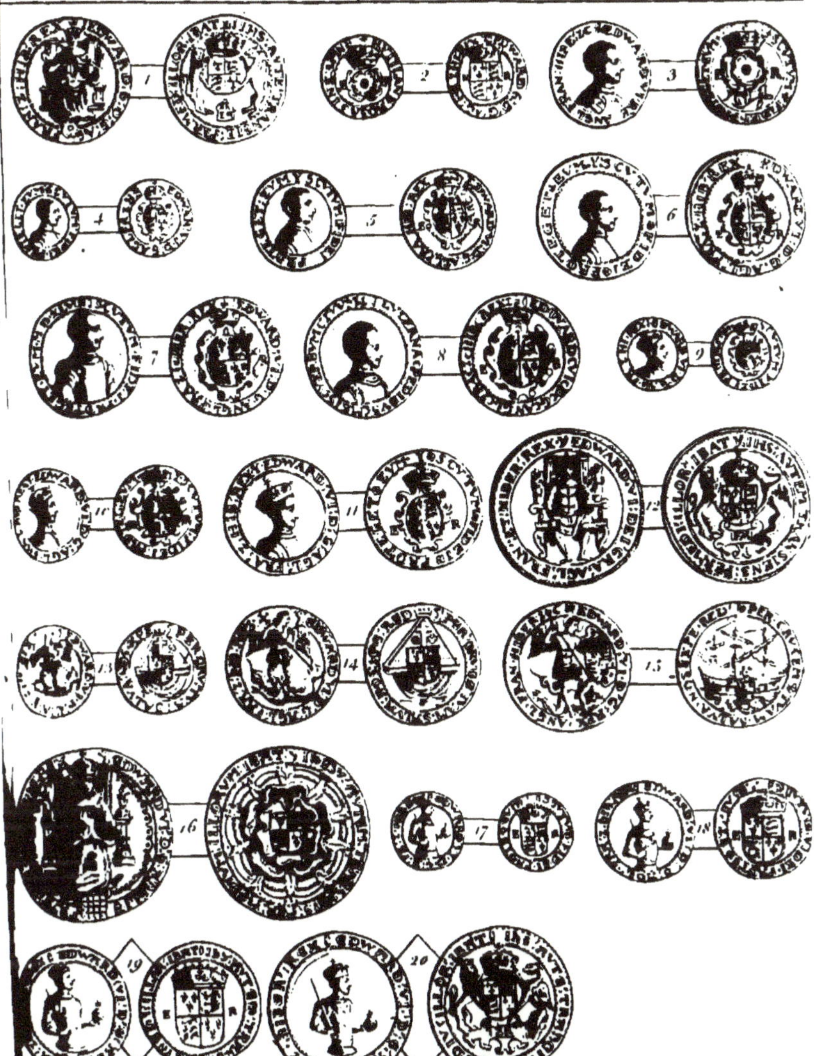

of France and England quarterly, and a rose on the side of the ship, also an M, the initial of her name on the flag at the stern of the ship, and near her head appears a furled sail with its yard. MARY.

It is inscribed nearly as the double Ryal, A DNO FACTUM EST INSTUD z EST MIRABI. Legend.

The reverse of the Ryal of Edward the Fourth is now again resumed, being the radiated rose in the center, surrounded with the lyons and crowns, the flourish'd points of the old cross, with their accompanying fleurs-de-lis, forming nearly a cross and saltyer, all within a compartment of eight leaves. REVERSE. Type.

The inscription differs but little from that of the double Ryal, being A DNO FACTUM EST ISTUD z EST MIRABI. Legend.

The type of the Angel and Angelet are the same as before, both obverse and reverse, those before her marriage, have an M. and a rose on each side the mast, but those after have a P. and an M. ANGEL. Type.

The inscription on the obverse of that before her marriage, is MARIA D. G. ANG. FRA. z HIB. REGIN. the half has A. FR. REGI; and that after her marriage is PHILIP z MARIA, D. G. REX z REGINA; on the reverse of both appears A DNO FACTUM EST ISTUD z EST MIRABILE, as on the other gold money of this queen.

Before her marriage she coin'd the Ryal, N. 3. the double Ryal or Sovereign, No. 4; and both before and after her marriage, the Angel, No. 2. and the Angelet, No. 1. all in plate 4. SORTS.

The Sovereign or double Ryal is common; the Angels and half Angels are very rare, especially the latter, but the Ryal is one of the rarest coins in the English collection. RARITY.

The sovereign weighs 240 gr. the Ryal 120 gr. the Angel weighs 80 gr. and the Angelet weighs 40 gr. Troy. WEIGHT.

They are all of the old standard for gold, or 23 carats, 3 grains and a half fine gold, and half a carat grain allay. FINENESS.

By indenture one pound weight Troy was cut into 24 Sovereigns, 48 Ryals, or 72 Angels, amounting to 36 pounds sterling in tale; and therefore the pound weight of fine gold was $36\frac{3}{16}$ pounds, or 36*l.* 3*s.* 9*d.* sterling. VALUE or PROPORTION.

One pound weight Troy of 11 oz. fine, contained 3 pounds sterling in tale, and therefore the pound weight of fine silver was at this time equal to $3\frac{3}{11}$ pounds sterling.

From hence it appears, that the proportion of fine silver to fine gold was as 1 to $11\frac{11}{191}$; and the true value of one pound weight of fine gold, was 11 lb. 13 dwt. 19 gr. of fine silver.

The fine Sovereign or double Noble of this queen, as usual, exhibit her on her throne, in her royal robes, crown'd, with a scepter in her right hand, the orbe in her left, and the portcullis at her feet; and the reverse has the large full-blown rose, charged with the shield and royal arms in the center. ELIZABETH, 1558. FINE SOVEREIGN. Type.

It is inscribed round the obverse ELIZAB. D. G. ANG. FR. ET Hib. REGINA; and on the reverse A DNO FACTU EST ISTUD ET EST MIRAB, or MIRA, like her sisters. Legend.

The queen appears on this piece, as usual, standing in a ship; but instead of a sword in her right hand, and shield in her left, she holds a scepter in one, and the orbe or globe in the other; there is a rose on the side of the ship, the head of which is more decorated than any of the preceding pieces of this sort. The RYAL Type.

reverse

ELIZABETH. reverse has the radiated rose with the lyons, crowns, and fleurs-de-lis enclosed within its compartment, as those of Edward the fourth, and her sister Mary.

Legend. The obverse is inscribed ELIZAB. D. G. ANG. FR. ET HIB. REGINA; on another sort, instead of ET HIB. it has Z M. P.R. AL. and again, one with M. P.R. C.AL. and a third sort with M. A. D G. PC. A. L. (z) The inscription on the reverse is the antient one, JHS AUT TRANSIENS PER MEDIU ILLORUM IBAT.

ANGEL. Type. This queen coined the Angel, Angelet, and quarter Angel, all of which have the usual type of St. Michael and the dragon on their obverse, and the ship with its mast charged with the royal shield of England, and the initial letter of her name E on one side of it, and a rose on the other, appears on the reverse.

Legend. There is inscribed round the obverse of the Angel ELIZABETH D. G. ANG. FR. ET HIB REGINA; on that of the Angelet, ELIZAB. D. G. ANG. FR. ET HI. REGI; and on the quarter, ELIZABETH D. G. ANG. FRANCIE, and this last has the remainder of the titles, ET HIBERNIE REGINA FIDEI on the reverse; but on that of the whole, and the half, there is A DNO FACTUM ET ISTUD ET EST MIRAB. or MIRABI.

POUND SOVERIGN. On the head side, or obverse of this piece, as also on the half, quarter and eighth, is the queen's bust crown'd in profile to the right, those of her first coinages very much resemble that on her silver money; but on those of her latter years, the bust is larger and more decorated, with dishevell'd hair, and the crown is double arched and higher, extending to the edge of the piece, whereas the former is within the inner circle, as are those which appear on the half, quarter, and eighth, No. 17, 18, 19. of the milled sort. The reverse exhibits the shield with the royal arms of France and England quarterly, with E. R. on the sides, and crown'd with the same sort of crown as is found on the obverse.

Legend. The inscription round the obverse of the whole and half Sovereigns are ELIZABETH D. G. Ang. Fr. ET HIB. REGINA; some have Fran. Hi. the quarter and eighth of the mill'd sort the same; but on those pieces of the hammer'd we see ELIZAB. D. G. ANG. FRA ET HIB. REG. some have FR. and REGI; the inscription on the reverse of all of them is SCUTUM FIDEI PROTEGET EUM, as on those of her brothers.

SORTS. There are the fine Sovereign, double Noble, or double Ryal, No. 11. the Ryal, No. 10. the Angel, No. 9. the Angelet, No. 8. the quarter Angel, No. 7. the pound Sovereign, No. 16. the half Sovereign, No. 12, 15, 19. the quarter Sovereign, No. 14, 18. and the eighth of the Sovereign or half Crown, N. 13, 17. all in plate 4.

RARITY. The money of this queen is, in general, frequent enough, if we except the quarter mill'd Sovereign, and the half quarters, or eighths, both of the mill'd and hammer'd, which are more rare, and the Ryal is extremely rare.

(z) These Ryals were counterfeited at Gorcum in Holland, as appears from a placart of the earl of Leicester's *, as follows: "Hunc sequitur accisa et improba moneta qua multi decipiuntur quamobrem. S. Extia monetariis suis hujus ratione habere jussit ut eam improbam monetam hominibus ab oculis penant scilicet ut ab ea sibi caveant nam talis moneta pro adulterina reputatur. Hujus farinæ est rosatus in Goricum sub nomine Don Anthonie excussus cujus unum latus a Nobile Anglico nihil differt, alteru vero hunc inscriptionem habet Elizabeth D. G. ANG. F. R. Z M. P. R. A. L. REGINA".

"Rosatus Nobilis in Goricom factus sub nomine principis a Summeii cujus alteru latus rosato Nobili Anglico convenit altera hunc inscriptionem habet Elizabeth ANGL. M. A D. G. P. C. A. L. REGINA."

And we suspect the following words in the proclamation of her 29th year † allude in particular to these sort of pieces, &c. many false pieces be counterfeited in foreign parts of the said coins, whereby great and intolerable loss and diminution of the riches of our realm doth daily grow and increase.

* MS. in our own possession. † Folkes, p. 73.

The

The fine Sovereign weighs 240 grains Troy, the Ryal 120 gr. the Angel before her 43d year weighs 80 gr. the Angelet 40 gr. and the quarter Angel 20 gr; and after her 43d year they weigh $78\frac{66}{73}$ gr. $39\frac{33}{73}$ gr. and $19\frac{53}{73}$ grains; the pound Sovereign, before her 43d year, weighs $174\frac{6}{11}$ gr. the half Sovereign $87\frac{3}{11}$ gr. the quarter Sovereign $43\frac{7}{11}$ gr. and the half quarter weighs $21\frac{9}{11}$ gr. but after her 43d year (*a*) they weigh $171\frac{63}{67}$ gr. $85\frac{65}{67}$ gr. $42\frac{66}{67}$ gr. and $21\frac{33}{67}$ gr. Troy (*b*). ELIZABETH. WEIGHT.

N. B. Those after her 43d year are known from all the rest, by their Mint marks 1 & 2.

The fine Sovereign, Ryal, and Angel, were all 23 carats, 3 grains and a half fine gold, and half a carat grain alloy; and the other Sovereign and its parts was 22 carats fine gold, and 2 carats alloy. FINENESS.

The fine Sovereign throughout this queen's reign was current for 30 shillings, the Ryal for 15 shillings, the Angel for 10 shillings, the half Angel for 5 shillings, the quarter Angel for 2*s.* 6*d*; the other Sovereign for one pound sterling, the half Sovereign for 10 shillings, the quarter Sovereign for 5 shillings, and the half quarter for 2*s.* 6*d.* VALUE or PROPORTION.

By several indentures (*c*) before her 43d year, one pound weight Troy was to be coined into 24 fine Sovereigns, 48 Ryals, 72 Angels, &c. amounting to 36 pounds sterling in tale, and therefore the nominal value of one pound weight of fine gold amounted to $36\frac{36}{191}$ pounds, or 36*l.* 3*s.* 9*d.* sterling. Before her 43d Year.

One pound weight of standard silver was, at this time, coined into 60 shillings in tale, or three pounds sterling; and therefore the said pound weight of fine silver was equal to $3\frac{9}{37}$ pounds sterling.

From whence it appears, that the proportion of fine silver to fine gold was as 1 to $11\frac{151}{955}$, and the true value of one pound weight of fine gold was 11 lb. 2 oz. 8 dwt. of fine silver.

There were at the same time 33 pound Sovereigns cut out of one pound weight of 22 carats fine, which gives the nominal value of the pound weight of fine gold 36 pounds sterling, and the pound of fine silver being as above $3\frac{9}{37}$ pounds sterling, therefore the proportion was as 1 to $11\frac{1}{10}$, and the true value of one pound weight of fine gold was 11 lb. 1 oz. 4 dwt. of fine silver.

By indenture of her 43d year (*d*), there was 73 Angels cut out of one pound weight Troy, amounting in tale to 36 pounds 10 shillings; and the nominal value of one pound weight of fine gold was $36\frac{132}{191}$ pounds, or 36*l.* 13*s.* 9*d.* 3*q.* sterling. In her 43d Year.

One pound weight of standard silver was to contain 62 shillings, or $3\frac{1}{10}$ pounds sterling in tale; and therefore the pound weight of fine silver contained $3\frac{13}{37}$ pounds sterling.

From whence it follows, that the proportion between fine silver and fine gold, was as 1 to $10\frac{5614}{5921}$, and the true value of one pound weight of fine gold was equal to 10 lb. 11 oz. 7 dwt. 13 grains of fine silver.

(*a*) The Sovereign coined by the archduke and archdutchess Albert and Elizabeth, and still in use in the catholick low countries to this day, is the same as this in weight, fineness, and value.

(*b*) By the proclamation of her 29th year, all counterfeited pieces were to have a hole struck through them; and likewise, all others that wanted in weight more than the following remedies, viz. double Ryal 4½ gr. Ryal 2¼ gr. Sovereign 3 gr. half Sovereign 2 gr. the quarter Sovereign 1 gr. and the eighth Sovereign half a grain.

(*c*) 2 Eliz. 19 Eliz. 25 Eliz. 26 Eliz. 35 Eliz. Lowndes, p. 49, 50, 51.

((*d* Lowndes, p. 51.

ELIZABETH. By the ſame indenture, one pound weight Troy was coin'd into $33\frac{1}{2}$ Sovereigns, or into 33 pounds 10 ſhillings in tale; and the nominal value of one pound weight of fine gold was $36\frac{6}{11}$ pounds, or 36*l.* 10*s.* 10*d.* 3*q.* ſterling; and the pound weight of fine ſilver being $3\frac{4}{11}$ pounds ſterling, therefore the proportion here is as 1 to $10\frac{905}{1000}$, and the true value of one pound weight of fine gold, is 10lb. 10oz. 17dwt. 3 grains of fine ſilver.

JAMES I. 1603. 1ſt Year. SOVEREIGN This piece has the king's buſt half bodied in armour, crown'd and looking to the left, with the ſcepter and orbe in his hands, on the whole, but on the ½, ¼ and ⅛, the buſt ſhews only the ſhoulders; on the reverſe is the royal ſhield crowned with J. R. on the ſides, exactly like the Unite, which immediately ſucceeded it, except in the inſcription, theſe have inſcribed round the head JACOBUS D. G. ANG. SCO. FRAN. ET HIB. REX, with ſome differences on the ſmaller pieces, as AN. ANGL. SC. FR. FRA. HI. HIBER. on the reverſe of the two largeſt pieces are inſcribed EXURGAT DEUS DISSIPENTUR INIMICI, (Pſalm lxviii. 1.) and the two ſmaller ones have TUEATUR UNITA DEUS.

2d Year. UNITIE or UNITE. This piece which was made current for one pound ſterling, ſucceeded the Sovereign of that value, and had its name, no doubt, from the union of the two crowns, which had juſt taken place in the perſon of this king; it is alſo frequently called a ſcepter, from the ſcepter in the king's hand, in diſtinction to thoſe of his 17th year, which are called Laurels, from the laureated head, both ſorts being in the indentures called by the ſame name of the Unitie or Unite.

Type. There is exhibited on this piece the king's profile buſt to the middle in armour crown'd, and regarding the left, having a ſcepter in his right hand, and the orbe in his left; the half Unite, called a double Crown, the quarter, called a Britain Crown, and the half quarter, called the half Crown, have the buſt only to the ſhoulder, without either ſcepter or orbe; the reverſe has the ſhield, with the royal arms crown'd, having the letters J. R. on the ſides of it, on the two largeſt pieces, but on the others they are over it; beſides the above pieces of the ½, ¼ and ⅛, there was alſo now for the firſt time one coined to be current for ⅕ of the Unite, or for four ſhillings named a Thiſtle Crown, which had on its obverſe a roſe crown'd between the letters J. R; and on the reverſe, the ſame letters on the ſides of a crowned thiſtle.

The Unite, double Crown, and Britain Crown, have all of them inſcribed round the head JACOBUS D. G. MAG. BRIT. FRAN. ET HIB. REX, and on the reverſe of the largeſt of them, or the Unite, there is FACIAM EOS IN GENTEM UNAM, and on the half and quarter HENRICUS ROSAS REGNA JACOBUS; the half Crown has for its legend on the head ſide, J. D. G. ROSA SINE SPINA, and on the reverſes of both are TUEATUR UNITA DEUS, as on the firſt coinage; and each of them regard the union of the two crowns.

3d Year ROSE RYAL. Type. On this fine Sovereign, which is now for the firſt time called a Roſe Ryal, the king is ſeated on his throne or chair of ſtate in his royal robes crowned, with a ſcepter in his right hand, and a globe in his left, having the portcullis at his feet; the reverſe has the full blown roſe, having on its center the royal ſhield, charg'd with the arms of France and England quarterly in the 1ſt and 4th quarters, Scotland in the 2d quarter, and Ireland in the 3d quarter, in which manner they were bore till the introduction of the milled money at the reſtoration.

Legend. The obverſe has inſcribed round it JACOBUS D. G. MAG. BRIT. FRAN. ET HIBER.

Coins of Mary and Elizabeth.

HIBER. REX; and on the reverse there is, A DNO FACTUM EST ISTUD ET EST MIRAB. IN OCULIS NRS. JAMES I.

The king on this Noble or Ryal appears standing in a ship as usual, with a sword in his right hand, and a large shield with the royal arms in his left; there is also his initial, an J on the flag, and a rose on the side of the ship. The reverse has the radiated rose, surrounded with the lyons and crowns, the flourish'd points, and fleurs-de-lis, all enclos'd within its usual compartment, as those of Edward the fourth, Mary, and Elizabeth, and is the last piece on which they appear in this manner. SPURRYAL. Type.

The obverse is inscribed round JACOBUS D. G. MAG. BRIT. FRAN. ET HIB. REX, and on the reverse, A DNO FACTUM EST ISTUD ET EST MIRABILIS. Legend.

The Angel and Angelet of this coinage differ but little from those of the former reigns, but have no cross near the top of the mast of the ship on the reverse, as all the former have; and the shield, with the royal arms which is fixed thereon, is much larger than on any of those. ANGEL. Type.

It has inscribed round the obverse JACOBUS D. G. MAG. BRIT. FRA. ET HI REX, and on the reverse there is A DNO FACTUM EST ISTUD. Legend.

This fine Sovereign exhibits the king sitting in his chair of state, the back of which, as well as the ground, is adorned with roses and fleurs-de-lis; he is in his royal robes, with a ruff about his neck, and the collar of the garter appears on his breast, has a scepter in his right hand, the globe in his left, and rests his feet on a portcullis; it has no compartment or ornament within the inner circle, as on the preceding ones, since Henry the Eighth. The reverse is entirely different from what had hitherto appeared on these pieces; having the old cross with the royal shield, on the top of which stands XXX for thirty shillings, its value, and is incircled with a kind of orle charg'd with lyons, roses, and fleurs-de-lis. 17th Year. 1619. ROSERYAL. Type.

The inscription round the obverse is JACOBUS D. G. MA. BRI. FR. ET HIB. REX, and on the reverse it is, A DNS FACTUM EST ISTUD ET EST MIRAB. IN OC NRIS. Legend.

The figure on the obverse of this piece is entirely new in the English series, as it exhibits a setting lyon, or lyon sejant crown'd, holding in his right paw a scepter, and his left supports the shield, with the royal arms, on each side of which appears X. V. for its value fifteen shillings; on the reverse appears the radiated rose, as on the former, having the lyons, crowns, and fleurs-de-lis within the usual compartment; but here the fleurs-de-lis are crown'd as the lyons, instead of being at the extremity of the flourished ends of the old cross, which remained after the cross was taken away. SPURRYAL. Type.

JACOBUS D. G. MAG. BRIT. FRA. ET HIB. REX, is the legend on its obverse; and on its reverse we read, A DNO FACTUM EST ISTUD ET EST MIRABI, which does not begin to read at top, as in general, but about the middle of the dexter side of the piece. Legend.

There is no material difference in the type or figure of St. Michael and the dragon on the obverse of this piece, from that on those of the preceding princes; but that of the reverse is very different, and both the design and performance are much preferable to any hitherto coined; the royal arms appear now on a full swelling sail; the side of the ship is ornamented with lyons and fleurs-de-lis, as on the old Noble; there is a lyon sejant holding a sword on the head and stern of the ship, (both of which are very much in the taste of that on his spur ryal) and has a flag flying, with a lyon of England on it. ANGEL. Type.

We

JAMES I. Legend. We read round the obverse JACOBUS D. G. MAG. BRI. FRA. ET HIB REX, and on the reverse, A DNO FACTUM EST ISTUD.

UNITE. Type. This piece, with its half and quarter, shew the profile head of the king laureated (from which they frequently are called laurels) and regarding the right the contrary way to the former, and has the value behind the head, viz. xx, x, and v, for twenty shillings, ten and five shillings sterling.

Legend. They have the same inscription both on the head and reverse as the last coinage, that is, JACOBUS D. G. MAG. BRI. FRAN. ET HIB. REX on the head side, FACIAM EOS IN GENTEM UNAM on the reverse of the whole, and HENRICUS ROSAS REGNA JACOBUS on the half and quarter

SORTS. There are the Rose Ryal, or fine Sovereign of his first coinage, No. 10, the Spur Ryal, No. 9, the Angel, No. 8, the Angelet, No. 7, the Sovereign or Scepter with ANG. SCO, the half ditto, No. 5, the quarter ditto, No. 3, and the half Crown ditto, No. 1, which were coined before the proclamation, and there are the same pieces coined afterwards till his 17th year, with MAG. BRIT. (as No. 6.). In his 17th year, and until his death, there are the Rose Ryal, No. 16, the Spur Ryal, No. 15, the Angel, No. 14, the Unite or Laurel, No. 13, the double Crown, No. 12, and the Britain Crown, No. 11, all in plate 5.

RARITY. The Sovereign and its parts, with ANG. SCO. are scarce, especially the two smallest; the Unites are very common, as are also the Rose and Spur Ryals; the Angel is not quite so common, and the Angelet is very rare.

WEIGHT. The Sovereign with ANG. SCO. weighs 171 [illegible] gr. and the half 85 [illegible] gr. the quarter 42 [illegible] gr. and the eighth 21 [illegible] grains; and the Unite with MAG. BRIT. weighs 154 [illegible] gr. the double Crown 77 [illegible] gr. the Britain Crown 38 [illegible] gr. the Thistle Crown 30 [illegible] gr. and the half Crown weighs 19 [illegible] grains Troy. The Rose Ryal, before his 17th year with MAG. BRIT. (having never seen one with ANG. SCO.) weighs 213 [illegible] gr. the Spur Ryal 106 [illegible] gr. the Angel 71 [illegible] gr. and the Angelet 35 [illegible] grains Troy. The Unite or Laurel, coined after his 17th year, weighs 140 [illegible] gr. the double Crown 70 [illegible] gr. and the Britain Crown 35 [illegible], the Rose Ryal weighs 194 [illegible] gr. the Spur Ryal 97 [illegible] gr. and the Angel 64 [illegible] grains Troy (*e*).

FINENESS. The Rose Ryals, Spur Ryals, and Angels, were all 23 carats, 3 grains and a half fine gold, and half a carat grain alloy; the Unites and their parts were all of 22 carats fine gold, and 2 carats alloy.

VALUE OF PROPORTION. Until the 9th year of this king's reign, the Rose Ryal was current for 30 shillings, the Spur Ryal for 15 shillings, the Angel for 10 shillings, the Angelet for 5 shillings, the Unite for 20 shillings, the double Crown for 10 shillings, the Britain Crown for 5 shillings, the Thistle Crown for 4 shillings, and the half Crown for 2 shillings and six-pence; but the augmentation in that year brought the Rose Ryal to 33 shillings, the Spur Ryal to 16 shillings and six-pence, the Angel to 11 shillings, the Angelet to 5 shillings and six-pence, the Unite to 22 shillings, the double Crown to 11 shillings, the Britain Crown to five shillings and six-pence, the Thistle Crown to 4 shillings and four-pence three farthings, and the half Crown to 2 shillings and 9 pence, at which rates they were current all the rest of his reign.

(*e*) By a proclamation of the 4th of February 1619, the same remedies are allow'd on the old coins, as by that of the 29th Eliz; and for the new Rose Ryal 3 gr. Spur Ryal $1\frac{1}{2}$ gr. Angel 1 gr. Unite 2 gr. double Crown 1 gr. and the British Crown $\frac{1}{2}$ grain, and were to be current (upon allowing two-pence for each grain) if they did not want more than the double remedy, but then to be broken or defaced.

And

Coins of James the First. Pl.

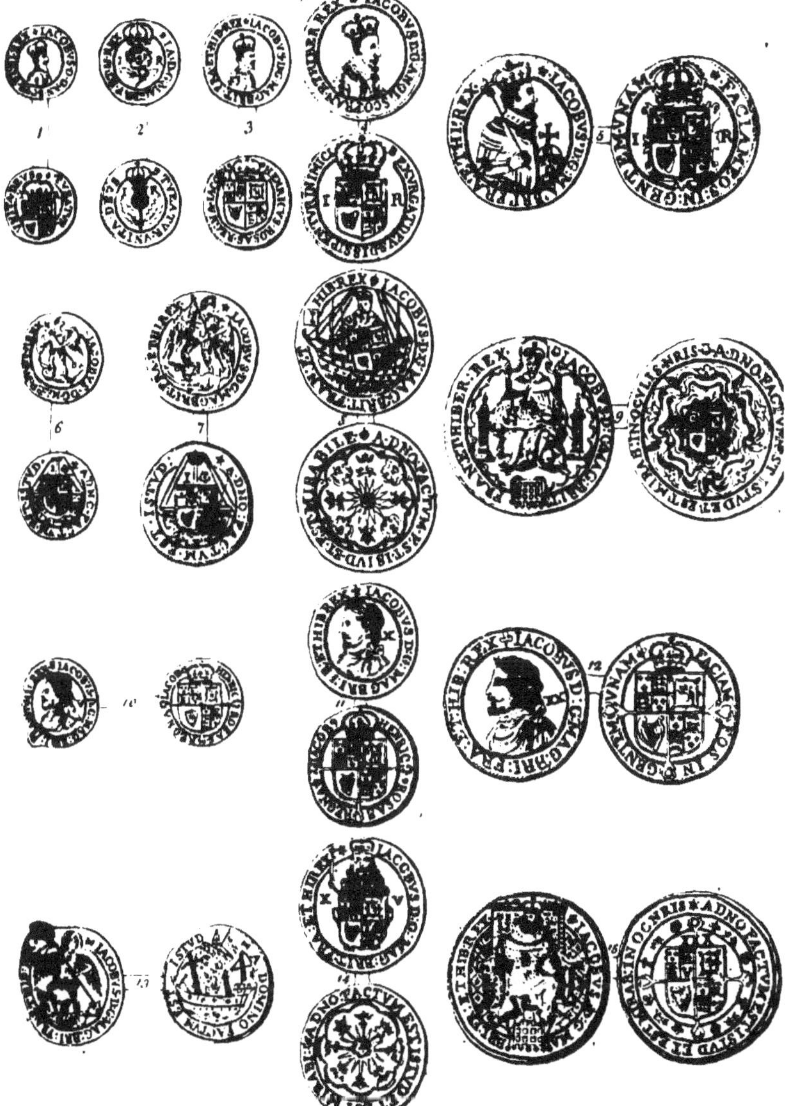

And the Rose Ryal, Spur Ryal, Angel, Unite, double Crown, Britain Crown and half Crown coined in his 17th year, were made current for 30*s.* 15*s.* 10*s.* 20*s.* 10*s.* 5*s.* and 2*s.* 6*d.* as the others had passed for before the augmentation. JAMES I.

The indenture of the first year * was the same as the 43d of Elizabeth.

By an indenture † of his 2d year, there was cut out of one pound weight Troy 37 [illegible] Unites, amounting to 37 pounds, 4 shillings in tale; and the nominal value of one pound weight of fine gold, was 40 [illegible] pounds, or 40*l.* 11*s.* 7*d.* 2*q.* sterling.

One pound weight Troy of fine silver was still at this time 3 [illegible] pounds sterling.

From hence it appears, that the proportion between fine silver and fine gold was as 1 to 12 [illegible], and the true value of one pound weight of fine gold, was equal to 12 lb. 1 oz. 6 dwt. 4 gr. of fine silver.

By another indenture of his 3d year, the pound weight was to contain 27 Rose Ryals, amounting to 40 pounds, 10 shillings sterling in tale; and therefore the nominal value of one pound weight of fine gold was equal to 40 [illegible] pounds, or to 40*l.* 14*s.* 2*d.* 3*q.* sterling.

One pound weight of fine silver remaining as before at 3 [illegible] pound sterling.

Therefore the proportion between fine silver and fine gold was as 1 to 12 [illegible], and the true value of one pound weight of fine gold was equal to 12 lb. 1 oz. 15 dwt. 12 gr. of fine silver (*f*).

This was a rise of about 11 per cent, and the first since the silver has been on the present foot.

By proclamation of the 23d of November 1611, or in his 9th year, the nominal and true value of gold was raised 10 *per cent.*

This brought the nominal value of the pound weight of fine gold (deduced from the rose Ryal) to 44 [illegible] pounds, or 44*l.* 15*s.* 7*d.* 3*q.* sterling; and the proportion of fine silver to fine gold was now as 1 to 13 [illegible], and the true value of one pound weight of fine gold was 13 lb. 3 oz. 16 dwt. 18 grains of fine silver.

The nominal value of one pound weight of fine gold (deduced from the Unite) was 44 [illegible] pounds, or 44*l.* 12*s.* 9*d.* 2*d.* and the proportion was as 1 to 13 [illegible], and the true value of the pound weight of fine gold was 13 lb. 3 oz. 16 dwt. 19 gr. of fine silver (*g*).

(*f*) By the ordonnance of the French king ‖ in September 1602, the Quart d'Ecu being 16 Sous, and the Ecu d'Or 65, the proportion was about 11 [illegible]. By the placart of the States dated December 19 1603 ‡, the Rix Dollar was 47 stivers, and the Ducat 74, therefore the proportion was about 12. In Germany, anno 1603 §, the Rix Dollar was 75 creutzers, and the Ducat 121, therefore the proportion about 12 [illegible]. And in Spain the Ryal was 34 Maravedis, and the Escudo or Pistole 400, as in in 1566 **, therefore the proportion was about 12 [illegible].

(*g*) By a placart of the States, July 6. 1610 ††, the Rix Dollar is 48 stivers, and the Ryder 212 stivers, therefore the proportion about 12 [illegible], Anno 1611. In France, the Quart d'Ecu was still 16 Sous, but the Ecu d'Or was risen to 72 ‖‖, therefore the proportion about 12 [illegible]. In Germany this same year, the Rix Dollar was 84 Creutzers, and the Ducat 140, therefore the proportion about 12. And in Spain 1609, the Pistole was raised from 400 to 440 §§ Maravedies, and the proportion was about 13 [illegible]. From whence it appears, that the proportion was higher than any of our neighbours, (except Spain) and no doubt was the principal cause of the great scarcity of silver, which appear'd a few years afterwards ‡‡.

* Mint books, Leake, p. 271. † Lowndes, p. 53. ‖ Conference des Ordonnances Royaux par Guenois, Lib. xi. Tit. vii. p. 781. ‡ Nederlantsche Munt Boeck, p. 781. § Hoffman's Muntz Schlussel, p. 160. ** Recopilacion de las Leyes, Part 5. Tit. 21. Ley xiii. Vol. 1. p. 347. †† Munt Boeck, p. 86. ‖‖ Advis presente a la Royne, par Godefroy, p. 130. §§ El Ajustamiento I proporcion de las Monedas de Oro, Plata, J. Cobre, p. 117. ‡‡ Malynes, p. 323. Mun, cap. 8. Folkes, p. 69.

JAMES I. By indenture of the 10th year * of this king, and a commiſſion of his 13th year, the pound weight Troy in Ryals was to contain 44*l.* 10*s.* in tale, and that of Unites (Scepters) 40*l.* 18*s* 4*d.* 3*q.*

By another indenture of his 21ſt year †, the ſaid pound weight in Ryals (i. e. 29 $\frac{3}{4}$) was to amount to 44*l.* 10*s.* as before; and that of Unites (laurels) to 41*l.* and this laſt exactly agrees with that of the 2d of Charles the Firſt.

This was the ſecond advance of the gold upon the ſilver, after it had been fixed on the preſent foot, and both together amounted to about 21 per cent.

CHARLES I. 1625. There are not ſo great a variety of the gold money coined by this king, as there is of the ſilver, he having but two mints wherein any gold were coined, which were thoſe in the Tower of London, and at Oxford.

TOWER MINT. By an indenture of his 2d year, Roſe Ryals, Spur Ryals, and Angels were to be coined; but we ſuſpect that neither of the two firſt ſorts were minted, as none of them are to be found in any cabinet.

ANGEL. Type. The Angel which we have of this king is like that of the laſt coinage of his father's, both on the obverſe and reverſe, only it has an x for 10 ſhillings, its value put on it, and is the laſt Angel coined by any king of England.

Legend. The legenda on its obverſe is CAROLUS D. G. MAG. BRIT. FRA. ET HI. REX; and that on the reverſe is peculiar to this piece, AMOR POPULI PRÆSIDIUM REGIS.

UNITIE. OBVERSE Type. The Unitie, or 20 ſhilling piece, the half Unitie, double Crown, or 10 ſhilling piece, and the Britain Crown, or 5 ſhilling piece, have each of them on their obverſe the profile buſt of the king looking to the right, as the laſt coinage of his father's. On thoſe of the two firſt years of his reign he is repreſented in a ſtiff ruff, and in his robes with the collar of the order of the garter about his neck; thoſe of the four or five next years exhibit him with a different ſort of a ruff, and in armour; but on all after, to the end of his reign, he appears in a falling laced band.

Legend. They are inſcribed CAROLUS D. G. MAG. BRIT. FR. ET HIB. REX, with ſome little differences, as BR. BRI. & HI.

REVERSE. Type. The reverſe has the ſhield with the royal arms, as have alſo the ſilver coins of this king, but on them it is not crowned; but on the gold it always is, and this is what they principally differ in; and like them alſo, the firſt coinage has the ſquare ſhield garniſh'd (but no croſs) which was chang'd for an oval ſhield, with the letters C. R. on the ſides, and this was continued with very little alteration during the remainder of the king's reign.

Legend. The Unite has inſcribed round it, FLORENT CONCORDIA REGNA; and the half and quarter Unites have CULTORES SUI DEUS PROTEGIT.

BRIOT'S MINT. UNITIE. OBVERSE. The Unite and half Unite of this mint have a very neat profile head of this king crown'd and regarding the right, and with a laced band round his neck, and a roman mantle on his ſhoulders, which extends no farther than to the inner circle, having xx and x behind the head, for 20 and 10 ſhillings, their reſpective values. The inſcription round the head is CAROLUS D. G. MAGN. BRIT. FRAN. ET HIB. REX.

REVERSE. The reverſe has a ſquare garniſh'd ſhield which is crown'd, and has the letters C. R. which are alſo crown'd on the ſides of it, in which and in the croſs are

* Lowndes, p. 53. Rymer, T. 17. p. 19. Leake, p. 279.

† 21 Jam. I. 19 Pt. Clauſ. No. 2.

the

the differences between the XX and X shilling pieces in gold, and the XII and VI penny pieces in silver. It has inscribed round the shield of the Unitie, FLORENT CONCORDIA REGNA; and on that of the half, CULTORES SUI DEUS PROTEGIT. CHARLES I.

This Angel has on its obverse the figure of St. Michael and the dragon, and has also the value X; the ship on the reverse appears of a neater construction, and has 17 guns on her side; she has only a flag-staff at her head, near which is the letter B, but on her prow there is St. George's flag flying, and on her main sail are the royal arms quartered. ANGEL.

This mint produced the Unité, or XX shilling piece; the treble Unité, or three pound piece; and the half Unité, or 10 shilling piece: the two first of which pieces exhibit a large bust of the king in profile crown'd, and regarding the right, having a sword erect in his right hand, and in his left hand he holds a branch of laurel. The largest piece has the feathers behind the bust, and on the other there is XX for its value, the half Unité has also an X; the bust on which piece only shews the shoulders, and extends to the edge of the coin; but the other two are within the circle. There is another sort of ruder workmanship, the bust on the largest of which though longer, yet does not touch the inner circle either at top or bottom; the other two pieces likewise differ from those we have been just describing. OXFORD MINT. UNITIE. OBVERSE Type.

The treble Unité, or 3 pound piece, is inscribed, CAROLUS D. G. MAG. BRI. FRA. ET HIBER. REX, another of them has BRIT. FRAN; the Unité reads BR. FR. HI. the half has AN. BR. FR. HI. Legend.

The reverse has its area filled with three scrolls, on which are RELIG. PROT. LEG. ANG. LIB. PAR, on some it is ANGL. and LIBER, over which are plac'd 3 feathers, and on the largest there is also III for 3 pounds sterling, the value of the piece; at the bottom of all of them is the date 1642, 1643, and 1644. OX. REVERSE Type.

All the three pieces have for their legend, EXURGAT DEUS DISSIPENTUR INIMICI. Legend.

There are of the Tower mint, the Angel, No. 1, the Britain Crown, No. 2, the double Crown, No. 3, the Unitie, No. 4; From Briot's mint, the Angel, No. 5, the double Crown, No. 6, and the Unitie, No. 7; and out of the Oxford mint, the double Crown, N. 8, the Unitie, No. 9, and the treble Unitie, No. 10. SORTS.

The gold money of this king are in general very common; however, we must except Briot's Angel, which is extremely rare. RARITY.

The Unitie weighs 140$\frac{20}{41}$ grains, the double Crown 70$\frac{10}{41}$ gr. the British Crown 35$\frac{5}{41}$ gr. the treble Unitie 421$\frac{19}{41}$ gr. and the Angel 64$\frac{64}{89}$ grains Troy. WEIGHT.

The Angel was 23 carats 3 grains and a half fine gold, and half a grain alloy, and is the last time this sort of gold has been used in our mints; all the other pieces are 22 carats fine, and 2 carats alloy, as at present. FINENESS.

The Unite was current for one pound sterling, the double crown and Angel for 10 shillings, and the Britain Crown for 5 shillings. VALUE OF PROPORTION.

By indenture of his 2d year, one pound weight Troy was cut into 41 Unites, or 41 pounds sterling in tale; and therefore the nominal value of one pound weight of fine gold, amounted to 44$\frac{8}{11}$ pounds, or 44*l.* 14*s.* 6*d.* 2*q.* sterling.

The same pound weight was cut into 89 Angels, amounting to 44 pounds 10 shillings sterling in tale; and the nominal value of one pound weight of fine gold amounted to 44$\frac{140}{191}$ pounds, or 44*l.* 14*s.* 7*d.* 3*q.* sterling.

One

CHARLES I. One pound weight of fine silver remained atthe value of $3\frac{13}{37}$ pounds sterling.

Therefore the proportion between fine silver and fine gold, in the first case, was as 1 to 13 [illegible], and in the second case as 1 to 13 [illegible]; and the true value of one pound weight of fine gold was 13lb. 4 oz. 3 dwt. 16 gr, and 13lb. 4 oz. 3dwt. 11 gr. of fine silver.

SIEGE MONEY. The only piece we have ever heard of struck in gold in any of the castles, is No. 11. pl. 6. which was struck at Pontefract, and appears to be a Unite, or 20 shilling piece; it is octagonal, and like the shilling.

COMMONWEALTH. 1649. xx Shilling Piece. The gold money of the Commonwealth is exactly like their silver money, both in type and inscription, differing only in the values put over the shield on the reverse.

Type. Legend. The obverse has the antique shield, with the cross of St. George encircled with a laurel, and a palm branch, and inscribed the COMMONWEALTH OF ENGLAND. The reverse has two antique shields joined together, containing St. George's cross and the Irish harp, with the respective values over them, as xx, x, and v, for so many shillings. Round them are inscribed GOD WITH US, and the date; which is from 1649 to 1660 inclusive.

SORTS. There are only three, the xx, the x, and the v, as above expressed.

RARITY. All the three sorts are very common (*k*).

WEIGHT. FINENESS. VALUE. Weight, fineness and value as those of Charles the First.

OLIVER PROT. 1656. There are of the Protector a twenty shilling piece, also a piece that weighs just two and an half of that, and therefore commonly supposed to be designed for a coin of fifty shillings; but we should rather suspect it was intended only as a proof of the 20 shilling piece, it being of the same size, and not different in the least either in type or legend, only in the thickness of the piece, and the inscription on its rim, both of which strengthen our conjecture of its being a proof-piece; there are likewise ten shilling pieces, but not struck in his time; but since the discovery of the dye or puncheon by Mr. Folkes (*l*), at whose instance chiefly we presume, those we have at present, owe their being.

OBVERSE These pieces are the performance of that excellent artist SIMON, and exhibit a fine profile bust of the protector, laureated and regarding the right, his neck being quite bare; but on the silver money it appears a la Romain, covered with a kind of roman mantle, and is what constitutes the chief difference observable between the two sorts of monies: round the head is inscribed OLIVAR D. G. R.P. ANG. SCO. ET HIB. &c. PRO. the &c. on the ten shilling piece, is wanting.

REVERSE. On the reverse is a neat plain square shield, crowned, different from that on the silver, with the cross of St. George in its 1st and 4th quarters for England, that of St. Andrew in the 2d for Scotland, the Irish harp in the 3d for Ireland, and on the center a lyon rampant his paternal coat. The inscription round it is PAX QUÆRITUR BELLO, as on the silver; and on the rim of the fifty shilling

(*k*) After the coining of the guineas, the Unites coined in the two foregoing reigns, and those of the commonwealth, got the name of BROADS and BROAD PIECES; also those of king James were called JACOBUS's, and those of king Charles·CAROLUS's; they continued in currency the scepters at 25*s.* and all the others at 23*s.* (although the former were worth 25*s.* 1*d.* 1*q.* and the latter but 22*s.* 9*d.* 3*q.*) until 1732, in which year, by a proclamation of February 1, they were forbid to be current, and received at the mint at the rate of 4*l.* 1*s.* per ounce.

(*l*) Table of silver coins, p. 102. Gold coins, p. 9.

piece

Coins of Charles I, The Common-wealth, Oliver Cromwell and Charles II.

OLIVER PROT.

piece there is inscribed, PROTECTOR LITERIS LITERAE NUMMIS CORÔNA ET SALUS.

RARITY.

The gold money of the protector is all of it rare, but the fifty shilling piece is extremely rare.

WEIGHT. FINENESS. VALUE.

Weight, fineness and value as those of Charles the First.

CHARLES II. 1660. HAMMER'D MONEY. xx Shilling Piece.

The first money coined by this king, after his restoration, in gold as well as in silver, was that struck with the hammer, and like them are of two sorts, with and without the value, and neither of them have an inner circle.

OBVERSE.

They exhibit the profile head of the king laurel'd, and looking to the right. Those coin'd first have no value behind the head, but the others have xx, x, and v, for so many shillings, and are inscribed CAROLUS II. D. G. MAG. BRIT. FRAN. ET HIB. REX.

REVERSE.

The reverse has an oval garnish'd shield crown'd with the letters C. R. on the sides, and there is inscribed on all the three pieces, FLORENT CONCORDIA REGNA; whereas this legend was only on the largest, or xx shilling piece of his father's, the two lesser pieces having a different legend. There is also a very neat milled 20 shilling piece, or pattern for one (No. 24.) which has the same legend as above, but the shield is square, and has the date 1662 on the top, over the crown. The legend round the head is CAR. II. D. G. M. BR. FR. ET HI. REX.

MILLED MONEY. xx Shilling Piece, or GUINEA.

This excellent method of coining by the mill and press took place in consequence of a warrant from the king, dated the 5th of November 1662, and another of January the 19th following, and were made current by a proclamation of the 27th of March 1663.

The term of twenty shilling piece is still kept in the indentures; the appellation of GUINEA given to it, was because great quantities of them were coined out of gold brought from that coast by the Royal African Company, which are distinguish'd by an Elephant under the head, some a castle, and others without, which was continued under each reign, until George I. However, but a few are to be seen, either of him or queen Anne, thus mark'd (*m*).

HEAD-SIDE

A very neat profile head of the king looking to the left, appears on all the pieces; it is laureated and has the neck bare, whereas the bust on the silver money is in the roman taste, with the toga or mantle gather'd on the shoulder; this distinction was first used by Simon on the pieces of Oliver Cromwell, and has been followed in every reign to the present, except on that of queen Anne, who was so delicate as not to suffer her portrait to be exhibited on the money with her neck uncovered, and therefore her bust on the gold money is the same as on the silver. It is inscribed round the head CAROLUS II. DEI GRATIA, as on the silver.

(*m*) An account of the number of Guineas coined out of gold imported by the Royal African Company *.

1675	12271	1681	24852	1687	32440	1693	7506	1699	2214	1708	2918	1721	2962
1676	15278	1682	23235	1688	39371	1694	15801	1701	4984	1709	11155	1722	12284
1677	83871	1683	25589	1689	25493	1695	21504	1703	397	1710	10382	1723	5427
1678	5005	1684	20684	1690	1562	1696	2410	1704	1836	1712	2925	1724	14388
1679	25277	1685	46066	1691	26700	1697	11443	1705	1358	1713	146	1725	4916
1680	17147	1686	23434	1692	19036	1698	17828	1707	5568	1715	591	Tot.	578754

* Gazetteer and London Daily Advertiser, 23 January 1755.

CHARLES II. REVERSE. The reverse exhibits the four crown'd shields of England, Scotland, France, and Ireland, in a new method, or in cross; that of England at the top, Ireland on the dexter side or 2d place, Scotland on the sinister side or 3d place, and France at bottom. The center is fill'd with interlink'd C's, and there are two scepters in saltier, which appear in the void spaces between the shields, and these scepters are what form the principal difference between the silver and gold monies on the reverse. They are inscribed as the silver with the title MAG. BR. FR. ET HIB. REX; and round the rim of the five pound piece is, DECUS ET TUTAMEN, with the year of the king's reign, as on the half Crown and Crown in silver.

SORTS. There are the half Guinea, No. 4, the Guinea, No. 3, the two Guinea piece, No. 2, and five Guinea piece, No. 1, all of which have continued to be coined to the present time.

WEIGHT. The half Guinea weighs 64 [illegible] gr. the Guinea 129 [illegible], the two Guinea piece 258 [illegible], and the five Guinea piece 647 [illegible] grains Troy.

FINENESS. They are all of twenty-two carats of fine gold, and two carats of alloy.

VALUE OR PROPORTION. The Guinea was coined for and current at 20 shillings, or one pound sterling, the half Guinea for 10 shillings, the double Guinea for 40 shillings, and the five Guinea piece for five pounds.

By indenture of his 13th year *, one pound weight Troy, was to contain 44 [illegible] guineas, or 44 pounds 10 shillings sterling in tale; and therefore the nominal value of one pound weight of fine gold was equal to 48 [illegible] pounds, or 48 *l.* 10 *s.* 10 *d.* 3 *q.* sterling.

One pound weight of fine silver was coined into 3 [illegible] pounds sterling, as in the 43d of Eliz.

From whence it appears, that the proportion between fine silver and fine gold was as 1 to 14 [illegible], and the true value of one pound weight of fine gold was equal to 14 lb. 5 oz. 16 dwt. 11 gr. of fine silver.

This was the third rise of the gold after the silver had been fixed on the present foot, and amounted to about 8+ per cent. and all three advances to near 33 per cent.

But they had not been long in currency before common consent had raised them to 21 shillings; and therefore the nominal value of one pound weight Troy of fine gold, was now equal to 50 [illegible] pounds, or 50 *l.* 19 *s.* 5 *d.* 3 *q.* sterling, the proportion was increased to 15 [illegible]; and the true value of one pound weight of fine gold was 15 lb. 2 oz. 10 dwt. 7 gr. of fine silver, which was an advance of 5 per cent; and the 4th rise, since the silver was fixed on the present foot, and all four advances amounted to about 39 per cent.

JAMES II. 1685. GUINEA. HEAD-SIDE. The gold money of this king present his profile bust laureated, and looking to the right the contrary way to his brother; a lock of hair flows over the neck. They are inscribed JACOBUS DEI GRATIA.

REVERSE. The reverse has the four shields in cross, as that of Charles the Second, as also the two scepters in saltier; but the center has no interlink'd letters in it as that has. They are inscribed round with the title MAG. BR. FRA. ET HIB. REX, and on the rim of the five Guinea, DECUS ET TUTAMEN.

SORTS. There are the half Guinea, No. 5, the Guinea, No. 6, the two Guinea piece, No. 7, and the five Guinea piece, No. 8.

WEIGHT. FINENESS. VALUE. The weight, fineness and value are the same as Charles the Second.

* Lowndes, p. 56.

The

Will. and Mary. 1689. Head-Side

The profile busts of the king and queen appear together, regarding the left; that of the king is laureated, and the queen has only her hair. They are inscribed GULIELMUS ET MARIA DEI GRATIA.

Reverse.

On the reverse there is the royal arms in a square shield, ornamented and crown'd; in the first and fourth quarters are France and England quarterly, in the second is Scotland, and Ireland is in the third quarter, having the arms of Nassau on the center. They are inscribed MAG. BR. FR. ET HI. REX ET REGINA; and on the rim of the five guinea piece is DECUS ET TUTAMEN, with the year of their reign.

Sorts.

There are the half Guinea, No. 12, the Guinea, No. 11, the piece of two Guineas, No. 10, and the piece of five Guineas, No. 9.

Weight. Fineness. Value.

Weight, fineness and value as those of Charles the Second.

William III 1694. Head-Side

The laureated bust of this king appears on his gold money looking to the right, with the neck bare as usual; it has inscribed round it GULIELMUS III. DEI GRATIA.

Reverse.

The reverse has the four crowned shields in cross, as on those of Charles and James the Second, together with the two scepters, and over the center the arms of Nassau; and has inscribed round them MAG. BR. FRA. ET HIB. REX, and on the rim of the five Guinea piece DECUS ET TUTAMEN.

Sorts.

There are the half Guinea, No. 13, the Guinea, No. 14, the two Guinea, No. 15, and the five Guinea piece, No. 16.

Weight. Fineness.

Weight and fineness as those of Charles the second.

Value or Proportion.

About the famous æra of the revolution, or a little while before or after, the Guinea, by common consent, was paid and received at 21 shillings and sixpence; which was an advance of about $2\frac{1}{2}$ per cent, and was the fifth rise of the gold after that the silver had been fixed on the present foot, and all five advances amounted to near 43 per cent.

The nominal value of one pound weight Troy of fine gold was now raised to 52[illegible] pounds, or 52*l.* 3*s.* 8*d.* 3*q.* sterling, the proportion was increased to 15[illegible], and the true value of one pound weight of fine gold was 15 lb. 6 oz. 17 dwt. 8 gr. of fine silver.

The gold money remaining without alteration in weight and fineness, and the silver money growing daily of less value by clipping and counterfeiting, occasioned 25 shillings, then 28 shillings, and at last 30 shillings to be given for a guinea; but no sooner was the silver money restored to its just value by the grand recoinage, than the guinea was again reduced, first to 28 shillings *, then to 26 shillings †, and finally to 22 shillings ‖; and soon after, by common consent, was paid and received as before, at 21*s.* 6*d.* and continued at that price for twenty years after.

Anne. 1702. Guinea. Head-Side

This queen is exhibited on her gold money with a profile bust turned to the right in her hair, which is tied up behind with a fillet, and has her breast and shoulders covered; whereas on all the gold milled money, both before and since, the neck and breast are naked. There is inscribed round it ANNA DEI GRATIA.

Reverse.

The reverse, as usual, has the four shields in cross, and the two scepters in saltier; those before the union have England at top, Ireland on the dexter side,

* 15 Feb. † 28 Feb. ‖ 26 March 1697. Journals of the House of Commons, Vol. XI. p. 451, 476 and 533.

Scotland

ANNE. Scotland on the finifter, and France at bottom; but after the union, Englaud and Scotland impaled are at top and bottom, France on the dexter fide, and Ireland on the finifter. There is alfo commonly the radiated crofs of St. George in the center, but there are a few with a rofe; and we once remember to have feen a Guinea with the figure of St. George in the fame place, and a very neat pattern Guinea has A. R. It has infcribed round it, as ufual, the titles MAG. BR. FRA. ET HIB. REG. On the rim of the five Guinea piece there is DECUS ET TUTAMEN.

SORTS. There is the half Guinea, No. 20, the Guinea, No. 19, the two Guinea, No. 18. and the five Guinea pieces, No. 17.

WEIGHT. FINENESS. The weight and finenefs the fame as all fince Charles the fecond.

VALUE. The Guinea paffed current all this reign for twenty-one fhillings and fixpence, and therefore the proportion between fine filver and gold was as 1 to 15[illegible], and the true value of one pound weight of fine gold was 15lb. 6oz. 17dwt. 5gr. of fine filver.

GEORGE I. 1714. GUINEA. HEAD-SIDE This king's buft is in profile to the left, and crowned with laurel, as all fince the reftoration. It has infcribed round it GEORGIUS D. G. M. BR. FR. ET HIB. REX. F. D.

REVERSE. The reverfe has four crowned fhields in crofs, as ufual, but that of his majefty as elector of Hanover is introduced, and England and Scotland, inftead of two places, have here but one; that is, at top are England and Scotland, on the dexter fide are thofe of Brunfwick, Lunenburgh, and Weftphalia; on the finifter fide is France, and Ireland is at bottom. There is the radiated crofs likewife, and crofs fcepters.

It is infcribed BRUN. ET L. DUX. S. R. J. A. T. H. ET E. L; and on a Guinea of his firft year there was added P. R. for Princeps Elector.

SORTS. This king, befides the ufual forts, that is, the half Guinea, the Guinea, the two Guinea, and the five Guinea piece, coined alfo a quarter Guinea (*n*).

WEIGHT. FINENESS. Weight and finenefs as thofe of Charles the fecond.

VALUE OF PROPORTION. The Guinea had continued to be current for 21*s.* 6*d.* ever fince the grand recoinage, until the year 1717, in which year there was a remarkable fcarcity of filver, which by Sir Ifaac Newton, at that time mafter of the mint, in a memorial dated the 21ft of September, by him delivered to the treafury, was partly imputed to the overvaluing of gold, or the too high proportion it was at in this kingdom, more than it was abroad; and therefore by a proclamation of December 20. 1717 (*o*), the proportion was lower'd, that is, the Guinea was reduced to 21 fhillings, as it has continued at ever fince, although it ftill left the gold at a higher value than amongft moft of our neighbours, and occafioned a continual drain of our filver coin from us ever fince.

This was a fall of $2\frac{1}{3}$ per cent. and the proportion became now again as 1 to

(*n*) Thefe pieces were coined immediately after the reduction of the Guinea, and therefore, no doubt, intended to help the great fcarcity of filver at that time; but there being no more tha 210 lb. weight of them coined, or 37380, and the firft time of this fort of money's being minted, they were moftly laid up as foon as delivered, and by that means the defign fruftrated, and none has been coined fince till this prefent year. when they have again been brought into the affiftance of the filver, in much greater numbers than before, as there has been coined 400000 of them, or 105000 pounds fterling.

(*o*) After this proclamation a Guinea at 21*s.* 6*d.* is found in the indentures, inftead of a piece for 20 fhillings, as had been in all of them fince 1663.

MILLED COINS from CHARLES II. to GEORGE II.

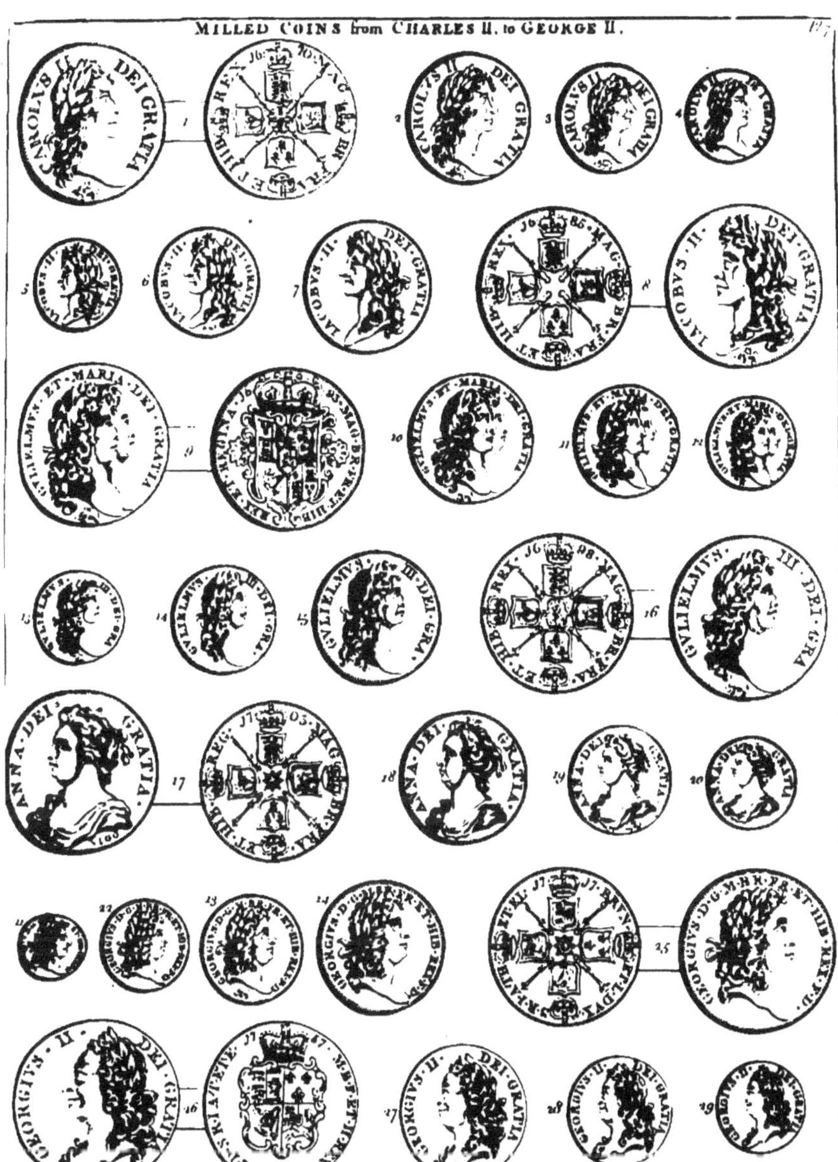

15[illegible], and the true value of one pound weight of fine gold was 15 lb. 2 oz. 10 dwt. 7 gr. of fine silver. **GEORGE I.**

This king is exhibited with a profile head laureated, and looking to the right. It has inscribed round it, GEORGIUS II. DEI GRATIA. Those coined of the gold, sent to the mint by the East India Company, have E. I. C. under the head. **GEORGE II. 1727. HEAD-SIDE**

The reverse of this king's money has not the shields in cross, but all in one escutcheon, in which England and Scotland are in the first quarter, France in the second quarter, Ireland in the third, and Brunswick, Lunenburgh and Westphalia in the fourth quarter. **REVERSE**

It is inscribed M. B. F. ET H. REX. F. D. B. ET L. D. S. R. J. A. T. ET E. for MAGNÆ BRITANNIÆ, FRANCIÆ ET HIBERNIÆ REX, FIDEI DEFENSOR; BRUNSWIGÆ ET LUNENBERGÆ DUX SACRI ROMANI IMPERII ARCHI THESAURARIUS ET ELECTOR.

SORTS, WEIGHT (*p*), FINENESS and VALUE as before.

The bust of his present majesty is laurel'd, and regards the left, having inscribed round it GEORGIUS III. REX. **GEORGE III. 1760. HEAD-SIDE**

The reverse has the shield, with the royal arms, as that of George the IId, and like that is inscribed, M. B. F. ET H. REX. F. D. B. ET L. D. S. R. J. A. T. ET E. **REVERSE.**

The only sorts at present current are the Guinea and the quarter Guinea. **SORTS.**

Weight and fineness as all since Charles the Second. **WEIGHT. FINENESS.**

The proportion as 1 to 15[illegible] (*q*), and the value 15 lb. 2 oz. 10 dwt. 7 gr. **VALUE.**

(*p*) By proclamation of James I. and Charles I, if the Unite wanted more than four grains, it was to be bored; but at present the Guinea passes without scruple, even if it wants 9 grains, or more than double what they were formerly defaced at, which deficiencies are occasioned more by filing †, than by wear, that pernicious practice being carried to an excessive heigth, during the first 13 years of this king.

(*q*) The proportion of fine silver to fine gold in the undermentioned kingdoms, and states stood as follows, anno 1754, as we are informed by a celebrated Italian author *. *N. B.* He has put our silver at 11 oz. fine, instead of 11 oz. 2dwt. which causes the difference between his proportion and ours: France 14[illegible], Flanders 14[illegible], Holland 14[illegible], England 15[illegible], Spain 14[illegible] 15[illegible], Portugal 13[illegible] 13[illegible], Russia 14[illegible], Austria 14[illegible], Turin 14[illegible], Genoa 14[illegible] 15[illegible], Naples 13[illegible] 14[illegible], Florence 14[illegible], Milan 14[illegible] 15[illegible], Venice 14[illegible], Rome 14[illegible], Lucca 13[illegible].

* Delle Monete E delle Instituzioni delle Zecche d'Italia Di Don. Gianrinaldo Carli Rubbi, Tom. 3, Dissert. 6. cap. 4. 4to. Lucca 1760.

† See Vallevine's Observations on the present state of the current coin.

COINS OF GEORGE III.

A Table of the Nominal Values of one Pound Weight of fine Silver and fine Gold; and the Proportion, true Value, or Number of Pounds Weight of fine Silver in one Pound Weight of fine Gold. *N. B.* The Pound Weight till 18 Hen. VIII. is that of the Tower, and fince that Time the Pound Troy.

Name of the King and Year of his Reign.	Nominal Value of one Pound Weight of fine Silver, in Pounds Sterling.	£.	s.	d.	Nominal Value of one Pound Weight of fine Gold in Pounds Sterling.	£.	s.	d.	True Value of one Pound Weight of fine Gold, or the Proportion of fine Silver to fine Gold.	lb.	oz.	dwt.	gr.
18 Edward III. 1344	1[illegible]	1	3	11[illegible]	15[illegible]	15	1	6[illegible]	12[illegible]	12	8	14	7[illegible]
					13[illegible]	13	4	8[illegible]	11[illegible]	11	0	11	2
20 ———— 1346	1[illegible]	1	4	3[illegible]	14[illegible]	14	1	5	11[illegible]	11	6	16	7
27 ———— 1353	1[illegible]	1	7	0[illegible]	15[illegible]	15	1	6[illegible]	11[illegible]	11	1	17	22
13 Henry IV. 1412	1[illegible]	1	11	10[illegible]	16[illegible]	16	15	0[illegible]	10[illegible]	10	3	19	13[illegible]
4 Edward IV. 1464	2[illegible]	1	0	6[illegible]	22[illegible]	22	17	7[illegible]					
18 Henry VIII. 1527	2[illegible]	2	8	8[illegible]	27[illegible]	27	8	2	11[illegible]	11	1	17	22
34 ———— 1543	2[illegible]	2	17	7[illegible]	30[illegible]	30	1	0[illegible]	10[illegible]	10	3	19	13
36 ———— 1545	4[illegible]	4	16	0	32[illegible]	32	14	6[illegible]	6[illegible]	6	9	16	13
37 ———— 1546					36	36	0	0	5	5	0	0	0
3 Edward VI. 1549	7[illegible]	7	4	0	37[illegible]	37	1	9[illegible]	5[illegible]	5	1	16	8
4 ———— 1550					34[illegible]	34	14	9	4[illegible]	4	9	17	22
5 ———— 1551	14[illegible]	14	8	0	34[illegible]	34	14	9	2[illegible]	2	4	18	23
6 ———— 1552	3[illegible]	3	5	1[illegible]	36	36	0	0	11[illegible]	11	0	12	0
1 Mary 1553	3[illegible]	3	5	5	36[illegible]	36	3	9[illegible]	11[illegible]	11	0	13	19
2 Elizabeth 1560	3[illegible]	3	4	10[illegible]	36	36	0	0	11[illegible]	11	1	4	0
					36[illegible]	36	3	9[illegible]	11[illegible]	11	1	17	22
43 ———— 1601	——	——			36[illegible]	36	10	10[illegible]	10[illegible]	10	10	17	3
					36[illegible]	36	7	7[illegible]	10[illegible]	10	11	7	13
2 and 3 James I. 1604	——	——			40[illegible]	40	11	7[illegible]	12[illegible]	12	1	6	4
					40[illegible]	40	14	2[illegible]	12[illegible]	12	1	15	12
9 ———— 1611	3[illegible]	3	7	0[illegible]	44[illegible]	44	12	9[illegible]	13[illegible]	13	3	16	19
					44[illegible]	44	15	7[illegible]	13[illegible]	13	4	7	1
15 Charles II. 1663	——	——			48[illegible]	48	10	10[illegible]	14[illegible]	14	5	16	11
					50[illegible]	50	19	6[illegible]	15[illegible]	15	2	10	7
William and Mary.	——	——			52[illegible]	52	3	8[illegible]	15[illegible]	15	6	17	5
3 George I. 1717	——	——			50[illegible]	50	19	5[illegible]	15[illegible]	15	2	10	7

By this table is appears, that on the first coinage of guineas in 1663, the proportion was about 14½, which is the proportion nearly kept at prefent by the neighbouring ftates, and therefore is that now contended for, by reducing the guinea again to 20 fhillings, as it was at that time. The fame proportion would likewife be obtained by falling the guinea to 20*s.* 6*d.* or fomething more than 1½ per cent. and altering the filver in the fame ratio, or coining it at 5*s.* 3*d.* 2*qr.* per ounce inftead of 5*s.* 2*d.*

The proportions above are thofe arifing between the two metals in coin; but as the price of filver uncoin'd has varied very much, or from 5*s.* 2*d* to 5*s.* 3*d*: 5*s.* 4*d*: 5*s.* 5*d.* &c. to 5*s.* 8*d.* and more per ounce, whilft the gold has continued nearly at £3. 17*s.* 10*d.* 2*qr.* per ounce; therefore the proportion between the metals uncoin'd or in bullion have ftood as follows.

A Table of the Proportion between Silver and Gold in Bullion.

St. Silv. per Oz. s.	d.	One Pound Weight of fine Silver.	£.	s.	d.	One Pound Weight of fine Gold.	£.	s.	d.	Proportion.	lb.	oz.	dwt.	gr.
5	3	3[illegible]	3	8	1[illegible]	50[illegible]	50	19	5[illegible]	14[illegible]	14	11	12	1
5	4	3[illegible]	3	9	2[illegible]					14[illegible]	14	8	16	6
5	5	3[illegible]	3	10	3[illegible]					14[illegible]	14	7	3	4
5	6	3[illegible]	3	11	4					14[illegible]	14	3	9	1
5	7	3[illegible]	3	12	5					14[illegible]	14	0	17	21
5	8	3[illegible]	3	13	6					14	13	10	8	5

A Table of the King's Seignorage, the Master of the Mints Allowance for Workmanship, and what the Merchant had paid him back; also the Quantity of fine Gold and Alloy, and the Remedy allowed the Master, both in Weight and in Fineness, each of them estimated on the Pound Weight †.

	One Pound Weight.			To the King.			To the Master.			To the King and the Master.			To the Merchant.			Fine Gold.		Alloy.		Remedy W. & F.
	l.	s.	d.	l.	s.	d.	l.	s.	d.	l.	s.	d.	l.	s.	d.	Car.	gr.	Car.	gr.	Carat.
18 Edw. III.	15	0	0	1	0	0	0	3	6	1	3	6	13	16	6					1/8
	13	3	4	0	5	0	0	3	4	0	8	4	12	15	0					1/12
19 ——							0	2	0	0	7	0	12	16	4					1/8
20. 23. ——	14	0	0	0	10	0	0	1	8	0	11	8	13	8	4					1/8
27 ——	-	-	-	0	7	3	0	2	0	0	9	3	14	10	9					1/8
30 ——	15	0	0	0	5	6	0	1	2	0	6	8	14	13	4					1/8
18 Rich. II.	-	-	-	0	3	6	0	1	6	0	5	0	14	15	0					1/8
3 Hen. IV.	-	-	-													23	3½	0	0½	1/12
13 —— / 9 Hen V. / 4. 24. H. VI.	16	13	4	0	3	6	0	1	6	0	5	0	16	8	4					
4 Edw. IV.	20	16	8	2	7	8	0	2	4	2	10	0	18	6	8					1/8
8 ——				0	12	0	0	2	6	0	14	6	21	15	6					
22 ——	22	10	0	0	5	0	0	2	6	0	7	6	22	2	6					
19 Hen. VII.				0	3	2	0	1	10											
18. 22 H. VIII	27	0	0	0	0	8	0	2	1	0	2	9	26	17	3					
	25	2	6	0	0	8	0	2	4	0	3	0	24	19	6	22	0	2	0	1/8
34 (r) ——	28	16	0	1	0	8	0	3	4	1	4	0	27	12	0	23	0	1	0	1/8
36 ——				-	-	-	-	-	-	2	10	0	27	10	0	22	0	2	0	1/8
37 ——	30	0	0	-	-	-	-	-	-	5	2	0	24	18	0	20	0	4	0	1/4
1 Edw. VI.				-	-	-	-	-	-	1	10	0	28	10	0					
3 ——	34	0	0	-	-	-	-	-	-	1	0	0	33	0	0	22	0	2	0	1/8
4 ——	28	16	0	-	-	-	-	-	-	0	2	9	28	13	3	23	3½	0	0½	1/8
6 ——	36	0	0	-	-	-	-	-	-	0	2	9	35	17	3	23	3½	0	0½	1/8
	33	0	0	-	-	-	-	-	-	0	3	0	32	17	0	22	0	2	0	1/8
1 Eliz.	36	0	0	-	-	-	-	-	-	0	5	0	35	15	0	23	3½	0	0½	1/8
	33	0	0	-	-	-	-	-	-	0	4	0	32	16	0	22	0	2	0	1/8
19 ——	36	0	0	0	2	6	0	1	6	0	4	0	35	16	0	23	3½	0	0½	1/8
25. 26. ——				0	1	3	0	4	9	0	6	0	35	14	0					
27 — - -	33	0	0	0	1	3	0	5	9	0	7	0	32	13	0	22	0	2	0	1/8
43 - - -	36	10	0	0	5	3	0	4	9	0	10	0	36	0	0	23	3½	0	0½	1/8
	33	10	0	0	4	3	0	5	9	0	10	0	33	0	0	22	0	2	0	1/8
2 James I.	40	10	0	1	3	7	0	6	5	1	10	0	39	0	0	23	3½	0	0½	1/8
	37	4	0	1	4	0	0	6	0	1	10	0	35	14	0	22	0	2	0	1/8
10 - - -	44	10	0	1	19	0	0	6	0	2	5	0	42	5	0	23	3½	0	0½	1/8
	40	18	4½	1	18	7	0	6	5				38	13	4½	22	0	2	0	1/8
	44	10	0	2	5	6	0	6	0	2	11	6	42	18	6	23	3½	0	0½	1/8
	40	18	4½	0	19	11½	0	6	5	1	6	4	39	12	0	22	0	2	0	1/8
17 James I.	44	10	0	0	15	0	0	6	0	1	1	0	43	9	0	23	3½	0	0½	1/8
2 Cha. I.	41	0	0	0	15	0	0	6	5	1	1	5	39	18	7					
13 Char. II.	44	10	0	0	13	9	0	8	0	1	1	9	43	9	[illegible]	22	0	2	0	1/8
17 - - - -				-	-	-	-	-	-	-	-	-	44	10	0					

† The king, this year, had but 24 *s.* for his Carat of fine gold, but it was worth 25 *s.* 7 *d.* 2 *qr.* (also his 2 ounces of fine silver was worth 9 *s.* 7 *d.* for which he had but 8 *s.*) In his 36th year he had but £ 2. 10 *s.* for 2 Carats, instead of £ 2. 14 *s.* 7 *d.* 2 *qr.* and the next year but £ 5. 2 *s.* for 4 Carats, instead of £ 6. and Milward informs us *, he could give twenty more instances to the same purpose.

(*r*) A brefe collection of alterations, which have been made in the monies of this realm, since Edw. I. MS. Sir Julius Cæsar's collect. of papers relating to mint affairs. MS.

* Short discourse touching the monies of this realm. MS.

An Account of the Gold Monies, coined from the 20th of July, 1660, to the 31st of December, 1748, Year by Year; made out from the Comptrollment Rolls and Books remaining in the Mint.

From July 20 to 31 Dec.	Weight. lb.	oz.	dwt.	gr.	Value. £.	s.	d.		Weight. lb.	oz.	dwt.	Value. £.	s.	d.
1660	110	3	12	12	5153	17	1½	1705	104	0	0	4859	8	0
1661	95	2	17	12	4450	1	2½	1706	537	0	0	25091	6	6
1662	713	1	13	0	33321	6	11½	1707	607	0	0	28362	1	6
1663	27	8	0	0	1292	14	6	1708	1010	0	0	47192	5	0
1664	1191	3	3	6	55649	9	6	1709	2468	0	0	115307	6	0
1665	1965	2	19	6	91824	4	0	1710	3716	0	0	173630	2	0
1666	1465	6	19	6	68479	4	4½	1711	9324	0	0	435663	18	0
1667	2824	4	10	1	131968	18	7	1712	2865	0	0	133399	17	6
1668	4449	11	4	7	207923	3	9½	1713	13187	0	0	6[illegible]3826	6	6
1669	2619	11	7	14	122417	1	5½	1714	29526	0	0	1379602	7	0
1670	2737	9	14	14	127923	15	8	1715	39090	0	0	1826480	5	0
1671	3853	11	17	6	180077	12	2½	1716	23765	0	0	1110419	12	6
1672	1880	0	3	5	87834	11	9½	1717	15186	0	0	709565	17	0
1673	2693	3	13	16	125844	9	3½	1718	3010	0	0	140642	5	0
1674	1844	11	11	16	86206	0	0	1719	14745	0	0	688960	4	6
1675	1162	8	13	3	54328	4	7	1720	18959	0	0	885859	5	6
1676	5249	8	7	7	245292	1	9½	1721	5832	0	0	272500	4	0
1677	5135	11	16	18	239979	19	2	1722	12728	0	0	594715	16	0
1678	3075	5	0	12	143698	18	7½	1723	8306	0	0	388097	17	0
1679	12009	2	5	6	561129	6	7½	1724	5860	0	0	273808	10	0
1680	12854	11	14	15	600648	16	6½	1725	1249	0	0	58359	10	6
1681	6721	9	8	9	314075	7	11	1726	18683	0	0	872963	3	6
1682	4124	4	12	6	192711	17	7½	1727	6266	0	0	292778	17	0
1683	8299	3	11	12	387782	14	9½	1728	1153	0	0	53878	18	6
1684	6392	11	15	0	298661	17	0½	1729	Nil					
1685	12075	0	0	0	564204	7	6	1730	1961	0	0	91627	14	6
1686	13874	4	15	0	648281	2	11	1731	6544	0	0	305768	8	0
1687	9018	1	0	0	421369	18	10½	1732	7993	0	0	372487	8	6
1688	12613	8	6	0	589374	14	10½	1733	17848	0	0	833947	16	0
1689	2886	4	0	0	134863	18	6	1734	10425	0	0	487108	2	6
1690	1094	10	13	0	51158	12	7½	1735	2295	0	0	107233	17	6
1691	1224	7	15	0	57221	11	6½	1736	7075	0	0	330579	7	6
1692	2573	0	10	0	120225	8	6	1737	1440	0	0	67284	0	0
1693	1157	8	12	14	54094	8	3½	1738	5775	0	0	269836	17	6
1694	1386	5	0	0	64780	6	4½	1739	6075	0	0	283854	7	6
1695	16117	3	0	0	753078	10	1½	1740	4200	0	0	196245	0	0
1696	3115	0	0	0	145548	7	6	1741	540	0	0	25231	10	0
1697	2706	8	0	0	126469	0	0	1742	Nil					
1698	10597	0	0	0	495144	16	6	1743	Nil					
1699	3177	0	0	0	148445	16	6	1744	210	0	0	9811	7	0
1700	2701	4	14	11	126222	11	7½	1745	6270	0	0	292965	15	0
1701	26740	0	10	0	1249519	19	0	1746	10155	0	0	474492	7	6
1702	3642	0	10	0	170172	9	0	1747	795	0	0	37146	7	6
1703	34	2	0	0	1159	8	6	1748	7245	0	0	338552	18	6
1704	Nil													

N. B. All these Values are at £3. 17s. 10d. 2 grs per Ounce.

COINED

COINED in each REIGN.

	Weight. lb.	oz.	dwt.	gr.	Value. £.	s.	d.
By King Charles II. -	93943	1	11	13	4389492	16	2
——— James II. - -	47497	6	1	0	2219320	13	10½
——— Will. and Mary	9962	8	0	14	465505	14	1¼
——— William III. -	66866	3	14	11	3124328	6	2½
— Queen Anne - - -	55832	2	0	0	2608757	19	9
— King George I. - -	181763	0	0	0	8492876	3	6
——— George II. to the 31ſt of Dec. 1748.	99333	0	0	0	4641334	8	6
	555197	9	7	14	25941616	2	1¾

The quantity coined at a medium each year of the reign of Charles the ſecond, was about 3834 lb. under James II. three times as much, or about 11375 lb. under William and Mary but 1660 lb. William III. about 8850 lb. Queen Anne 4137 lb. George I. about 13981 lb. and George II. 'till 1748, about 4620 lb. and, during the entire century, between 1658 and 1668 (by taking the medium of the 21 years of George II. for thoſe between 1748 and 1758) it was about 6000 lb. wt. per annum.

This was treble the quantity coined during the preceding century, or between 1558 and 1658, or during the reigns of Queen Elizabeth, James I. and Charles I. as appears by the table below (a). Queen Elizabeth coined but little; about 518 lb. per annum at a medium, and her whole coinage of 44 years did not amount to what was coined in each of the ſingle years of 1714 and 1716, and not more than ⅔ths of the year 1716. King James's annual medium coinage was about 4137 lb. or 8 times that of Elizabeth's. That of Charles the firſt was about 6¼ times of her's, or 3360 lb. That of the Commonwealth was very ſmall, and the total coinage of the whole century but 199457 lb. whereas that of the 13 years of George the firſt only was ⅞ths of it, or 181763 lb. The great increaſe of the quantity in this laſt period aroſe, very probably, from the high proportion and free coinage.

In regard to the quantity of fine ſilver that was coined more than fine gold, in theſe two periods, it appears that, in the firſt, there was about 2⅔ as much, and, during the ſecond, about 3⅓'s (b).

A Table of the Quantity of Gold coined between 1558 and 1658.

	Crown Gold. Weight. lb.	oz.	dwt.	gr.	Value. £.	s.	d.	Fine Gold. Weight. lb.	oz.	dwt.	gr.	Value. £.	s.	d.
1558 to 1601	10086	3	18	17	332846	16	5½	12201	8	0	22	439260	2	9
1601 to 1603	643	10	8	21	21737	3	1¼	35	4	17	8	1292	6	0½
Total Crown.	10730	2	7	14	354583	19	6½	12237	0	18	6	440552	8	9½
Total Fine.	12237	0	18	6	440552	8	9½							
Total Elizab.	22967	3	5	20	795136	8	4½	518	0	14	0	ann. med. for 44½ yrs.		
1603 to 1611	23258	3	14	0	853704	2	0	152	2	4	19	6163	17	0
1611 to 1625	67819	3	15	15	2780591	11	2	582	8	7	0	25930	0	9
Total Crown.	91077	7	9	15	3634295	13	2	734	10	11	19	32093	17	9
Total Fine.	734	10	11	19	32093	17	9							
Total James I.	91812	6	1	10	3666389	10	11	4173	3	11	0	ann. med. for 22 yrs.		
1625 to 1641	68832	11	11	4	2822151	9	10	284	5	9	9	12688	5	9
1641 to 1649	11826	0	8	20	484867	10	2							
Total Crown.	80659	0	0	0	3307019	0	0							
Total Fine.	284	5	9	9	12658	5	0							
Total Cha. I.	80943	5	9	9	3319677	5	0	3372	7	14	13	ann. med. for 24 yrs.		
1649 to 1653	1768	7	17	16	72514	18	8¼							
1653 to 1658	1965	2	2	8	81996	16	1½	this computed from				the med. of the forego.		
Tot. Com. wlth.	3733	10	0	0	154511	14	9½	393	0	0	0	ann. med. for 9½ yrs.		
Grand Total. 1558 to 1658	199457	0	16	15	7935714	19	1	1994	6	10	19	annual medium for 100 years.		

(a) Folkes, p. 65. 66, 74, 78, 96. A brief note of all the monies of gold and ſilver coined in the reign of queen Elizabeth and James I. till the laſt day of Dec. 1611, by John Milward. MS.

(b) See our View of the Silver Coin, pag. 55.

A Table of the Weights of the English Gold Coins in Troy Grains.

		¼ Noble.	½ Noble.	Noble or Ryal.	Double Noble or Rose Ryal.	¼ Angel.	½ Angel.	Angel.	¼ Sovereign. ½ Crown.	½ Sovereign. Crown. ½ Guinea.	½ Sovereign. Double Crown. ½ Guin.	Sovereign. Unite. Guinea.
18	Edward III. 1344	34	$68\frac{1}{4}$	$136\frac{1}{2}$	—	—	—	—	—	—	—	—
20	———— 1346	32	$64\frac{1}{4}$	$128\frac{1}{2}$	—	—	—	—	—	—	—	—
27	———— 1353	30	60	120	—	—	—	—	—	—	—	—
13	Henry IV. 1412	27	54	108	—	—	—	—	—	—	—	—
4	Edward IV. 1464	30	60	120	—	—	40	80	—	—	—	—
	Hen VII.	—	—	120	240	—	40	80	—	—	—	—
18	Hen. VIII. 1527	—	—	—	240	—	40	80	$28\frac{1}{2}$	$57\frac{1}{4}$	—	—
34	———— 1543	—	—	—	—	20	40	80	—	—	—	200
36	and 37 —— 1545	—	—	—	—	—	—	—	24	48	96	192
1	Edward VI. 1547	—	—	—	—	—	—	—	24	—	96	—
3	———— 1549	—	—	—	—	—	—	—	21	$42\frac{1}{4}$	$84\frac{1}{2}$	$169\frac{3}{7}$
4	———— 1550	—	—	—	240	—	40	80	—	—	—	—
6	———— 1552	—	—	—	240	—	40	80	$21\frac{7}{8}$	$43\frac{3}{7}$	$87\frac{1}{2}$	$174\frac{4}{7}$
1	Mary 1553	—	—	120	240	—	40	80	—	—	—	—
2	Elizabeth 1560	—	—	120	240	20	40	80	$21\frac{7}{7}$	$43\frac{3}{7}$	$87\frac{1}{2}$	$171\frac{6}{7}$
43	———— 1601	—	—	—	—	$19\frac{3}{4}$	39	$78\frac{7}{7}$	$21\frac{1}{4}$	$42\frac{7}{7}$	$85\frac{7}{7}$	$171\frac{7}{7}$
1	James I. 1603	—	—	—	—	—	—	—	$21\frac{1}{4}$	$42\frac{7}{7}$	$85\frac{7}{7}$	$171\frac{7}{7}$
2	and 3 —— 1604	—	—	$106\frac{1}{2}$	$213\frac{1}{4}$	—	$35\frac{1}{2}$	71	$19\frac{1}{7}$	$38\frac{3}{7}$	$77\frac{1}{7}$	$154\frac{2}{7}$
17	———— 1619	—	—	97	$194\frac{1}{2}$	—	—	$64\frac{3}{4}$	—	$35\frac{1}{2}$	$70\frac{1}{4}$	$140\frac{1}{2}$
15	Charles II. 1663	—	—	—	—	—	—	—	—	—	$64\frac{1}{2}$	$129\frac{3}{7}$
4	George I. 1718	—	—	—	—	—	—	—	—	$32\frac{2}{7}$	—	—
2	George III. 1762	—	—	—	—	—	—	—	—	$32\frac{2}{7}$	—	$129\frac{3}{7}$

N. B. The quarter, half and whole Florin weighs the ſame as the quarter, half and whole Noble of 13 Henry IV. The Double Sovereign of Henry VII. weighs 480 grains, or 1 ounce Troy; the George Noble 71 grains, and the Thiſtle Crown 31 grains feré.

F I N I S.

E R R A T A.

PAGE 2. line 25. *omit* or proportion. P. 3. l. 17. for 138 [illegible] read 136 [illegible], for 69 [illegible] read 68 [illegible], and for [illegible] read [illegible]. P. 12. l. 29. for 120 read 240. P. 17. l. 24. for 28 [illegible] Sovereigns r. 34 [illegible] £. l. 29. for [illegible] r. [illegible]. l. 30. for 5 dwt. r. 9 oz. 17 dwt. 22 gr. l. 32. for $\frac{1}{4}$ or 20 r. [illegible] or 6 [illegible]. l. 35. for 270 r. 230. l. 40. for 2 dwt. 12 gr. r. 4 oz. 18 dwt. 23 gr. l. 42. for 550 r. 460. P. 18. l. 19. for 178 r. 174. l. 37. for firſt r. ſecond. P. 32. l. penult. *omit* 6d. P. 34. l. ult. for 14 r. 13 [illegible].

A

V I E W

OF THE

COPPER COIN

AND

COINAGE

OF

E N G L A N D,

INCLUDING

The Leaden, Tin and Laton Tokens made by Tradesmen during the Reigns of ELIZABETH and JAMES I; the Farthing Tokens of JAMES I and CHARLES I; those of Towns and Corporations under the Commonwealth and CHARLES II; and the Tin Farthings and Halfpence of CHARLES II, JAMES II, and WILLIAM and MARY.

With COPPER-PLATES.

By THOMAS SNELLING.

L O N D O N:

Printed for T. SNELLING, next the *Horn Tavern*, in *Fleet-Street*.

MDCCLXVI.

Who buys and sells all Sorts of Coins and Medals.

PREFACE.

In all well regulated governments it is found to be as requisite, that there should be money of small value for the use of the market and the poorer sort of subjects, as of the larger species for the other purposes of trade and commutation; and what the value of the smallest piece should be, is pointed out by the proportion the price of provisions bears to that of labour, and to the abilities of the lower class of people to purchase them.

A farthing, or the fourth part of a penny, and its double, or an Halfpenny, are those of the least value we ever had in England, and began to be coined about the year 1270, under Edward the first, of standard silver, and continued to be minted in this manner the former for near 300 years, and the latter a century longer, or till the restoration of Charles the second.

At their first introduction, the farthing weighed about 5½, and the Halfpenny about 11 gr. troy, and therefore on account of their lightness were inconvenient in their use, and liable to be lost, which was the reason of the frequent complaints of their scarcity and of the petitions for new coinages of them, and also a principal cause of the base black coins of foreign countries, obtaining a currency among us, and we find by Stat. 1 H. 4, that this deficiency of our small money prevented the laws made to prohibit those base coins from having the desired effect.

Every rise in the denomination of our money, lessened the weight of these pieces, so that in the year 1464, the 4 Ed. 4, the farthing weighed but 3 gr. and the Halfpenny 6 gr. tr., and they continued to coin them many years of these weights, though in small quantities. These farthings are almost all lost, as well as those which had been coined for near an hundred years before, our best furnished cabinets hardly producing any but of the three first Edwards.

As the farthing could be minted no longer of good silver, being lost almost as fast as coined, no other method remained of striking them but of base silver, or pure copper, and the legislature not taking

As

either, and they being much wanted for many purposes, shopkeepers and tradesmen made *Tokens* for themselves, which, altho' it was a notorious abuse of the royal prerogative, was however winked at; though many complaints were made by projectors who were endeavouring to get the sole coinage of them into their own hands.

The coining of these tokens in such quantities and for so long a time, we presume, is the only instance to be found of this sort in any state, and appears very strange to foreigners; and when a certain author * gives an account of these tokens, Mr. Misson † affirms, that every word he says on this subject is false from one end to the other; but that author is only mistaken where he says, that they purchased leave from the king to coin them, which we cannot find to have been the case.

The first person that appears to have made a collection of these tokens, was the late Brown Willis, Esq., which is now in the Bodleian library at Oxford, and is the compleatest that has come under our notice. The next was Dr. Gifford, one of the Librarians of the Museum, whose collection is now dispersed, except the *Town pieces*, which are in the King's cabinet. The most copious collection we know of at present, is that of Mark Cephas Tutett, Esq. and several of the finest specimens are in the collection of Thomas Hollis, Esq. of Pall Mall. Upon the whole, there are few English collections, to which some of them are not joined; and on being considered with attention, they will be found not the least interesting part of them.

* On bat presque dans tous les Villages, de petite monnoie de cuivre qu'on nomme Fardins; ce qu'il y a d'incommode c'est que ces Fardins n'ont cours que dans le Village, & quelquefois dans la rue ou ils ont été fabriquez ils sont marques du nom des particuliers que achettent la permission du Roi pour les faire battre. *Voyages Historiques Tom.* 4. *p.* 17. 12mo. *Bruss.* 1704.

† Travels over England, p. 63.

3

A VIEW OF THE COPPER COIN AND COINAGE OF *ENGLAND.*

WE ſhall conſider this ſubject under four diſtinct heads, in the firſt, the Leaden, Tin and Latten tokens will be treated of, which were current during the reign of queen Elizabeth, and the firſt ten years of James the firſt. The ſecond will contain an account of the royal farthing tokens ſtruck in 1613, and which continued during the remainder of James the firſt, and that of Charles the firſt. Under the third will be found what we have been able to gather concerning the private tradeſmen and town farthings which paſſed from the death of Charles the firſt, or from about 1648 to 1672. And the ſubject matter of the fourth, is the copper money by authority which began in 1672, and is continued to the preſent time, including thoſe of tin of Charles II. James II. and William and Mary. SUMMARY.

B SECTION

SECTION I.

Of the LEADEN TOKENS under QUEEN ELIZABETH and JAMES I.

LEADEN TOKENS under HEN. VIII.

THE great scarcity of silver farthings and halfpence was the cause no doubt of the private tokens in lead, &c. first making their appearance, but in what king's reign they began this practice is uncertain; however, we find that they were in use in Henry the eighth's time, when Erasmus was here in England, for without dispute, it is these tokens he must mean by his (a) *Plumbeos Angliæ*, and from him it is that (b) Hoste and (c) Patin have said that we have had leaden money; Budelius (d) likewise mentions the leaden money current in England, whereas these were only pieces of necessity, tickets, tokens or pledges for money, but not money themselves.

Complained of under ELIZABETH

In queen Elizabeth's time we are informed that there were frequent complaints made of private persons, such as grocers, vintners, chandlers, alehousekeepers and others stamping and using tokens of lead, tin, latten, and even of leather for farthings and halfpence, to the great derogation of the princely honour and dignity, and as great loss to the poor, since they were only to be repaid to the same shop from whence they were first received, and no where else; of which abuse that great queen, who was singularly attentive to the coinage, was very sensible, as also that there was a great want of farthings and halfpence.

Farthings of base silver proposed.

To remedy these wants and disorders, proposals † were made to the queen for coining farthings and halfpence of base silver 7oz. 6dw. 16gr. fine, and 4oz. 13dw.

* The pieces in this plate are in the collection of Thomas Hollis, Esq; of Lincoln's Inne, F.R.S. F.S.A.

† The projectors of this scheme were Mr. Wickliffe and Mr. Humphry, as appears from a paper drawn up in defence of these proposals, and addressed (as we think) to lord Berleigh; and from a letter of Sir Richard Martin to the said lord, dated Oct. 1, 1576, (e) we learn that they were offered in 1574, or about two years before. Had this coinage taken place the lb. wt. troy of fine silver would have been coined into no more than 3l. 5s. 5d. ½. exceeding that of the queen's silver money but by 7d. farthing; and therefore preferable by far to the copper tokens which were so near taking effect soon after, wherein 11s. 6d. per lb. wt. were to be allowed for expences of coinage; but the very name of *Base Money*, and the remembrance of the confusion lately occasioned by it, was the reason, it is probable, of its not being attended to.

(a) Adagia p. 130. edit. Wechel 1639. idem Opera omnia, vol. 2, p. 1183. (b) Historia Rei Nummaria, B. 1. C. 7. S. 2. (c) Histoire des Medailles, Cap. 6. (d) de Monetis, p. 5. "licet apud anglos adhuc hodie plumbei numi dicantur esse recepti. (e) Collect. of papers on exchange, &c. MSS. p. 148, 149.

8 gr.

8gr. alloy, the weight 6gr. and 12gr. but the queen would by no means give ear to embasing the coin again, but was resolved to continue it on the footing it then was, and to which she had brought it in the beginning of her reign with the greatest difficulty.

Other proposals were made to the queen to coin copper pledges for farthings and halfpence, the first to weigh 12 gr. and the other 24 gr. by which the lb. weight troy would be coined into 10s. these proposals were so far approved on as to have a proclamation drawn up to make them current, in which the private tokens are forbid to be made or used without a warrant or commission first obtained for that purpose, on pain of imprisonment of the person who made them, for one year, and to be fined also at pleasure; the new pledges of an halfpenny and a farthing are ordered to be made current in all the queen's dominions, and every person was obliged to receive them under pain of her displeasure, and such other punishment as should be thought meet in that case; that no person should be obliged to receive them in any payments above twenty shillings, and in all sums under twenty shillings no more than one groat to be paid in them; an officer was likewise to be appointed to reside in some noted place in the city of London to exchange to every person who required it, two thirds of any sum in silver pennies (which were to be coined for that purpose) and one third in these pledges, that no more of those pledges should be coined than were thought barely necessary for the present ease of the subject; the queen's intent being to take away the private tokens so prejudicial to her royal estate and dignity, and to give in exchange for them a far more convenient pledge, universally payable in all small payments, and particularly in changing of threepences, threehalfpences and pence.

Copper pledges proposed.

Proclamation concerning them.

This proclamation (f) we apprehend was never published, nor did the coinage spoken of in it ever take place; all that we think was done in it was the sinking a die and striking off some pieces as patterns; that for the farthing we have never seen, but a few of those for the halfpenny are still remaining in some cabinets, but are very scarce, it has on one side the letters of the queen's name in a monogram crowned, and on the other a rose crowned, the inscription round it is (g) The Pledge of—a Halfpenny, (marked D in the small plate) it is found both in silver and copper.

Their type.

In this coinage a lb. wt. avoirdupoise of copper worth at that time about eightpence would have been coined into twelve shillings and two pence, whereby there would have been too great a temptation for the counterfeiter, to let slip such a favourable opportunity, and the whole affair, we apprehend, ended in the coining of silver halfpence, (h) which, though weighing but four grains, and therefore

(f) There is no date to it, but it certainly was intended to be published between the years 1576 and 1582, for lord Burleigh's letter (just mentioned) to Sir Richard Martin concerning these tokens, is dated Sept. 30, 1576, and the coinage of the silver halfpennies did not take place 'till the last mentioned year. A copy of this proclamation is among the Harleian MSS. in the British Museum, and in our appendix, No. 1.

(g) Besides this pledge of an halfpenny, there is also another of a penny, (marked F) which has the Queen's head on one side, and the same monogram as the halfpenny on the other, and withal the date 1601, and therefore probably might be made in consequence of other proposals offered on the same subject in or about that year, when the halfpenny and penny were coined for Ireland.

(h) One sort of the base half-groats and groats were made current in the year 1560, at three-farthings and three-halfpennies each, and the queen rechanged these pieces for others of the same value, which she had caused to be coined of standard silver, according to her proclamation of Dec. 23. 1560, observing, no doubt, that the want of farthings and halfpence was less sensibly felt, by the mutual interchange of them, with the pennies and twopences, the coinage of which continued till 1582, when these halfpennies were also coined with the same intent. See pl. 6, No. 17. of our silver coin.

very

JAMES I. very inconvenient and troublesome in their use, were esteemed more eligible than those of copper above, which carried so great a temptation with them.

Bristol farthing tokens. After this the city of Bristol struck a copper farthing token by authority, and as several persons in the said city did strike tokens also in lead and brass without any authority, uttering them to their private use, and which many times were refused to be accepted again by them, whereby many inconveniencies did grow to the poor; therefore an order [k] was sent from the lords of the privy council to the mayor and aldermen for the time being, to call in all the said tokens, and to require those that uttered them to change them for current money, to the value they were first uttered at, and none to make any for the future without licence from the mayor, who is directed to take care that the former abuses be reformed; this order is dated May 12, 1594.

This farthing token of the city of Bristol was not only current in the city, but in the country for ten miles round, to the great benefit of those places, [l] and the projectors in the succeeding reign of James the first urge very strongly, that this city ought not alone to enjoy this priviledge, but that it should be communicated to all the rest of the kingdom by the making of a general token.

In the sixth year of James the first, two persons, Thomas Moze, ordinary yeoman of the king's chamber, and William Edgely, groom of the same, petitioned [m] his majesty to grant them a patent for the sole making of the Bristol farthings; as also another for Glocester, which petition his majesty refers to the commissioners for sutes.

The only cities which we have been able to learn that did strike farthing tokens at this time were those of Bristol, Worcester and Oxford.

In London we are informed by Sir Robert Cotton [n] that there were no less than 3000 persons who made their own tokens, * and there were other places besides in which they were likewise struck, but he does not mention their names.

We know but little what were the types on the pieces during this interval, but are told that on the first of those struck by the city of Bristol, which was of lead or latten, there was a coney, and on that of Worcester of the same metal was a death's head, but we have never seen either.

The copper farthing of Bristol, as we are informed by Malynes in his Lex Mercatoria, chap. 5, had on one side a ship, and on the other C. B. for Civitas Bristolie, See plate, letter G.

Those of the private traders were made without any form or fashion, as might at that time be seen in every tavern and chandler shop, [o] and the only pieces which we have seen that appear to answer this description are those in the small plate marked A, B, C, D, and have more the appearance of dumps than money.

* We must confess we do not understand what he means by their costing each person 5l. a piece, unless it is that there were uttered as many as amounted to that sum every year.

[k] Sir Julius Cæsar's collect. of MSS. on coin, p. 102. Appendix, No. 2. [l] ibid. p. 9, 12. [m] ibid. p. 101. Appendix, No. 3. [n] Posthuma 12mo, p. 199. edit. 1679. [o] Sir J. Cæsar, p. 21.

SECTION

Section II.

The Royal Farthing Tokens of James I. and Charles I.

THERE had been several proposals and schemes made, for coining farthing tokens upon the coming of king James to the crown, nay even three years before the death of queen Elizabeth, she was again press'd upon this head, but to no purpose, as she declared [a] she never would consent to a currency of copper money. James I. Different projects.

The reasons now given were still the same as before, that is, the infringment of the prerogative, by private persons making of them, the loss to the poor by their being not universally current, and the want of them to bestow in charity.

One of the schemes [b] was to make 30s. in farthings out of a lb. wt. of copper, and to deliver these 30s. in farthings to the warden of the mint for 6s. sterling, so here was to be a profit of 24s. in each lb. wt. Anno 1607.

Another proposal was made [c] to coin halfpence, farthings, and half-farthings, to weigh 24, 12 and 6 gr. each, in equal quantities; here the lb. wt. Troy was to make 10s. but as the computation was made on the lb. wt. Avoirdupoise, that amounted to 12s. and 2d. A list was likewise added of the price of copper, and the salaries to the requisite officers belonging to such a coinage; and supposing that 100,000 lb. was coined in a year, the whole charges would amount to 3s. 8d. per lb. Avoir. which is nearly 3s. per lb. Troy, that is, about 7s. in a lb. wt. gained. Anno 1608.

Some of the proposals were likewise on the same footing as those which were intended to be coined by the queen about 30 years before, that is, to make the farthing to weigh 12 gr. Troy, and the halfpenny 24 gr. and Sir Richard Martin's opinion being asked concerning the king's profit on these terms, he said, [d] that 1 lb. weight of copper being worth 12 pence, and the charge of workmanship 22 pence, therefore there would be 7s. and 2d. profit in every pound weight, and in 100,000 lb. wt. 35,863 l. 6s. 8d.

The next year another proposal which had been made, was laid before him, [e] wherein they were to be but half the weight of the former, that is, the farthing Anno 1609.

[a] Sir Richard Martin's letter to Sir Julius Cæsar, in Sir Julius Cæsar's MSS. p. 282. [b] Sir Julius Cæsar's brother Tho. Cæsar, was concerned in this project, whose original letter is here, dated Sept. 1, 1607. p. 9, 10. [c] dated April 1, 1608. Idem p. 19. see our appendix No. 4. [d] ibid. p. 29, 33. [e] dated May 27, 1609. ibid. p. 39.

5 gr. and the halfpenny 12 gr. so the lb. wt. to be coined into 20 shillings, the value of the copper being 12 d. as before. But Sir Richard now makes the charge of coinage 2 shillings, and therefore the king here would gain 17s. per lb. wt. and if 120,000 lb. wt. was coin'd, it would be 102,000l. clear. These same proposals were made and the same answer was again given: about three years afterwards, (ᶠ) and about five months after that, in another letter (ᵍ) to Sir Julius Cæsar, Sir Richard thinks the upper mint in the Tower would be the properest place to coin them in, and to be performed by his majesties officers, by which the king will always know what quantity were coined; he likewise submits it to his majesty rather to reward any suitor for the coinage, with a particular sum out of it, than to part with the coinage out of his own hands.

Anno 1612.

We now come to that project which, with some alteration, at last took place, which had for its title, a modest proposal for the making of farthing tokens, (ʰ) in which it is desired, that full power might be given to some sufficient persons to make such a competent quantity of farthing tokens, as might conveniently be issued among his majesties subjects, according to their own desire, within the term of three years. Secondly, the said farthing tokens to be made exactly, having on one side, two scepters crossing under a diadem, and on the other side I R. crown'd, weighing 6 gr. (that is, 24s. 3d. per lb. wt.) Thirdly, his majesty to receive half of the profit every quarter without being at any charge. Fourthly, that they shall be made at any place where his majesty shall appoint, and under the inspection of a surveyor. Lastly, every person that desired it, might have 21s. in farthings for 20s. sterling, and be at liberty, if at any time they should have too many of them, to rechange them at the same rate.

These proposals were often debated on by the privy council, and at last were consented to, with a clause of revocation, and Lord Harrington did obtain the king's half of the profit, and the grant did pass in his name; but whilst his lordship's patent was under privy seal, his majesty was informed that the grant was worth 60000l. shewing that if 100,000 lb. wt. was coined, they might be worth 90400l. and deducting 24450l. for copper and charges, there would remain 65000l. profit. His majesty therefore allowed lord Harrington 25000l. as it should be raised by issuing of these tokens, and the surplus, if any, to come to the king.

Ld. Harrington obtains the patent, 10 Apr. 1713

Lord Harrington having thus obtained the patent, entered into covenant with the king to account quarterly, and to pay into the exchequer whatever the profit should amount to more than 20000l. all charges deducted, and entered into a recognizance of 20000l. to perform the same, and Edward Doubleday, Esq; was appointed surveyor of the said accompt.

He then assigned the patent over to Gerard Malynes and William Cockayne, in consequence of an agreement heretofore made with the former. And after the articles of the said contract had been examined by the king's surveyor, an abstract of them was laid before the privy council, who referred it to the perusal of Sir Francis Bacon, and he certified to their lordships it was no way prejudicial to his majesty.

William Cockayne soon after not liking the clauses of revocation, and accompting to his Majesty, fell off, and it was sometime before they could find another

(ᶠ) Sir Richard's Letter is dated Aug. 13, 1612. ibid. p. 83. (ᵍ) ibid. p. 84, dated Feb. 19, 1612-13. (ʰ) dated 7 Aug. 1612, ibid. p. 83.

person

person who would join with Gerard Malynes, until one John Couchman, merchant, did at last come in on the same conditions as before.

Lord Harrington and Simon Chambers (who bore the rechange) then contracted with Christ. Warwick, Peter Malynes and Samuel Malynes, for the making of the tokens for the said three years, who gave a bond of 3000l. to perform the same; and they immediately contracted with an engineer, a graver, and other workmen; as likewise for the copper; and lastly, chose several deputies for the dispersing them in different parts of the kingdom.

The proposals as we have just now seen, were to make about 25s. out of 1 lb. of copper, of which 5s. was for copper and workmanship; 1s. for the subject, 1s. to bear the rechange, 9s. to lord Harrington, 2s. for the deputies for issuing, and the other 7s. were for the contractor to bear other contingent expences and losses, and by agreement they were to coin 400lb. a week, and therefore it would be something more than two years before lord Harrington would receive his 20000l.

Duke of Lenox wants the patent.

But the duke of Lenox being very desirous of getting the patent from lord Harrington, offered (k) to pay him his 20000l. in 18 months; that is 13s. 4d. per week, to give him the same or better security for performance thereof than he then had; to pay what had been expended for engines and instruments touching their business, and not then discharged; and to give 3000l. to his contractors for their trouble; informing lord Harrington likewise, that by the conditions of his patent, he might be freed from his contractors, without any prejudice to himself. The duke further also said, he had better opportunities of issuing them as alnager, since his deputies could perform both services.

Malynes's observations thereon.

But Gerard Malynes, lord Harrington's contractor, in answer to the duke, alledges (l) that his offer of paying 400l. in the same time as he was to pay lord Harrington 300l. was imaginary, since both payments depended on the quantity of tokens issued, which he apprehends he can increase more than they, and which requires great policy and cunning to perform; and recites some of the methods he had hitherto used to perform the same; as first, that he had found means to dissolve the combination among the chandlers in London, who had resolved to refuse the tokens, and was in hopes of doing the same in other parts of the kingdom. Secondly, in giving 21s. in farthings for 20s. sterling; thirdly, in rechanging them; fourthly, by the neat minting of them, to satisfy the subject of the difficulty of counterfeiting of them; fifthly, in a proper choice of deputies, whose dexterity consisted mostly in their pleasing manner of issuing them, and which would be much more distasteful if done by the duke's officers as deputy alnager; sixthly, in giving tradesmen three or four months credit to disperse them; which, seventhly, incouraged them to give credit to their customers, and so on to others; eighthly, in giving instructions properly timed to the deputies, how to act between the retailer and their customers; ninthly, by changing farthing tokens for commodities not very saleable in England, which commodities were afterwards exported; tenthly, several foreign merchants, who were used to such small coins, were engaged to give their assistance; eleventhly, to exchange these tokens for foreign coins of gold and silver, and clipt ryals of plate; and lastly, the usurers themselves were to be dealt with to forward their utterance. All which means were accomplished by policy, labour and industry, without the assistance of authority.

(k) The duke of Lenox his offer and exceptions, touching farthing tokens, Harleian MSS. No. 451, p. 106. and our MSS. of exchange, and the coin and coinage of England, p. 171. (l) ibid. p. 176.

It

It is certain, these tokens at first were circulated with great difficulty, and in several counties, as Derbyshire, Staffordshire, Flintshire and Denbighshire, they absolutely refused to take them, although they were countenanced by the magistrates, and dispersed printed bills; and even in those counties where they did then take them, it was but in small quantities; so that in six months time they had hardly uttered 600l. the rechange likewise at first was very heavy; and a report being spread that they were to be altered, and that the old ones would not be taken, it increased to 40l. and 50l. a week.

Proclamations concerning them.

They were ushered in with the king's proclamation of May 19, 1613, which forbids the currency of all private tokens whatever then made, or thereafter to be made, or of any other but these made by his majesties authority: also, strictly forbidding any persons from counterfeiting them, or any engines made use of in the making of them. There were likewise other proclamations of June 20, 1614; of April 26, 1615, and of 17 March, 1616, to the said purpose; besides which, the deputies for circulating in every county, were provided with recommendatory letters (k) from the king and council, directed to all mayors, sheriffs, justices of peace, bailiffs, constables and headboroughs, as much as in them lay to forward their currency.

Lord Harrington died Feb. 27, 1614, (l) and his son, the second lord Harrington, a few months after him, * and we cannot learn into whose hands the patent came afterwards, but we suspect it was the duke of Lenox that had it; for in 1622, we find, by the king's recommendatory letter, that it was possessed by him and James marquiss of Hamilton, and that their ministers or contracters were Tho. Woodward and Edward Garret, which is the last we hear of this affair during this reign.

Type
Legend

The type of the farthings are, on one side, two scepters in saltier, through a crown, and on the other, a harp crowned (instead of J. R.) the legend is JACO. D. G. MAG. BRI. or BRIT.—FRA. ET HIB. REX. (mark'd A) which inscription, in all those we remember to have seen, always begins at top; whereas that ingraved by Simon (pl. 6, No. 128) begins at bottom; we have them with the 16 following mint marks,

Annulet	Cinquefoil	Coronet	Cross	Fleurdelis
Fret	Grapes	Key	Lozenge	Lyon Rampant
Martlett	Rose	Ton	Tower	Triangle
Thistle				

The small one marked b in the plate, appears to have been intended for an half farthing.

CHARLES I. Proclamations.

King Charles the first, soon after his accession to the throne, published a proclamation, May 30, 1625, to continue their currency; and another June 4, 1626; also another dated May 30, 1630, and a fourth, published June 20, 1634; the principal purport of the publication of which appears to be, to put a stop to the counterfeiting of them, which was now become a common practice both at home and abroad, and afterwards disposing of them at the rate of 24s. nay 25s.

* John lord Harrington of Exton, so created 1 Jam. I. was tutor to the princess Elizabeth, and on her marriage with Frederick count Palatine of the Rhine, attended her into that country, and died at Wormes in Germany; leaving issue, by Anne his wife, daughter and heir to Robert Kelway, Esq; John, his son and heir, who survived him but a few months, and Elizabeth, a daughter, who became heir to her brother, and was married to Edward earl of Bedford. (m)

(k) A copy of one of them is among the Harl. MSS. in the musæum, No. 4888, see our append. No. 5. (l) Sir Jul. Cæsar's MSS. p. 90. (m) Collins ext. peer. v. ii. p. 336.

and

and 26s. in these farthing tokens, for 20s. sterling; which, although under the patentees price (viz. 21s.) yet left a sufficient profit for them to persevere in doing of it. However, there were several prosecuted for it in the star chamber; by a decree of which court, in Hill. term, 6 Car. I. (m) two persons were fined and set in the pillory; and others again in Mich. term, 7 Car. I. (n) and 9 Car. I. (o) and lastly, Will. Hawks and others in East. term, 10 Car. I. (p) were again fined and set in the pillory.

At the making this last decree Ap. 25, 1634. (q) the court having taken into consideration the complaints made from several parts of the kingdom concerning the stop and refusal of farthing tokens, proceeding as well from the abuse in counterfeiting, as in causing the same to pass in payments to workmen for wages, and likewise for commodities in greater quantities than was at first intended. It was likewise ordered, that thenceforth no man should pay above 2 d. in farthings at any one time, nor buy any farthings at a less rate than they are usually vended by the patentees: and by another decree of the star chamber, dated June 4, 1634, (the same day the proclamation † was published) it was ordered to be printed; the same things are again enforced by another proclamation, published Mar. 1, 1634/5, (r) wherein the farthing tokens were directed, for the future, to be made with such a distinction of brass, as will readily make them known from all others, and thereby prevent the people from being deceived by counterfeits; and that the patentees shall rechange all that shall be brought to them for that purpose; not only of these, but likewise those of allcopper, made by his present majesty and his father.

A patent was granted, July 11, 1626, for 17 years, to Frances, dutchess dowager of Richmond and Lenox; and to Sir Francis Crane, Kt. (s) and by the last proclamation, we find it was, at that time, possessed by Henry lord Maltravers and the said Sir Francis Crane. Patentees in this reign.

What we could gather farther on this subject, is from a scarce pamphlet of 6 pages in quarto, printed 1644, entitled, A Remedy against the Losse of the subject by Farthing Tokens, wherein the author complains loudly against the abuse of them.

Our projectors (says he) soon found the advantage that accrued to a private tradesman by his farthings being sometimes lost, and under pretence of the good of the subject and of the poor, obtained a patent to make thousands of pounds worth; and amongst other ways to get rid of them, some merchants would sell unvendible commodities for tokens, and then would press them upon their workmen whom they dealt with, and by that means, even chandlers, bakers and victuallers had their hands full. Their profit was exorbitant, as out of 1oz. of copper, which cost them one penny, they made 20 pence in tokens. This could not hold long, but others, more eminent persons, must have a share, and so the first makers were dismissed, and their patent disanulled, and all the tokens left on the subjects hands, who were to sell them to the braziers at 10 or 12 pence a pound, for they had a patent to make and distribute them, but the poor subjects had no patent to force the makers to take them again. Substance of a tract on this subject.

The next token makers, we all know who they were, the public farthing token offices in London do witness it, and this was done with a more large

† These farthings being current in Ireland as well as England, a proclamation, (t) to the same purpose as this, was published by the lord Deputy Wentworth, Sept. 16, 1634.

(m) Rushworth, vol. 3, appendix, p. 33. (n) Ibid p. 41 (o) Ibid p. 70. (p) Ibid vol. 2, p. 202. (q) Ibid vol. 2, p. 250. (r) Rymer, T. 19. p. 760. (t) Simon, p. 46 and 114. (s) Rymer, T. 18, p. 743.

profit to the makers; they had their officers to attend the sale of them daily, and had a pretty way to vent them, by giving one shilling over in twenty to those that came to buy them, which occasioned many to fetch them, and force 5, 10, yea 20 shillings at a time away; so that in a short time there was an infinite quantity dispersed abroad, to the excessive profit of the makers, but the excessive loss of the takers, as shortly after did appear, as it inticed many that had no patent to become farthing makers; but the city of London, and the adjacent counties of Kent, Essex, Suffolk and Norfolk were so loaded with them, that there was scarce any silver or gold coin left, but all was farthing tokens. But when farthings began to come in faster than they went out, the patentees did not like it, but soon found out a device; that is, that none was theirs but double ringed; a pretty device, for very few were double rings, most single, and not theirs; and who could prove the contrary? and so upon a sudden, all farthings were left upon the subject's hands. This was the second cheat, and a grievous one it was, many poor persons lost all they had; for they who got their living by selling of fruit, herbs, fish and other commodities, had all their stock in farthings, some 6, 8, 10, to 20 shillings; which was all lost to their utter undoing. Tradesmen of a higher degree, had, at that time, 10, 20, 40, yea 60l. worth of farthing tokens in their hands; which almost all proved clear loss, or single rings. It was conceived that there was, at least 100,000 l. dispersed throughout the kingdom, which was all lost, and no remedy could be had against the farthing makers. And this was the lamentable issue of making farthing tokens for the good of the subject.

But these pretenders, who do all for the good of the subject, would by no means forsake that excessive profit, but constructed another sort of tokens, that none should be able to counterfeit, as they pretended, and that was with a little yellow spot in the copper; a good mark to know their own, but a better mark to make another cheat of 100,000l. more upon the poor subject; but all for their good, as is pretended. This has gone on certain years, but at first they could not vend so many as was expected. In the mean time, this, now sitting parliament, began; and all patents were put down, because they were so illegal and pressing to the subject; but, to the great admiration of many, this, so illegal and pressing a patent, did stand upright, in its full power, and they have dispersed an infinite quantity of them; by which means they are become so plenty, that every retailing tradesman is so pester'd with them, that almost half of what they receive is farthing tokens; and all adjacent counties are become full of them, nay, more than ever they were before; so that, of necessity, these tokens must go down again; which will prove a greater loss than those formerly, except the parliament do compel the token makers to attend at the offices, with ready money, to exchange all their tokens for good ready money.

It is very true that farthings are useful and necessary, both for rich and poor, we cannot well be without them; and in silver, they are so small, that many cannot feel them between their fingers; therefore, we ought to have farthings, either in copper or some mettal mixed with copper, and they ought to be so much in value as may be worth a farthing; all copper without any mixture is likely to be best, to prevent counterfeiting of them; for it is certain, if it be so big and so weighty, as with the coining and other charges, they cost a farthing, we are sure none shall be counterfeited, nor brought in from foreign parts; for it was the great profit that made the increase. Therefore, we ought to make our farthings worth a farthing.

a farthing, that the subject may be no more deceived with unlawful tokens. These farthings will be very beneficial to all tradesmen, especially retailers, and very comfortable to the poor people

The first farthings of this king's are like those of his fathers (only CARO. instead of JACO.) having the inscription beginning at the top generally, like them, therefore we have not engraved one of this sort; others there are, but not so common, where it begins at bottom (as D) and both these sorts, we apprehend, are those which are called the single rings. There is another sort, which has an inner circle (as C) and, it is very probable, are those called the double rings, they are inscribed CAROLUS D. G. MAG. BRIT.—FRAN. ET HIB. REX. of these sorts, the following mint-marks have come under our notice. Type. Legend.

Mynt marks

Annulet	Cinquefoil	3 Daggers	Lozenge	Ton
Ball	Coronet	Fleur de lis	Martlet	Trefoil
Billet	Crescent	Harp	Rose	Woolpack
Castle	Cross	Lyon	Sword.	

Those that were minted after the alteration in 1635, are smaller, thicker and heavier than the other, and have an appearance of brass in some part of them: they have the same type on one side as the former, but on the other, they have a rose crown'd, instead of the harp (mark'd E). Some read CAROLU. D. G. MA. BRI.—FRA. ET HI. REX. others, CAROLUS D. G. MAG. BRIT. —FRAN. ET HIB. REX. We have only observed a mullet, crescent, and fleur de lis on these, as mint marks.

SECTION III.

Of the TOWN and TRADESMEN'S TOKENS between 1648 and 1672.

THE great quantity of royal tokens uttered by the patentees, the numbers of counterfeits which were also mixed with them, and the patentees refusing to rechange them, at last put an intire stop to their currency. Currency of royal tokens stopped.

But their being almost an absolute necessity for some such sort of money, for small change, and the badness of the times preventing the legislature from paying a proper attention to this affair; were the reasons that private tradesmen once more began to avail themselves of these pieces, in which they were soon after followed by those struck for the use of a whole village, borough, town or city. Farthings greatly wanted.

We apprehend this practice was resumed in, or about, the year 1648, as we have never met with any of these pieces with an earlier date, or even more than two or three of this year, and not many of 1649; but they appear to have increased every year more and more, until 1672, and are found with every date on them within that interval; but in that year, they were all cryed down by proclamation. Tokens resumed again, 1648 by tradesmen.

The earliest of the town pieces which are dated, are those of Bristol and Oxford, in 1652; there are no others 'till 1657, then two more in 1659; and between that And towns that year and 1666, there were 8 others; but after that year they multiplied prodigiously, there being 9 in 1667, 11 in 1668, 19 in 1669, and 12 in 1670; that is, 51 in those 4 years; whereas, in the 20 years preceeding, there were no more than about 14; and, it is very probable, it was this great increase of them which roused the legislature to put a stop to them, and to coin a common farthing and halfpenny by authority.

But without authority.

It has been observed in the first section, that the mayor and aldermen of the city of Bristol, were authorised by the privy council, to strike a farthing token; but this does not appear to be the case, during this interval, either with that, or any other place (much less any private tradesman) and we think that Mr. Thoresby was mistaken, in asserting that such a priviledge was obtained, (') by several towns, during the usurpation, the contrary appearing from the following instances, and that the striking of these tokens, was an abuse of, and not a release (') from the royal authority.

Norwich obtains a pardon for making them.

The city of Norwich, in 1669, had a pardon granted them for all transgressions in general, and in particular for their coining of * halfpence and farthings, (') by which they had forfeited their charter, all coinage being determined the king's prerogative; upon which they were all called in.

Yarmouth the same.

The next year, 1670, the town of Yarmouth was very desirous, likewise, of obtaining a pardon for the same offence, and employed the solicitor of Norwich, to prevail with lord Townshend, that he would petition his majesty on their behalf; which was accordingly done, and their pardon procured, the charges of which amounted to 80l. and he had also 10l. given him for his trouble; after which they ordered the bellman to go round the town, and give notice, that every one might have the value in silver for their farthings, if they would bring them in. (')

Published by act of common council.

The towns which used these tokens, published them by an act of common council of those places; the mayor, or other magistrate, being impowered, either by himself or with others of the court, to procure a dye to be made, and a certain quantity of them to be struck for the use of the town. Certain persons were also appointed to deliver them out, and likewise to rechange, for silver, all that should be brought to them again. (')

What quantity first uttered at Dover and Poole.

By the particulars we have procured, in relation to the town of Yarmouth, it does not appear what sum was ordered to be laid out for this purpose; but, at Dover, (') we find it was 32l. and at Poole, (') no more than 10l. for which 10l. there was paid, into the mayor's hands, 19l. 10s. in farthings; and the mayor, at the close of his mayoralty, was to deliver over to his successor, this 19l. 10s. either in silver, if the farthings were all uttered, in order to exchange them, or the farthings themselves, if they had not been delivered; and so on to the next mayor, until his majesty should prohibit their currrency. †

* We have never seen any halfpenny of this place, but there are two farthings, dated 1667 and 1668.

† The papers relating to Yarmouth were communicated by Mr. Thomas Barber, of that town; those which relate to Dover, by Mr. Edward Jacob, of Feversham; and those of Poole, by Sir Peter Thompson.

(') Thoresby ducat. leod. p. 381. (') Drake's antiq. of York, cx. (') Blomfield's hist. of Norfolk, vol. 2, p.290 (') See our Appendix, No. 6. (') See Appendix, No. 6, 7, 8. (') Appendix, No. 7. (') Appendix, No. 8.

The

The following liſt contains the names of all the places which have come to our knowledge, where they ſtruck a common town farthing or halfpenny; of which, thoſe with † are cities, thoſe with * are Burroughs (*i. e.* ſend members) thoſe with ‡ are corporations; and all the reſt are not incorporated.

List of the places which ſtruck a common token.

*Andover	Caer Lyon	*Grantham	Loweſtoff	*Nottingham	Tamworth
*Aſhburton	Chard	Guilford	Lowth	Owndle	‡Taunton
Axmiſter	Chepſtow	‡Henley up-	*Lyme Regis	†Oxford	Tetbury
†Bath	Chertſey	on Thames	*Lynn	†Peterbor.	Thornbury
Beccles	Cirenceſter	†Hereford	*Marlbor.	*Poole	‡Gt. Torrin.
*Bewdley	Claye	Illmiſter	*Midhurſt	‡Romſey	†Wells
Bigleſworth	†Coventry	*Ipſwich	*Minehead	*Rye	*Weymouth
‡Blandford	Croyland	*Ivilcheſter	Morton	†Saliſbury	Wimborne
*Boſton	*Dartmouth	*St Ives	St Neot's	*Shaftſbury	†Wincheſter
Brewton	Diſs	King's Cliff	(Eed's)	Sherborne	Woodbridge
*Bridgnorth	*Dorcheſter	Langford	‡Newbury	*Southamp.	†Worceſter
*Bridgwater	*Dover	‡Langport	*Newport	‡Southwolde	Wotton un-
†Briſtol	*Eveſham	†Lincoln	Iſle of wight	Spalding	der Edge
‡Burford	Froome	†Litchfield	*Northampt.	*Stamford	*Yarmouth
Burlington	†Glouceſter	Littleport	†Norwich	Stourbridge	Yeovill
		Iſle of Ely			

We find, in this liſt, but few places in the neighbourhood of London, which ſtruck theſe pieces, any more than that great metropolis itſelf; not one in either of the counties of Middleſex or Eſſex, and but one in Kent. There were 13 Places in Somerſetſhire which uttered them, being more than in any other county in the Kingdom; there were 8 in Dorſetſhire, 5 in Lincolnſhire, 5 in Glouceſterſhire, 5 in Devonſhire, 5 in Norfolk, 5 in Suffolk, 4 in Hampſhire, 4 in Northamptonſhire, &c. and, what is very remarkable, no more than one in the large populous county of York, although there were ſo many manufacturing and trading towns, which were thoſe in which they were moſt wanted.

There are four different dates on the Briſtol farthings; that is, 1652, 1660, 1666 and 1670; three on thoſe of Glouceſter, 1657, 1660 and 1667; two on thoſe of Bath, 1659 and 1670; the ſame number on thoſe of Andover, 1664 and 1666; Lynn has 1668 and 1669; and on thoſe of Norwich, 1667 and 1668.

Types on the town pieces.

The town pieces of thoſe places which are incorporated, have, in common, their arms, on one ſide; and the non-incorporate (as having no arms) a device inſtead thereof; both ſorts of which, on many of them, are without any inſcription round them, as thoſe of Beccles, Bewdley, Burford, Cirenceſter, Coventry, Croyland, Dartmouth, Diſs, Ipſwich, Lincoln, Lynn, Newport, Nottingham, Norwich, Peterborough, Southampton, Weymouth and Wincheſter; that of Burford has B-B, that of Coventry has C-C on the ſide of the arms, and that of Wincheſter, C-W at top; all of which, have generally the other ſide filled with an inſcription, A Beccles &c. Farthing &c.

Another ſort have an inſcription round the arms, to inform us they are, the arms of Bath, Bridgewater, Briſtol, Coventry, Dorcheſter, Glouceſter, Hereford, Ivilcheſter, Lyme, Southwoulde and Shaftſbury. This ſort have, in the area, on the other ſide, in general, the initial letter of the name of the place; with B for Burgus, or C for Civitas, with the date at bottom; we do not know the meaning of the H in that of Dorchester, that of Shaftsbury has only an inscription, but we are ignorant of the meaning of the words MOUNT PA LA DORE, of which it consists.

A third sort have, likewise, their arms on one side, as the last, but with different inscriptions round them; as those of Andover, Boston, Bridgenorth, Chard, Dover, Evesham, Grantham, Guilford, Henley, Langport, Marlborough, Newbery, Northampton, Pool, Romsey, Salisbury, Stamford, Tamworth, Wells, Worcester and Yarmouth; this last place has the arms on both sides, as have also two or three of the preceeding ones; those of Boston and Salisbury have their crest on one side, some their initial letter, with C or B as before, but we are at a loss for the meaning of the E in that of Langport.

Types on those not incorporated.

Some of the devices on the non-incorporate places, are relative to the intention of their being struck, *i. e.* for the use of the poor, as a cripple on that of Andover; another on that of Biglesworth, having, on its reverse, a spinning wheel; on those of St. Ives and Wimborne, there are two washerwomen at the washing-tub; and on that of St. Eeds, two women spinning.

Others again, exhibit something relative to the chief trade or manufacture carried on in those places; as on that of Thornbury, those of Minehead and Wotton under edge have a Woolpack, and on the reverse of the former a ship, as being a sea port; that of Stourbridge has the ironmonger's arms on one side, and the cloth-workers on the other; being, perhaps, the two principal manufactures carried on there at that time; on that of Beccles is a sheep-fold, regarding probably, the extensive common of 1400 acres belonging to this town.

Some have a sort of rebus relating to the name of the place; as on Brewton a B and a ton, and on that of Taunton, a T through a ton; that of Burlington has 3 B's on it; and that of Diss, has on it, the noted meer, near that place; those of Chertsey, Motton, and Spalding, have their churches, that of Sherburn has a mitre, as having been formerly an episcopal city, and on Croyland, the abbey arms.

There are some others of these places have types, which we do not know for what reason they were carried, as the flower-pot, on one side of that of Axmister, and the T W on the other; the armed man on one side, and the feathers on the other of Caerlyon; the portcullis on that of Chepstow; we are ignorant, likewise, what offices those persons bore whose names are inscribed round those two last pieces; we should be glad, likewise, to be better informed in relation to the cross-swords and legg on that of Illmister, and what officers T P and T S were. We are under the same uncertainty as to the anchor and horshoe on that of Claye, the crown and fleur de lis on King's Cliff, the talbot and griffin on Owndle, and the tree and two female figures on that of Midhurst.

Legends on the town pieces.

The inscriptions on some of these pieces have the name of the place where struck, but do not declare what they were to pass for, as BRIDGEWATER, GREAT TORRINGTON, p. 3, No. 10, NEWPORT IN THE ISLE OF WIGHT, p. 2, No. 27; GUILFORD F M. F S. p. 1, No. 39: BOROUGH OF NEWBRY IN COUNTY OF BERKS, p 2, No. 25; CITTY OF WELLS IN THE COUNTY OF SUMMERSET, p. 3, No 11; but the value is generally added also, as a BECCLES FARTHING, p. 1, No. 6; an ASHBURTON HALFPENNY, p. 1, No. 3; and a BURFORD TOKEN, p. 1, No. 16; and many more have it in the area of the piece; others have the same inscription, but in the legendary circle, as in the ILLMISTER FARTHING, p. 2, No. 3. Others again, besides the place and value, add the county, as a MARLBOROUGH FARTHING IN THE COUNTY OF WILTS,

Have the name of the place, and value.

WILTS, p. 2, No. 20; a FROOM FARTHING IN THE COUNTY OF SUMMERSET, p. 1, No. 34; a CHARD FARTHING IN SUMMERSETSHEIRE, p. 1, No. 19; a THORNBURY FARTHING IN GLOUCESTERSHEIRE, p. 3, No. 9; and a CLAYE FARTHING IN HOULT HUNDRED (Norfolk) p. 1, No. 23. On several of them we find it declared, whether the place is a corporation, borough, or city, as those of Wells and Newbury, just mentioned; others, also FOR THE CORPORATION OF RYE, p. 2, No. 32; THE CORPORATION OF SOUTHAMPTON'S FARTHING, p. 2, No. 40; THE CORPORATION OF HENLEY UPON THAMES THEIR HALFPENNY, p. 2, No. 1; TOKENS SET FORTH BY THE CORPORATION OF THE TOWN OF ROMSEY, p. 2, No. 36; THE BOROUGH OF BLANDFORD THEIR CORPORATION FARTHING, p. 1, No. 9; THE CITTY OF COVENTRY THEYRE HALFEPENNY, p. 1. No. 26; and VILLA LOWESTOFF SUFFOLK, p. 2, No. 15. Besides these, Lincoln and New-Sarum are called CITTIES; Pool, a TOWNE and COUNTY; Chard, Evesham, Ilchester, Tetbury and Yeovil, declare themselves BOROUGHS; † and Brewton and St. Eeds, TOWNS.

The legends on some of them, shew by what magistrates or officers they were uttered, whether mayor, portreeve, bailiff, constable, chamberlain, church-warden, overseer or rector, as follows, — *By what magistrate or officer uttered.*

For the maior of the town and county of Poole, p. 2, No. 35. — *Maior.*
For the maior of the city of New Sarum, p. 2, No. 37.
The maior of Oxford's token, p. 2, No. 38.
Luke Nourse, maior (Gloucester) p. 1, No. 36.
Thomas Price, maior, p. 1, No. 37.
This farthing will be owned by the maior and aldermen (Wotton) p. 3, No. 17.
Made by the portreeve of the borough of Yeovill, p. 3, No. 19. — *Portreeve*
A Langport farthing, made by the portreeve, p. 2, No. 10.
The borough of Chard, made by the portrife, for the poor, p. 1, No. 20
By the bayliff of the borough (Ivilchester) p. 2, No. 5. — *Bailiff.*
By the Constables, a Taunton farthing, p. 3, No. 7. — *Constable.*
The chamberlains of Bridgenorth, their halfpenny, p. 1, No. 12. — *Chamberlain.*
Tamworth's chamberlains, for change and charity, p. 3, No. 10.
R. S. in Northampton, chamberlain, p. 2, No. 33.
The warden's halfpenny of Bewdley, p. 1, No. 7. — *Church warden.*
Jos. Smithson, Rob. Barker, church wardens (Lowestoff) 1669, p. 2, No. 18.
The overseer's farthing of St. Ives, p. 2, No. 6. — *Overseer.*
The overseer's halfpenny of Peterborough, p. 2, No. 33.
The overseers of the town of St. Eeds, their halfpenny, p. 2, No. 24.
The overseers of the poor, Littleport, Isle of Ely, p. 2, No. 14.
Joseph Sayer, rector of Newbery, p. 2, No. 26. — *Rector.*
Henry Jones, sword berer. — *Sword berer.*
The 8 men and Feefees of Morton, p. 2, No. 23. — *Feefees.*

We are at a loss to determine what magistrates those are whose names stand upon those of Caerlyon, p. 1, No. 18, and Chepstow, p. 1, No. 21, or whether the piece of Newbery is a town piece, although placed among them. We appre-

† Chard is a borough in the strictest sense of the word, as having formerly sent members to parliament; and Tetbury is such, in its largest signification, as having had formerly a castle, and being a strong place, having never sent a member to parliament; but Yeovill cannot be called such on either of those accounts

hend that the I N, in p. 2, No. 32, as well as the I T on another we have seen, are both initials of the names of other chamberlains of that place. The sword-bearer, we think, likewise, was appointed by the mayor to superintend this business.

Many of them also declare, that the intent of striking them was to serve the poor.

Made for the use of the poor.

The poor's farthing of Minehead, pl. 2, No. 22.
The poor's halfpenny, of Croyland, pl. 1, No. 27.
A halfpenny for the use of the poor of Dover, pl. 1, No. 33.
A Weymouth farthing, for the poor, pl. 3, No. 12.
Sherborne farthing, for the poor, pl. 2, No. 39.
Midhurst farthing, in Surry, for the use of the poor, pl. 2, No. 21.
A Woodbridge halfpenny, the poor's advantage, pl. 3, No. 15.
A halfpenny for the poor's Advantage (Southwould) pl. 3, No. 1.
For the Use of the poor of Wimborne, pl. 3, No. 13.
For the use of the poor of Burlington, pl. 1, No. 17.
For the use of the poor, Great Yarmouth, pl. 3, No. 18.
For the poor's benefit help O Andover, pl. 1, No. 2.
To supplie the poor's need——Is charity indeed (Litchfield) pl. 2, No. 13.

Those likewise of Blandford and Romsey declare, they were for the use and benefit of the poor.

By others we are informed, that they were intended for the ease and conveniency of change.

For necessary change.

A Stowrbridge halfpenny, for necessary chainge, pl. 3, No. 4.
A Worcester farthing, for necessary change, pl. 3, No. 16.
The Burrow of Evesham, for necessary exchange, pl. 1, No. 33.
Luke Nourse, maior, for necessary change, pl. 1, No. 36.
Necessary change for the towne of Brewton, pl. 1, No. 11.
Tamworth chamberlains, their halfpenny for change and charitie, pl. 3. No. 1.

Lastly, others inform us what magistrate's office it was to rechange them, when any person required it.

By whom exchanged.

Lincoln citty halfpenny, changed by the maior, pl. 2, No. 12.
Peterburg halfpenny, to be changed by the town bailife, pl. 2 No. 34.
Nottingham halfpenny, to be changed by the chamberlains, pl. 2, No. 31.
A Biglesworth halfpenny, to be changed by the overseer, pl. 1, No. 8.
A Stamford halfpenny, to be changed by the overseers, pl. 3, No. 3.
A Boston halfpenny, to be changed by the overseers, pl. 1, No. 10.
King's Cliffe halfpenny, changed by the overseers, pl. 2 No. 8.
Langford halfpenny, changed by the overseers, pl. 2, No. 9.
Lowth halfpenny, to be changed by the overseers of the poor, pl. 2, No. 31.
A halfpenny to be exchanged by the overseers of the poor, Grantham, pl. 1, No. 38.

The three following places have something singular in their legends.

A farthing for Axmister and no other place, p. 1, No. 2.
This farthing is owned in Tetbury, the arms * of that borough, p. 3, No. 8.
This farthing will be owned in Wotton under edge, p. 3, No. 17.

* We apprehend that the arms bore by any corporation, are derived from those on their common seal; and therefore, those places which are not incorporated have not any; however, here is an instance of a non-incorporate place with arms.

The

The Tokens struck by private tradesmen and shopkeepers were either farthings, halfpennies or pennies, but not near so many of the last as the two first sorts. *Tradesmen's tokens.*

The farthings have for their type generally, on one side, the tradesman's sign, and on the other, the initial letters of their christian and surnames; and on many is added a third for that of their wifes; some, instead thereof, have the date of the year; others their trade, or the name of the place where they live; others again, have initial letters on both sides, and some, tho' very few, have their names at length. Several of the farthings have inscribed round them, only their sign and place of abode, viz. at the D. and Dunstan's, within Temple-bar—at the cole-house, in Barking;—the tallow chandler in Smithfield;—the willow tree, Cloak-lane;—at the corner house in little Queen-street;—the bell tavern, in Distaff-lane;—the gun without Aldgate, &c. But in general they have their names also on them. There are very few which have their value, that is, HIS or HER FARTHING, on them; whereas there are as few of the halfpennies or pennies without it. *Farthings their type.* *Legend.*

The halfpence have usually, like the farthings, on one side, the tradesman's sign, but on the other side, HIS or HER HALFPENNY. Some of them, however, have instead thereof, either the initial letters as before, or the date of the year, their trade, or the name of the place, or the town, and sometimes their names at length; and some few of them have both their sides filled with an inscription only. *Halfpennies, their type.*

The legend round them is the name of the person, and that of the place of his residence, and sometimes their trade, also the value, where it is not in the area. *Legend.*

There are great numbers, both of farthings and halfpence, which have the grocer's arms on them, sometimes instead of their sign, and often when that is on the piece also; many others, again, have a sugar loaf; and many tallow-chandlers have a man at work, dipping of candles, on theirs.

We have observed the arms of the following companies on these pieces. *Companies arms.*

Apothecaries	Butchers	Fishmongers	Mercers	Smiths
Armourers	Carpenters	Girdlers	Merchant Taylors	Stationers
Bakers	Clothworkers	Goldsmiths	Pewterers	Tallow chandlers
Barber-Surgeons	Coopers	Grocers	Plaisterers	Vintners
Brewers	Distillers	Haberdashers	Salters	Weavers
Bricklayers	Drapers	Ironmongers	Skinners	Woolpackers
	Dyers	Joyners		

The following list contains, also, the trades and professions we have found mentioned in these tokens. *Trades mentioned on these pieces.*

Apothecary	Bookbinder	Chirurgeon	Distiller	Goldsmith
Artizan Skinner	Bookseller	Clockmaker	Draper	Grocer
Baker	Brewer	Clothier	Dyer	Gunner
Barber	Bricklayer	Clothman	Farthing-changer	Haberdasher
Bankesman	Broker	Coalman	Fishmonger	Haberdasher of small wares
Bailiff	Capmaker	Comfit maker	Gardener	Hatter
Baytemaker	Carrier	Confectioner	Girdler	Hosier
Beare brewer	Chandler	Cook	Glassman	Inn-keeper
Bellman	Chapman	Cornchandler	Glover	Joyner
Bodismaker	Cheesemonger	Cutler		

Ironmonger
Lether-cutter
Lether-ſeller
Limeman
Linnen draper
Linnen weaver
Lockſmith
Marſhal
Malſter
Mealman
Merchant
Mariner
Millener
Miller
Oylman
Pewterer
Pinner
Poſtmaſter
Poulterer
Rugmaker
Sadler
Salter
Silkman
Silkweaver
Shoomaker
Smoker
Starchmaker
Stationer
Sutler
Tallow chandler
Tapſter
Taylor
Tobacconiſt
Trunkmaker
Truſſmaker
Vintner
Vitler
Upholſterer
Watchmaker
Weaver
Wine cooper
Woolen draper
Woollman
Woodmonger

The ſurnames contained in the following liſt are all that have come under our notice, but we are very ſenſible what great additions may be made to it.

Abbits
Abbot
Able
Ablet
Abraham
Ackley
Acton
Adams
Adamſend
Adamſon
Adcocke
Adderley
Adſe
Adkines
Adlington
Adſon
Aeris
Albert
Alchorne
Alchurche
Alcocke
Alder
Alderſon
Aldread
Aldridge
Alexander
Aleyne
Alezander
Alford
Algar
Allanſon
Alldridge
Allembridge
Allen
Allercy
Alliſon
Allmond
Allott
Allſop
Alſtor
Alſtrop
Ambler
America
Ames
Amond
Amps
Anderton
Andrews
Annis
Anniſon
Annker
Anſley
Anſlow
Anſty
Antrobus
Applebee
Apthorpe
Archer
Ardley
Armiſtead
Arnold
Aſhby
Aſhe
Aſhfield
Aſhmead
Aſke
Aſkew
Aſkugh
Aſpray
Aſtrup
Athy
Atkines
Athwood
Atkinſon
Atton
Attow
Attwood
Avery
Aungier
Auſtin
Axtell
Aylett
Ayliffe
Ayſley
Aynſworth
Aylward
Aylwin
Backer
Backery
Backler
Bacon
Bedget
Badcock
Bagg
Baggot
Baggs
Bailey
Bailsford
Baker
Bakewell
Balet
Ball
Ballard
Balley
Banat
Bandy
Banick
Banniſter
Bancraft
Banes
Barewhit
Barker
Barkett
Barlow
Barnard
Barnes
Barnwell
Baradell
Barrett
Barriff
Barron
Barrowes
Barſlow
Barſtow
Bartholemew
Barwell
Barwick
Baſſet
Batch
Bate
Baten
Bates
Bateman
Batsford
Batſon
Bavet
Baxter
Baylef
Bales
Bayne
Bayneham
Baythorne
Bazell
Beadingfield
Beale
Beales
Bearde
Bearne
Beaumond
Beaumont
Beawell
Becham
Becke
Beckford
Becket
Beckwith
Beddingfield
Bedford
Bedoe
Bedoes
Beech
Beere
Behtha
Belcher
Bele
Bell
Benett
Benington
Benn
Bennet
Benſon
Bentham
Berriffe
Berry
Bethel
Betes
Betts
Beverly
Bigg
Biggs
Billing
Billinges
Birch
Bird
Birkbeck
Birkby
Biſhop
Biſſel
Biſſi
Blachford
Blakett
Blackden
Blackmore
Blackwell
Blagrewe
Blake
Blanchard
Bland
Blanden
Blatchford
Blofeld
Blomer
Blooner
Blundell
Blyth
Boad
Bodicote
Bodycott
Bodington
Boddington
Boheyne
Bold
Bolton
Bond
Bono
Bonyfield
Bonner
Bonnick
Bonney
Boone
Booſey
Booth
Boram
Boſtock
Boſwell
Bothell
Boughton
Boulter

Boulton

Boulton
Boulden
Boulderoe
Bound
Bourne
Bowdler
Bowe
Bowell
Bowker
Bowtell
Boyce
Boyes
Bradbury
Braine
Bramble
Brand
Brands
Braſſier
Bratherick
Bray
Brayne
Breight
Bremredge
Brenn
Brent
Brewer
Brian
Briant
Bribriſt
Bricdell
Brich
Brides
Bridgell
Bridgeman
Bridgman
Bridges
Bridgs
Briggs
Bright
Briſenden
Broad
Brock
Brockden
Brockett
Bromfield
Bromhall
Bromles
Bronſon
Brookes
Broome
Brotherſt
Brothers
Browne
Bryan
Brydon
Bucher
Buckeuk
Budd
Bugg
Buggin
Buicher
Bulmer
Bull
Bumſtead
Burche
Burcombe
Burfey
Burgas
Burges
Burgis
Burle
Burly
Burnham
Burner
Burrel
Burredge
Burroughs
Burrowes
Burry
Burted
Burſton
Burſtow
Burſted
Burten
Buſby
Buſh
Buſhel
Buſhop
Buſtard
Buttall
Butter
Butterfeild
Buttrey
Butts
Byard
Byat
Bybee
Bye
Cab
Cadd
Cadman
Cadmer
Cagworth
Calloway
Calvert
Cam
Camfield
Cammoch
Campe
Campion
Cane
Canner
Cannon
Capon
Cardon
Carforth
Carnatt
Carr
Cart
Carter
Carvell
Cary
Caſtle
Caſtleman
Cater
Catt
Catten
Cauldry
Cauterey
Cawdron
Chambers
Champe
Chance
Chandler
Chanler
Chaplyn
Chapman
Charwell
Chaton
Chayton
Chaytor
Cheapman
Chebſey
Cheetham
Cheeſman
Cheſham
Cheever
Cheves
Cheney
Cheſton
Cheſter
Cherry
Cherieholme
Cheval
Chick
Chidley
Child
Chittenden
Chitty
Chriſtopher
Church
Churchell
Churchey
Clarke
Clayton
Cleare
Cleaver
Clement
Cler
Clery
Clifford
Clifton
Clithero
Clough
Coates
Coarſon
Cobb
Cobbet
Cobham
Cock
Cockes
Cockee
Cockell
Codington
Coddington
Coke
Coker
Coldewell
Cole
Coleman
Coles
Collet
Collin
Collins
Collis
Colliſon
Coltman
Combes
Condley
Complyn
Comynt
Connington
Conry
Conway
Conſtable
Cony
Conyers
Cooke
Cooper
Cope
Corbett
Cordall
Cordey
Corfie
Corfield
Corie
Corney
Corniſh
Cornwill
Coſhey
Coſton
Cotton
Covallin
Coudry
Coverdale
Coulſell
Cowpland
Cowley
Cox
Coxall
Coxon
Coyde
Crabb
Crafts
Crane
Cranfield
Cranbroo
Crannidgo
Crannts
Crapp
Craven
Crawley
Craycroft
Creſſwell
Creed
Creever
Crewes
Crichelowe
Criſpe
Crocker
Cromus
Croſland
Croſbie
Croſs
Crouch
Crowe
Crown
Cryer
Cully
Cullyer
Cupp
Cupdell
Cundell
Curle
Curtis
Cutterbank
Cutler
Cutt
Dagnal
Dale
Dalling
Dance
Daniel
Danſie
Darker
Darkin
Darrant
Darrel
Daſhwood
Davie
Davies
Davidge
Davis
Daws
Dawſon
Day
Deale
Deare
Dearmer
Deben
Debert
Debnam
Deighton
Delamaine

Deluke

Deluke
Demonci
Dennis
Dent
Derin
Deveniſh
Deveral
Deverrel
Dewat
Dew
Dewes
Dickens
Dickinſon
Dichfield
Dill
Dimarſh
Dimbleby
Dinn
Diplak
Diſton
Dix
Dixon
Dixſon
Dobſon
Doe
Dolle
Dolliffe
Doman
Donne
Doughty
Dowding
Dowley
Dowlings
Downs
Downing
Draper
Dring
Drury
Dry
Duncombe
Dune
Duory
Durell
Dutton
Dyer
Eagleſton
Eaſton
Eaton
Ede

Edgell
Edmonds
Edmun
Edwards
Eedes
Eeles
Elderfeld
Eldridge
Ellfry
Elie
Elliot
Ellis
Ellwood
Elm
Elmes
Elvis
Ely
Emett
Emperor
Endon
Enfield
Engelfield
Englefield
Engliſh
Ering
Erwin
Etherige
Evanes
Eve
Everard
Everel
Eveſham
Ewing
Exley
Exton
Eyre
Faerley
Fagg
Faircloth
Faldo
Fallowfield
Farbecke
Farley
Farmer
Farnehill
Farrand
Farre
Farrer
Farſhal

Faſſon
Faulkingham
Falkoner
Feild
Feilder
Feillder
Felkingham
Fellowes
Fellſted
Fellwell
Fenford
Fereby
Ferebee
Ferris
Fidge
Fidoe
Field
Filbee
Finall
Finch
Fiſh
Fiſher
Fichat
Fitchet
Flatman
Fletcher
Flint
Flower
Flumer
Fockard
Folkard
Fooke
Foorde
Forcet
Forder
Forfeit
Foreman
Foſſet
Foſſey
Foſſon
Foſter
Foulſum
Fountain
Fowler
Fox
Francis
Franklyn
Fray
Freeman

Freke
French
Fricy
Frolock
Froſt
Fuller
Fullthorp
Fullwood
Furrill
Furzer
Gagworth
Gale
Galloway
Gamblyn
Gardener
Gardiner
Gardner
Garforth
Garthwaite
Garnan
Garnatt
Gaſley
Gaſtquon
Gaunt
Gaylard
Gaynes
Gent
Gerſed
Gibben
Gibbons
Gibbs
Gifford
Gilbart
Giles
Gillat
Gilman
Gimbart
Ginn
Glanfield
Gladman
Glover
Godbee
Goddard
Goderey
Godfray
Godleman
Godſel
Godwin
Godwyn

Gold
Goldfinch
Golightly
Goldſton
Goldſmith
Good
Goodacre
Goodare
Goode
Goodeve
Goodmay
Goodwyn
Gooſey
Gorge
Gorham
Gorſuch
Goſs
Goſſley
Goſling
Gott
Gothridge
Goulgag
Gould
Goulding
Gouldley
Gramphorn
Grandy
Granger
Grape
Graſt
Graves
Grayſon
Greathead
Greedier
Green
Greendune
Greenewood
Greenedow
Greveſon
Gregory
Grenway
Grene
Grible
Grice
Griffith
Grimes
Groome
Groſter
Growſe

Grundy
Gryer
Guilbert
Gunthorpe
Gurden
Gurdon
Gutch
Gutteridge
Guy
Guyon
Hackluyt
Hackny
Hadley
Hadye
Hackton
Hagley
Hailme
Haiſted
Haiten
Hale
Halford
Haley
Hall
Hallet
Hallſey
Hammerton
Hamper
Hancock
Hand
Hannam
Hannell
Hanſon
Harding
Hardy
Hardmeat
Hardwicke
Harford
Harrinton
Harley
Harman
Harper
Harrice
Harrindine
Harrington
Harris
Harriſon
Harrold
Hart
Hartley

Hartenup
Harvell
Harvey
Harvie
Harviling
Haruyn
Harwick
Harwood
Haſard
Haſell
Haſleden
Hatley
Hatton
Hauſon
Hauton
Hawke
Hawrmood
Haydcocke
Hayes
Hayne
Headach
Healey
Hearn
Heater
Heath
Hebb
Heckes
Heffield
Hellow
Henley
Herbert
Herring
Hewes
Hey
Heynes
Heyward
Hibberdine
Hickman
Hide
Higgs
Hill
Hind
Hinde
Hinckes
Hinckly
Hird
Hiſcock
Hoad
Hoare
Hoard
Hobbs
Hobſon
Hodd
Hodges
Hodgkin
Hodgſon
Hogben
Hoggard
Holbrough
Holland
Hollaway
Holloway
Holmes
Homes
Homeſby
Honit
Honner
Hopfeild
Hopkins
Hopton
Hooke
Hooker
Hookham
Hooper
Hoopes
Horler
Horne
Horton
Horwood
Hovdgben
Houlcroft
Houting
Howes
Howgrave
Howſon
Hoyles
Hubbard
Hubbart
Hubbold
Huckerſon
Huff
Huffatt
Hugh
Hughes
Hulett
Hull
Humpherls
Humfre
Hunſdon
Hunt
Hunter
Hurdman
Hurſt
Hutcherſon
Hutchins
Hutchinſon
Hutheſon
Huthinſon
Hutten
Hutton
Hyde
Jackſon
Jacob
Jacobs
Jaes
James
Jaques
Jarman
Jarvis
Ibanes
Iberee
Ibbeitſon
Jbbot
Ibbotſon
Jebb
Jeenes
Jefferies
Jeffrſon
Jeffry
Jeffes
Jemmet
Jenings
Jennens
Jenkinſon
Jenman
Jerman
Jerwell
Jewell
Ilife
Inner
Inns
Ingleby
Ingram
Ingrom
Johns
Johnſell
Johnſon
Jollie
Jonas
Jones
Jordan
Joyce
Joydell
Ireland
Iſaac
Iſard
Ivard
Jues
Iveſon
Juffrum
Juninge
Juſon
Juſtice
Juxon
Izard
Kam
Keate
Keatchere
Keen
Kellet
Kemble
Kemp
Kempeton
Kerin
Kenſie
Kent
Keribb
Kerop
Kettlewell
Kichener
Kichley
Kider
Kightley
Kilderbee
Kindon
King
Kinge
Kinger
Kingsford
Kingdon
Kingtun
Kirton
Kitchin
Kite
Knapp
Kneeſbane
Knibb
Knighton
Knight
Knights
Knightſ-bridge
Labrain
Lacke
Ladbrook
Laight
Laithwait
Lambe
Lambert
Lamkin
Lamplugh
Lane
Langdon
Langham
Langley
Langthorne
Langthoral
Lanaſtone
Langriſh
Lankford
Lardner
Laret
Lark
Latch
Lawſon
Lax
Leadbeatter
Leader
Leager
Leames
Lee
Leddle
Leech
Leeds
Leeſe
Legg
Leightly
Leit
Lem
Lemon
Lekeux
Leonard
Leſcaillet
Lewis
Ley
Lichford
Lidendall
Liſord
Lightmaker
Lightwood
Limber
Lintott
Lione
Liſle
Litchfield
Lithford
Livinge
Locke
Lodge
Looger
Love
Lorie
Lord
Lovinge
Lovell
Lucas
Ludington
Ludwell
Luffe
Lumbard
Lumpkin
Luſher
Lye
Lule
Lyon
Lyng
Lyne
Macham
Mackrish
Mackeris
Mackers
Macks
Madell
Madocks
Malhis
Malls
Malvos
Man
Markendale
Manklins
Mander
Maning
Manninge
Manley

Manyringe
Manſuar
Mansfield
Manſer
Maples
March
Marchant
Marefield
Marke
Marken
Markendale
Markham
Marlow
Marsfield
Marſhall
Marſton
Marſh
Marriot
Martin
Martyn
Marvell
Maſcall
Maſlin
Maſmore
Maſon
Maſſone
Maſteres
Maſters
Maſterſon
Mathew
Mathorpe
Mathus
Mawbs
May
Maycocke
Mayer
Mayes
Mayne
Mayu
Mead
Meale
Meales
Meaſeley
Meekes
Meggs
Mehew
Merill
Meſſinger
Metcalfe
Mewes
Meyrick
Mibouch
Michel
Michill
Mickell
Midleditch
Midlaton
Midleborah
Midwinter
Mierdoch
Milbanck
Miles
Mileſon
Millgate
Millard
Miller
Milliard
Millington
Mills
Milner
Minifie
Minſhew
Minty
Moare
Modell
Molby
Molldy
Monuet
Moody
Mooer
Moore
Moortier
More
Morgan
Morley
Morrell
Morſe
Morrys
Mortimer
Moſelye
Moſlye
Moſs
Moſſye
Moulton
Mountaine
Mumford
Munn
Murdok
Muſcut
Mynn
Mynſhal
Nailer
Naiſh
Naſh
Nayler
Naylor
Neau
Nelme
Nevell
Neur
Newbery
Newman
Newlove
Newld
Nickls
Nicholas
Nicholls
Nicholſon
Nightingale
Nunn
Noble
Noldred
Norborne
Noris
Normanile
Norman
Northover
Norwood
Nourſe
Nowell
Nuce
Nuriſh
Nutby
Nutt
Nuttall
Nuttett
Nutton
Oborne
Oaker
Odden
Ofum
Ogdey
Oke
Okes
Ogle
Ollive
Ores
Ormes
Orpin
Orter
Orton
Orum
Orwell
Oſborne
Oſburne
Oſgooby
Oſman
Ottley
Overing
Overond
Owarne
Oxnam
Oxon
Oyle
Owen
Owſley
Pace
Packman
Page
Paice
Paige
Paine
Painter
Pallant
Palmer
Papworth
Parat
Pares
Parfit
Park
Parker
Parkes
Parkinſon
Parkman
Parmenter
Parnell
Parrot
Parſon
Parry
Parteſhall
Partington
Partrick
Paſkall
Paſke
Paſhley
Patmer
Patey
Paton
Patten
Paulin
Payton
Peachey
Peacock
Peale
Peare
Pearce
Pearſon
Peeke
Peele
Peirce
Peile
Peiſley
Pelly
Pemberton
Pemble
Penden
Pengſtone
Penford
Pennoc
Pennington
Penny
Perce
Percy
Perfet
Perkins
Perſnell
Perſmore
Perrett
Perris
Perry
Perſor
Peſtle
Peterſon
Pettitt
Petty
Peyton
Phillipes
Phillips
Phithy
Pidgeon
Pierſon
Pile
Pilman
Pinock
Pinden
Pingſton
Pinkney
Pinnell
Pinniſney
Pitman
Pittock
Pittway
Platt
Platten
Plimton
Plomer
Plumer
Pochin
Pocock
Poley
Polham
Poole
Poore
Ponder
Pont
Port
Pore
Porter
Potter
Power
Powning
Prai
Pratt
Prence
Preſton
Pricke
Prince
Princet
Priſs
Prittell
Prockter
Proper
Proſſer
Pruce
Puceridge
Puckeridge
Pudeford
Purcell
Purdue
Purratt
Purſſell
Putnam
Quaterman
Quelch
Quingbrow

Quingbrow
Rabie
Radcliffe
Rachell
Radford
Ragg
Railton
Rallin
Rammage
Rance
Randall
Randell
Randolph
Rands
Ranger
Raſine
Raſin
Raſtell
Ravens
Ray
Raylton
Rayner
Rayment
Rayſin
Read
Reader
Redman
Redmayne
Reeca
Reed
Reeve
Reeves
Remnant
Rennals
Renolds
Reſby
Reſtall
Reve
Reveil
Reves
Rewſe
Reynolds
Rhodes
Rice
Rich
Richards
Richardſon
Richeſon
Richmond

Riddal
Riddeſdale
Ridelſdale
Rider
Ridge
Ridley
Ridout
Ridſon
Righton
Ringer
Rixon
Roaſe
Roberts
Robertſon
Robins
Robinſon
Robottom
Robotham
Rocke
Rodd
Roe
Rogerman
Rogers
Rolfe
Rollingſon
Rolph
Rolſton
Rome
Roome
Rooſey
Rope
Roper
Roſendall
Roſſendall
Round
Rouſe
Rowe
Rowell
Rowland
Rowlandſon
Rowley
Royd
Ruddock
Rudg
Rudge
Rudgeley
Rumham
Runham
Ruſe

Ruſhell
Ruſſell
Rutt
Ryland
Rymer
Rythe
Sae
Salmon
Salterſwake
Salter
Sam
Samethurſt
Sammon
Samſon
Samway
Samworth
Sanddcrs
Sanders
Sanderſon
Sandes
Sapp
Sapcot
Sare
Sargent
Sarjent
Sarten
Satchell
Savidge
Saul
Saxbee
Scaiſe
Scavinton
Scholes
Scott
Scory
Seaborne
Seale
Sealy
Searle
Seayre
Seddon
Seeley
Seeling
Selby
Seldred
Sellam
Senior
Sevitt
Seward

Sewell
Seymor
Shakeſpeer
Sharp
Shaller
Shaw
Shebbear
Sheene
Sheldon
Shengold
Sherley
Sherward
Shiers
Shiver
Shipton
Short
Shortner
Shrawley
Shropſhire
Shrouch
Sibley
Sidey
Sidnor
Sikes
Silke
Silveſter
Simons
Simpſon
Simſon
Sindry
Skelſon
Skenge
Skedmore
Skinner
Slye
Smalaber
Small
Smallſhaw
Smart
Smeeth
Smethurſt
Smith
Smithſon
Snary
Snealton
Snell
Snelling
Snowden
Sorell

Soreſbie
Sole
Solley
Somes
Somner
Souch
Southern
Sowle
Sowerby
Speere
Spencer
Springe
Spry
Squier
Stanyard
Stanforth
Stamp
Stanard
Standbrooke
Stanhope
Stanton
Stanſby
Starkey
Statham
Stationer
Stayner
Stearne
Stebbing
Stedman
Steevens
Steale
Stell
Stevenſon
Stevinſon
Stinton
Stiver
Stolbart
Stockton
Stokeld
Stokins
Ston
Stone
Stowe
Stranger
Stringfellow
Stringer
Street
Stubbs
Stud

Studly
Stutſbery
Stutly
Sudbury
Sugden
Sugder
Summer
Sury
Sutton
Swallow
Swan
Sweet
Swetnam
Swiſt
Swinerton
Swinton
Symonds
Sylveſter
Tabor
Taler
Tallbot
Tampſell
Tamptor
Tanner
Tart
Taſt
Tate
Taylcott
Tayler
Taylor
Taynton
Tayſpell
Temple
Templeman
Tench
Teper
Terrill
Terry
Tetberry
Tibbenham
Tidde
Tillard
Timberlake
Tindall
Tippets
Tilberry
Tiddalle
Tiwill
Tizard

Thacker

Thacker
Tharle
Tharpe
Thomlinſon
Thomas
Thomſen
Thonton
Thorne
Thornback
Thornum
Thornton
Thorpe
Thring
Throwley
Thurman
Todd
Token
Tomfran
Tompkins
Tompſon
Toms
Tongue
Toomer
Toplady
Touthaker
Touchin
Towle
Toy
Tracey
Tracy
Travers
Treagle
Tredway
Trenes
Trevet
Trimmer
Triplet
Tripp

Trotter
Troughton
Trowan
Trowell
Trubſhaw
Tuchin
Tucker
Tuer
Tuil
Tunard
Tunſtable
Tunſtale
Turbery
Turges
Turkinton
Turnagain
Turney
Turll
Turrill
Turtly
Tutheld
Tuthill
Twigden
Twiſtleton
Tyzard
Valer
Valle
Vaſton
Vickry
Vincent
Vivers
Vol
Voll
Underwood
Ungle
Unrin
Uſher
Wade

Wafford
Waggoner
Waiter
Wake
Wakelin
Waker
Walden
Waldron
Walford
Walker
Wallcher
Waller
Wallet
Wallis
Wallton
Wand
Wandrick
Waple
Waples
Ward
Warff
Warington
Waringe
Warke
Warmall
Warmer
Warner
Warren
Warwell
Waſhbourne
Waſſe
Waſtal
Waterſall
Waterman
Watere
Watford
Wathing

Watmough
Wats
Watters
Watts
Waud
Waye
Weale
Wearg
Web
Webb
Weber
Weedin
Weedon
Weeks
Weker
Welch
Welchman
Welde
Wells
Wern
Weſt
Weſterman
Weſton
Wethered
Wethrel
Wetſon
Whaght
Whale
Whedda
Wheeler
Wheſton
Whiſton
Whitcombe
Whitchurche
White
Whitebread
Wolrick

Whiternam
Whitman
Whittaker
Whitingham
Whittman
Whitton
Whitty
Wickenden
Wickings
Wickins
Widdope
Widmere
Wighton
Wike
Wilberfoſs
Wilock
Wilcocks
Wilder
Wildham
Wildinge
Willmer
Wildman
Wilking
Wilkins
Wilkinſon
Willet
Williams
Williamſon
Willmer
Willmatt
Wilmot
Wills
Willſon
Willy
Winbery
Winechuſt
Winckell

Winte
Wiſe
Witchell
Witherlin
Withers
Wood
Woodgreen
Woodman
Woodroofe
Woodward
Woolman
Woore
Woorenum
Wolball
Wolkrich
Wollaſton
Wolterton
Worale
Worrall
Worth
Worwood
Wraighte
Wriggleſ-worth
Wright
Yanſborough
Yardley
Yarford
Yarnold
Yate
Yatts
Yeats
Yeelds
Yould
Young
Younge
Youngeſt

The following liſt contains the names of all thoſe places we have found noted on theſe pieces, ſeveral of which have added to them the county in which they are ſituate: for where that is wanting, and there are ſeveral towns which bear the ſame name, it cannot be determined to which they belong, unleſs it is known where the pieces have been found.

Abby Milton
Abergavenny
Abingdon
Acton

Acton in Hampſhire
Ageiche
St. Albans

Albern
Albom in Wiltſhire
Alborough

Alceſter
Aldborough
Aleiſbury
Alford

Alfreton
Aliſham
Alington
Alſeſter

Alton

Alton in Hampſhire
Amerſam in Buckinghamſhire
Amerford in Kent
Ampthill
Andover in Hampſhire
Angmoring
Apleby
Appledore
Apſum
Arlington
Arundele
Aſhborne
Aſhburton
Aſhcote
Aſhford
Aſhford in Kent
Aſhley
Aſhwell
Attarcliffe
Axbridge
Axmiſter
Aynho upon the hill
Ayno on the hill
Bacons Inn
Backwell
Bagſhot
Baldock
Bamton
Bamton the Buſh
Banbury
Bangor Faur
Great Barford
Barkhampſted
Barkin
Barkley
Barkway
Barley
Barnards Caſtle
Barnes
Barneſley Yorkſhire
Barneſley
Barnet
Barnſtable
Barrow upon Humber
Barton
Barton in the Clay
Barton upon Humber
Barton hundred Gloſterſhire
Baſingſtoke
Batterſea
Battell
Batley
Beadle
Beare Regis
Beaumaris
Beckington
Beckles
Beckonsfield
Beckensfeild in Buckinghamſhire
Bedal
Bedford
Great Bedwin
Belton
Bemeſter
Bemiſter
Bengworth
Bentham
Betley and Laſterley
Beverley
Biddenden in Kent
Biddeford
Bigleſwade
Bigleſworth
Billerkey in Eſſex
Bilrekey in Eſſex
Billingham
Biſley
Bpp. Aukland
Biſhops Caſtle
Biſhopſton
Biſhop Storford
Biſhops Wallton
Blackborne
Blackmore in Eſſex
Blackwater
Blakey
Bletſoe
Blockley
Bocking
Bocking in Eſſex
Bodmin
Bolney
Borntwood in Eſſex
Borow Bridge
Boſton
Boulton
Bourne
Bourton on the water
Bow
Bowerne
Bowldoake
Bowden
Boxford
Brackley
Bradford
Bradnege
Bradſtock
Brailes
Braintree in Eſſex
Bramyard
Old Brandford
Brandon
Branſton
Branton
Old Brentford
Brentwood
Breylas
Brill Buxes
Bridgewater
Bridlington
Bridgeſtock
Bridport
Brinkley
Brithelſome
Broadwater in Suſſex
Broadway
Brockley in Shropſhire
Bromſgrove
Bromley in Kent
Brookland
Buckingham
Budſdell
Bullingbrook
Bulwiter
Bungay
Buntingford
Burford
Burgh
Burnham
Burntwood
Burrow
Burten on Trent
St Edmonds Bury
Cailham
Calne
Cambridge
Camdin
Camelton
Canterbury
Canſtby
Great Carden
Carmarthen
Carleton
Carlile
Carline
Carteſley
Carouſe
Caſtle Cary
Caſtil Henningham
Carreſbie
Catworth
Caxton and Elſworth
Cavendiſh
Cawood
Cerne Abbis
Chard in Sumer.
Charing
Chanderton near Manch
Charlton Kings
Chatam
Chatepis in the Iſle of Ely
Cheddon near Taunton
Chelmesford
Chelſea
Cheltenham
Cheſham
Cheſhunt in Harfordſhire
Cheſter
Cheſterfield
Great Cheſterford
Chiceſter
Chiddingford
Chillom in Kent
Chinner
Chippingham
Chipping Norton
Chipping Ongar
Chipen Sadbury
Chiperfield
Chiſwick
Chorley
Chriſt Church
Churchey
Chulmley
Church Stretton
Cirenceſter
Clack
Clapton in Hackney
Clifton
Clinton upon Team
Clophill
Cobham
Cockermouth

Coggeſhal in Eſſex
Colcheſter
Colebroke
Coleſhill
Collingborne
Collingham
Comunhill
Conway
Cophill
Corfe Caſtle
Cornwell
Coſell
Coſham
Couldekeſter
Cowbridge
Coxhal
Weſt Cowes Iſle of Wight
Cranbrooke
Cratfield
Crayden inSurry
Crayfield
Creaditon
Crewkerne
Cricklade
Crofford
Crofte Caſtle
Cropready
Croſcomb
Crowland
Culliton
St. Cullum
Cullumpton
Daintry
Daſie Hillock in Weſt Houghton
Dalham
Darby
Darford in Kent
Darking
Darlington
Dartmouth
Daventree
Deadford
Deal
Lower Deal
Debinham
Dedington
Dell
Dennington
Deptford in Kent
Dertford in Kent
The Deviſes
Dinchurch
Doncaſter
Dorcheſter
Dover
Downham Market in Norfolk
Dranfield
Draton in Shropſhire
Droitwich
Dudley in Worceſterſhire
Dunſden in Oxford
Dunmow in Eſſex
Dunnington
Dunſtabel
Dunwich
Durham
Durſeley
Great Ealing
Eariff
Earith in Kent
Eaſtborne in Suſſex
Eaſtwick
Great Eaſon
Eaton
Ebiſham
Edgham
Edgeworth
Eaſt Church
Eaſt Dereham
Eaſt Grinſtead
Egam
Egham
Elham
Ellerton
Elltham
Elſworth
Ely
Eynſbury and Poten
Eppin
Epworth in the Iſle of Axholme
Eſt Church in the Iſle of Shipway
Evercrick Sumerſet
Everſhot
Eveſham
Exeter
Exon
Eye
Eyeovell
Falkingham
Falmouth
Faringham in Kent
Farnham
Farnham in Surrey
Felſtead in Eſſex
Fenny Stanton
Fenny Stratford
Feverſham
Feverſham in Kent
Finſtocke
Framlingham
Framlington
Freſhford
Froume
Fulham
Gainſbrough
Gallingham
Gamlingay
Gamlingham
Garſtang and Preſton
Gateſhead
Gedington
Gilford
Giſbrough
Glaſton
Glaſtonbury
Godmancheſter
Glouceſter
Goſport
Goudhurſt
Gragric in Kendal pariſh
Grantham
Graveſend
Great Grimſby
Greenwich
Groton
Hackney
Hadlich
Hallifax
Hallſham in Suſſex
Halongton Loſtſhire
Halſted in Eſſex
Halſworth
Halton
Hamerſmith
Hampton Road in Glouceſterſhire
Hamton Road
Hamſted
Harborough
Harleſton
Harlow
Harlow in Eſſex
Harmworth
Harrow Hill
Harrow on the Hill
Hartlepool
Hartwell
Haſlingden
Harty in the Iſle of Shepey
Harwell Berks
Harwich in Eſſex
Harley Row
Hatfield.
Hatfield in Yorkſh.
Haverford Weſt
Hawworth
The Haye
Hecleft near Luems
Hedingham Caſtle
Hedingham Caſtle Sidney
Helpringham
Helſton
Hemel Hempſted
Hempſted
Hendon
Henley upon Thames
Hereford
Herion
Heth
Highgate
Higham Ferrers
Highworth and Abingdon
Hinckley
Hitchin
Hiworth
Hoddnit
Hodſdon.
Holbee near Leeds
Holbeck
Holbidge
Holmford
Holy Head
Holſworth
Hooke Norton
Honiton
Horn Caſtle
Hornchurch
Horſam
Houldback
Houldon.
Hounſlow
Huchenden
Hull
Hungerford
Huſborne Crawley
Huthersfield
Hythe

Hythe

Hythe in Kent
Igtham in Kent
Itham in Kent
Great Ilford
Ilſley in Berkſhire
Infield and St. Ives
Ingatſtone
Ipſwich
Iſſleworth
Itmiſter
Ivingoe
Iver
St. Ives
St. Ives county of Huntington
Kempſon
Kemsford
Kendall
Kenton in Warwickſh. par.
Kerkham
Kettering
Kidderminſter
Killham
Kilmerſdon in Somerſetſhire
Kilve
Kimbolton
Kingſton upon Hull
Kingſton in Surrey
Kingſton
Kington
Kingſwood
Kirby
Kirby Kendal
Kirby Moneſyde
Kirkby Stephen in Weſtmorland
Kirkland
Kirton upon Thames
Knaeſborough
Knutsford
Laighton

Lamborne
Lambeth
Lancaſter
Langport
Laneham
Lanrooſtpence
Lavenham
Lavington
Llannidloes
Llanvillinge
Launceſton
Lechlade
Leeds
Leckhampſted
Ledbury
Leiceſter
Leitliſe
Leitchfield
Leigh
Lemſter
Lenham
Leominſter
Leonards Stanley
Leſtithall
Leverpool
Lewiſham
Licham
Lidd
Liddington in Rutlandſhire
Lightcliff near Hallifax
Limehouſe
Lincoln
Linton
Liphant in Hampſhire
Lipruck in Ham
Liſcard
Liverpool
Longcutt
Longworth
Loughborough
Louth
Loweſtoff
Ludbury
Ludham
Ludlow

Luton Bedfordſhire
Lutterworth
Lyme
Lymington
Lynn
Lynn Regis
Maborow
Macclesfield
Madely in Shropſhire
Malden
Malden in Eſſex
Malmeſbury
Malton
Malvedon
Mancheſter
Mansfield
Marazoon
March
Margret in the Ile of Thanet
Margat in Thanet
Marget in Kent
Market Boſworth
Market Deeping
Market Reaſon
Market Street
Great Marlow
St. Mary Cray
Marſhfield
Maſk in the Iſle of Ely
St. Maws
Maydenhead
Mayfield
Maydſton
Maymudine
Meere
Long Melford
Melkeſham
Mells
Melton in Kent
Melton Mowbray
Merſham

Michall Deane
Micham
Middlewich
Milbrook
Mildenhal
Mildenhal in Suffolk
Milderſhal
Mile End
Milſden
Milton
Milton Abbey
Milton near Graveſend
Mims
Minſter in Kent
Molthy
Moltby
Monmouth
Moorton in Hampſhire
Moreclac
Mortlacke
Morton
Morton Henmarſh
South Moulton
Moulſham
Mountogeu
Montſoriel
Mutcer in Monmouth
Much Wenlock
Muchbuddow
Namptwich
Nayland
St. Neots
St. Neots in Cornwall
St. Neots in Huntingtonſhire
Nettlebed
Neunham in Gloſterſhier
Newant
Newark
Newbery
Newborough

Newcaſtle
Newcaſtle under Lyne
Newington
Newington Butts
Newington Green
New Malton
Newmarket
Newport
Newport Iſle of Wight
Newportpagnel
Newport pond
Newton Abot
Newton near Mancheſter
Noneaton
Northall
Northallerton
Northampton
Northapp
Northleach
Norlege
Northleigh
Norwich
Great Norwood
Little Norwood
Notteſberry
Oakham
Ockley
Okeham in Rutland
Ockhamton
Ockingham
Olney
Ormſkirke
Orpington in Kent
Oſtenfield
Oſwalſtry
Ottley
Ottery St. Mary
Ovenden
Oundle
Outwell
Outwell in Norfolk

Ouburn

Ouburn
Oxford
Painſwick
Pancridge
Parſhore
Parſons Green
Partington
Pavenham
Paynſwick
Pebmarſh in Eſſex
Eaſt Pelham
Pemſie
Penhurſt
Penhurſt in Kent
Peterborough
Petersfield
St. Peters Chalfont
St. Peters Shalford
Petworth in Suſſex
Pull Hely
Pinner
Plaſtow
Pleſhey in Eſſex
Plymouth
Pocklinton
Pontefract
Poole
Poole in Dorſet.
Poplar
Portchmouth
Potterſpery
Potton in Middleſex
Preſcott
Preſteigne
Preſton
Preſton and Garſton
Princes Riſborough
Puckridge
Pulburrough
Pulham market
Purbick
Putney
Pyrton
Queen Hive in Kent
Rachdale
Ragby
Ramſbury
Ramſey
Ramſgate
Raſton
Reading
Redbury
Red Rutt in Cornwall
Retford
Retherhead in Kent
Richmond
Richmond in Surrey
Rickmanſworth
Ringwood
Ripley in Surrey
Rippon
Riſenden
Robin Hood Bay
Rocheſter
Rochford
Rodwell
Romanſgate in Thanet
Romanſgate in the Iſle of Tennet
Romford
Roſſe
Rotherham
Rotherhithe
Rowell
Rowhampton
Rowley
Royſton
Rudgeley
Rudham
Rugby
Rumſey in Hampſhire
Ruſden
Rye
Ryegate
Sadbery
Saddington
Saffron Walden
Salop
Saltaſh
Samford in Eſſex
Sandwich
Sapcott
Sarum
Sawtry
Saxmundham
Scarbrough
Seaford
Sedbridge
Selby
Sevenoakes in Kent
Shanſted
Shaſton
Shaſton in Dorſetſhire
Shatford
Sheffield
Shenley
Sheereborne
Sherborne
Shifnall
Shipſon
Shipſon upon Stower
Shipton Mallet
Shrewſbury
Shiver
Sibton
Silferton in Devonſhire
Sittingborne in Kent
Skipton
Sleaford
Slocombe
Smerden in Kent
Soham
Somerton
South near Hull
Southam
Southampton
Southminſter
South Moulton
South Petherton
South Town
Southwell
Southwould
Spackſtone
Spalding
Springfield in Eſſex
Stafford
Stainland
Stainland in Yorkſhire
Stamford
Stamford Baron
Stanes
Staple Grove
Starton
Steavenidge
Stebbing in Eſſex
Stepel Gladon
Stewtley
Steyning
Stilton
Stoake Norf.
Stobbart
Stoberry
Stock
Stockport
Stoke next Clare
Stoke in Kent
Stoke by Nailon
Stoke Newington
Stoke in Pelham
Stony Middelton
Stony Stratford
Stone upon Hull
Stow Bridge
Stow
Stowry
Stoxley
Stowerbridge in Norfolk
Stratford
Stratford upon Avon
Streode in Kent
Stroude
Sturrey in Kent
Styſted in Kent
Sudberie
Sumerſham
Sumerſet
Sunning Town
Sutton
Kings Sutton
Long Sutton
Swaſham in Norfolk
Swainton Abbey
Swanton
Swaſey
Swindon
Old Swinford
Swinſhead
Tackley in Eſſex
Tame
Tamworth
Tarring
Tatenham High Croſs
Tatnam
Taunton
Taunton in Somerſet
Tedbury
Tenbury
Tenterden
Tenterden in Kent
Great Terrington
Tewkſberry
Tewxbury in Gloceſterſhire
Thame
Thetford
Thindon
Thirſke
Thiſelworth
Thornborough
Thorney Abbey
Thorpe in Eſſex
Thrapſton
Tideſwall

Tidſwell

Tidswell
Tinhead
Tiverton
Tolshon Dacey
Toncester
Tooting
Lower Tooting
Topsham in Coun. Devon
Totness in Devon
Towcester
Tring
Trowbridge
Truroe
Tunbridge in Kent
Turton
Tuxford
Uckfield in Sussex
Uppingham in Rutland
Upton
Uttoxeter
Upwell
Uxbridge
Wainflett
Wakefield
Walkham
Wallingford
Wallom Green
Walpole
Waltham le Willows
Little Walsingham
North Walsham
Waltham Abbey
Waltham Green
Waltham Magney
Waltone in Surrey
Walton upon Thames
Little Walton
Wansford
Wantage
Wanting
Ware
Warington
Warmister
Warrington
Wardenton in the county of Oxon
North Washam
Waterman
Watford
Watleton
Watlington
Watsall
Watton
Waynford in Suffolk
Waymouth
Weatherbe
Webley
Weding in Kent
Wednesbury
Wecvor in Glocestershire
Welden
Wellington
Wells
Welles in Norfolk
Wendover
Wenlock
Wesbury
Wesbury in county Wilts
Westgate
West Ham
West Mean
Westminster
Westerham in Kent
Wevenhoe
Wexworth in Suffolk
Weymouth in Dorset
Weymouth Mel Regis
Whitchurch
Whitehaven
Whitley
Whitney
Whittlesey
Wickham
Wickham in Essex
Great Wickham
Hie Wickham
West Wickham
Widesley
Wigan
Little Wilbram
Wildin
Willstone in Wiltsh.
Willton
Wilton in Wiltsheere
Winborne
Winchcombe
Wincombe
Windham
Windham in Norfolk
North Windham
Windsor
Little Windsor
New Windsor
Wingham in Kent
Winslow
Winston
Winton
Wisbech
Witham
Witham in Essex
Wittney
Wokingham
Wolverhampton
Wooburne
Woodbridge
Woodchester in Glocest.
Woodchurch in Kent
Woodham Morton
Woodhurst
Woodstock
Wooton Basset
Wooton under Hedge
Worcester
Workingham
Woxbridge
Wrexham
Wrotham
Wye
Yalden in Kent
Yatley
Yarme
Yarmouth
Great Yarmouth
North Yarmouth
South Yarmouth
Yeavell
Yeovell
Yeovil in Sumer.
Yoghill
Yoxal

It is observable, that some towns stand in this list which are also among those which uttered a common farthing or halfpenny, but this was generally done either before or after those took place; however, it does not appear that this ever was the case at Bristol, as we never saw a single tradesman's token of that place.

In the fourth and fifth plates are engraved some of the most remarkable pieces which have come under our notice.

The first was struck FOR NECESSARY CHANGE IN GLOCESTERSHEIRE No. 1.
HUNDRED, but we do not know who uttered this, or what officer T L was, pl. 4.
except he was the baylife, for we find that the same year 1669, EDWARD
TAYLOR BAYLIFFE OF HEMLINGFORD HUNDRED in Warwickshire did No. 16.
make use of one, and has put his head upon it, being the only instance we have met with of this kind. We have next some for the use of coal mines, as HIGH
PEAKE COLE MINES IN DARBYSHEIRE, with the coat and crest of No. 2.

No. 3 Shalcrosse of Shalcrosse in this county; another FOR THE USE OF THE COLE
No. 7 PITS of Midleton in Yorkshire; MR. THO. ADDISON'S COALS, TAKE GOOD
No. 19 MEASURE, * but we do not know where those pits lay; also Richard Kippax,
bankesman of MARSDEN COAL PITT. Besides which we have seen of John
Keynorr, MERRY VALE PITS, and another of John Lamplugh, BROUGHTON
COAL PITTS.

No. 4 Some hospitals and companies of tradesmen struck them; as, THIS HALFPEN-
No. 5 NY BELONGS TO THE HOSPITAL OF BRIDEWELL, LONDON; — MERCER'S
No. 6 COMPANY IN KENDAL; — COMPANY OF SHEREMEN IN KENDAL; — THE
No. 8 4 YEOMEN OF THE WATERSIDE TOKENS; here are two different farthings
No. 9 10 11 of A MERCHANT OF THE STAPLE OF ENGLAND, on one side of each are the
arms of that company, on the reverse of one of them is a ship, and on that of the
other a fleece; a third sort is much in the taste of several town farthings, being
inscribed A STAPLE FARTHING on one side, and THE ARMES OF THE STAPLE
on the other, but we cannot determine whether it was for the use of the com-
No. 12 pany; we are informed by No. 12 that AT THE WARDROBE IS WORK FOR
THE POOR,—HEMP AND FLAX, 1653. but what place that was is uncertain,
perhaps a seminary for industry of Mrs. Cromwell's.

We think it can admit of little doubt that tradesmen and shopkeepers in the same town, agreed, in some manner, to take and circulate each others tokens; and for that purpose might have a particular box, with several partitions, called a parting box, † to keep them separate; and when full, make a rechange of them for silver, or probably for such of their own as were in those other persons hands. And in London and its environs, we find there were also persons who made a
trade of it, to exchange tokens, as H. M. AT THE WHITE BEARE IN
No. 13 KENT STREET, A FARTHING CHANGER, and RICHARD RICH IN LITEL
No. 14 DRURY LANE, CHANGER OF FARTHINGS; but in what manner this business
was carried on we cannot determine; neither can we tell what was the
No. 15 profession of JEREMY BUSHER AT SHOOE LANE END, SMOKER; besides that
No. 18 of ROBERT WATMOUGH CARRIER FOR HALLYFAX; we have seen one of
JOHN LOADMAN, RICHMOND CARIER, but never any other TOLEMAN
No. 20 but ROBERT FLOWER OF STILTON.

Pl. 5, No. 1 The first piece in this plate declares for what purpose struck, I PASS TO AND
No. 2 3 FRO FOR A HALFPENNY IN LEEDS; the utility of the two next are also taken
notice of, I AM FOR A PUBLICK GOOD IN COCKERMOUTH; and I AM FOR
BETTER CHENG COCKERMOUTH; until we saw this last we were not certain
whether the first was not a town piece, and A B put for the name of the
magistrate.

Every person that uttered these sort of pieces were obliged to rechange them
for silver when required, that such was their intent we are informed by several
No. 4 of them, but in a different way, as by THOMAS OGDEN OF HAWWORTH, I WILL
No. 5 EXCHANGE MY I^d. — THOMAS DAWSON IN LEEDS WILL EXCHANGE THIS
No. 6 PENNY. ‡ — SEND ME TO THE MERCER OF KNOSS HALL—IN LIEU OF THIS
No. 7 TO THE BEARER A PENNY IS DUE; on the next there is EDWARD NOURSE,
No. 8 HIS FARTHING WORTH OF COPPER, and an honest farthingworth it was,

* This is made of lead, and we are not certain whether it is not rather of the ticket kind.

† See Mr. Pegge's Letter, in Gent. Mag. 1757, p. 498.

‡ Mr. Thoresby had the dye of the reverse of this piece with the Bear, given him by one of the family, Ducat. Leod. p. 492.

requiring

requiring no promiſe of repayment, and carrying its value along with it, and certainly would have been taken in any part of the kingdom without ſcruple.

The two following declare, they were FOR NECESSARY CHANGE; alſo No. 1. No. 9 10
pl. 4. and two more we have ſeen of the name of MOSSE OF STAFFORD, and
HARRISON OF OXFORD. The only piece which has come under our notice with
its value expreſs'd fraction wiſe ¼ is No. 10, and only the next thus wrote A FAR-
THING; thoſe with his or her farthing we have already obſerved are not common,
having only ſeen thoſe of CROW OF WANDSWORTH, HAY OF THAMES
DITTON, Hoart of Weckover, LWIS OF ABERGAVENNY, MADELL OF OXON,
Rogers of Woodcheſter, SMITH AT CHEPING SUDBURY, and two others with
the names of APLEBEE and YOUNGE JUNIOR. The manner of expreſſing the
value A ¼d. and Ob. (for Obolus) are ſeldom ſeen. No. 12 was ſtruck by two No. 13 14
partners, John Cocke and William Balley. We have other partnerſhips, viz. No. 12
FOR JOHN BROOK AND WILLIAM COUDRY; alſo JOHN HARDY, EDWARD
DALE, BOTH OF STAMFORD; JOHN MERE, EXON; DAVID HART, EXON;
and RICHARD MATHEW AND JOHN POTTERIL OF OAKHAM: it is
probable ſome of theſe perſons only joined to ſtrike a token between them,
without being in partnerſhip; and ſuch appears to be that of JOHN ADFE OF
ALBORNE, I CLARKE, BISHOPSTON.

The word Token is ſeldom met with upon theſe pieces, we find it but upon
three town pieces, Burford, Oxford and Romſey; and here are three more, No. 16 17
A HALFPENNY TOKEN, TOKEN, and DOUBLE TOKEN FOR A ½d. beſides 18
which we have ſeen double tokens of Baker of Canterbury, Pearce of Dover,
Ungle of Brantre, an halfpenny token of Roys, near Newgate; and with
¼ thoſe of Williams of Longcutt and Knight, In Alderſgate ſtreet, we ſhould ſuſpect that the token paſſed for a farthing (but we never ſaw a piece with farthing token on it) and the double token for a halfpenny.

Here are three poetical ones, viz. No. 19, 20 and 21.

Although but braſs	The pump runs clear	Welcome you be
Yet let me paſs.	With ale and beer.	To trade with me.

There is alſo a caſt one, for a coffee houſe, with a turk's head, and round it

Morat the great men did me call,
Where'er I came I conquer'd all.

the inſcription on No. 22 is the ſhorteſt we have met with, being, WELCOM— SHERBORNE; and we have been informed, that there is ſtill in that town, the ſame white hart inn as this piece is ſuppoſed once to have belonged to.

We are informed by Anthony Search of Tenbury, that PLAINE DEALING IS No. 23
BEST, and Thomas Dedicot, grocer in Bewdley, recommends SQUARE DEAL- No. 24
ING on a ſquare piece; and the ſame is done by Richard Ambler, Apothecary in
Biſhopſcaſtle. No. 33, is very remarkable for its double ſquare, formed by the No. 33
legend.

There are many pieces with different companies arms on them, but this is the No. 25
only one with the motto alſo; the CREDE SED CAVE on No. 26, and VIVE LE
ROY IN UTTOXETER, are ſingular; as alſo POARE NED IN FEVERSHAM, and No. 28 29
OLD PHAROH IN BARLEY; who, no doubt, were well known in thoſe places
at that time. EDWARD WILLIAMSON it is probable was a draper, but he only No. 30
informs us he was ALDERMAN OF LIVERPOOL, and HENRY CHAPMAN only No. 31
QUONDAM ESQ.; RICHARD SMITH IN POLL, (Poole) prides himſelf in being No. 32
FREEMAN OF ENGLAND; and probably on the parliament ſide, and had fought
againſt

No. 34 against the king. Besides this piece of EDWARD TOMSON IN THE BAILE OF LINCOLN (which we suppose is some particular jurisdiction or priviledged place in that city) we have seen two others of the same place.

We have already observed, two tradesmen's names on one piece, here is one piece,
No. 35 viz. of Thomas Hartwell, which serves for two places, HIWORTH and AHINGDON; we have seen likewise of this sort, one of ANDREW SELBY, OF ENSBURY AND POTEN; JOHN CODMEN, OF PRESTON AND GARSTANG; JOHN WILLIAMS, OF ST. IVES AND RAMSEY; THO. JOHNSTON, OF INFIELD AND ST. IVES; THOMAS RICH, IN BETTLEY AND LASTERLEY; WILL. KEMP, IN PUTNEY, OR AT PARSON'S GREEN; but we cannot think what was the business
No. 36 of JOHN PITMAN OF DORSET AND SOMERSETSHIRE, in two counties instead of towns. The Robin Hood and Little John on No. 28, alludes to the name of the place; we have seen several which regarded the name of the person, as on those of Samson, Hancock, Bolton, &c. we apprehend the last piece, No. 40, was certainly made at Nuremberg, it being of the same metal and thickness, and intirely in the same taste of those which come from the counter makers at that place, not only on the reverse but likewise the head-side, as may be seen by comparing it with No. 24, 30, of pl. 4, of those counters.

Weight. These tokens are generally of brass or copper, a leaden one being very rarely to be met with; the generality of the tradesmen's farthings may weigh about 13, 14, or 15 gr. each; and the halfpence about 26, 28, or 30 gr. and therefore on a medium struck at half a guinea per lb. wt. avoirdupoise: but the town pieces are from 14 gr. to 70. gr. and the farthings of some places as heavy as the halfpence of others.

SECTION IV.

Of the COPPER FARTHINGS and HALFPENCE from 1672 to the present Time, including those of TIN between 1684 and 1692.

BY what has been said in the three former sections, it appears that the royal farthing tokens were current from 1613 'till about 1646 or 1648, in which year those of private tradesmen and corporations began, which continued for 24 years, or until the year 1672.

Pattern farthings of Cha. I. It is certain that during the first interval, there were pieces struck as patterns for a larger sized farthing, agreeing nearly with those which afterwards took place by authority; and we think the first of these may be put as far back as the year 1640, if not sooner; the type of which agrees very much with those of the
No. 1 royal tokens then current, having on one side the crown and scepters, with the addition of three lyons of England; and the other side has the crowned rose, with the addition of two scepters and three fleurs de lis; the legend on one side is FARTHING TOAKENS, and on the other TYPUS MONETA ANGL. ÆRIS, corresponding with the pattern shilling of Briots, dated 1638; and therefore, it is probable, came from the hands of the same artist.

Of the Commonwealth. Those struck during the time of the commonwealth are next in order; the four first of which have on one side, the English shield with the cross, and on the

the reverse that of Ireland with the harp; the two last have also a wreath or garland over the shields, their inscriptions * declare the purport of their intended currency, either to facilitate small commutations, or to help the poor, viz.
FARTHING TOKENS OF ENGLAND—FOR NECESSARY CHANGE 1649, THE No. 2
FARTHING TOKENS FOR—THE RELEIF OF THE PORE, ENGLANDS FAR- No. 3 No. 4
DING—FOR NECESSARY CHA. ¼ OUNCE OF FINE PEWTER—FOR NECESSA- No. 5
RY CHANGE. † The next, we apprehend, may have been struck from the dye No. 6
of the pattern sixpence of Ramage, with TRUTH AND PEACE.

On No. 7. appears a ship in full sail, representing the commonwealth, No. 7
inscribed AND GOD DIRECT OUR CORSE. The reverse has the three kingdoms of England, Scotland and Ireland, represented by three pillars tyed together, ‡ and round them, THUS UNITED INVINCIBLE. a well chosen motto for those distracted times, had it been properly attended to.

We come next to those of Oliver Cromwell, each of which have, on one Oliver Cromwell.
side, his head and titles, OLIVAR PRO. ENG. SC. IRL. the reverse of the first No. 8,9,10.
of them has the three pillars exactly like the preceding one, and with the same inscription; the next has the same arms and shield as are on his silver money, but is inscribed CONVENIENT CHANGE 1651.

If there is no mistake in this date, we should suspect the protectorship had been long concerted before it was effected. The last of them round the same reverse has CHARITIE AND CHANGE.

Among the pieces belonging to Charles II. the two first have the head of Charles II.
his father, inscribed SUCH GOD LOVES, a legend by no means suiting a piece of money. One of the reverses is a crown'd rose between C. R. with the date 1660 at bottom, and round it TRUTH AND PEACE; therefore it is plain the reverse was struck after the restoration; but whether intended for that head, we cannot determine, and we see both the reverses together on No. 15. We find the same reverse of a ship on No. 16, 18 and 19, but they have different legends; that of No. 18 is NUMORUM FAMULUS, the same as was afterwards used on the edge of the tin money; that of No. 19 is QUATUOR MARIA VINDICO, and this was afterwards put round the Britannia on the pattern farthings and halfpence struck in 1665, and the inscription round the head of the same pieces was CAROLUS A CAROLO, the same as upon these three numbers, but the types are different; the two last being a rose, thistle, harp, fleur de lis, crown'd and formed into a cross (as the shields on his silver money) and on the other a crown'd rose. There is a crown for the types of No. 20, 21 and 27, the two first differently inscribed, the last without any; the reverse of the first is four C's interlink'd, the second the royal oak, and the third two ƆC's crown'd. There is a double CR crown'd on the obverse sides of No. 22, 23, and 24; and on the next three is a double ƆC crown'd. The reverses of No. 23. 24 and 25 are cross scepters; on No 26 there are 3 scepters, and on No. 28 a rose. The legends on the reverse of No. 20 and 22, and both sides of No. 21, have an affinity to each other, as TERRAS CHARITAS REVISIT, THE KING'S GRACE IS—THE POORES RELEIFE, and on the

* These patterns were certainly prior to the town pieces, and therefore those of them with parallel inscriptions, it is very probable, were taken from these.

† We should almost suspect from the T K. and the different cross on this piece, that it might rather belong to a private tradesman.

‡ There is an R under the pillars on this piece, as also on No. 15. and the same appears on the town piece of Oxford, and that of Bristol, 1652, which we think were done by Rawlins.

last, round the figure of Charity with two children is, THE POORES RELEIFE.

Quatuor Maria Vindico. Pattern farthings.

The last pattern pieces were the QUATUOR MARIA VINDICO farthings, to which were also added, for the first time, halfpence also, and are sometimes called Lord Lucas's farthings; not because he was concerned as a projector in their coinage, but on account of a spirited speech ‡ made by him in parliament. These were what had the preference to all the others, and the same as those coined by authority in 1672; only putting the word BRITANNIA round the reverse instead of QUATUOR MARIA VINDICO, to oblige the king of France; and taking the date 1665 from under the head, and placing it in the exergue on the reverse, where the word Britannia stood before. On one of the farthings, the king's head is adorned with a larger flowing head of hair than on the other; and there is one with this head, which is something broader than common, and which has the date 1676 under the head; but with what intent this could be struck we cannot think, as the currency of the other farthings had been established for four years: there is a little difference likewise on the reverse, as the spear of the Britannia but just touches the bottom of the letters in the legend; we have never seen this piece in any other metal than silver.

Metals in which the patterns are struck.

The major part of the pattern pieces are usually met with in copper, as No. 1, 2, 3, 4, 7, 8, 9, 10, 11, 12, 14, 15, 18, 19 and 24, pl. 6; and No. 1, 2 and 3, pl. 7. We have seen also, No. 15 in silver, and No. 13 never in any other metal; and the QUATUOR MARIA farthings are much commoner in this metal than in copper, but not the halfpence: No. 21, 26, 27 and 28 are a sort of mixed metal; and No. 5, 16, 17, 20, 22, 23, 24, and 25, are in pewter or tin.

Methods to prevent counterfeiting.

As the price of the materials, and the expence of the workmanship in most of these pieces did not come up by far to the value, they were to be current for, and therefore great encouragement given to counterfeit them, from the profit to be made thereby; for this reason several methods were contrived to render this more difficult, and with this view, the last sort of the royal tokens were brased. Among these patterns there is a small sort of No. 4, which has the middle part brass and the outer circumference copper; there is a beautifull specimen of No. 3 in the British museum, having a small central circle of a silver colour, a second circle of copper, and the legendary circle of brass; and some of No. 1, p. 7, have a circle of brass through the copper.

Many of the farthings proposed to be struck in tin or pewter, have a small circle of copper through them, as those of No. 22, 23, 24 and 25.

Another method to prevent their being counterfeited, was to edge them, § either by putting an upright or slope line upon the edge, or an inscription; there are several done in the first manner, the neatest of which sort that we

‡ "And it is evident that there is a scarcity of money, for all the parliament money, called breeches "(a fit stamp for the coyn of the rump) is wholly vanished, the king's proclamation and the Dutch "have swept it all away; and, of his now majesties coin, there appears but very little, so that in "effect, we have none left for common use, but a little old lean coyned money of the late three "former princes; and what supply is preparing for it my lords? I hear of none unless it be of "COPPER FARTHINGS, and this is the metal that is to VINDICATE, according to the inscription, "THE DOMINION OF THE FOUR SEAS." (*)

§ By Blondeau's warrant Nov. 3, 1662, to be engineer of the mint, he is to enjoy the benefits arising from his edging engines for 14 years, and no persons belonging to the mint were to be permitted to make use of them, "either in the coining of farthings of any base metal, or of any other small money whatever." and the same prohibition is also expresly enjoined in the indenture of Henry Slingsby Esq; 8 Oct. 1670.

(*) My lord Lucas his speech in the house of peers, Feb. 22, 1670-1. Middleburg, printed in the year 1673, 4to. p. 3.

have

have ſeen, is one of No. 1. p. 7, which has a ſmall neat cordon running round the middle of the edge over the lines. There is an inſcription round No. 21, but not perfect, which appears to have conſiſted of the king's name and titles; thoſe of MONETA INSTAURATOR, 1662, on No. 18, and ISTA FAMA PER ÆTHERA VOLAT on No. 19, and alſo on one of No. 2, p. 7, were not intended, we think, for common farthings, but rather as finiſhed proofs, or in the nature of the PIED FORTS in France,* as we apprehend they were propoſed to be ſtruck in copper, and are of a moderate weight; beſides, we have ſeen ſeveral of No. 18 only with the lines on them; the firſt common farthing with an inſcription being that of tin, 1684.

It is very probable that moſt of theſe pieces were ſtruck in conſequence of projects formed by different perſons, to obtain a patent for the ſole coining of them, but we have never been ſo fortunate as to meet with any of them before the year 1659, which were thoſe made by Violet, to the protector Richard Cromwell. No propoſals till Violet's 1659.

Violet had been ſome years petitioning to obtain 1100l which had been promiſed him for ſervice done the commonwealth, in getting the 300000l. which was on board the Sampſon and Salvador for them, and in conſideration of ſeveral loſſes he had ſuſtained; but not ſucceeding, he therefore petitioned Richard Cromwell, † after the death of his father, to have a patent for to coin FARTHING TOKENS for 31 years.

His propoſals were to coin 22 ſhillings in farthings out of 8 lb. avoirdupoiſe, of fine copper, each farthing to weigh half a quarter of an ounce, to be allowed a remedy of ſixpence under or over, for which liberty he propoſed to pay one ſhilling out of the ſaid 22 ſhillings, to be applied to the uſe of the maimed ſoldiers. To coin them at 2s. 9d. per lb.

And if the ſtate choſe to have farthings made of a ſmaller proportion, and yet more than as heavy again as the tradeſmens, he would then allow 5 ſhillings out of the ſaid 22 ſhillings, which he ſaid would bring in about 300l. per month, for ſeveral years. Theſe propoſals were not made in his own name, but in that of Edward Johnſon, junior, and others.

The protector Richard, in conſequence of this petition, iſſued out his warrant dated April 19, 1659, to the ſollicitor general, Sir William Ellis, Baronet, to prepare a book ready, to be ſigned by him, for the erecting an office for the ſole making and vending of a common farthing in England, Scotland, Ireland and Wales, for 31 years, in conſideration of one ſhilling in every 22 ſhillings, according to the propoſitions; with ſuch rules to be obſerved in relation to the ſtamps, figures and arms, as he or his ſucceſſor ſhould appoint. he is likewiſe ordered to attend the parliament with the ſaid petition and warrant, who are deſired to appoint ſuch rules, prohibitions and penalties, for the effectual and better management of this ſervice, the remedying all former abuſes, and preventing their being imported from beyond ſea, or any thing elſe they think proper for the better carrying on the ſame. Richard iſſues out a warrant in his favour.

The change of government which followed ſoon after, it is probable, prevented any thing farther being done in this affair; and, although Violet, after the reſtoration, ſtill continued to petition the king in relation to the gold and ſilver thread, exportation of bullion, &c. yet he makes not the leaſt mention of this project for farthings.

* One of Henry IV. 1607, has PERENNITATE GALLIÆ RESTITUTORES; and there are of theſe ſorts with EXEMPLUM PROBATI NUMISMATIS and EXEMPLAR PROBATÆ MONETÆ.

† Violet's true narrative of the proceedings in the court of admiraltie, 4to. p. 118, 119, 120, 121.

As the money of the commonwealth was current at the time these proposals were made, it is not improbable but that some of those above, as No. 3, 4, 6 or 7, might have been struck to accompany this petition.

Proposals by Pr. Rupert and ld. Henry Howard. 1668.

No other proposals have come to our knowledge after these, until the year 1668, when propositions were made to coin a common farthing, by prince Rupert and lord Henry Howard; and the next year others by Mr. Elias Palmer; § but we are ignorant what articles either of them consisted of, and therefore cannot determine whether they had any affinity to, or agreed with the patterns of 1665, or the farthing which took place by authority soon after.

Charles II. farthings and halfpence. 1672.

At last a copper farthing and halfpenny were made current, by a proclamation dated August 16, 1672, which were to pass in all payments, bargains and exchanges to be made under the value of sixpence, and no otherwise; and the making of tokens were strictly forbidden after the first of September following.

But this not having the desired effect, as the tokens still continued to be current, especially in places remote from London; therefore a second proclamation was published Oct. 17, 1673; and a third Dec. 12, 1674: by this last their currency is prolonged until Feb. 5. following; after which, if any person or corporation presumed to make or vend them, strict orders were to be given to prosecute, as it hindered the farthings from being dispersed in those parts.

Type. Legend.

These pieces have the king's head laureat looking to the right, contrary to those on his silver and gold money, where it is turned to the left; and the same circumstance is to be observed on those of his brothers. His bust is in armour, whereas on the silver there appears the top of the mantle, and on the gold the neck is bare; and this was always attended to in the following reigns, the only exceptions being the halfpenny of his brother, and the patterns of Queen Anne. The legend round it is CAROLUS A CAROLO. On the reverse is a woman sitting with a palm branch in her right hand, and a spear in her left, which is on a shield, with the united crosses of St. George and St. Andrew; the legend informs us it is BRITANNIA; in the exergue is the date of the year. All those we remember to have seen are 1671, 1672, 1673, 1674, 1675 and 1679 on the farthings; and only those of 1672, 1673 and 1675 on the halfpence.

Were coined by patent.

This appears to have been a coinage by patent, but we do not know the terms of it, nor to whom it was granted, only that it was of pure Swedish copper, and at the rate of 20 pence to the lb. weight, avoirdupoise; that his majesty advanced 1500l. to pay for copper blocks, which were delivered free from customs and excise; * and that the dyes were engraven by Rotier at one penny per lb. weight.

A project in 1680 to make tin farthings

About the year 1679 or 1680 it appears there was a project on foot to make them of tin, it being at that time cheaper than ever known to have been before; so that his majesty had reaped no advantage from his prerogative of præemption after 1666, which was used to be farmed for 12000l. per annum. †

§ May it please your Majesty. In obedience to your majestie's order of reference of 11th of March, 1667, we have considered the proposition of his highness prince Rupert and the Ld. Henry Howard, for making a general farthing; and in obedience of your majesties order of reference of the 13th of January, 1669, we have considered the proposal of Elias Palmer, for making such a farthing, and have heard the officers of your majesties mint upon both, and finding it to be a matter too great for our determination, we humbly submit the same to your majestie, with the several papers of the proposers and of your majesties officers of the mint thereupon.

Treasury chamber, 9th of August, 1669. Ashley, T. Clifford.

* Simon's Irish coins, append. No. 61. † Collins's plea for bringing in of Irish cattle, 4to. 1680, p. 13, 14. Ibid. salt and fishery, 4to. 1682, p. 155, 156.

In

In order to reſtore this branch of the royal revenue, endeavours were uſed to come to a compoſition with the miners of Cornwall, to take of all the tin yielded by the mines, or at leaſt 1200 tons per annum: but in the firſt place, the convocation could not come to ſuch an agreement without an act of parliament, which ſhould bind all particular miners to ſtand to ſuch contract as the convention ſhould make. And, ſecondly, the farmers would not make ſuch a bargain without covenanting with his majeſty to ſupply England, Ireland and the plantations, with TIN FARTHINGS at 16 pence a pound, that by the profit ariſing from thence they might be enabled to pay their rent.

But this deſign was oppoſed by the mint as a groſs cheat upon the nation. As firſt, that a metal might be made white, and harder than tin, of ſpelter, arſenick, regulus of antimony, &c. which, when worn, would not yield twopence a pound, and no pewterer durſt uſe it. Secondly, that theſe farthings might be coined with a hammer, mold or vice; and counterfeited by any tinker, plumber, ſmith, glazier, tinman, watchmaker, &c. Thirdly, a query being put to the farmers; whether they would change all that were brought to them, good or bad, made by themſelves or others; and if they agreed to that, who ſhould allow the country and city brewers the charge in ſending them to London, in drays and waggons with tellers. Both which being refuſed by them, it was thence infered, that if the tin farthings were eſtabliſhed, his majeſty muſt receive his revenue of exciſe, and the duke of York his poſtage in them; thereſore this ruined the project for the preſent.

In the laſt year of this king, propoſals were made to the commiſſioners of the treaſury, by the commiſſioners of the mint, to coin a halfpenny and farthing of tin upon his majeſties own account, by authority from his majeſty under the great ſeal of England; to be made of the weight of thoſe of copper, being about 20 pence per pound, exactly ſtamped, and a motto to be put about their edge; the charge of making, coining and iſſuing the ſame, about 4 pence per pound, and one lb. weight of tin about 8 pence; in all about 12 pence per lb. weight; ſo that if coined at 20 pence, there would ariſe a profit of about forty per cent. *Propoſals for tin farthings from the mint.*

This being reported to his majeſty in council at Hampton-Court, May 28, 1684, was approved of by him; and Sir Robert Sawyer, attorney general, was ordered to prepare a warrant for his majeſties royal ſignature, to paſs the great ſeal of England; containing a commiſſion and full authority to the commiſſioners of his majeſties mint to make them, according to the ſaid report, during his majeſties pleaſure; the attorney general to inſert all ſuch clauſes, proviſions and non obſtantes in the ſaid commiſſion as are uſual in ſuch caſes. *Coinage of tin farthings 1684.*

This coinage conſiſted of no other ſort but farthings, which did not differ from thoſe of the copper, neither in type or legend; but they have a ſtud of copper ſtruck through the center of them, and on their edge NUMMORUM FAMULUS 1684, both which methods were taken to render the counterfeiting of them more difficult, as we have already obſerved; however, they were counterfeited in great numbers. *Type. Legend.*

This coinage conſiſted of farthings as before, to which halfpence alſo were now added, with the ſame ſtud of copper through them, and inſcription on their edge; the uſual dates on which are 1685 on the farthing, and 1687 on that of the halfpenny. We have before obſerved, that his head on theſe pieces ſtands the contrary way to that on his gold and ſilver money, but after him *Tin farthings of James II.*

 they

they look the ſame way upon thoſe of gold, ſilver and copper. The legend round it is JACOBUS SECUNDUS.

This king granted a patent ‡ to Thomas Neale, * Hoare and Charles Duncombe, Eſqrs; who were allowed 20 pence per lb. weight for coining and milling them in the Tower, and to pay 40l. per cent. out of the profits, to the king; being the ſame terms as thoſe of his brothers.

Tin farthings of William and Mary. In the beginning of the reign of William and Mary a commiſſion, dated Oct. 12, 1689, † was granted to Charles Godolphin, James Hoare and Andrew Corbet, Eſq; for the coining tin farthings; and by a warrant from the treaſury, dated April 18, 1691, it appears that they had under them a treaſurer at 120l. per annum, two engravers ‖ at 100l. each, a ſurveyor of the meltings at 60l. and three tellers at 40l. per ann. each.

Type. Legend. Theſe pieces have on one ſide both their heads, regarding the left, inſcribed GULIELMUS ET MARIA; the reverſe as before, with the date in the exergue, as well as on the edge upon the farthings, which are 1690, 1691 and 1692: the halfpence generally have it only on the edge; the only one we have ſeen with it in the exergue being of 1689, which we think is rare, and a few of 1691.

Quantity of tin Money coined. Theſe tin farthings and halfpence continued to be coined till the year 1692, in which year ſeveral propoſals were made to coin them of a different metal again; and we learn from one of thoſe papers, that there had been coined in this metal, between March 1684 and January 1692, the quantity of 344 ton, amounting to 65929l. 15s. 9d. which is very near 21d. per lb. weight; it is alſo ſaid, that tin was 65l. per ton (or near 7d. per lb.) and 344 ton; at that rate is 21960l. being not one fourth of the coinage duty, which we have juſt now ſeen was eſtimated at about 12000l. per annum.

Allowance for circulation. We are likewiſe informed in the ſame papers, that a propoſal had been made in May 1691, to have ſent theſe pieces into different parts of England at his majeſties expence, and that it would not have amounted to one third of the 10 per cent. which was allowed to circulate them, and which made a great clamour.

Propoſals for a new coinage. 1692. One of theſe propoſals, dated Auguſt 3, 1692, was firſt, to coin theſe pieces of tin mixed with copper, which would be expenſive in working, and was to have different letters on each ſide and on the edge, from the former. Secondly, it was deſired, that a proclamation might be iſſued to call in the old ones within ſix months, to the farthing-office to be exchanged for new ones, but not in leſs ſums than 5s. Thirdly, the propoſers to be appointed commiſſioners to manage the coinage at 300l. per annum; and if any one of the commiſſioners died in the 9 years this patent was to laſt, then another to be choſen by the remaining commiſſioners. Fourthly, as an inducement to grant the patent, the propoſers to lend the government 12000l. of which they deſire 2000l. might be left with them to enable them to put it in execution. Fifthly, no other to be coined till they were repaid the 12000l. There is no name to this paper, but another to the ſame purpoſe has that of John Hall for the petitioner, but on the back is put Mr. Germain's propoſals. There was alſo another made by Mr. Slaney, but all of them without effect.

‡ Journals of the houſe of commons, vol. 11, p. 753.
† MSS. Britiſh Muſeum, No. 6886, p. 94.
‖ George Bowers was firſt employed from Nov. 1, 1689, for 4 months, at 150l. per ann. and upon his death, Henry Harris and James Roetier.

In

In the beginning of the following year 1693, Andrew Corbet, Esq; endeavoured to get a patent for coining farthings and halfpence of copper, and the members of the county of Cornwall petitioned against the granting of it; whereupon the commissioners of the treasury, by an order dated March 9, 1692, direct the officers of the mint to consider whether the copper or tin farthings, then proposed to be made might most easily be counterfeited, and with most advantage to the counterfeiters; their answer we have never seen, but Mr. Corbet obtained his patent, § with power of making copper farthings for the term of 9 years from Lady day, 1693, under the yearly rent of 1000l.

Mr. Corbet gets a patent to coin copper for 9 years.

In a paper from the mint, dated May 12, 1693, the purport of which was to shew the profit to be made by this patent, we are informed, that there was to be coined 780 ton in the 9 years; that is, 120 ton per annum, for the first four years, and 60 tons per annum during the other five years; but they suppose that only 700 tons could be uttered, and upon that quantity raise the following calculation.

Profit arising there from.

700 tons, at 24d. or 2s. per lb. or 224l. per ton, amount to, in coin,		£156800
Patentee's charges.		
1st. 700 ton, at 112l. per ton, is	78400	
2d. Charges of coining, &c. at 40l. per ton	28000	
3d. Incidents, Rent, &c. at 7l. per ton	4900	
4th. Exchanging tin farthings	10000	
5th. To circulate them at 5 per Ct. or 12l. per ton	8400	
6th. Paid to the government 1000l. per annum	9000	138700
Profit remaining to the patentee in 9 years		£18100

In a representation made by Mr. Neale, master of the mint, dated June 9, 1693, he says, that he wanted presence of mind when he agreed that to make 24d. to the lb. and allow 1000l. per annum, was the same as his proposal to coin them at only 21d. per lb. without that allowance; whereas 3d. per lb. the difference, on 780 tons is 21840l. but 1000 per annum for 9 years, or 9000l. is what they give, and the difference or 12840l. is what they gain by it.

Mr. Neale's representation.

Whether it was in consequence of these two last papers, or from any other cause, we cannot determine, but we find that Mr. Corbet did not long enjoy his patent; for the next year a grant ¶ was made unto Sir John Herne and others, * of the licence and authority of making farthings and halfpence of copper for 7 years, from midsummer 1694; paying therefore to a comptroller to be appointed by his majesty (which appears to have been Mr. Corbet) 200l. per ann. and changing all the tin farthings and halfpence.

Sir John Herne's patent for 7 years, 1694.

The principal terms of this patent were to coin 700 tons in 7 years, to make 21d. to 1 lb. weight, with a remedy of two farthings which were to be of the best English copper, rolled and milled; and to exchange 200l. per week of tin farthings for copper farthings, to any person that should bring them, and should melt down the same within fourteen days.

Conditions of the patent

* We learn from a printed sheet entitled "the case of several tradesmen and dealers in and about the city of London on behalf of themselves and their country chapmen, aggrieved by the patentees of the copper farthings; humbly offered to the consideration of the honourable house of commons in parliament assembled." that these other persons were Abel Slaney and Daniel Barton, who bid more for the patent than the copper company, who were endeavouring to procure one at the same time, for which reason they were joined by the copper miners each bearing their own charges. ‡

§ Journals of the house of commons, vol. 13, p. 195. ¶ Ibid. p. 108. ‡ Ibid. vol, 11, p. 549.

But

William III. Complaints againſt the patentees, 1696.

But great complaints were made againſt the patentees, † as that they did not make their farthings of good copper, but what was ¼ part worſe; neither were they rolled and cutt but caſt; that they were made too light, or after the rate of 26 pence and many 28 pence to the lb. weight; by which they would gain 45000l. if they coined the whole quantity of 700 tons.

That they refuſed to exchange the tin farthings brought to them, but wearied out the bringers with tedious delays, employing their ſervants to buy up great quantities at 8s. and 10s. for a pound Sterling; and have permitted ſuch only as belonged to themſelves or their ſervants to be exchanged; that in order to colour their fraud with ſome ſhew of public juſtice, they had ordered that every perſon having any quantities, ſhould enter their name and quantities in their office, promiſing to exchange thoſe perſons firſt who ſtood prior in their books; but that they had put many hundred ſham names there, in order to abuſe ſuch perſons who ſhould inſpect their books, with a beliefe that there were greater quantities to be exchanged than there was in reality; and had made uſe of as great frauds alſo to prevent melting them down, and groſly deceived the king's comptroller, whoſe duty it was to ſee the ſame done; and that they had made agreements in writing to have 20 and 30 per cent. for exchanging.

Proceedings in the houſe of commons upon it.

Theſe complaints being laid before the houſe of commons it was reſolved, Jan. 30, 1695-6, that a committee be appointed to examine into the matter of them, and to report the ſame with their opinion thereon to the houſe; and on the 20 Feb. it was ordered, that the report be made in a full houſe; which report being made it was reſolved, April 6, that the patentees had made the farthings and halfpence of good copper according to the direction of their patent; that they had delivered them out for gold and current ſilver money at the common value, without farther recompence; and that they had exchanged 200l. a week of tin farthings and halfpence, for 200l. of the like value in copper farthings and halfpence, in purſuance to their patent. ‡

It appeared from this report that the patentees had bound their ſervants in bonds of 200l. a piece, not to buy any tin halfpence and farthings, or make any advantage by changing them, that the copper was furniſhed by the copper company, and was near as fine as Swediſh copper, and would not bear a worſe alloy than as the patentees received it; that if it was not fine it would not roll, that thoſe that were caſt were as fine and as heavy and better coloured, than thoſe that were rolled, and coſt the patentees 5 pence a pound ⸸ making as well as them; it likewiſe appeared that theſe complaints were managed by Mr. Lock, Mr, Laurence and others.

Coined in too great quantities.

We hear no more of this matter for about two years, when great clamours were again made againſt them on account of the great numbers which had been coined, and the badneſs of the copper, which were laid before the parliament.

Complaints again laid before the parliament, 1698.

A petition of the grocers, cheeſemongers, mealmen, bakers, victuallers, market-people, and retailers of the borough of Southwark, was preſented to the houſe * and read; ſetting forth that the patentees refuſed to change white farthings, that they have coined extravagant quantities of copper halfpence and farthings,

⸸ Out of this the graving of the dyes coſt no more than a farthing per lb. weight, inſtead of one penny as at firſt, the patentees having been offered to have them done at that price by ſome foreign engravers.

† Caſe of ſeveral tradeſmen, &c. aggreived by the patentees of the copper farthings.

‡ Journals of the houſe of commons, vol. 11, p. 388, 458, 510, 543, 549. * Ibid. vol. 12, p. 136.

which

which were become a greater clog than the white farthings, and pray a stop to the copper coinage. There were other petitions to the same purpose afterwards from Ware, Bedford, St. Botolph's Aldgate, East-Smithfield, Whitechapel, St. Giles, Great Marlow in Bucks, Litchfield, St. Botolph without Bishopsgate (who say the patentees allow 4 per cent. to any person who would take them) Coventry, Tamworth, Warwick and Stamford.*

All which petitions being referred to a committee, Mr. Manley reported † that the committee do find, that the patentees for coining copper halfpence and farthings were empowered by his majesties letters patents, bearing date June 24, 1694, to coin 700 tons of English copper in seven years, and that the same patentees had already coined 460 ton; but there being a great glut in several parts of the kingdom, especially in and about London, of halfpence and farthings; resolved that it was the opinion of the committee, that the execution of the patent be suspended for 6 months, which on the second reading was altered to 12 months, and the house agreeing with the committee therein, ordered that a bill be brought in upon the said resolution, and Mr. Lowndes was ordered to bring in the bill; upon the second reading of which it was resolved,‡ that it be an instruction to the said committee that they do provide, that when halfpence and farthings should be coined again, that the same be at the true value, except the charge of coinage.

Which clause being read a second time, the same was amended; and was, that after the 24th of June, 1699, it shall not be lawfull for any persons to coin any farthings or halfpence but of fine English copper, and of the real value of what the same shall be taken for in payment, with allowance only for coining at five pence per lb. weight. ‖ The question being put it passed in the negative, ordered that the bill be engrossed. The engrossed bill being read a third time, ordered that the bill do pass; and that it be entituled, An act to stop the coinage of farthings and halfpence for one year.

By this act it was 5l. penalty for every lb. weight that should be coined within the limited time, one half of which to go to the informer, and the patentees are freed from the obligation of changing the tin money during the same time. *An act 10. W. III. to stop the coinage for one year.*

In the next session of parliament a bill was brought in to prevent the patentees coining for one year longer (or from 24 June 1699 to 24 June, 1700) which bill was read three times, ordered to pass and be sent up to the house of lords; after which we hear no more of it.

The contractors at the same time petitioning the house that they might be permitted to perform their contract, or have reliefe given them for the losses they shall sustain. It was ordered that they should be heard before the said committee; who having heard them, Mr. Lowther was directed to move the house that their accounts might be stated and made up, and if it appeared that they were loosers by their contract, a compensation to be made them. An engrossed clause offered as a ryder that their accounts should be settled by the lords of the treasury, passed in the negative. § *Endeavours to continue the prohibition another year, 1699.*

The next year another bill was brought into the house, to put a stop to any farther coinage of halfpence and farthings, which was twice read ¶ and then dropt, as we think, there being no farther mention of it. *Another attempt. 1700.*

* Ibid. p. 154, 160, 167, 180, 194, 196, 208, 238, 262. † Ib. p. 267. ‡ Ib. p. 273. ‖ Ib. p. 278, 283, 324. § Ib. p. 585, 592, 615, 619, 640, 651. ¶ Ib. vol. 13, p. 126, 130, 131, 141.

The farthings and halfpence we generally meet with of William and Mary are all dated 1694, but there are a very few of them, and those only farthings, dated 1692, and 1693; there are of both sorts of William the Third every year after, as 1695, 1696, 1697, 1698, 1699, 1700 and 1701; some in the exergue, as had been usual, and others at the end of the legend.

Patterns for farthings and halfpence of W. and M. No. 1, 2, 3, pl. 8.

There was also a pattern piece for a farthing of William and Mary which has his head in profile to the left on one side, inscribed GULIELMUS III. DEI GRATIA, and on the reverse the head of the queen inscribed MARIA II. DEI GRATIA. There is also a halfpenny of the same sort, and another wherein the busts both of the king and queen are larger, and inscribed GULIELMUS REX and MARIA REGINA. The farthing we have seen in silver but never the halfpenny.

Of Queen Anne.

There could be no want of this sort of money during the reign of queen Anne, as there had been such large quantities coined under the last patent. However, towards the close of her reign, we find several patterns for farthings and halfpence were engraved; and it is probable, at the instance of some person suing for another patent: but of this we are not certain.

Farthings. No. 5, 8, 10, 12, pl. 8.

Of these pattern pieces we have seen four different ones for farthings; which have the queen's head on one side, with her hair adorned with pearls and her breast covered, as on her other money: three of them are inscribed ANNA DEI GRATIA, and the other ANNA AUGUSTA. On the reverse of No. 5 and 8 is the figure of Britannia as usual, the usual legend and the date; but on No. 5, it is in the inscription, and on No. 8 in the exergue: No. 5 is broader than No. 8, and has a very neat grained and dotted edge; on No. 10 Britannia is seated under a sort of portal or arch; the figure of peace in a car appears on No. 12, inscribed PAX MISSA PER ORBEM, and was the design and thought of the late Mr. Sadler.

Halfpennies. No. 4, 6, 7, 9.

There are four halfpennies which have all the same head and inscription, shewing no pearls on her hair as the farthing, and a different inscription from that, being ANNA D. G. MAG. BR. FR. ET HIB. REG. on the reverses of No. 4 and 6 is the figure of Britannia with a crown over her, without any legend, holding a branch of laurel in the first, and in the other a rose and thistle on the same branch; No. 7 and 9 have only the said branch with the rose and thistle, but with different leaves. We sometimes meet with the reverses of No. 4 or 6 on one side, and those of No. 7 or 9 on the other; but they must be accidental or pieces de plaisir, and not intended as patterns: and the same may be said of No. 11 with her head on both sides, as it is probable a reverse was never made to it, and therefore her head put on both sides, which is in the same taste with that on the farthings, and the same legend of ANNA AUGUSTA; it sometimes has an inscription upon its edge ANNO REGNI DUODECIM.

No. 11

The dyes for all those pieces were engraved by Mr. Croker, and those of the halfpence afterwards came into the hands of Mr. Bush of the office of ordnance in the Tower, who had several of them struck off, until Mr. Arundel by warrant, ordered the dyes to be destroyed.

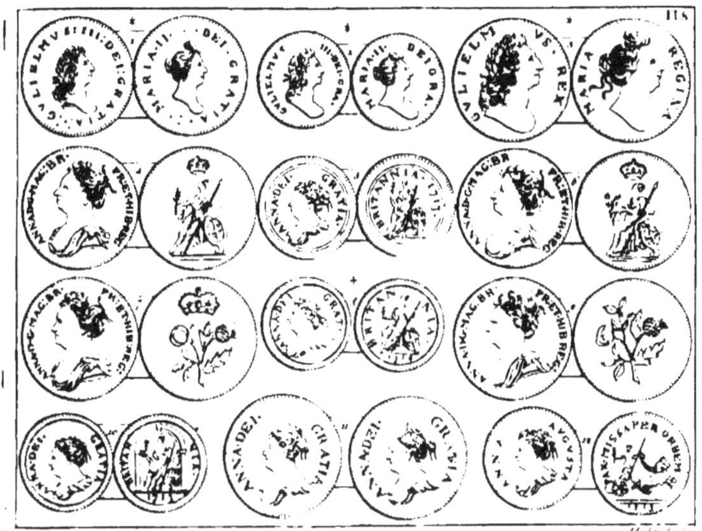

* Besides these pieces of Will. and Mary, we have seen a pattern halfpenny like the common one, but finer work, especially the Britannia; also a tin one, with the copper in the center radiated.

† This is the farthing usually met with of this queen, and is common enough, although many believe there were only 3 or 4 of them struck; but No. 10 and 12 are very scarce, especially the last.

After the troubles which disturbed the beginning of the reign of George the first, were blown over, or in the year 1717, the subject of the copper money was again taken into consideration; and they proceeded to coin again in the Tower, and we suspect that it was by warrant as in the following reign, but are not certain. These were made lighter than those of king Williams, there being now 28 pence to one lb. Avoirdupoize instead of 21 pence, which was the number before; the Bars or Fillets were delivered into the mint at 18 pence pr. lb; * and there appears to have been coined to the amount of 46000 £ sterl. † or about 213½ tons; and these are all the particulars we have been able to come at in relation to this coinage. George I. 1717.

There are both ½ pence and farthings of every year from 1717 to 1724 inclusive; but we have met with none after. Those of 1717 and 1718 are remarkably small and thick, and are frequently called by the name of dumps.

Under the reign of George the second we are at more certainty than before, that they were first coined by a warrant under the sign manual of queen Caroline when guardian of the realm, dated July 21, 1729, which was afterwards confirmed and continued by another warrant of Aug. 17, 1738. George II. 1729. coined by Warrant.

By these warrants there were to be 46 halfpence and 92 farthings cut out of 1 pound Avoirdupoize, the copper at such a rate and in such quantities as should the Substance of the Warrant

N

* Leake p. 415.

† Defence of the conduct of the people of Ireland in their unanimous refusal of Wood's copper money, p. 12.

be directed by the commissioners of the treasury; 4½ pence per lb. was allowed for bearing and sustaining all manner of waste, provision, necessaries, &c.; the master and worker to accompt annually before the auditor, and to be answerable to his majesty for the profits thereof above the charges; the auditor to have the same power as in auditing the accompts of the gold and silver; the king's clerk to be appointed by his majesty or the treasury to make out a roll upon oath of the weight and price of every parcel of new money coined and delivered from time to time from the moniers to the master; also to examine and sign all bills of charges, repairs, &c. and all sums of money paid for copper imported; for which service he was to receive 20 Shillings pr. ton of all the money coined.

Substance of the Contract with the English Cop. Comp. The lords of the treasury, in consequence of the power given them by these warrants, have impowered the masters of the mint to enter into contract with the governor and company of the copper miners of England for copper, which they have accordingly done; the first quantity of which was for 100 tons, and all the succeeding ones have been for 200 tons each; which copper was to be melted and refined with pit coal from ore, that was to be of the produce of Great Britain, Ireland or the Plantations, an affidavit of which to be made at each delivery, they were to be delivered in bars or fillets nealed of such a fineness as to spread thin under the hammer when heated red hot without cracking, and of such a width and thickness, that 46 halfpence and 92 farthings (without erring in excess or defect above the 40 part of a lb. wt.) were to make 1 lb. Avoirdup. to be supplied with cutters from the mint, the quantity of fillets to be sufficient to coin 180 tons of halfpence and 20 tons of farthings; the master was to pay half the value at each delivery at the rate of 15¼ pence pr. lb.; the other half to be paid for after the blancs have been cut out, in money, sciffell and brokage, reckoning the sciffell and brokage at the same price as the copper imported into the mint. The company oblige themselves to deliver 2 tons per week, until the demand from the public for halfpence and farthings shall cease, and after having had one months notice from the master in writing, they are not to send any more to the mint; and if upon trial it is found, that the copper does not answer in fineness, or that the excess or defect in one lb. is more than the 40th part, then they were obliged to take it away at their own expence.

Counterfeited in great Numbers. The counterfeiting and casting of this sort of money had been long carried on, and complaints had been frequently made against it, which occasioned an act of parliament to be made in 1741, 16 G. 2, c. 28, in which coiners and counterfeiters, when discovered, were to suffer 2 months imprisonment, and to find sureties for their good behaviour for 2 years more; and a reward of 10l. was to be paid upon their conviction. But the practice still continuing, a proclamation was published July 12, 1751, to enforce the said act. However, this did not stop the evil, so that in the beginning of the year 1753 it was computed, that near ½ (or ⅔) of the current copper money were counterfeits, and a resolution was taken by several persons absolutely to refuse taking of them; and about a twelvemonth afterwards a petition and representation was made to the lords of the treasury by several bakers, butchers and other dealers in provision and the necessaries of life, praying a suspension of the copper coinage for a few years, and that some laws might be enacted and enforced to prevent its being counterfeited; both of which were sent down to the officers of the mint, ordering likewise a stoppage to be put to the coinage, which was accordingly done, and the company ordered to send no more fillets after one month; nor has any more halfpence been made since but from those fillets.

Coinage stopped.

Some

Some time after a proposal was made to call in and recoin all the copper money; and the beginning of the year 1755 the lords of the treasury laid before his majesty in council a report from the mint on this subject, together with their opinion, that it would greatly prevent the counterfeiting the same, if the genuine halfpence and farthings were ordered to be current at 6 and 3 to a penny; but as to the calling in the copper coin, as it would be attended with many inconveniencies and a very great expence, their lordships could not advise his majesty to give any orders in relation thereto.

But this reduction was opposed, and another representation and petition laid before the privy council and several of his majesty's dutiful and loyal subjects, loaded with copper money (whose chairman was John Whalley) together with a scheme, shewing how the re-coinage might take place at the rate of 16 pence per lb. wt. avoir, and to oblige all those possessed of the old to bring it to the mint, where they were to receive 21 pence per lb. for it; therefore they would lose 3 pence per lb. and the public 10 pence (1 lb. being estimated at 11 pence) they supposed, that ⅓ might be brought in as above, and the other ⅔ exchanged for new coin at 16 pence per lb; therefore the subject in this case would lose ⅓ or 4 pence per lbwt., and the government 5 pence; and as the total currency is by them supposed to be 1800 tons, the loss sustained by the publick will be 126000£, besides 4000 more expended in coining; and the loss to individuals would be 92400£ Sterling, and the whole loss sustained 222400£. However, the matter rested here; nor can we find any thing more was done in relation thereto.

The laws relating to coining and counterfeiting were also looked into, a difficult point being now started, whether the copper coin was to be considered strictly as current money, and to be protected as such, or whether it was not only so to a special purpose? the latter of which opinions does appear to have obtained; for tho' the Stat. 16 *G.* 2. cap. 28. inflicts punishment in several degrees on utterers of any *false and counterfeit money*, yet it was construed not to extend to the uttering of counterfeit halfpence or farthings.

Upon the whole, it has been seen in the prosecution of this work, that such coins as those of farthings and halfpence are absolutely necessary, and cannot be dispensed with, and that copper is the properest metal they can be made of, and the quantities such as the wants and occasions of the publick may require; but the misfortune has been, that the publick utility has scarcely ever been attended to; that the very great profits left to the patentees have been an inducement to them to utter such quantities of them as to become a great burthen on the publick; and at present the price of 1 lbwt. of copper before coining being but 10 pence, and when coined current for 23 pence, or more than double its first value, is the cause of the great numbers of counterfeits lately uttered; whereas in several of the neighbouring kingdoms and states * 1 lbwt. avoir. appears to be coined into no more than 18 pence, or 5 pence per lb. less than here in England.

* In France 20 Sols to a Markwt. *Prix de Monnoies de France*, 4to. *Paris* 1736, p. 73. In Spain 51 Quartos to 1 lbwt. *Cavallero Breve Cotejo y Valance de las Pesas y medidas de varias Naciones*, 4to. *Mad.* 1731, p. 190.

P. S. To the list of Town pieces in page 13 should be added Kidwelly and Kendal.

An

An Account of the particular Distribution of the Allowance for coining one ton of copper.

The Master of the Mint is allowed 4½*d.* per lbwt. for coinage, &c. per ton		£ 42: 00: 00
Out of which he pays		
To the Moneyers for coining, per lbwt. 2*d.*, which is per ton		18: 13: 4
To them for barrelling	¾	7: 00: 0
To the Graver per lbwt.	¼	2: 06: 8
To the Die Forger	¼	2: 06: 8
He allows the Deputy Warden per ton		16: 0
His own Deputy per ton		1: 00: 0
His Assayer per ton		5: 0
The Weigher of the Copper per ton		5: 0
For mixing to the Clerk of the Irons		5: 0
The Master's Profit per ton		9: 02: 4
		£ 42

One Ton of Copper Halfpence, which per hdwt. is 1 £. 10*s.* 6*d.* on an Average		210: 05: 0
One Ton of Fillets out of which the Halfpence are cut, at 1*s.* 3¼*d.* per lbwt.	£ 147	
Charge of Coinage, as above	42	
To the King's Clerk for this Coinage	1	
To the Purchasers	3: 16: 8	
		193: 16: 8
Profit to the Crown per ton		16: 8: 4

As of late Years the Fillets have been more equally sized, and produced more Halfpence nearer to the Standard than formerly, this Profit for 6 Years to Christmas 1750 was upon an Average to the Crown per ton £ 22: 6: 0

An Account of the copper monies coined between Nov. 20, 1729, and Dec. 23, 1753, as it appears from the particular Rolls made up for the Auditors, and sworn before the Barons of the Exchequer.

		Tons	hd.	qr.	£.	s.	d.
Coined between 20th Nov. 1729, and 1st Jan.	1732	100	9		21,392	14	6
between 2d Jan. 1732-3, and 23d May	1737	171	12		36,257	14	
between 23d May 1737, and 24th June	1738	28	8		6,014	7	7½
between 24th June 1738, and 24th June	1739	34	13		7,322	6	
between 24th June 1739, and 31st Dec.	1739	27	7		5,773	3	
to do.	1740	42	6		8,852	4	4
to do.	1741	8	12		1,824	4	8
to do.	1742	8	17		1,850	6	4
to do.	1743	36	6		7,707	0	8
to do.	1744	27	19		6,007	4	
to do.	1745	30	18		6,600	14	8
to do.	1746	34	18		7,410	6	6½
to do.	1747	42	16		9,082	2	8
to do.	1748	28	10		6,044	3	4
to do.	1749	42	14		9,049	13	
to do.	1750	22	7	2	4,705	18	2
to do.	1751	32	4	2	6,800	13	
to do.	1752	37	18	2	8,020	11	4
to do.	1753	40	6		8,544	14	8
		799	1	2	169,260	2	6
		£.	s.	d.			
Price of Fillets at 1*s.* 3¼*d.* per lbwt.		117,464	0	6			
Coinage at 4½*d.* per lbwt.		33,561	3				
King's Clerk's All. 20*s.* per ton		799	1	6			
					151,824	5	
				Profit to the Crown	17,435	17	6

Except that out of this Profit some small Expences, such as Royal Sign Manuals, Treasury Warrants, and the Fees of passing the Accounts of this Coinage, &c. are to be deducted, the Amount of which will appear by the several Accounts of the Masters of the Mint.

Mint-Office, Jan. 19th, 1754. ANT. POLLET, King's Clerk for the Copper Coinage.

During the next half year, or till June 1754, there was coined more 19 tons 13 hd. 3 qr. 25¼ lb; and since the accession of his present majesty, in 1762, 10 to. 8 hd. 2 qr., and in 1763, 7 to. 5 hd. 3 qr. in farthings, from the dies of his late majesty of 1754, no die of copper money for his present majesty having yet been sunk.

APPENDIX.

NUMBER I.

Harl. MSS. Brit. Muſe. No 698, p. 117.

WHEREAS in the beginninge of our reigne, to the greate honour and profytt of us and all our people, we did reſtore and reduce the moneys of our realme from droſſe and baſe matter unto fyne gould and fyne ſilver, which by God's ſavor we entend to contynue and maynteyn; yet becauſe the rate and diviſion of our ſilver money is ſuche, and as the preſent tyme requiereth, cannot well be altered, as that with any convenyencye any ſmaller money maye be made thereof than a penny or threefarthinge; nevertheleſs we have been often informed, and doo perceyve what greate neceſſytie our lovinge ſubjects have of ſmaller moneys, halfpence and farthings, and cheifly what loſſe and hendraunce the poor ſorte doo ſuſteyne by the lacke thereof, whereof we have pytifull confyderation, and bendynge ourſelfe to the remedy of the ſame, diverſe deviſes have been tendered to us and our previe councell, as well ſhewing meanes howe the ſame ſmall moneys might be made both fayer in ſhewe and ſufiycyent in quantitie; as alſo complaninge of a longe contynued and yet a very intollerable and arrogant diſorder uſed by private perſons in makinge of tokens of leade and tynne, and generally coyned and put out inſtead of ſuch ſmalle monys by grocers, vintners, chandlers and alehouſe-keepers, and diverſe other perſons, therein manyfeſtly derogatinge from our princelye honour and royale dignytie, which complaint we have conſidered as very juſte and reſonable; but becauſe the devyces offered therewith have all tendyd to the breach of the fyne ſtanderd of our coyne in ſuch ſmall moneys ſo required and wanted, have a mixture for the ſame, of courſe and baſe aleaye, to the ſlander and diſcredit of our fyne ſilver moneys. Now being we have rejected all the ſame devices, and yet waying with ourſelves the greate diſorder uſed in the ſayde tokens, and howe that our ſayde ſubjects have greate loſſe, and no manner of profytable eaſe thereby, whileſt they ſerve not in anywiſe to be utterred or payde agayne but only at that ſhoppe or place where they were firſt receved. Therefore we doo, by theſe preſents, ſtreightly forbid and command that none of the ſayde former tokens, or any ſuch like of what deviſe or invention ſoever from or after the feaſt of all Saints nexte cominge, ſhall be made or uſed without our ſpecyall warrent and comyſſion in that behalfe, upon payne that the perſon or perſons makinge or uſinge the ſame ſhall ſuffer impriſonmente of their bodies by the ſpace of one whole year; and ſhall moreover paye ſuch fyne to our uſe as ſhall be ſettled by our previe councell in the ſtar chamber at Weſtminſter. And foraſmuch as upon great deliberation we well perceyve that of neceſſitie our ſaid ſubjects muſt either have halfpence and farthings, or elſe tokens to ſupplie the ſted thereof; and becauſe that ſuch ſmall moneys cannot be made of the fyne ſilver of our moneys whilſt the ſame are at 5s the oz: but that they will be ſo ſmall as that they can neither be well kept or uſed in payment. Wherefore, for the eaſe of our ſayde ſubjects, and to ſerve their neceſſitie in this caſe, we have taken order that by our authoritie there ſhall be pledges or tokens made of pure and fyne copper of halfpence and farthings, whereof every *pledge of an halfpenny* ſhall waie 24 gr. and that of the farthing 12 gr.. In the making thereof we entend to employ ſuche coſte and charge as that anye so evill disposed shall hardly attayne to counterfayte the same; and yet more suerly to avoyde such counterfaiting, we not only in that respect, and not otherwise, do as well rate and value by authority hereof every of the saide pledges of xxiiii gr. in weit to passe and be current as aforesaid, in place and sted of an halfpenny throughout all our realme and domynions, to and amongst all persons whatsoever; and likewise every of the sayde pledges of xii gr. in weit to passe and be current as aforesaide, in place and sted of a farthinge. As also, do previledge all and every of the sayde pledges so by our authoritie and comyssion to be made with the name of our coyne, and so to passe and be current from one to another amongeste all persons throughout all our realmes and domynions, from and after the saide feast of all saints next comynge; and doo streightly charge and comande all our loving subjects, and all other persons whatsoever from thenceforth to take and receyve the saide several pledges for their several values set as aforesaide, upon payne of our high displeasure, and suche further punishment as we by the lawes of our realme maye impose upon them if they offende in that behalfe: provided alwaies, and yett our pleasure is, and by these presents we doo expresly commande, that after the first deliverie of the saide pledges, any of the same shall not be used in any payment whereas the saide payment shall exceed xx s. of our current money. And that in any such payment being xx s. as aforesaide, or under, there shall not be above one grote in value of the pledges aforesaide. And for the further ease and use of our said loving subjects, and for the preservation of all our moneys of gold and silver, truly and uprightly to their standerd, whereof they are nowe appointed to be by the ordinances by us made in our mynte; and to remove all occasyons which might in anywise be to the alteration thereof, we will presently take order that there shall be coined suche a competent nomber of pence of the fyne standard of our saide silver monies as to us shall seem mete. And we will also, before the saide feast of all saintes, appoint especyal workmen which shall make so many only of the saide pledges as we shall think necessarie to the use of our people; and will also appoint our special officer to be resyant in some notorious place to be assigned to that purpose in the citie of London, which there shall be redy at all tymes, from and after the said feaste of all saintes, to make exchange to all our loving subjects for other, delivering to every man which shall have need thereof, two parts of his payment in the saide silver pence, and a third parte of the pledges aforesaide, according to suche somme as any person or persons shall be disposed to exchange in that behalfe; for we will take such present order herein, that no greater quantitie shall be made of the pledges aforesaide then shall be barely necessarie for the ease and use of our said loveing subjects. Neither have we devised the same for any other entent, but that whilst we doo abandon and take away these former tokens which without prejudice of our royale estate and dignitie we may not longer endure. That our loveing subjects by our warrant and comission for the common ease, and much more benefit of them all, might in sted thereof have farr more convenient pledge universally payable in all petyt payments and receytes, and specyally in chaunging of threepences, threehalfpences and such like, in all places throughout all our realms and domynions.

Given &c.

To the mayor and Aldermen of Bristol for the time being.

Sir Julius Cæsar's MS. p. 102.

No. II. Whereas we are credibly informed of divers persons within that citie of Bristol that sell and utter small wares; and of themselves, without any manner of authority, do frame and stamp in lead and brasse, certain farthing tokens of sundry sortes and making, uttering them to their private use in exchange of monies in their several trades and occupations, which many times are refused to be accepted againe by those who first utter the same, whereby many inconveniencies do growe to the poor and otherwise. We have therefore thought good to require you forthwith, by authoritie hereof, to call in all the said tokens so stamped by them, and to take order, that all such persons who have without authority framed and stamped anie tokens, be from henceforth restrained by you, and in our names streightlie charged and required to chaunge the same for some current money, to the value they were first

first uttered by them, and none to make the same without special licence from you the maior, and wherein you shall take special care, that the former abuses be duly reformed for requiring your extraordinary care hereof. wee &c.

Dated the xiith. of May 1594

Present the

Lord Arch B. of Cant.	Ld. Chamberlain.
Ld. Keeper	Ld. Buckhurst,
Ld. Ther.	Sir Ro. Cecil.
Ld. Admiral.	Sir Jo. Wolley

Concordat cum regist.
John Corbet.

To the King's most excellent majesty. The humble petition of Thomas Moze, one of the ordinary yeomen of your majestie's chamber, and of William Edgely, groom of the same. Ibid. p. 101.

No. III. Humbly sheweth, That whereas that within the citie of Bristol there hath been a custom this manie years past, authorized by the queen of famous memory, for stamping of farthing tokens in copper, for the behalfe as well of the citizens and country people, as also for the furtheraunce of the poore, who recieve very often a farthing from them who would not give a halfpenny or more. And this authority seasing ever since your majesties coming to the crowne. That your majesty would be pleased to authorise your poor servants for the stamping and working of the same farthing tokens, for the cities of Bristol and Glocester by us and our deputy or deputies, and that no other tokens shall go current but such as are stamped by us, and, as in dutie bound, we shall ever pray for your majestie's long and happie reigne.

At the court of Whitehall the 2d of April, 1609.

The king's majesty doth refer the consideration of this petition to the commissioners appointed by his highness for sutes.

Roger Willbraham.

A Benefytt by coyninge Copper Money.

No. IV. One pound of fine copper being haberdepoyes weight, which is 16 oz. will make a pound of troy weight, which is but 14 oz. 12 dwt. to the pound, and there will be made thereof, in half penny peeces, farthing peeces and half farthing peeces, being equally proportionate in thirds as well in weight as in peeces. 686, that is to say the halfpenny peece to contain 24 gr. the farthing 12 gr. and the half farthing 6 gr. which being once made current, after this rate, the pound of copper will yield in value to be worth — s. 12 d. 2 Ibid. p. 19, 20.

		s.	d.
100 lb. weight in third, as before.	68	2	8
1000 ditto	681	6	8
10000 ditto	6813	6	8
20000 ditto	13636	13	4
30000 ditto	20440	—	—

which 30000 lb. weight of copper being quoyned, will scarcely give contentment to every parish throughout the realme, as it will yield then little more than 20s. a piece and therefore of necessity there must be supplies made dayly, which will encrease the more benefyt.

A Brevyatt

A Breviatt of what charge will ensue yearly to effect the coinage of 10000 lb. weight as before.

To the Master of the copper mynte, for his fee per ann.	66	13	4
To his Clerk ditto	6	13	4
To the comptroler of the said copper mynte	60	0	0
To his clerk, ditto	6	13	4
To two melters ditto	33	6	8
To a graver of the iron stamps	26	13	4
To a Tynker of the said stamps,	6	13	4
To the porter,	10	0	0
To the keeper of the irons,	15	0	0
To the blauncher,	6	13	4
For the diet of those officers above mentioned per ann. so as they be nowe permitted to the diett, but by the consent of the master and comptroller of the said mynte,	100		
For the wages of 30 workmen, which are yearly to be employed, allowing each man for his wages and diet 18d. a day, which is 9s. a week for one man, in the whole	754		
For sundry implements, tools, and other furniture requisite yearly for this service, as furnisses, melting-pots, ansields, great and small hammers, trays, tongs, ballencers, copper-pans, chests, planks, coles, &c. may amount to yearly	200		
Some totall	£1292	6	8

Ten thousand weight of fine copper, at 5l. 6s. 8d. the hundred weight, is 53l. 6s. 8d. the 1000 lb. wt. at which rate the 10000 lb. weight	533	6	8
The waste which will fall out to be in this 10000 lb. wt. of copper, in the cliping and melting thereof may be in value	60		
Sum total	593	9	8

A briefe ballance for the chardge and dischardge of the said 10000 lb. wt. of copper as follows,

Received by the benefit of coinage of the said 10000 lb. wt. of copper abovementioned	6813	6	8
Whereof is to be paid out yearly as followeth,			
For the fees, wages, dyets of the officers and workmen, with the charge of sundry implements, as per contra appeareth	1292	6	8
For the charge of 10000 wt. of copper, with the waste thereof as aforesaid,	593	6	8
Some total	1885	13	4
So resteth yearly all charges defalced	4927	13	4

A True coppie of the Lo. letters of assistance.

Harl. MSS. Brit. Muse. No. 4888.

No. V. Whereas it pleased the king's majestie, by his highness letters patents, under the great seal of England, to appoint Edward Woodward, Esq; and Thomas Garret, of London, Goldsmith, to make a convenyent quantity of farthing tokens, to passe between man and man, for the use of his majesties subjects, in bartering and exchange; and also, did accordingly publish his highnesses will and pleasure, by diverse proclamations, to establish the currency of them, and prohibition of the use of all other tokens, or things in the nature of tokens, whatsoever; and whereas, it being found by almost six years experience, that the use of the said farthing tokens is very necessary, and generally pleasing to the subjects, in regard there is a continual current exchaunge mayntayned; whereby all just cause of complaint is taken away, and by the use of them charitie to the poor hath much increased. His majestie hath been bin farther pleased, by his lettres patents, under the great seale of England, to make a new graunt of the same privilege unto our very good lord Lodovicke duke of Lenox, and James marquis of Hamilton; with command, there be from time to time, a convenient quantitie of the same farthing tokens, sent to the several citties and burroughs corporate, and market townes, within the realmes of England and Ireland, and dominions of Wales; and the same to be left (with the sufficient meanes for the exchaunge of them) in the hands of some discrete person, to be issued, with a like commaund, to the cheefe officers and governors, with the ministers and constables of those places, to endeavour the disposing and free passage of the same tokens, for the value of farthings, both which letters and proclamations being published for the common good of his majesties subjects, ought, according to the intent thereof, in all points be put in due execution. These are therefore to will and requier you, in his majesties name, to charge and commaund you and every of you, from tyme to tyme, to be ayding and assisting to the said Edward Woodward and Thomas Garrett, and to the said Lodovicke, duke of Lenox, and James Marques of Hamilton, or any of them or any of their deputies or assignes (shewing forth this our lettre) in the due execution of the said lettres patents and proclamations, according to the true intent and meaning thereof; and if you, or any of you, shall fynde any person or persons so obstinate or refractory, as to disobey or obstruct the same, or any deputie or assignes of the said Edward Woodward and Thomas Garrett, or of the said Lodovicke, duke of Lenox, and James Marquis of Hamilton, or to misdemeane themselves in or about the execution of the said lettres patents and proclamations, contrary to the true meaning of the same; that then you take bonde, with sufficient surities, of any such person or persons so wise demeaning themselves, or offending against the said lettres patents, or proclamations, in the execution thereof, for their appearance, to answer their contempt, in that behalfe, before us; certefying, under your hande, their particular misdemeanors or offences; whereof you nor any of you may faile, as you will aunswer the contrary.

Dated at Whitehall, the 28th of June, 1622.

To all maiers, sheriffs, Justices of peace, bayliffs, constables, headboroughes and all other his majesties officers and loving subjects whom it may concern, and to every of them.

C. Cant. Jo. Lincoln, C. S. Mandeuill, E. Worcester, Arundell Surrey, Pembroke, Falkland,
T. Edmondes G. Calvert, Jul. Cæsar, Jo. Suckling, G. Carew.

No. VI. Extracts from the town books of Yarmouth, 6 June, 1667.

"At this assembly it is approved of, what the overseers have done in getting a stamp for farthings, for payment of the poor; and that the overseers from time to time, shall give for those farthings the value in silver, to any that shall bring the same unto them to be changed."

October 10, 1670. 22. Car IId.

"It is ordered at this assembly, that Mr. Deering, the sollicitor for the city of Norwich, be writ unto, imployed and impowered, on behalf of our corporation, to petition his majesty by the lord Townshend, for his gracious pardon for coyning our towne farthings; and Mr. Richard Huntington and Mr. George Ward be desired to journey to the lord Townshend, to crave his honours assistance on our town's behalf, to move his majesty in it."

April 14, 1671. 23, Car. IId.

At this assembly Mr. Deering's Letter and bill of charges about passing the pardon for coyneing the towne farthings amounting to 80l. which this house do order shall be paid him by the chamberlyns, and likewise 10l. for paines.

August 31, 1672. 24 Car. IId.

"Ordered at this assembly, that the bellman goe about and give notice, that whosoever bring in any of the towne farthings, before 6 of the clock of Wednesday at night next, to Mr. Abr. Havett and Mr. John Crow, shall have the value in silver; and that what money they shall take up for payment thereof at interest, shall be allowed them againe, out of the money they gather for the relief of the poor."

Feb.

Feb. 14, 1672-3. 25 Car. IId,

"It is ordered that Mr. Crow make sale of the town farthings, which he hath now in his hands, to the best advantage."

No. VII. Extracts from the books of the corporation of Dover, as to the coining of farthings and halfpence there, 1657 and 1658.

Dovor.

At a common assembly holden the 13th. day of January, 1667.

"It is ordered and decreed that a certain quantity of farthings and halfpence be provided and stamped by the corporation, for the use of the overseers of the poor and others; and to be stamped in manner and form as shall be advised and directed by Mr. Mayor, Mr. John Golder, Mr. George West, Mr. John Carlile, Mr. William Pepper, Mr. John Matson, Mr. Richard Barley, Jurats; the chamberlains for the time being, Warren Hugeson and Bartholomew Anderson; or as any five or more of them shall think fit upon the account of this corporation."

Examined,

Alexander Wellarde, common clerke.

Dovor.

At a common assembly holden the 30th. day of March, 1668.

"Whereas according to a late decree, there is provided and put in the chamberlain's hands the value of [illegible] or thereabouts, in farthings and halfpence for the use of the corporation. It is thought fit, and so ordered, that the chamberlains do, upon all occasions, exchange so much of them as hath or shall, at any time hereafter, be delivered out to any person or persons whatsoever of the said town and port."

Examined,

Alex. Wellard, common clerk.

August 22d. 1667.

No. VIII. Whereas Moses Durell, mayor of this town and county, have by the consent of us whose names are hereunder subscribed, disbursed the sum of ten pounds in copper farthings, with the stamp of the towne armes in them; with the inscription (for the mayor of the town and county of Poole) and hath received in farthings, at four farthings to the penny, the sum of Nineteen pounds and four shillings, to be dispersed and to pass in exchange, betwixt man and man, as current money, until it shall be prohibited, by his majesties order. It is this day at a common hall agreed on, agreed upon, that if his majestie shall not, during the time of his mayoralty, prohibit the said farthings, then he the said Moses Durell, shall deliver over unto the next succeeding mayor of this town and county, the sum of nine pounds and four shillings in current money, or the same farthings; to exchange so many of the said farthings as shall be brought unto him during the time of his mayoralty, into silver, by any person or persons whatsoever. And farther, that the like sum of nine pounds and four shillings in the like money, or the same farthings, shall, from year to year, be paid over by the mayor for the time being unto the next succeeding mayor of this town and county, untill his majestie shall prohibit the same farthings; and then the mayor for the time being, shall still exchange all the said farthings which shall be brought unto him to be exchanged upon the account of the corporation, not exceeding the said sum of nineteen pounds and four shillings sterling, which the mayor shall be reimbursed out of the town revenue.

Nicholas Efford
John Willie

Moses Durell, Mayor
Robert Cleeves
Steph. Street, sen. Bailef
Peter Heiley
Edward Man
John Carter
John Gigger
Ri. Albert, Scr. and town clerke.

F I N I S.

Town Pieces.

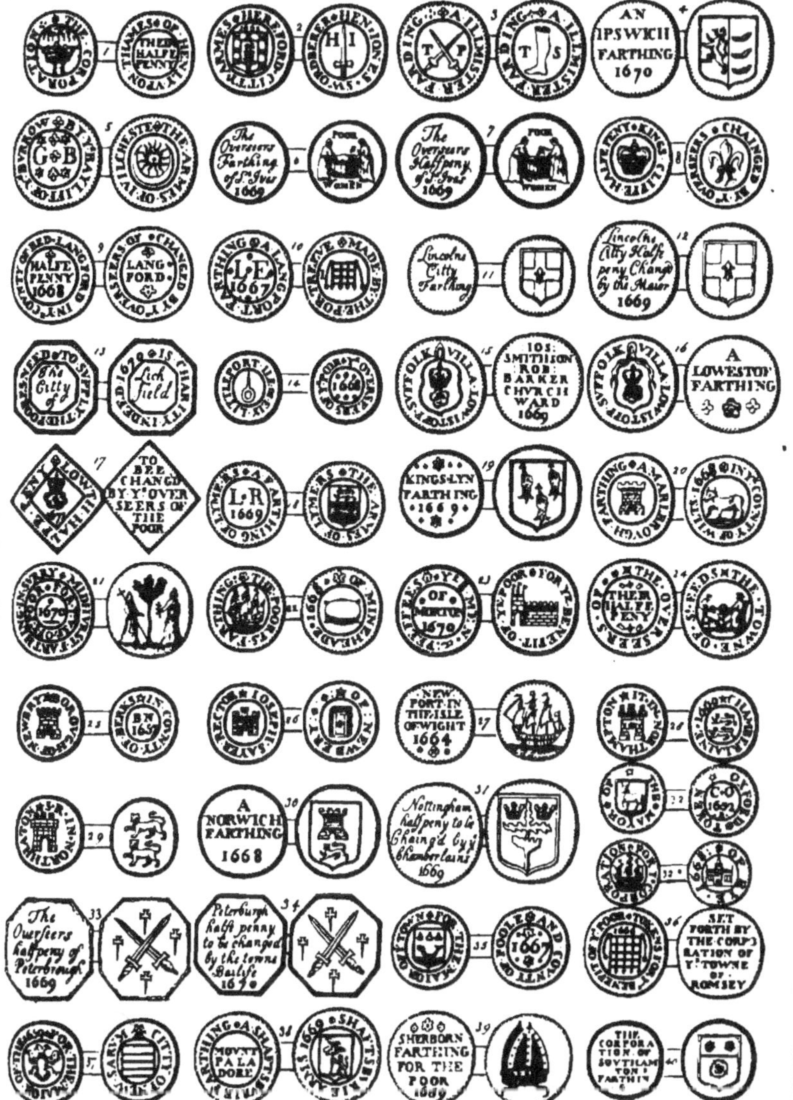

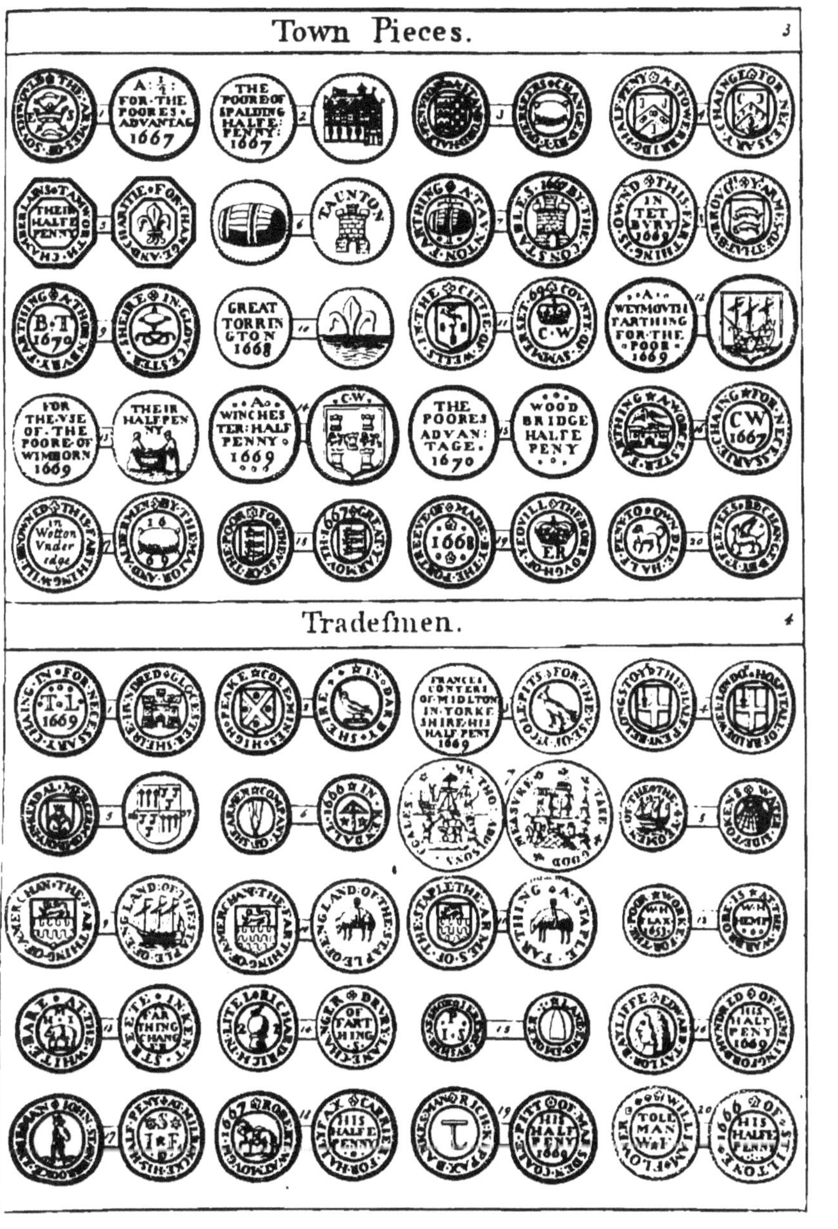
Town Pieces.
3
Tradesmen.
4

PATTERN PIECES FOR FARTHINGS

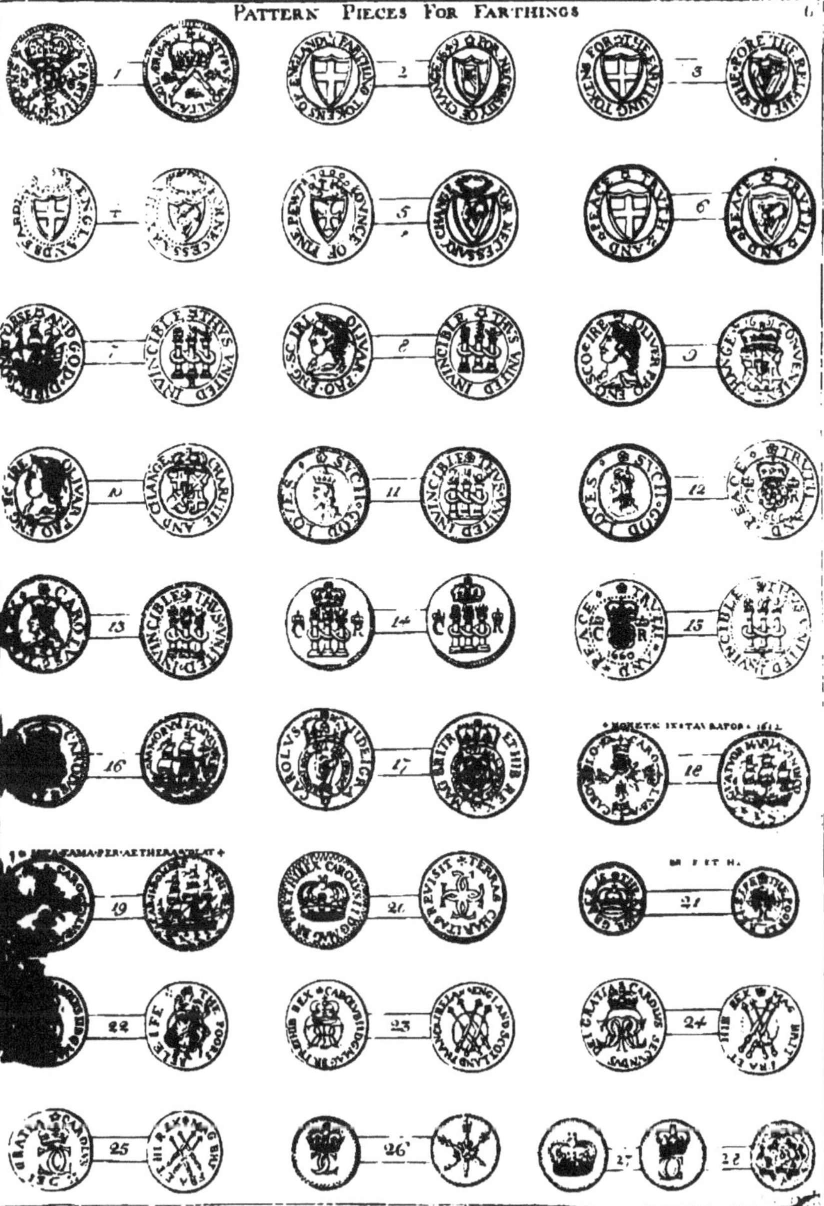

Farthings and Halfpennies, from Charles II. to George II.

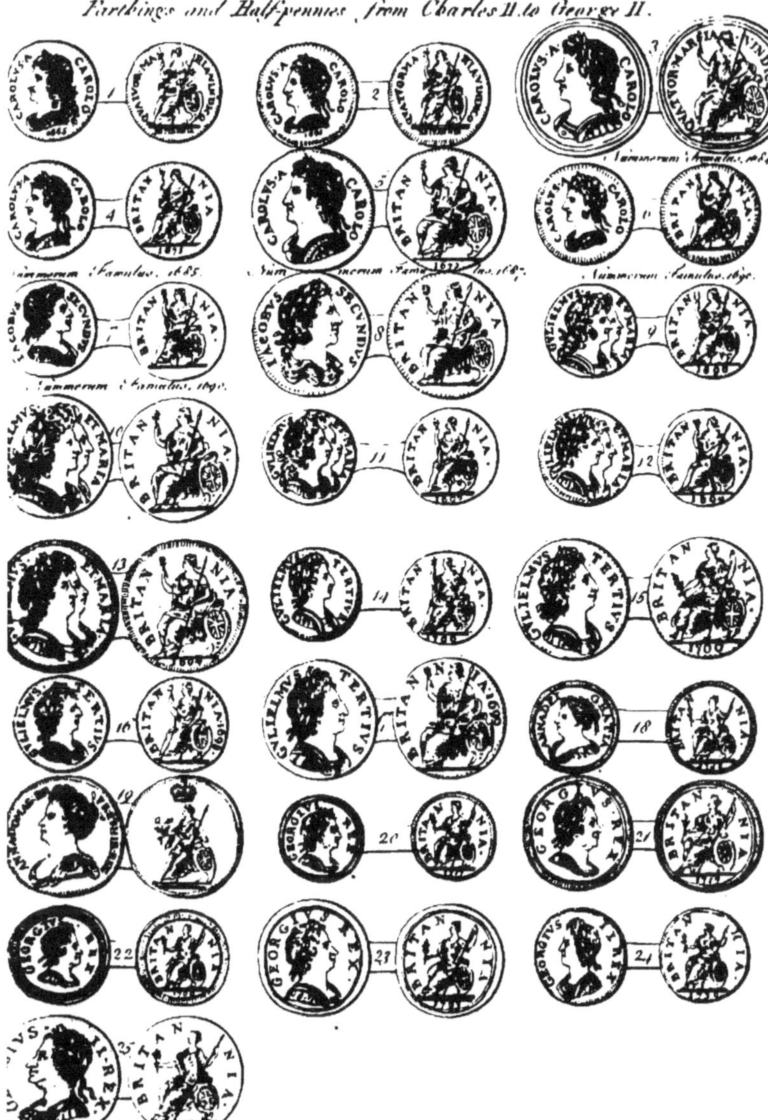

Hall sculp.

A VIEW OF THE ORIGIN, NATURE, and USE OF JETTONS OR COUNTERS.

ESPECIALLY

Those commonly known by the Name of BLACK MONEY and ABBEY PIECES;

WITH

A Sketch of the Manner of Reckoning with them, and its Affinity with that of the Roman ABACUS, the Chinese SOAN PAN, and the Russian SHTCHOTA.

With COPPER-PLATES.

By THOMAS SNELLING.

LONDON:

Printed for T. SNELLING, (No. 163.) next the *Horn Tavern*, in *Fleet-Street*.
MDCCLXIX.

Who buys and sells all Sorts of Coins and Medals.

PREFACE.

IN considering the origin and use of Jettons, we were led naturally to take notice of those struck by the authority of the prince, or of the states in France and the Low Countries; the early ones of that sort generally having on them the purpose they were struck for, and the Office they were to be used in; we have also related a few particulars in regard to their distribution, and the expences attending them; observing that the custom is laid down in some places, and still continued in others; likewise, the great difference betwixt the purposes of those at present made in France, from those formerly used there; but have not concerned ourselves with their types and historical inscriptions, those which regard the Low Countries having been done in Van Loons Histoire Metallique des Pais Bas, and Mieres's Nederlandshe Vorsten, and it would give us great pleasure to see those of France described in the same manner. We have the rather chose to touch on these things from the novelty of the subject, and the little knowledge we have of these matters here in England.

We cannot learn it ever was the practise with us to make any Jettons or Counters for the purpose of calculation; the few we have of Queen Anne, George I. and some others since, being intended for play, and always found in silver: However, it is certain we used them here for computation, as well as abroad, Madox † mentioning them in the 17 John and 12 Ed. 2. both times tells us they were Venetian money; the first time he says they were shillings, and that 10 of them were equal to 15 shillings sterling; but I should judge they were rather Grossi or Matapani; which had about the year 1194 been first coined under Henry Danduli ‡, and weighed about 35 gr. troy, or 1½ of our sterlings or pennies, 10 of them making 15 sterlings, and not so many shillings.

The

† History of the Exchequer, p. 711, Cap.xxIII. §xxix. ‡ Rubbi delle Moneta, 4to. a l'Aja 1754. p.406.

PREFACE.

The pieces exhibited in the following plates, differ widely from those just mentioned, having nothing in their types nor their workmanship to recommend them to the curious, neither is there any erudition contained in their inscriptions; or information to be gathered from them; this being the case, it will be naturally asked; for what purpose they are published? and in what consists the utility of this work? to which we shall answer, It is published with an intent that Gentlemen when they meet with them among other brass pieces in parcels, (as is almost always the case) may know what they are, and to what class they belong, and either turn them out, or keep them, as agrees best with their mode of collecting.

The pieces in the first plate are usually called Black Money, but if it be considered, that on the generality of them, there is not so much as a single letter to denote what prince or state they belong to; this alone will be sufficient to overthrow that opinion, to which we have added some others, where they are described; those in the second and third plates, and many of those in the fourth, are named Abbey Pieces, and have this appellation, probably from their being so frequently met with in their ruins; or, it is likely, the pious sentences found on them, may be also a motive for their being thus called; be that as it will, it is certain that in those religious foundations, their use were better understood, than any where else, or by any other persons, before the manner of working the present Arabick figures with the pen, was so well known as now; besides, the settling the revenues of their respective houses, required more of them, than most at that time; and this we imagine was then the only use of them; nor do we conceive they were ever in the nature of Tessera's or Ticket's, as some have thought; and as there are others again, that have supposed them ancient brass money of our Saxon ancestors, or belonging to some Gothic princes, and such like opinions; to correct these mistakes, and shew what they really are, is our purpose in the following sheets.

We have given a slight sketch of the manner of using them in calculation; and as the principles in working them, and the Roman Abacus, the Chinese Soan Pan, and the Russian Shtchota, are the same; we have performed the same sums all four ways. There are several ways of disposing of counters in adding and substracting of mixed numbers; as pounds, shillings, pence, &c. besides what we have chosen, which differs from that used in the Exchequer, in setling the Sheriffs, and some other accompts, which we have been informed is done there once a year with such sort of pieces.

A VIEW OF THE ORIGIN, NATURE, and USE OF JETTONS OR COUNTERS.

A Celebrated author(*a*) is of opinion, that the uſe of pieces to compute with, was too natural and ſimple not to be ancient, and probably were prior to Arithmetick itſelf; ſmall ſtones, ſhells, kernels, &c. ſerved thoſe nations for common uſe, who either knew not, or deſpiſed gold and ſilver, and is ſtill followed by many nations of ſavages: he carries the invention as far back as the ſons of Noah, who to eaſe their memory, and ſettle among themſelves the increaſe of their

Computing with Pieces ancient. as ſmall ſtones, &c.

(*a*) Mahudel de l'Origine & de l'Uſage des Jettons. Hiſt. de l'Academie Royale des Inſcript. tom. 3. p. 388; alſo Patin's hiſt. des Medailles, cap. 14. Van Loons Hedendaagſche Penninkunde, 8vo. cap. 4. folio, cap. 11.

flocks, made use of this sort of calculation, the Egyptians used no other method, which Josephus informs us they learnt from Abraham, and Herodotus had before said that the Egyptians, as well as the Greeks, made use of this sort of computing, besides that with characters, with this difference, that they placed them from the left to the right, but the Egyptians from the right to the left.

Called by the Greeks Ψηφοι. By the Romans Calculi.

The Greeks called the little flat, rounded and polished stones, they used for these purposes Ψηφοι, and the art itself Ψηφοφορια, and from hence we have our terms of, *Cyphering*, to *Cypher*, &c. these same sort of stones were by the Romans called *Calculi*; hence our expressions, of *Calculating*, to *Calculate*, &c. and its probable were a long time used by them, as the words *Lapillus* and *Calculus* are sometimes used in the same sense; when luxury increased amongst them, they used ivory counters, as appears from Juvenal, Sat. 11. V. 131. and although no cabinet can at present shew one of these pieces, yet an hundred proverbial expressions prove that this manner of reckoning was very common, as *ponere calculos*, a train of reasons, *hic calculus accedat*, the addition of a new proof added to several others, *calculum detrahere*, when they endeavoured to suppress an article, and a thousand others which alluded to addition or substraction of Jettons in accompts. It was the first Arithmetick that children of every condition learnt; Capitolin, speaking of Pertinax in his youth, says, *puer litteris elementariis & calculo imbutus*; those which taught children this art, are by Tertullian, Ulp. l. 7. de oper. named *primi numerorum arenarii*, the lawyers called them Calculones, if slaves or lately made free; but if they were of a more elevated condition, then they were called *Calculatores*, or *Numerarii*; it was usual to have one of these masters in every considerable family, and the title of the employ was, *a calculis, a rationibus*.

Passages in Classic Authors alluding to them.

Those in metal used by the Moderns, called Jettons.

The pieces of metal used by the moderns for the same purpose, are called by the French, at present, JETTONS, and receive this name from the manner of *their being used, that is cast or moved upwards, downwards or sideways; being derived from the verb *Jetter*, to cast or throw, and from this original came our expressions of, *Casting Accompts, to cast up a sum*, and such like. The words LEGPENNING, LEGGELT, the names given by the Dutch to these pieces, have also these appellations for the same reason, that is, from being *Laid*, or put in different manners on the Board, as shall be related. Whereas the word used by the Germans, viz. RECHEN PFENNING, or Reckoning Penny, has relation only to its use in general, and not to the manner of using it; and it is the same with the word used with us, viz. COUNTER, its original use being to Count, Accompt, Compute, Calculate or Reckon. In the same sense the French, Italians and Spaniards use their verb Conter, Contaire and Contar, from whence the latter have their *Contadore*, or *Counter*, as with us.

Legpenny.

Rechen Pfenning.

Counter.

* But on the old ones we find great variety in the spelling as Gects, Gectz, Getoers, Getoirs, [illegible]teirs, Getteurs, Jectoer, Jectoir, Jetoir, Giets, Gietons, and Gitones.

The inſcriptions on the oldeſt of the pieces are relative to the purpoſe of ſtriking them, as *pour les Comtes, pour les Finances*, and ſuch like.

LEGENDS regard the purpoſe ſtruck for.

Many of them had Legends alſo that admoniſhed thoſe concerned in accompts to be careful in their computations, the advantage and benefit accruing from exactneſs in calculation, and adviſing thoſe who have made an error, to examine and caſt it up again, and ſuch like expreſſions, as follows:

Exhort to exactneſs in accompts.

Geſtez, Entendez au Compte.
Entendez bien & loyaument aux Comtes.
Gardez vous de Meſcomptes.
Bon Compte Ne Font a Nulle Honte.
Qui Bien Jettra le Compte Trouvera.
Jettez bien, que vous ne perdre Rien.
Qui Tien Bon conte pais luis reſta.
Comptes & Jettes juſtement, craignant le divine Jugement.
Se vous Failles, le Recomptes.
Redde Rationem Villicationis Tua.
Subducendis Rationibus.
Bene Subductis Rationibus.
Numeris Eſt Diſcretio Rerum Omnia.
Contes, Peſes, meſures juſtement, car Conte rendres au jugement.

We find alſo on ſome, what Prince or great Officers they were made for, of which thoſe which follow are a ſpecimen.

Declare for whoſe uſe they were made.

Calculi ad Numerandum Reg. Juſſu Lud. XII.
Gectoirs du Prince de Caſtelle.
Jectoirs pour Monſoer de Berg.
Jettoirs pour le Seignieur de Berſſele.
Jett pour Monſieur le Chanſelier.

We have a much greater variety on which are found the names of the ſeveral Bureaus, Chambers, Offices, and Departments about the court, in which the publick buſineſs was adminiſtered, and to aſſiſt the officers of which in their calculations was the intent they were ſtruck for.

And for what departments.

Ject pour ceulx des Finances.
Gettoirs au Gens des Finances.
Jett pour des Maitre des Fina.
Gectoirs du Bureau de Finances du Roy.
Calculus Rationum Financiarum.
Nummi Rationum Financiarum

Gects du Bureau de Madame.
Gitones del Bureo de ſu Mageſtad.
Contadores del Bureau de ſu Alteza.
Jectoers du Bureau des Maiſtres Doſtel des Meſdames.

Gects des Comtes de Lorrain.
Gettons pour le Chambre des Comptes a Lille.
Jectoirs de la Cambre des Compts du Duc.
Jetoirs de Meſſinnurs de Conte a Lille.
Gectoirs pour le Chambre en Gueldre.
Calculi Camera Computorium Ducatus Gelria.
Calculi Camera Rationum Zelandia.
Nummus Calculus Camera Rationibus Brabantia.
Numiſma Camer. Comp. Hollan.
Gect de la Chambre des Aides.

Jett

Jett pour le Monnoie de Flandre.
Ject. pour le Maist. de la Mon. a Brux.

Calculus Clere Hannonie.
Gectiors des Estats de Namur.
Calculi Ordinum Belgia.
Jectoirs pour le Chambre Eschevinale.

Leggelt van de Munters van Holland.

Calculi Civitatis Bruxellensis.
Leggelt der Stadt van Brussel.
Calculi Ærari Bruxellensis.
Calculi Fossæ Bruxellensis.
Leggelt de Vaert van Brussel (*b*).

Some have not the words Gectoir, Calculis, &c.

There were others without the words Gectoir, Calculus, &c. but the sense in other respects nearly the same.

Pro Camerum Computorum Bressiæ.
Pro Gentibus Computorum.
Camera Computorum Regiorum.
Curia Monetarum Franciæ.
Suprema Repetundarum Curia.
Ad Usum Cancellaria Clivensis.
Ad Usum Camera Rationum Insulensis.
Pour l'Ecurie de la Royne.

Les Cinq Gross Fermes de France.
Fermes des Aides.
Domaines du Roy.
Alienation des Domaines.
Chambere aux Deniers du Roy.
Conseillers du Roy & Notaires.
Advocats aux Conseils.
Experts & Greffiers des Batimens.
Cavallerie Legere.

Others have the names of the Officers on them

Finally, many of them have the names of the officers on them, for whose use they were intended, as follows:

Raoul de Refuge, Maistre des Comptes of Charles VII.
Jean de St. Amadour, Maitre d'Hotel of Louis XII.
Thomas Boyer, General de Finances under Charles VIII.
Jean Testu, Conseiller & Argentier to Francis I.
Antoine de Corbie, Controlleur under Henry II.
Jehan Stanley, Tresorier de Normandy under Lewis XII.

Many the office without the name.

The title of the office, but without the name of any officer, is also found on some, as Tresor. Gnal. des Fermes de France. Tresorier Gnal. des Guerres, and no doubt a great number of other varieties, which never came under our notice.

Type. First plain, then with Flowers, lastly heads, and Devices.

The pieces of metal first used by the moderns for the purposes of computation, were round, flat, well polished, and quite plain; they afterwards began to engrave on them Flowers, Leaves, and other ornaments, to which succeeded that of the Head, Device, and Arms of the Prince, who caused them to be struck; this sort, we are told, had their origin in France in the 14th century*; but

(*b*) Vidé Histoire der Nederlandsche Vorsten, fol. Sgraavenhage 1722, 3 deel. Van Loon's Histoire Metallique des Pays Bas, 5 tom. fol. Ams. 1738.

* A fine Jetton of our Edward the Third, struck as we apprehend in France; will be found the most ancient of these pieces, which has yet come to light, and may be regarded as an Historical one, the King being exhibited thereon with his sword and shield, as asserting his right to the crown of that kingdom, the field is also semy of Fleurs de lis, and the inscription *Edwardus Rex Regratis*; on the reverse is four crowned Lyons in cross, with four fleurs de lis in the vacancies, all within an ancient

but, however, the oldeſt Jetton of this ſort, in the King of France's cabinet, is one of Charles VII. who lived about the middle of the next, or 15th century; the moſt ancient among thoſe of the Low Countries, are thoſe of Philip the Good, Duke of Burgundy, about the ſame time. After which, towards the cloſe of the ſame century, or under Philip the Fair, but principally under his ſon, Charles V. they began to mark the principal events of the ſtate on them, from which time Jettons began to be monuments conſecrated by ſovereign authority; for the choice of the Emblems and Inſcriptions, did not depend upon the Graver, but every year they preſented to the States General, to thoſe of particular provinces, and to the Council of State divers deſigns, of which that was choſen, which they thought was moſt agreeable to the conjuncture of the times(c). Under ſuch regulations were ſtruck in the Low Countries the moſt intereſting collection of Jettons that have ever appeared, commencing with their defection from the Spaniards, about anno 1563, and continuing until the truce in 1609, by which the Dutch became a free State, after which they are fewer in number, and not ſo ingenious.

Become hiſtorical.

Regulated by the States in the Low Countries.

This cuſtom of making them hiſtorical, obtained alſo in France, upon great numbers of which, are found many ingenious and intereſting Devices, Emblems and Inſcriptions, eſpecially ſince the eſtabliſhment of the Academie Royale des Inſcriptions, one of the principal functions of whoſe members related to theſe matters, and which they continue to perform till this day.

In France by the Academy of Inſcript.

The practice of giving, or diſtributing Jettons, as Etrennes or New Year's Gifts, at the publick expence, in the Low Countries, began towards the cloſe of the 15th century, when a certain number of Silver and Copper Jettons were given to each member of the ſtate, as the Governor General, thoſe of particular provinces, the members of the eſtates of each province, thoſe of the Chamber of Accompts at Bruſſels, Flanders, Holland, and Gelderland; the Inſpector of the Canal of Bruſſels, and other publick Officers, which were put into a magnificent purſe, or a ſilver box, the top of which was ornamented with the Arms of the Province, the City, or the Aſſembly; there was alſo an officer eſtabliſhed on purpoſe to diſtribute them in the order, and conformable to the Arrets of the Council, as the number of Jettons was proportioned to the dignity and quality of each officer, and varied according to the number of perſons who aſſiſted at the Aſſemblies.

Preſented as New Year's Gifts in the Low Countries.

The expence of theſe Jettons, in the United Provinces, amounted anno 1596, to near 700 l. ſterl. but in the year 1619 to 2770 l. ſterl. what occaſioned ſo great a difference, was in part owing to their being given to a greater, or a leſſer number of members, one year than another, but moſtly in the numbers given to the ſame members, which ſometimes, as in 1589, was 50 or 60 in ſilver; in 1694, it was as many as weighed 1½ mark (about 11 oz. 16 dwt. 6 gr. troy) in 1596 there was an hundred in ſilver, each worth about 11 pence, beſides what they called a *Jet*, or a neceſſary number of Jettons for calculation, was in 1330 e-

To what Amount.

ancient compartment, and inſcribed *Garde Robe Regis*, having on both ſides ſmall open crowns between each word, and ſeems to have been ſtruck for the uſe of the King's Wardrobe. It is engraved in our View of the Coins ſtruck by Engliſh Princes in France, p. 5.

(c) Van Loon's Preface.

ſtimated at 48 guilders, or about 4l. 8s. ſterling; but in 1672, and ever ſince, worth 81 guild. or 7 l. 8 s. 6d. ſterling.

Laid aſide in the United Provinces.

This cuſtom of giving Jettons having ceaſed in the United Provinces many years, (but their uſe in calculation a long time before) a method has been introduced of giving, in lieu of them, their value in money, which appears to have been done anno 1654, and is ſtill continued; thus every year towards the end of December, the ſame day they regulate the Etrennes, the Agent of the States General receives a formal order to take 2061 guil. 12 ſt. to make the uſual reports on, according to the Ordonannce eſtabliſhed for ever; the States of Holland give alſo every year to the Counſellor Deputé a certain ſum on the ſame account, which, anno 1723, according to the ancient cuſtom, amounted to 972 guild. about 89 l. 2s. or 12 Jets, each of value of 81 guild. which were diſtributed to the Counſellor, Deputy Counſellor, Secretary, and two Counſellers of the Finances, the officers of the Mint at the Hague are allowed alſo annually a Mark weight of ſilver.

Still continued in the Auſtrian Low Countries.

In the Catholick Low Countries, the old cuſtom of giving Jettons is ſtill continued in its full extent, for under the reign of Charles II. every New Year's Day, the Counſel of Finances ordered the Receiver General, to preſent to the Governor General, then reſiding at Bruſſels, a magnificent embroidered purſe, containing 100 ſilver Jettons, the Emblem and Device of which differed according to conjunctures; the ſame was practiſed under Philip V. when each member of the council royal, that was added to the privy counſel, received alſo yearly 100 ſilver Jettons, and ſince anno 1717, theſe Etrennes have been doubled, and the Governor General has received 200 annually, inſtead of 100; the ſame thing is alſo obſerved at Tournay, at Ghent, and the territory of Oſtend, in the Chatellany of Courtray, in that of Ipres, in the City and Franc of Bruges, and at Namur; in which laſt province they diſtribute beſides, a great number at the arrival of every new Governor General and Grand Bailey, in memory of his taking poſſeſſion of that charge, having on one ſide his Arms, Device, and Titles, and on the other the arms of the province; thus in 1715 they amounted to 1303 ſilver, and 2616 copper, that is 168 ſilver, and 363 copper to the Governor General, and half as many to each member of the Aſſembly, of the Eſtates, this cuſtom has produced, for a great many years, an uninterrupted ſeries of governors of this province, their titles, and the year of their inſtalment.

Formerly done in France.

The Kings of France formerly, when the uſe of Jettons was well eſtabliſhed cauſed purſes to be made and diſtributed to the Officers of their Houſhold, which were charged with the care of the publick expences, to thoſe who were appointed to examine them, and to thoſe who had the management of the publick money, but at preſent, and for a long while paſt, the original method of giving them to the publick offices has been laid aſide, they being at this time preſented to the King, to the Royal Family, to the Princes of the Blood, the Chancellor, the Miniſters and Secretaries of State, in magnificent purſes of 100 Jettons each, ſome gold, ſome ſilver, according to their quality or cuſtom, which is done by the Prevot des Marchands, and Echevins of the City of Paris; alſo ſeveral other officers, as the Gardes des Treſors Royale, les Treſoriers de l'Extraordinaire

At preſent given to the King and Miniſters of State.

traordinaire and Ordinaire des Guerres, those of the Marine and Partes Casuelles, & les Tresoriers des Batimens du Roy; nor is there scarcely in Paris a publick Body, either in the superior or inferior Magistracies, the Faculties or in the companies of Marchands, or those of any Arts or Trades, which have not their silver Jettons ornamented with their device, and struck for their particular uses, to be distributed at Receptions or Assemblies; the three Academies likewise, which have their sittings in the Louvre, as also that of Painting and Sculpture, which assemble in the same place, have their Jettons to distribute to the Academists which assist there, and this is at the King's expence, a fund being established for that purpose(*d*). Also by publick Bodies, Companies, &c. to their Members.

What has hitherto been said, principally regards those Jettons made by publick authority in the Low Countries and in France; we shall now proceed to what is our principal intention, that is those which have no such plea, but made by them whose employment it was, for the use of private persons, or rather for Communities, Abbies, Monasteries, Churches, &c. whose revenues required a good deal of computation. Jettons by authority not the design of this work, only private ones.

We think the pieces in pl. 1. are some of the earliest counters made use on for this purpose, and prior to those we have already been treating of, and among them those with the head on one side, and the cross on the other, to be as ancient as any, but can determine nothing in regard to their age, or where struck; we can only say the English Sterlings, with this head, first appeared in 1272, and continued till 1500, different sorts of crosses make up the generality of the other types; as for legends, we are of opinion they were a long while before they were introduced, but its place filled with dots, pellets, mullets, roses, &c. as may be seen by turning to the pieces in the plate, better than by any description. Those in pl. 1. the most ancient. Those supposed the oldest with the head. Are without legends.

The pieces with the head, in the first plate, which we have been just mentioning, are by many esteemed, and usually called *Black Money*, but that they have no right to be admitted into this class, we think is clear for the following reasons; 1st, It does not appear from any of our records, we ever had any Base or Black Money till Henry the Eighth's time; 2dly, No other country in Europe at the time these are supposed to be struck, had such a head upon any of their coins, or indeed any head at all; besides, if we even grant they had, it would prove nothing, as these pieces have no pretence to be thus called, on account of the metal they are made of, which is *Brass*, and a bad sort also, with a larger mixture of lapis calaminaris than usual, and very thin withal. Usually called Black Money, but falsely, are a bad sort of brass.

Now we think there is hardly a single instance to be given, or a piece to be produced of any money thus circumstanced, they being all that have come to our knowledge, made of a mixture of copper and silver, but so little of that as not after being ometime in currency, to be distinguished by their colour, whether there is any silver or not in their composition, and on this accuont generally called *Black Money*, from their colour, and to this sort of money is to be referred the *Monnoye Noire* of the French, and *Moneta Nigra* of Latin, authors. Black money has always a little silver in it.

(*d*) Savary Dictionnaire de Commerce.

We

We will now proceed to describe the pieces in the second and third plates, not as they ſtand, but firſt their types, and afterwards their inſcriptions.

Types on pl. 2, 3. Almoſt all the pieces in plate 2, and 3. have on one of their ſides a Croſs, but widely differing from each other, according to the capacity and ſkill of the graver; thus ſome of them are plain, others are fleur de liſſé, many of them are narrow, others again are broad; on ſome the bars of the croſs conſiſt but of one line, ſome of two, and others of three, and on many they are dotted, ſeveral are voided or open, forming a ſort of fuſil, a ſort of compartment of 4 Arches or Leaves ſurround many of them, the vacant ſpaces or interſtices are embelliſhed or ornamented with letters, leaves, fleurs de lis, ſtars, &c. moſt of which iſſue from the inner circle or points of the compartment.

variety of Croſſes.

differently ornamented.

rude Shields with fleurs de lis. On ſeveral of them we find fleurs de lis in ſhields of different forms, ſome having three, ſome four, others again have ſix and eight, but on No. 24. pl. 3. they are ſemeé in the area of the piece without any ſhield, and we think the major part both of theſe and the croſſes have been copied, though in a barbarous manner, from French coins.

Tower. The type of the Groſs Tournois ſeems to be that meant on No. 24. pl. 3. but whether a Tower or Shakles we cannot ſay, it is very probable thoſe with the Dolphin on No. 12, 13. pl. 2. and No. 24. pl. 3. were intended for Dauphiny, if not made there, as they much reſemble the money ſtruck in that province; there are many French Doubles and Deniers alſo, which have a crown on them, as No. 14, 15. pl. 2, thoſe with the Holy Lamb, as No. 8, 9, 10, and 22. pl. 3. ſeem to be taken in part from the French Gold coins, called by them Moutons and Aignels, as thoſe with the king ſtanding in his royal robes crowned, with a ſword or ſcepter, No. 16, 17, 18, 19, 20. appear to be rude imitations of another gold coin of theirs, called a Royall; there is a Lyon rampart on No. 13, 15. pl. 2. the former within a compartment, its probable theſe may have belonged to Flanders and Brabant; the head on No. 12. pl. 3. is the only one that looks in the Engliſh taſte, but that much reſembles that on our Engliſh Sterlings, as they were for above 200 years, we know of no money with a profile head, from which thoſe of No. 22, 23. pl. 3. can be taken.

Dolphin. Crown. Lamb. King. Lyon. Head.

No. 2, 3, 11, pl. 2. very ancient. No. 19. pl. 3. We apprehend that No. 1. pl. 2. is very ancient, the ſhield on which, as alſo on No. 3, and 11. carry no meaning with them; No. 2. we alſo think very ancient, and the ſcales on it very ſingular and proper for a Jetton, the type of No. 17. pl. 3. reſembles a ſaſh or ſcarf, as does No. 19. a creſt, but both extremely rude, the three letters IHS for the word Jeſus, on No. 27, 28, 29, 30. pl. 2. and No. 20. pl. 3, ſeem to be peculiar to theſe pieces, and owing to the piety of the age; what is meant by the three circles on No. 9. pl. 2. No. 9, and 14. pl. 3. we dont know.

The

The moſt ancient of theſe pieces, we apprehend, had no legends on them, but the circle where they uſually are, was filled with dots, roſes, ſtrait ſtrokes, coronets, ſtars, &c. as all thoſe in pl. 1. No. 1, 2. pl. 2. and No. 21, 22. pl. 4. and afterwards when they began to put letters, they ſeemed rather for ornament than information, as ſometimes a ſingle letter was repeated till it filled the circle, as No. 13. pl. 3. others have two or more, and thoſe conſonants and on many, altho' there are many different letters, yet appear to be without any meaning, and quite unintelligible, ſuch as No. 2, 3, 4, 5, 6, 8. pl. 2, one ſide of No. 3. pl. 3. alſo of No. 4, 6, 11, 15, 16 and 17. pl. 4. all which are copied as near as poſſible, and with great exactneſs.

Legends on pl. 2, 3. The moſt ancient have none. Or unmeaning ones.

Thoſe whoſe legends we are able to read, for the moſt part contain ſome religious or moral ſentence, but in a moſt ſad, careleſs, and blundered manner; thus on No. 9. pl. 2. is *Sit No-Men*, No. 10, 11, have *Sit Nomen Domini*, on both ſides, but No. 28. on one ſide only: from No. 12, to 26 incluſive, alſo No. 1. pl. 3. although they differ ſo much in their types, have *Ave Maria Gracia Plena*, or part of it, ſome only on one ſide, others on both; No. 18. has *Rex Gra*, ſeveral alſo have *Ave M.* in the external Angles of the Croſs; and on No. 22 pl. 3. ſtands *Ave Maria Mater*; on No. 27, 28, and 31. pl. 2. is *Ave Maria Stella Dei Mater*, in whole or in part. No. 29. has *xpa Dns Laudet Vi*, on one ſide, and *Domini Reſurexit*. on the other; round No. 30. is *xpa Deus Dns Ibs—Autem Tranciens*, and on No. 32. *Gloria Tibi Domine*; we have alſo one with *Pater Nos. Qui*, another with *Pater Noſter, Ave Maria Credo*, round No. 9. ſtands *Agnus Dei Qu Tolis—Peccati Mundi Miſe*; we are ignorant what is meant by *Pierar Durar Adelie Derme*, on No. 7. pl. 2.

The legible ones moſtly religious or moral. But very inaccurate, blundered, and on many unintelligible.

On No. 1. pl. 3. we find *Vive Le Roi Ave M.* on others, as No. 2, 3. pl. 3. *Vive le Bon Roy de France*; on No. 18. and 21. it is twice repeated, ſometimes we alſo find *Vive le Roy Vive le Royne*, and *Vive le Noble Duc*; on both ſides of No. 4. are *Vive Amant, Vive Amours*; and on No. 6. *Amor, Amor, Amor, Amours*, many more as unintelligible as this we find; thus on No. 5. *Je Suis de la Tount*, on No. 9. and 12. *De la Ton Sui Noume*, round the lamb on No. 9. is *Heurte Rien Moutoun*, and on No. 10. *Mouton Sul De Bri*, round No. 7. *Le Noble Espieri*, and No. 11. *Ceſt Madalle Beſlet*, on No. 16. *Loenge Adieu Avant Tout Eu*.

Vive le bon, Roi, &c. Unintelligible.

We learn from No. 14, to 24 incluſive, although their figures are ſo very different, yet that they are all intended for Jettons, we find by their inſcriptions, as on No. 15. *Getoers de la Tor B.* the word Getoers is likewiſe on No. 12. round No. 16. and 18. are *Gettes Seurement Gettes*; on both ſides of No. 19. *Gettes Rien Paie Rien*, but only on one ſide of No. 17. and 21. on No. 14. *Gettes Sil Vous Plais*; on No. 20. *Gettes Paies Rendes Rien*; on No. 22. *Getter Sans Failir*; on No. 23. *Icy Comptes Et Geotes Bien —Car La Trouvera Le Compte*, and finally on No. 24. *Gettes Entendes au Compte—Gardes Vous de Meſcomptes*, we have alſo one inſcribed as follows, *Ces Sont Les Getoers De la C...— Aus Treſories Le Roi*.

Appear from many of their legends that they are Jettons.

D There

Where made not known, but many probably at Nurembergh.

There are no lights left us, which we have been able to come at, from whence we can judge where, or by whom, the Jettons in the three first plates were made, but we think it is not improbable but many of them were the productions of Nurembergh, as well as those which follow, and we are inclined to think so from the likeness of the first four in pl. 4. to No. 3. pl. 3. the reverse of No. 11. pl. 4. is also in the same taste; however, that be, we are at more certainty in relation to those which follow.

Where are mills on purpose, and it is a particular business.

They have had for a long time at Nurembergh mills for the making of Jettons, called by them Rechen Phennings, which business is one of those called in Germany *Gesparred*, or *Locked up*, that is, those who are brought up to it, cannot after they served their apprenticeship, quit that city to follow it for a certain time in some other place, and return again there and settle. It is very probable that most parts of Europe wherein they were used, especially formerly, were supplied with them from hence, but whether those with the fleur de lis were intended for France, those with the lyon of St. Mark, No. 15, 16, 17, 18. for Venice, and those with what the Germans call the Reichs Apple, or Monde and Cross on one side, and on the other side 3 fleur de lis, and 3 crowns placed circularly round a rose, as No. 21, 22, 25, 26, 27, 28, 31, 32, were designed for Germany; or whether all the sorts were sent promiscuously, we cannot tell; but, however, at present they are frequently found together.

Types, whimsical and without design.

Heads of the makers.

The types upon these pieces seem to be directed by whim, humour, or accident, without any certain design or scheme that they followed; there are heads upon No. 9, 10, 11 and 12. but whom they are intended to represent does not appear; round the first is a German inscription, the English of which is, *The word of God endures for ever*; No. 10. has *Sancti Domi*, that round No. 11. we cannot read, under the head on the last is *Egidi*, I suppose for *Egidius Krawinckle*, whose head we imagine it is; as also that on No. 10. to be *Damianus Krawinckel*, as we have one like that so inscribed, it is therefore probable the other two heads are also those of the makers; that on No. 20. we think to be intended for the Emperor Charles V. and we have seen one with that of his son Philip II. crowned, with *Soli Deo Gloria* round it. On No. 13, and 14. there is a person with a table before him, having many counters on it, and on one side a sort of Abacus or counting board; the last has no inscription, and the first the maker's name, but there is one sort which has *Rechen Meister*, or Cyphering Master round it; we think the alphabet on the reverse of No. 14. might be intended also as a sort of a Horn Book for children, it is sometimes contained in a square; on No. 6. is a figure with a sort of cup in her right hand, said by some to be Pandora with her box.

A cyphering master with his counting board.

The alphabet.

A Venus appears on No. 8. with a flaming heart in her left, and three arrows in her right hand; a piece like No. 6. made as we suppose for the use of the Duchy of Burgundy, is found in great numbers, the legends of which are seldom to be read, any more than that is; the type is found on many in Meris, Nederlandisch Vorsten, vol. 1. the first as ancient as 1496, we suspect they are all made at Nurembergh, as we have one which has Macht Zu Nurembergh on it.

The

The winged Lyon of St. Mark is on one side of No. 14, 15, 16, 17, and 18. a sort of Turk's Head on No. 24. and that of Mercury on No. 30. the reverses of all which, viz. from No. 15. to 32. are a Globe or monde surmounted with a Cross within a double compartment, and is taken from the ancient Rhenish Gold Gulden, of which it continued to be the common type for many years. Lyon of St. Mark. Type of the Gold Gulden,

The Makers of these Pieces at Nurembergh, seem at first to have been confined to a very few families only, for we find but the name of four families from between the middle of the 16th to the middle of the 17th century, viz. that of *Schultz*, of which were *Jog* and *Hans*, one of *Koeb*, viz. *Kilianus*; 3 of *Krawincle*, viz. *Egidius*, *Damianus* and *Hans*, which last made more than all the others taken together; of the *Laufers* there were six, viz. *Hans*, *Matthew*, *Wolfgang*, *Chonradt*, *Cornelius* and *Laz Gotlieb*; there are some pieces with C. K. but whether for *Kocb* or *Krawinckle* we don't know, but since the above mentioned time, there seems to have been a great many more, as we shall observe when we come to the last plates.

The legends on No. 1, 2, 4, 6, 9, 13, 15, 16, 17, 19, 23, 24, 25, 26. and from 27 to 32. are the maker's names, and place where made in Nurembergh; No. 8 has only K. K. and No. 12. Egidi; No. 7, 8, 9, 12, 18, 20, 25, 29, and 32. declare they are Rechen Phenige, or Counter; No. 2. a Ship Counter, No. 18. Counters to Compute, and No. 13. which is also German, we think may properly enough be englished by *Right Reckoning makes long Friends*; most of the remaining legends consist of moral sentences in German, but those of No. 26, and 28. are in Latin, viz. *Soli Deo Gloria*, and *Verbum Domini Manet in Aeternum*, and there are others also, especially of Hans Krauwincle. Legends often the maker's name.

Almost all the pieces in pl. 5. are of Hans Krawincle, and made in Nurembergh, having either his name at length or H. K. on them, most of them probably of his own invention; among the types many of them are drawn from sacred history, as Adam and Eve, with the reverse of our Saviour on the cross. On No. 30; David and Jonathan, Joab and Amasia. On No. 4; Haman and Mordecai, and the hanging of Haman on the reverse. Of No. 1; Judith. On No. 2; also others not engraved; as Saul and Samuel, Samuel and David, the Beast in the Revelations, &c. on many others are represented the Heathen Gods, Goddesses, and Heroes, as Jupiter and Ganymede; No. 5. Jupiter and Europa, the reverse Pallas, Juno, and Venus; No. 11. Pluto with Cerberus; No. 15. Neptune, Hercules and Pallas; No. 8. Mars and Venus, No. 10. Apollo and Diana, Meleager and Atalanta; No. 13. Perseus, No. 14. Cephalus and Procris, No. 16. Pyramus and Thisbe, No. 17. there is also one, but not engraved, inscribed, *Honos Et Virtus*, with the figures of those two deities. We find also many great captains of Greece, Carthage and Rome, as Alexander the Great on No. 19. Hannibal on No. 20. also another nearly like those; of Scipio Africanus, all with the same reverse; Romulus and Remus is on some, Curtius leaping into the fiery lake, No. 21. with Popilius the Roman legate, drawing a circle round Antiochus IV. king of Syria. Also many of the modern Princes, as the Emperor Charles V. No. 22. the Grand Signior, No. 23. Queen Elizabeth on Horseback, as she appeared at the camp All in pl. 5. are Hans Krawincle. Types. Bible Histories. Heathen Gods, Goddesses, and Heroes. Heroes of Greece, Rome, and Carthage. Modern Princes.

camp at Tilbury 1588; besides which there is another of her in a standing posture, as also of the King of the Romans, of Bohemia and Spain, with their respective arms on the reverse.

Some copied from French Jettons

Besides the above mentioned Types of his own invention, there are others copied from Medals and Jettons done in France, as No. 27, 29. as also the reverses of No. 9, 12, 14, and 18. No. 16. is taken from one of Maximilian, Archduke of Austria, administrator of the Teutonick Order, the device of Charles IX. is found on No. 7. besides which there are others also which we have not engraved, as one of Charles IX. with three figures, *Amans Famanque*, another of Henry III. semeé of fleurs de lis; 2 branches between 3 crowns, *Manet Ultimo Cælo*; Henry IV. with a sword between two scepters, *Duo Protegit Uno*; others again perhaps his own chusing, as Minerva standing, *Seu Pacem Seu Bella Geras*, the same type, but with *Quos Vult Minerva Beat*; an armed man, *Nec Ignis, Nec Terra Cedens*, another, No. 17. *Aut Cæsar, Aut Nihil*, a Horseman, *Per Saxa Per Ignis*, a figure burning implements of war, *Ex Pace Ubertas*; another, *Mater Pacis Concordia*; Apollo sitting crowned by a standing figure, *Honor Alit Artes*, Hercules and Diomedes's mare, *Assuritate Et Tolerantia*, two figures, *Concedat Laurea Linguæ*, an Unicorn, *Nihil in Explorat*; a man stoning a dog, *Alius Peccat Alius Plectit*; a man fettering a lyon, *Ingenium Vires Superatus*; an Eagle with a crab in its bill, *Justa Ultio*; another *Animus Quoque Timendum*; and no doubt many others we have not seen, there are some of them with a little difference, done by Matthew and Wolfgang Laufer, C. K. and others.

Others of his own chusing.

PLATE VI. the first 10 made for France by the Laufer's

The first eleven pieces in plate 6. (except No. 10.) are done by the Laufers, and relate entirely to France, having the heads of Henry IV. Mary de Medicis, Lewis XIII. and Anne of Austria; several of the reverses are taken from French Jettons relating to the birth of the Dauphin and such like. No. 11. is the first we meet with done in the manner they are at present; the reverse having the single shield of France, the makers name and that of the piece, they are also much thinner and made of Brass, whereas the former ones were sometimes copper, No. 17. is a Spanish one of *Cornelius Laufers*, in the old manner, we have seen but another different sort of the King of Spain, No. 18, and 19. are of Joseph King of the Romans, afterwards Emperor, the first made by *J. M. Lindner*, the other by *John Weidinger*, No. 20. is of the Czarina Anna, and made by *John Adam Vogel*; No. 13, 14, 15, and 16. are of the present King of France, Lewis XV. by *John Conrad Hoger*, *Michael Leykauf*, and *John Jacob Dietzel*, who were all Counter Makers at Nurembergh, but whether are there at present cannot determine.

Others by Weidinger, Lindner, Vogel, Hoger, Leykauf, Dietzel.

Charles II. James II. William and Mary, William III. Anne, George I. George II.

All the other pieces in this plate are made for England, beginning with Charles II. and continued to the present time, there being of James II. William and Mary, William III. Anne, George I. George II. and his present Majesty, No. 21 and 22. have the heads of Charles and Catherine, the royal arms supported on the reverse of the first, and the Royal Oak appear on the other; No. 23. has only the king's head, and for its reverse that of a well known medal with *Favente Deo*. No. 24. and No. 25. have the royal arms, one in a single shield, the other in cross, as on his coin with the ɔc between them, which we we find also upon No. 27. of William and Mary, No. 31. of Queen Anne, No. 33. and 39. of George I. and George II. but whether put on them by way of ornament, or for want of knowing the true reason of their being put on those of Charles, we do not know, the inscription on these and all the remaining ones, except No. 32. is the name of the maker and that of piece, as *Lazarus Gotlieb Laufer, Cornelius Laufer, John Michael Lindner, John Henry Meisger, John Weidinger, John Jacob Deitzel, John Conrad Heger, Wolfgang Hieron Hoffman* and *Christian Sig. Anert.*

The words *Rechen Pfenning*, in whole or in part stands upon all of them; to which is also added the English word *Counter*, answering to it, but the word Jetton we have never observed to have been upon any of the French. There is a sort of these pieces which are more like the old ones, or much thicker than usual; in this manner is No. 32. of Queen Anne, another of her's on the taking the Spanish Galleons at Vigo; also one on the successes in Germany, having Minerva standing near a trophy, with *Res In German. Feliciter Gesta*, and in the exergue *Virtute Et Prudent Reginæ*; others of George I. like No. 32. and 37. and one with the figure of St. George, *Fidei Defensor Aque*; also one of Charles III. on the relieving of Barcelona 1706. and no doubt many more. Reckoning penny on all the reverses, and counter also on those for England.

We will now, by way of Addenda, cursorily shew the manner in which they used to compute with Jettons and Counters, as they were at first made for this purpose, and received their name from it. Manner of computing with Counters.

It is done by laying them on lines, increasing in their value from the bottom, which is a line of Units; the second, or next above it, is a line of Tens; the third a line of Hundreds, the fourth of Thousands, and so on. A Counter laid on the first line is only 1, being laid on the second line it is 10, on the third it is a hundred, on the fourth it is a 1000, on the 5th it is 10,000, &c. A counter laid in the space between the first and second line is 5; between the second and third it is 50; between the third and fourth it is 500, and so on; being in all cases equal to five, of those which lay on the line under it, and half of one of those on the line over it. By this contrivance, less room is required to perform the operations in, and they are done by half the number; that is, four counters on each line, and one above it, are sufficient, instead of nine, which would otherwise have been wanted on each line. A tablett, or partition with its lines, and their values as just described, ready for the purpose of calculation, is marked with (a); many of which are usually made on a table, or rather a green cloth to put on a table, or other contrivance for the purpose of computing in this manner; we shall only give examples in addition and substraction, which they seem to be particularly adapted for. are laid upon lines. those on the bottom line of least value between the lines are 5, 50, 500, &c. pl. 7. (a)

To lay down any number upon these Tables, as for example, 6327 is done in the same manner as it is reckoned; that is, the highest number first, and ending with the least, or units. Thus you lay a counter over the fifth line for 50,000, and another on it for 10,000, which makes 60,000; then lay three counters on the fourth line for 3000, two others being laid on the third line is 200; lay one over the second line for 50, and two on it for 20, is together 70; lastly, put a counter on the bottom line, and it compleats the number 63271. Notation, with counters. to lay down 63271 (b) pl. 7.

Addition with Counters. Addition may be performed by beginning to add the highest number first, and probably may be in some cases preferred, to the method at present in use with the pen, in commencing with the least; however, as we think it will be sooner comprehended this way, we have pursued that method in adding 26526 to 63271, the number just laid on.

to 63271(b)
add 26526
89797(c)

First lay a counter over the bottom line, and another upon it for 6; then 2 on the second line for 20; lay one over the third line for 500; also one over the fourth line, and one upon it for 6000; lastly, lay 2 on the fifth line for 20,000, the sum will be 89797, as in (c); in this example, no two numbers when added together amount to ten; therefore it is performed by laying on the 26526, without taking off any of those already there; but when the added number amounts to ten or more, the counters which are there must be shifted; in doing which, the general rule is, to take off as many counters as the number to be added wants of 10, and adding a 10; that is, putting down one on the line above, but if there is already 4 on it, instead of laying it down, take off all 4, and lay one above the line; and if there should be one there before, then take it off, and put one down on the next line, which is in fact taking off 99 and putting on 100, and in this manner all the following examples are worked.

general rule

to 89797(c)
add 4624
94421(d)

to 94421(d)
add 8679
103100(e)

Thus, to add 4624 to 89797, first the 4 is added by taking off 5 and 1; also 40 and 50; and laying on 100; then lay 2 counters on the 2d line for the 20; to add the 600, take off 500 and put on 100; take off 4000 and 5000 and lay down 10000; lastly, put 4 single ones on the line of thousands, the amount being 94421, as in (d). Again, to 94421 add 8679; the 9 is added by taking off 1 and putting down 10; the 70 is done by taking off 30 and 400, and putting down 500; the 600 is added by taking off 500 and laying on 100; taking off 4000 and 5000 and putting down 10000; lastly, take off 5000 and put down 3000, take off 40000 and 50000 and lay down 100000, and the sum is 103100, as in (e). That this manner of working may be easier understood, those counters which have been shifted are left on, but are scratched, and must not be reckoned in summing up, and those which have been first taken off and then put on again, are made black, and the same will be done in what follows.

Addition of different denominations. What has already been done, has been with Integers or numbers of one denomination only; but if there are more than one, as suppose pounds, shillings, and pence, or any other; the operation is the same, only in 3 such partitions, as (a) instead of one; that on the left being for the integer, and the other two for the parts; which last never require more than the two bottom lines for unites and tens, as we have no integer divided into an hundred or more parts; for in that case, a third would likewise be necessary; for example, to lay down 7632l. 17s. 10d. put on the pounds as before; then lay in the next partition a counter above the bottom line, and 2 on it for 7 shillings; lastly, a counter laid on the 2d line of the 3d partition is the 10 pence, as in (f). And if to this we add 4759l. 3s. 8d. the sum is 12391l. 11s. 6d; as it stands in (g). The 8d is added by taking off 4, and putting down one on the bottom line of the 2d partition; the 3s. by taking off 7 and laying on 10s. in the same partition; the rest is

7632	7	10
4759	3	8
12391	11	6

is done as before. *N. B.* there are many other ways of working these mixed numbers.

Substraction may likewise be performed as numeration and addition, by commencing with the highest numbers first; but we shall proceed as we begun, with the least; as for example, substract 54363 from 76894. having laid down the 76894 as in (h). In this example, as in the first; in addition there is no occasion to shift any counters, only to take off those to be substracted, which are scratched, and must not be reckoned, the remainder being 22531, as (i). Again, substract 57688 from 81454, in this example, as the figures to be substracted (all but the highest) are more than these they are to be taken from, you must observe always to take off 10, and to lay down as many as the number to be substracted wants of 10; as first to substract 8, lay down 5 and take off 3 and 10, the 80 is substracted by putting on 20 and taking off 100; the 600 by laying on 500 and taking off 100 and 1000; the 7000 by laying on 3000 and taking off 10000; and lastly, take off the 50000 and the remainder is 23766, as in (l). If mixed numbers are to be substracted, as suppose 78330 l. 1 s. 8d. from 91764 l. 11 s. 9 d. lay down the last sum, as in (m); then you first substract the 8d. by putting off the 5 and 3 single pence, and taking 1s. off from the bottom line of the shillings; proceed with the pounds as before, and the remainder will be found to be 13434 l. 10 s 1 d. as in (n).

Substraction of Integers.

76894 (h)
54363
22531 (i)

General rule

81454 (k)
57688
23766 (l)

ditto of mixed numbers.

It is on the same principles, that addition and substraction are performed by Counters, and upon Counting Boards; the laying down a Counter being to the same purpose, as pushing forward a Bead on a Counting Board, and taking one off, by a Bead's being shoved back; to make this the plainer, after a short description of each board, which are the *Abacus* of the Romans, the *Soan Pan* of the Chinese, and the *Shchota* of the Russians; we have worked the same examples on them, as we have done with counters, and distinguished them by the same letters, (b), (c), &c. the beads are also scratched, which have been shoved back, and those made black which have been first shoved back, and then forward again.

Affinity between Counters and Counting Boards.

as the Abacus, Soan Pan, and Shchota.

The Roman Abacus has 7 wires or lines for Integers, each having 4 Beads running on them, separated by a Partition, from 7 other lines, which have only one Bead on them, each in value 5 of those under it. The lines increase in their value from right to left, the 1st being Units, the 2d Tens, the 3d hundreds, and so on; these values are marked on the partition. There is also another line to the right of these, for 12th parts of an Integer, the bead at top being $\frac{6}{12}$, and the 5 under it each $\frac{1}{12}$ together $\frac{11}{12}$; which is the same number as the 4 beads on the 3 small lines, as that at top is $\frac{1}{24}$; that in the middle $\frac{1}{48}$, and each of the two at bottom $\frac{1}{72}$. (Vide Phil. Transf. Abridg. Vol. XI. p. 380.) the manner of working on this board, is by pushing the beads forward and backward, to and from the partition, and it is only those which lay close to it, are to be reckoned when the work is done. The Abacus ready for working is marked, (a) in pl. 7. and (b), (c), &c. are the same examples, as were worked by counters.

Roman Abacus. pl. 7. (a)

The Chinese Soan Pan differs principally from the Abacus in its having 2 fives at top, instead of one as that has, and in having 5 single ones at the bottom under the partition, the Abacus having but four; so that the 2 lines together make 15 instead of 9; by which means a sum is added or substracted with more ease, and fewer

Chinese Soan Pan. pl. 7. (a)

fewer moves, but the notation afterwards does not appear quite fo plain. Parts of an integer, under 16, may be work'd by taking one more line to the right, and under 31, by taking two; and by this method are worked the fhillings and pence in (f), (g), (m), (n), their boards have not always the fame number of lines but generally about 13; one of them with 8 is reprefented in (a), ready for ufe.

Ruffian Shtchota. pl. 7. (a)

The Ruffian Shtchota has 9 beads on each line, and no partition, inftead of 4 fingle ones, and a 5 with a partition between them; before you begin to work them, they are all on the left fide of the board, as in (a), with a fufficient fpace left to work them in, which is done by pufhing them forward and backward from left to right, and from right to left, and not upwards and downwards as on the Abacus, and Soan Pan. It is only thofe on the right fide are to be reckoned; when the operation is finifhed. We apprehend the Ruffians reckon the top line, a line of Units; and increafe the value in defcending, but the refult of any operation being the fame; if we begin to compute from the bottom upwards, we have worked them that way, as we did the counters, and for the fame reafon. Mixed numbers are worked by taking anothertablette as (a), for the parts, the 2 bottom lines for the leaft Denomination. Suppofe pence, and the 2 next above for fhillings, as in (g), (h), (i), (k). This Board ready for ufe is feen under (a), which is followed by the fame examples as before.

The Beads on each line of this Board are often of feveral colours, thofe at bottom being black, the 2d or next above Green, the 3d Yellow, the 4th Blue, the 5th Red, and thofe at top White; fome of thefe reckoning Boards have a partition from top to bottom, with four fmall ones, fuch as (a) on each fide; they have others again larger ftill, having fix partitions, as above, inftead of one, and 6 fuch fmall ones as (a) between each * of them.

* Peter Van Hagen Reife in Rufland, p. 524. Copenhagen 1744, 8vo.

FINIS.

Old Jettons or Counters commonly called Black money

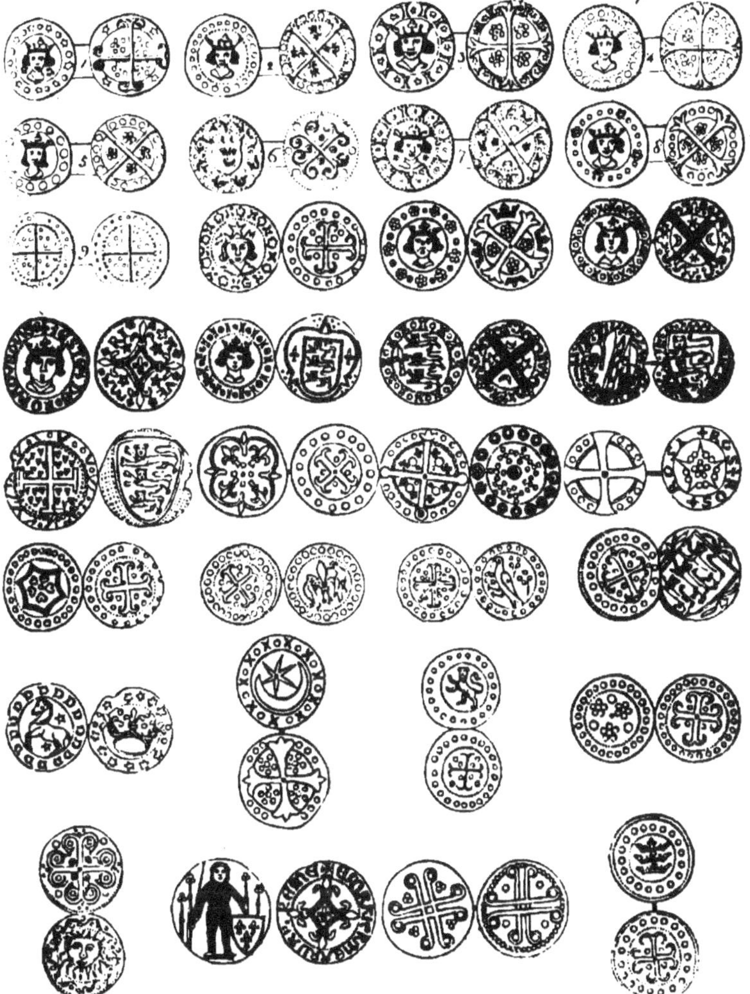

Ancient Jettons or Counters

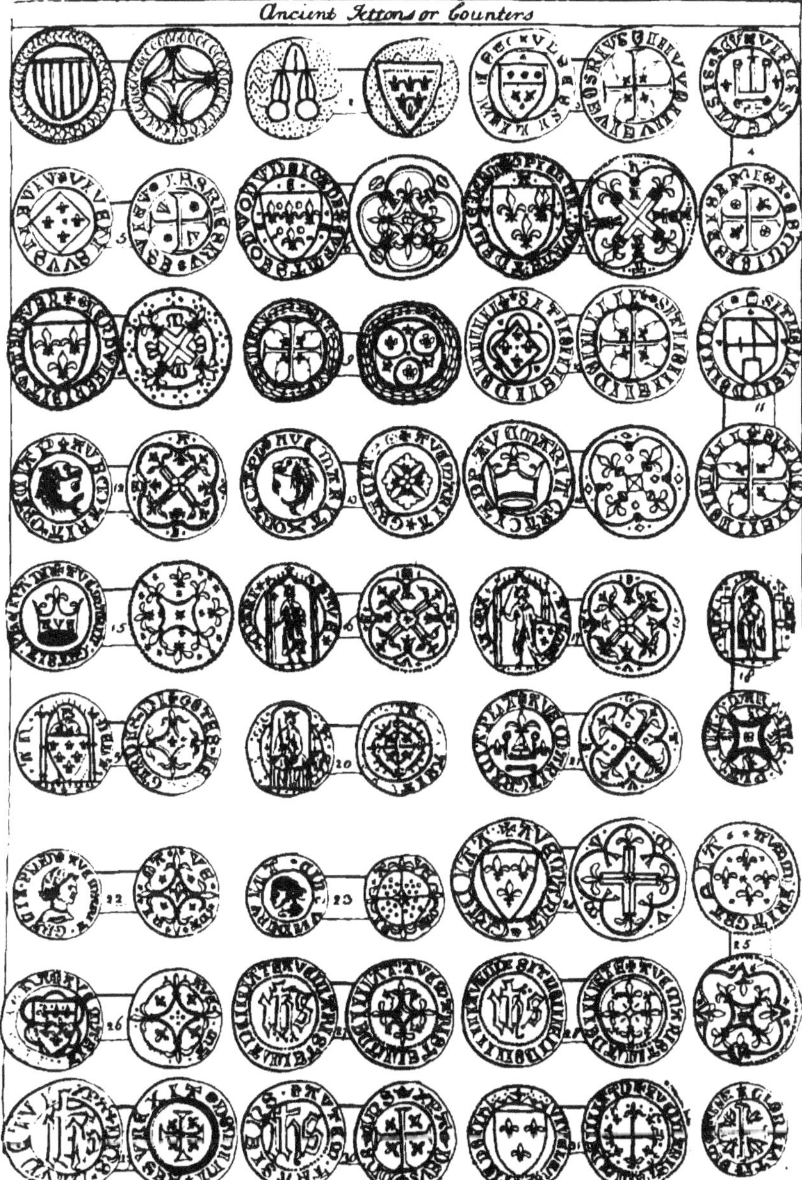

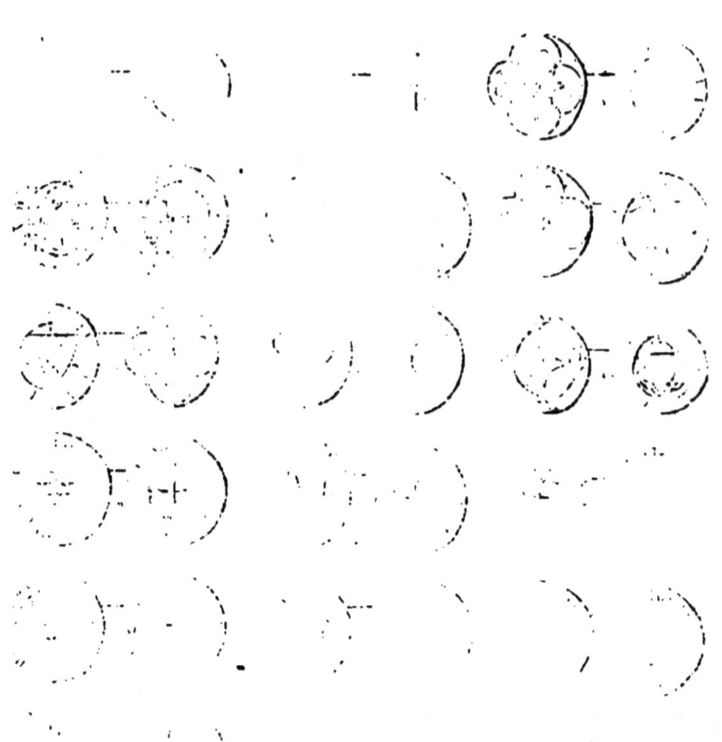

Reckoning Pennies or Counters made at Nuremberg

Reckoning Pennies or Counters made at Nuremberg

Reckoning Pennies or Counters made at Nuremberg

Counters.

a. | b. 63271 | c. 80707 | d. 94481 | e. 103100 | f. 7632

g. | h. 76894 | i. 22531 | k. 81454 | l. 23766 | m. 91764.4 | n.

Roman Abacus.

a. The Abacus | b. 63271 | c. 80707 | d. 9441

g. 13391 u. 6 | h. 76894 | i. 22531 | k. 81454 | l.

Chinese Soan Pan.

a. Chinese Soan Pan | b. 63271 | c. 80707 | d. 9444

g. 13391 u. 6 | h. 76894 | i. 22531 | k. 81454 | l.

Rufsian Shtchota.

a. Rufsian Shtchota | b. 63271 | c. 80707 | d. 94481 | e. 103100 | f. 763

h. 76894 | i. 22531 | k. 81454 | l. 23766 | m. 91764.4

MISCELLANEOUS

V I E W S

OF THE COINS

Struck by ENGLISH PRINCES in FRANCE,

COUNTERFEIT STERLINGS,

COINS ſtruck by the EAST INDIA COMPANY,

Thoſe in the WEST INDIA COLONIES,

And in the ISLE of MAN.

ALSO OF

PATTERN PIECES for GOLD and SILVER COINS,

AND

GOLD NOBLES ſtruck ABROAD in Imitation of ENGLISH.

With COPPER-PLATES.

By THOMAS SNELLING.

LONDON:

Printed for T. SNELLING, (No. 163.) next the *Horn Tavern*, in *Fleet-Street.*
MDCCLXIX.

Who buys and ſells all Sorts of Coins and Medals.

ASHMOLEAN
OXFORD
MUSEUM

P R E F A C E.

IN our View of the Gold, Silver and Copper Coins of this kingdom we have confined ourselves to speak of those alone, which were not only struck in England, but also the true and lawful currency of it, and that for full seven Centuries. Those contained in the following pages, although struck by English princes, or under their authority, yet were not the proper money of this realm.

The Anglo-Gallic series is fine and interesting, in particular those of Edward the Third, and his Son the Black Prince; the former as duke, the latter as prince of Aquitain, and of equal importance also, are such as were struck by Henry the Fifth, as Heir to the crown, and those of his son Henry the Sixth, as king of France, minted in Paris, its capital. The compleatest collection of these coins that ever came under our notice, are in the possession of Sir Charles Frederick, Knight of the Bath, and Surveyor General of the Ordnance; many doubts and difficulties which have occurred to us in treating this subject, we suspect may be cleared up by properly examining that fine Suite; however, in the king of France's cabinet at Paris, there are some pieces not in the above collection; which M. l'Abbé Barthelemy, keeper of that cabinet, permitted us to take the designs of; and we seize this opportunity to express our obligations to that Gentleman for that, and many other favours, we received at his hands, whilst we were in Paris.

The Counterfeit Sterlings, we are of opinion, were made during the reigns of the three first Edwards; yet we have met with very few which carry their names, or titles on them, but generally those of some princes in the Low Countries or Germany; and what is still more extraordinary, is, that as few even of them were struck in the mints of the princes, whose name they bear, and some of them we suspect had no mint at all belonging to them, whilst on others there appears an inscription designedly blundered; all this seems to have arose from the little probability of their being detected, as very few were the number in those days able to read an inscription at all. They seem to have been uttered from the mints of some petty princes, which were farmed out, a thing not very uncommon at that time, ; and we find sometimes those who farmed them, had the permission to coin other money, besides that of the prince to whom the mint belonged, and even the liberty to chuse their own types.

It

It is to the noble ſpirit of Queen Elizabeth to ſpread the fame of the Engliſh nation in foreign parts, that collectors are obliged for the Portcullis money of that princeſs; the only intereſting pieces to them, beſides, of the Eaſt Indian, are the Rupees and Pice of Bombay, with Engliſh and Latin inſcriptions, and the Fanams, Doudoos, and Caſh of Madraſs. In the Weſt Indies the principal money was that of New England, which they continued to ſtrike for 30 Years; but we are of opinion, many of the others never obtained a currency at all.

Among the pattern pieces will be found ſome of the fineſt performances of *Briot* and *Simon*, as alſo of the artiſt employed in the Tower, whoſe name we do not know, that produced patterns againſt thoſe of Briots. We have our doubts whether ſome we have given may not be rather Jettons then patterns, by which word we would not be underſtood to mean, pieces made for computation or play, which is the true acceptation of the word; but a ſmall medal called thus, as being about the ſize of ſuch a piece, or leſs, and its work in the ſame taſte; that is, flat, and with little relief, differing in this from a medal, and of this ſort it is probable may be No. 15, 20, 26, 27, 28 and 36. pl. 5. and No. 15, 16, pl. 6.

The Gold Nobles were very noted, and Computations frequently made in them, in the Northern parts of Europe, but they coined none, any where elſe but in the Low Countries; firſt by the Duke of Burgundy, and then by ſeveral of the States, after their revolting from the Spaniards, and it was one of the firſt coins, ſtruck by the Dutch, as a Sovereign State. We do not know how to diſtinguiſh thoſe of Elizabeth's, which we are informed, were ſtruck by the Earl of Leiceſter when Governor there, from thoſe coined in the Tower, no more than we can the double ones, both ſorts were ſtruck at Amſterdam, he infringing thereby the excluſive privilege, that the City of Dort had always enjoyed, of coining in South Holland, and ſince the Year 1600, the Cities of Horn, Enckhuſen and Medemblich, by rotation, have obtained the ſame privilege for North Holland, or Weſt Frieſland.

A

VIEW

OF THE

COINS

STRUCK BY

ENGLISH PRINCES

IN

FRANCE.

WILLIAM, surnamed the *Bastard*, succeeded his father Robert, as Duke of Normandy, *anno* 1035; and on the defeat and death of Harold, became King of England, *anno* 1066. He died in 1087.

WILLIAM I. 1035.

The first figure in the plate is supposed to be a Coin of this Prince, and has on both sides a cross inclosed within the legendary circle; and between the arms of the cross on one side are four pellets, and in the same place on the other side are three crescents, and a sort of quatterfoil; it is inscribed, WILELMUS & ROTOMACIS. There is another sort, which only differs in having four crescents instead of three, and reads ROTOMACIL.

No. 1. Type. Legend.

B It

WILLIAM I. It is probable that both these pieces were struck at Rouen before he was King of England, and they are the only ones to be met with till after the recovery of that duchy again by Henry V.

They are both in the cabinet of Sir Charles Frederick, and in the plates of Mr. De Boze (*a*); the latter of them is in Venuti (*b*), and said to be from Sir Charles's: but the pellets and crescents being omitted, has occasioned it since to be engraven as a different piece (*c*).

HENRY II. 1151. This great Prince, upon the death of his father Geoffry, in 1151, came into possession of the earldoms of Anjou, Touraine, and Maine. Also, the same year, by his marriage with Eleanor, sole daughter and heiress of William Duke of Aquitaine, he obtained Guienne, Poitou, Zantoinge, Limosin, Perigord, and Augumois; and lastly of the duchy of Normandy, upon the death of Stephen, in 1154: all which his son Richard succeeded to upon his death, in 1189.

No. 4. Type. Legend. The only piece known at present of this King is No. 4. having a cross within a circle, with HENRICUS REX on one side, and on the other side the word AQUI—TANI—E in three lines fills the area between a + and two pellets at top, and two pellets at the bottom.

We know of no other but Sir Charles's, and one that Venuti was possessed of (*d*).

ELEANOR. No. 2. There is also a Coin of Eleanora, Duchess of Aquitaine, struck before her marriage with Lewis the Young, King of France (from whom she had been divorced but six weeks before she was married to our Henry) which has on one side a sort of Monkish M at top, two + + in fess, and an A at bottom, inscribed, DUCISIA; and on the other side a plain cross, and AQUITANIE.

Besides this of Sir Charles Frederick's, there is another in the collection of Thomas Dummer, Esq; which was formerly Mr. Fairfax's; and a third published by Mr. De Boze (*e*), which has a T instead of an A in DUCISIA, and a C instead of a Q in AQUITANIE.

No. 3. Another of this same Princess, coined, it is probable, during her marriage with Lewis, has on one side a + between three annulets, and a sort of semicircle, and inscribed, LIONORA; and on the other side is a plain cross with LODOICUS. This was first published by Clairac *, and from him by Venuti (*f*). There is one published by De Boze (*g*), with the name of LEWIS only on it.

RICHARD I. 1089. Richard I. succeeded his father in 1089, and died in 1099.

No. 5. On one side of No. 5. is a plain cross and RICARDUS REX A. and in the area on the other is a cross between two O O's, having the word DUX at top, and AQUIT at bottom. This Coin was published with some English Coins of this Prince (*h*); and was Mr. Locker's, late master of the free school of Farringdon Within, but since lost. Nor is it either in the cabinet of Sir Charles Frederick, or the plates of De Boze.

No. 6. Type. Legend. The next piece, or No. 6, has, as the last, RICARDUS REX inscribed round a plain cross on one side, and the area of the other is filled with PIC TAVIE-NSIS in three lines, and was struck at Poitou. This Coin is in Sir Charles Frederick's Collection, and has been also published by Mr. De Boze (*i*), who both of them

(*a*) Monnoyes des Barons de France, pl. 26. No. 7, 8. (*b*) Dissertations sur ses anciens monumens de la ville de Bourdeaux, F. viii. (*c*) Ducarel, Series of Anglo-Gallic Coins, pl. 8. No. 99. (*d*) F. xii. (*e*) Pl. 19. No. 2. * Usance du Negoce ou Commerce de la Banque. (*f*) F. x. (*g*) Pl. 19. No. 3. (*h*) Twelve plates of English Silver Coins, pl. 3. No. 7. (*i*) Pl. 34. No. 9, 10.

have

have alſo another much ſmaller, with the ſame type and inſcription (except a ſmall creſcent in one quarter of the croſs); but whether ¦ of the other, we cannot ſay.

The obverſe of No. 7. is filled with RICA—RDUS in two lines between a croſs at top, and two creſcents or ſemicircles at bottom. The reverſe has a croſs and four fleurs-de-lis iſſuing from the inner circle into the quarters of it, and is inſcribed, AQUITANIE. Sir Charles Frederick has this piece, and it is alſo publiſhed by De Boze (*k*), but without the fleurs-de-lis; and Venuti's (*l*) alſo wants them, though he ſays it is Sir Charles's. No. 7. Type. Legend.

The next piece, No. 8. was publiſhed (*m*) from a drawing of Mr. Hodſol's, which we always imagined was taken from one in the collection of Sir Charles Frederick; but this differs from it (*i. e.* No. 7.) as it has in the firſt place R A under RICARDUS; and, 2dly, in the form of the D, which is thus Ō, we ſhould rather ſuſpect it to be a miſtake in the drawing, than a different Coin; but, however, cannot determine. No. 8. Type. Legend.

Edward I. ſucceeded his father Henry III. *anno* 1273. By his Queen Eleanor of Caſtile he acquired Ponthieu, and became poſſeſſed of the ſaid earldom on the death of her mother Joan in 1279. His other poſſeſſions in France were but ſmall; for Normandy, Anjou, Touraine, and Maine, were confiſcated by Philip Auguſtus, upon John's refuſing to appear before the court of peers at Paris, to anſwer for the murder of his nephew Arthur; after which nothing remained to the Engliſh but Guienne. And in 1223, under Henry III. all that duchy on this ſide the Garonne was loſt; as Limouſin, Perigord, Pays d'Aunis, St. Jean d'Angely, Nicort, Rochelle, &c. moſt of which places were, however, ceded to him again in 1259, and confirmed to Edward in 1279. EDWARD I. 1273. EDW. II. 1308.

The Coins uſually aſcribed to this King are No. 9. which has on one ſide a croſs, and in one of the quarters a creſcent, inſcribed, EDOARDUS REX. On the reverſe is, MONETA PONT, in two lines; and at top and bottom is a + between two pellets. There is another ſort, which only differs in its inſcription of EDVARDUS and PONTI, inſtead of EDOARDUS and PONT; and having a creſcent in one quarter, inſtead of the two pellets. No. 10. beſides the two pellets, has alſo two creſcents in the quarters, and is inſcribed EDWARDUS REX; and on the reverſe is a lion paſſant, guardant, crown'd; over which is MONETA, and under it is POTIV. All theſe pieces are in Sir Charles Frederick's cabinet, and in the collection publiſhed by Mr. De Boze (*n*). No. 9, 10. Type. Legend.

On No. 11. is a plain croſs circumſcribed with EDVARD REX ANGLIE, and on the reverſe is a lion couchant, inſcribed, DUX AQUITANIE. On No. 12, in the area, are the letters AGL—E in two lines, and over them a lion paſſant, guardant, inſcribed, EDWARDUS REX; and on the reverſe is a croſs with two creſcents in the two upper quarters, inſcribed, DUX AQVIT BURD. Mr. Hodſol has drawn a piece like this (*o*), but of the ſize of No. 11. which is inſcribed, EDWARDUS DEI GRA REX; and on the reverſe, DUX AQUITANIE. Both No. 11. and 12. are in no other collection but that of Sir Charles Frederick, that we can learn; nor do we know where the Coin lies from which that drawing was made, or the other before mentioned of Richard. No. 11, 12. Type. Legend.

The obverſe of No. 13. has a lion paſſant, guardant, and round it, EDVARDUS R. ANG; on the reverſe is a croſs different from all the foregoing, as it extends to the edge of the piece quite through the legendary circle, and is not ſeen No. 13. Type. Legend.

(*k*) Pl. 19. No. 4. (*l*) F. xxviii. (*m*) Ducarel, pl. 13. No. 3. (*n*) Pl. 38. No. 4, 5, 6. (*o*) Ducarel, pl. 13. No. 5.

so broad: it is inscribed, DUX AQIT. BURDE. This is in Sir Charles Frederick's collection, and no other, that have come to our knowledge (*p*).

EDW. III. 1326. This Prince came to the crown in 1326, his possessions in France being at that time part of Aquitaine, and the earldom of Ponthieu in Picardy; and by the treaty of Bretigny, 1360, he had ceded what had been taken from Henry III. part of which, however, was again lost before he died, which was in 1377.

No. 14, 15. Type. Legend. We have in No. 14, 15. the nearest approach to the taste of the English Sterling, than any either before, or indeed afterwards, as they shew the King's head, but not quite full-fac'd, having the Aquitaine lion on his breast, and inscribed, EDWARD REX ANGL. On the reverse is a cross extending to the edge of the piece between four coronets, and inscribed, DUX AQUITANIE. They are the whole and the half, weighing about 21 Troy grains, and the half about 11. There are some of these in the English cabinets of Mr. West, Mr. White, Mr. Hollis, Mr. Bartlet, Mr. Foote, Mr. Brent, *&c.* but not one in Haultin ‡, or De Boze.

VALUE. These two pieces likewise approach the nearest to the values of the English Sterling, and $\frac{1}{2}$ Sterling, of any of the Aquitaine Coins, and are therefore usually called the Aquitaine penny, and $\frac{1}{2}$ penny; but it will be a difficult matter to ascertain what they were current for there. However, we think we may fix the value of the largest between 4 and 6 deniers, and the other between 2 and 3; for the English penny had been, for above a century before, worth 4 deniers, and we should suspect it was now of more value, in respect to the denier, and therefore that of Aquitaine nearly as we have set it above.

No. 16. Type. Legend. The next, No. 16. has the King standing in his royal robes crowned, under a sort of Gothic arch, his sword in his right hand, and pointing with his left: it is inscribed, EDVARDUS REX ANGLIE; on the reverse, a cross of double lines extending to the edge of the piece, and in the spaces are two lions and two fleurs-de-lis, inscribed, FRACIE DNS AQITANIF.

This is the first piece with the type of what is generally called the Hardy, Ardit, or Hardit, or piece of 3 deniers; but this, by its appearance, should be a double one; and there is another of his son's, No. 26. the same: and if so, they should be about the value of 6 deniers. As for the Hardy (*q*) itself, we find it first struck by the Black Prince, then Richard II. and Henry IV. but it is a doubt with us, if there are any of Henry V. at least we cannot distinguish it from his father's; for that usually given to him with HÆRES FRANC is certainly a mistake.

The gold pieces with this type of the Black Prince, Richard II. and Henry IV. are therefore called Gold Hardies; and we find one likewise of Charles, brother to Lewis XI. There are also silver ones of both Lewis and Charles.

(*p*) Great difficulties occur in regard to the value of the Anglo-Gallic Coins, as we are often destitute of all the three requisites which constitute value, viz. weight, fineness, and currency. Some judgment may be formed of the two first, from the balance and the touchstone, when we have the pieces before us; but even these assistances (from their great rarity) have mostly been wanting; and the only method we can bring to help us in this case, is by considering the cotemporary Coins of the Kings of France, and supposing them nearly on the same footing.

Deniers, or pennies, were the only pieces current during the two first centuries of our period above; the obole, maille, or halfpenny, being first mentioned under Lewis VIII. 1225; the pougoise, pite, $\frac{1}{4}$ denier or farthing, in 1273; and the double denier in 1293. The gross weight of these deniers were about 20 gr. Troy; but the weight of fine silver in them at first about 14, afterwards 10, and lastly about 7 gr. Troy; as they contained $\frac{2}{3}$, $\frac{1}{2}$, and $\frac{1}{3}$ fine, and $\frac{1}{3}$, $\frac{1}{2}$, and $\frac{2}{3}$ alloy. Under St. Lewis, which is the famous epocha of the French money, the gross weight of the denier was about 14 Troy gr. and fine silver in it about 5 gr. Troy.

(*q*) It was a Coin peculiar to Guienne, and of ancient use in that province, and thus called from Philip the Hardy *, who began to reign *anno* 1220. *Le Blanc* † promised to treat at large of this money, when he came to those of Aquitaine.

‡ *Figures des monnoyes de France.*

* Borel Tresor de Recherches et Antiquitez Gauloises et Françoises. † P. 252.

This

This piece might either pass for 6 deniers, as we have just observed, if it was billon; but if good silver, it might have been current for 10 deniers. It is only in Sir Charles's cabinet. VALUE.

The pieces No. 17. 18. 19. and 20. are much in the taste of the gross tournois. No. 17. has a long cross within a double legendary circle; the outermost is inscribed, BENEDICTUM CIT NOMEN DOMINI; and the inner, ED DNE IBER REX ANG; and on the reverse a lion couchant, crown'd, within a border of fleurs-de-lis, and under the lion, AQUITANIE DUX. No. 17. 18. 19. 20. Type. Legend.

The obverse of No. 18. is nearly the same as the last; but the cross is contained within the inner circle, round which is inscribed, ED DNE IBE ANGLIE. The reverse has the common type of the gross tournois, with the addition of a coronet below, and a lion at top, and inscribed, REX ANGLIE—DUX AQUITANIE.

The type of No. 19. is the same as the last on both sides, only the lion the contrary way, and inscribed, ED REX ANGLIE—DUX AQUITANIE.

No. 20. appears to be the half of the three last, and differs from them only in the lion and coronet's being wanting: it is inscribed, ED REX ANGLIE—DUX AQUITANIE.

We should suspect by the agreement both in type and size (for we do not know either their weight or fineness) that these might be struck in imitation of the gross tournois of this time, which was of very good silver, weighed about 65 grains Troy, and was current for 15 deniers, when the money was *fort*, or good, and not when debased, or *foible*. This is upon a supposition that they are silver; but if it should happen that they are of a sort I have seen with this type, but thick, and of a composition of copper and calamine, wherein the latter predominates, (that is, a bad sort of brass) they then will turn out only of the ticket or jetton kind, and can have no plea to be called money. VALUE.

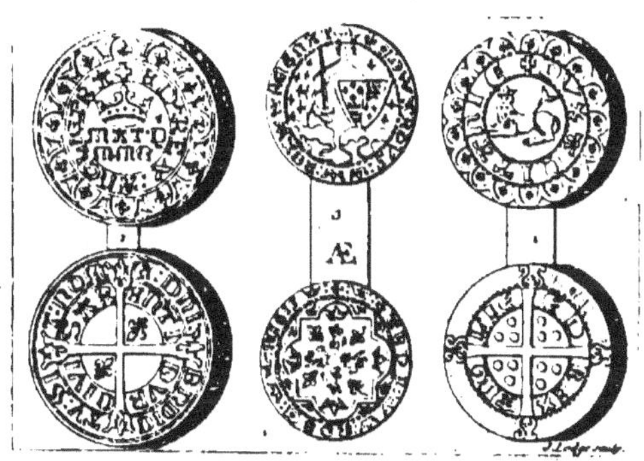

Of this kind we think is No. 1. of Sir Charles Frederick's, having on one side a crown, and under it, MAT. D. M. ME, perhaps for MATER DOMINE MISERERE ME. The inscription round is, ED REX ANGLIE FRA; on the other side, a flourished cross with a fleur-de-lis in two of its spaces, inscribed, CIVIS

 ARENTIBUS;

EDWA. III. ARENTIBUS; on the inner circle, and on the outermost one, SIT NOME DNI BNDIC. No. 2. is Dr. Ducarel's, which, round a cross and pellets, has inscribed, ED REX ANGLIE; on the inner circle and on the outer one only BEN is legible of SIT NOME DNI, *&c.* The other side has a couchant lion, as No. 17. with the remainder of the King's title, DUX AQUITANIE, within another circle of crosses. To these we have added a third, probably the oldest jetton extant, which is in the collection of Thomas Hollis, Esq; of Lincoln's-Inn, F. R. S. F. S. A. representing on one side this magnanimous King with his sword and shield, in a field fleury, as asserting his right to the crown of France. Two lions appear at his feet. The inscription is, EDWARDVS REX REGNAT. The reverse has, within a compartment of right lines and arches, four crown'd lions in cross between four fleurs-de-lis, inscribed round, GARDE ROBE REGIS, being intended, we apprehend, for the use of the King's wardrobe.

GOLD. This Prince is the first that coined gold abroad, of which we have No. 21. called a Guiennois, wherein he is represented in compleat armour, all but his head, which is crowned: he holds a sword in his right hand, and a shield with the quartered arms of France and England in his left, and seems to stand upon two lions, having a B between his feet, and is under a grand Gothic portico. On the reverse is an ornamented cross within a compartment something like that on his noble.

GUIENNOIS. Type. Legend.

The inscription on the obverse is, ED D GRA REX ALIE DO AQUITANIE; and and on the reverse is, GLIA IN EXCELSIS DEO ET IN TERRA PAX HOIBUS; that is, *Gloria in Excelsis Deo et in Terra Pax Hominibus.* Luke xi. 14.

No. 22. LEOPARD. Type. Legend. The next, No. 22. called a Leopard, has on the obverse a lion passant, guardant, crown'd, within a compartment; and on the reverse a cross, whose ends terminate in acorns with leaves, within a rose or compartment of four arches, and four angles. The inscription is, EDWARDUS DEI GRA ANGLI FRANCIE REX, and XPC VINCIT XPC REGNAT XPC IMPERAT.

No. 23. ECU. Type. Legend. The last, No. 23. called an Ecu, the King is represented sitting on an ornamented throne or seat within a compartment, with his sword erect in his right hand, and a shield with some fleurs-de-lis in his left. The reverse has a curious ornamented cross within a rose of four leaves, whose ornamented angular points terminate in the quarters, and the same leaves issue also from the legendary circle into the angles.

The inscription on the obverse is, EDWARDUS DEI GRA AGLE & FRANCIE REX; and on the reverse, XPC VINCIT XPC REGNAT XPC IMPERAT.

Gold coined in Aquitaine before it was in England. When Edward made his first expeditions to France, we had no gold money in England; and what sorts those were he coined during his sojourning at Antwerp, 1338, does not appear. And as for the gold money at that time struck in France, it was upon no regular foot; for Philip de Valois, in about twelve years, or between 1330 and 1342, struck seven different sorts, which had not been seen before, as the Paris of 32½ to the mark, Ecu 54, Lion 50, Pavillon 48, Couronne 45, Anges 38½, and Florins; besides the Royal Double 58, which had been minted under the last reign, and which he struck till he began to coin the others; and a Chaise, 52, different from that of his predecessors, which he struck in 1346 and 1347. Not one of all these pieces were of the same weight, being between our Noble and half Noble, or the heaviest about 113 Tr. gr. and the lightest about 64. There was but one of these that was continued by his son John, and that only in the beginning of his reign, which was the Ecu, of the same weight; but at first 22, then 20, and at last but 18 carats fine, or but ¾ of the value of those of Philip.

This

This Ecu was one of those struck by Edward, and appears also to have been the first, as Le Blanc informs us it was coined in 1339, which was five years before he began to coin in that metal in England. It is the only one of the three sorts that he coined in imitation of those of France, being of the same weight also, that is, about 70 grains Troy, which that in the King of France's cabinet weighs; but that at Southampton weighs only 66 grains, and it was worth about 15½ *d.* more than our half Noble, or 55½ *d.* or 4 *s.* 7½ *d.* The Leopard exactly answers the description of the half Florin of this King, which was to have one Leopard on it, and the whole was to have two. From the weight, as given by Hautin (for we do not know that of Sir Charles's) it answers also exactly; that is, 54 Troy grains, or that of the common Florin and Ducat. But however, from the inscription on the reverse of XPC. VINC. XPC. *&c.* we think it cannot be one of those half Florins. EDW. III.

The type of the Guiennois is likewise entirely different from any either before or since, except that struck by his son; and I think that the name in old French has some allusion to the armed figure it carries on it, by the weight of that in the King's cabinet at Paris, that in the Duke of Devonshire's collection, and that of Sir Peter Thompson's; that is, 60 grains Troy, we suspect it might be struck on the footing of the half Noble, whose weight was the same.

Besides the Guiennois of Sir Charles, we know of no other than the Duke of Devonshire's, that of Sir Peter Thompson's at Poole, and that in De Boze; of the Leopard only Sir Charles's, and one in Hautin; and of the Ecu that of Sir Charles, one at the free school at Southampton, and one in the King's cabinet at Paris, tho' not in De Boze.

This great Prince, called frequently also the *Black Prince*, was declared Prince of Aquitaine by his father in 1362, which he held for ten years, or until 1372, when he again resigned it into his father's hands, and died about four years afterwards, or in 1376. EDWARD, Prince of Wales and Aquitaine, 1362.

The first piece of this Prince, No. 24. shews him in armour to the knee under a canopy, with a sword in his right hand, and his left on his breast, as No. 16. The reverse also is just like that, a cross between two lions, and two fleurs-de-lis. The inscription on the head side is, ED PO GNS REG AGLE B; and on the reverse, PRNCPS AQUITANIE, for EDVARDUS PRIMO GENITUS REGIS ANGLIE PRINCEPS AQUITANIE. No. 25. only differs from the last in being covered with a royal mantle, and within a sort of compartment, and on the reverse has AQUITA. HARDY. Type. Legend.

No. 26. appears to be double the value of the two last, and has the Prince in his royal robes, which are adorned with fleurs-de-lis below the waste, holding his sword in his left hand, differing in this from No. 16. of his father's, but in all other respects like that, both head and reverse. The inscription on the head side is, ED PRIMO GENITUS ANG; and on the reverse, PRINCEPS AQUITANIE. Type. Legend.

No. 27. and 28. have the Prince in profile, with a sword in his right hand, as before; and the last is within a rose or compartment; some of which have him bare-headed, on others he has a sort of chaplet, and is crown'd on another; and the reverses are exactly agreeable to those on the English money, *viz.* the cross and pellets. The inscription on the first is, ED PO GN REG ANGLI, and PRICPS AQUITE; and on the other, ED PO GNS REGIS ANGLIE; and on the outer circle of the reverse, GLIA IN EXCELSIS DEO E IN TRA PAX; and on the inner circle, PRNCPS AQUITAN. On some of No. 27. are found, EDW. PRIM. GENITUS; and on that of Hautin, the word REX, instead of REGIS. GROAT. HALF GROAT. Type. Legend.

The

EDWARD, the Black Prince. The largest of these pieces is called a Silver Sterling, in the ordonnance of the Black Prince taken out of the Livres de Bouillions (*q*). Venuti calls it a Silver Sol, and a little lower infers it was the same as the Gross Tournois. It is called a Silver Hardy by De Boze (*r*); by Ducarel (*s*), a Bourdeaux Groat; and with us here its usual name is an Aquitaine Groat. The weight of the largest is generally comprised between 33 and 24 Troy grains, and the half in proportion. Besides these of Sir Charles's, they are in the cabinets of James West, Esq; of Mr. Edward Hodsoll, Mr. John White, and perhaps other gentlemen.

VALUE. We are told it was 8 oz. fine; that the mark was coined into 5 livres 5 sols; but are not informed, whether the mark of 8 oz. or 12 oz. is of this value. However, we think it is the former; and if so, and that they were current for 12 deniers, or a sol, their weight would be about 36 grains Troy; but if only a Grand Blanc, or 10 deniers, not more than 30 grains, which is against experience. On the contrary, by supposing it a sol, the fine mark would be 7 *l.* 17 *s.* which is worse than that of Charles V. during this interval, which was but 6 *l.* that is, Blanc of 4 den. fine, and of 96 to the mark.

Venuti (*t*) says, it was of the same fabric, size, and weight of the Gross a la Couronne of Philip de Valois; but he is mistaken in all three articles. That being different in type, was larger, and but one half as fine, weighing 57 grains Troy, and coined at 9 *l.* 8 *s.* the fine mark.

GOLD. There are five sorts of gold money of this Prince, two of which had been before struck by his father.

CHAISE. Type. Legend. On the first, No. 29. he appears sitting in a Gothic chair, or throne, with a scepter in his right hand. On the obverse is a cross within a compartment of four roses and four angles, much like No. 22. and 23. It has two lions and two fleurs de-lis in the quarters. On the head side of it is inscribed, ED PO GNS REGIS ANGLIE PNS AQUITANIE; and on the reverse, DEUS JUDEX JUSTUS FORTIS PACIENS B. From this inscription De Boze (*u*) calls it a *Juste*, or *Fort*. That in the King of France's cabinet weighs about 54 grains Troy, or that of the florin and ducat; and that of Mr. Hollis the same.

HARDY. Type. Legend. On No. 30. he is in his robes to his waist, with his sword in his right hand, within a compartment. On the reverse is a cross with the lions and fleurs-de-lis. It is inscribed on the obverse as the last; but on the reverse, AUXILIUM MEUM A DOMINO B. That in the King of France's cabinet weighs 75 French grains, or about 61 grains Troy; the Duke of Devonshire's 60, or that of the half noble. Hautin, p. cxxxiii. has one a little different, he being crowned. His robes are open so as to shew his armour, and it has only AQT instead of AQUITANIE. Mr. John White never had a piece in silver of this sort in his collection, as is reported by Dr. Ducarel (*w*).

GUIENNOIS. Type. Legend. No. 31. is exactly like No. 21. of his father's, being completely armed with his sword and shield. It is inscribed, ED P GNS REGIS ANGLIE PINCPS AQUITANIE; and on the reverse, as No. 21. that is, GLIA IN EXCELSIS DEO ET IN TER PAX HOMINIB.

LEOPARD. Type. Legend. No. 32. is also exactly like No. 22. of his father's, with the leopard, and inscribed, ED PMO GNS REGIS ANGLIE PNCEPS AQUITANIE; and on the reverse also as his father's, XPC VINCIT XPC REGNAT XPC IMPERAT.

PAVILLON. Type. Legend. No. 33. is the last of the gold pieces of this Prince, in which he is represented standing in his robes under a spacious portico, with his sword as usual, and has two ostrich feathers on each side of him. On the reverse is a cross formed of leaved acorns, inclosed within a sort of curved lozenge, out of the middle of the four sides of which issue the four angles of a square. It is inscribed round the obverse,

(*q*) Venuti, p. 173, 175. (*r*) Pl. 20. No. 1. (*s*) Page 22. (*t*) P. 173. (*u*) Pl. 19. No 7. (*w*) P. 23.

ED

Coins struck by English Princes in France from Will. I. to Rich. II.

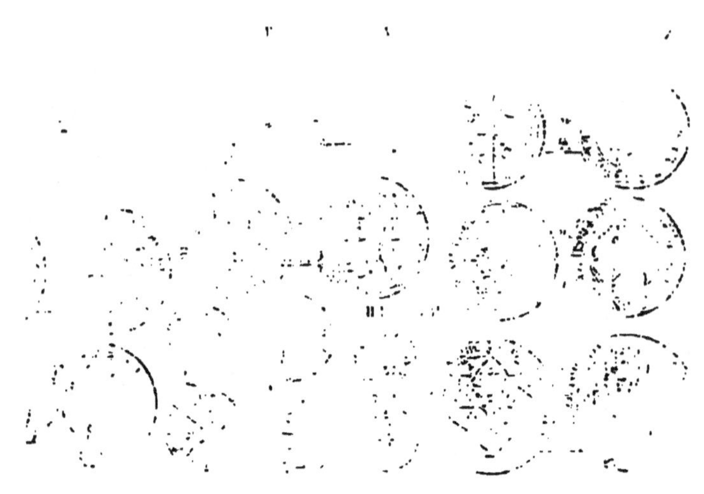

ED PO GNS REO ANGL PNPS AQUI; and on the reverſe, DNS AJUTO PTECIO EDWARD,
ME IIPO SPAVIT COR MEUM B; that is, *Dominus adjutor protector meus, in eo* the Black
ſperavit cor meum, Pſ. xxviii. 7. The King's, and that of the Duke of Devonſhire's, Prince.
weigh 69 gr. Troy, that at Paris about 73 gr. Troy, and Mr. Knight's 83 gr. Troy, differing more in their weight than any of the Aquitanian gold coins.

All the gold money of this Prince are very rare. Of Chaiſes, beſides this of Sir Charles's, there is one in the collection of the Duke of Devonſhire, and one in that of the Earl of Pembroke (*a*); another is in that of Thomas Hollis, Eſq; formerly Mr. Thomas Grainger's (*b*), and one in the King of France's cabinet at Paris (*c*). We know of no other Guiennois or Leopard than this of Sir Charles's, and that in De Boze (*d*). There is a Hardy in De Boze (*e*), and the Duke of Devonſhire has another. Of Pavillons, there is one in the King's cabinet, formerly Dr. Andrew Gifford's (*f*); one in the Devonſhire, and another in the Pembroke collections (*g*); another is in that of Thomas Knight, Eſq; of Godmerſham, near Canterbury, formerly poſſeſſed by Bryan Fairfax, Eſq; (*h*); one in De Boze (*i*) (named by him a Double) and a bad print of one in ſeveral old Dutch placarts.

This Prince ſucceeded his grandfather, Edward III. He was called of Bour- RICH. II.
deaux, as being born there, and exceedingly beloved by them; to which city and 1377.
its territory, Bayonne and Calais, all our dominions in France were now reduced. He was dethroned in 1399, and ſoon after died, or was murdered.

There is a lion paſſant, gardant, on the obverſe of No. 34. and under him a No. 34.
G, and on the other ſide a plain croſs, inſcribed, RICARDUS REX ANGL—DUX Type.
AQUITANIE. This appears to be a denier; but by Venuti, who publiſhed one Legend.
from Clairac, it is falſely called an Ardit, or Hardy, or 3 deniers.

No. 35. is much like No. 24. of his father, as is No. 36. like No. 25. but he No. 35, 36.
is crowned in both, and is entirely covered with his robes. The inſcription on HARDIES.
No. 35. is, RICARD REX AGLI—FRACIE DNS AQITANE; and on No. 36. it Type. Legend.
is, RIC REX ANGLIE—FRACIE DNS AQUI.

The only ſort of Gold Coin of this Prince is No. 37. and like No. 30. of his GOLD.
father's; but he is here again crowned, which his father is not: it is inſcribed, HARDY.
RICARD D GRA ANGL REX D AQIT; and on the reverſe, AUXILIUM MEUM Type.
A DOMINO (Pſalm cxxvii. 2.) Beſides that in Sir Charles's collection, Venuti Legend.
(F. xxvi.) publiſhed one he took from Clairac; and there is another in De Boze, pl. 20. No. 3. which lies in the French King's cabinet at Paris, weighing 70 French grains, or about 57 grains Troy, or between 3 and 4 grains more than his father's. There is alſo one publiſhed by Speed.

This Prince's dominions in France were likewiſe little more than Bourdeaux, HENRY IV.
Bayonne, Calais, &c. with their territories. He came to the crown *anno* 1399, 1399.
and died *anno* 1413.

This ſmall piece is much in the taſte of No. 11. 13. and 34. pl. 1. it has the No. 1. pl. 2.
lion paſſant, guardant, on one ſide, and a plain croſs on the other: it is inſcribed, Type.
ERICUS REX ANG—DUX AQUITANIE. Although it is here put to this Prince, Legend.
yet we are not clear it does not belong to one of the former Henries: it is probably like thoſe juſt mentioned, a Denier.

Theſe pieces agree nearly in type with thoſe of Edward III. No. 16. pl. 1. the No. 2, 3, 4.
Black Prince, No. 24. and 25. and thoſe of Richard II. No. 35. and 36. The HARDIES. Type. Legend.

(*a*) P. 4. T. 19. Fig. 2. (*b*) Ant. Soc. pl. 43. (*c*) De Boze, pl. 19. No. 7. (*d*) Ibid. No. 9. 11. (*e*) Ibid. No. 8. (*f*) Ducarel, pl. 4. No. 58. (*g*) P. 4. T. 19. Fig. 1. (*h*) Ant. Soc. pl. 36. (*i*) Pl. 19. No. 10.

D inſcription

HENRY IV. 1399. inſcription on No. 2. is, HENRIC REX ANGLIE—FRANCIE D AQUITANIE: the reverſe differs from the reſt, as the croſs is incloſed within the inner circle, and inſtead of two fleurs-de-lis in the interſtices, has ſomething unknown to us. No. 3. reads, ENRIC R ANGLIE—FRACIE DNS AQI; and No. 4. HENRICUS ANGLIE—REX FRANCIE DVS. This reading on the reverſe ſeems to be tranſpoſed, and ſhould ſtand thus: FRANCIE REX DVS. The type of both theſe laſt are nearly the ſame, both head and reverſe, and like No. 25. and 36. pl. 1.

The figure on No. 4. will, upon examination, be found to be the ſame as that upon the Aquitaine Coin in the Bodleian collection, from whence it will appear how different the figure of it in pl. xxi. p. 291. is from the Coin itſelf: the legend likewiſe, which remains, will be found to anſwer to that of No. 4. or FRAN—CIE—RE, the quarter where HER is ſuppoſed to ſtand being obliterated: but if it had not, it would have been, we think, DVS, as it is upon No. 4. We therefore judge it to be one of Henry IV. at leaſt, if it ſhould be Henry V. it has not HERRES FRANCIE on it.

No. 5, 6, 7. Type. Legend. The Numbers 5. 6. 7. be the pieces what they will, either Groſſes Tournois, or only a jetton or ticket, as we have given our opinion under thoſe of Edw. III. No. 17. 18. 19. 20. pl. 1. we ſuſpect were of a ſimilar kind, and for the ſame purpoſe as thoſe. They have all on one ſide a croſs incloſed within a double circle, and No 5. has beſides a fleur-de-lis in one of the quarters, on the reverſe of which is the lion with a crown over his head, but does not touch it. No. 6. has the common type of the Groſs, with the addition of the lion, which is alſo on No. 7. but he is on ſomething entirely different from what we have before met with on theſe or any other pieces. The inſcription on the obverſe of No. 5. is, CIT NOMEN DOMINI BENEDICTUM, on the outer circle, and the ſame on No. 7. but on No. 6. the word BENEDICTUM ſtands firſt. On the inner circle of No. 5. is, ERI REX ANGLIE—DUX AQUITANIE. No. 6. has ERIC, and No. 7. EN DNS IBRACIIE—DUX NANCIE, which is unintelligible, and certainly a blundered inſcription.

No. 8. Type. Legend. No. 8. is very ſingular in its type, and we have nothing like it before or afterwards, having a buſt full faced and crowned, and on the reverſe a caſtle within a compartment of eight leaves, with a B at bottom: it is inſcribed round the head, ENRICUS DUX ET DEI GRACIA REX—ANGLIE DNS IBERNIE ET AQUITANIE ELESI. Here again is a legend very different from thoſe commonly found on theſe ſort of Coins; the type is borrowed from thoſe of the Henries, Kings of Caſtile, and we ſhould almoſt ſuſpect it to be one of thoſe, and the inſcription not quite legible. The Coin given by Venuti, F. xxv. to the father of this Prince, is likewiſe Spaniſh, and belongs to one of the Johns, King of Caſtile.

GOLD. HARDY. There are two different pieces of gold money of this King: the type of No. 9. is in imitation of thoſe of the Black Prince, No. 30. and of Richard II. No. 37. pl. 1. having a three quarter length of the King in his royal robes, with his ſword in his right hand, and a fleur-de-lis and lion on his ſides, all within a compartment: the reverſe has the ornamented croſs, like the above-mentioned Coins: it is inſcribed, HERIC D GRA R ANGLIE F. D. AQITA; and on the reverſe, XPC VINCIT XPC REGNAT XPC IMPERAT, as uſual. This piece is Sir Charles's, and has already been publiſhed by Venuti, F. xxxii. who calls it an Ecu d'Or, the only one beſides being that of Hautin, and is ſaid to weigh 70 French grains, or about 58 grains Troy, and called a Talbot. The other piece, No. 10. differs principally from the foregoing, in having the two beaſts on his ſhoulders (which has puzzled ſo many) but has no compartment, lion, or fleur-de-lis: it is inſcribed, HENRIC DEI GRA R ANGLIE F. D. AQIT; and on the reverſe, AUXI-

LIUM

LIUM MEUM A DOMINO, as No. 30. and 37. pl. 1. Besides this of Sir Charles's, which Venuti has also published, F. xxxiii. but falsely calls it an Half Noble, there is one in De Boze, pl. 20. No. 5.

This great Prince succeeded his father *anno* 1413; he invaded France in 1415, HENRY V.
and mastered the dutchy of Normandy; was married to Catherine, daughter of 1413.
Charles VI. King of France, June 1420, and declared Regent of, and heir to the kingdom of France, but died about two months before his father-in-law, or August 31, 1422.

The first silver, or rather billon Coin of this King, was a Gross or Grand Blanc, current for 20 deniers, having on the pile side his name, HENRICUS, with a cross and leopard, being all the description given of it, and agreeing so far with that of his son's, No. 14. with which we think it corresponded in type and legend, but not in nominal value, and are not at present easily to be distinguished from each other. It seems to have been uttered soon after his taking of Roan, which was in January 1419; for the ordonnance dated at Gisors, 25th September, this same year, takes notice of its prior currency; by which order (*k*) the four following pieces were to take place. GROSS, or GRAND BLANC.

An Half Gross at 10 deniers, and a Quarter Gross at 5 deniers, both of which were to have on the pile side a shield with three fleurs-de-lis; also a Double, or Mansois, at 2 deniers, to have but two fleurs-de-lis; and a Single Denier, which was to have only one. All these pieces were to have an H in the middle of the cross, which we suppose was to be on the other side. However, not one of these pieces have reached our days, nor do we know any cabinet where any of them lies, or any author come under our notice who pretends to have seen them. HALF GROSS. QUARTER GROSS. DOUBLE. DENIER.

The *Pes Moneta*, or *Money Foot*, in this Coinage, was 15 livres, the Quarter Gross being $2\frac{2}{3}$ oz. fine, and 13 *s.* 4 *d.* or 160 to the mark *, each piece weighing $28\frac{4}{5}$ Paris, or about 23 Troy grains: the Double was $1\frac{1}{3}$ oz. fine, and 16 *s.* 4 *d.* or 200 to the mark, each weighing 23 Paris, or 19 Troy grains: the Denier was 1 oz. fine, and 25 *s.* or 300 to the mark, the weight of each being 15 Paris, or 12 Troy grains. We are informed the Gross was on the same foot with the above, but not told its weight and fineness: however, it is highly probable these were the same as those his son afterwards coined, *viz.* 5 oz. fine, and 75 to the mark, or weighing $61\frac{1}{2}$ Paris, or near 50 Troy grains, which brings the fine mark to 15 livres. VALUE.

By another ordonnance (*l*), dated at Roan, Jan. 12, 1420, or about four months after the last, a new sort of Gross, No. 11. is made current for 20 deniers, which on the pile side is to have three fleurs-de-lis crown'd, and supported by two leopards, round which was to be HENRICUS FRANCORU REX, and on the other side to have a grand cross, with an H in the middle, and round it, SIT NOMEN DOMINE BENEDICTU, which corresponds with that in Le Blanc (*m*); whereas this of Sir Charles Frederick's (No. 11.) has besides a lion and fleur-de-lis in two of the quarters. Another, published by Hautin (*n*) and Du Fresne (*o*), has two coronets in those places, as has also a third in Molinet (*p*), which is also otherwise GROSS. Type. Legend.

* Mr. Leake, p. 140. has mistaken the fineness of the silver for the absolute weight of the piece, and the number of pieces in the mark for the value of a mark of such silver in the two first; but in the last he calls the fineness, the weight of alloy, and the number of pieces, the value of a mark of such alloy.

(*k*) Rymer, tom. 9. p. 798. (*l*) Ibid. tom. 9. p. 847. (*m*) P. 244. (*n*) cxxix.
(*o*) Glossarium, tom. 2. p. 643. (*p*) Le Cabinet de la Bibliotheque de St. Genevieve, p. 148.

very

HENRY V. 1412. very remarkable, as the H in the middle of the cross reads with the legend round it of FRANCIE ET ANGLIE REX; and that round the supported arms is, SIT NOMEN DOMINI BENEDICTI.

VALUE. Here is an advance in the denomination of 60 per cent. the fine mark being increased from 15 to 24 livres, the Gross being $3\frac{1}{2}$ oz. fine, and 6 *s.* 8 *d.* or 80 to the mark *; each therefore weighing $57\frac{1}{2}$ Paris, or 48 Troy grains. This Coinage is enforced by another order of Feb. 1. following (*q*), wherein they are called *Royaux*, and other pieces of Quars de Gros, Mansois or Doubles, and Deniers, are to have course. The currency of those of France and Brittanny are forbidden, there being many false and bad among them. This is again enforced by a third ordonnance of April 18. (*r*) directed to the wardens of the mint at St. Looe.

No. 12. After his marriage with Catherine, and being made heir to the crown of France, Henry published another ordonnance (*s*), dated at Braye sur Seine, June 14. 1420, directed to the wardens of the mints at Roan and St. Looe, for making current a new Groz, or Blanc Denier, which was to have the usual type of three fleurs-de-lis crowned, and supported by two leopards, *&c.* but the inscription was to be, HENRICUS REX ANGL ET HERES FRANCIA. This is only in the cabinet of Sir Charles Frederick, and reads, H REX ANGLIE & HERES FRANCIE.

VALUE. The Gross is here only $2\frac{1}{2}$ oz. fine, 8 *s.* 4 *d.* or 100 to the mark, and therefore its weight 46 Paris, or about 38 Troy grains, the King ordering the *Money Foot* to be that of the *Huit Vientiesme* †, or 40 livres, and the last being only of 26 livres, here was a nominal rise of $66\frac{2}{3}$ per cent.

No. 13. Another piece struck about this time is No. 13. having on one side a lion passant, guardant, with a fleur de-lis over it, and inscribed, H. REX ANGL. HERES FRANC. On the reverse is a cross, with a small compartment in the center, whose angles end in four fleurs-de-lis, inscribed, SIT NOMEN DNI BENEDICT. On some the fleurs-de-lis are larger, and project farther than on others. There is one in Haultin (*t*), and another in Du Fresne (*u*), (but the last we suspect to be taken from the former) both of which are inscribed, H REX ANGL ET REX FRANC. We should be inclined to think, that the words ET REX are not legible on the piece; for if they are, it must belong to his son, and the order for its coinage could not be June 28, 1422, as in the MS. notes to Haultin (*x*). Besides this of Sir Charles's, there is one in the collection of Mr. Dummer, which had been first Mr. Fairfax's, and afterwards Mr. Folkes's. Mr. White has also one, and another is possessed by Sir Thomas Fludyer. +

VALUE. We are at a loss in relation to the value of these pieces, but think that with HERES to have been a Gross as the last, but not so heavy, weighing 30, $26\frac{1}{2}$ grains,

* The same mistake as above, in giving that for the weight of the piece, which expresses the fineness of the silver, and instead of the number of pieces, the value of a mark of that silver, is here again committed by Mr. Leake, p. 142. as also by Dr. Ducarel, p. 36.

† The *Money Foot* is here called the 160th, which we think was the highest of our Henries, and which, about two years afterwards, was reduced more than four parts in five, or to that of the 30th. During the time that the French King, John, was prisoner in England, it rose to the 500th, or 125 livres the fine mark. In this manner of computing the *Money Foot* by the ordinal numbers, the basis, or first Foot, is supposed 5 sols; but for what reason, no where appears; for the lowest it ever could have been in fact, and from which the others should be reckoned, is that of $13\frac{1}{3}$ sols, or 13 sols 4 deniers, or 160 deniers, by the old method still used in England, or of 16 sols or 192 deniers, according to the method of computation made use of in France.

(*q*) Rymer, tom. 9. p. 860. (*r*) Ibid. p. 888. (*s*) Ibid. p. 926. (*t*) P. cxxvii. (*u*) Tom. 11. p. 643. (*x*) Ducarel, p. 36.

+ another different in Dr. Ducarel's Collection 1773

grains, &c. Thoſe with Rex are ſaid, in the MS. notes to Haultin, to be 3 oz. fine, 150 to the mark, and to paſs for 3 deniers; which therefore was after the reformation of the coin, or when the fine mark was 7 *l.* 10 *s.* but they muſt be lighter, as weighing not more than 30½ Paris, or 25 grains Troy, when unworn. HENRY V.

We find by the ordonnance of this King, dated at Giſors, Sept. 25. 1419, that he had cauſed Gold Moutons to be coined ſome time before; and he now orders, that thoſe which ſhall be hereafter made, ſhall have an H in the middle of the croſs: they were 22 carats fine, 96 to the mark; therefore weighed 48 Paris, or about 39 grains Troy, paſſing at firſt for 20 ſols, or one livre or frank, but were now raiſed to 30; and by an ordonnance of Charles VI. dated 17th Jan. 1420 (*y*) they were permitted to be current in other places beſides Normandy, but their value was then but 15 ſols. GOLD. MOUTON.

By the ordonnance of Jan. 12. 1420, a Petit Florin d'Or is to be coined, which on the pile ſide was to have a ſhield with the quartered arms of France and England, inſcribed, HENRICUS DEI GRATIA REX FRANCIÆ ET ANGLIÆ; the reverſe to have a croſs with an H in the center, alſo two leopards and two fleurs-de-lis in the quarters, inſcribed, CHRISTUS VINCIT, CHRISTUS REGNAT, CHRISTUS IMPERAT: it was to be of the ſame weight and fineneſs as the Mouton, but to paſs for 40 ſols, or 2 franks. FLEURIN.

All the intelligence we have in relation to the above two pieces, is gathered from the orders publiſhed concerning them; for, upon the ſtricteſt inquiry, we cannot learn that a ſingle one of either of them is now to be found in any cabinet.

The laſt gold money of this King was the Salute *, and Half Salute, being a new ſpecies of coin minted and made current towards the cloſe of the year 1421, by Charles VI. by his ordonnances of Aug. 11. Oct. 12. and Nov. 8. and ſoon after, Henry, during the time he was at Paris, or about Chriſtmas, coined them likewiſe, which Charles VI. by another ordonnance of January 17th following, gave a currency to in his dominions, for the ſame values as his own, or 25 ſols the whole, and 12 ſols 6 deniers the half. Neither of theſe are in De Boze, nor does it appear that Le Blanc had ever ſeen one, Dr. Ducarel being miſtaken in making that author ſay, that Salutes and Demy Salutes were coined by this King with HERES FRANCIA on them; for he only affirms, that thoſe titles are found on two ſilver coins; not one of theſe, any more than the former, being depoſited in any cabinet we have any knowledge of. SALUTE. None of either now remaining.

This Prince ſucceeded his father, Auguſt 31, 1422, being but nine months old: he was crowned King of France at Paris, November 12, 1422, his uncle, John Duke of Bedford, being appointed Regent of that kingdom. The Engliſh continued maſters of Paris during the firſt thirteen years of his reign, but were obliged to quit it, April 3, 1435, and in his 32d year, or *anno* 1454, all the other places poſſeſſed by the Engliſh in France were loſt, except Calais and Guiſnes. This King died *anno* 1469. HENRY VI. 1422.

* The old Engliſh chronicles of Hall (*a*), Grafton (*b*), and Hollingſhed (*c*), take notice of the ſtriking of this Salute when the King was at Paris, about Chriſtmas this year. The firſt and laſt of thoſe authors tell us it has two ſhields on it, and the ſame had been aſſerted before by Monſtrelet (*d*); but however, it will appear preſently that Grafton was in the right, in ſaying it had no more than one on it, or that of France and England, quarterly.

(*y*) Le Blanc, p. 243.

(*a*) P. 163. (*b*) P. 44. (*c*) Vol. 2. p. 1211. (*d*) Vol. 1. p. 251. Du Freſne, T. 2. p. 648.

E On

GRAND BLANC. Type. Legend.

On the same day this King was crowned at Paris, November 12, 1423, the Blanc (No. 14.) received its currency, and continued to be coined as long as the English were masters of Paris, which was near fourteen years, and is the reason of so many being still remaining, as it is almost the only silver coin now to be met with, of the many that were struck in France by our Princes. On its obverse, over the two shields, with the arms of France alone, and France and England quarterly, is HERICUS; and round them, FRANCORUM ET ANGLIE REX: the reverse has HERICUS under a cross between a fleur-de-lis and a lion, and inscribed, SIT NOMEN DNI BENEDICTU. We suspect that these were nearly, if not altogether, of the same type as the first Gross of Henry V. but have no criterion whereby we can distinguish them. However, it is probable the major part of those now remaining are of the last sort.

VALUE.

The money foot on which these were coined was that of 7 livres 10 sols, to which it had been reduced from 40 livres, some time before his father's death: they were 5 oz. fine, and 75 to the mark, or weighed $61\frac{11}{25}$ Paris grains, or about 50 grains Troy. The pound Troy of standard silver in England at this time was 32 *s.* and of fine 34 *s.* $0\frac{1}{4}$ *d.* at which rate the Paris mark is 22 *s.* $0\frac{1}{4}$ *d.* the livre 3 *s.* $0\frac{1}{2}$ *d.* the sol $1\frac{1}{2}$ *d.* and this Blanc was worth $1\frac{1}{4}$ *d.* Sterling.

PETIT BLANC. Type. Legend.

The Petit Blanc, No. 15. or half the Grand Blanc, has, like that, the two shields; but instead of the word HERICUS over them, has a crown, and inscribed, HENRICUS REX. The same word is omitted under the cross on the reverse, having round it the remainder of the titles, FRANCORUM ET ANGLIE. The MS. notes to Haultin make this of the St. Looe coinage of 1420; but that piece was No. 11. quite different in all respects. No. 16. is also an Half Blanc, which has neither the word HERICUS, nor a crown over the two shields, like the other; but reads, HENRICUS REX, as that does. The reverse has the cross, like the other; but it is between H. R. instead of the fleur-de-lis, and inscribed, SIT NOMEN DNI BENEDICTU.

VALUE.

Both these pieces are in Haultin (*z*) and Le Blanc (*a*), but the last is only in Du Fresne (*b*), who says it is like the whole; and the MS. to Haultin (*c*) makes it 5 oz. fine, 150 to the mark, or weighing $30\frac{18}{25}$ Paris grains, or about 25 grains Troy; but those notes are wrong in making the former like those struck at St. Looe.

DOUBLE PARISIS. Type. Legend.

On the obverse of No. 17. is the word HERI crowned, and under it a fleur-de-lis and lion, with the inscription, FRANCORUM & AGL REX: its reverse shews a cross fleury, inscribed, CIVIS PARISIUS. This piece is engraved in Le Blanc as a Double Parisis; it is also in Du Fresne's plate, T. 2. p. 643. but in his description of it, he says its value was a Denier Parisis, that it was $1\frac{1}{2}$ oz. fine, and weighed 23 Paris grains, or 19 grains Troy; therefore the fine mark is $6\frac{2}{3}$ livres Paris, or about 8 livres Tournois; agreeing nearly with the money foot of Henry VI. and, if this data is right, makes us suspect it rather to be a denier than a double: it is also in Haultin.

VALUE.

DENIER PARISIS. Type. Legend.

The obverse of No. 18. is like the last, only has not the fleur-de-lis and lion, and in the inscription has ET ANGL, instead of & AGL: the reverse has the same cross also as that, but is within the inner circle, and not extended to the edge of the piece, as that is. This stands in Le Blanc as a Denier Parisis, as also in Du Fresne, but no name to it on the plate; nor does he mention or describe it at all: it is likewise in Haultin, the MS. notes to which make it $1\frac{1}{2}$ oz. fine, 180 to the

VALUE.

(*z*) P. cxxv. (*a*) P. 144. (*b*) T. 11. p. 643. (*c*) Ducarel, p. 42.

mark,

mark, or weighing 25¼ Paris, or about 21 grains Troy; therefore the Money Foot 7 livres 4 sols. HENRY VI.

We are of opinion that No. 19. is a Double Tournois. On one side is a lion passant, guardant, inscribed, HENRICUS REX; on the other side, round a plain cross, with an H in the center, is TURONUS CIVIS. We know nothing of its weight or fineness, nor any other besides this of Sir Charles Frederick's. DOUBLE TOURNOIS.

A lion passant, guardant, with a fleur-de-lis over its back, is on the obverse of No. 20. much like No. 13. it is inscribed, H REX FRANC ET ANGL: the reverse has TURONUS CIVIS round a plain cross, which has an H in its center. This piece is in Le Blanc, as also in Du Fresne, who calls it a Petit Denier Tournois, and is made to be 2½ oz. fine, and to weigh 20 grains Paris (about 16 Troy); therefore the *Foot* would be but about 4 livres 12 sols, which must be a mistake. I should therefore rather suppose the fineness to be 1½, instead of 2½ oz. by which the Foot will be 7 livres 13½ sols, or near the true one of this time. Haultin has one in his work. DENIER TOURNOIS.

The last piece of this King is the Maille, No. 21. having on one side a lion, with a fleur-de-lis before him, inscribed, H FRANC ET ANGL REX; and on the reverse, round a plain cross, is OBOLUS CIVIS. Le Blanc and Du Fresne both have it; called by the latter a Petit Maille Tournois, being 1 oz. fine, weighing 15 Paris grains (12½ Troy) therefore the Foot about 7 livres 13½ sols. Haultin likewise has this piece. Dr. Ducarel would prove these two last pieces to be of Henry V. and struck in consequence of the ordonnance of September 25, 1419; but it is there expresly said, that the former had three fleurs-de-lis, and the latter two. MAILLE, or OBOLE.

The first gold coined by this Prince was a Salute (No. 22.) which was either minted, or a currency given to it, by an ordonnance of Feb. 1423: the obverse had on it the Salutation; the hands of the angel are lifted up, and those of the Virgin folded over her breast. The word AVE is in a scroll over a crowned shield, with the arms of France and England quartered together, which stands between them, the inscription being, HENRICUS REX ANGLIE ET FRAN. The reverse has a long cross between a lion and a fleur-de-lis, within a compartment, and is inscribed, XPC VINCIT XPC REGNAT XPC IMPERAT. It is very probable that the Salute of his father was in every part like this, but the word HÆRES instead of REX, and both of them nearly like that of Charles VI. (*d*) except the titles, arms, and a lion instead of a fleur-de-lis, on the left side of the cross. It was first published by Haultin, p. 129. then by Du Fresne, T. 2. p. 630. which is all the intelligence we have concerning it; nor do we know where any one of them is now to be found. GOLD. 1st SALUTE. Type. Legend.

It appears from Le Blanc, p. 330. that they were fine gold, and that there was 63 to the mark, weighed each 73 Paris, or 60 Troy grains, which corresponds with that of the half of our Edward's noble: it was current for 25 sols, therefore the fine mark was coined into 78 livres 15 sols, and the proportion about 10½ to 1. VALUE.

The gold money generally met with of this King, is that Salute (No. 23.) coined in consequence of the ordonnance of September 6, 1423; the principal difference of which in its type from the other, is, that the scroll with AVE is held by the angel, the Virgin has her hands elevated instead of folded, and there are two shields, neither of them crowned; one at the feet of the Virgin, with the arms of France alone, and the other contains France and England quarterly, and 2d SALUTE. Type. Legend.

(*d*) Haultin, p. 121. Le Blanc, p. 238.

round

HENRY VI. round it, HENRICUS DEI GRA FRANCORU & AGLIE REX: the reverse is the same as the other, and has an H at the bottom of the cross, which it is probable was also on that, but by accident omitted. There was also an Half Salute coined, but it is probable only a few, as we never heard of but one, which is in the cabinet of the late Hugh Howard, Esq;

VALUE. This was also fine gold, but was lighter than the first, there being 70 to the mark, weighing 65$\frac{5}{6}$ Paris, or 54 grains Troy, equal to that of the half noble of this King and his father's: it was current for 22$\frac{1}{2}$ sols, which was exactly in proportion to the first, or seven eighths of it, both in weight and value, and therefore no alteration made in that of the fine mark. The livre was worth near 3 shillings, and about 6$\frac{2}{3}$ to one pound Sterling, but at present the pound Sterling is worth near 23 French livres.

ANGELOT. Type. Legend. This King likewise afterwards caused another sort of Coin, called an Angelot (No. 24.) to be minted, probably by an ordonnance of June 24, 1427 (*e*): it is thus called from its type, which is an angel with the two shields of France alone, and France and England quarterly, which are before him: the inscription is, HENRICUS FRANCORUM ET ANGLIE REX. The reverse is like the two last, both in type and inscription, except the H under the cross, and the compartment:

VALUE. it was fine gold, 105 to the mark, or weighs near 44 Paris, or 36 Troy grains, and was current for 15 sols, being $\frac{2}{3}$ of the Salute; or the Salute was 1$\frac{1}{2}$ Angelots, answering exactly to each other, according to these values: it is a very rare piece, as we know of no other but this of Sir Charles's, that in the collection of the Earl of Pembroke, and one in the King of France's cabinet at Paris: it has been engraved also in Haultin and Du Fresne.

FRANK. Type. Legend. We are informed by Le Blanc (*f*), that it was the general opinion the English coined no other sorts of money in France than the Salute and Angelot; but, however, it appears they also struck a Frank (No. 25.) on whose obverse there is the King on horseback, armed cap-a-pie, a crown upon his helmet, his sword drawn ready to strike, and his armour and that of his horse semeé of fleurs-de-lis and lions: it is inscribed, HENRICUS D G FRANC & ANGLIE REX: on the reverse an ornamented cross within a compartment of four arches, inscribed, XPS VINCIT XPS REGNAT XPS IMPERAT.

VALUE. This sort of Coin was first struck by John, King of France *, upon his return from England, and were so called from their value of a frank, livre, or 20 sols: their weight was the same as that of the first Salute; that is, 60 grains, or half the Edward's noble. I find there was another sort, of 80 to the mark, in 1423, or weighing but 48 Troy grains. As to the weight of Henry's, Le Blanc himself could not determine (*g*); neither do we know that of Sir Charles Frederick's.

NOBLE. That this King struck such a piece as this in France, as also the $\frac{1}{2}$ and $\frac{1}{4}$, appears expressly from an ordonnance of his, published in January 1426; but we are sorry to say, we have no criterion by which we can discover these from those that were struck in England, any more than we are able to distinguish these last, when struck in different towns of England, from one another; and the case is the same in regard to those formerly struck in different parts of the Low Coun-

* Several Princes coined pieces nearly of this type, as those of Flanders, Burgundy, Guelders, Brittany, Bearn, Arragon, Savoy, Milan, &c. all which were usually called Ryders; and in 1606 the same was done by the states of the United Provinces, and, after being discontinued for some time, was again revived, *anno* 1749, of the same intrinsic, but a higher nominal value; that is, 14 guilders instead of 10$\frac{1}{8}$.

(*e*) Le Blanc, p. 330. (*f*) Ibid. p. 244. (*g*) Ibid. p. 7.

tries,

tries, in the time of Edward the Third as at Ghent, Ipres, and it is probable many more places; and it would give us great pleasure could the curious enquirers into antiquities, in those parts, help us to any anecdotes that would lead us to discover those that were made abroad, from such as were struck in England*.

Calais Money, mostly of Hen. VI.

The money coined at Calais, being in all respects English, tho' struck at that place, is the reason we have not taken notice of it in this work; however, we would observe in this place, that it is highly probable very little, if any, appertains to Henry V. as no notice is to be found relating to this mint, till a statute of his 9th year†, which parliament did not meet till December 1, 1422, and the King died the August following; as this is the case, and the money usually supposed to belong to him, with an annulet on each side the head, are all of the Calais mint; this distinction appears to have little weight, and we must look out for one better founded, to know the Father from the Son.

Henry VIII 1513.

We meet with no other coins minted in France by any of our princes till Henry VIII. (for we do not think the singularity of the arms of France only, on the Ryal of his fathers(*k*), is sufficient to support an opinion of its being coined there) who undertook an expedition to France Anno 1513, and took Tournay Sept. 21 that same year, which he kept for near four years, it being not yielded to them again till Oct. 6. 1517, on consideration of being paid 400,000 crowns. No materials have reached our time, from which it could be inferred, we had a mint there during the time we were in possession of it, had not three different coins, with the name of this place on them, put it past dispute

The first of these pieces, No. 25. is more in the French taste than either of Tournay
them, having on its obverse a crowned shield, with the arms of France and Groats.
England quarterly, between a fleur-de-lis and a lyon, and round it Henricus 8 Type.
Di Gra Francie et Anglie Rex; on the reverse is an open cross formed Legend. No. 25.
of double lines, with an H in the center of it and two fleurs-de-lis, and the same
number of lyons in the spaces, inscribed Civitat Tornacensis 1513. It is
very observable, that the letters on both sides are Roman, and not Monkish, like
the two others, which do not appear on his English money till his 34th year.
The 2d, No. 26. has its obverse much like the other, only wants the fleur-de- No. 26.
lis and lyon, inscribed, Henric 8 Di Gra Franc z Anglie R. the type of
the reverse is very singular, having a large rose on the center of a plain cross,
and Civitas Tornacensis 1513. The 3d. or No. 27, is exactly like his No. 27.
English groat, with his head, and Henric Di Gra Rex Franc z Anglie round
it, and round the cross and shield on the reverse Civitas Tornacen. this Rarity.
last, tho' far from being common, is oftner met with than the others; we know
of no other of No. 26. but the Duke of Devonshire's, and one we were formerly
possessed of, but now in the possession of Mr. Benjamin Bartlet; and of No. 25.
only Sir Charles Frederick's, and one in the collection of the late Hugh Howard,
Esq;

F

* There is frequent mention made in the ordonnances of the Counts of Flanders of a Noble coined by them of fine gold, and 32½ to the mark, which answers to the weight of the Edward Noble, and Mr. Leake (*h*) says differed in nothing from the English but in the arms, the names and the titles; but we know not any cabinet that has one, nor have seen the figure of any printed, the only one of this sort being of Philip the Good, duke of Burgundy and earl of Flanders which is not of the weight of the Edward, but the Henry Noble, and therefore must have been struck after the year 1412 (*i*).

† An act was made, to endure for the King's pleasure, that a mint should be made at Calais, An. 9. H. V. Cap. 6. Item, that the king's mint be coined and made at Calice, in the manner it has been made and governed in the Tower of London. 9 H. V. Stat. 2. Cap. 5. Rastal, article money, Sect. 35, 36, p. 278.

(*h*) Page 115. (*i*) View of the Gold Coin, page 6. *k* Ibid. pl. 2. No. 5.

Since the printing of the former sheets of this work, we have been so fortunate as to discover several rare coins, both in gold and silver, struck in France, none of which have yet been published.

EDW. III. HALF GROAT. First, an half Aquitain groat, as it is usually called, of Edward III. (D) which has on one side a three quarter length of the king crowned, regarding the right, having in his right hand a sword, and in his left something like a globe, but without a cross, inscribed, ED REX ANGLIE; the reverse has a cross and pellets as an English sterling, and is inscribed, DNS AQUITANIE B. Another piece of same value (E) has also the king's bust crowned, but extends only to the waist, and confined within the legendary circle; he holds a sword in his right hand, and the left is extended, inscribed, EDWART REX ANGLIE; the reverse as the last, and, DNS AQUITANIE, the half groat of the Black Prince, No. 27. pl. 1. is in imitation of this; the weight also of those which are best preserved, agree nearly with these of Edw. III. which are 17 tr. gr. and 16½ tr. gr. it is probable a groat of this sort, like that of his son, No. 28. may hereafter be discovered.

There are some reasons to conjecture, that the Aquitain coins of this prince, with DUX AQUIT. as No. 14, 15, 17, 18, 19, 20. were struck some of the earliest, and prior to his asserting his title to the crown of France, after which we think they have, DNS AQUIT. we also suspect that the above-mentioned pieces, all but the two first, were rather struck in imitation of the Gross Tournois, having seen one lately of good silver, and weighing 36 tr. gr. although much worn.

GOLD MOUTON. Besides the three sorts of gold money of this prince, viz. No. 21, 22, and 23, pl. 1. there is in the French king's cabinet at Paris a Mouton of Edw. III. (F) much like those of John, king of France, who coined some about Anno 1368, having on the obverse the holy lamb, under which is the king's name, ED-WARD, and inscribed, AGN DEI QVI TOLLI PECCA MVNDI. MIS NOS. and round an ornamented cross are, XPC VINCIT, XPC REGNAT XPC IMPERAT. this piece differs from the other Moutons principally in having the king's name at length, under the lamb, instead of the first, or the two first letters of it, and the word, REX, which is here wanting; it weighs about 1 grain tr. more than those of the French king, that is 71 gr. troy.

BLACK PRINCE DENIER. We have seen also a small billon coin of the Black Prince, having on one side a lyon within a compartment, in that differing from No. 11, 12, 13, and 34. pl 1. all of which we esteem to be of the same value as this, viz. a denier; the inscription is, ED PMO...... the reverse has a cross, extending only to the legendary circle, as No. 11, 12, and 34. all that remains of the inscription is, ACQUE.

RICH. II. ½ GOLD. HARDY. In the French king's cabinet at Paris, there is also a fine half gold Hardy of Richard II. (G) having on the obverse his bust only to the shoulders, inscribed, RICARD RX ANGLIE FRACI; the reverse is like the whole one, No. 87. pl. 1. and like that inscribed, AVXILIVM MEUM A DNO B. its weight is also in proportion, 36 paris gr. or about 29¼ tr.

Coins struck by English Princes in France from Hen. IV. to Hen. VIII. Pl. 2.

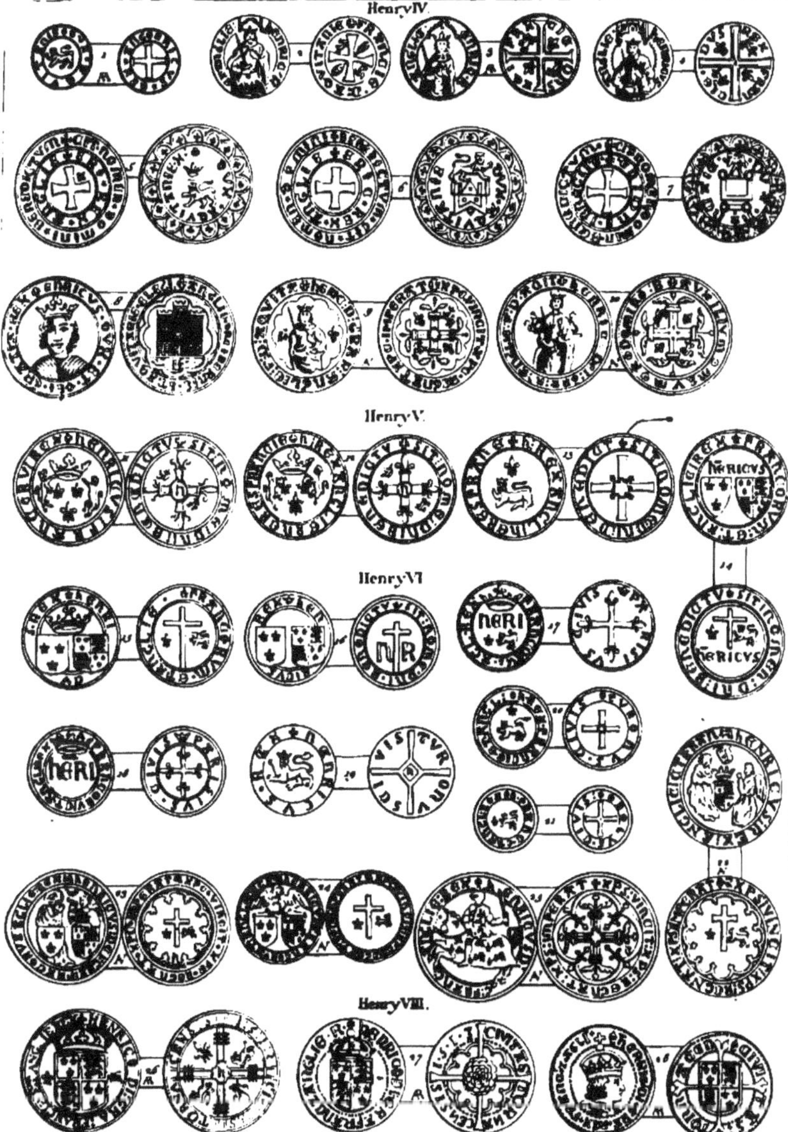

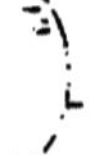

In the fine collection of French coins, kept in the mint at Paris, late belonging to Monf. Bizot, there is a fine Grofs of Henry V. probably ftruck about the time that No. 13, pl. 2. was, as it has the title of HERES on it; but it differs in the type on one of its fides, having a lyon between three fleurs-de-lis, inftead of one, it is of good filver. HENRY V. GROSS.

We have obferved, page 12. that no Salute had hitherto been publifhed of Henry V. with the title of *Heres Francie*, but we have lately difcovered one in the king of France's cabinet at Paris (H) having the fingle fhield, like that of the firft of his fons, No. 22. pl. 2. it is infcribed, HENR DEI GRA REX ANGL HERES FRANC; and on the reverfe XPC VINCIT, XPC REGNAT, XPC IMP. RAT, as ufual; the weight of it likewife anfwers what I there faid it fhould, viz. 60 tr. gr. the fame as the half Edward's noble, whereas all thofe of the double fhield are of the weight of the half Henry's noble, or 54 troy grains. SALUTE.

We fhall now add two tables of the proportion of the Englifh troy weight, to the mark weight of Paris and the contrary, fuch tables, we apprehend, being much wanted, as the weights of many coins are fometimes given in one, and fometimes in the other, and the not paying a proper attention to the difference, has occafioned many miftakes on that account*. Thefe tables are calculated from 1 mark or 8 ounces of Paris, being equal to 7 ounces 17 pennyweights, 12 grains troy; it muft be obferved alfo, that the French oftner reckon by ½ grofs and grofs, than by denier weights; thus, 62 grains is equal to ¼ a grofs, 26 grains, and 125 gains is equal 1½ grofs, 17 grains, &c.

* As in Dr. Ducarrel's Table, No. 21. Supplem. where the firft five pieces are given too heavy by more than ½ part.

A TABLE of the Agreement of the English Troy Weight, with the Paris Mark Weight. N. B. 24 Grains is 1 Pennyweight (dwt.) 20 dwts. 1 Ounce, (oz.) and 12 oz. is 1 Pound Weight Troy.

Troy Grains.	Paris gr. parts	Troy Grains.	Paris gr. parts	Troy Grains.	Paris gr. parts	Troy Grains.	Paris gr. parts	Troy Grains.	Paris gr. parts	Dwts.	Paris gr. parts
1	1. 219	26	31. 694	51	62. 171	75	91. 427	99	120. 685	8	234. 056
2	2. 438	27	32. 913	52	63. 389	76	92. 646	100	121. 904	9	263. 314
3	3. 657	28	34. 133	53	64. 606	77	93. 865	101	123. 123	10	292. 571
4	4. 876	29	35. 352	54	65. 827	78	95. 084	102	124. 342	11	321. 829
5	6. 095	30	36. 571	55	67. 046	79	96. 303	103	125. 562	12	351. 086
6	7. 314	31	37. 790	56	68. 265	80	97. 523	104	126. 781	13	380. 344
7	8. 533	32	39. 00[illegible]	57	69. 484	81	98. 742	105	128.	14	409. 598
8	9. 752	33	40. 22[illegible]	58	70. 703	82	99. 960	106	129. 210	15	438. 856
9	10. 971	34	41. 447	59	71. 923	83	101. 179	107	130. 438	16	468. 112
10	12. 190	35	42. 666	60	73. 142	84	102. 397	108	131. 657	17	497. 370
11	13. 409	36	43. 884	61	74. 361	85	103. 616	109	132. 876	18	526. 628
12	14. 628	37	45. 103	62	75. 580	86	104. 835	110	134. 095	19	555. 886
13	15. 847	38	46. 323	63	76. 799	87	106. 054	111	135. 314	1 oz.	585. 144
14	17. 066	39	47. 542	64	78. 018	88	107. 273	112	136. 533	2 oz.	2oz. de. 18gr.
15	18. 285	40	48. 761	65	79. 237	89	108. 492	113	137. 752	3	3 : 1 : 3
16	19. 504	41	49. 980	66	80. 456	90	109. 712	114	138. 971	4	4 : 1 : 12
17	20. 723	42	51. 198	67	81. 675	91	110. 932	115	140. 190	5	5 : 1 : 21
18	21. 942	43	52. 417	68	82. 894	92	112. 151	116	141. 409	6	6 : 2 : 6
19	23. 161	44	53. 636	69	84. 113	93	113. 370	117	142. 628	7	7 : 2 : 16
20	24. 380	45	54. 856	70	85. 332	94	114. 589	118	143. 847	8	8 : 3 : 1
21	25. 599	46	56. 075	71	86. 551	95	115. 808	119	145. 066	9	9 : 3 : 10
22	26. 818	47	57. 294	1 dwt.	87. 770	4 dwt.	117. 027	5 dwt.	146. 285	10	10 : 3 : 19
23	28. 037	2 dwt.	58. 513	73	88. 989	97	118. 247	6	175. 543	11	11 : 4 : 4
1 dwt.	29. 258	49	59. 732	74	90. 208	98	119. 466	7	204. 799	1 lb.	12 : 4 : 13
25	30. 476	50	60. 952								

A TABLE of the Agreement of the Paris Mark Weights, with the English Troy Weight. N. B. 24 Grains is 1 Denier Weight; 72 Grains, or 3 Denier wt. is 1 Grofs; 576 Grains, 24 Denier wt. or 8 Grofs is 1 Ounce, and 8 Ounces is 1 Mark.

Paris Grains.	Troy gr. parts	Paris Grains.	Troy gr. parts	Paris Grains.	Troy gr. parts	Paris Grains.	Troy gr. parts	Paris Grains.	Troy gr. parts	Paris Grains.	Paris gr. parts
1	0. 820	27	22. 148	52	42. 656	77	63. 163	102	83. 671	127	104. 179
2	1. 640	28	22. 968	53	43. 476	78	63. 984	103	84. 491	128	105
3	2. 460	29	23. 789	54	44. 296	79	64. 804	104	85. 312	2 gro.	118. 125
4	3. 281	30	24. 609	55	45. 116	80	65. 624	105	86. 132	2½ gro.	147. 655
5	4. 101	31	25. 429	56	45. 937	81	66. 445	105	86. 952	3 gro.	177. 187
7	4. 921	32	26. 249	57	46. 757	82	67. 264	107	87. 773	3½ gro.	206. 718
6	5. 742	33	27. 070	58	47. 577	83	68. 085	1½ gro	88. 593	4 gro.	236. 25
8	6. 562	34	27. 890	59	48. 398	84	68. 905	109	89. 413	4½ gro.	265. 779
9	7. 382	35	28. 710	60	49. 218	85	69. 726	110	90. 234	5 gro.	295. 310
10	8. 203	½ gro.	29. 531	61	50. 038	86	70. 546	111	91. 054	5½ gro.	324. 842
11	9. 023	37	30. 351	62	50. 859	87	71. 366	112	91. 874	6 gro.	354. 375
12	9. 843	38	31. 171	63	51. 679	88	72. 187	113	92. 695	6½ gro.	383. 905
13	10. 664	39	31. 992	64	52. 499	89	73. 007	114	93. 515	7 gro.	413. 436
14	11. 484	40	32. 812	65	53. 320	90	73. 827	115	94. 335	7½ gro.	442. 957
15	12. 304	41	33. 632	66	54. 140	91	74. 648	116	95. 155	1 oz.	472. 5
16	13. 124	42	34. 453	67	54. 96	92	75. 468	117	95. 976	2 oz.	1oz. 19dwt. 9gr.
17	13. 945	43	35. 273	68	55. 781	93	76. 288	118	96. 796	3 oz.	2 : 19 : 1½
18	14. 765	44	36. 093	69	56. 601	94	77. 109	119	97. 616	4 oz.	3 : 18 : 18
19	15. 585	45	36. 913	70	57. 421	95	77. 929	120	98. 437	5 oz.	4 : 18 : 10½
20	16. 406	46	37. 734	71	58. 242	4 den	78. 749	121	99. 257	6 oz.	5 : 18 : 3
21	17. 226	47	38. 554	1 gro.	59. 062	97	79. 57	122	100. 077	7 oz.	6 : 17 : 19½
22	18. 046	2 den.	39. 374	73	59. 882	98	80. 39	123	100. 898	1 Mark	7 : 17 : 12
23	18. 867	49	40. 195	74	60. 702	99	81. 21	124	101. 718		
1 den.	19. 687	50	41. 015	75	61. 523	100	82. 031	125	102. 538		
25	20. 507	51	41. 835	76	62. 343	101	82. 851	126	103. 359		
26	21. 328										

A VIEW OF COUNTERFEIT STERLINGS.

BEFORE we proceed to describe the counterfeit sterlings, as they stand in plate 3. we would first mention a few imitations of the English sterling, but not in the nature of counterfeits, prior to the Edwards, that is, of Henry the Third's first coinage, which we have put together in the small plate.

The two first are of Otho IV. Emperor of Germany, son to Henry Duke of Saxony, and Maud, eldest daughter of Henry II. king of England; he was educated in the court of his uncle Richard I. was elected emperor in 1198, crowned the same year at Aix la Chapelle, but at Rome not till *anno* 1210, married Mary, daughter of Henry duke of Brabant, *anno* 1215, was defeated at the famous

battle

battle of Bovines in Flanders *anno* 1214, he afterwards went to Brunswick that same year, and died in 1218, the 3d of Henry III.

He is represented full faced on the first (A), with pearls in his ears, and a scepter in his hand, inscribed, *Otto Impator*, and round the cross and pellets on the reverse *Tremonia Reia*, struck at Dortmund*, in the county of Marc; he is also full faced on (B), and crowned, but no scepter, inscribed, *Otto Imperator*; and on the reverse, *Colonia Teucia*, or Cologne, where it was coined. The third (C), we take to be a coin of Munster in Westphalia, having on its obverse the head of their patron Saint Paul, and inscribed, *Sanctus Pauls*; on the reverse, round the cross and pellets is inscribed, *Henri.on London*. It will, we think, be a difficult matter to assign the reason for this legend, on a coin of the bishop of Munster's, as we certainly think it must be, from another of this sort, having the same head and inscription, but on the reverse a church, which we suppose to be that of Munster, with *Monasterium* round it. There is the whole and the half, all three of which are in the collection of Mr. Duane; the 4th piece in the small plate has a place here, not from its type, but its name, which is an *Angli* or *English*. Schlegelius has published (*a*) a Franckforter English, called so I should think from its being of the value of the English sterling or penny, it being entirely different in type, having on one side a cross between four eagles, inscribed, *Moneta Nova*, and on the other a small cross terminated with large flowers, with *Angli Francofur*; which he informs us is a very rare coin. Joachim, in his Groschen cabinet, (*b*) has also given one like this of Gerlace, archbishop of Mentz, only four lyons instead of eagles, inscribed, *Glac Archies*, and *Moneta Moguntina*, that marked (D) in the plate, is of a duke of Brabant, having like the last four lyons between the cross, on its obverse inscribed, *Dux Braban*, reverse, *Moneta Lovanens*, this piece, and the first, are in our own possession.

* Dortmund was burnt a few years before this, and to make up its loss had a grant of a fair; and there are many old coins of the emperor Otho, Henry, Rudolph, and Lewis IV. with *Thier* upon them; in Joachim Ertes's supplement, p. 28, 38, 76 and 88.

(*a*) De Nummis Antiquis Gothanis, &c. 4to. Gotha 1717, page 30. pl. 1. N. 26.

(*b*) Neuntes Fach. Ta. 2. N. 20.

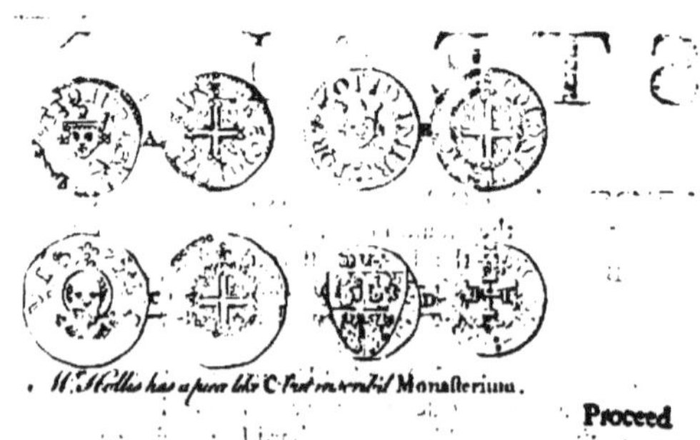

Mr. Hollis has a piece like C but inscribed Monasterium.

Proceed

Proceed we now to the principal intent of this work, that is, fuch pieces as were ftruck in imitation of the Englifh fterlings, or pennies, in order to run current with them (as being a famous well known coin) but were either lighter or bafer than them.

Coin debafed under Ed. I.

Among the many abufes and corruptions crept into the Englifh money, in the reign of Edward the Firft, fuch as clipping or rounding the good, making fome of copper, and then blanching it, others again with lead or pewter, and cafing them with fine filver; befides thefe different methods of debafing the coin, there were feveral foreign pieces that were brought over and run current for a fterling or penny, but were not worth fo much, and fome of them but little more than an halfpenny; the names of which, as *Mitres*, *Lions*, or *Leonnies*, *Eagles*, *Rofaries*, *Crocards*, *Pollards*, *Staldings* and *Steepings*, is almoft all we know of them, as none of the pieces themfelves have come to our knowledge, nor do we know with certainty where, or by what princes, they were ftruck.

Many foreign pieces introduced.

Mitres.

One pound (i. e. 20 fhilling) of the Mitres, we are informed, weighed but 16 *s.* 4 *d.* of the money of England, that is, about 18 troy gr. and therefore it is probable the filver of thefe were nearly as good as the fterling; the Leonnies or Lyons were as light as the Mitres, and there were two forts of them, one of them with a bend and one without. The *Eagles* and *Rofaries*, it is probable took their names from their types, but we are at a lofs for what reafon the *Crocards* and *Pollards* were fo called, as well as the Staldings and Steepings, but fufpect that thefe two laft were money of the Hans Towns, and the name of the former, borrowed from the name of their principal commodity, fteel or ftahl, and their warehoufe in London, called the fteel yard, for the fame reafon.

Leonnies.

Are cried down.

(*c*) Rot. Pat. 18 Ed. I. m. 5 in cedula.

These pieces were all cried down and put out of currency, 7 Ed. I. however, in his 28th year, the *Crokards* and *Pollards* are allowed to pafs for an half-penny each. It was thought requifite likewife to have it publifhed in every market town, that no other money fhould pafs but that of England, Ireland, and Scotland; alfo that none fhould import more money into the realm, than what ferved for his neceffary expences, nor be fo bold as to arrive at any other place than Dover, Sandwich, London, St. Botoph, and Southampton, unlefs driven thither, and that by proof of fufficient witneffes (for it had been cuftomary with the merchants not to land at Dover or Sandwich, as they knew there was a fearch made there, but to come to London from Effex, or Suffolk, or Norfolk, or Linfey, or other parts of England, where they could not be found out) and when he came to any of thofe places, he was to fhew his money to thofe who fhould be affigned on the behalf of the king, upon forfeiture of body and goods, nor was he to depart or difpofe of the money by himfelf, or by another, until the money was feen and examined by him that the king fhould affign.

Many regulations.

It

(*c*) De quibufdam Remediis Provifis contra retonfionem & falfificacoem moneta.

The articles of this record are in old French, the fubftance of which, if carefully compared together, will be found the fame as what is contained in the Articuli de Moneta, & Statuum de Moneta Magnum, both of which are without date, and appear to be no more than certain propofals which were made to the king and his council by the moneyers, for preventing the deceipts of clypt, counterfeit, and debafed money, which were afterwards approved and ordered to be obferved by proclamation, to avoid thofe mifchiefs. The *Statuta de Moneta Parva*, directed to the fheriffs of Lincoln, 20 Ed. I. appears to be no ftatute neither, but only a writ or proclamation, to proclaim among other things, what had been ordained by a former law concerning clypt and counterfeit money, and may well

2 be

It was forbidden likewise to conceal any money in bales, cloaths, or bundles, upon forfeiture of body and goods, and if any such was found, the finder to have 4d in the pound, the rest to go to the king; and if any should find any other money than English, or clipped money, that it should be bored and returned; but if any false money was found, it was to be detained, and the person on whom found to give security; and in order to know one money from another, and those which are weighty from those clipped, it was thought proper that he which shall receive or pay money, shall do the same by even weight of five shillings by the Tumberel; and any person that is willing, may have Tumberel delivered to him by a person whom the king shall assign, or by the warden of the Exchange, to be marked with the king's mark, as his measures; and it shall be lawful to pierce the money which will not pass the Tumbrel; if a pound is found to weigh less than twenty shillings by four pence, the deficiency is to be found out by the Tumberel; and if a pound of twenty shillings want but sixpence, it was to be delivered to him that brought it, but if more, it was to be served as the rest.

Counterfeits with the name of EDWARD.

Besides the above sorts of money imported from abroad, this record informs us there was yet another, which had the name of Edward King of England, made in Germany, that weighed more or less than the Mitres, and could not be known but by weight; these are what are called counterfeit sterlings, and are strictly so,
No. 1. as No. 1. whose inscription round the head is exactly like those of Edw. the First, only AGNL. instead of ANGL. it being EDW. R. AGNL. DNS HYB; but then that on the reverse proves it a counterfeit, being MONETA MONTES, or money of Mons in Hainault. There are others with EDW. E M E POLON REX, reverse, JOHNES DEY GRA; also one in the Bodleian collection, inscribed, EDW.
No. 37. SAIWATTONAS, and on the reverse, COMES TULE*. And a 4th, No. 37. with EWANESDNS REX; reverse, LUCENBGENSIS; this is called in our statute book† a Lushburg, and I believe coined later than the others.

Counterfeits with other names.

But the far greatest number of these sort of pieces, are only made with the type of Edward's pennies, and not with his name, and counterfeits only in that particular; we having them with the names of the dukes of Brabant and Limburgh, the earls of Flanders, Hainault, Namur, Ligny, Loos, Porcien; the seigneurs or lords of Harstel and Ligny, the emperor Henry VII. of Luxemburgh, and Lewis IV. of Bavaria, John, king of Bohemia, the bishop of Cambray; also many have not the name of any prince, &c. on them, as No. 33, 34. Others again, which have blundered inscriptions, as we think designedly, and several whose place of mintage does not agree with the name of the prince, or are not now to be discovered; besides, there is reason to believe, that the major part of those which have the name of a prince on them, have never been struck by his moniers, but came out of other private mints. And as this age was remarkable for its want of literature, so

be referred to what was done in the parliament held at London in the 11th or 12th Ed. I. and tho' this proclamation is not in the rolls of Edw. I. yet in the 8 Ed. II. Rot. Claus, m. 7. dorso, is a writ to every sheriff in England to proclaim the foregoing articles of Ed. I. and to cause them to be kept and observed; and in 27 Ed. I. Rot. Claus, m. 10. pro Mercatoribus Brabantia; several writs were sent to the sheriffs of Lincoln, Nottingham, Northampton, Leicester, and to the mayor and sheriffs of London, on behalf of the merchants of Brabant and Flanders, wherein notice is taken of proclaiming an ordinance, which had before that time been made; in which, among other things, it was ordained, that no bad money should be received or paid in the sale of wool, &c. but only good and lawful money. See also stat. 9. Ed. 3. ca. 5, 10. concerning counterfeit sterlings.

* Wise Nummorum Antiquor. Scrin. Bodleianis. Tab. 19.

† 25. E. 3. stat. 5. ch. 2.

few

few being able even to read the inscriptions; these deceptions were not so easily detected or discovered, whilst the type appeared nearly the same, differing only in the ornament of the head, as some are not crowned, viz. No. 2, 3, 4, 6, 7, 8, 9, 11, 15, 16 and 30. that of No. 14. is like the Scotch, and No. 29. like the Irish, No. 38, 39 and 40. have only the reverse of the cross and pellets like the sterling, the obverse being entirely different.

John II. Count of Hainault and Holland, was grandson of Bochart d'Avesnes, **John, count of Hainault.** the first husband of Margaret countess of Flanders and Hainault; he succeeded her in the year 1280, and died *anno* 1305. He was father of John of Beaumont, often mentioned in our chronicles, and grandfather to Philippa queen to Edward III. whose sister Margaret, being married to the emperor, Lewis of Bavaria, carried these counties into that family.

On No. 2, 3, 4. pl. 3. is the head of John, with a diadem adorned with two **No. 2, 3, 4.** or three roses, and inscribed, J. COMES HANONIE, on the reverse is the cross and pellets, and round it, MONETA MONTES. No. 3. has MELBODIENSIS, and No. 4. VALENCHENSIS, being struck at Mons, Maubeuge, and Valenciennes, all in Hainault. Alkemade(*d*) has given us the first and last of these, but does not inform us whether true coins or counterfeits; however, be that as it will, it is certain they have coined nothing like those before or since†.

John I. John II. and John III. dukes of Brabant, succeeded each other between **John, duke of Brabant.** the years 1260 and 1356, and Jane, daughter of the last, reigned till 1399; we do not know to which of them appertains No. 5 and 6. John II. married Eleanor, daughter of our Edward I. whose son, John, made an alliance with our Edward III. and assisted him in his expeditions into France in 1339 and 1340; he died *anno* 1356.

The head on No. 5. is crowned, and inscribed, J. DUC BRABANTIE; and on **No. 5, 6, 40.** the reverse, BRUXELLENSIS, that on No. 6. is not crowned; round it is, J. DUX LIMBURGI, and on the reverse, DUX BRABANTIE, we think it is probable, a coin of John I. struck upon his purchasing Limburg, which was in 1282.(*e*) No. 40. instead of the head has a castle, and round it, J. DUX BRABANTIE, and on the reverse, MONETA BRUXEL, we think these two last have much the appearance of true coins of the Dukes and not counterfeits*.

H God-

† D'Outreman(*f*) informs us, that the money of Valenciennes was one of the *Mother Coins* of Christendom, the others being those of France, England, Venice, and Mets in Lorrain, and thus called, as serving for patterns to all others, as those of that city had proved in a process of Mortesmains. He also says that Blancs have taken their name from the Blanch or white money of this city, for when fine silver or good money was mentioned, it was compared to the ancient money of Valencienne, and has brought many proofs of its being mentioned in the year 1119, 1158, 1182, 1212 and 1226, but we have never heard of any of this money being published.

* We have also a coin of one of these princes, with a lyon rampant, in an ancient shield, on one side, inscribed, *J. Dei Gratia*; on the reverse the four letters WALC, between the bars of a cross, inscribed, *Dux Brab.* we have the half also the same; these, and the *Angli*, or English, mentioned p. 2. are the oldest coins of the duke of Brabant come to our knowledge. John III. is likewise said to have struck a coin when he, and Lewis count of Flanders, entered into an alliance with Edw. III. they agreeing to strike money in common; that of John to have the arms of Brabant on one side, [illegible] inscribed

(*d*) Munte der Graven van Holland, fol. Delft 1700, Tab. 21.
(*e*) Butkens Trophies de Brabant, fol. Anv. 1641. To. 1. p. 298.
(*f*) Histoire de Valentiennes, fol. Valen. 1681. part 2. chap. de la monnoie.

JOHN, Seigneur of Louvain. Godfrey, Sieur de Louvain, Liere, and Gaesbeke, son of Henry I. and brother of Henry II. dukes of Brabant, died 1253, whose son Henry, called Tristan, was the prince who we think struck No. 7, 8. pl. 3. he was left young by his father, married Felicitas of Luxemburgh, sister to the emperor Henry VII. and died *anno* 1318, leaving two sons, Henry and John, the last died 1324, aged 16 years(*g*), whose aunt marrying a Count de Hornes, these estates went into that family.

No. 7, 8. The heads of No. 7 and 8. are both diadem'd and adorn'd with roses; round the former is, JOHES DE LOUVAIN, and the reverse MONETA HASTEL: on No. 8. is, JOANES DE LOANIO, and the reverse is, DNS DE HAESTEL.

GUY and ROBERT Counts of Flanders. Guy, count of Flanders, was son of Margaret countess of Flanders and Hanault, by William of Dampierre; his first wife was Machtild, daughter of Robert Avoyer of Arras, and Lord of Bethune and Dendermonde, upon whose death, in 1248, he took those titles; and after the death of his brother, William, *anno* 1251, that of Count of Flanders, jointly with his mother, and after her death, in 1280, alone. In 1264 he married Isabella of Luxemburg, who brought him the county of Namur, of which he took the title, as appears by No. 9. he afterwards resigned it to the eldest son he had by her, viz. John, in 1290, in whose race it continued, and we have a coin, No. 10. of his great grandson, William.

GUY, Marq. of Namur.

No. 39, 9, 10, 11. We have no coin of Guy, as count of Flanders, with the head, but we have one with a spread eagle, No. 39. inscribed, G. COMES FLANDRIÆ, and on the reverse, CIVITAS ALOST; No. 9. is struck as marquis of Namur, the inscription begins on the reverse, G. COMES FLANDRIA; and round the head, MARCHIA NAMUR; besides which we have seen one, in which, like the others, the inscription begins on the head side. No. 11. is exactly like No. 9. in the head and inscription; but on the reverse is MONETA NAMUR, without any name or initial. No. 10. is of the grandson of John, to whom he have observed, Guy resigned it; he lived between 1335 and 1391, it is inscribed, GULIEL. COME. Namurcensis.

No. 12, 13, 14. Number 12. is of Robert, son of Guy, the head crowned and inscribed, R. COMES FLANDRIE; and on the reverse, MONETA ALOTEN. No. 13. has, EDL. ROBERTUS COMES, and the reverse, MONETA GANDES; the head on No. 14. is in profile, like those of Alexander III. of Scotland, but no scepter, inscribed, ROB. COMES FLAND. reverse, MONETA ALOSTEN.

inscribed, *Jacobus Dux Brabantie*, and on the reverse, *Gandensis*; that of Lewis was to have *Ludovicus Comes Flandrie*; and on the reverse, *Lovanie* (*h*). ——— It is certain by the valuation made in 1288, still in being, that John I. had, prior to that year, coined a grand and a petit lyon d'or, and a tournois d'or, but neither of them have yet been discovered; but there is a mouton d'or of John III. struck in 1313. In *anno* 1291, the moneyers in Brabant had several privileges granted them, and their number increased to 90, that is 50 at Brussels, and 40 at Louvain, which were confirmed by Anthony in 1411, and were in force when Butkens wrote; however, they were infringed by Jane in 1395, who set up mints at Maestrich, Oyen and Vilvorden, but were soon discontinued. (*i*)

(*g*) Butkens, p. 610, 611, 615. (*h*) Ibid. p. 428. (*i*) Ibid, p. 567.

The

The Barons of France, one of the principal of which the Count of Flanders was, had liberty to strike no other sort of money but Deniers and half Deniers, or Mailles, and we find that Guy's immediate predecessor, Margaret, by an indenture with her mint master, Nicholas Deckin, *anno* 1275, actually coined only Mailles, Artesianas, Redondas o Valencienescs, (*k*) what regulations they were under in the Imperial Flanders, of which Alost was the capital, and a fief of the Empire, and what sorts they were by the Emperor permitted to strike we do not know; however, we think No. 32. with the spread eagle has some plea to be admitted as a true coin, whereas No. 12 and 14. tho' struck at the same place, it is probable were intended for counterfeit sterlings, as well as the rest above described; however, we apprehend, they are the only coins of Guy and Robert now to be found.

The first count of Loos or Loz was Rodolph of Hainault, count of Hasbaye, the 17th in succession from him was Arnou or Arnold VIII. who came to the succession 1280, and died 1328, who is the person under whom, or under whose name was struck No. 15. and 16. his third successor Thierry, or Thiebaut, died *anno* 1361; and in 1366, after several disputes with Arnold de Hurle and William de Hamal, the bishop of Liege, gave them an annuity of 3000 florins per annum, uniting it to his other possessions, and still carries the title and arms in their money. ARNOLD Count of Loos 1280.

Round the head of No. 15. is inscribed, MONETA COMIT DE LO; and on the reverse COMES ARNOLDUS; No. 16. has on the head side, COMES ARNOLDUS, and on the reverse, MONETA COMITIS; we apprehend both to be rather struck with their name, than in their mint if they had one. No. 15, 16.

We must confess ourselves ignorant to whom appertains No. 16. as we can make nothing of the inscription, EDNSIOHS DE FLAD; on the reverse we find MONETA ARLEUS, the place which approaches nearest to this in its reading is ARLEUX, a small town in Artois, on the borders of Hainault, upon the little river Senset, but which no author we have met with has thought worth describing; and is more famous for the operations of the Allied and French armies near it in 1710 and 1711, than on any other account. No. 17. Incerta.

Henry IV. count of Luxemburgh, succeeded his father Henry III. in 1288, who was killed, together with his brother Gualeran de Ligny, in the battle of Vara, near Cologne, against John I. duke of Brabant, whose daughter, Margaret, Henry afterwards married, he was chosen emperor in November 1308, on the death of Albert of Austria, was crowned at Aix la Chapelle, January 6, 1309, by his brother Baldwin, archbishop of Triers, and at Rome, August 1, 1312, and died, as supposed by poison, at Benevento in August 1313. Henry VII. Emperor 1308.

On the head side of No. 23. is inscribed, HENRICUS DEI GRA; and on the reverse is, ROMANORUM REX; there is an eagle after the word HENRICUS, and another after Rex, but no place of mintage; however, it is probable it was struck at Aix la Chapelle, by comparing this and No. 18. together, No. 24. has round the head HENRICUS DEI GRA, and on the reverse, MON TORRENCIS, we have put this with the preceding one, the work in both being much alike, but are not certain it belongs to this prince, nor what place it was struck in. No. 23, 24.

(*k*) Sueyero annales de Flandes, fol. Ant. 1624. lib. 8. to. 1. page 307.

We

We have never met with any coin of the counts of Luxemburgh so ancient as this of No. 23. nor is this properly to be called so, but rather, as we just now observed, a coin of Aix la Chapelle, and no counterfeit; nor do we apprehend that Joachim (*l*) had ever seen one, or he would have given it among those of the other German emperors.

JOHN, king of Bohemia. 1310. John of Luxemburgh was the only son of the emperor Henry VII. he married Elizabeth, youngest daughter of Wenceslaus II. king of Bohemia, and by the assistance of his father, was himself crowned king at Prague, February 1310, when the emperor went into Italy, he left him vicar of the empire, and he arrived in Italy with an army to his assistance just at the time of his death. He took Silesia from the Poles in 1321, and after a long war with them, it was at last agreed, in 1345. that he should keep Silesia, but at the same time to renounce his right to the kingdom of Poland, and the next year he was killed at the battle of Cressy, August 26, 1346.

No. 20, 21, 22. We have seen many pieces of this king, and as we think, all counterfeits in his name; † thus No. 20. has JOHAES DEI GRA REX B. and on the reverse, MONETA MERAUDE; we have seen another also with Moneta Florins, neither of which places we know any thing of; the inscription on No. 21. is, JOHANNES DEI GRA —BOE ET POLO REX; that on No. 22. JOHNES DEI GRA— BOEMI ET POLONIE REX, but it begins on the reverse; there is also another that appears to be designedly blundered reading, EDWEME POLON REX—IOHNES DEY GRAC.

LEWIS IV. Emperor, 1314. Lewis of Bavaria, second son of Lewis, called the severe Elector Palatine, whom he succeeded in Bavaria, *anno* 1294, and was elected emperor in 1314, after the death of Henry VII. and a fourteen months interregnum, together with Frederick of Austria, both of them reigning in different parts of the empire till 1322, when Frederick lost a battle to Lewis, and was taken prisoner, after which Lewis reigned alone; he married Margaret of Hainault eldest sister to Philippia, queen to Edward III. in 1326, and when Edward invaded France 1339, he sided with him, and made him his vicar general*. He had great broils with John king of Bohemia, with pope John XXII. and Benedict XII. but the independency of the empire on the see of Rome was established under him, by the famous constitution made in 1337; he died in 1347, having reigned 33 years.

No. 18, 19. We have two pieces of his, both struck at Aix la Chapelle; the first, No. 18. as king of the Romans, struck between 1314 and 1322; and the other, No. 19. after his being crowned at Rome in 1329, they both have an eagle at the commencement of the inscription on the head side, and another in one of the quarters of the reverse, round which are inscribed, Moneta Aquensis; on the head side of No. 18. is,

† We have the Bohemian Gross of this king in Praun (*m*) Ta. 1. No. 2. but have never seen any coined by him for Luxemburgh or Poland; however, we are told by Calmet (*n*) that a treaty was concluded 1342, between him and Henry count of Bar, in which it was agreed to strike money of the same weight, alloy and value, with the names and arms of both on it, to be current in their counties of Luxemburgh and Bar, that of John to be struck in Luxemburgh and Damviller, and those of the latter in St. Mihell and Estain, but not one of either sort is at present remaining.

* Upon which occasion, Butkens says, p. 425. that Edward caused money, both of gold and silver, to be struck in Antwerp, with his effigie, and that of Lewis on it, but we have never seen any such.

(*l*) Groschen's cabinet zwetes fach. Ibid. Esstes's supplement.

(*m*) Grunliche Nachricht von dener Groschen (*n*) Histoire de Lorain, fol. Nan. 1748. tom. 3. p. CXIII.

is, LUDOVICUS ROM REX; and on No. 19. is, LUDOVICUS ROM IMPR. Tileman Friesens (*o*) has published the first with a little difference in the legend, viz. LUDEWICUS ROMANO REX, but he has given it too great an antiquity, assigning it to Lewis the Pius; Joachim (*p*) has given the second for a coin of Lewis IV, as it most certainly is. We have a fine piece, about double the value of these, exactly the same in type, which has round the head, AQUIS GRANI CAPUT IMPE; and on the reverse, URBS AQUEN. REGA SEDS, but know not when struck.

Gualeran, or Walleran of Luxemburgh, the first lord of Ligny or Liney, in the Barrois, was killed, anno 1288, with his brother Henry, called Blondel, father of Henry VII. emperor, as we just now observed; he was succeeded by his son Gualeran II. whose grandson, Guy, was made count of Ligny, and by his marriage with Mahault, heiress of St. Paul, became count of St. Paul also; he served against the English in France in the years 1368, 1369, and 1371; in which last year assisting Wenceslaus, duke of Brabant, against the count of Juliers, he was killed in battle, and his son Gualeran III. taken prisoner, (*q*) which Gualeran III. after being released, serving against the English in France, was again taken prisoner 1374, and detained in England until 1379, when he was ransomed for 120,000 franks, half of which were paid down, and the other half remitted on his marrying Mahault of Holland, sister, by the mother, to Ric. II. (*r*) He was greatly esteemed by Charles VI. of France, and by him sent to England, in 1396, to treat concerning a peace, and in 1402. he wrote a congratulatory letter to Henry IV. on his coming to the crown. GUALERAN seigneur of Ligny.

We apprehend it is to Gualeran II. we must attribute the No. 27, 28, 29, that it is his name made use of, for we think them all counterfeited to pass for English Sterlings; on No. 27. round the head is G. DOMINUS DE LUNY; on No. 28. is GUALER DE LUSEMB; and on No. 29. the head of which is in a triangle, in imitation of the Irish money of Edward I. and which were allowed a currency the same as the English; is, G. DOMINUS LY. on the reverse of the two first is, MONETA SERENE, and on No. 29. MONETA SERAIN; there is also in Mr. de Boze, pl. 32. another of Gualeran, inscribed, MONETA NOVA SERENENSIS; in the same plate there also is two pieces in silver, and a St. Peter in gold of John, son of Gualeran II. and father of Guy, and of Guy himself, a gold Ryal, and three silver pieces, the latter struck at Elincourt. No. 27, 28, 29.

Galcher of Chatillon, constable of France, had the county of Porcien, or Chateaux Porcien, in Rethelois, given him by Philip king of France, *anno* 1308, and by his marriage, in 1314, with Isabella or Elizabeth, of Rumigny and Floriens, widow of Thiebaut or Theobald II. duke of Lorrain, he acquired as her dowry the city of Neufschatel in Lorrain, by virtue whereof he insisted on a right of coining money there, independent of her son Ferry, or Frederick IV. however, the matter was compromised between them, the profits arising from the coinage to be equally divided, the duke to give them a currency in his dominions, and the count promising, if possible, to obtain a currency for them in GALCHER, count of Porcien, 1308.

(*o*) Muntz Spiegel, p. 106. 4to. Franc. 1592. (*p*) Groschen Cabinet, Erst. Supplem. Tab. VIII. No. 91.
(*q*) Histoire de la Maison de Luxemburgh, par Vigner, 8vo. Par. 1617. page 157, 201, 224. Butkens, page 489. (*r*) Froisart, cap. cccxx. Vigner, p. 224.

 France,

France, this was in 1318 (s). It is proper also here to observe that the dukes of Lorrain coined principally at Nancy and Neufchatel (t), yet not one piece coined at the last mentioned place is now to be found. The emperor, Albert, in 1298, granted to Frederick II. duke of Lorrain, the privilege of coining at *Ivé*; money which was to be current not only in Lorrain, but also in the places of the empire bordering thereon, tho' not in France; there are none of these coins of the dukes now to be found neither, nor are the learned agreed where *Ivé* itself was situate; however, we have them both of Neufchatel and Ivé, with the name of Galcher.

No. 25, 26. There is inscribed round the head on No. 25. GALCHS COMES PORC; and on the reverse, MONET NOV. IVE; on No. 26. is, GAL. COMES PORCI; and on the reverse, MONETA NOVI CA; this last being of Neufchatel, and the other Ivé; in plate 32. of De Boze, there is one of No. 26. and three others of different types, all struck at Neufchatel; the small one agrees exactly with No. 9. pl. 1. the two others are Riders, a very common type abroad at that time, and much like No. 18. pl. 1. of the money of Lorrain (u), for on fresh differences arising after the above cited treaty in 1318, it was at last adjusted in 1321, that his money should be of the same type as that of Lorrain; but Baleicourt, p. 122. says, that in 1318 he had a right to strike it, with the effigies of himself and his dutchess.

No. 38. The above pieces were struck in right of his wife Isabella, but it is probable that No. 38. might be as count of Porcien; it has on the obverse two lyons rampant, inscribed, GUAL COME POR, and on the reverse, which has a rose in one quarter instead of three pellets, inscribed, MONETA PORCI, we have also seen another nearly like this, only round the reverse is inscribed, MONETA FLORINS; we would just observe, that Florins was one of the titles that Isabella brought to the house of Lorrain by her marriage, and after the death of the duke her husband, was given to her second son by him, Matthew, and therefore did not belong to Gualcher; we are at a loss likewise to what family belongs the lyons, for his arms were gules, 3 pallets vairé, a chief Or, with a martlet for distinction.

WILLIAM, bishop of Cambray, No. 30. William D'Avesnes was brother to John II. count of Hainault, he was chosen bishop of Cambray in 1292, and died *anno* 1295, on a journey to the Holy Land, he is represented on No. 30. exactly like his brother on No. 2, 3, 4. it is inscribed GUILLS EPISCOPUS, and on the reverse CAMERACENSIS. On No. 31. is a head crowned, but it is inscribed, THOMAS EPISCOPUS, and from its contrariety undoubtedly a counterfeit; on the reverse is inscribed, SIGNUM CRUCIS, the same inscription (w) is found also on the reverse of the next, and round the head, which is also crowned, JUS DE LOTHORENCIE, probably a counterfeit as well

THOMAS No. 31. as the last. We have also one with a mitred head within a triangle, as No. 29.

(s) Baleicourt Traite Historique de Lorrain, 8vo. Berl. 1711. p. 120. lxxxviii. Calmet, tom. 3. p. 104, 249.

(t) The count of Bar coined at Clarmont, in Argonne, St. Mihell, and Stain or Estain, the bishop of Toul, at Ivoy, Liverdun and Brixey, and the bishop of Metz at Metz, Marsal, Vic and Epinal, vide Calmet, tom. 3. pa. 114, 122, 130.

(u) Ibid. pa. 71.

(w) A piece of John II. count of Hainault, is found thus inscribed in Alkemade, p. 21. N. 4, 5. and another of his great grand-daughter Margaret, p. 24. No. 2. also in the plates of Mr. De Boze, there are others of Peter, bishop of Cambray, Raimond, prince of Orange, Walerand, count of Ligny, and Guy, count of St. Poll; we have also one of Utrecht the same, which is not in Mieres, having on its obverse a castle, as No. 40. with *Trajectum*.

the

Counterfiet Sterlings Pl 3

the inſcription not quite ſo perfect as we could wiſh, but appears to be HENR ARCH; the reverſe has not the three pellets in each quarter of the croſs, as thoſe of England, but inſtead thereof a Mullet, as in thoſe of Scotland, and we think inſcribed MONETA BUREN, or ſomething like it. No. 33, 34.

No. 33. and 34. have each a head crowned and inſcribed EG or EC MONETA NOSTRE; on the reverſe of the firſt is, CIVITAS TOLLO, and on the ſecond is, TOL-LEN-GEN-LUN, or LUN-TOL-LEN-GEN, for it may be read either way but neither of them intelligible, being both counterfeits, and deſignedly blundered, as are alſo, as we imagine, the two next, No. 35, 36. eſpecially the laſt of them, both which have crowned heads, the former inſcribed, HANS DNS SONEK, on the reverſe is, MONET DE LISE; round the head of No. 36. is, LUDEIO DTSAOI; and the reverſe, SOIVCIATIM. We can only find one Schoneck, in the electorate of Triers of little conſequence, and another in Upper Alſace, which formerly had its own barons till about 15.... No. 35. 36.

During the time of the ſtriking theſe pieces, there were a great number of Biſhops, Abbots, Barons, &c. who had their own mints, which were often farmed of them by their mint maſters, or others, many of whom coined the money of other princes, beſides their own; nay, even there is an inſtance of their having the liberty to chuſe what type they pleaſed to put on it (x). It is therefore very probable, that many of our ſterlings had their birth in ſome of theſe ſort of mints, and that there are many more ſorts than have come to our knowledge. Probably made in a Biſhop's Abbot's, or Baron's mint.

The Engliſh Sterlings were allowed a currency in France for many centuries, and it is probable alſo in thoſe places out of France, where the French money itſelf was permitted to paſs, as in Flanders, Hainault, Luxemburgh, &c. their value being well known, and for 117 years together were worth four deniers or pennies tournois each, but we ſhould be inclined to think that the greateſt number of them were made for England, as they are ſo frequently found among the Engliſh coins, as all thoſe we have here given came to us in this manner at different times, particularly in the parcel found near Newbury ſome years ſince, in which there was 50 (y) of them, they continued nearly the ſame type, with the full face, for more than 200 years, or from 1272, till the beginning of the 15th century. Engliſh Sterlings Current in France many Centuries.

We have never met with more than one ſingle piece of the numbers 1, 7, 8, 10, 14, 15, 16, 17, 24, 27, 28, 29, 30, 31, 35, 36, 38, and 39. thoſe which are the commoneſt are No. 2, 4, 9, 21, 25 and 26, altho' ſome of them are not met with every day; thoſe four which we publiſhed in our View of the Silver Coin, viz. No. 1, 14, 27, and 29. are now in the collection of Thomas Hollis, Eſq; No. 38. is in Mr. Duby's cabinet at Paris, and all the others in our own poſſeſſion.

(x) Calmet Diſſertat. ſur les Monnoyes, Tom. 3. page 113.
(y) View of the Silver Coin and Coinage, page 13.

A

A
VIEW
OF THE
COINS
STRUCK BY THE
EAST INDIA COMPANY,
AND IN THE
WEST INDIA COLONIES.

Spanish Pieces of Eight, the best for the East India trade.

THE English and Dutch in their first voyages to the East Indies, found the Spanish dollars, or pieces of eight, the best specie they could carry thither, being better than bullion, as the natives were well acquainted with them, and liked them better than any other sorts. Upon the East India Company's being incorporated by Queen Elizabeth, she was often pressed by them for liberty to export a certain quantity of these pieces yearly, alledging that her own money was

was not known there, for which very reason the queen refused to grant it, being determined, that if they were not acquainted with her coin, they should be, and informed by that means she was as great a sovereign as the king of Spain: therefore she ordered a particular sort of money to be struck on purpose for this trade, of the same weight and fineness as the Spanish, but with her royal arms and device of the Portcullis, called from thence the Portcullis money.

Elizabeth's Portcullis money.

No. 1, 2, 3, 4.

There are four sorts of them, generally called by collectors, the crown, half crown, shilling, and sixpence; but in reality, as we have just observed, were pieces of eight ryals, four ryals, two ryals, and a single ryal, being worth about 4 *s.* 6*d.* 2 *s.* 3 *d.* 1 *s.* 1 ½*d.* and 6 *d*¾. and weighing 420, 210, 105, and 52½ troy grains each when full weight. On the obverse side there is the royal arms between E. R. all crowned, and inscribed, ELIZABETH D. G. ANG. FRA. ET HIBER. REGINA; on the reverse is a Portcullis crowned, and round it the usual motto on the English silver money, POSUI DEUM ADJUT. MEUM. the mint mark is an Annulet, and shews they were struck *anno* 1600. We do not think there was any more coined afterwards, as Violet (*a*) tells us that the East India Company bought off the restriction of exporting Spanish money, in the beginning of the reign of James I. the Dutch also, in 1601, struck pieces at Dort (*b*) for the same purpose, having on one side the Holland Lyon, with the value as to IIII-IIII, II-II, I-I, &c. and on the other the arms of Amsterdam, but we think these were also soon discontinued.

Bombay ceded to Cha. II. 1662.

and by him to the East India company 1668.

Upon the marriage of Charles II. with the Infanta Catherine of Portugal, in 1662, the island and port of Bombay were ceded to him as part of her portion, by Art. XI. and lord Marlborough with Sir Abraham Shipman were sent with five men of war and 500 soldiers to take possession, but before it could be effected, the former was returned, and the latter dead, it being delivered to Mr. Humphrey Cook, Sir Abraham's Secretary, the articles being dated 14 Jan. 1665, which were deemed derogatory and contradictory in almost all their parts, to the treaty entered into by the two crowns, and Sir Jervas Lucas was sent over to succeed him: soon after which, the king by his royal charter, dated 27 March 1668, granted it to the East India Company, making them absolute lords proprietors thereof (*c*).

We are not certain when the mint was first erected at Bombay; however, the first money they coined were not current in trade, but only among themselves, not going at Surat, or in any part of the Mogul's dominions, or in the territories of the Indian Raja's (*d*), and of this sort we think are all which follow.

(*a*) Appeal to Cæsar, p. 25, 26. 4to. 1660. in the same place he also gives a plate with the figures of the standard weights of the three largest pieces, being square and marked India VIII Testernes, India IIII Testernes, and India II. which were then in custody of Sir William Parkhurst, warden of the Mint.

(*b*) Van Loon Histoire Metallique des Pais Bas, Tom. I. p. 539.

(*c*) A description of the port and island of Bombay, 8vo. 1724.

(*d*) Tavernier's travels, part 2. page 5.

Bombay Rupee, No. 5, 7. Among the first of them we apprehend was the Rupee, No. 7. which in the area on one side, THE RUPEE OF BOMBAIM; and round it, BY AUTHORITY OF CHARLES THE SECOND 1678; on the reverse is the royal arms crowned, and the remainder of the inscription, KING OF GREAT BRITAIN FRANCE AND IRELAND, it is broader than the rupees in general are, and very well done. No. 5. has on one side the arms of the company without any inscription, and in the center of the reverse, PAX DEO, and inscribed MONETA BOMBAIENSIS, this is smaller and thicker like those of the Mogul's. These are the only sorts of Rupees we have ever seen, but we are informed by Mr. Folkes (*e*) that there are two more, one having like the last, on one of its sides the arms of the company, but the other side filled with an Arabic inscription; the other sort has inscribed in the area on one side, MON BOMBAY ANGLIC REGIMS AO. 7. and round this, INCREMENTUM A DEO ET PAX; on the reverse, round the company's arms, inscribed, HON. SOC. ANG. IND. ORI. we would recommend to the curious collectors to discover in what cabinets these pieces are now to be found. At the present, and we think for a long time, the company have struck Rupees like those of the Moguls, with an Arabick inscription on both sides, which brings them in something considerable, for the coinage, which is to the companies servants 1½ per cent. and 2½ to all others.

Copper Pice. The company had also a sort of money in copper for small change, called Pice, consisting of 5 Rees, 80 of which make a Rupee; that is, about one-third of a penny in value, the old ones were struck in a very careless manner, neither round nor square, and seldom have surface enough to contain the whole legend; and besides that generally struck on one side, not in the center, and very thick.

No. 8. On No. 8. all that can be read round the arms of the company is, INCREMEN, and on the reverse, only SOC. ANG. round MOET BOMBAY ANGLIE REGUM AO. D.... in the center; on another we have seen the arms without a single word round them, and in the area, on the other side, only .... VM 74 A D... both of which appear to be nearly in the same manner as the last of the four rupees just mentioned.

No. 10. There is another sort much neater, being round and better work, having on one side a crown, with G. R. at top, and at bottom, BOMB. and on the reverse, AUSPICIO REGIS ET SENATUS ANGLIE 1720, 1728, &c. fills the piece: there are others of them also which are struck in Tutanague, or a sort of tin, which

Tutanague Pice. No. 9. being of less value are much larger, as No. 9. these are dated 1717, 1718, &c. there appear to be the whole and the half of each sort, if not other varieties; we have also an half pice in Tutanague, as we think, which has on one side 1739 ½P. and on the other E I as on some copper ones of Madrass.

C

Madrass, or Chinapatam goldPagoda, No. 5. We have no account when the mint was first set up at Madrass, but it is probable nearly as soon as at Bombay, for Tavernier (*f*) tells us, that the gold pagoda's struck at Madrass were in great esteem when he was in the East Indies,

(*e*) Table of the English silver coins, p. 113.

(*f*) Travels, part 2, page 5. Indian coin.

and

and are ſtruck there ſtill in great quantities; however, theſe are pieces that ſeldom are noticed by an Engliſh collector, any more than their Rupees, as having an Arabick inſcription on both ſides, which they ſtrike in great numbers, and receive a conſiderable profit therefrom (g); the piece moſt generally known here, is the ſilver Fanam, No. 6. firſt ſtruck in the time of Charles II. having an Indian pagod or idol on one ſide, and two croſſed C's on the other; and we think have been continued to be coined with the ſame type ever ſince, there are alſo double fanams. Silver Fanam, No. 6.

They have alſo two ſorts of copper coin ſtruck here, viz. Caſh, and Doudoos of 10 Caſh, having on one ſide a croſs between C C, and on the other a date, E as 1695, 1705, &c. others again have Arabick characters inſtead of the date. There is alſo another ſort which has a kind of a ſaltier between E I on one ſide, C and a date on the other, viz. 1734, 1739; there are ten Caſh to one Doudoo, and eight Doudoos to a fanam, or about two-pence ſterling. Copper Caſh and Doudoos No. 7*. No. 8*.

We now come to thoſe coins we have been able to diſcover, that have been ſtruck in our Weſt India Colonies.

The firſt of them, in order of time, appertains to the Sommer or Summer Iſlands, which received their name from Sir George Sommers who was ſhipwrecked there, *anno* 1609. A colony was endeavoured to be ſettled there under the Virginia Company in 1612, Mr. John More being ſent for that purpoſe; he was ſucceeded by Capt. Daniel Tuckar, in whoſe time it was our piece, No. 19. had a currency, as we are informed by Capt. Smith(*b*). His words are theſe, "beſides meat and drink, and cloaths, they had for a time a certaine kind "of braſſe money, with a Hogge on one ſide, in memory of the abundance "of hogges which were found at their firſt landing." Over the Hog on No. 19. is XII. the ſignification of which we do not know. It has on its reverſe a Ship. We have never ſeen any other than this ſingle piece, which is in the collection of Mr. Hollis. Sommer Iſlands. No. 19.

What firſt gave riſe to the coinage of ſilver in New England, was great quantities of ſilver being taken about this time by the Bucaniers from the Spaniards, and bringing it there, it was thought prudent to coin it for prevention of frauds, and therefore a mint was erected in Boſton for that purpoſe(*i*). New England, 1651.

The firſt pieces coined at this time, or rather ſtamped, were ſix-pences and ſhillings, like No. 17. 18. having on one ſide NE, and on the other VI and XII for their reſpective values; we are alſo told there was another ſort ſtruck with III. for three-pence, but we have never yet met with it in any cabinet, and even the other two are very ſcarce. No. 17, 18.

(*g*) A mint has within a few years been erected at Calcutta in Bengal, in which numbers of Rupees are alſo coined with Arabick inſcriptions, as thoſe of Bombay and Madraſs, but broader and not ſo thick.

(*b*) Hiſtory of Virginia, p. 183. Purchas, vol. 4. p. 1803.

(*i*) Hutchinſon's hiſtory of the colony of Maſſachuſet's Bay, vol. 1. p. 177.

In

No. 11, 12, 13, 14, and 15. In October 1651 the type was altered, the court ordering they should have a double ring, with the inscription, MASSACHUSETT, round a tree, in the center, and on the reverse, NEW ENGLAND, with the year of our lord (i. e. 1652) the value is also under it, as XII, VI, III, II and I. we hear of no other pieces but the three first, viz. shillings, six-pences, and three-pences, which were struck at that time; but there are also two-pences and pennies, but we have not seen any of the last sort, nor the shilling, No. 14. with the story of the good Samaritan on one of its sides, instead of the tree, which is said to be in the Pembroke collection, and is engraved in tab. 14, p. 4. of that museum.

Struck for 30 years with the same date. The first money being struck in 1652, the same date was continued upon all that was struck for 30 years afterwards, and altho' there are a great variety of dies, it cannot now be determined in what years the pieces were coined; no other colony ever presumed to coin any metal into money. It must be considered, that at this time there was no king in Israel, no notice was taken of it by the Parliament, or by Cromwell; and having been thus indulged, there was a tacit allowance of it afterwards, even by Charles II. for more than twenty years; and altho' it was made one of the charges against the colony, when their charter was called in question, yet no great stress was laid upon it. It appeared to have been so beneficial, that during Sir Edmund Andross's administration, endeavours were used to obtain leave for continuing it, and the objections against it seems not to have proceeded from an encroachment on the prerogative (*k*), for the matter was referred to the master of the mint, and the report against it was upon mere prudential considerations; it is certain that great care was taken to preserve the purity of the coin. I don't find, notwithstanding that it obtained a currency, any where otherwise than as bullion, except in the New England colonies (*k*); Douglas (*l*) farther says, that no other money besides, but English, were to be current, that the exportation of it was prohibited, except twenty shillings for necessary expences, on pain of confiscation of all visible estate; he also observes that "coinage is the prerogative of the sovereignty, not of a colony.

Value. These shillings, we are told by Douglas (*m*), were struck at 6 to the piece of eight, therefore weighed 2 dwt. 22 gr. each, and worth about nine-pence sterling; in another place (*n*) he says, that they were coined at two-pence in the shilling less than the English coin; he says also, that five per cent. for charges of coining was to be allowed by the owners of the silver brought into the mint to be coined; Hutchinson says fifteen pence in every 20 s. was allowed (*o*) (6 ¼ per cent.) for all charges which should attend melting, refining and coining. The court was afterwards sensible that this was too advantageous a contract, and the mint master, John Hull, was offered a sum of money by the court to release them from it, but he refused to do it; it was to be coined of the just alloy of the then new sterling English money. He raised a large fortune from it, leaving a large pater-

(*k*) Hutchinson, vol. 1. page 178.

(*k*) Summary Hist. and Polit. of the British Settlements in North America, vol. 1. p. 433.

(*m*) Discourse concerning the currencies of the British Plantations in North America, p. 9.

(*n*) Summary, vol. 1. p. 433. (*o*) Vol. 1. p. 178.

nal

nal estate, and one of the best real estates in the county; Samuel Sewall, Esq; who married his daughter received with her, as is reported, 30,000 l. in New England shillings; he was the son of a poor woman, but dutiful and tender of his mother, which Mr. Wilson, his minister, observing, pronounced that God would bless him, and although then poor, yet he should raise a great estate.

30,000l. in these Shillings given by the Mint Master as his daughter's portion.

At the first settling the New England colonies, their medium of trade, or currency, was sterling coin, at sterling value, five shillings denomination for an English crown, and 4 s. 6 d. a piece of eight, when they got into trade a heavy piece of eight passed for five shillings (5 s. 8 d ¼ per oz.) in 1652 they coined at 6 s. the piece of eight (6s. 10½ per oz.) on this footing it continued upwards of 50 years (p), and at this value it was also fixed by a general assembly of the Leeward Islands in 1694 (q), and became the current value throughout all the Plantations, by a proclamation dated 18 June 1704, which was again enforced by an act of parliament of the 6th of queen Anne, but the abuse of taking them without weighing, brought light pieces to pass for 6 s. the price of the heavy ones, which occasioned these last to be fixed at 8 s. (9s. 1½ per oz); between these two last valuations generally, but sometimes a little higher, Jamaica, Barbadoes, and the Leeward Islands have still continued, at the former till 1723 in Pensylvania, and in Maryland until 1734; Virginia is better than either.

Different values of the piece of Eight.

The prodigious rise of silver, from the above values, has been occasioned by large emissions of paper money currency from time to time, more than could be circulated by the usual trade of the provinces that uttered them, the distant periods of payment of them, and often also postponing those periods, have been the cause of the depreciating these bills, and consequently of the rising of the exchange and value of silver, which has been more severely felt in New England, than in any of the other plantations, where their bills began to depreciate about the year 1713, being then nearly at par with silver at 8s. per ounce, and it was supposed that their currency at that time consisted of ¼ silver and ¾ in Bills, but between that and 1718, the silver was drove away by the money bills, of which all their currency was then made up, and silver valued at 12s. per oz. (r) after that the bills depreciating more and more, till in 1741 the exchange was 550 per cent. and silver 29 s. per oz. and lastly, in 1749, were doubled, or 1100 per cent. and 60 s. per oz. their bills amounting unto 3,748,000 l. when the parliament reimbursed them the expences they had been at in the taking of Louisbourg, amounting to 183,649l. sterl. which was sent over in pieces of eight, and at the same time a stop put to any more emissions of paper money; and finally, it was entirely set aside by the acts of 24 Geo. II. C. 51. and 4 Geo. III. C. 34. and a silver currency again introduced on the old footing of 133 exchange for 100 l. ster. or silver at 6 s. 10d. ¼ per. oz.

Paper currencies occasions great rise in the value of silver.

Are all abolished in the plantations.

Here are added the form of some of these paper money bills that we have at present by us.

(p) Douglass's Essay concerning silver and paper currencies, p. 4.

(q) Two letters to Mr. Wood on the coin and currency of the Leewards Islands, p. 12.

(r) Discourse concerning the currencies, p. 25.

Maryland paper money bill. 1. Two Shillings and Six-pence, No. 80034—This Indented Bill of one Shilling shall pass current for the *Sum* herein mentioned in all payments according to the Directions of an Act of Assembly of *Maryland*, dated at *Annapolis* the 4 Day of May Anno Dom. 1734 11S viD W. Hammond, R. Gordon, B. Young.

Virginia. 2. 1 *Shilling & 3 Pence* (No 7921) ONE SHILLING & THREE-PENCE Current Money of VIRGINIA According to ACT of *Assembly* passed *May* 24, 1760. Fifteen Pence.—Pistereen—*James Cocke—One Pistereen.*

Massachusett's Bay. 3. 4d 4d THIS BILL OF FOUR PENCE *due to the Possessor thereof from the Province of the* Massachusetts Bay *shall be equal to Twenty-One grs coined Silver Troyweight of Sterling Alley or Gold Coin at the Rate of Five Pounds ten shillings & three pence per Ounce and shall be so accepted in all Payments in the* Treasury *agreeably to Act of Assembly June 20th 1744. By Order of the* General Court of ASSEMBLY (11656)—*S. Wall—P. Hale*—1742; on the other side is, *Sixteen Pence,* Old Tenor. *Twenty-one Grains of* SILVER, *Four Pence, Or* Gold at 5/ 10 *Shillings &* 3 *Pence* an Ounce, 1744.

Maryland, or Lord Baltimore's money. Cæcilius Calvert, Lord Baltimore, obtained his patent as proprietor of Maryland June 20, 1632, and in the autumn of the next year he sent thither a colony of about 200 persons, during the civil war lord Baltimore was deprived of his government, or jurisdiction of Maryland, but the grant was restored again to his son Charles in the year 1661; we have not been able to learn any thing in regard to the striking of these pieces, or when they were struck, nor whether they ever obtained a currency there, but we are rather inclined to think they did not.

Groat. Six pence Shilling, No. 19, 20, 21. Value. There are three sorts of them, the groat, the six-pence, and the shilling, No. 19, 20, 21, all of them have his head in profile to the right on one side inscribed, CÆCILIUS DNS TERRÆ MARIÆ, &c. and on the reverse, his arms crowned with an imperial crown between the values XII, VI, and IV, and round it, CRESCITE ET MULTIPLICAMINI; the work is that of a very good artist, and their weight approaches to that of the English.

JAMES II. No. 24. It is from the inscription on the reverse of this piece, viz. VAL 24 PART REAL HISPAN. that we have placed it among the coins of the plantations, as their currency consisted chiefly of Spanish silver, and in particular in Pistareens, Reals and half Reals, the two last usually called Bits and half Bits; and this piece was intended that 24 should make the first, and 12 the latter, but we cannot tell where struck, nor for what place intended; it is made of tin, as his farthing and halfpenny are, but has neither the stud of copper in the center, nor inscription on the edge; it has on its obverse the equestrian figure of the king, but different from that on his Irish crown, as are the shields on the reverse, there being a sort of chain which holds them together.

Carolina 1694, No. 23 It is for the sake of information that we have inserted No. 23. as we cannot ourselves conceive the intent of striking it, or for what purpose it was intended; however, we think it has no claim to be admitted as a piece of money, but rather is of the ticket kind, and we are of the same opinion in regard to another piece, which is certainly of the same class with this; be it what it will, it is what

what we call the London Halfpenny, one side of both, that is the Elephant, we apprehend was struck from the same dye, which is still remaining in the Tower, and appears to be the work of Rotiers; on the other side instead of GOD PRESERVE CAROLINA AND THE LORDS PROPRIETORS 1694, as upon this; there is upon that, round the city arms, GOD PRESERVE LONDON; we have heard two or three opinions concerning the intent of uttering this piece, as that it was for the London Workhouse; also, that its inscription alludes to the plague, and was struck whilst it raged in London; and we have likewise heard it was intended to be made current at Tangier in Africa, but never took place; if this had been the case it would have been very proper to have introduced it here.

In the year 1722, a project took place of supplying the British plantations in America with brass money, such as two-pences, pence, and halfpence; the projector was the noted Mr. William Wood, whose copper money for Ireland made so great a noise at that time, but we have never met with an American *Swift*, who has analysed this project for America, as the Dean has done that for Ireland; one of his Irish adversaries has informed us of a few particulars in relation to this coinage, which we could never meet with any where else (*f*), viz. "Mr. Wood obtained a patent for coining small money for the English plantations in America; in pursuance of which he had the conscience to make 13 shillings out of a pound of brass; this money they rejected, in a manner not so decent as that of Ireland, but he has never called it popular fury, and we hear nothing of the patent itself," all that we know farther of it is, that the patent was for 14 years. Wood's Plantation Money, 1722. 1 lb. of brass made into 13 Shillings.

We have also been informed that Kingsmill Eyres, Esq; Mr. Marsland, a Hardwareman in Cornhill, and several others were concerned in the scheme, the last mentioned person had great quantities of them in his cellar, was ruined by it, and died housekeeper at Gresham College; the dyes were engraved by Mr. Lammas, Mr. Standbroke, and Mr. Harold, some of which were in the possession of Mr. Winthorpe, who went to New-York, his father lies buried at Rockingham; they were struck at the French Change, in Hogg Lane, Seven Dials, by an engine that raised and let fall an heavy weight upon them when made hot, which is the most expeditious way of striking Bath metal, which was the sort of metal they were made of.

There are three sizes of them, No. 25, 26, 27. made for an halfpenny, twopence, and a penny; the largest has round the King's head, GEORGIUS D. G. MAG. BRI. FRA. ET HIB. REX. the other only GEORGIUS D. G. REX. there are two different reverses, viz. a rose, and a rose and crown, both sorts inscribed, ROSA AMERICANA—UTILE DULCI, sometimes also the dates 1722 and 1723. *N. B.* If these were made only for 2d, 1d and ½d of their currency, and not sterling, they were not worth but a trifle more than ⅓ of those values in sterling, as the exchange in those years was 270 per Cent. and silver 14 s. per oz. We have a piece much like the penny in size, struck in the same metal, the head also nearly the same, inscribed, GEORGIUS D. G. FRA. ET HIB. REX. and on the reverse Type, Legend No. 25, 26, 27. Value.

(*f*) A defence of the people of Ireland in the unanimous refusal of Mr. Wood's copper money. p. 37.

verse, the figure I crowned between two laurel branches, inscribed, BRUN ET LUN DUX SA ROM MI ARC THE ET PR. ELEC.

George II. 1733. No 28 We never heard of any proposals made about the year 1733, for an American coinage; however, No. 28. has the appearance of a pattern piece for some such scheme; it has the king's head laureat, inscribed, GEORGIUS II. D. G. REX. and on the reverse a leafed rose crowned, inscribed, ROSA AMERICANA 1733 —UTILE DULCI. The only piece we know of, is in the collection of Thomas Hollis, Esq; we have also seen a proof of the head in steel, said to be struck on that metal to shew how malleable they could make it by smelting it with pit coal, by a scheme then on foot.

North Carolina 1754. Proposals for coining 2d, 1d, and ½d in copper. In 1754 a proposal was sent over here for approbation, from Arthur Dobbs, Esq; Governor of North Carolina, for to coin copper money for that colony, to consist of pieces of the value of two-pence, one penny and an halfpenny of their currency, which was in proportion to that of England as four to three; the quantity proposed to be coined to be such as the Governor and Council of Carolina should think proper, but not to exceed 50 tons; they delivering the copper into the mint, paying all expences and fees attending the coinage, and to have such a device on them as should be thought proper. His letter with the proposals were sent down from the treasury, June 24, to the officers of the mint to consider of them, and give their opinion on the most proper method to put them in execution; in answer to which it was proposed, that one half of what should be coined should be in halfpence of such a size, that 61 pieces was to make 1 lb. weight avoir. one fourth should consist of two-penny pieces, and the other fourth of penny pieces, of a proportional weight to the halfpence, the remedy to be $\frac{1}{41}$ part of a lb. wt. avoirdupoize, and this not by design, but accident; to perform them at the same price as those for Ireland, five-pence per lb. wt. for the master, and 20s. per hund. to the deputy comptroller; the proportion as to the number of each sort to be kept, as an increase in the number of halfpence, would increase the expence, one side to have the king's effigies, with GEORGIUS II. REX. on the reverse the arms of North Carolina, inscribed, SEPT. CAROLINA, and under it the date of the year; we apprehend it rested here, and was never put in execution. But does not succeed.

A VIEW of the COINS struck in the ISLE of MAN.

Norwegian race of the Kings of Man. THE Isle of Man lies between England and Ireland, nearly equidistant from both; it became subject to the Kings of Norway very early, and was governed by kings dependent upon them; as 1, Godred, the son of Sirric, who died 1066; 2, Fingal; 3, Godred Crovan, who died 1082; 4, Lagman, who died 1089; 5, Dopnald, sent from Ireland; 6, Olave, son of Godred, from 1111 to 1144; 7, Godred his son till 1187; he was also king of Ireland; 8, Raignald; and 9, Olave his son till 1237. Vide Speed's theatre of Great Britain, p. 92.

Supposed to have struck No. 1, 2, 3, 4, 5. Under some of these princes we apprehend were struck the five first pieces in the small plate annexed, but to which to ascribe them is uncertain, as we cannot make out any name upon them, and the greatest presumption we have of their belonging to these kings, is, that they were found in that Island. The time when published we think was included between the years 1100 and 1200, and

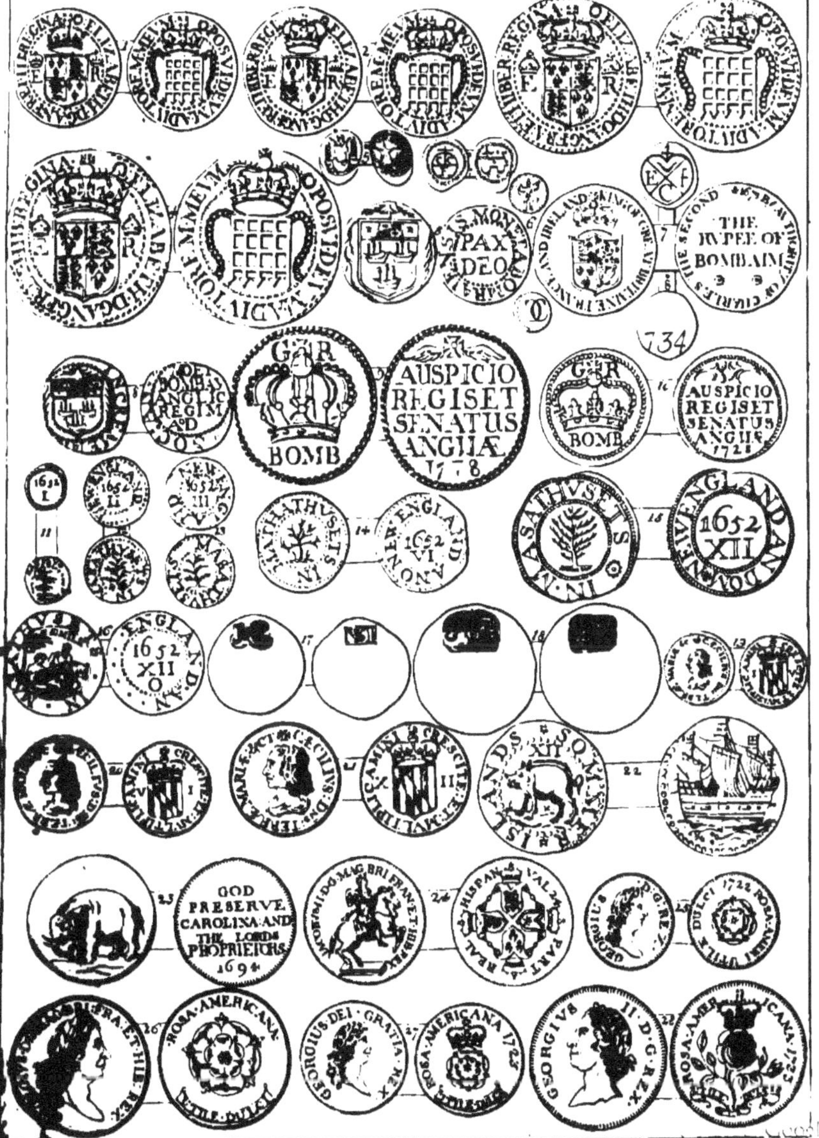
THE RUPEE OF BOMBAIM
PAX DEO
BOMB
AUSPICIO REGIS ET SENATUS ANGLIÆ
1652 XII
GOD PRESERVE CAROLINA AND THE LORDS PROPRIETORS 1694
ROSA AMERICANA
GEORGIUS DEI GRATIA REX
GEORGIUS II D G REX

and moſt probably by Olave, or Godred his ſon; we have heard of many other ancient pieces which were lately found there, and ſaid to be Daniſh, but not having ſeen any, can determine nothing concerning them.

The head of No. 1. is much in the taſte of No. 25. pl. 1. of our ſilver coin, of Stephen, the reverſe exactly the ſame; the only letters on it are MITA; there is ſomething in the head of No. 2. which reſembles the work of that time, but the reverſe quite ſingular, as is alſo the reverſe of No. 3. the head of which is worn away, having round it only MMI'.. we have two other pieces with the ſame reverſe, one of which has a profile head, apparently with a helmet; the reverſe likewiſe of No. 4. is like the laſt, but the head exactly as No. 29. of Stephen, as is alſo the next, No. 5. only looks the contrary way, and it's reverſe much like No. 19, 20. of Henry the Firſt. This laſt is in the collection of the Earl of Bute, all the reſt are our own. Type.

In the 7th year of Henry IV. or 1406, Sir John Stanley, Knight, had a grant in fee of the Iſle of Man, with all its regalities; his grandſon, Thomas, was created Earl of Darby, Oct. 27, 1485, by the marriage of Amelia, daughter to James, the 7th Earl, to John, Earl of Athol, the ſame regalities came into that family, from whom they were purchaſed, by act of parliament, 5 Geo. III. c. 26, anno 1765, for 70,000 l. ſterling. The Iſle granted to the Stanley family.

The earlieſt pieces made by this family, are dated 1709, and are caſt, being in other reſpects the ſame as No. 7, 8. the next is an halfpenny, dated 1723, a neat dye, and ſtruck, as are alſo thoſe in the plate, having on one ſide three legs, the arms of the iſland, inſcribed, QUOCUNQUE JECERIS STABIT, alſo I-D for JACOBUS DARBIENSIS, and under it the value ½d, or 1; the reverſe has the creſt and motto of the Earls of Darby, and under it the date 1733 No. 9. and 10. are thoſe ſtruck by the Duke of Athol, differing from the others only on the reverſe, which has the duke's cypher crowned, and 1758, inſtead of the creſt of the Stanley family. Money ſtruck by the Earls of Darby. No. 7, 8. and the Duke of Athol.

We find by No. 6. the cuſtom of tradeſmen making their own money, was introduced into this Iſland, it being a penny of John Murray 1668, its obverſe having the three legs as the four laſt pieces. A tradeſman's token.

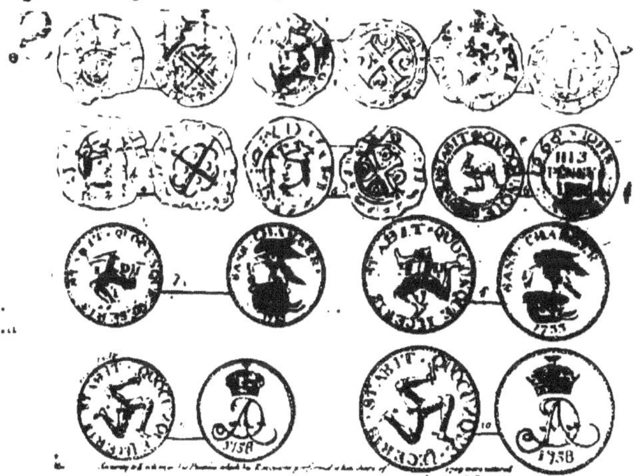

A VIEW OF PATTERN PIECES, FOR ENGLISH GOLD and SILVER COINS.

What is meant by Pattern Pieces.

BY Pattern pieces, or Tryal Pieces, we would be understood to mean designs, that have at different times been drawn and engraven as specimens, presented to the prince and legislature for their approbation, but which, for reasons at present mostly unknown, were not liked or carried into execution.

Often not known for what coin intended.

We are often at a loss to ascertain what sort of coin many of the following pieces were intended for, as it often happens we meet with some of them both in in gold and silver, other sorts again in silver and copper, nor will the weight always help us out, as it seems often not attended to, especially where only the type and inscription, and not the value was varied, as we think was the case of most, if not all the pieces under consideration.

Besides the above difficulties, we cannot be certain that many of them were really intended as patterns for any sorts of money, but rather jettons, nay, whether some of them may not even be of the ticket kind, as there are many of both sorts, the purposes for which they were made, we are unacquainted with, nor can it be discovered either by the Type or Inscription found upon them. *Or Patterns, Jettons, Tickets.*

The first piece, in plate 5. in Mr. Folkes's opinion, was intended for a groat of Henry VIII. after his 18th year, 1527; his reason for judging thus, was its weighing near 43 gr. which was their weight at that time, but we are rather inclined to think it a pattern groat of Henry VII. and struck about the time of the great change in the type of the silver money in 1504, from the full face, cross and pellets, to the profile one, and royal arms, and Mr. Folkes himself has placed it at the head of that coinage in his own plates. *Henry VII. or VIII. [illegible] No. 1. pl. 5.*

On the obverse, the king appears sitting in his chair of state, having a scepter in his right hand, and a globe in his left, as on his sovereign, of fine gold, No. 2. pl. 2. from which, it is probable, the thought was borrowed, and that of the pennies of this reign the same; its greatest singularity is the word LONDON, which is under him, and is found thus on no other piece, the inscription on both sides is the usual one, except the number after the king's name, which is not here; it is also wanting on one of his shillings, it is an Unique, formerly in the collection of Mr. Thomas Grainger; but at present, in that of Mr. John White. *Type. Rarity.*

The second piece is commonly known by the name of Henry VIII's crown, but its weight will by no means support such an opinion; Mr. Folkes, from its mint mark of a fleur de lis, supposes it to have been struck in his 34th year, 1542, and that its full weight should be 480 gr. (its real weight being only 464, as being much worn) and therefore a pattern for a Quadruple Testernes, or piece of 4 Shillings; but if we suppose it to be struck before that year, and after 1527, as is highly probable it might, its value will then be but three shillings and nine-pence. However, we rather judge it to a medal, struck upon his assuming the supremacy in 1530, which is strongly corroborated by the legend on the reverse of it. *Henry VIII. supposed crown. No. 2.*

The king is portraited to the waist, and crowned, has a sword in his right hand, and the monde in his left; it is inscribed HENRI 8. DEI GRATIA ANGLIE, FRANCI Z HIBERN REX; the reverse has the royal arms crowned, and supported by a lyon and a dragon; inscribed, ANGLICE Z HIBERNICE ECCLESIE SUPREMUM CAPUT; the reverse of the pound sovereign, published some years afterwards, was an imitation of this; we know of but two of these, that in the Bodleian collection at Oxford, and that in the Pembroke museum. *Type. Legend. Rarity.*

It

Edw. VI. 1547. Testoon, No. 3.

It was during the unsettled state of the coin, in the beginning of this king's reign, that the Testoon, No. 3. was struck; it is what is usually called Bishop Latimer's Shilling, from the mention he makes of it in one of his sermons†, for its rarity, we should rather suppose it a pattern for a Testoon, than in common currency; it is very probable that the silver it is made of is 10 oz. fine; if this is a fact, its true weight should be 48 gr. to which they approach very near; the most material difference between this and the common one of 1549, as No. 10. pl. 4. besides its weight and fineness, is in its having the Arabick 7, instead of the Roman VII. in the dates, as also in the, &c. after the king's stile on the reverse.

No. 4. also a pattern piece for a Testoon

The next piece, No. 4. we are of opinion was intended also as a pattern for a Testoon, as well as the last, and that those we have remaining of them are proof pieces, some weighing about an ounce, and others about half an ounce, the value of which at that time was 10 shillings and 5 shillings, and has occasioned such pieces to be called patterns for those species of money, but we have many instances of proofs being struck upon pieces of metal very different in weight, from what they were to be of when made current; as among others, a fine Aquitain penny of Henry II. (*a*) a Canterbury penny of Edward II. (*b*) a Durham penny of Henry VIII. (*c*) and two Dublin Groats of the same kings (*d*) we therefore are of opinion that No. 4. which is found both of the weight of 1 oz. and ½ an oz. to be of this class; besides, there were no coins at that time current abroad of this value, but were much broader and thinner, like the crown coined by this king four years afterwards.

And not for a piece of 5 or 10 shillings.

Type.

The principal difference between this and the common ones, besides the goodness of the silver, is the ZC after the king's titles, and the date XLVII, instead of XLIX, L & LI. Horace Walpole, Esq; has that which was Lord Oxford's of the weight of an oz. and Mr. John White has one of half that weight.

Half Crown, with leafed Rose. No. 5.

The first gold piece in this plate is No. 5. a fine half crown from the cabinet of the Duke of Devonshire, the same type and legend exactly, as the crown of this sort in pl. 3. No. 3. of our Gold Coinage, having the king's titles round the head, and scutum &c. on the reverse, round the rose; we know of three of these crowns, that of Lord Oxford's, which was afterwards Mr. Fairfax's, and at present Mr. Hanbury's, weighing 50 grains; one of Mr. Dummer's of 48 grains, formerly Dr. Mead's, and Mr. Barret has one nearly the same weight, once Mr. Beachcroft's; we do not know any half sovereign of this sort, but only that which has the motto Scutum, &c. round the head, and the king's name and titles on the reverse, as No. 6. which is in the collection of Dr. Ducarel, and weighs 117 grains; Mr. Fairfax had one which weighed more than the double, that is 240 grains, bought at his sale by Mr. Gardiner, the true weight

Half sovereign ditto. No. 6.

† We have now a pretty little shilling, indeed a very pretty one, I have but one I think in my purse, and the last day I had put it away almost for an old groat, and so I trust some will take them. The fineness of the silver I cannot see, but therein is printed a fine sentence, *Timor Domini Fons Vitæ vel Sapientiæ*; the fear of the Lord is the fountain of life or wisdom; I would God this sentence were always printed in the heart of the king. Folkes, p. 32.

(*a*) Mr. Hollis's. (*b*) Dr. Bettesworth's. (*c*) Mr. Hollis's. (*d*) Dr. Sharpe's and Mr. Dummer's.

of this piece ſhould be but 84½ grains, and therefore both of them are undoubtedly proofs; we have never heard of the Crown and half Crown of it. The reverſe of No. 6. was engraved in the year 1547, as it is uſed as an obverſe to the jetton of this king, with the inſcription, Inſignia Potentiſſime Regis Angliæ 1547.

Six Angel Piece. No. 7. The pattern for a piece of 6 angels, as No. 7. from its weight is ſuppoſed to be, we think, was made before his 4th year, when the Angel and half Angel were coined, for it has the roſe or emony flower for its mint mark, and the &c. after the titles, as in the Teſtoon of 1547; and the gold crowns and half crowns, which it is very probable were ſtruck that year alſo. It is in the Pembroke collection. We have engraved and deſcribed it before in our Gold Coinage, pl. 3. No. 15. but obſerved it was not in its proper place.

ELIZABETH's Pound Sovereign, No. 8. Edward the Sixth was the firſt of our princes that has his head in profile on our gold money, as the half Sovereign and ſmaller pieces, which ſort of pieces were alſo minted by Queen Elizabeth, from the beginning of her reign, as the milled ones, with the mullet and fleur de lis, and the hammered ones with thoſe of the croſs croſlet, lyon, coronet, &c. but we not remember to have ſeen any Sovereign till after the year 1590, the firſt being with the Ton MM, which correſponds with Mr. Lowndes's indenture of her 35th year; however, from this piece, which was certainly intended as a pattern for a Sovereign, there were thoughts of ſtriking them as early as the year 1565.

Type. Legend. It is fine work, and much in the taſte of the halves juſt mentioned, only ſhe has a royal mantle covered with ermins, and is not in armour, as moſt of the others appear to be; the legend nearly the ſame, as upon the Sovereign of her brother, IHS AUTEM TRANS. PER MEDIU ILLOR. IBAT. whereas thoſe that were afterwards coined had Scutum, &c. as upon the half, quarter, and eighth; it has a fine full blown roſe for its mint mark; this piece is an Unique, formerly in the collection of Thomas Sawbridge, Eſq; but at preſent in the collection of Thomas Knight, Eſq; who purchaſed the whole cabinet. *An Unique.*

No. 9, 10. Probably ſilver half pence. We conjecture that No. 9. with the queen's head on one ſide, and her crowned cypher on the other, as alſo No. 10. with E. R. crowned with a bell between them, and on the reverſe a roſe, were both intended for half-pence, none of which ſort of money were coined by her till the 24th year, 1582, the bell being the mint mark for that year (t), and No. 12. having it alſo, might probably be ſtruck at that time, and intended for a groat, the coinage of three-pences being diſcontinued after that year; the fleur de lis behind the queen's head is very ſingular; we have no where met with this, or No. 10. but in the Devonſhire muſeum. *No. 12. a Groat.*

A copper token, or pledge for a halfpenny, No. 14. The four remaining pieces of this Queen have, like No. 10. on one of their ſides the crowned cypher, or Monogram, but we are not certain for what any of them were deſigned, except No. 14. which is THE PLEDGE OF A HALF-PENNY (u), and prior by many years to the other three, that were all ſtruck

(t) View of the ſilver coin, p. 31.   (u) View of the copper coin, page 3.

in 1601, not long before the queen's death; however, it is not improbable No. 11. might be intended for an halfpenny Token or Pledge in copper, like No. 14. the intent of No. 13. we read on one side being, THE PLEDGE OF A PENNY; on No. 15. is inscribed UNUM A DEO DUOBUS SUSTINEO—AFFLICTORUM CONSERVATRIX, and has, we think, more the appearance of a Jetton, than a Pattern for a Two-pence in copper, as Mr. Folkes thought might have been its intent (*w*); we have seen No. 13, and 14. in copper, as well as in silver, but never No. 15.

A Penny, No. 13. A Two-pence, No. 15.

JAMES I. Laurel or Unite. No. 16.

Upon examining No. 16. which is in gold, with a little attention, it appears to have been intended for a laurell'd Unite or XX Shilling piece of this King, which were introduced in his 18th year 1621, it is better work than those are in general, the bust more in relief, the legend is JACOBUS D.G. MAG. BRI. FRA. ET HIB. REX; that on the reverse was never put in, as it was, we apprehend, never finished, the arms and cross, much the same as those on the laurels. It is in the collection of Mr. Hollis. The I R crowned between a rose and thistle on one side, and the crowned portcullis on the other; on No. 17. is clearly an imitation of No. 12. of Elizabeth, and probably intended for the same sort of money.

No. 17.

CHARLES I. Silver Halfpennies, No. 18, 19. No. 21.

We think it may safely be conjectured, that No. 18. having C R crowned on one side, and a rose on the other, was intended for an halfpenny, the work is Briot's and very neat; the next, No. 19. has a rose crowned on each side, inscribed, CAROLUS REX—A HALF-PENNY, we judge No. 21. from C ✠D R on its reverse, designed also for an halfpenny, not in silver, but in a mixed metal, which this piece consists of; the king has a radiated crown, being the only one we remember to have met with, and makes us suspect it was done after his death, the inscription is, CAROLUS D. G. MAG. BRIT.—FRAN. ET HIBER. REX; we have never seen but one of each of the above pieces, which are in the cabinets of Mrs. Cavendish, Mr. Hodsol, and Mr. Hollis.

Farthing Token, No. 25.

It is probable that No. 25. was intended as a pattern for a Farthing Token, and as such its proper place, one of the first in plate 6. of our copper coin, the helmeted head of this king is the only one we have seen, it is very neatly performed, and in copper; we should judge from the form of the shield, and the small roses, it is done by an artist of the Tower Mint about 1631; Dr. Mead had one, and Mr. Dummer has another of them; No. 22. is a two-pence of Briot's, done by him pretty early, as we think from the ruff round the king's neck, like those on No. 26. and 28. the inscription on the reverse is, FIDEI DEFENSOR, as on No. 36. it is highly probable from the manner of No. 29. that is, the Feathers between C. R. with ✱ II ✱ at bottom, that it came out of the Aberistwith mint, and was intended for a two-pence, the CHIRSTO AUSPICE REGNO on this and No. 24. are singular, on pieces less in value than the three-pence, we are possessed of this last piece.

Briot's Two-pence No. 22.

Aberistwith Two pence. No. 29.

Briot's Penny No. 23.

The most material difference between No. 23. and the common penny of Briot (No. 2. pl. 10. of our Silver Coin) is the small rose over the I. No. 31.

(*w*) Tables of silver coin, p. 64.

and

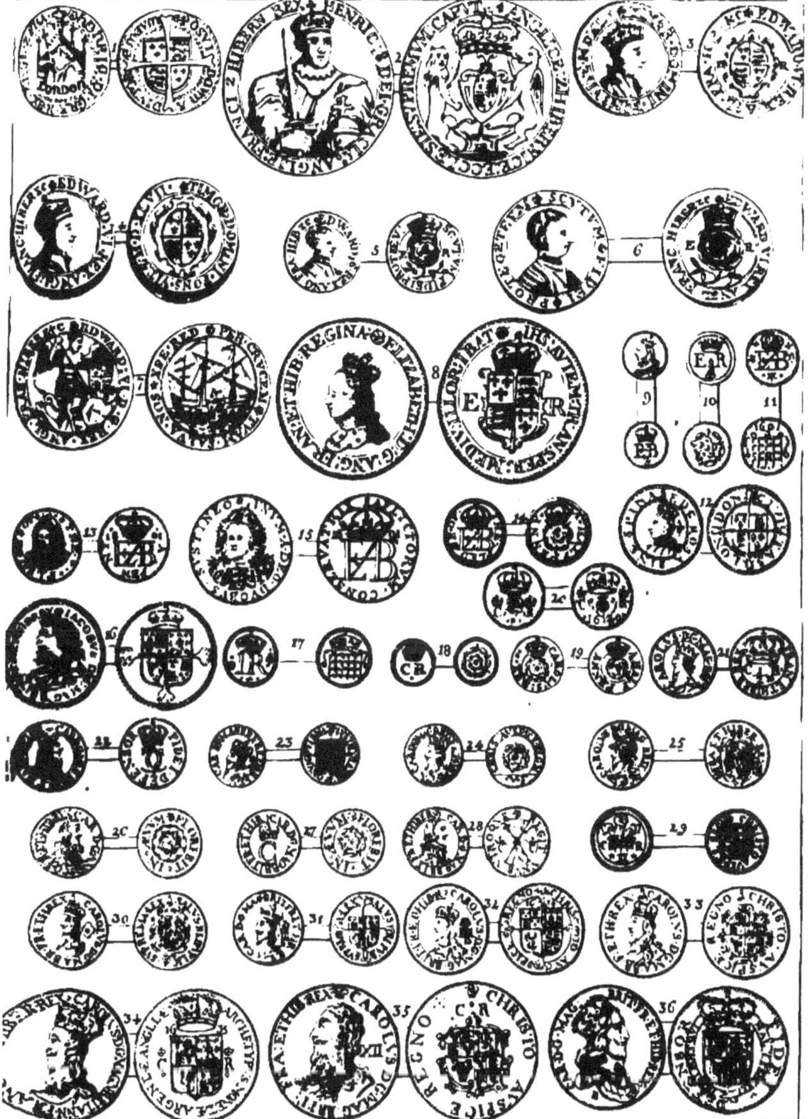

Threepence Groat. No. 31, 32.

and 32. have alſo the ſame ſmall roſe and a D likewiſe added under the figures, being undoubtedly intended for a three-pence, and groat; the firſt of them is farther remarkable in the legend on the reverſe, SALUS REPUB. SUPREMA LEX, which is that on his Scotch XL penny piece of this king; No. 32. is ſingular in the date 1634, over the ſhield.

Tower Threepence Groat, No 30, 33. No. 24. Briot's.

The ſame date is found alſo on No. 30. which has alſo the like inſcription as No. 31. altho' the ſhield is plainly that of the Tower Mint, as is that on No. 33. both which appear clearly to have been done the ſame year in the Tower, and intended as Briot's, for a three-pence and groat; No. 24. is certainly Briot's, but for what intended we do not know, neither can we tell the meaning of the V. F. in the exergue on the reverſe; it is in the collection of Loftus Jones, Eſq; as is No. 23. in that of William Sotheby, Eſq;

No. 26, 28. have the ſame head as No. 22. No. 20. Briot's.

We ſee the ſame head nearly on No. 22. (which was certainly intended for a two-pence) as upon No. 26. and 28. but then from the reverſes we ſhould rather think them of the Jetton kind, the former has a roſe with FLOREBIT IN ÆVUM, and we find the ſame on the next, No. 27. which inſtead of the head has a C crowned on the obverſe; the reverſe of No. 28. has a ſcepter and trident in ſaltier, between C-C crowned; another ſort has not the C-C, it is inſcribed, REGIT UNUS UTROQUE*. No. 26. is ſingular in having ANG. SCO. round the head, as all the reſt have MAG. BRIT. No. 20. we are inclined to think rather of the ticket or jetton claſs, than a coin, having a crowned roſe between C-R crowned, with 16-40 on one ſide, and a crowned thiſtle on the other, it is the performance of the ingenious and induſtrious Briot.

Shillings. No. 35. not Briot's, but an artiſt of the Tower mint, at preſent unknown. No money of this king with a bare head.

The three laſt pieces in plate 5. we are of opinion were all intended for ſhillings, of which No. 35. as we apprehend, was firſt in time, or done 1630, the feathers being the mint mark uſed that year in the Tower mint, and this piece a ſpecimen of the art of an engraver, at that time employed there, perhaps the ſame as did No. 25, 30, and 33. in this plate, and No. 4 and 5. pl. 6. whoſe name has not reached us; for if we except Rawlins, we have had the name of no other engraver of this time tranſmitted down to us, and we think it was too early for him. The king is bare headed, as on No. 22, 26, 28. and No. 2 and 4. pl. 6. but never appears thus on his current money, being always crowned, as had been the ancient cuſtom, the XII behind the head is for the value; this has no inner circle, but there is another ſort which has, and the ſhield on the reverſe is ſomething longer and narrower, in other reſpects the ſame.

No. 34. Briot's.

Number 34. is clearly a pattern for a piece of money, and probably a ſhilling, as we learn from the inſcription on the reverſe, ARCHETYPUS MONETÆ ARGENTÆ ANGLIÆ 16-35; the principal difference between this and Briot's current Shilling (No. 4. pl. 10. of our Silver Coin) beſides the above inſcription, is the C-R on the ſides of the ſhield, and the omiſſion of the croſs, which runs thro' it.

* There is a jetton alſo about the ſize of a ſhilling with this reverſe, the obverſe having the royal arms, and dated 1628, and Mr. Knight has a very fine gold medal with this type, and the head of the king on the other ſide.

We

No. 36 Briot's. We have more doubt concerning No. 36. being intended for a ſhilling, than either of the laſt, altho' there is nothing either in its type or legend, which is inconſiſtent with ſuch a ſuppoſition; the head looks a different way from that on any of his common money, and the poſition of the crown on the king's head is very ſingular; on the reverſe is a neat ſquare ſhield, with the royal arms incircled with the garter and motto, HONI SOIT QUI MAL Y PENSE, and another circle with FIDEI DEFENSOR, as on No. 22. the head of which alſo ſtands the ſame way, but that is with a ruff, but this with a band.

Unite or Broad Piece. No. 4, 5. pl 6. We think it will not be diſputed that No. 4. and No. 5. in pl. 6. were intended as patterns for Unites, or Broad pieces; on the firſt of them the King appears bare headed, as in No. 35. pl. 5. and No. 2. on pl. 6. on the other he is crowned as uſual, both of them have the value, viz. XX. behind the head; there is nothing ſingular in the inſcription round the head, any more than that on the reverſe, FLORENT CONCORDIA REGNA, from thoſe on the then current Unites, the ſhield on the reverſes is alſo the ſame as thoſe ſtruck in the year 1630, which year we think they were done, from the band on the king's neck; the form of the ſhield and the mint mark of the feathers, being ſpecimens that the moneyers in the Tower produced, againſt thoſe engraved this ſame year by Briot. The former of theſe is in the collection of the Duke of Devonſhire, and the latter in that of Mr. Hollis. *N. B.* Many of No. 4. are met with in ſilver, but without the XX. which together with the inſcription on the reverſe appears at firſt puzling.

Type, Legend.

Are of the Tower Mint.

No. 1. 2, 3. ſuppoſed to be deſigned for Broad Pieces alſo. The three firſt pieces in plate 6. are all by Briot, and if we ſuppoſe them patterns for coins, as we reaſonably may do from their type ſhould think were intended for Broad Pieces, as well as No. 4, and 5. which are ſmaller and thicker. The head on No. 3. is nearly the ſame as that on No. 34. of the laſt plate; that on No. 1. is larger, fuller, and extends to the edge, not being included within the inner circle, as thoſe laſt mentioned; the ſame difference is obſervable between No. 2. and No. 35. of plate 5. both of which are alſo bare headed; the inſcription on No. 1. and 2. begin at bottom, and are CAR. D. G. MAGN. BRITAN. FR. ET HIB. REX; No. 3. begins at top, CAROLUS D. G. MAGN. BRITANN. FRANC ET HIBE. REX.

Head ſide.

Reverſe. They have all three the ſame reverſe of the ſquare ſhield, with the royal arms, garniſhed and crowned between C—R, crowned alſo, the date is over it, and on No. 3. is divided 16-30. but not on the other two; near which is a ſmall neat St. George for a mint mark; they all have the ſame inſcription of AUSPICIIS REX MAGNE TUIS; had theſe patterns been approved on, ſome other motto muſt have been put to them, this being by no means proper, as it only declares that the royal protection and encouragement gave birth to theſe pieces. No. 1. is an Unique, in the collection of Joſeph Browne, Eſq; of Shepton Mallet, the other two are in Mr. Bartlet's; they are uſually met with in ſilver, but ſometimes in gold.

Rarity.

We uſually call No. 6. Briot's half crown, as having the common type of the king on horſe back on one ſide, and the royal arms on the other, it differs

differs from the half crowns at that time minted in the Tower, in having the horse's head the contrary way, and the shield on the reverse being crowned between 16-28; however, we think it never could be intended for a coin without the name of the king, and his titles being on it, neither of which are, but instead thereof is, O REX DA FACILEM CURSUM — ATQUE AUDACIBUS ANNUE COEPTIS. from which inscription it has more the appearance of a medal struck on the unfortunate expedition of the Duke of Buckingham to the Isle of Rhee (which took place this year) than a coin.

By its legend rather of the medal kind.

It is proper to consider No. 7. here, tho' put out of its place, which has nothing in its type but what is consistent with the supposition of its being intended for a pattern crown. It has on one side the king's head crowned, and inscribed CAROLUS D. G. ANGLIÆ SCOT. FRAN. ET HIB. REX FIDE DEFENSOR. The legend on the other side is the king's Equestrian figure inscribed, HAUD ULLI VETERUM VIRTUTE SECUNDUS; here again, as in the two last sorts, the inscription is not suitable to a current coin, but Briot herein makes his court and flatters the king, it is struck both in gold and silver, the latter in the collection of Mr. Hodsol.

Briot's pattern crown, No. 7.

The legend on the reverse not proper for a coin.

The Commonwealth began very soon to take into consideration the state of the money, and how much it had suffered by clipping, owing to the irregularity of its form, and inequality in the weight of the pieces; judging that the coining them rounder and neater, would in a great measure remove this evil; and hearing that Peter Blondeau was a famous artist in this way, the council of state procured from him patterns of some coins made after a new invention of his, and informed themselves at the same time of the quantity he could coin in a week, and the expence attending them; they therefore invited him to come to London, in order to agree verbally with him for coining the money of the Commonwealth. He arrived at London, Sept. 3, 1649, and had 40 pound given him on his arrival, with a promise that if they should not agree with him in regard to price, to indemnify him for his journey coming and going, and besides make him a gratuity for his trouble†.

The Commonwealth to prevent clipping, and counterfeiting their coin, send for Blondeau to coin it by his new method.

The master, the officers, and workmen of the mint, not liking to have any new method introduced, informed the committee, it was not likely that those pieces they had of Blondeau, were of his doing; besides, they said, it was an old invention‡, which they knew themselves; that such pieces were only made

It is opposed by those of the Mint.

for

† The corporation of Moniers answers to Blondeau, fol. 1653. page 15, &c.

‡ The first milled money was made in France, anno 1553, and many pieces of Henry II. are to be seen fabricated in this manner, it was the invention of an engraver named Anthony Brucher, and under the direction of Aubry Olivier, and continued in use till 1585, when it was forbidden. It was introduced into England in the beginning of Queen Elizabeth's reign, or from 1561 to 1568; the performer, Philip Mestrille, suffering in 1569 for privately coining; it was dropt here also, however, these had only a graining or grenelle on the flat edges, but no inscription.

The inscription on the edge appears first on the French Pied Forts, or finished proofs, which were generally quadruple, the weight of the current piece; there is one dated 1573 of Charles IX. and others also of Henry III. Henry IV. Lewis XIII. and Lewis XIV. of different sorts of coin, and with different inscriptions.

The earliest medal come under our notice thus distinguished, is a fine gold one of Ferdinand, Grand Duke of Tuscany, having his head on one side, and that of his duchess, Christiana of Lorrain, on the other, and on the edge FERDINANDUS MEDICES MAGNUS DUX ETRURIA III. ANNO MDXCIII. we

do

for curiosity, with great time and expence, and that it was impossible that it could be introduced in the ordinary current coin, as being very thin. They desired also, that Blondeau might be ordered to make a fresh trial of his skill, by making some more pieces, and that they would do them as well as him.

Ramage and Blondeau ordered to make patterns.

In consequence of this, on the 18th of May 1651, the committee for the mint, issue their orders to Mr. David Ramage (on the part of the mint) and Blondeau, to make patterns for a tryal, and present them to the committee, having for a motto TRUTH AND PEACE 1651, the impression to be the states armes, as on the twenty shilling piece, also two in silver for an half crown piece, and two with graining about the edges, without the motto, to be brought in; as also their propositions by July the third. Mr. Simon is also ordered at the same time to send to Ramage's office in the mint on the Monday following, 2 rollers and a drawing mill; and in case he does not, Violet is ordered to go to him for them, the day after, or on the Tuesday.

Ramage willing to put the states arms, or a device of his own on them.

On the 27th of May, Ramage complains (I should think to Sir James Harrington, for there is no name) that he had been twice to obtain a warrant from him, to get the puncheons of the states arms, the harpe and crosse, in order to make his trials; however, declaring at the same time, it was intirely indifferent to him, whether he put in the states arms, or a device of his own, only desiring to know which he chose; for if he put his own phantasie, he needed not the puncheons from Mr. Simon, otherwise he did.

A second order to Ramage.

The last order we meet with concerning the tryal, is dated June 14th, and directed to Ramage alone; whereas that above of May 8th, was to both him and Blondeau, the substance is much the same as that authorizing him to make some patterns as broad as a shilling, a half crown, and a twenty shilling piece in gold, in a mill, and with letters about the edge, if he can do it; or otherwise according to Queen Elizabeth's milled money, or any other models.

Both produce their pieces, but nothing determined.

The affair ended in both parties making their trials, and producing the patterns before the committee on July 3, as ordered, without coming to any determination in favour of either party; Blondeau's pieces were left with them, and remained in the hands of Sir James Harrington near two years, but those of Ramage's were delivered back to the moniers by Violet; who declares that in regard to the milled money, he thinks *It is faire to the Eye, but not safe for the Commonwealth*; whereas we are of opinion, that no motto was ever more justly

do not remember any other with an inscription, till the gold coronation medal of Charles I. done by Briot, which is certainly the first specimen among us; it is inscribed, EX AURO UT IN SCOTIA REPERITUR BRIOT FECIT EDINBURGII 1633; there are also some so inscribed in silver, though with great impropriety. A Teston of Cosmus II. Grand Duke of Tuscany*, between 1608 and 1621, having on its edge, HAS NISI PERITURUS MIHI ADIMAT NEMO (afterwards adopted by Oliver Cromwell, on his crown and half crown) is the first coin, and we have never heard of any piece of money after this piece, with an inscribed edge, until those trials we have been mentioning, between Blondeau and Ramage; it was first in common on the current coin of Charles II. 1662; it was imitated in Sweden in 1670, and soon after in Denmark, and by several princes in Germany, but none of the emperors till Joseph; the first French piece found with it, is the 4 Livres of Flanders 1684; there are a few of the Flemish cross dollars which have it, and we have a 3 guilder piece of Deventer, with IN TE DOMINE SPERAVI...CONFUNDAR IN ÆTERNUM; a fine ducaton of Cosmos III. has IPSA SUI CUSTOS FORMA DECORIS ERIT; a piece of Eight of Philip V. 1709. the only one either with a head or inscription, has AUXILIUM MEUM A DOMINO.

* Orsini Storia delle Monete de Granduci, 4to. 1760.

justly applied than the DECUS ET TUTAMEN, on its edge; which certainly is as much a security as an ornament to it.

There are three pieces of Ramage, No. 8, 9, 10. the first usually supposed to have been intended for a six-pence, has TRUTH AND PEACE on both sides, and likewise on its edge, being pretty thick; but there is one in the Devonshire cabinet, which instead of these words, has the edge filled with 22 pierced mullets like those in the legend; the obverse of No. 8. differs a little in the form of the shield, and is entirely encircled with laurels; but the reverse is quite different, having an Angel holding the two shields of England and Ireland, inscribed, GUARDED WITH ANGELES 1651; this is the shilling, and appears to be exactly the same dye as No. 10. which is the half crown, only that it is thicker, and has inscribed on its edge, TRUTH AND PEACE 1651. It was the fancy, we may suppose, of Ramage, and borrowed from the Angelot of Henry VI. but who engraved by does no where appear; however, probably by John East, the colleague of Simon, in the mint, if we will not give it to Simon himself. Ramage's patterns, No. 8, 9, 10, six-pence, shilling, and half crown.

The pieces of Blondeau are No. 11, 12, 13 and 14. designed for a six-pence, shilling, and half crown; they no way differ from the current money, but in their superior neatness and beauty, and the inscription on the edges of the two last; on the former of which we see TRUTH AND PEACE 1651, PETRUS BLONDEUS INVENTOR FECIT; and on No. 13. IN THE THIRD YEAR OF FREEDOME BY GOD'S BLESSING RESTORED 1651. Blondeau's six-pence, shilling, and half crown. No. 11, 12, 13, 14.

The above are all very rare, especially those of Ramage's, for we are informed he produced but a dozen pieces, whereas of Blondeau's there were 300; the collections of the Duke of Devonshire and the Earl of Pembroke, have each the half crown of Ramage; Mr. Browne has both that and the shilling, formerly Mr. Folkes's; they are likewise in the cabinet of Mr. Tutett, heretofore in the collection of Mr. Matthew Beachcroft, and perhaps in others that we are not acquainted with. None of the gold pieces have yet appeared, altho' they were both ordered to make some; we find the gold charged in Ramage's account, and that Blondeau actually delivered some of his twenty shilling pieces. Rarity. No 20 shilling pieces yet found.

The fine pieces of Oliver Cromwell should now follow, but we have already given them among the current coin; however, we think there is a much greater probability of their being rather pattern pieces, than otherwise, and to be classed among the most curious of them; and some of the finest specimens of the superior genius both of *Simon* and *Blondeau*, in their particular branches, although we find no mention made of the latter, as being concerned therein. Oliver Cromwell's rather patterns than money. Blondeau concerned in their fabrication.

There appears the same difficulties in regard to the intention of striking No. 15. and 16. of Charles II. as in many of his father's; for the types both of the head and reverse would incline us to imagine they were designed for money, but their inscriptions are of the medal kind, and plainly allude to the restoration of this prince; especially those of the last, which have an inscription on their edge. They are met with both in gold and silver, and some of the earliest pieces done after the king's return. CHARLES II. No. 15, 16. by Simon, may be either patterns or medals.

They have both the laurelled head of this prince in profile to the left; No. 15. is inscribed CAROLUS II. D. G. MAG. BR. FR. ET HI. REX; on No. 16. only CAROLUS II. REX. both have an S under the head; the reverse of the first has the royal arms crowned in a plain square shield; inscribed, MAGNA OPERA DOMINI 1660. the other has four ɔc II crowned, and put in form of a cross between the four shields of England, Scotland, France and Ireland, and a mullet of 8 points in the center; Type, Legend.

center; it is inscribed, MAGNALIA DEI 1660, and some of them on their edges, REVERSUS SINE CLADE VICTOR T. S.

Shilling, No. 17.

We apprehend that No. 17. was intended for a Shilling, (altho' we never saw any but in Copper) the head and inscription round it being exactly like the current one of 1663, the first of this kings; the inscription on the reverse is the same also on both, but differently placed, the date filling the last quarter, instead of being on each side the crown at top, and a rose, thistle, fleur de lis, and harp, each crowned stand in this, where the shields are in that, and the ɔc's are in the center, and not in the interstices of the cross.

Simon's Petition Crown, No. 18.

The famous contention between *Simon* and *Roettiers* gave birth to the finest Pattern piece to be met with in the English, or perhaps in any other series, especially in regard to the inscription on its edge; from whence it receives its name of the *Petition Crown*, which is, without dispute, the most curious specimen of this kind, ever exhibited by any artist, it makes a double row as follows:

Thomas Simon, most humbly prays your Majesty to compare this his Tryal piece with the Dutch, and if more truly drawn and embossed, more gracefully ordered and more accurately engraven to relieve him.

there are some of these pieces, which instead of the petition, have another inscription on the edge, viz. REDDITE QUÆ CÆSARIS CÆSARI, &c. POST, and a sun appearing out of a cloud to express Nubila Phœbus. Another sort, being a translation of the last, viz. RENDER TO CÆSAR THE THINGS WHICH ARE CÆSAR'S; we have no where seen, but in the cabinet of Thomas Dummer, Esq; the name of this excellent artist stands under the king's head, and in the center of the reverse is the figure of St. George, surrounded with the garter, and HONI SOIT QUI MAL Y PENSE.

Queen Anne's Guinea, No. 19.

We meet with no other pattern piece till the curious guinea of Queen Anne, having her neck bare all but a lock of hair brought over it; which, as we have once before observed, she thought immodest, and expressed a dislike at being represented in that manner, although it had been the constant practice on all the milled gold coin of her predecessors for them to be thus represented; nor could the gold be distinguished from the silver coin any other way but this, and the cross scepters on the reverse. In the center of the reverse stands AR, instead of the garter star, which is most usually found there, and on a few of them a rose; we have never seen but two of these pieces, one of them formerly Mr. Folkes's, then Mr. Samm's, and now in the collection of Mr. Bartlet; the other was once Mr. Hannott's, but at present in Mr. Browne's cabinet.

Geo. I. II. No. 20. 21.

The first Guinea of George I. being very particular in regard to the PR. EL. on the reverse, as also in its being much better performed than any other of this king, altho' not properly a pattern piece, we have added here, as having a little room, and for the same reason the first guinea of George II. as the manner differs, we think, from all the rest of his guineas, and is withal remarkably small and thick.

* There were three different edging tools or engines used on the first current crowns of this king, or those with the rose under the head; two of them have only DECUS ET TUTAMEN, which words on the first are so disposed as to fill the whole circumference; on the second sort, between the beginning and end, are a cross and two stars thus ● + ●, the letters being put closer together; to the last sort is added the date 1662, and 2 crosses + +, that of the next year, viz. 1663, instead of the date has the year of the reign, viz. ANNO REGNO XV. and the three following years the same, that is XVI, XVII and XVIII; but in 1667, instead of being in roman numerals, it is put in words at length, or DECIMO NONO, and in this manner it continued to the end of his reign, and ever since. Besides the crown with the rose, there is another dated 1662, which we think was coined after those with the rose, as that has the II behind the king's head; this, on the contrary, having it before the head, as is found on all afterwards; the inscription on the edge of this is the second sort with the ● + ●.

Pattern Pieces for Gold and Silver Coins

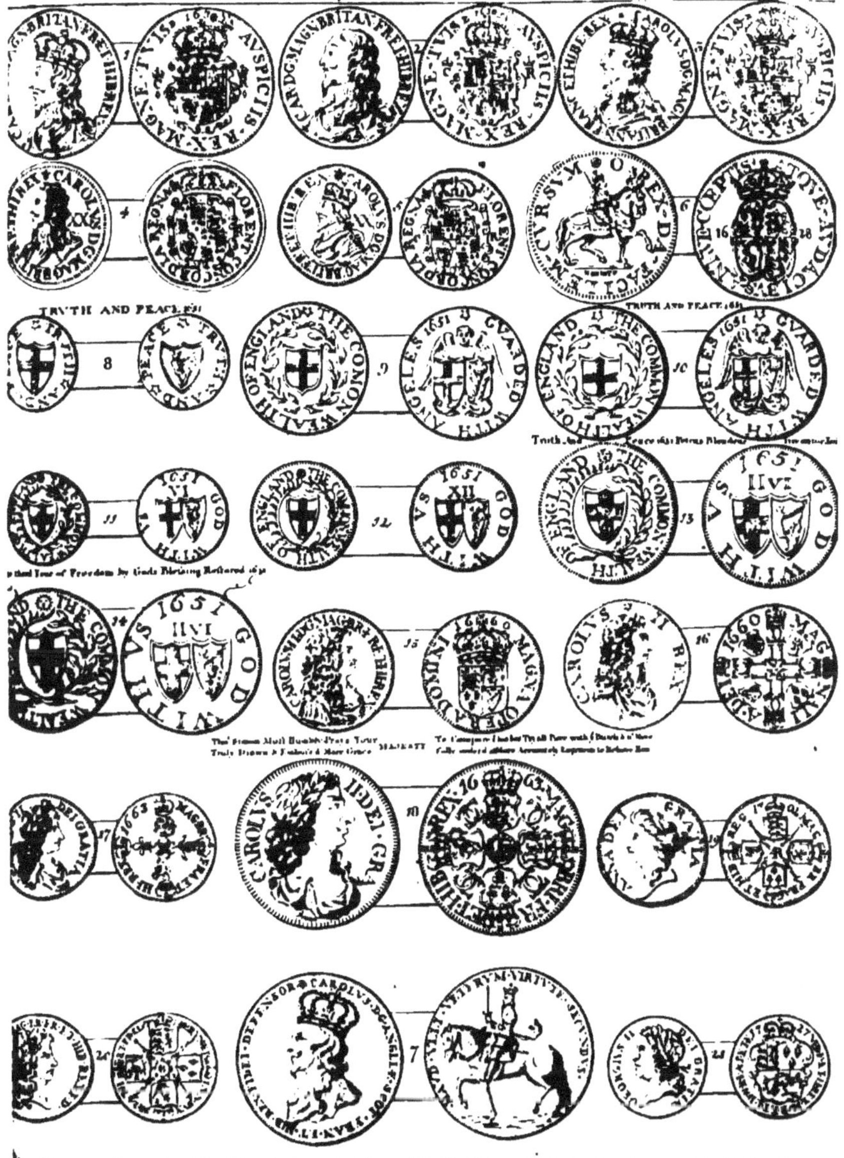

Mr. Dummer has a piece like No 3 which on the Sides of the Shield towards the top, has 16–30 and for M.M. a Heart.

A View of NOBLES ſtruck Abroad, in Imitation of Engliſh.

THE Engliſh Noble was as famous formerly among the gold coins, as the Engliſh Sterling had been among thoſe of ſilver, and we think it to have been a long while, of near double the weight and value of any other coin then uſually current; eſpecially in the Northern parts of Europe, and of as much note as the Florin and Ducat in the Southern parts. Obligations, payments, &c. were often ſtipulated to be fulfilled with theſe pieces, inſtead of being in Marks of ſilver, as had been the cuſtom before; and among other potentates this was adopted, as well by the maſter of the Teutonick Knights in Pruſſia, as head and protector of the grand confederacy of the Hans Towns, as by many of thoſe cities themſelves. Engliſh Noble of great note in the northern parts of Europe.

There are two ſorts of theſe nobles in reſpect to their value: as firſt, thoſe ſtruck by Edward III, &c. between 1353 and 1412, when they were altered, but coined of their old weight again 1464, and continued ſo till the cloſe of the 16th century; both ſorts are commonly called Roſe Nobles, although it is only the latter ſort which are ſtrictly ſo, as the former are properly Edward's, a few of Richard's being included among them. They weigh 5 dwt. or ¼ oz. troy; and thoſe that belong to this ſort among the following are, No. 4, 6, 7, 8, 9, 10, 11, 12, 19 and 20. The ſecond ſort of Nobles, are thoſe uſually called Henry Nobles, as being coined only by Henry V. and VI. between 1412 and 1464, and are 10 per cent. lighter than the others, weighing only 4½ dwt. troy; of this ſort, among the following, are No. 1, 2, 3, 5, 13, 14, 15, 16, 17 and 18. It muſt be obſerved, that although there were the ſame number of Nobles of each ſort ſtruck out of the Flemiſh Mark Troy, as there were of ours, out of the Engliſh Troy Mark, yet that being lighter than the other, theſe pieces are ſo likewiſe, by a few grains, and therefore ſomething leſs in value than ours; beſides, we think very few of them were quite ſo fine as thoſe ſtruck here. Are of two ſorts; the Edward, or Roſe Noble, and the Henry Noble. Thoſe of the Low Countries not quite ſo heavy nor ſo fine as thoſe of England.

The oldeſt Noble now to be met with, ſtruck in imitation of the Engliſh, is of Philip the Good, duke of Burgundy; however, it appears from the old placart of Maximilian of 1489; that there was alſo a Joannes Noble of the ſame value; therefore, probably one of Philip's father's, who died in 1419. The quarter No. 1. the half, No. 2. and the whole No. 3. are all alike as to type, and on the obverſe of each, with a little variety, is PHS DEI GRA DUX BURG COMES ET DNS FLAND; on the reverſe of No. 1 and 3. are IHS AUTEM TRANSIENS PER MEDIUM ILLOR IBAT; and on No. 2. DOMINE NE IN FURORE TUO ARGUAS ME. Although we never had in England a quarter Noble like this of Phillip's, as may be ſeen in pl. 1. of our Gold coin; yet there is a print of one like it (No. 21) in ſeveral placarts, which muſt have been occaſioned by their not having ſeen any of ours, and if ſo, is not eaſily accounted for, as they are common enough, eſpecially thoſe of Edward the Third's. Philip, or old Flemiſh Noble, with its half and quarter. No. 1, 2, 3. pl. 7. No Engliſh quarter Noble like No. 21.

Maximilian, king of the Romans, cauſed No. 4. to be ſtruck anno 1487, as guardian to the archduke, Philip his ſon, duke of Burgundy, it was called an half Ryal, and is inſcribed, M. D. G. RO REX ET PHS ARCHDUCES AU. CO. HO. on the reverſe is MO AUREA RO REGIS ET PHI ARCHD. AU. B. CO. HO. No. 5. was alſo ſtruck by him in 1488, and in a placart of 1489, is called the half Maximilian's Noble, or half Ryal, No. 4.

but generally a Schuytken, from the Ship, its legend is MO. RDUC.AUS. BO. BR. CO. H. reverse, REFORMATIO POST GUERRA

no other imitation of our Noble, for near a century after, or s of the Low Countries, when between 1579 and 1584, the 18 were struck. On the obverse of No. 6, 7, and 8, which ler of the States of Gelderland, Utrecht and Overyssel, is in-. HISP. ZC REX DUX GEL C Z. —PHS DG HISPANIÆ REX DNS D G HISPANIAR REX DO TRANSISL; but on the reverses of RES PARVÆ CRESCUNT. This same inscription is also found No. 9. and 10. struck at Utrecht and Campen, but on the ob-he name of Phillip, is MON NOV ORDIN TRAJEC, and MON IN VALO TRANSISULAN; nearly the same we find on No. 11. viz. MON NOVA AUR COMITAT ZEL; as also on No. 12. of ON AUR DUC GEL ET COM ZUT; but on the reverse of the OBISCUM QUIS CONTRA NOS; and on the last, ADJUTORIUM DOM. The three following, No. 13, 14 and 15. were struck tropolis of Flanders, and called the new Flemish Noble; on whole, No. 13. is, MO AUREA RESTAUR METROPOL GAND he reverse the inscription is NISI DNS CUSTOD. CIVIT. FRUST I; the half and quarter No. 13 and 14. want the two last word RESTAUR on the obverse, in other respects nearly the same. in Gelderland, round its obverse is inscribed MO AUREA DUC TFANIÆ, and on its reverse, NISI QUIA DNS ERAT IN NOBIS s. No. 17. was struck in Zealand, having on its obverse for ERVA NOS PERIMUS, and on its reverse, MONETA NOVA AU- No. 18. is of Overyssel, and reads on its obverse, MONETA IN TRANSISLANIÆ, and on the reverse, NISI TU DOM NOS STRA; the last of these sort of pieces struck in the Low Coun-being the first gold money of the United Provinces in 1586; d of having the head crowned, has it with a close helmet; and d in the left hand, is a bundle of arrows; the arms of the the side of the ship, and a bundle of arrows is in the center of erse; it is inscribed, MO ORDIN PROVIN FOEDER BELGIÆ 1586. ARVÆ CRESCUNT; it was made current for 7 Guildrs, increa-11 Guilders, but have been long out of currency; the last in 20. is that of Scotland of James VI. and the only one they ever ed JACOBUS 6. DEI GRATIA REX SCOTORUM; reverse, FLO-IIS REGNA HIS JOVA DAT NUMERA.

FINIS.

Nobles struck abroad in imitation of English
Pl: 7
1
2
3
4
5
6
7
8
9
10
11
12
13
14
15
16
17
18
20
21

A

V I E W

OF THE

SILVER COIN

AND

COINAGE

OF

SCOTLAND,

FROM ALEXANDER THE FIRST

TO THE UNION OF THE TWO KINGDOMS;

Confidered with Regard to

TYPE, LEGEND, SORTS, WEIGHT, FINENESS AND VALUE.

With COPPER PLATES.

By the late Mr. THOMAS SNELLING.

TO WHICH ARE ADDED,

FOUR PLATES of the GOLD, BILLON and COPPER COINS of the fame Kingdom.

LONDON:

Printed for *Thomas Snelling*, Printfeller, in *Fleet-Street*.

M,DCC,LXXIV.

Advertiſement to the READER.

THE following Work was nearly finiſhed, the Plates engraved, and the greateſt Part printed, before the Author's Death; the three Plates of the Gold Coins, and one of the Billon and Copper, were alſo engraved; but no Materials ſufficient for a compleat Illuſtration being left, we muſt confeſs our Inability to explain them, and with the Lovers of this Branch of Antiquity deplore the Loſs of ſo valuable a Man.

Auguſt 21, 1774.

The EDITORS.

A VIEW OF THE SILVER COIN OF *SCOTLAND.*

WE commence the series of the silver coin of Scotland with Alexander the First, as Mr. Anderson has done, upon the credit of a piece or two which he has caused to be engraved, and supposes to belong to this king; but we are of opinion they do not appertain to him, but rather to Alexander the Second. The piece which he has also given to David the First, taken from the Pembroke Museum, is still more suspicious, being a very imperfect coin, and, we fear, is badly drawn, therefore suspect it to be rather a blundered one of William, of that sort inscribed LA REI WILAM, we having often met with such, the letters of which were misplaced, and out of their true order. We have, however, put the abovementioned coins at the head of the series, yet do not think they were struck by those princes, and until some better proofs are produced, that William the Lyon must stand at the head of the Scotch collection, as William the Conqueror does in that of England after the Saxon.

 Alexander

ALEX. I. 1107. Alexander the First was son of Malcolm III. called Canmoir, and of Margaret grand-daughter to Edmund king of England, sister to Edgar Atheling: He married Sybilla, daughter to the Conqueror, succeeding his brother Edgar in the crown of Scotland, anno 1107, he reigned near 17 years, and died anno 1124.

Type. Legend. No. 1 & 2. Plate I. A rude profile head, regarding the left, appears on No. 1, 2, having a scepter before it; there is a sort of circle formed of dots or pearls round it, and inscribed ALEXANDER REX. On the reverse of No. 1. there is a short voided cross, extending only to the legendary circle, whereas that on No. 2. runs through it to the edge of the coin; the legends on the reverses of neither can be made out.

These two pieces are copied from Anderson, Tab. CLVII. No. 2, 3. only in the position of the reverses the bars of the crosses stand upright, which we think is their true position, whereas there they are put so as to form a St. Andrew's cross, or in saltier. It is probable one of these pieces is that mentioned by Nicholson *(a)*, to have been in Mr. Sutherland's collection, which, although he thought it appertained to Alexander the First, yet was not sure whether it might not be attributed to one of the other princes of that name.

DAVID I. 1124. David the First, called also the Saint, succeeded his brother Alexander; he married Matilda, daughter of Waltheof Earl of Northumberland; and his sister of the same name (Matilda) was wife to Henry the First, and mother of the empress Matilda, or Maud.

Type. Legend. No. 3. Pl. I. The king is here represented with a profile head turned to the left, with a scepter, as the last; the head is bare, without any ornament, and the work rude and barbarous; it is inscribed DAUID . R . . . m. The reverse has a short cross voided, formed only of single lines, instead of double ones, as the others; the mullets in the quarters have only five points instead of six, and much larger than usual, the legend round it is, HVE WAT n . . R.

The piece here given is no where else to be found but in the Pembroke collection, among which it is engraved in Part 4. Tab. 24 of that cabinet, and copied from thence by Anderson, Tab. CLVII. We should suspect the letters round the head are not so plain on the coin as to read the word DAUID seen in the print, and that it is very likely to be a blundered coin of William's, of his rudest sort, as No. 11, 12, 13, 14, Plate 1. from which it is otherwise but little different, viz. in having his head the contrary way; however, William is thus represented on some other coins, as No. 15 and 16.

MALCOLM. IV. 1153. This prince was son of Henry prince of Scotland, and grandson of David, whom he succeeded, was called the Maiden, because he would never marry; he died in the 12th year of his reign.

No coin found of him. Although he reigned so many years, yet no coin of his was ever discovered; this would be difficult to account for, if we were not almost assured, that those coins already given to his grandfather and great uncle, did not with much greater probability belong to his brother William and his nephew Alexander the Second.

WILLIAM I 1165. William the First, called the Lyon, succeeded his brother Malcolm IV. during his long reign of near 49 years, he had many disputes with our king Henry II. Richard I. and John; he was taken prisoner by the first, and forced to pay 50,000 marks of silver, or 750,000l. for his ransom, one half down, and to pawn four castles, for payment of the remainder, which Richard afterwards gave him up for 10,000 marks. The silver coin of Scotland cannot with any sort of certainty be carried higher than this king's reign, as we have already observed.

(a) Scotch Historical Library, p. 326.

The

HEAD SIDE. Type. No. 4. to No. 16. Pl. I.

The head of this king, on his coin, is always in profile, and generally regards the right, as on No. 4, 5, 6, 7, 8, 9, 10, 11, 12, 13 and 14; but on No. 15 and 16, it looks the contrary way, or to the left; the heads themselves are also very different, though all very rude, especially No. 11, 12, 13 and 14. Some appear to be ornamented only with a sort of circle of pearls, others again have besides, over that, four other pearls, in form of a cross: All of them have an erect scepter before them, surmounted with four dots or pearls in cross, that goes through the legendary circle to the edge of the piece, except the two last, No. 15 and 16, which are contained within the circle.

Inscription.

The inscriptions round the head on No. 4, 5, 6, 7, 8, 9, 10. 15 and 16. is WILELMVS RX, or REX; but on No. 11, 12, 13 and 14, it is LE REI WILA, or WILAM; this last has induced several authors to suppose them not Scotch, but Norman coins, and minted by the Conqueror in Normandy. Our famous antiquary and historian, Stowe *(a)*, mentions these last pieces, and ascribes them to William the Conqueror.

REVERSE. Type.

On the reverse we discover a short voided cross confined within the legendary circle, with a mullet of six points in each quarter, which are put very close, as the space allowed for the cross is too small, and that for the legend very large.

Legend.

The inscriptions on the reverse, like those on the English, have the name of the moneyer, and that of the town where it was coined; three different ones appear on the coins of this king, viz. Edinburgh, Roxborough, and Perth. On No. 4. we see HUE ON EDNEBUR; on No. 5. HUE ON EDENBUR; on No. 6. WTAR (probably for Walter) ON PERT; on No. 7. WTAR ON PRET (here the R is transposed) on No. 8. HUE ON RO; on No. 9. is DERISADAM ON ROCI; on No. 10. RAUL ON ROCE; on No. 11. RAUL ON ROCEBUR *(b)*; on No. 12. HVE . . . . . . RO; No. 14. ADAMDERIS ON . . . . No. 15. DERISADAM ON RO. on No. 13. which is one of LE REI WILA, we read HUE WALTER, and this is the usual one found on this sort, with a small difference sometimes in a letter or two, and is that found on No. 3. which is given to David the First, which strengthens the presumption, that it is rather an imperfect blundered coin of this king. We should surmise that these two words stand for both names of the monier, or *Hugh Walter*, and perhaps the same circumstance may attend the monier's name on No. 9. 14 and 15.

Although it is very certain that the Scots in general copied after the English, in their coinages, yet this was not the case in their first setting out, the work of those being much ruder than what was then done in England, where although no fixed manner had been followed in regard to the heads of their kings, yet not any of them like what we find on these; the same may be said of their reverses, none of which are found any thing like these, except one of Stephen, who died a year before William came to the crown; but the money of our Henry III. is quite in the rude taste of these, and we should almost think was borrowed from the Scots, as they had coined in this manner 40 years before.

WEIGHT.

These pennies usually weigh about 22½ grains troy, some only 21½ or 22, and No. 6 weighs 23 grains.

(a) Survey of London, B. I. p. 82. Edit. 1720.

(b) By comparing No. 10 and 11 together, the former of which has *Willelmus Rex*, and the latter *Le Rei Wila*, and both of them coined by *Raul*, or *Ralph*, of Roxborough, the ingenious Mr. Leake's doubts are cleared up*; 1st, That those with *Le Rei Wila*, are not Norman or English, but Scotch coins; and, 2d, That William of Scotland did coin money: However, the reason of such an inscription as that above, on a Scotch coin, is as inexplicable as before. No. 10 and 11 are in the collection of Thomas Hollis, Esq; and all the rest in that of Dr. Hunter.

* Hist. Account of Eng. Money, p. 42. Nicholson, p. 308.

Eleven

Fineness. Eleven ounces two pennyweights of fine ſilver, and eighteen pennyweights of alloy, as in England *(c)*, was the fineneſs of the coins of Scotland at this time, and remained ſo till the reign of James the Fifth.

Value. The money of Scotland being at this time of the ſame value as in England, therefore the pound weight Tower of 12 ounces, of the ſtandard juſt mentioned, *(d)* was of the ſame value as the pound tale, or twenty ſhillings in money. The pound weight here is made up of 240 pennies of the weight of 22½ troy grains each; that is, of 5400 troy grains, or 11 oz. 5 dwts. troy, or lighter by one-ſixteenth than the pound weight troy *(e)*.

Alex. II. 1214. Alexander II. ſucceeded his father in 1214; his firſt wife was Joan, daughter of John king of England; his ſecond wife was Mary, daughter to the Earl of Coucy, who was mother to his ſucceſſor; he reigned with reputation near 35 years.

Type. Head Side. No. 17, 18, 19. Plate 1. He is repreſented on his money with a profile head looking to the right, in general; on ſome it is adorned, as his father's, with a circle of pearls, which we ſhould ſuppoſe were his firſt coins, and agree with thoſe given by Anderſon to Alexander the Firſt, only the head is turned the contrary way, but on others, and thoſe the greateſt number, his head is crowned with an open crown fleury, which was followed by all his ſucceſſors, and ſo is that given to Alexander the Firſt, (in Pembroke, p. 4. Tab. 24. No. 1.) and afterwards copied by Anderſon, Tab. 157. No. 1. which however is undoubtedly one of this king's.

Reverse. The only material difference in the reverſe of the coins of this king from thoſe of his father, is in the croſs being extended quite through the circle of letters to the edge of the piece, inſtead of being confined within the legendary circle, as the others all are; however, we are inclinable to believe that he might and did coin ſome in the beginning of his reign, with the ſhort croſs like his father's, and that No. 1. is probably one of that ſort, and not of Alexander I. in which point, and the contra poſition and ornament of the head, conſiſted the difference of that and the ſubſequent coinages.

Legend. The inſcription round the head is uniformly ALEXANDER REX, upon all of them; and on the reverſe, the names of the moniers and towns, of which we have met with the following, viz. No. 17. ROBER. ON RO; No. 18. WAL. ON BER; and on No. 19. JOHAN ON BER; others we have ſeen with ADAM ON RO, RENAUD DE PER, WALTER ON PRET, ALEXANDER ON EDEN, ION ON BERWI, WALTER ON BERWI, WILLEM ON BERWI, and no doubt there are many others.

Weight. Fineness. Value. His money, in theſe articles, like his father's, and as they ſtood in England, viz. about 22½ grains troy, of 11 oz. 2 dwts. fine ſilver, and the pound in tale equal the pound weight.

Alex. III. 1249. This king ſucceeded his father in the year 1249; he married Margaret daughter to Henry III. king of England, to whom he gave aſſiſtance on many occa-

(c) Ruddimanni Præfat. ad Anderſon. § 59. p. 15. et Tab. 2. p. 30. *(d)* Ib. Tab. 2. p. 30.

(e) The pound weight Tower being that for many centuries uſed in the mint of England, and the value of the Scots coin a long time of the ſame value as that, was the reaſon, no doubt, of Mr. Ruddiman's making it the ground-work of his tables of the value of the Scots coins at different periods; the ounce of this pound, however, ſeems to have been very nearly the ſame with that of the pound then uſed in Scotland, which conſiſted of 15 ounces *.

* Ruddimanni Præfat. et Tab. ut ſupra.—Stat. Rob. III. cap. 22. Regiam Majeſtatem, fol. Edin. 1613. p. 68.

ſions;

Silver Coins from Alexander I.st to Robert II. IV.

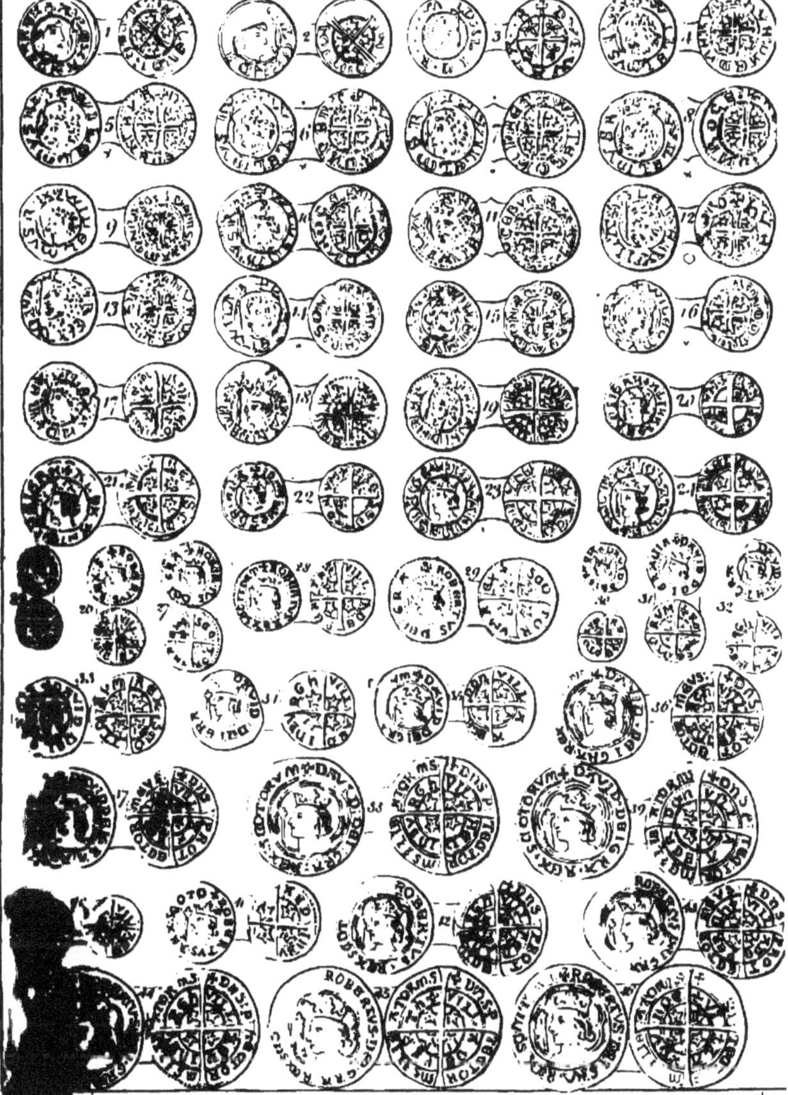

ſions; he was killed by a fall with his horſe from a precipice, in his 37th year, anno 1285, leaving only a grand-daughter, who died unmarried. ALEX. III.

The coins uſually given to this prince have his head in profile, to the right, as thoſe of his father and grandfather, in general; and, like them alſo, there is a ſcepter before it; but it muſt be obſerved, that it is contained within the letter circle, and does not run through it as formerly; the head is always crowned fleury, the croſs on the reverſe is quite different from the ancient ones, being cloſe and broad, and continued quite to the edge, which was followed with little alteration till the time of James V. and, with reſpect to the head, till Robert the Second. Type. No. 20, 21. Pl. I.

Round the head, inſtead of Alexander Rex, as before, it is ALEXANDER DEI GRA; (one ſort has ALEXSANDER) and on the reverſe, inſtead of the names of the mint-maſter and town, it is REX SCOTORVM. Legend.

We find a great improvement in regard to the workmanſhip in the money here attributed to this king; the head, the croſs, the letters are all better done, and the diſpoſition of the whole more regular and uniform than before; and we ſhall venture a conjecture, that theſe improvements came from England, and followed that great one made there in the monies of Edward I. anno 1270.

If this be the caſe, it will be aſked, What coins have we of him before this period? The queſtion is very proper, and we think can be no otherwiſe got clear of, than by ſuppoſing that many of thoſe given by us to his father, were ſtruck by this king before this æra; and, at this time, it is not poſſible to diſtinguiſh one from the other.

Before this king's time we only find pennies; but under him we firſt meet likewiſe with the half penny (No. 20.) the coinage of which had been introduced in England about the middle of this king's reign. SORTS.

Theſe articles ſtand as before, the penny weighing 22½ gr. troy; the ſtandard 11 oz. 2 dwt. fine; and a pound in weight paſſing for no more than one pound in tale. WEIGHT. FINENESS. VALUE.

Alexander III. dying without iſſue, John Baliol, deſcended from Margaret, eldeſt daughter of David Earl of Huntingdon, youngeſt brother to William king of Scotland, after an interregnum of about ſeven years, was choſen king; he reſigned the kingdom to Edward I. in his 4th year, when a ſecond interregnum followed of nine years, and more. JOHN BALIOL. 1292.

Little difference is to be found between the types of the coins of this king and the laſt, they having the profile head crown'd, with the ſcepter on one ſide, and the croſs between four mullets on the other. Type. No. 22, 23, 24. Pl. I.

The inſcription round the head of the money of this king, is JOHANNES DEI GRA; and on the reverſe of No. 22, 23, is REX SCOTORVM; but on No. 24, with the name of the town only, viz. CIVITAS SANDRE, or St. Andrew's, in the new Engliſh mode introduced there about the year 1270. Legend.

Pennies, No. 23 and 24. and half pennies, No. 21. were the only ſorts hitherto met with of this king. SORTS.

Theſe articles as before, viz. Weight 22½ gr. troy, 11 oz. 2 dwt. fine, and the pound tale equal the pound weight. WEIGHT. FINENESS. VALUE.

This prince was deſcended from the ſecond daughter of David Earl of Huntingdon above-mentioned, and, after many ſtruggles with our Edward I. obtained the crown, and held it glorioufly for Scotland during 24 years. ROBERT BRUCE. 1306.

Type. No. 25, 26, 27, 28, 29. Pl. 1. No alteration in the type from the two former kings, viz. the crown'd head in profile on one side, and the cross and mullets on the reverse.

Legend. On No. 25. 27. 29. we read round the head ROBERTVS DEI GRA. and on the reverse SCOTORVM REX; but on No. 26. is ROBERTVS REX S. and on the reverse VILLA EDINBVG. No. 28. has round the head ROBERTVS REX SCOTORVM, and reverse VILLA DE PERTH.

Sorts. We have, as before, his penny, No. 28, 29. his halfpenny, No. 26, 27. and now, for the first time, a farthing, No. 25.

Weight. The penny weighs now but 17 gr. troy, the halfpenny 8½, and the farthing 4¼; but if there were 21 pennies in the ounce, it should weigh 21⅓ troy gr.

Fineness. Eleven ounces two pennyweights fine silver, and 18 pennyweights alloy.

Value. From the Stat. Rob. III. cap. 22. *(f)* as being there said that the ounce consisted of 21 den. and at this value it likewise stands in the table *(g)*, it is inferred, the pound tale, under this king, was 21s. The penny, on this supposition, should weigh nearly 21 troy grains; but we have just now observed, it seldom weighs more than 17, never 18 grains; this brings the pound tale to 24s.

DAVID BRUCE. 1329. Succeeded his father when an infant, and was forced to fly into France, being outed of his kingdom by Edward Baliol, son of the late king John Baliol, assisted by Edward III. who held it about four years; returning from France he was afterwards taken prisoner and carried into England, where he remained above eleven years, and was released on agreeing to pay 100,000 marks of silver for his ransom. He died in the 41st year of a very troublesome reign.

Type. No. 30 to 39. Pl. 1. The types of the penny, halfpenny, and farthing, are the same as before; those of the groats and half groats which were now first struck, have the head circumscribed within a sort of rose, or compartment; and the reverse, instead of one has two literary circles, following in both these articles the manner just before introduced in England in these species. From the mullet or spur in the quarters of the cross of this and the two following kings, they were afterwards called *Spurred Groats*.

Legend. The inscriptions on No. 30, 31. 33, are DAVID DEI GRACIA, and on the reverse REX SCOTORVM. No. 32. 34. 35, have DAVID DEI GRA. R. SCOTORVM (and sometimes contracted to SCO, SCOT, and SCOTOR; on the reverse of the 1st and 2d is VILLA EDINBVRGH; on the 3d, VILLA ABERDON. The inscriptions round the heads of No. 36, 37. 38 and 39, are like the last, only have REX instead of R; on the outer circle of the two first is DNS PROTECTOR MEVS; and on the 3d, DNS PTECT MS Z LIBATOR MS (Dominus Protector Meus et Liberator Meus) No. 39 is the same, except instead of the first MS is ME; the inner circle contains the name of the city, as No. 36 and 38. VILLA EDINBVRGH; and No. 35 and 39. VILLA ABERDON.

Weight. The groats of this king are of 72 troy grains, or approach nearly to it, being the weight of those in England at this time; the half groat 36 troy grains, the penny 18 troy grains, the halfpenny 9 troy grains, and the farthing about 4½ troy gr.

Value. In his 37th year, anno 1366, his money is ordered to be coined of the same value as in England *(h)*, which was 25 shillings the pound tale; and the weight of those pieces of his now generally found, answer to this order; but the next year 1367, it appears this standard was altered, and the pound tale advanced to 29s. 4d. *(i)*; this reduces the weight of the groat to 61 troy grains, but we

(f) Regiam Majestatem, p. 68. b. and our Appendix, No. 6. *(g)* Ruddiman, Praefat. p. 30.
(h) Stat. David II. cap. 38. Reg. Majestatem, p. 56. b. Append. No. 3.
(i) Stat. cap. 35. 46. Ibid. p. 55. Append. No. 1. 4.

have

have never met with any near so light, which would make us suspect that they were not so fine as before; but it is expresly said they were to be made as fine as those of England *(k)*, therefore a doubt arises here whether this coinage ever took place. DAVID BRUCE.

The last king dying without issue, Robert Steward, son of Walter Steward and Marjerie Bruce, sister to Robert the First, succeeded, and reigned about 19 years. ROBERT II. 1371.

The types of this king's coins, are the same as the last, and those of the half-penny and penny not to be distinguish'd from those of Robert Bruce. Type. No. 40 to 46. Pl. 1.

All the money of this king that we have seen contain his name and titles on the head side; thus, on No. 40. ROBERTVS REX; No. 41. ROBERTVS REX SCOTO; No. 42. ROBERTVS REX SCOTORVM; and the rest, ROBERTVS DEI GRA. REX SCOTORVM. On the reverse is the name of the town, as No. 40, 41, 42 and 44 have VILLA EDINBVRGH; No. 43 and 45, VILLA DE PERTH; and No. 46. for the first time, VILLA DVNDE; on the outer circle are DNS PROTECTOR MEVS, as on the half groats of the last reign; and, on the groats, DNS PTECTOR MS z LIBATOR MS. as before. Legend.

This king's groats some of them weigh 64½ troy gr. and others no more than 56 troy gr. the half groat and penny in proportion. WEIGHT.

We do not find the value of the money pound is to be gathered from any of the old statutes, but is usually supposed to be the same as that of his father, viz. 29s. 4d. *(m)*; but the heaviest groats of this king will support an opinion of its being at first not so much as this; however that be, we think it continued but a short time at either of those values, as in his second year, 1371, the Scotch money is in England all called in *(n)*, and two years afterwards their currency is reduced to three-fourths of that of England *(o)*, which still continued at 25 shillings) this brings the pound to 33s. 4d. and the weight of the groat to about 54 troy gr. however, few are found so light as that. VALUE.

This prince succeeded his father, and was called *Farne Zeir*; that is, John of another year, as having been baptized John, and not changed his name to Robert till his coronation. ROBERT III. 1390.

We now meet with a considerable change in the type of the Scotch coins, that is, from the profile face to the full one; and on the reverse, the single mullet in each quarter is altered for three pellets, as in the English, to which these converge more than those of any other prince. Type.

Round the head ROBERTVS REX Sc. & SCOTOR; others, ROBERTVS DEI GRA. or GRACIA REX SC. SCOTOR. SCOTORV. SCOTTORV. SCOTORVM, and probably with other little differences. The reverses have the names of the towns; thus on No. 3, 4, 5, 6, 7, are VILLA EDINBVRGH; on No. 2. VILLA DE PERTH; No. 8. VILLA ABERDENE; and on No. 9. we first meet with VILLA DVNBERTAN. We encounter some little differences in the legend on the outer circle; thus, No. 8. has DNS PTECTOR MS z LIBERATOR; but on Legend.

(k) Stat. cap. 46. Ibid. p. 55. b.—Append. No. 4.

No person, native or foreigner, to carry more money out of the kingdom than will serve his necessary expences, without paying for each pound half a mark, or six shillings and eight pence to the king. At the same time the gold and silver coins of England are permitted to a currency at their full value *.

(m) Ruddiman. Prefat. Tab. 2. p. 30. *(n)* 45 E. III.—Cott. Abr. p. 114. *(o)* 47 E. III. cap. 2.

* Stat. cap. 37. c. 49. Ibid. Append. No. 2, 5.

No. 9.

ROBERT III. No. 9. it is LIBERAT. The halfpenny, No. 1. has REX SCOTORVM in the ancient manner on its reverſe, and no town.

WEIGHT. His groats at heavieſt about 50 troy gr. and many of them not more than 32 or 33; the half groats and pence in proportion; but there are ſmall pennies which appear like halfpence, weigh 9 troy gr. and 10 troy gr. a-piece, anſwering nearly the light groats, being too heavy for any ſort of halfpence, if as fine as the larger pieces.

VALUE. In the Stat. Rob. III. cap. 22. *(p)* the pound tale is ſaid to conſiſt of 32 ſhillings; at this value the groat ſhould weigh 56 troy grains, but none are found of that weight; in the table *(q)* it ſtands at 29s. 4d. as his father's. In his ſecond year, or 1391, the Scotch groat is cryed down in England to two-pence ſterling *(r)*; this brings the pound tale to 50s. and the weight of the groat to 36 troy gr. in his fourth year, 1393, they were forbid any longer to be current in England: *(s)* It appears from hence, nothing certain can be gathered of the true value of the pound tale.

JAMES I. 1405. This prince ſucceeded his father, being then a priſoner in England, where he continued for 18 years, or till 1424, in which year he was ſet at liberty, having married Joan, daughter to Henry Earl of Somerſet, for whoſe portion 10,000l. was deducted out of the 40,000l. agreed to be paid by him for his entertainment in England. He was killed by a conſpiracy at Perth, in his 11th year, after he returned from his captivity.

Type. No. 10, 11, 12, 13, 14 and 15. The firſt coins here given to this king, we conjecture were coined in his minority, whilſt he was a priſoner in England, and affairs were in great confuſion; they exhibit him with a full face with a ſcepter on the right ſide uſually, but No. 15 has it on the left; the ſcepter had been firſt omitted during the laſt reign, nor does it appear after this. On ſome the breaſt is naked, on others there is a fleur de lis, a croſs, &c. and frequently both, only two of the interſtices between the croſs on the reverſe have three pellets in them, the other two having a fleur de lis in each; from thence, in the following reigns, called *Fleur de lis Groats*.

Legend. On the head ſide are IACOBVS DEI GRACIA REX SCO. or SCOT, SCOTOR, &c. The towns we meet with on the reverſes of this king are VILLA EDINBVRGH, on No. 10 and 15. VILLA ABERDEN on No. 11. VILLA DE PERTH on No. 12. VILLA STREVELI on No. 13. VILLA LINLITHC. on No. 14. Theſe two laſt of Sterling and Linlithgow now firſt occur in the Scotch ſeries.

WEIGHT. Theſe ſort of groats are uſually very light, ſeldom weighing more than 37½ troy grains, and oftner much leſs.

FINENESS. Eleven ounces two dwts. of fine ſilver, and 18 dwts. of alloy, as before.

VALUE. The value of the pound tale ariſing from the uſual weight of the groat above, is brought to about 48 ſhillings; but in the table of the different values of the money pound, we find under this king it was 37s. 6d. *(t)* or 25 per cent. more than in England, but are not informed how it is made out, nor can we diſcover it.

(p) Regiam Majeſtatem, p. 68.—b. *(q)* Ruddiman. Prefat. p. 30. *(r)* 14 Ric. II. cap. 12.
(s) 17 Ric. II. cap. 1. *(t)* Ruddiman. ut ſupra.

Forty pence to be paid cuſtom to the king for every pound in money that is exported *, under pain of forfeiting what is found upon him, and 10l. to the king for the unlaw. Alſo ſtrangers bringing and ſelling their merchandize in the realm, their hoſt to witneſs that the money had been laid out in other purchaſes, or elſe to pay cuſtom for it to the king. Ja. I. Parl. 13. cap. 143. Append. No. 9. Again, "None have out of Scotland, gold, ſilver, nor jewels, cunzeit, nor uncunzeit, under pain of eſcheit." Jam. I. P. 13. c. 149. Append. No. 10. See alſo Jam. II. P. 1. c. 8. P. 3. c. 61. Jam. IV. P. 11. c. 68. Jam. V. P. 7. c. 108. Mary, P. 9. c. 70. Jam. VI. P. 15. c. 249.

Three ounces of bullion ſhall be imported by every merchant for each ſack of wool he exports, alſo for each laſt of hides as much as three ſacks of wool, and for five Hamburgh barrels as much as one ſack of wool; alſo for every ſerplaith (i. e. 80 ſtone, each 16lb.) in freight of other goods. P. 13. c. 143. See alſo Ja. III. P. 7. c. 50. P. 8. c. 61. Ja. IV. P. 2. c. 14. Ja. VI. P. 7. c. 107.

* Stat. Jam. I. Parl. 3. cap. 49. App. No. 8. Lawes and Actes of Parliament, by Skene, fol. Edin. 1597.

Silver Coins from Robert III to James V. Plate II.

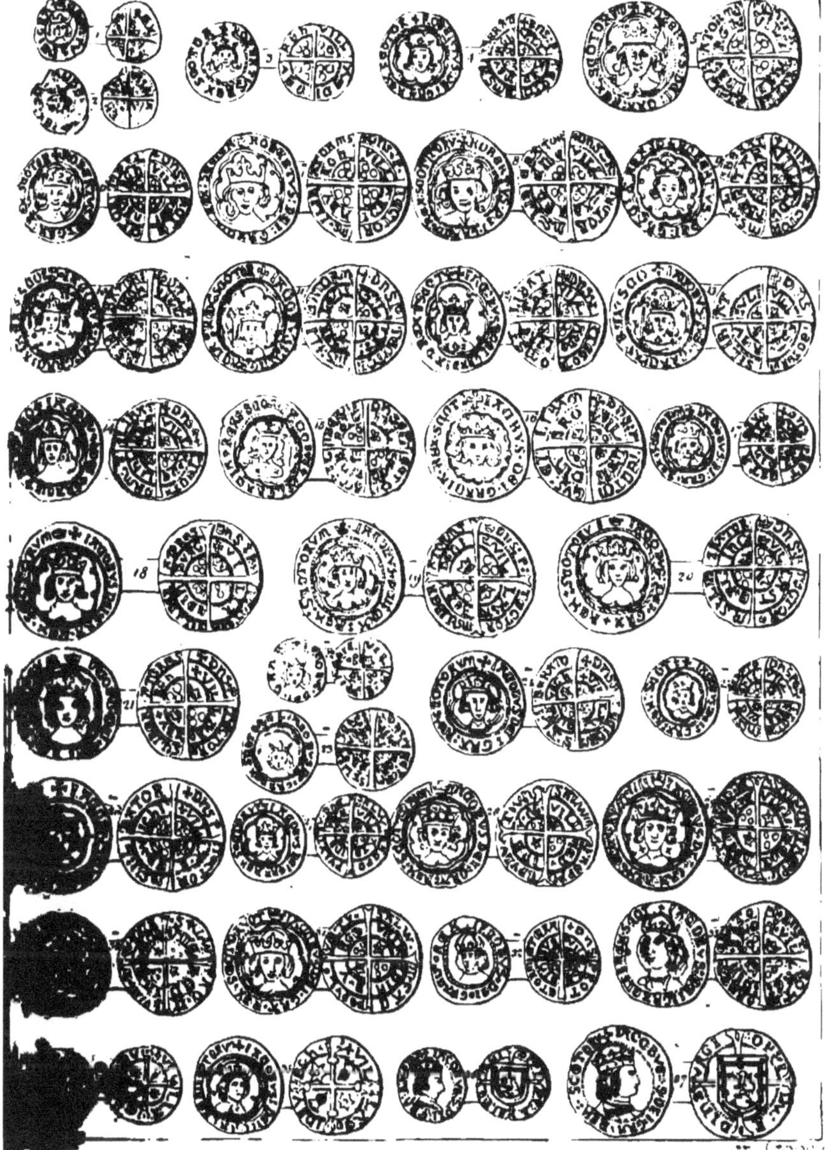

Upon the return of this king to Scotland, it was ordered by act of parliament, the coin of the kingdom should be mended, and made of the same weight and fineness as that of England, where, at this time, the groat weighed 60 grains troy; and as those with the crowns on the reverse, viz. No. 16 to 21. approach nearer to this weight than any other, we think it highly probable that they were struck pursuant to the above act, and that they were coined also by James II. and possibly in the beginning of the reign of James III. JAMES I. 1424.

The only material difference in the type between these and the last, is in the want of the scepter on the head side; and on the reverse, having in two of the interstices of the cross two crowns (from thence afterwards called *Crown Groats)* instead of two fleurs de lis; only on No. 16. there is but one crown and one fleur de lis, and was probably the first attempt towards the change which followed. Type. No. 16. to No. 21.

IACOBUS DEI GRA. REX SCOTORVM usually is found on all the groats, but the half groat, No. 17. has DI instead of DEI. On the reverses we find VILLA EDINBVRGH, on No. 18; and on No. 17. it is EDINBVG; on No. 19. VILLA ABERDEN; on No. 20. VILLA STERLINO; and on No. 21. for the first time since Alexander II. VILLA ROXBVRGH.—The inscription on the outer circle as usual, DNS PROTECTR MEVS & DNS PTECTOR MS Z LIBERATOR MS. attended with the usual little differences. Legend.

These groats weigh at most about 56 troy grains, but often not that, and though ordered to be struck of the same weight as in England; however they generally want 4 grains of the weight of the English groat: They were continued to be coined by James II. and the only sort he struck. WEIGHT.

Eleven ounces two pennyweights of fine silver, and 18 pennyweights of alloy, as before. FINENESS.

The value of the pound tale, as brought out by these groats, is about 32 shillings, whereas in England, with which the abovementioned act required it should conform, it was only 30 shillings *(a)*; the difference between them being the same as between the pound Tower and the pound troy. VALUE.

James II. succeeded his father very young; married Mary, daughter of Arnold duke of Gelders, and in the 24th year of his reign was killed by the bursting of a piece of cannon at the siege of Roxborough. JAMES II. 1437.

We find no other groats but those last described, or those which have a crown in two of the quarters on the reverse, and three pellets in the other two, that can be ascribed to this king, therefore must refer back for what regards their type and legend, to what is there said, but we have no criterion by which we can distinguish those of this king from his father. No. 16. to No. 21.

There is an half groat, No. 17. and groats, No. 18. to 21. besides which the Act mentions *(b)* pence, halfpence and farthings, but we have seen neither. SORTS.

We have, under the last reign, observed, these groats seldom weigh 56 troy grains, yet are said to be equal to those of England, which weigh 60 troy grains, or ⅛ of an ounce; however, there are many of the last that weigh no more than 56 grains, though seemingly well preserved, therefore it cannot be determined what the weight of the former were at first from what they weigh at present. WEIGHT.

Eleven ounces two pennyweights of fine silver, and 18 pennyweights of alloy. FINENESS.

The pound tale, upon the coining the above groats, in 1451, is valued at 64 shillings, or 3l. 4s. (that is, 96 groats, each eight-pence) which is more than double the nominal value of the pound sterling, which was only 30 shillings. In his 13th parliament, or about four years after, in 1455, by raising the groat VALUE.

(a) Silver coin and coinage of England; Tab. p. 51. *(b)* Parl. 8. cap. 33.

JAMES II. from eight-pence to twelve-pence *(c)*, the nominal pound is increaſed 50 per cent. or from 3l. 4s. to 4l. 16s.

JAMES III. 1460. This prince ſucceeded to the crown on the death of his father; he reigned near 29 years, and was murdered in his flight after the loſs of the battle of Bannock-burn. He was in poſſeſſion of Berwick, from 1460 to 1482.

Type. No. 22. to No. 28. The coins firſt ſtruck by this prince, anno 1475, like the former James's, have on one ſide the head full faced, within a roſe or compartment of five leaves, and on the reverſe is a croſs, as uſual, running to the edge of the piece, in the ſpaces of which, incloſed within the inner circle, two of them are filled with three pellets, as in all the James's, and in the other, inſtead of fleurs de lis and crowns, as on the former, there are mullets of five or ſix points.

Legend. Round the head, as uſual, we find his name and titles, IACOBVS DEI GRA. REX SCOTORVM, with the difference ſometimes of a few letters, more or leſs; the outer circle of the reverſe has the common legend of DNS PTECTOR MS. z LIBATOR, or LIBERAT. with little differences as before. On others, for the firſt time, are found SALVVM FAC PPVLVM TVVM DNE. The inner circle is filled with the name of the town or city, VILLA EDENBEOVRGE, No. 29. EDINBVRG, No. 28. and now, for the firſt time ſince Alexander II. VILLA BERVICHI, No. 25, 26. We have never ſeen No. 25. with four mullets.

SORTS. There is a penny, No. 22. half groat, No. 23. 25. 27. and the groat, No. 24. 26. 28. We cannot tell what groat is meant by the Borage groat under this reign, nor how to diſtinguiſh the new ſixpenny groat of the fleur de lis from the old one.

WEIGHT. Theſe groats generally weigh about 36 troy grains, ſeldom more, but very often leſs, the other pieces in proportion.

FINENESS. Eleven ounces two pennyweights of fine ſilver, and 18 pennyweights of alloy.

Type. No. 32, 33. On the king's ſecond coinage, in 1483, he appears with a three quarters face to the left, with buſhy hair, and is now firſt crowned with an imperial arched crown inſtead of an open one as formerly, the reverſe continues nearly as on

(c) Parl. 13. Cap. 59. Skene's Actes, p. 39. Append. No. 13.

JAMES II. The Engliſh groat of 8 to the oz. to have courſe for eight-pence, the half groat in proportion, but no Engliſh penny but at the will of the receiver.——After the new groat is ſtruck, the new groat then current for ſix-pence, to paſs for four-pence, and the half groat for two-pence.——No more than twelve pence in the pound to be taken of the pennies ſtruck by the king's coiners, Robert Gray, John of Dalrympill, Alexander Todd, and John Spethey; all other pennies, ſtruck by Henry Goldſmith, or other falſe coiners, either in Inverneſs, Dyſart, or Forfare, or other place, ſhall not be current from this time.—The maſter of the mint to be anſwerable for all the gold and ſilver ſtruck under him, which the warden has taken an aſſay of, and put it into his box, and to have power to chuſe all ſervants under him, and puniſh them if they treſpaſs. None of the coiners to be goldſmiths, if others can be found.—No perſon to take money if burled or clipped, but at his own will.—Proviſion to be made for the gravers of the irons, and truſty perſons to receive all the irons of the king's, ſtricken both in gold and ſilver, together with the graving letters from the graver, and deſtroy them before the king and council. Parl. 8. cap. 33. App. No. 12.—The ſix-penny groat to have courſe as before.—That there be coined one ſhilling in a pound of ſmall pennies.—None to coin, under pain of death, any money then current, nor ſix-penny groats. Parl. 13. cap. 59. Append. No. 14.

It is referred to the actes made by the 24 perſons choſen for that purpoſe, what concerns the bringing in of bullion by the merchants, and ſtrict ſearch to be made at all ports, and alſo on the borders, that no perſon carry money out of the kingdom.—All counterfeiters of gold, ſilver, groats and pennies, be taken and puniſhed for the ſame. Parl. 6. cap. 29. Append. No. 11.—That no perſon export gold, ſilver, or bullion, under pain of eſcheating thereof, one half to the king, the other to the informer. Parl. 8. cap. 34. App. No. 13. Parl. 13. cap. 59. Append. No. 14.

A deacon to be ordained in each town where there are goldſmiths, to examine the fineneſs of the gold work, and to ſet his mark to it, and to have a penny for each ounce ſo marked; and if found not good, both the deacon and goldſmith's goods to be forfeited to the king. Parl. 14. c. 66. Append. No. 15.

No

on those of James I. II. and III. which have in two of the spaces of the cross, JAMES III.
a crown, and in the other two are four pellets instead of three, as before, which is the only difference between these reverses and those on No. 16. to No. 21. and we suppose this coinage was continued from the return of James I. 1424, till 15th James III. 1475, when those with the mullets took place of them.

These pieces are appropriated to this king on account of their weight, as no other of all the James's answer to the 10th of an ounce, as we are expressly told those coined this year did; otherwise, to judge from their type, we should rather have supposed them to have belonged to James IV. and coined after his 14th year, as it was about that time the change in the English coinage, in regard to the profile head, took place, and that this improvement had been soon after adopted in Scotland: However, the weight determines it to have been prior by 20 years to that alteration. There is another novelty, in respect to the type, viz. the arched crown, which we think might have been as old on the English, at least within two years, especially if we confine this to have taken place no sooner than Henry VII. in 1485.

Round the head of the king we read JACOBVS DEI GRACIA REX COT, Legend.
(without an S.) COTRV, COTTO, and, no doubt, other readings; one half groat has only REX; others, REX COT, as the groats.

These groats usually weigh about 47 grains troy; but had the use of the Tower WEIGHT.
pound still continued, at 10 to the ounce they would have weighed but 45 troy grains. The ounce weight deduc'd from the groat above answers that afterwards introduced into Scotland, very probably from France, as being equal to it, or 63 parts in 64 of the pound troy; that is, the ounce has 472½ grains troy, and the pound 11 ounces 17 pennyweights 12 grains troy.

Eleven ounces two pennyweights of fine silver, and 18 pennyweights of FINENESS.
alloy.

We should surmise that till his third parliament, the money continued as at VALUE.
his father's death, viz. the pound tale at 4l. 16s. but in that year *(d)* it was raised ⅙ or 16⅔ per cent. or the groat from twelve pence to fourteen pence, and the pound weight to 5l. 12s. in tale. On coining those with the mullets (1475) at 12 to the ounce, to pass for twelve pence, or a shilling, *(e)* the pound tale was then increased to 7l. 4s. And again, when he coined the new sort, of 10 to the ounce, (Anno 1483) current for fourteen pence, *(f)* the money *foot* was then but 7l. tale for one pound weight, and we should suppose it stood thus at his death.

No person to have money out of the realme under pain of forfeiting 10l. unremittable to the king, and of as much money as he takes or sends out of the kingdom, saving moderate expences, to the value of an English noble, to be allowed each person. Parl. 1. c. 8. App. No. 16.

The Edward groat to pass for ten-pence, and no more; and the lords who were to be appointed to take care of the affairs of the mint, &c. to take orders in regard to the six-penny groat of the fleur de lis. Parl. 1. c. 9. App. No. 17.

The old English groat to pass for sixteen pence, the borage groat as the new, the new Edward groat for twelve-pence, the spurred groat as the old English, for sixteen pence, the English penny for three-pence, and the new English penny in proportion; the crown groat to pass for fourteen pence, the half groat for seven-pence, the fleur de lis groat for eight-pence; the white Scotch penny and halfpenny to have course as before; no more black pennies to be struck, and search to be made after any such. Parl: 3. c. 18. App. No. 18.

All contracts, &c. made between creditor and debtor, buyer and seller, borrower and lender, lord and tenant, to be satisfied, and payment to be made in the same substance and value as at the time of making the contract, before the raising of the coin by the parliament. Parl. 3. c. 19, 20. Append. No. 19, 20.

(d) Parl. 3. c. 18. *(e)* Parl. 8. c. 64. *(f)* Parl. 13. c. 93.

This

JAMES IV. 1488.

This prince succeeded his father, and married Margaret eldest daughter of Henry VII. He was killed at the battle of Flowden Field, in the 25th year of his reign.

The same as his Father's in Type LEGEND. WEIGHT, and VALUE.

No. 32. 33.

No. 29, 30, 31.

It does not appear from any intelligence we have been able to come at, or from any pieces now remaining, that this king coined money of a different type from those of his father's, that is groats of 12 to the ounce with the mullets, and others of 10 to the ounce with the bushy hair or wig, both described under that reign, nor do we know how to distinguish this last sort struck by him, from what were struck by his father, although it is expresly order'd a particular mark should be put upon those of this king, to know them from the former; *(g)* and this sort (viz. 10 to the ounce) is the only one mentioned under this reign, therefore should not have suspected any of those with the mullets had been his, but for having IIII. QRA, and QT. on them, which fixes them to him and is the first instance of this sort in the Scotch series. The weight, fineness and value, as in the last reign, without any alteration that we can find. *(h)*

Suc-

JAMES III.

The crown groat, to pass for fourteen pence, and the half groat for seven pence; the old English penny after the old English groat, or for four-pence, and the new English penny after the new groat, at three-pence; the white Scotch penny to go till the next parliament, and then to be remedied, if occasion require; no more than 12d. in a pound to be taken of the black money. Parl. 4. c. 21. 23. Append. No. 21, 22.

The old English groat to pass for thirteen pence, the new English groat for eleven pence, the English penny three-pence, spurred groat for thirteen pence, the crown groat for twelve pence, the fleur de lis groat for six-pence halfpenny, Scotch pennies as before, and of farthings two shillings in the pound. Obligations to be satisfied as when contracted. Parl. 4. c. 23. App. No. 22.

No denier of France, mailzies, cortes, mites, nor other counterfeit of black money, to be took in payment but the king's own black money, on pain of death. Parl. 5. c. 40. Append. No. 23.

Money to have course as at present, until the continuation of parliament.—The new alloyed groat, passing for seven-pence, to pass for six-pence, and the half groat in proportion. Parl. 6. c. 46. Append. No. 24.

The acts for the bringing in of bullion to be strictly observed; that is, for each *serplaith*, two ounces of burnt silver, and other goods in proportion; the last of herrings, four ounces; last of salt, two ounces, under forfeiture of 10l. Parl. 7. c. 50. App. No. 25.—Merchants to receive for each ounce of bullion brought in 12 shillings, and the coiners to make an ounce into 12 groats of the same type as the new groat, and of the same fineness as the English; also a penny and halfpenny, the penny to pass for three-pence. Parl. 8. c. 64. App. No. 26.

No money, on which any impression is to be seen, is to be melted, either at the mint or by goldsmiths, without the king's special licence. Parl. 8. c. 65. App. No. 27.

Merchants to bring into the kingdom for each serplaith of wool, skin, hides, cloth, &c. four ounces of burnt silver, and to have for each ounce 10 groats, of 10 to the ounce. Parl. 13. c. 93. Append. No. 29.

Deacons to be appointed in each town where there are goldsmiths; all the work to be marked with the marks of the deacon, of the workman, and the town, and to be 12 den. fine; none to keep open shop till admitted by the whole craft. Parl. 13. c. 96. App. No. 30.

Great quantities of placks being counterfeited so like the true ones, as not to be distinguished from them, therefore the currency of those lately coined by authority, are stopt, and both true and false are called in before May next, and to be paid for by Thomas Todd and Alexander Levingston, at two-pence each, or a fourteen penny groat for seven placks, to be new coined into fourteen penny groats, at 10 to the ounce, and fine as the English, and to be repaid by the last of September. Parl. 13. cap. 97. App. No. 31.

(g) Parl. 2. c. 17.

JAMES IV.

(h) The king to appoint one master, viz. Alexander Levingstoun, and a wise and loyal man to be warden, that is James Creichtoun, of Ruchwendaun, for the space of one year, to assay the gold and silver, according to the rule made before by the parliament; the said warden and master to have the same fees as usual in the time of the king's progenitors, and the king's profits on the coinage the same.—The merchants to bring into the realm for each *serplaith* of wool, last of salmon, each 400 cloths, 4 oz. of burnt silver; each last of hides, 6 oz. and each last of herrings, 2 oz. and so in proportion for all other goods that pay custom.—The said merchants shall be paid by the warden for each oz. of the said silver, 12 shillings. Parl. 1. c. 2. App: No. 32.

No goldsmith shall put more alloy into his work than it ought to have, and to put his mark upon all he makes, and the same work to be of the fineness of the new silver work of *Bruges*, and that there be

Coins of Mary and her two Husbands. Pl.

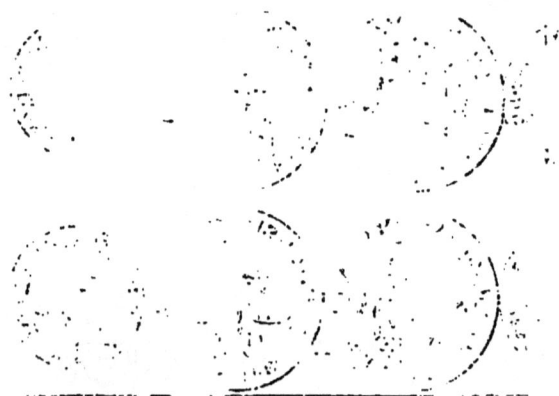

Succeeded his father anno 1514; his first wife was Magdalen, daughter of Francis I. king of France, and his second was Mary, daughter of Claude duke of Guise; he reigned near 29 years, and died in 1543. JAMES V. 1514.

The head of the king shews a three quarters face regarding the left, crowned with an open crown, and inclosed within the customary rose or five-leav'd compartment, inscribed IACOBVS DEI GRA. REX SCOTOR; on the reverse is a sort of a cross bottony, terminated with leaves, having in two of the spaces a mullet of six points, and in the other two a thistle; the outer circle is taken away, as has been the manner ever since, and is inscribed VILLA EDINBVRGH; the half groat the same, with a few contractions in the legend round the head. Type. Legend. No. 34. 35.

These pieces are lighter than any in the Scotch series, weighing about 30 grains troy, and 15 grains the half; being about [illegible] of those of this king, with the 5 after his name. WEIGHT.

We cannot get any information either of its fineness, or for what current, for without which, its value, and that of the pound tale, cannot be known. If it could be carried so high as James III. we should have suspected it to have been one of the seven penny groats, afterwards reduced to sixpence. FINENESS. VALUE.

The king's head is here in profile to the right, crowned with an imperial or arched crown; the compartment is also taken away; on the reverse the old cross is still continued, but it has the arms of Scotland on the center; these pieces, both head and reverse, are plainly borrowed from the improvements made by Henry VII. anno 1503. No. 36. 37. Type. Legend.

The inscription round the head is IACOBVS DEI GRA. REX SCOTORV, or SCOTOR; and on the reverse, OPPIDVM EDINBVRGI; and one sort has VILLA instead of Oppidum. WEIGHT.

The groat usually found of this king (No. 37.) weighs about 42 grains, and

E the

be a *deacon* that shall examine the same, who is likewise to put his mark to the said work, and to answer thereto upon his life and goods. Parl. 2. c. 13.—The act relating to the bringing in of bullion to be put in strict execution. P. 2. c. 14. App. No. 33.

A true and substantial man to be master of the mint, and to make a groat of 10 to the oz. to be of the same fineness as the Edward groat of England, who is to pay for each ounce of burnt silver 11s 6d, and the same for the silver work of *Paris* or *Bruges*, and what any work wants of the said fineness to be deducted; and if the coiner and seller cannot agree about the price, then two goldsmiths to be chosen to determine the value, by which both of them shall abide—and to discover whether the said coinage be kept up in weight and fineness to the Edward's groat, the coiner shall have a particular mark to distinguish it from the first coinage; and if any are found defective in weight or fineness, the coiner to forfeit life and goods, to be examined at the next parliament, or sooner if it is the king's pleasure.—Gold and silver coin shall not be refused by any body, if it is of just weight and fineness, although it should be be cracked, flawed, or solder'd. Parl. 2. c. 17. App. No. 35.

All persons obliged to take the several different sorts of the king's money, if it be of just fineness, and bears the figure of the king on it, notwithstanding the diversity of types, and struck by several moniers, as well those of Gilbert Fish, commonly called *Berwick groats*, as also of Levingston, and John Currour; and if any refuse the said money, the possessor to apply to the proper officer, who finding it good, the refuser to forfeit the value of it to the king, and the goods he refused to sell for it to the possessor, but if found bad, to be chop'd to pieces, and returned to the owner. Parl. 4. c. 40. App. No. 37.

An understanding person to be chosen master of the mint, who is to overlook the coinage, the fineness and the currency, also what concerns the bringing in of bullion by the merchants, and to give them for each ounce what is fixed by parliament, to take care of its not being transported out of the realm. Parl. 5. c. 55. Appen. No. 38.

The statutes against carrying money out of the realm to be enforced, searchers to be appointed to every town which has a port, with power to search all persons going out of the realm — One quarter of the money discovered to be for himself, and the other three fourths for the king. No person to carry more than forty shillings. Par. 6. c. 68. Appen. No. 39.

No flawed or cracked money to be refused in payment, the refuser to forfeit the value refused to the king, and the tenderer to have the commodity which it was to have purchased for nothing. Par. 6. c. 97. App. No. 40.

the half groat (No. 36.) in proportion; the other piece of this king (No. 35.) about 30 troy grains, or ⅔ of the groat, and the half (No. 34.) in proportion.

FINENESS. In the table, the silver money of this king is put at 11 ounces fine silver, and one ounce alloy, but we are informed by Nicholson, *(i)* that the *Douglas* groat, which we think was No. 37. and the common one of this reign was only 10 ounces fine.

VALUE. We find in the table (so often referred to,) that a pound weight of silver was coined into 9l 12s in tale, now the groat generally in use appears to have been that called the *Douglas* groat, which we think was No. 37. weighing about 42 gr. tr. and must have been current for about 17 pence, to bring out the above value, but if it was current for 18 pence, as Lindsay *(k)* informs us, and was but 10 ounces fine, the pound tale will be increased to more than 11l. and Mr. Balfour, in his account of the Cunzie, *(l)* tells us, that at the death of this king, the ounce was worth 19s 9d, and consequently the pound 11l 17s, which of these is the justest, we must leave to better judges.

We hear no more after this reign of the groat, which had been the largest piece coined in Scotland, from the time of David Bruce, or near two centuries; at its first introduction, it was of the same intrinsick and nominal value as in England, that is four pennies, at this time it was reduced to about ⅓ of the old weight, yet passed for between four and five times its first value, as was the manner in France, Germany, and Italy, where the *grost*, *grosch*, and *grosso*, were continually raised in their *nominal* value, whereas in England, notwithstanding the groat has been diminished in its *intrinsick* value, yet the *nominal* has always been four-pence.

MARY, 1544. This unhappy princess came to the crown upon the death of her father, being but a few days old, was married in her 16th year to Francis, then Dauphin, afterwards king of France; her second husband was Henry, Lord Darnley, she was deposed in 1567, and beheaded in Fotheringay Castle, in February 1586-7, where she had been imprisoned near 18 years.

Pl. 3. No. 1. Type. Legend. Weight. The first silver coin we have of hers, was in her tenth year, which has her head crowned, and regarding the right, inscribed MARIA DEI GRA. R. SCOTORUM, on the reverse is the royal shield of Scotland crowned, between two stars or mullets of five points, and round it DA PACEM DOMINE 1553. We should think from the weight of this piece, some of them being as heavy as 66 or 68 tr. gr. that it is an half testoon.

No. 2. Type. Legend. Weight. We conjecture that No. 2. may have been the next piece minted by her, but cannot be certain, as it is not dated, and being nearly of the same weight, usually about 64 tr. gr. it might have been likewise an half testoon; it has on its obverse an M crowned between two crowned thistles, and inscribed MARIA DEI G. SCOTOR. REGINA, the reverse has the royal shield of Scotland crowned, and extending to the edge of the piece, the legend DELICIE DNI COR HVMILE.

No. 3. 4. Type. Legend. Weight. Number 3. and No. 4. have the M crown'd, between two crowned thistles, on the obverse as the last, and inscribed exactly like that, with the addition of the date, viz. 1555, the reverse shews the royal arms of Scotland, but not crowned, fixed on a cross potence, extending through the literary circle, inscribed COR HVMILE DELICIE.

(i) Lindsay's Hist. of Scotland, p. 176. *(k)* Page 292. *(l)* ibid.

DELICIÆ DNI. there are half testoons, and testoons weighing about 4 dwt. 20 gr. and 2 dwt. 10 gr. or 116 and 58 tr. gr.

The royal shield of Scotland crowned, between an M and an R, is found on the obverses of No. 5. and No. 6. within a circle, with MARIA DEI G. R. SCOTORUM 1558 on it, and on their reverse a cross potence, with 4 small ones in the interstices of it, and inscribed IN VIRTUTA TUA LIBERA ME 1558, the former generally weighs about 45 tr. gr. and the other about 90, or something more or less, and appear likewise to be an half and whole testoon. No. 5, 6. Type, Legend, Weight.

On the obverse side of No. 7. and No. 8. is a cross potence, charged with a shield, party per pale, on the dexter side, the arms of the Dauphin in chief, and of Scotland in base, the sinister is filled with that of Scotland; the legend round it is FRAN. ET MA. DEI G. R. R. SCOTOR. D. D. VIEM; on the reverse is F M, crowned, between two double barr'd crosses, inscribed FECIT UTRAQUE UNUM 1558; these pieces are likewise the half testoon and testoon, weighing usually about 46 and 92 troy grains. No. 7, 8. Type, Legend, Weight.

The portraits of the Dauphin and Queen face to face, with a crown over them, as appears on No. 9. inscribed FRAN. ET MA. D. G. R. R. SCOTOR. DELPHIN. VIEN. the royal shield crowned, with the arms of the Dauphin impaled with those of Scotland between F M, crowned, and inscribed as the last, FECIT UTRAQUE VNVM 1558, forms the reverse, this rare piece was certainly a testoon, but we have never had an opportunity of knowing its weight. No. 9. Type, Legend.

The obverse of No. 10. and 11. exhibit a shield, with the royal arms of France impaled with those of Scotland, crowned with an imperial crown, having on the dexter side a cross, and on the sinister side a saltier, inscribed FRAN. ET MA. D. G. R. R. FRANCO. SCOTOR. the reverse has F M. crowned between a fleur de lis and a thistle, both crowned, the inscription is VICIT LEO DE TRIBV IVDA 1560, and some have 1559. They are the half and whole, and weigh nearly the same as the last. No. 10. 11. Type, Legend.

We have the widowed head of the Queen looking to the left on No. 12. and 13. it is inscribed MARIA DEI GRA. SCOTORVM REGINA, and under the head in a scroll 1561 or 1562, on the reverse, in a shield, the royal arms of France are half effaced on the dexter side, by those of Scotland on the sinister, having on each side an M crowned, the inscription is SALVVM FAC POPVLVM TVVM DOMINE. These are also an half and whole testoon, and the last coins of this sort in the Scotch series, and weigh near the same as the last and No. 7, 8, viz. 92 and 46 tr. grains. No. 12, 13. Type, Legend.

The heads of Henry and Mary, regarding each other, appear on the obverse of No. 14, and under them the date 1565, round their head is inscribed HENRICUS & MARIA D. GRA. R. & R. SCOTORVM; on the reverse is the royal arms of Scotland, crowned between two leaved thistles, inscribed QVOS DEVS CONIVNXIT NEMO SEPARET. No. 14. Type, Legend.

This rare piece was certainly struck upon the Queen's marriage with Lord Darnley, and in all probability, as a pattern for a coin of XXX shillings, as we have some of that value, but with different impressions coined that year; it must be observed also, that on this piece his name stands before that of the Queen, but on all the others her name is first.

The obverses of No. 15, 16, 17, are exactly like the reverse of the last, viz. the royal shield of Scotland, crowned between two leaved thistles, it is inscribed MARIA & HENRIC. DEI GRA. R. & R. SCOTORV. on the reverse is a palm tree, crowned on a scroll, is fasten'd to it DAT GLORIA VIRES, and under the No. 15, 16, 17. Type, Legend, Weight, the date 1565, 1566 or 1567. Bishop Nicholson observes, p. 323. That the tree on the reverses of these pieces is by some taken for a yew tree, and to have been put on these pieces in allusion to a famous one of this sort, that formerly grew in the park or garden of the Earl of Lenox, which gave occasion to the thought; the tree being crowned, denotes the advancement of the Lenox family by Lord Darnley's marriage with the Queen, and the inscription on the scroll confirms this conjecture.

No. 18. 19. 20. Type, Legend, Weight. The only difference between these three last coins in plate 3, and those just described, is in the inscription round the obverse, as being struck after the death of her second husband Darnley, his name is omitted, being only MARIA DEI GRA. SCOTORVM REGINA; and on the reverse no other date but 1567. These pieces weigh the same as the last, that is, the largest one ounce Scotch, and the others in proportion to their value, that is ⅔ and ⅓ of the same.

SORTS. In silver, there appears to be only the testoon and half testoon, at five shillings and thirty pence each, and the pieces of x, xx and xxx shillings each.

FINENESS. Eleven ounces of fine silver, and one ounce alloy.

VALUE. In the table, we find a pound weight of silver, at the beginning of her reign, was coined into 9l 12s in tale, and as the testoons and half testoons are said to be current for 5s and 30 pence, they should have weighed about 147 and 73 tr. grains. Of the testoons, there are none found of this time, and the heaviest half testoons are only 66 gr. In her 13th year, there was 13 pound tale to one pound weight. No. 3 and 4 agree in their weight to this *foot*. The pound tale appears to have been increased to 15l 15s or 16l, when No. 5, 6, 7, 8, 10 and 11 were coined, or between 1555 and 1562 inclusive, and in the year 1565, and the remaining part of her reign, we are certain it was 18 pound.

JAMES VI. 1567. This prince came to the crown when an infant; the Earl of Murray was the first regent till 1570; 2d. the Earl of Lennox till July 1571; 3d. the Earl of Mar, until October 1572; the 4th. and last was the Earl of Morton, until Feb. 1578; when the king took the reins himself, he married Anne, daughter to Frederick III. King of Denmark, he succeeded Queen Elizabeth in the crown of England 1603, and died at Theobalds, March 27, 1625, in the 48th year of his reign over Scotland, and 22d over England.

No. 1, 2, 3. pl. 4. Type, Legend. The obverse of these pieces are like the last coins of his mother's, the royal shield of Scotland, crowned with an I and an R, crowned on the sides, instead of the crowned thistle as was on hers, they are inscribed IACOBVS 6. DEI GRATIA REX SCOTORVM, on the reverse is a sword erect in pale, crowned, having on the dexter side a finger or index pointing to the value xxx, xx or x on the other side; and a little lower the date 1567, 1568, 1569, 1570, or 1571, the famous speech of Trajan on delivering the Prætor's sword, is inscribed round, viz. PRO ME SI MEREOR IN ME.

Weight, Fineness, Value. The articles of weight, fineness, and value, the same as the last coins of Mary, viz. the weight 472½, 315 and 157½ tr. grains, the fineness, 11 oz. fine silver, and one ounce alloy, and the pound weight cut into 18 pound tale.

No. 4, 5, Type, Legend. The pieces, No. 4 and 5, are an half noble, and noble, having their obverse like the last, the royal shield of Scotland crowned, with their value, viz. 3—4 and 6—8 on the sides, and round it IACOBVS 6. DEI GRATIA REX SCOTORUM; on the reverse is a cross form'd of I's, the initial of the king's name ornamented at the ends, those of No. 5. are surmounted with a coronet, the spaces of the cross are filled with an arch'd crown and thistles, the inscription round it is

SALVVM

Hodge Sculp.

SALVVM FAC POPVLVM TVVM DOMINE 1572, there are others likewise of 1573, 1574, 1575 and 1577.

The half noble usually weighs about 2 dwt. 6 gr. tr. and the noble 4 dwt. 12 gr. a little more or less.

In the table against 1571, the fineness is 8 oz. and in 1577, it is 9 oz. but we do not remember to have seen any of the pieces just described, which were those struck during the above period, to have been of such bad silver.

The pound weight of silver being valued at 16l 14s in tale, as in the table, will arise from the noble's weighing 4 dwt. 17 gr. tr. supposing this is its value at 11 oz. fine, if it was 9 oz. fine, it would amount to about 20l 5s; and if but 8 oz. fine, to 23l; nor can we determine which of these values was the true one.

The royal shield of Scotland, crowned, appears on the obverse of these pieces, and the inscription round is IACOBUS 6, DEI GRATIA REX SCOTORVM, some have only G. instead of Gratia, on the reverse is a leaved thistle between I R, which is crowned on No. 6, but not on the other; they are both inscribed IACOBVS 6, DEI GRATIA REX SCOTORVM, and on the rev. NEMO ME IMPVNE LACESSET, 1579 and 1581, and perhaps of other dates. No. 6, 7.

The portrait of the young king, regarding the right, in armour, crowned, with a sword erect in his band, appears on all those pieces, — IACOBVS. DEI. GRATIA. REX. SCOTORVM. and on the rev. the royal arms of Scotland between I R. which letters are the value of XS. XXS. XXXS. and XLS. round the shield, HONOR. REGIS. IVDICIVM. DILIGIT. 1582. there is one sort of No. 10. with XXX in one line, they are dated in 1581, 1582, 83, 84, and 85. No. 8, 9, 10, 11.

The weight ¼, ½, ¾, and one ounce Scots, or about 4 dwt. 22 grs. 9 dwt. 20 grs. and 19 dwt. 16 grs. troy; they hold 11 ounces fine silver, and one ounce alloy, and the value of a pound weight amounts to 24 pounds in tale. Weight, Fineness, and Value.

On the obverse of No. 12 and 13, are the royal shield of Scotland, crowned, a thistle on each side on the largest piece, but not on the other. IACOBVS D. G. R. SCOTORVM. 1591; on the reverse, a sword and ballance, HIS. DIFFERT REGE TYRANNVS. No. 12, 13. Type, Legend.

We find no account what was the fineness or value of the money in the years 1591 or 1592; now as the largest of these coins weigh about 3 dwt. or 72 grs. if we suppose it was current for 6s 8d. or a mark, the pound weight will amount to something more than 26l in tale. WEIGHT, FINENESS, VALUE.

The king's bust bare-headed, looking to the right, with his usual title, viz. IACOBVS, D. G. R. SCOTORVM. and on the other side, a three-headed thistle, crowned, and circumscribed NEMO ME IMPVNE LACESSIT, 1591; on the largest piece we have 1594, 1598, 1599 and 1601; on No. 16, from 1593 to 1599, but on the two smallest only 1602. No. 14, 15, 16, 17. Type, &c.

The largest of these pieces, No. 17, weighs 3 dwt. 22 grs. or 98 grs. and the others, the half, quarter, and eighth, in proportion, or 49. 24½ and 12 grs. the fineness as usual 11 oz. fine silver, and one ounce alloy; and the pound weight was cut into 30 pounds tale, or 60 pieces of 10s each. WEIGHT, FINENESS, VALUE.

These pieces have on their obverse the royal arms of Scotland, crowned, and inscribed IAÇOBVS. D. G. R. SCOTORVM. and on the reverse a leaved thistle, crowned, and circumscribed REGEM IOVA PROTEGIT. 160 . in which year they were mostly struck, but there is one of the largest dated 1603. No. 18, 19, 20, 21.

The largest of these pieces, No. 21. is a mark or 13s 4d. the other three are a noble or 6s 8d. and the two smallest, the half and quarter noble. SORTS.

 The

WEIGHT, FINENESS, VALUE. The largest of these pieces, No. 21. usually weighs about 4 dwts. 12 to 8 grs. and the other three in proportion, or 54, 27 and 13 grs. the fineness as before, and the pound weight cut into 36 pounds tale, or 82 ½ mark pieces, and so in proportion.

On the demise of Elizabeth, James being advanced to the throne of England, the arms of both kingdoms, with those of Ireland, were quartered in one shield; viz. Scotland in the first and fourth quarter; France and England quarterly in the second quarter; and Ireland in the third; when pieces of six-pence, one shilling, half a crown and a crown, were struck; the two first have his head in profile, crowned, to the right, the value VI. and XII. behind; the larger pieces have the king on horseback, looking as the others to the right, a sword in his hand, and a thistle head crowned, on the horses caparison. IACOBVS. D. G. MAG. BRIT. FRAN. & HIB. REX. on the rev. the royal arms as now used, on No. 1 and 2, in ornamented shields, and on No. 3. and 4. in plain ones. None of these pieces are dated, except the sixpences, on which the date is placed over the shield, viz. 1622, &c.

Type. Legend. No. 1, 2, 3, 4. pl. 5.

No. 5. pl. 5. The crowns and half crowns made their first appearance in 1605, and were continued the remainder of his reign; there is a two-pence the same as coined in England, which with the penny and halfpenny, being impressed with a rose on the obverse and a thistle on the reverse, were current in both kingdoms.

FINENESS. The same as in England, viz. 11 oz. 2 pennyweights fine silver, and 18 pennyweights alloy.

CHARLES I. 1625. No. 6, 7, 8, 9. pl. 5. His first coinage seems to be from the same dies with his father's, the name only changed; of these are the six-pence, No. 6. the shilling, No. 7. the half crown and crown, No. 8. and 9. and as they are so exactly alike shall refer to the description of them, their fineness, &c.

No. 10, 11, 12, 13. BRIOT'S. Are of much finer workmanship than the preceding ones, and are the productions of the celebrated Briot, who accompanied the king in his journey into Scotland in 1632; on the six-pence, No. 10, the shilling, No. 11, the head is turned to the left, and the shield on the reverse, crowned betwixt C. R. crowned; they are inscribed on the obverse, CAROLVS D. G. MAGN. BRITANN. FRANC. & HIBERN. REX. arms crowned QVÆ DEVS, &c.

Mint Marks. The small marigold and B on one side, and a thistle, sometimes single, sometimes with three heads.

No. 14, 15, 16, 17. On the six-pence, No. 14, and shilling, No. 15, the heads stand to the edge of the coin, and the inscription begins on the right side of the neck, and have an F or a T for a mint mark; the half crown, No. 16, and crown, No. 17, having the same mint marks, appear to be the produce of the same mint, but excepting that particular alteration, do not appear to have any other difference from No. 12 and 13.

No. 18, 19, 20, 21, 22, 23. Now were introduced several species of coins, viz. the piece of twenty pennies, the two shillings, the piece of forty pennies, or quarter mark, and the half mark.

TYPE. The twenty pennies, No. 18, has the king's head, crowned, and extending to the edge of the coin, with XX behind CAR. D. G. SCOT. ANG. FR. & HIB. R. rev. a leaved thistle, crowned, IVSTITIA THRONVM FIRMAT. No. 19. has the busts within the circle, and wants the ET in the legend on the obverse.

Fineness, Weight. The same as the crown, &c.

The,

Coins of James VI and Charles I.　I

J. Lizars Sculp.

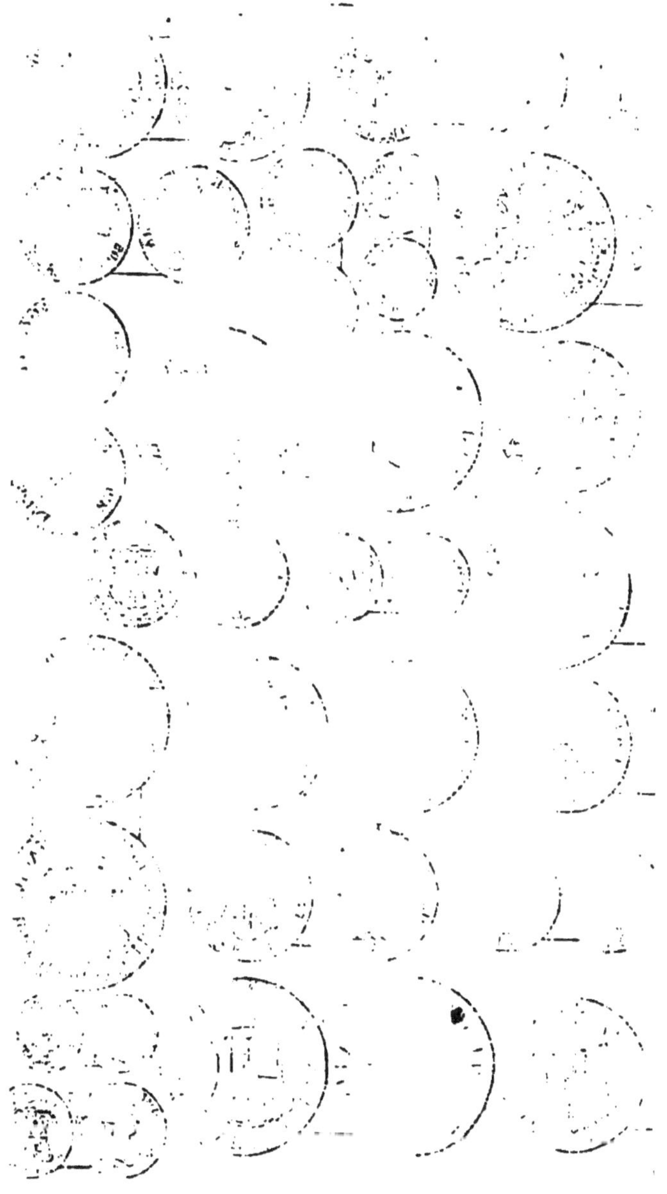

Lodge Sculp

The two shillings, No. 20, gives the head crowned, with 11 behind CAR. G. D. SCOT. AN. FR. & HIB. R. rev. the Scots arms crowned, IVSTITIA, &c. No. 21. differs from the former, in that the head extends to the edge of the coin, and wants the numerals behind, the other parts as before. Type.

The forty penny piece, or quarter mark, No. 22. has the king's head extending to the edge of the coin, with XL behind, CAR. D. G. SCOT. ANG. & HIB. R. rev. a leaved thistle crowned, SALVS REIPVB. SVPREMA LEX. No. 23. has the head confined in the letter'd limb, and a thistle head behind, instead of the numerals. Type.

The noble or half mark, No. 24. gives the crowned bust, with VI behind, CAROLVS D. G. ANG. FR. & HIB. R. rev. the arms crowned, CHRISTO AVSPICE REGNO. No. 25. has C. R. crowned on each side the arms. Type. No. 24, 25.

The half mark 51 grs. the forty penny piece 30 grs. and the piece of twenty pence 12 grs. WEIGHT.

These coins, from No. 18. to No. 25. inclusive, seem to have been the work of Briot, or his disciple; and such as have any mint marks, carry those of that great artist. Mint Mark.

The use of the hammer being laid aside in England, Charles introduced the press into Scotland, but without the graining on the edges of the smaller pieces, or the letters on the larger. He also laid aside the crown and parts thereof, and coined the four mark piece, the two mark, the mark, and the half mark; these have his busto laureat, with long hair, looking to the right, in Roman drapery, with the George dependent, CAROLVS II. DEI GRATIA; on the rev. the arms in four seperate shields, the value of each piece in the centre, as LII. XXVI. XIII. VI. in the interstices ☧ crowned; round are the king's titles, MAG. BRI. FRA. & HIB. REX. 1664, &c. to 1765. On the obverse of the four mark of 1764, there is a large thistle at the end of Carolus; on that of 1674, and under the bust, an (a) F. on the three smaller pieces, a small thistle under the head. CHARLES II 1660. No. 1, 2, 3, 4.

These were succeeded by the dollar, its half, quarter, and half quarter, No. 6, 7, 8 and 9, the king's head laureat turned to the left, and are inscribed CAROLVS II. DEI GRA. rev. the arms in four shields crowned, with a leaved thistle in the interstices, and the ☧ in the centre, SCO. ANG. FR. & HIB. REX. 1675 to 1681. The half quarter, on the rev. has a saltier cross, with a crown on the centre, between a thistle, rose, flower de lis, and a harp. No. 5, 6, 7, 8, 9.

The dollar 4 pennyweights 12 grs. and the parts in the same proportion; the standard silver in these coins was computed at three pounds four shillings Scots, and were current for 28 shillings, 14 shillings, seven shillings, and three shillings and six-pence. Weight. Fineness. Value.

He altered the value of the coin, and laying aside the mark and dollar, published two coins, No. 10. of 10 shillings, and No. 11. of 40. They have his head laureat, looking to the right, IACOBVS II. DEI GRA. the value 40 and 10 under the busto; on the rev. the royal arms in one shield, crowned, and inscribed MAG. BRIT. FRA. & HIB. REX. 1687. On the rev. of the ten shilling, the arms are in four seperate shields, crowned, a St. Andrew's cross in the centre, with JAMES II. 1684. No. 10, 11

(a) This was John Faulkner of Balmaker, the master; or, James Faulkner of Plaisley, the Warden of the mint.

with a thistle, rose, flower de lis, and harp in the vacancies, inscribed MAG. BR. &c. 1678.

WILLIAM and MARY. 1688. No. 12, 13, 14. 15, 16. Coined pieces of 60, 40, 20, 10, and 5 shillings, their heads conjoined, and turned to the left, the king's laureat, with the value of each piece underneath, GVLIELMVS & MARIA DEI GRA. rev. on the four larger pieces, the arms in one shield, crowned, MAG. BR. &c. The smallest piece, No. 12. has on the rev. a cypher of W. M. crowned. Titles as the others.

WILLIAM alone. No. 17, 18, 19, 20, 21. He coined the same pieces, with his head laureat, and value under, GVLIELMVS DEI GRA. reverse, the arms in one shield, and titles as before; on No. 17, the reverse presents us with a three headed thistle, crowned, and inscribed NEMO ME IMPVNE LACESSIT. 1697.

ANNE. 1701. No. 22, 23. Only coined two pieces of 10 and 5 shillings, these have her bust, ANNA DEI GRATIA. No. 23. gives her arms in a crowned shield on the rev. with the usual titles; and No. 22. the three headed thistle.

FINIS.

ERRATA.

Page 1. line 13. (that) must be left out.
Page 10. line 5. for Berwiok read Berwick.

Gold Coins of Scotland, from Robert III to James IV.

Gold Coins of Scotland from James V. to James VI. Pl. 2

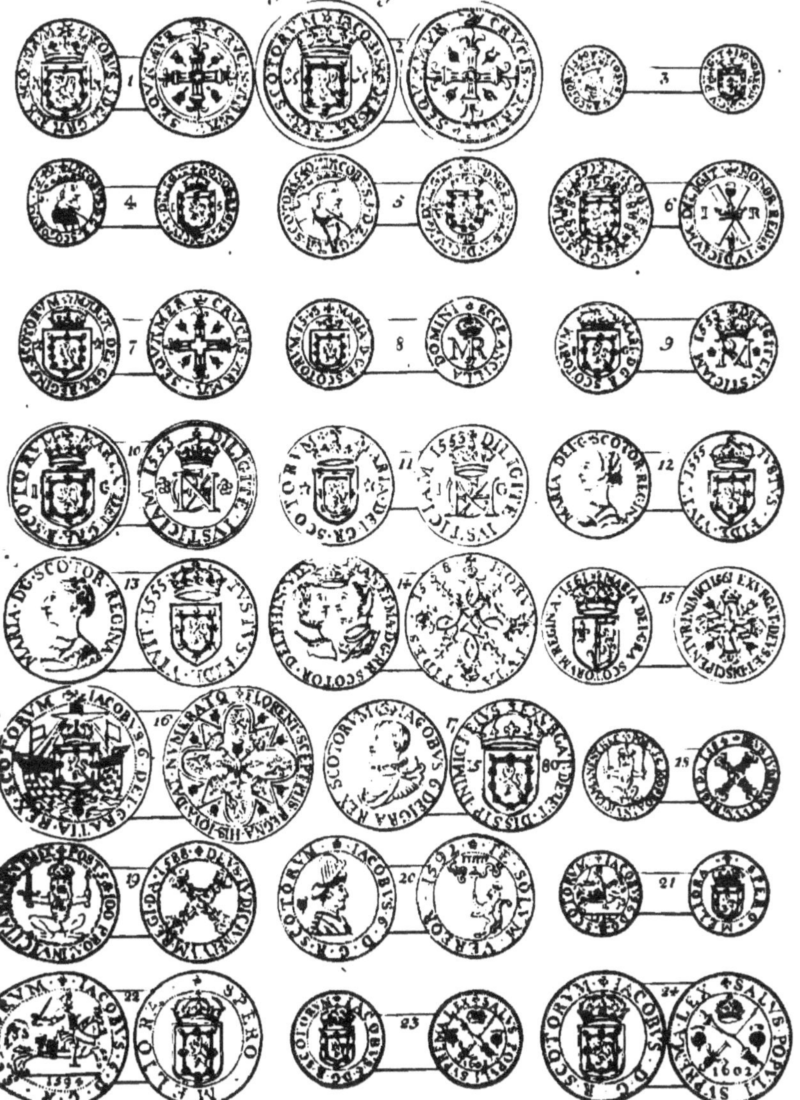

Coins of James VI, Charles I, & Will.m III. Pl 3

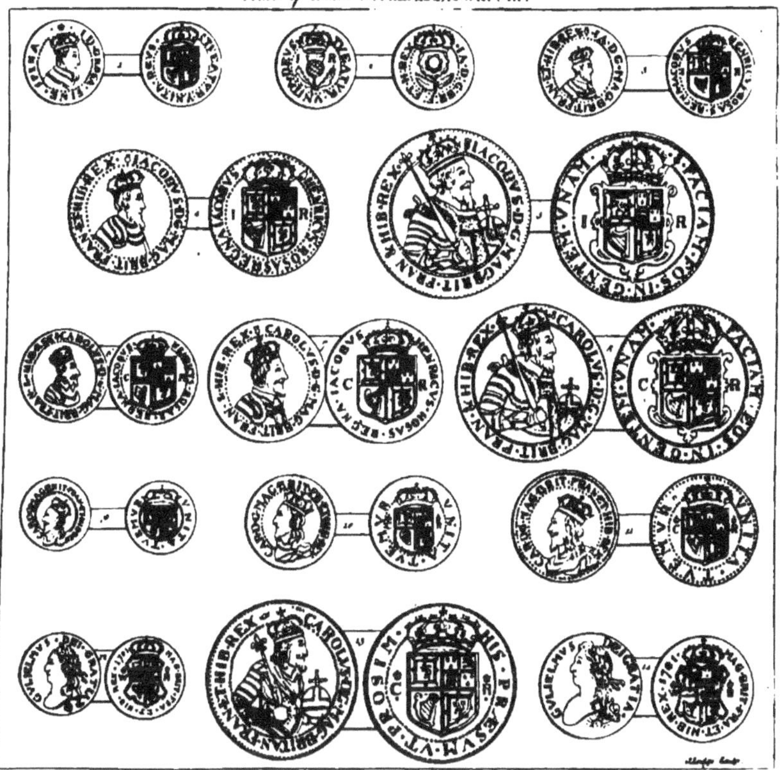

Billon Coins of Scotland until James VI.

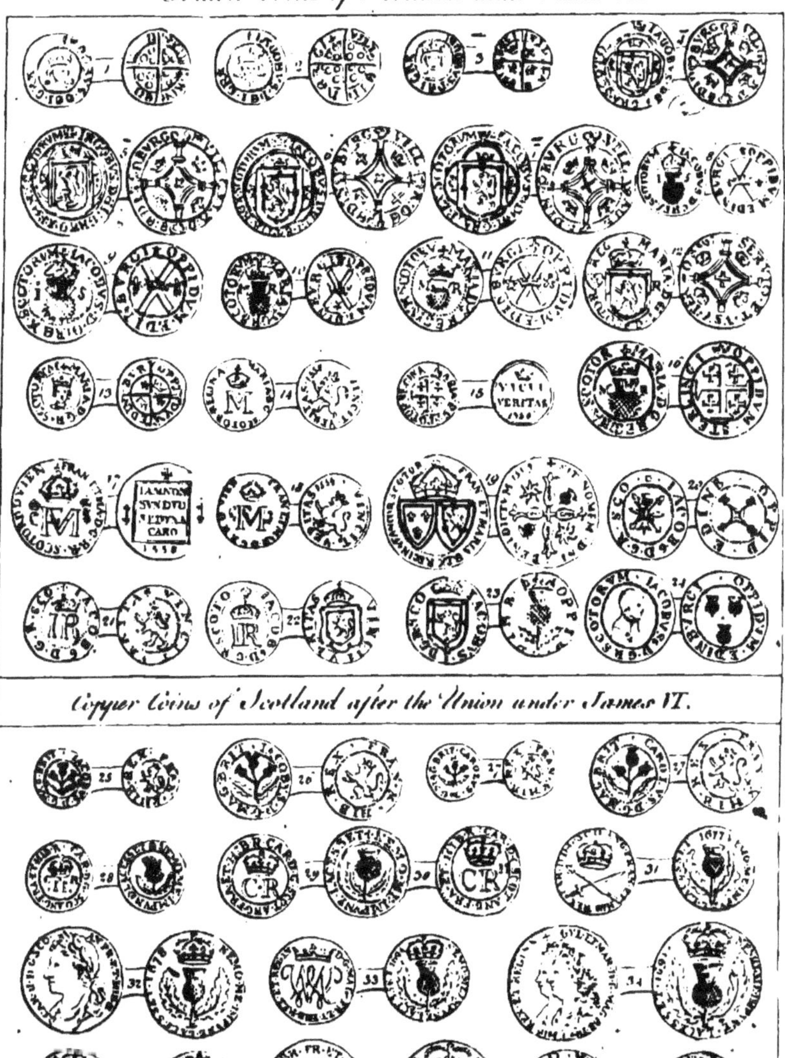

Copper Coins of Scotland after the Union under James VI.

Francis Wheeler
1797.

THIRTY THREE PLATES, OF ENGLISH MEDALS

By the late

MR. THOMAS SNELLING.

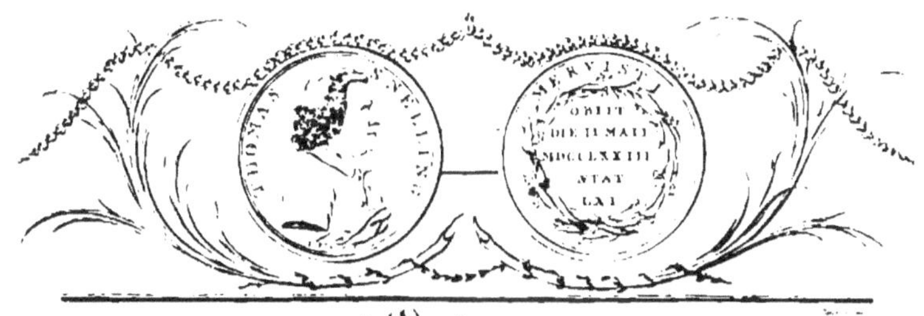

London:

SOLD BY THOMAS SNELLING,

Printseller in Fleet Street.

MDCCLXXVI.

ASHMOLEAN
OXFORD
MUSEUM

English Medals, William I to Edward II.

J. C. Burk sculp.

Plate II. ENGLISH MEDALS. Edward III to Henry VIII.

ENGLISH MEDALS Henry VIII & Edward VI.

Plate V.

English Medals. Elizabeth.

ENGLISH MEDALS. Elizabeth & Leicester.

Plate VII. ENGLISH MEDALS. James I & Family.

ENGLISH MEDALS, James's Queen & Daughter

ENGLISH MEDALS, Charles I.

Plate IX.

Charles I. ENGLISH MEDALS. Plate II.

CAR·I·MAR·D·G·ANGL·FRANC·ET HIBER·RR
16 36
IVSTITIA ET PAX OSCVLATAE SVNT
PSAL·84
SIMON BEAL AE SVÆ
1641
1644
GVIL·LAVD·ARCHIEPISC·CANTVAR·X·IAN·1644
ÆGIDIVS·STRANGWAYS·DE·MELBVRY IN COM·DORCESTR·ARM
DECVSQVE ADVERSA DEDERVNT

THO · CARY · R · CAROL · CVBICVLAR · ETATIS · 1633
ENDYMION PORTER R CAROLI A CVBICVLIS
EGO VIDEO · ET · RECIPIO · ILLE QVE VIDET · RECIPIT
TH · DE · MAYERNE · EQ · AVR · BA · MB · REG · GAL · ET ANGL · ARCHIA
NON · HÆC · SINE · NVMINE

Illustrious Persons. ENGLISH MEDALS. Plate 14

CAROLUS·II·D·G·MAGNÆ·BRIT·FRA·ET·HIB·REX
PSAL 89 IN NOMINE MEO EXALTABITUR CORNU EIUS
AUGUSTISS CAROLO SECUNDO·I·P
NULLUM NUMEN ABEST
BRITANNIA
CAROLUS·II·DEI·GRATIA·MAG·BR·FRA·ET·HIB·REX
CAROLUS II·REX
MAGNA·OPERA·DOMINI
1660

CAROLUS SECUNDUS D·G MAG·BRIT·FRAN·ET·HIB·REX
FELICITAS·BRITANNIÆ,
29·MAII 1660.
IN
ÆTERMEMOR
CAROLI II MAGBR
FRANC·ET HIBER
CLEMENTISSIMI
REGIS·RED!
29·MAII:
1660:
INVIDIA MAIOR

1
2
3
4
5
6
NEC MINOR IN TERRIS
NOS PENES IMPERIVM
CAROLVS·SECVNDVS·DEI·GRATIA·MAG·BRI·FRAN·ET·HIB·REX
CAROLVS·SECVNDVS·D·G·MAG·BRI·FRAN·ET·HIB·REX
GENVS ANTIQVVM
PRO·TALIBVS AVSIS
PRO·TALIBVS·AVSIS·

Hall sc.

DEO
FAVENTE
BRITANNIA
CAROLVS ET CATHARINA REX ET REGIN
DEO
FAVENTE
1666
RELIGIONIS REFORMATAE PROTECTORI
FIDEI DEFENSORI
LIBERTAS
CAROLVS SECVNDVS D G MAG BRI FRAN ET HIB REX
1
2
3
4
5

CAROLVS ET CATHARINA REX ET REGINA
1670 DIFFVSVS IN ORBE BRITANNVS
IACOBVS · DVX EBORACENSIS
MARIA · DVCISSA EBORACENSIS · 16·80
CAROL II·D·G·ANGL SCOT·FRAN·ET·HIB·REX
CAROLVS·SECVNDVS·DEI·GRATIA·MAG·BRI·FRAN·ET·HIB·REX
A QVADRATO AD LINEAM RECTAM EXTRORSVM
ABD . DEG
A PENTAGONO AD LINEAM RECTAM INTRORSVM
PRO QVADRATO
INPAVIDVM FERIENT

C. Hall sculp

ENGLISH MEDALS.

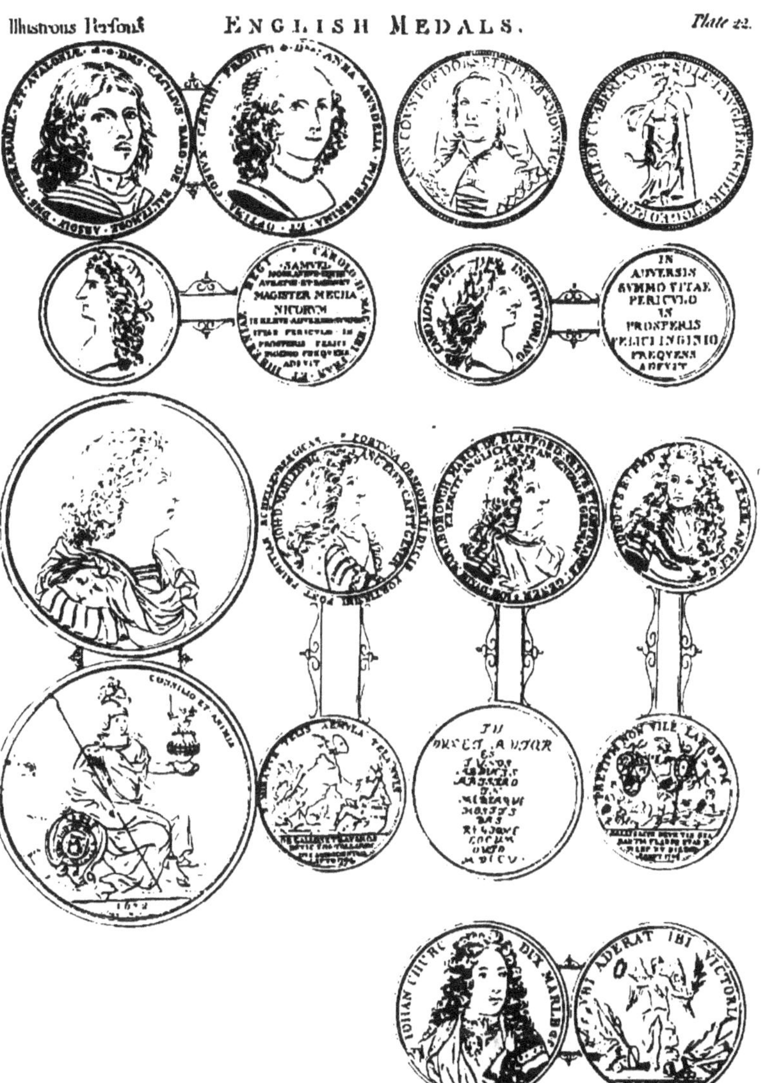
IN
ADVERSIS
SVMMO VITAE
PERICVLO
IN
PROSPERIS
FELICI INGINIO
FREQVENS
ADFVIT
MAGISTER MECHA
NICORVM
CONSILIO ET ARMIS
IBI ADERAT IBI VICTORIA

le

IACOBVS·II·D·G·ANG
IACOBVS·II·ET·MARIA·D·G·MAG·BRI·FRAN·ET·HIB·REX·ET·REGINA
1685 FORTES RADII SED BENIGNI
MARIA·D·G·ANG
O·DEA·CERTE
IACOBVS·II·D·G·MAG·BRI·FRAN·ET·HIB·REX
IACOBVS·II·D·G·MAG·BRI·FRAN·ET·HIB·REX·
NEMO·ME·IMPUNE·LACESSET
MDCLXXXV.
IACOBVS·II·DEI·GRA·ANG·SCOT·FRAN·ET·HIB·REX
GENVS·ANTIQVVM
IACOBVS·II·D·G·MAG·BRI·FRAN·ET·HIB·REX
MARIA·D·G·MAG·BRI·FRAN·ET·HIB·REG
2
5
6
7
8
9
10

SEMPER TIBI PENDEAT HAMUS
IACOBUS II REX ANG SCO FRA ET HIB NAT 15 OCT BAPT 24 NOV ANNO 1633. PRIMA SUI REGNI DIE 6 FEB ANNO 1685.
SPERANDUM ET FERENDUM
EXPERIENTIA FULCITUR
ADEO CONSONANT MAIORA MINORIBUS
O DIVINI AMBO SI QUID MEA CARMINA POSSUNT NULLA DIES UNQUAM MEMORI VOS EXIMET AEVO DUM TUA BANCHO DOMUS CAPITOLI IMMOBILE SAXUM EDINI IMPERIUMQUE PATER STUARTUS HABEBIT
A · P
PROVIDENTIA
IMPROVIDENTIA
IACOBUS DUX MONMOUTHENSIS
MDCLXXXV

MORIENDO RESTITVIT REM E. GODFREY
TANTVM RELLIGIO POTVIT
MORIENDO RESTITVIT REM E. GODFREY
EQVO CREDITE TEVCRI
MORIENDO RESTITVIT REM E. GODFREY
ECCLESIA PERVERSA TENET FACIEM DIABOLI
O WHY SO FICKLE
THE POPES SLAVGHTERHOVS ROMES REVENGE
16 7 8
BIRDS OF A FEATHER FLOCK TOGETHER
EDMUND BURY GODFREY MORIENDO RESTITUIT REM
TANTUM RELLIGIO POTERAT SUADERE MALORUM
THE POPISH PLOT
1
2
3
4
5
6
5
7
8

OLIVARIUS CROMWELL
JOANNES MILTON
E
MARMORE
IN ECCLESIA
ERECTORE
RYSBRACHIUS
JOHANNES LOCKE
GULIELMUS WARE ARCH CANT
ICONES VERISSIMAS
GULIELMO WARE
JOANNES DASSIER
SAMUEL CLARKE
GULIELMUS WINDHAM ARMIGER

Hall sc

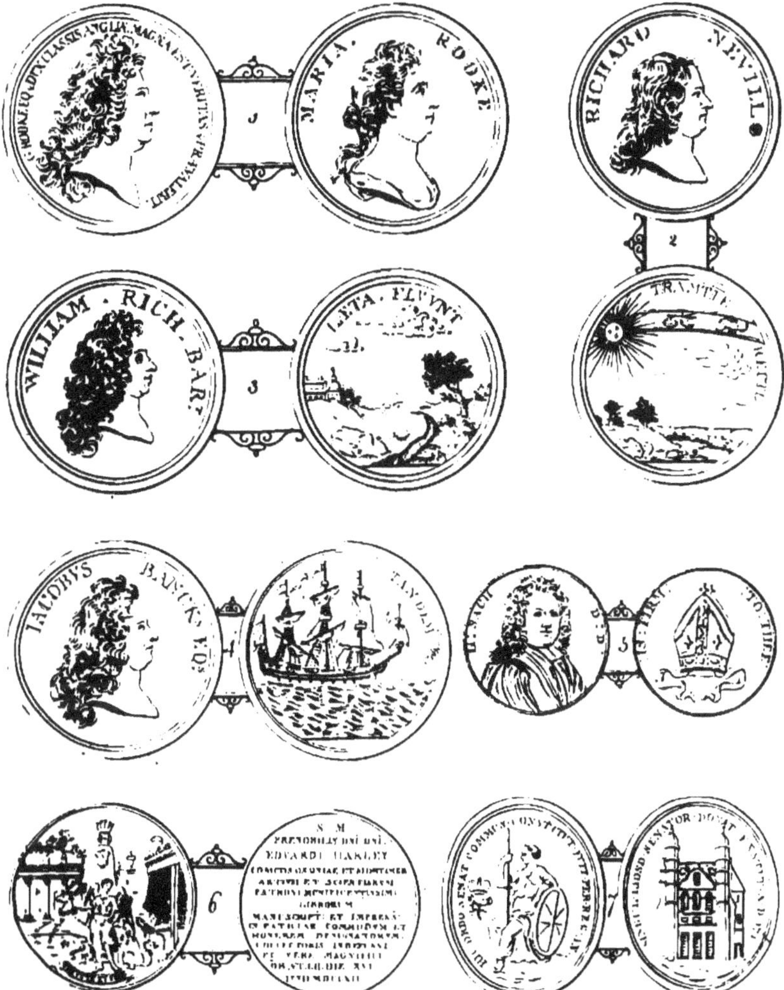
MARIA · ROOKE
RICHARD · NEVILL
WILLIAM · RICH · BAR.T
LÆTA · FLUUNT
IACOBUS BANCKS EQ.
S · M
EDVARDI HARLEY

Wall sc.

ABLEG·EXT·BRIT·AD·
ULTERIUS·ALTERA·POSCIT·
IO·MOLESWORTH·ABLEG·EXT·BRIT·AD·
GLORIA·PRINCIPUM
MOLES·WORTH·BRIT·TRIB·
PER ARDUA
1
2
3

1

2

3

4

5

6

7

8

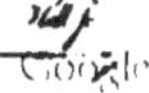

ANDREAS · FOVNTAINE · EQVES · AVRATVS · ANGLVS ·
A · SELVI · F
CONYERS · MIDDLETON · S · T · P ·
NIL ACTVM REPVTANS CVM QVID SVPERESSET AGENDVM
DANIEL · WRAY · ANGLVS · AET · XXI ·

IOHANNES BERNARD EQUES
ALDERMANUS
CIVITATIS LONDINI
MDCCXLIV
ROBERTUS BARKER
DOCTOR MEDICUS
SOCIUS REGIÆ SOCIET
LONDINENSIS
MDCCXLIV
ALEXANDER POPE
POETA
ANGLUS
MDCCXLI
POETA
ANGLUS
ABRAHAMUS DE MOIVRE
UTRIUSQUE
SOCIETATIS REGALIS
LOND ET BEROL
SODALIS
MDCCXLI
RADULPHI BRIDEOAKE ARCHIDIACONUS WINTON
EDMUNDUS HALLEY
ASTRONOMUS
REGIS MAGNÆ
BRITANNIÆ
MDCCXLIV
ECCLESIA BEATÆ MARIÆ SOUTHTON RESTITUTA 1722
NAT 13 IUN 1663 OB 15 MART 1742/3

IOHANN CAMPBELL.

DUX DE ARGYLE ET DE GREENWICH MDCCXLIII

1

IOHANNES CARTERET.

2

BARO DE CARTERET MDCCXLIV.

GUILIELMUS PULTENEY.

3

COMES DE BATH MDCCXLIV.

ROBERTUS WALPOLE.

4

COMES DE ORFORD MDCCXLIV

ROBERTUS. WALPOLE. ORD. PERISCELIDIS ROVES

5

REGIT. DICTIS. ANIMOS.

THE RIGHT HON. ROBERT EARL OF ORFORD

6

ENVY SHALL NOT PREVAIL AGAINST THEE

PHILIPPUS STANHOPE
COMES DE CHESTERFIELD MDCCXLIII
1
CAROLUS SPENCER
2
DUX DE MARLBOROUGH MDCCXLII
HANS SLOANE EQ. BARONETTUS
3
PRÆSES SOCIETATIS REGIÆ LONDINENSIS MDCCXLIV
ANDREAS FOUNTAINE EQ. AURAT.
4
A A A F F IIIVIR
MDCCXLV
I. A. DASSIER
MARTINUS FOLKES
5
MARTINUS FOLKES ARM.
6
SOCIETATIS REGALIS LONDINI SODALIS
M.DCCXL.

Hall sc.

www.ingramcontent.com/pod-product-compliance
Lightning Source LLC
Chambersburg PA
CBHW032300280326
41932CB00009B/641
* 9 7 8 3 3 3 7 1 7 3 3 5 7 *